W9-CCL-964

For Reference

Not to be taken from this room

GALE
ENCYCLOPEDIA OF
MULTICULTURAL
AMERICA PRIMARY DOCUMENTS

RENFRO LIBRARY
MARS HILL COLLEGE
MARS HILL, N.C. 28754
DISCARD

GALE
ENCYCLOPEDIA OF
MULTICULTURAL
AMERICA PRIMARY DOCUMENTS

volume 2

Jamaican Americans – Vietnamese Americans

Edited by

JEFFREY LEHMAN

GALE GROUP

Detroit
San Francisco
London
Boston
Woodbridge, CT

R
305.800973
G(5)ma
V. 2

Jeffrey Lehman, *Editor*
Elizabeth Shaw, *Associate Editor*
Gloria Lam, *Assistant Editor*
Linda S. Hubbard, *Managing Editor*

Contributing editors: Brian Koski, Ashyia N. Henderson,
Allison McClintic Marion, Mark F. Mikula, Joseph M. Palmisano, Patrick Politano

Maria Franklin, *Permissions Manager*
Edna Hedblad and Keryl Stanley, *Permissions Specialists*

Mary Beth Trimper, *Production Director*
Evi Seoud, *Assistant Production Manager*

Cynthia Baldwin, *Product Design Manager*
Martha Schiebold, *Art Director*

Barbara J. Yarrow, *Imaging and Multimedia Content Manager*
Randy Bassett, *Image Database Supervisor*
Pamela A. Reed, *Imaging Coordinator*
Mike Logusz, *Senior Imaging Specialist*

While every effort has been made to ensure the reliability of the information presented in this publication, the Gale Group does not guarantee the accuracy of the data contained herein. The Gale Group accepts no payment for listing; and inclusion in the publication of any organization, agency, institution, publication, service, or individual does not imply endorsement of the editors or publisher. Errors brought to the attention of the publisher and verified to the satisfaction of the publisher will be corrected in future editions.

This publication is a creative work fully protected by all applicable copyright laws, as well as by misappropriation, trade secret, unfair competition, and other applicable laws. The authors and editors of this work have added value to the underlying factual material herein through one or more of the following: unique and original selection, coordination, expression, arrangement, and classification of the information. All rights to this publication will be vigorously defended.

Copyright © 1999
The Gale Group
27500 Drake Road
Farmington Hills, MI 48331-3535
http://www.galegroup.com
800-877-4253
248-699-4253

All rights reserved including the right of reproduction in whole or in part in any form.

ISBN (set) 0-7876-3990-7
ISBN (Vol 1) 0-7876-3991-5
ISBN (Vol 2) 0-7876-3992-3

Library of Congress Cataloging-in-Publication Data

Gale encyclopedia of multicultural America. Primary documents / edited by Jeffrey Lehman.
    p. cm.
    Includes bibliographical references and index.
    Summary: Primary documents, including letters, articles, cartoons, photos, and songs,
illuminate the experience of culture groups in the U.S. from colonial times to the present.
    ISBN 0-7876-3990-7 (set : alk. Paper) — ISBN 0-7876-3991-5 (v. 1) —ISBN
0-7876-3992-3 (v. 2)
    1. Pluralism (Social sciences)—United States—History—Sources—Juvenile literature. 2.
Minorities—United States—History—Sources—Juvenile literature. 3. Ethnology—United
States—History—Sources—Juvenile literature. 4. United States—Ethnic
relations—Sources—Juvenile literature. 5. United States—Race
relations—Sources—Juvenile literature. [1. Ethnology. 2. Minorities. 3. United
States—History—Sources.] I. Title: Encyclopedia of multicultural America. Primary
documents. II. Lehman, Jeffrey, 1969-
E184.A1 G15 1999
305.8'00973—dc21   99-044219

10 9 8 7 6 5 4 3 2 1

JUL 19 2000

CONTENTS

PREFACE

The *Gale Encyclopedia of Multicultural America: Primary Documents* was created as a companion to the award-winning *Gale Encyclopedia of Multicultural America*. Each ethnic group represented in *Primary Documents* has an essay in the second edition of *Gale Encyclopedia of Multicultural America*. The 210 primary documents included in this book bring history to life by providing insight into key events as well as the everyday lives of 90 different cultures. Students and teachers of U.S. history, social studies, and literature will find this book an indispensable tool for research projects, time period exploration, and independent analysis and critical thinking about historical evidence.

SCOPE

Unlike many compilations of primary documents, the *Gale Encyclopedia of Multicultural America: Primary Documents* is not limited to one type of document, one group of people, or a small period of time. We have chosen almost 20 document types, including letters, poems, oral histories, autobiographies, political cartoons, recipes, speeches, and photographs. They represent 90 national, ethnoreligious, and Native American groups. The documents originated throughout the history of North America, from transcriptions of Native American legends—which date from long before European arrival—to periodical articles from 1999.

Each item was chosen for one of the following reasons: it expands upon an individual's American experience or the general immigrant/minority experience in America; or it records the treatment of an entire group. The 198 text documents average a little more than 2,000 words each. The graphical documents have been enlarged to nearly full-page size to maximize legibility. With the exception of articles from scholarly journals, the majority of documents were created by members of the group being highlighted.

FORMAT

The *Gale Encyclopedia of Multicultural America: Primary Documents* is arranged alphabetically by group name. When a group has more than one item, they appear chronologically from oldest to newest date of creation. A commentary of about 800 words introduces each document to provide historical, literary, and/or biographical context.

For more information on the group's experiences in the United States—specifically in the areas of acculturation and assimilation; family and community; language; religion; employment and economics; politics and government; and significant contributions to American society—please consult the second edition of the *Gale Encyclopedia of Multicultural America*.

ADDITIONAL FEATURES

More than 80 photographs, maps, and other illustrations provide visual cues to the groups and their experiences. A two-level general index follows the last document in the second volume. It cites specific documents by title as well as ethnic groups, concepts, people, and places.

ACKNOWLEDGMENTS

This book would not have seen publication in as fine a form as it has without the intelligent guidance and unflagging persistence of Liz Shaw. See the separate "Credits" section for acknowledgment of the copyright holders when cooperation made this collection possible.

SUGGESTIONS ARE WELCOME

The editor welcomes your suggestions on any aspect of this work. Please mail comments and suggestions to: The Editor, *Gale Encyclopedia of Multicultural America: Primary Documents*, The Gale Group, 27500 Drake Road, Farmington Hills, MI 48331-3535; call 1-800-877-GALE [877-4253]; fax to (248) 699-8062; or e-mail galegroup.com.

CREDITS

The editors wish to thank the copyright holders of the excerpted criticism included in this volume and the permissions managers of many book and magazine publishing companies for assisting us in securing reproduction rights. We are also grateful to the staffs of the Detroit Public Library, the University of Detroit Mercy Library, Wayne State University Purdy/Kresge Library Complex, and the University of Michigan Libraries for making their resources available to us. Following is a list of the copyright holders who have granted us permission to reproduce material in these volumes of *Gale Encyclopedia of Multicultural America: Primary Documents*. Every effort has been made to trace copyright, but if omissions have been made, please let us know.

Copyrighted excerpts in the *Gale Encyclopedia of Multicultural America: Primary Documents*, were reproduced from the following periodicals:

Ethnicity, v. 2, September, 1975. Copyright © 1975 by Academic Press, Inc. Reproduced by permission.—*Indiana Folklore: Journal of the Hoosier Folklore Society,* v. III, 1970. Reproduced by permission. —*New York Folklore Quarterly,* v. XX, September, 1964; v. XXI, September, 1965. Both reproduced by permission of the publisher./ v. XXIV, December, 1968 for "Polish Customs in New York Mills, N.Y." by Robert Maziarz. Reproduced by permission of the publisher and the author. —*The Nation,* New York, v. 253, September 23, 1991; v. 259, December 12, 1994; v.264, February 3, 1997; v. 266, May 18, 1998. © 1991, 1994, 1997, 1998 *The Nation* magazine/ The Nation Company, Inc. All reproduced by permission. —*The New Republic,* v. 217, November 24, 1997. © 1997 The New Republic, Inc. Reproduced by permission of *The New Republic.* —*The New York Times,* April 3, 1998; June 26, 1998; February 10, 1999; April 4, 1999; April 7, 1999; May 2, 1999; May 10, 1999. Copyright © 1998, 1999 by The New York Times Company. All reproduced by permission. —*Society,* v. 14, September-October, 1977. Reproduced by permission. —*Utah Historical Quarterly,* v. 43, Winter, 1975. © Copyright 1975 Utah State Historical Society. Reproduced by permission. —*Vital Speeches of the Day,* v. XI, August 1, 1945. Reproduced by permission. —Zia, Helen. From a speech delivered on January 29, 1994 at the 6th Annual Gay Asian Pacific Alliance in San Francisco. Copyright © 1994 by Helen Zia. Reproduced by permission.

Copyrighted excerpts in the *Gale Encyclopedia of Multicultural America: Primary Documents*, were reproduced from the following books:

Adamic, Louis. From *Laughing in the Jungle.* Harper & Brothers, 1932. Copyright 1932 by Louis Adamic. Renewed 1959 by Stella Adamic. Reproduced by permission of Harper-Collins Publishers. —Alvarez, Jaime. From *American Mosaic: The Immigrant Experience in the Words of Those Who Lived It,* by Joan Morrison and Charlotte Fox Zabusky. E. P. Dutton, 1980. Copyright © 1980 by Joan Morrison and Charlotte Fox Zabusky. All rights reserved. Reproduced by permission of Joan Morrison and Charlotte Zabusky. —Ayobami, Tunde. From *American Mosaic: The Immigrant Experience in the Words of Those Who Lived It,* by Joan Morrison and Charlotte Fox Zabusky. E. P. Dutton, 1980. Copyright © 1980 by Joan Morrison and Charlotte Fox Zabusky. All rights reserved. Reproduced by permission of Joan Morrison and Charlotte Zabusky. —Bode, Janet. From *New Kids on the Block: Oral Histories of Immigrant Teens.* Franklin Watts, 1989. Copyright © 1989 by Janet Bode. All rights reserved. Reproduced by permission. —Bray, Bill. From *First Person, First Peoples.* Edited by Andrew Garrod and Colleen Larimore. Cornell University Press, 1997. Copyright © 1997 by Cornell University. Reproduced by permission of Cornell University Press. —Burns, Allan F. From *Maya in Exile: Guatemalans in Florida.* Temple University Press, 1993. Copyright © 1993 by Temple University Press. All rights reserved. Reproduced by permission. —Chawla, Sudershan S. From *Asian American Experience in the United States,* by Joann Faung Jean Lee. McFarland & Company, Inc., 1991. Copyright © 1991 by Joann Faung Jean Lee. All rights reserved. Reproduced by permission. —Criddle, Joan D. From *Bamboo & Butterflies: From Refugee to Citizen.* East/West Bridge Publishing House, 1992. Copyright © 1992 by Joan D. Criddle. All rights reserved. Reproduced by permission. —El Saadawi, Nawal. From *Memoirs from the Women's Prison.* Translated by Marilyn Booth. University of California Press, 1994. Copyright © Nawal El Saadawi 1983. Translation © Marilyn Booth 1986. Afterward for the American edition © 1994 by The Regents of the University of California. Reproduced by permission of the publisher and the author. —Espada, Martin. From *Trumpets from the Island of Their Eviction.* Bilingual Press/Editorial Bilingue, 1987, 1994. Copyright © 1987, 1994 by Martin Espada. All rights reserved. Reproduced by permission. —Flores, Rita. From *American Mosaic: The Immigrant Experience in the Words of Those Who Lived It,* by Joan Morrison and Charlotte Fox Zabusky. E. P. Dutton 1980. Copyright © 1980 by Joan Morrison and Charlotte Fox Zabusky. All rights reserved. Reproduced by permission of Joan Morrison and Charlotte Zabusky. —From "Birth Chant for Kau-I-ke-ao-uli" in *The Echo of Our Song: Chants & Poems of the Hawaiians.* Edited and translated by Mary Kawena Pukui and Alfons L. Korn. University Press of Hawaii, 1973. Copyright © 1973 by The University Press of Hawaii. All rights reserved. Reproduced by permission. —From "The Pearl" in *The Echo of Our Song: Chants & Poems of the Hawaiians.* Edited and translated by Mary Kawena Pukui and Alfons L. Korn. University Press of Hawaii, 1973. Copyright © 1973 by The University Press of Hawaii. All rights reserved. Reproduced by permission. —Hadley, Su-Chu. From *American Mosaic: The Immigrant Experience in the Words of Those Who Lived It,* by Joan Morrison and Charlotte Fox Zabusky. E. P. Dutton, 1980. Copyright © 1980 by Joan Morrison and Charlotte Fox Zabusky. All rights reserved. Reproduced by permission of Joan Morrison and Charlotte Zabusky. —Haney, Michael. From a speech delivered on March 30, 1991 on the International Indian Treaty Council before the United Nations Subcommission on the Prevention of Discrimination Against Minorities, at the American Indian Community House in New York, NY. Reproduced by permission of the author. —Hassan, Ibrahim. From *American Mosaic: The Immigrant Experience in the Words of Those Who Lived It,* by Joan Morrison and Charlotte Fox Zabusky. E. P. Dutton, 1980. Copyright © 1980 by Joan Morrison and Charlotte Fox Zabusky. All rights reserved. Reproduced by permission of Joan Morrison and Charlotte Zabusky. —Hernandez, Antonia. From a speech delivered on October 5, 1994, on "Are We Compassion Fatigued?" at the Temple Isaiah in Los Angeles, CA. Reproduced by permission of the author. —Johanson, Gunnar. From *American Mosaic: The Immigrant Experience in the Words of Those Who Lived It,* by Joan Morrison and Charlotte Fox Zabusky. E. P. Dutton, 1980. Copyright © 1980 by Joan Morrison and Charlotte Fox Zabusky. All rights reserved. Reproduced by permission of Joan Morrison and Charlotte Zabusky. —Jordan, Barbara. From *"A New Beginning: A New Dedication."* Reproduced by permission of the Estate of Barbara C. Jordan. —Kanosky, Stella. Excerpt from *"Case Study in Family Relationships,"* August, 1941. Reproduced by permission of Stella McDermott. —Karenga, Maulana. In an introduction to *"The Million Man March/Day of Absence Mission Statement."* Reproduced by permission. —Kiet, Kim Huot. From *Asian American Experiences in the United States,* by Joann Faung Jean Lee. McFarland & Company, Inc., 1991. Copyright © 1991 by Joann Faung Jean Lee. All rights reserved. Reproduced by permission. —Kochiyama, Yuri. From *Asian American Experiences in the United States,* by Joann Faung Jean Lee. McFarland & Company, Inc., 1991. Copyright © 1991 by Joann Faung Jean Lee. All rights reserved. Reproduced by permission. —Laxalt, Robert. From *Sweet Promised Land.* Harper & Brothers Publishers, 1957. Copyright 1957, renewed 1985 by Robert Laxalt. Reproduced by permission of HarperCollins Publishers. —Lee, Li-Young. From *The City in Which I Love You.* BOA Editions, Ltd., 1990. Copyright © 1990 by Li-Young Lee. All rights reserved. Reproduced by permission. —Liadis, Nikos. From *American Mosaic: The*

Immigrant Experience in the Words of Those Who Lived It, by Joan Morrison and Charlotte Fox Zabusky. E. P. Dutton, 1980. Copyright © 1980 by Joan Morrison and Charlotte Fox Zabusky. All rights reserved. Reproduced by permission of Joan Morrison and Charlotte Zabusky. —Livo, Norma J., and Dia Cha. From *Folk Stories of the Hmong: Peoples of Laos, Thailand, and Vietnam.* Libraries Unlimited, Inc., 1991. Copyright © 1991 Libraries Unlimited, Inc. All rights reserved. Reproduced by permission. —Lor, Ge. From "Learning American Farming" in *Voices from Southeast Asia,* by John Tenhula. Holmes & Meier, 1991. Copyright © 1991 by Holmes & Meier Publishers, Inc. Reproduced by permission. —Mankiller, Wilma P. From "Inaugural Address," in *Native American Reader: Stories, Speeches and Poems.* Edited by Jerry D. Blanche. The Denali Press, 1990. Copyright © 1990 by Jerry D. Blanche. Reproduced by permission of the publisher. —Means, Russell. From "The State of Native America" in *Native American Reader: Stories, Speeches and Poems.* Edited by Jerry D. Blanche. The Denali Press, 1990. Copyright © 1990 by Jerry D. Blanche. Reproduced by permission of the publisher. —Mohammed, Karim and Aziza Mohammed. From *American Mosaic: The Immigrant Experience in the Words of Those Who Lived It,* by Joan Morrison and Charlotte Fox Zabusky. E. P. Dutton, 1980. Copyright © 1980 by Joan Morrison and Charlotte Fox Zabusky. All rights reserved. Reproduced by permission of Joan Morrison and Charlotte Zabusky. —Namias, June. From *First Generation: In The Words of Twentieth-Century American Immigrants.* Revised edition. University of Illinois Press, 1992. © 1992 by June Namias. Reproduced by permission. —Natividad, Irene. From a keynote address delivered on March 7, 1991, at the symposium of the National Museum of American History Smithsonian Institution in Washington, DC in Proceedings of Specializing in the Impossible: Women and Social Reform in America, 1890-1990 Conference. Reprinted by permission of the author. —Ngan, Lang. From *Asian American Experiences in the United States,* by Joann Faung Jean Lee. McFarland & Company, Inc., 1991. Copyright © 1991 by Joann Faung Jean Lee. All rights reserved. Reproduced by permission. —Phong, Hoang Khoi. From "Twilight" in *Thu Khong Nguoi Nhan.* Translated by Thai Tuyet Quan, Truong Hong Son, and Wayne Karlin. Thoi Van (California), 1991. Copyright © 1991 by Hoang Khoi Phong. Translation © 1995 by Thai Tuyet Quan, Truong Hong Son, and Wayne Karlin. Translated and reproduced by permission of the author. —Qoyawayma, Polingaysi. From *No Turning Back.* University of New Mexico Press, 1964. © The University of New Mexico Press, 1964. All rights reserved. Reproduced by permission. —Ramirez, Marta. From *American Mosaic: The Immigrant Experience in the Words of Those Who Lived It,* by Joan Morrison and Charlotte Fox Zabusky. E. P. Dutton, 1980. Copyright © 1980 by Joan Morrison and Charlotte Fox Zabusky. All rights reserved. Reproduced by permission of Joan Morrison and Charlotte Zabusky. —Rasmussen, Knud. From "The Story of Nuliajuk, Mother of the Sea, Ruler of All Beasts, The Most Dangerous and Terrible of All Spirits, to Whom Nothing Is Impossible" in *Eskimo Songs and Stories.* Translated by Edward Field. Delacorte Press, 1973. Copyright © 1973 by Dell Publishing Co., Inc. All rights reserved. Reproduced by permission of Edward Field. —Reina, Ernesto. From "Seven Days: Diary of a Rafter," in *The Documentary Archives: Multicultural America.* Translated by Beth Wellington. Primary Source Media, 1997. Copyright Primary Source Media 1997. All rights reserved. Reproduced by permission. —Ryu, Charles. From *Asian American Experiences in the United States,* by Joann Faung Jean Lee. McFarland & Company, Inc., 1991. Copyright © 1991 by Joann Faung Jean Lee. All rights reserved. Reproduced by permission. —Sakya, Labring. From *American Mosaic: The Immigrant Experience in the Words of Those Who Lived It,* by Joan Morrison and Charlotte Fox Zabusky. E. P. Dutton, 1980. Copyright © 1980 by Joan Morrison and Charlotte Fox Zabusky. All rights reserved. Reproduced by permission of Joan Morrison and Charlotte Zabusky. —Santoli, Al with M. Daud Nassery. From *New Americans, An Oral History: Immigrants and Refugees in the U.S. Today,* by Al Santoli. Viking Penguin, 1988. Copyright © Al Santoli, 1988. All rights reserved. Reproduced by permission of Penguin Putnam Inc. —Santoli, Al with Paulette Francius. From *New Americans, An Oral History: Immigrants and Refugees in the U.S. Today,* by Al Santoli. Viking Penguin, 1988. Copyright © Al Santoli, 1988. All rights reserved. Reproduced by permission of Penguin Putnam Inc. —

Santoli, Al with Tesfai Gebremariam and Lem Lem Gebremariam. From **New Americans, An Oral History: Immigrants and Refugees in the U.S. Today,** by Al Santoli. Viking Penguin, 1988. Copyright © Al Santoli, 1988. All rights reserved. Reproduced by permission of Penguin Putnam Inc. —Siu, Paul C. P. From **The Chinese Laundryman: A Study of Social Isolation.** Edited by John Kuo Wei Tchen. New York University Press, 1987. Copyright © 1987 by Paul C. Siu All rights reserved. Reproduced by permission. —Smith, Faith. From "I See an Incredible Force within Native People" in **Messengers of the Wind: Native American Women Tell Their Life Stories.** Edited by Jane Katz. Ballantine Books, 1995. Copyright © 1995 by Jane Katz. All rights reserved. Reproduced by permission of Random House, Inc. —Song, Cathy. From **Picture Bride.** Yale University Press, 1983. Copyright © 1983 by Cathy Song. All rights reserved. Reproduced by permission. —Stennett, Rennie. From **American Mosaic: The Immigrant Experience in the Words of Those Who Lived It,** by Joan Morrison and Charlotte Fox Zabusky. E. P. Dutton, 1980. Copyright © 1980 by Joan Morrison and Charlotte Fox Zabusky. All rights reserved. Reproduced by permission of Joan Morrison and Charlotte Zabusky. —Sue, Sam. From **Asian American Experiences in the United States,** by Joann Faung Jean Lee. McFarland & Company, Inc., 1991. Copyright © 1991 by Joann Faung Jean Lee. All rights reserved. Reproduced by permission. —Suettinger, Sue Jean Lee. From **Asian American Experiences in the United States,** by Joann Faung Jean Lee. McFarland & Company, Inc., 1991. Copyright © 1991 by Joann Faung Jean Lee. All rights reserved. Reproduced by permission. —Tracy, Deescheeny Nez. From "Deescheeny Nez Tracy" in **Stories of Traditional Navajo Life and Culture.** Edited by Broderick H. Johnson, translated by Casey Allison & others. Navajo Community College Press, 1977. Copyright © 1977 by Navajo Community College Press. All rights reserved. Reproduced by permission. —Valdez, Luis. From **Zoot Suit and Other Plays.** Copyright © 1992 by Luis Valdez. Arte Público Press—University of Houston. Reproduced by permission. —Whitehorse, Emmi. From "In My Family, The Women Ran Everything" in **Messengers of the Wind: Native American Women Tell Their Life Stories.** Edited by Jane Katz. Ballantine Books, 1995. Copyright © 1995 by Jane Katz. All rights reserved. Reproduced by permission of Random House, Inc. —Whiteman, Roberta Hill. From "Let Us Survive" in **Messengers of the Wind: Native American Women Tell Their Life Stories.** Edited by Jane Katz. Ballantine Books, 1995. Copyright © 1995 by Jane Katz. All rights reserved. Reproduced by permission of Random House, Inc. —Whiteman, Roberta Hill. From **Star Quilt.** Holy Cow Press, 1984. © 1984. Reproduced by permission. —Yamileth. From **Undocumented in L.A.: An Immigrant's Story.** Scholarly Resources Inc., 1997. © 1997 by Scholarly Resources Inc. Reproduced by permission. —Yau, Wong Chun. From **Asian American Experiences in the United States,** by Joann Faung Jean Lee. McFarland & Company, Inc., 1991. Copyright © 1991 by Joann Faung Jean Lee. All rights reserved. Reproduced by permission.

Photographs appearing in the *Gale Encyclopedia of Multicultural America: Primary Documents* were received from the following sources:

Albanian family waiting to board bus at McGuire Air Force Base, New Jersey, May 5, 1999, photograph by Charles Rex Arbogast. AP/Wide World Photos. Reproduced by permission. — Albanian refugee sitting on prayer rug, refugee village, Fort Dix, New Jersey, May 14, 1999, photograph by Charles Rex Arbogast. AP/Wide World Photos. Reproduced by permission. —Amish boys photograph. AP/Wide World Photos. Reproduced by permission. —Amish man in horse and buggy crossing traffic, Lancaster, Pennsylvania, July, 1998, photograph by Rusty Kennedy. AP/Wide World Photos. Reproduced by permission. —"Arapaho Ghost Dance," c. 1900, painting by Mary Irvin Wright based on photographs by James Mooney. National Archives and Records Administration. — Armenian immigrants on Ellis Island, photograph. Corbis-Bettmann. Reproduced by permission. —Barnes, Robert, II, hugs son at Million Man March, Washington, D.C., 1995, photograph. AP/Wide World Photos. Reproduced by permission. —Bates, Daisy, photograph. AP/Wide World Photos. Reproduced by permission. —Batik created in Djojakarta, Java, Indonesia, photograph by Charles Lenars. Corbis/Charles & Jossette Lenars.

Reproduced by permission. —Cherokee Indian scholar Sequoyah, holding his syllabary, lithograph. The Library of Congress. —Cherokee Syllabary, illustration. From *Beginning Cherokee*, by Ruth Bradley Holmes and Betty Sharp Smith. Second Edition. University of Oklahoma Press, 1977. Reproduced by permission. —Chief Joseph (Himaton-yalatkit), 1877, photograph. National Archives. —Chinese launderer, woodcut, photograph. Corbis-Bettmann. Reproduced by permission. —Chisholm, Shirley, photograph. AP/Wide World Photos. Reproduced by permission. —Corner grocery store Japanese American owners interned ("I Am An American"), photograph. National Archives and Records Administration. —Cuban exiles using mirrors to signal shoreline, Florida Straits, July 18, 1998, photograph by Joe Cavaretta. AP/Wide World Photos. Reproduced by permission. —Cuban refugees aboard freighter "Red Diamond," Straits of Florida, June 2, 1980, photograph. UPI/Corbis-Bettmann. Reproduced by permission. —Cuban refugees, June 4, 1980, photograph. Corbis-Bettmann. Reproduced by permission. —Cuban-American children carrying crosses in Patriotic Reaffirmation. March, December 6, 1997, photograph by Joe Cavaretta. AP/Wide World Photos. Reproduced by permission. —Customers waiting in line for zeppole on St. Joseph's Day, Scialo Bros. Bakery, March 19, 1999, photograph by Paul Connors. AP/Wide World Photos. Reproduced by permission. —Dim Sum Dumplings served at Ocean Star Restaurant, Los Angeles, California, photograph by Nik Wheeler. Corbis/Nik Wheeler. Reproduced by permission. —Echford, Elizabeth, photograph. AP/Wide World Photos. Reproduced by permission. —Espada, Martin, photograph by Terry Pitzner. Reproduced by permission of Martin Espada. —Field hands picking Ginseng, photograph by Richard Hamilton Smith. Corbis/Richard Hamilton Smith. Reproduced by permission. —Filipino laborers, Hawaii, 1920's, photograph by George Bacon. Hawaii State Archives. Reproduced by permission of Mrs. George Bacon. —Filipino migrant workers, 1939, photograph by Dorothea Lange. Corbis. Reproduced by permission. —Four Korean Americans, photograph. Reproduced by permission of Jamie Lew. —Funeral for Jorge Mas Canosa, November 25, 1997, Miami, Florida, photograph by Joe Cavaretta. AP/Wide World Photos. Reproduced by permission. —Garcia, David, adding cream topping to zeppole on St. Joseph's Day, Scialo Bros. Bakery, Providence, Rhode Island, March 19, 1999, photograph by Paul Connors. AP/Wide World Photos. Reproduced by permission. —Gelmu Sherpa rubbing "singing bowl," May 20, 1998, photograph by Suzanne Plunkett. AP/Wide World Photos. Reproduced by permission. —Geronimo, 1887, photograph by Ben Wittick. The Library of Congress. —Greek women (five women standing on ship deck), photograph. UPI/Corbis-Bettmann. Reproduced by permission. —Group of Chinese American women doing morning Tai Chi exercises, Washington Square, San Francisco, photograph by Alison Wright. Alison Wright Photography. Reproduced by permission. —Group representing traditional Greek soldiers march in Boston, March 28, 1999, photograph by Patricia McDonnell. AP/Wide World Photos. Reproduced by permission. —Guatemalan Indian woman weaving, photograph by Nik Wheeler. Corbis/Nik Wheeler. Reproduced by permission. —Hayakawa, S.I., photograph. UPI/Corbis-Bettmann. Reproduced by permission. —Hernandez, Antonia, photograph by George Rodriguez. Reproduced by permission of Antonia Hernandez. —Him Mark Lai, reading poetry on Angel Island wall, photograph. AP/Wide World Photos. Reproduced by permission. —I'ini, Lei Ku'u, performing Hawaiian dance, May 24, 1996, photograph by Lennox McLendon. AP/Wide World Photos. Reproduced by permission. —Inouye, Daniel, photograph. UPI/Corbis-Bettmann. Reproduced by permission. —Italian family celebrating Ferragosto, 1947, photograph. UPI/Corbis-Bettmann. Reproduced by permission. —Italian family gathering, 1936, photograph. Corbis-Bettmann. Reproduced by permission. —Japanese American girl standing, holding U. S. flag, Japanese internment camp, photograph. The Library of Congress. —Japanese American relocation (mother and child) during WWII, photograph. Archive Photos, Inc. Reproduced by permission. —Japanese mother and daughter, near Guadeloupe, California, March, 1937, photograph. Corbis. Reproduced by permission. —Jewish Americans celebrating Seder, March 22, 1989, photograph by Roger Ressmeyer. Corbis/Roger Ressmeyer. Reproduced by permission. —Jordan, Barbara, photograph. AP/Wide World Photos. Reproduced by permission. —Kanosky Family, August, 1941. Reproduced by permission of Stella McDermott. —Korean bride in red silk with large bouquet, photograph by Leslye Borden. Leslye Borden/PhotoEdit. Reproduced by permission. —Letter written by members of the Blackfoot tribe to the Honorable Franklin K. Lane, February 23, 1915. The Library of Congress. —Lord, Bette Bao, photograph. AP/Wide World Photos. Reproduced by permission. —Man and woman with kolaches at Kolache Festival, photograph. Kolache Festival. —Mankiller, Wilma 1985, photograph. AP/Wide World Photos. Reproduced by permission. —Mardi Gras float from Krewe of Troth, February, 1994, photograph by Drew Story. Reuters/Drew Story/ Archive Photos, Inc. Reproduced by permission. —Marti, Jose, photograph. Corbis-Bettmann. Reproduced by permission. —Mas Canosa, Jorge, photograph. UPI/Corbis-Bettmann. Reproduced by permission. —Matachine Dancers, Christmas Eve, 1996, photograph by Tom Bean. Corbis/Tom Bean. Reproduced by permission. —Means, Russell, photograph. AP/Wide World Photos. Reproduced by permission. —Million Man March, photograph by Greg Newton. Reuters/Greg Newton/Archive Photos, Inc. Reproduced by permission. —Mormon family in front of log cabin, 1875, photograph. Corbis-Bettmann. Reproduced by permission. —"My Country 'Tis of Thee," cartoon, Life, 1918. —Natividad, Irene, photograph. AP/Wide World Photos. Reproduced by permission. —Nicoloso family at dinner, November 23, 1948, Rome, Italy, photograph. UPI/Corbis-Bettmann. Reproduced by permission. —"No Haitians Need Apply," 1994, political cartoon by Neil R. King. Reproduced by permission of Neil R. King. —Omaq-kat-tsa, Chief of Blackfoot tribe photograph. The Library of Congress. —Paths of Early Europeans, map. National Park Service, Department of the Interior. — Personnel record of Japanese American, featured in exhibit on Ellis Island, April 2, 1998, photograph by Bebeto Matthews. AP/Wide World Photos. Reproduced by permission. —Plantation workers, 1930, photograph. —Proprietor of Greek coffee shop, Aliquippa, Pennsylvania, 1938, photograph by Arthur Rothstein. The Library of Congress. —Protestors, marching to the El Conquistador Hotel July 14, 1996, Fajardo, Puerto Rico, photograph by John McConnico. AP/Wide World Photos. Reproduced by permission. —Roshetsky, Oksana, photograph. UPI/Corbis-Bettmann. Reproduced by permission. —Sadawi, Nawal, October 3, 1993, photograph by Robert Maass. Corbis/Robert Maass. Reproduced by permission. — Seguin, Juan Nepomuceno (in 19th century officer's uniform), painting. U.S. Department of Defense. —Spitzer, Jeff and Carol, holding trays of Kuchen, Eureka Bakery, Eureka, South Dakota, March 15, 1999, photograph by Jill Kokesh. AP/Wide World Photos. Reproduced by permission. —Supporters (Governor Pedro Rossello addresses the crowd in Guanica, Puerto Rico) photograph by Lynne Sladky. AP/Wide World Photos. Reproduced by permission. —"The Good for Nothing in Miss Columbia's School," political cartoon by Thomas Nast. Harper's Weekly, 1871. —"The Water Carriers," 1874, photograph by John K. Hillers. Copyright © 1995-1999 Denver Public Library. Reproduced by permission. —Valdez, Luis, poster of "Zoot Suit" in the background, photograph. AP/Wide World Photos. Reproduced by permission. —Warum, Jodi, directing preparations of Purim baskets with students, Ramaz Hebrew Day School, March 1, 1999, photograph by Tina Fineberg. AP/Wide World Photos. Reproduced by permission. —Williams, Janine Caubit, wearing French resistance armband, May 10, 1999, photograph by Berry Craig. AP/Wide World Photos. Reproduced by permission. —Winnemucca, Sarah, photograph. Nevada Historical Society. Reproduced by permission. —Women on Mulberry Street, Italian Market, New York, circa 1910, photograph. Gift of State Historical Society of Colorado, 1949. The Library of Congress. —Wovoka, or Jack Wilson, photograph. Nevada Historical Society. Reproduced by permission. —Yellow Bird (lying dead on Wounded Knee battlefield), 1891, photograph by George Trager. The Library of Congress. —Zia, Helen, photograph. Reproduced by permission.

JAMAICAN AMERICANS

In an oral history interview taken in October of 1938, Wilbert J. Miller, a Jamaican immigrant, talks about Marcus Garvey and a speech he made at Madison Square Garden in 1920 inciting "the 400,000,000 Negroes of the World" to take back Africa for themselves. The informant quotes much of the speech made by Garvey and gives a thorough description of the meeting of delegates for the "Back to Africa Movement." The convention lasted a month and its climax was a parade of 50,000 people through the streets of Harlem. The interview gives an excellent account of Garvey's activism and downfall, and speaks to his importance as a symbol for all African Americans.

Garvey, a Jamaican immigrant himself, was a flamboyant character with strong opinions and the oratory and leadership skills to voice them. Born in St. Ann's Bay, Jamaica in 1887, he founded the Universal Negro Improvement and Conservation Association and African Communities League, also called the Universal Negro Improvement Association (UNIA). The organization was originally founded in Jamaica, but did not attract a following there, and so Garvey immigrated to the United States in 1916. Miller's account indicated that the movement was not officially organized in the United States until 1918. The primary goal of UNIA was the formation of an independent black nation in Africa. He brought branches of UNIA to Harlem and other black ghettos in cities throughout the Northeast. This followed the immigration patterns of Jamaicans who came primarily to New York City, with immigration beginning early in the twentieth century and peaking in the late 1910s and early 1920s. Almost three quarters of Jamaicans are located in New York City, with other large communities in Washington, D.C., Miami, and Hartford.

Garvey also founded a newspaper, Negro World, to promote his views. Using money from the Association, Garvey founded the Negro Factories Corporation, the Black Star Line, and a chain of restaurants, grocery stores, laundries, a hotel and a printing press, all of which were created specifically to serve blacks. Garvey's popularity began to dwindle in 1921, when his radical ideas began to alienate African Americans and the NAACP. Garvey's business ventures, especially the Black Star Line, became unstable, and he solicited investors via the U.S. Mail. This led to his conviction for mail fraud in 1923, his imprisonment and eventual deportation in 1927. Membership and interest in the UNIA flagged, and after Garvey's death in 1940, the organization disbanded entirely. Garvey, however, is remembered as an important figure in black history, and is traced as one of the predecessors of the black nationalism movement which was prominent in the late 1960s and early 1970s.

ALMOST MADE KING

FORM A: Circumstances of Interview

1. Date and time of interview: Oct. 4th, 5th, 10th, 12th, 19th

2. Place of interview: Informant's home, 224 W. 140th St.

3. Name and address of informant: Wilbert J. Miller, 224 W. 140th St. Apt 9

4. Name and address of person, if any, who put you in touch with informant:

5. Name and address of person, if any, accompanying:

6. Description of room, house, surroundings, etc.: Five room apartment, comfortably furnished, Neighborhood entirely Negro.

FORM B: Personal History of Informant

1. Ancestry:

2. Place and date of birth: Jamaica, B. W. I.—April 2nd 1870

3. Family: Wife and one daughter

4. Places lived in, with dates: Jamaica England and South Africa

5. Education, with dates: Elementary

6. Occupations and accomplishments, with dates: Interior Decorator

7. Special skills and interests:

8. Community and religious activities: Member of Seventh Day Adventist Church Universal Negro Improvement Association

9. Description of informant: About 5 ft 11 in, tall, Negro, mixed gray hair weight about 185 lbs.

10. Other Points gained in interview:

FORM C: Text of Interview (Unedited)

So you want me to tell you something about Negro Folklore well, here's a story about a strapping, jet-black Negro that will live as long as folk tales are handed down from generation to generation. To many, he was a clown; a jester who wanted to play at being king but, to hundreds of thousands of Negroes, he was a magnificent leader and martyr to a great cause; complete and unconditional social and economic freedom for Negroes everywhere. And, had it not been for one flaw in his plan of action, there would probably be no more than a handful us Negroes in America today.

His name was Marcus Garvey. He was born, so the records say, on the island of Jamaica in the British West Indies about 1887, but few people ever heard of him until he came to New York. He was a born orator and his power to attract and hold an audience was destined to make him famous.

I remember his first important speech.

"Wherever I go, whether it be France, Germany, England, or Spain, I am told that there is no room for a Negro. The other races have countries of their own and it is time for the 400,000,000 Negroes of the world to claim Africa for themselves. Therefore, we shall demand and expect of the world a Free Africa. The black man has been serf, a tool, a slave and peon long enough.

That day has ceased.

We have reached the time when every minute, every second must count for something done, something achieved in the cause for Africa. We need the freedom of Africa now. At this moment methinks, I see Ethiopia stretching forth her hands unto God, and methinks I see the Angel of God taking up the standard of the Red, the Black, and the Green, and sayings; Men of the Negro race, Men of Ethiopia, follow me:

"It falls to our lot to tear off the shackles that bind Mother Africa. Can you do it? You did it in the Revolutionary War. You did it in the Civil War. You did it in the battles of Maine and Verdum. You did it in the Mesopotamia. You can do it marching up the battle heights of Africa. Climb ye the heights of liberty and cease not in well-doing until you have planted the banner of the Red, the Black, and the Green upon the hilltops of Africa."

These, my child, were the very words of the man Marcus Garvey, whom many called the black Napoleon. I remember them well as you, perhaps, remember Lincoln's Gettysburg address. He was standing there, strong and forceful before a crowd of more than 25,000 Negroes who had assembled in Madison Square Garden to consider the problems of the Negro race. It was shortly after the World War, August 1920 I believe.

Well that was a sight to thrill you with pride. Imagine, huge spacious Madison Square Garden, rocking with the yells of 25,000 frenzied Negro patriots demanding a free Africa, from the Strait of Gibraltar to the cape of Good Hope—a Negro republic run exclusively by and for Negroes. Doesn't sound real, does it? Well, it happened—and it can happen again, but not until another leader with Marcus Garvey's strength, vision and courage comes along. Some people say that Father Divine is the answer to this need. Personally I doubt it. He is a good organizer but his Divinites are not to be compared with the powerful and vigorous following once commanded by the Universal Negro Improvement Association that Garvey founded and built single-handed. Why, he had such a magnetic personality that people flocked to see him wherever he went, and when he appeared on any platform to speak he'd have to wait sometimes five or ten minutes before the loud ovations an sounds of applause subsided. Then he would stride majestically forward in his cap and gown of purple, green and gold, and the hall, arena, square, or whatever it was, would become magically silent.

He was always an enigma to the white people who flocked, in great numbers, to hear him, They couldn't decide whether to consider him a political menace or a harmless buffoon. But to his several hundred thousand Negro followers he was a great leader with a wonderful idea, an unequaled program of emancipation. He did not claim to be a great intellectual, a Frederick Douglas or Booker T. Washington, but he was certainly endowed with color and originality; so much so that he caught the fancy and commanded the solid support of the Negro masses, as no other man has done before or since. He had the unusual happy faculty for stirring their race consciousness.

I can see him even now as he stood and exhorted his followers at that first organizational meeting.

He read a telegram of greeting to Eamon De Valera, President of the Irish Republic, wait a minute, I'll look among my papers and find a copy of it for you.

Here it is. It says; "25,000 Negro delegates assembled in Madison Square Garden in Mass Meeting, representing 1000,000,000 Negroes of the world, send you greetings as President of the Irish Republic Please accept sympathy of the Negroes of the world for your cause We believe Ireland should be free even as Africa shall be free for the Negroes of the world. Keep up the fight for a free Ireland."

After that, he spoke at length and if I remember correctly, his speech went something like this;

"We are descendants of a suffering people. We are descendants of a people determined to suffer no longer. Our forefathers suffered many years of abuse from an alien race.

It was claimed that the black man came from a backward people, not knowing and not awake to the bigger callings of civilization. That might have been true years ago, but it is not true today.

Fifty-five years ago the black man was set free from slavery on this continent. Now he declares that what is good for the white man of this age is also good for the Negro. They as a race, claim freedom, and claim the right to establish a democracy. We shall now organize the 400,000,000 Negroes of the World into a vast organization to plant the banner of freedom on the great continent of Africa. We have no apologies to make, and will make none. We do not desire what has belonged to others, though others have always sought to deprive us of that which belonged to us.

We new Negroes will dispute every inch of the way until we win.

We have no apologies to make, and will make none. We do not desire what has belonged to others, though others have always sought to deprive us of that which belonged to us.

We will begin by framing a bill of rights of the Negro race with a constitution to guide the life and destiny of the 400,000,000. The Constitution of the United States means that every white American would shed his blood to defend that Constitution. The constitution, of the Negro race will mean that every Negro will shed his blood to defend his Constitution.

If Europe is for the Europeans, then Africa shall be for the black peoples of the world, we say it. We mean it."

****

Following the thirty day organizational convention of the Universal Negro Improvement Association at Madison Square Garden, more than three thousand delegates and sympathizers of the group gathered in Harlem at Liberty Hall, 140 West 138 Street, where they gave their final approval of the declaration of rights of the Negro peoples of the world. Delegates were there from Africa as well as the West Indian and Bermuda Islands. It was a memorable occasion.

Decorating the huge hall were banners of the various delegations. Prominently displayed also were the red, black and green flags of the new African [Republic-to-be]. A colorful, forty piece band, a choir of fifty male and female voices and several quartets entertained the assembly all during the early part of the evening. Afterwards, Marcus Garvey, president general of the association, announced the business of the meeting and read the declaration.

Much applause greeted the reading of the preamble to the declaration which stated: "In order to encourage our race all over the world and to stimulate it to overcome the handicaps and difficulties surrounding it, and to push forward to a higher and grander destiny, we demand and insist upon the following declaration of rights."

Then followed the fifty four statements of rights that the association demanded for Negroes everywhere. The first was similar in form to the American Declaration of Independence. It read: "Whereas all men are created equal and entitled to the rights of life, liberty and the pursuits of happiness, and because of this, we, dully elected representatives of the Negro people of the world, invoking the aid of the just and almighty God, do declare all men, women and children of our blood throughout the world free denizens, and do claim them as free citizens of Africa, the motherland of all Negroes."

The first statement was greeted with loud and prolonged applause, as were many others that followed it, but there was so much enthusiasm, shouting, stamping of feet and other exhibitions of approval at the conclusion of the following statement that the chairman was forced to appeal, again and again for order. It read: "We declare that no Negro shall engage himself in battle for an alien race without first obtaining consent of the leader of the Negro peoples of the world, except in a matter of national self-defense."

Another statement which met with popular fancy was: "We assert that the Negro is entitled to even-handed justice before all courts of law and equity, in whatever country he may be found, and when this is denied him on account of his race or color, such denial is an insult to the race as a whole, and should be resented by the entire body of Negroes.

"We deprecate the use of the term 'nigger' as applied to Negroes and demand that the word 'negro' be written with a Capital 'N'.

"We demand a free and unfettered commercial intercourse[?] with all the Negro peoples of the world. We demand that the governments of the world recognize our leader and his representatives chosen by the race to look after the welfare of our people under such governments. We call upon the various governments to represent the general welfare of the Negro peoples of the world.

"We demand that our duly accredited representatives be given proper recognition in all leagues, conferences, conventions or courts of international arbitration whenever human rights are discussed.

"We proclaim the first day of August of each year to be an international holiday to be observed by all Negroes."

The thing that makes this ambitious adventure all the more remarkable, my child, is the fact that all these strong resolutions and gigantic plans were conceived entirely by this one man, Marcus Garvey, who, in the beginning, was just another underprivileged West Indian boy; a printer's apprentice. Fired with the idea of welding the divided black masses of the world together, however, he became an entirely different and revolutionary personality.

Garvey worked his way to London and studied, at night, at the University. His education was supplemented by travel and observations in the different European countries. He did not get to Africa but listened attentively to many fellow ships' passengers who told of the cruelty inflicted on the natives in many districts. Later, Garvey worked on freighters that touched several of the West Indian, Central and South American ports. He had many opportunities to observe the exploitation of the black workers of quite a few different countries who created vast fortunes for their white bosses while they lived in abject poverty. Once he is quoted as having said: "Poverty is a hellish state to be in. It is no virtue, it is a crime."

And so, it was this knowledge of unfavorable working conditions for black men everywhere that fired the wandering, giant Negro with his idea of a separate country and homeland for these oppressed peoples; a country with a civilization second to none. Africa, he felt, was the logical country. Thus was born the "Back to Africa" movement.

Nineteen seventeen saw the actual beginning of the Garvey movement but not until the Spring of nineteen eighteen did Marcus succeed in officially organizing the Universal Negro Improvement Association. Later, in the Fall, he established his own newspaper, "The Negro World" and began a systematic appeal for contributions to the movement. It was also his medium for preaching his doctrines to the out of town public. Week by week the paper's editorial pages aired his opinions.

Soon, money began pouring into the coffers of the Association, and it was not long before Garvey organized a steamship company, known as the Black Star Line, and scheduled to operate between the West Indies, Africa and the United States. During the winter of 1919 alone, more than half a million dollars worth of stock was sold to Negroes. One Negro college in the state of Louisiana was reputed to have raised seven thousand dollars for promotion of the scheme. Three ships, Garvey said, had been bought from the entire proceeds of the national fund: The Yarmouth, the Maceo and line Shadysiah. Another, the Phyllis Wheatley, was advertised weekly in the Negro World. It was claimed that she would ply between Cuba, St. Kitts, Barbados, Trinidad, Demerara, Dakar and Monrovia. The only hitch was, the date of sailing never came. In fact, the mass inspection of the Phyllis Wheatley that Garvey kept promising his followers, never came. Certain doubters in the organization then began to wonder whether there was any ship at all they went even further than that. They sent a delegation to His Highness, the President, with a demand to see the boat. Garvey, always at ease in the face of any difficult situation, that them that he would attend to it the next day. When the next day came, he put them off again. And so it went from day to day.

This difficult situation arose during the famous "first convention" that was held in August 1920 and lasted for thirty days. There was a grand and imposing parade through the streets of Harlem and the colorful, regal mass meetings at Madison Square Garden and Liberty Hall. Garvey said he was busy. There was nothing for the delegates to do but wait. The publicity that the movement received during this gigantic display of marching legions and blaring trumpets, skyrocketed the circulation of the "Negro World" to the amazing figure of 75,000 unprecedented in the field of weekly Negro journalism. It was one of the instruments that made Garvey the most powerful black man in America at that time. Harlem and black America were literally at his feet.

Garvey then bought a chain of grocery stores, restaurants, beauty and barber shops, laundries, women's wear shops, and a score or more of other small businesses. He instituted a one-man campaign to completely monopolize the small industries in Harlem and drive the white store-keepers out. His one big mistake came, however, when he printed and issued circulars asking for additional purchasers of Black Star Line stock and assuring prospective buyers of the financial soundness of the company. This was too much for the delegates who had been asking for a detailed accounting of the Associations' funds throughout the entire convention only to get the run around. They immediately petitioned the U.S. Post Office Department of Inspection to investigate the company's books. When the true state of affairs was brought to light, Garvey was immediately indicted for using the mails to defraud. The investigation also brought to light the fact that Garvey had collected thousand of dollars for his so called "defense fund".

Well, to make a long story short, by June 1924, instead of perching majestically on his golden throne in some far away jungle clearing, being waited and danced attendance upon by titled nobles, the erstwhile Black Napoleon and Provisional President of Africa, found himself sitting, disconsolate and alone, in a bare cell of the Tombs prison. It was the culmination of a 27 day trail in the United States District Court. The jury, after listening to testimony and arguments for practically the entire duration of that time, brought in a verdict of 'guilty'. Marcus, the great, had been duly and officially convicted of using the mails to defraud.

Loyal officers of the movement had a bail bondsman on hand, ready to secure the release of their idol but the Assistant U.S. District Attorney foiled this move by asking that Garvey be remained to prison without bail. His [request] was granted when the Court was told that Garvey's African Legion was well supplied with guns and ammunition and would probably help their chief to escape.

And so, in the midst of heavily armed U.S. Marshals and a detachment of New York City policemen, the "Leader of the Negro Peoples of the World", was marched off to the, anything but comfortable and homelike, atmosphere, of the Tombs. Later he was transferred to Atlanta. With him went his dreams of a great Black Empire, his visions of a final welding of all Negroes into one strong, powerful nation, with himself as dictator; his favorite supporters, elegant lords, princes, dukes and other personages of high-sounding title: like "High Commissioner", "His Highness and Royal Potentate", "Minister of the African Legion", "The Right Honorable High Chancellor", "His Excellency, Prince of Uganda", "Lord of the Nile" and so on.

Yes, there's no doubt about it, Garvey had grandiloquent ideas. Conceiving and attempting to put over big things was his specialty. But like most dreamers, he dreamed just a little too much. He was too little the realist. Otherwise, his story might have been different. As it was, few of his dreams ever came true; not, mind you, of their lack of soundness. I still feel that he was a great man, honest and sincere. But he was not practical. Conducting a business enterprise according to established rules meant very little to him. That was his undoing. But there was no denying the fact that he was a colorful personality. The way he thought up such grand titles for his subjects was only one manifestation of it. In defense of conferring these titles, by the way, Garvey said:

"It is human nature that when you make a man know that you are going to reward him and recognize and appreciate him for services rendered, and place him above others, he is going to do the best that is in him."

Garvey also called attention to the fact that the conferring of degrees by colleges and universities adopted from European customs, is only parallel to the conferring of titles by the Universal Negro Improvement Association. The only differ-ence being that one is scholastic, the other political. And, perhaps he was right.

Source:

Library of Congress. *American Life Histories: Manu-scripts from the Federal Writers' Project, 1936-1940* from the American Memory website: (http://memory.loc.gov/ammem/wpaintro/wpa-home.html).

JAPANESE AMERICANS

At the time Japan bombed Pearl Harbor on December 7, 1941, some 125,000 persons of Japanese birth (called Issei) or descent (Nisei) were living in the United States. The Nisei, as people born on American soil, were U.S. citizens, and many of the Issei had obtained citizenship. Certainly the vast majority of them considered themselves Americans, with all the loyalties that this implied; but in a wave of hysteria that followed the outbreak of World War II, they lost many of their civil liberties.

On February 19, 1942, President Franklin D. Roosevelt (1882-1945; President 1933-1945) signed Executive Order 9066, which led to the internment of thousands of Japanese in camps throughout the United States. Executive Order 9066 did not explicitly provide for such internment, nor did it even mention the Japanese Americans as such; rather, it "authorize[d] the Secretary of War, and the Military Commanders whom he may from time to time designate . . . to prescribe military areas . . . from which any or all persons may be excluded." The order went on to authorize all government agencies to assist in the necessary relocation of persons from sensitive areas.

Public Law 503 followed Executive Order 9066, and provided punishments for those who defied it. Again, the law made no mention of Japanese Americans, but its meaning had already become painfully clear to thousands of Issei and Nisei. The worst treatment occurred initially in Hawaii, where a state of martial law had been declared and habeas corpus suspended. This meant that persons arrested had no right to appeal their arrest or conviction, and within a short time, more than 3,000 Japanese Americans were herded into concentration camps.

Of course the term "concentration camp" requires some qualification, given the fact that during World War II, the term acquired a whole new meaning. Certainly the conditions applied to the Issei and Nisei were nowhere near as severe as those used by Nazi Germany, or even the Japanese forces, against civilians. People were not exterminated in America's camps, and in fact many thousands of babies were born in U.S. internment facilities during that time. In contrast to the torture meted out in German or Japanese prisons, the worst techniques used by the authorities at the camps in Hawaii included threats of violence and forcing people to eat in the rain.

The internment of Japanese Americans can only be evaluated properly by the standards of U.S. law and practice, not by those of its enemies; and by those standards it has been judged an appalling act. On the West Coast alone, persons of Japanese ancestry were deprived of nearly half a billion dollars in annual income, along with tens of millions of dollars more in personal property. Families were uprooted and forced to live in barracks-style housing, usually in desolate areas of the American West. They were treated, quite simply, as prisoners.

The War Relocation Authority (WRA), which had taken over the relocation of the Japanese Americans from the army, began in 1943 to begin returning former internees to civilian life—though far from their homes on the West Coast. Many communities refused to allow Japanese in their area, and several persons who relo-

cated became victims of vigilante attacks. Thus although the WRA managed to relocate some 55,000 persons by war's end, many more remained in the camps voluntarily, for fear of what awaited them outside.

The persons interned, the vast majority of the Japanese Americans living in America at the time, were threatened in the two areas of perhaps greatest importance to Americans and Japanese respectively: liberty and dignity. Their treatment seems particularly ironic in light of their professed patriotism, even in the face of mistreatment by their adopted country. Thus at the camp in Topaz, Utah, where internees were allowed to take adult education courses, the two most popular classes were the English language and American history.

Particularly notable was the performance of many thousands of Nisei in the U.S. armed forces. Most served in segregated units such as the 100th Infantry Battalion and the 442nd Regimental Combat Team. The latter fought in Italy, where its members earned literally thousands of decorations, including 3,600 Purple Hearts, which are awarded to soldiers wounded in combat. A few were even allowed to fight in the Pacific, where Staff Sergeant Kenny Yasui became a hero by posing as a Japanese colonel and taking 13 enemy soldiers prisoner.

Among the Japanese American soldiers who served with distinction was Daniel K. Inouye (1924-). In 1988 Inouye, as a senator from Hawaii, cosponsored a bill with several other Japanese American legislators which called for apologies and cash payments of $20,000 tax-free dollars to each of the 60,000 internment victims still living. This became the Civil Liberties Act of 1988, which also provided for people of the Aleutian Islands whose property had been seized during the war. In 1989, Congress passed a second bill to assure that the payments would be made.

EXECUTIVE ORDER 9066

WHEREAS the successful prosecution of the war requires every possible protection against espionage and against sabotage to national-defense material, national-defense premises, and national-defense utilities as defined in Section 4, Act of April 20, 1918, 40 Stat. 533, as amended by the Act of November 30, 1940, 54 Stat. 1220, and the Act of August 21, 1941, 55 Stat. 655 (U.S.C., Title 50, Sec 104):

NOW, THEREFORE, by virtue of the authority vested in me as President of the United States, and Commander in Chief of the Army and Navy, I hereby authorize and direct the Secretary of War, and the Military Commanders whom he may from time to time designate, whenever he or any designated Commander deems such action necessary or desirable, to prescribe military areas in such places and of such extent as he or the appropriate Military Commander may determine, from which any or all persons may be excluded, and with respect to which, the right of any person to enter, remain in,

or leave shall be subject to whatever restrictions the Secretary of War or the appropriate Military Commander may determine, from which any or all persons may be excluded, and with respect to which, the right of any person to enter, remaining, or leave shall be subject to whatever restrictions the Secretary of War or the appropriate Military Commander may impose in his discretion. The Secretary of War is hereby authorized to provide for residents of any such area who are excluded therefrom, such transportation, food, shelter, and other accommodations as may be necessary, in the judgment of the Secretary of War or the said Military Commander, and until other arrangements are made, to accomplish the purpose of this order. The designation of military areas in any region or locality shall supersede designations of prohibited and restricted areas by the Attorney General under the Proclamations of December 7 and 8, 1941, and shall supersede the responsibility and authority of the Attorney General under the said Proclamations in respect of such prohibited and restricted areas.

The patriotism of Japanese Americans was unfairly questioned during World War II.

I hereby further authorize and direct the Secretary of War and said Military Commanders to take such other Commander to take such other steps as he or the appropriate Military Commander may deem advisable to enforce compliance with the restrictions applicable to each Military area hereinabove authorized to be designated, including the use of Federal troops and other Federal Agencies, with authority to accept assistance of state and local agencies.

I hereby further authorize and direct all Executive Departments, independent establishments and other Federal Agencies, to assist the Secretary of War or the said Military Commanders in carrying out this Executive Order, including the furnishing of medical aid, hospitalization, food, clothing, transportation, use of land, shelter, and other supplies, equipment, utilities, facilities, and services.

This order shall not be construed as modifying or limiting in any way the authority heretofore granted under Executive Order No. 8972, dated December 12, 1941, nor shall it be construed as limiting or modifying the duty and responsibility of the Federal Bureau of Investigation, with respect to the investigation of alleged acts of sabotage or the duty and responsibility of the Attorney General and the Department of Justice under the Proclamations of December 7 and 8, 1941, prescribing regulations for the conduct and control of alien enemies, except as such duty and responsibility is superseded by the designation of military areas hereunder.

Franklin D. Roosevelt
The White House, February 19, 1942.

Source:

Asian American Almanac. Susan Gall, Managing Editor. Detroit: Gale Research, 1995. pp. 238-239.

I AM AN AMERICAN

Source:
Library of Congress.

PUBLIC LAW 503

Be it enacted by the Senate and House of Representatives of the United States of America in Congress assembled, That whoever shall enter, remain in, leave, or commit any act in any military area or military zone prescribed, under the authority of an Executive order of the President, by the Secretary of War, or by any military commander designated by the Secretary of War, contrary to the restrictions applicable to any such area or zone or contrary to the order of the Secretary of War or any such military commander, shall, if it appears that he knew or should have known of the existence and extent of the restrictions or order and that his act was in violation thereof, be guilty of a misdemeanor and upon conviction shall be liable to a fine of not to exceed $5,000 or to imprisonment for not more than one year, or both, for each offense.

Approved, March 21, 1942.

Source:

Asian American Almanac. Susan Gall, Managing Editor. Detroit: Gale Research, 1995. pp. 239.

CIVIL LIBERTIES ACT OF 1988

"Restitution for World War II internment of Japanese-Americans and Aleuts,"

50 App. USCA s 1989, 50 App. USCA s 1989

The purposes of this Act (sections 1989 to 1989d of this Appendix) are to—

(1) acknowledge the fundamental injustice of the evacuation, relocation, and internment of United States citizens and permanent resident aliens of Japanese ancestry during World War II;

(2) apologize on behalf of the people of the United States for the evacuation, relocation, and internment of such citizens and permanent resident aliens;

(3) provide for a public education fund to finance efforts to inform the public about the internment of such individuals so as to prevent the recurrence of any similar event;

(4) make restitution to those individuals of Japanese ancestry who were interned;

(5) make restitution to Aleut residents of the Pribilof Islands and the Aleutian Islands west of Unimak Island, in settlement of United States obligations in equity and at law, for—

(A) injustices suffered and unreasonable hardships endured while those Aleut residents were under United States control during World War II;

(B) personal property taken or destroyed by United States forces during World War II;

(C) community property, including community church property, taken or destroyed by United States forces during World War II; and

(D) traditional village lands on Attu Island not rehabilitated after World War II for Aleut occupation or other productive use;

(6) discourage the occurrence of similar injustices and violations of civil liberties in the future; and

(7) make more credible and sincere any declaration of concern by the United States over violations of human rights committed by other nations.

Source:

Public Law 100-383, Sec. 1, Aug. 10, 1988, 102 Stat. 903. Available online at http://www.udayton.edu/~race/japanam.htm (last accessed September 28, 1999).

This document consists of two identification records of Japanese Americans, part of a show subtitled "Alien Enemy or Prisoner of War." These identification records are displayed in an exhibit on Ellis Island in New York. Ellis Island was once the gateway to the New World and was also a detention center for many immigrants, including the Japanese. This exhibit records the poor treatment of Japanese Americans by their country during World War II.

IDENTIFICATION RECORDS

Source:
Library of Congress.

One of the most colorful—and controversial—public figures in recent American history was Samuel Ichiye Hayakawa (1906-1992), a noted educator and university administrator who burst onto the national scene in the late 1960s and later entered the realm of politics. Known as "Don" to family and friends, he was born in Vancouver, British Columbia, Canada, to parents who had immigrated from Japan. His father ran an import-export business and frequently moved his wife and four children from one Canadian city to another until he finally returned to his native country in 1929.

Unable to secure a teaching position in Canada after graduating from the University of Wisconsin, Hayakawa remained in Madison to teach adult students in the university's extension division. He left there in 1939 to take a job as instructor in English at the Illinois Institute of Technology in Chicago. He remained at the school throughout the 1940s, moving up to the rank of assistant professor of English in 1940 and associate professor in 1942.

At the same time he was advancing his academic career, Hayakawa was also making a name for himself outside the classroom. During the late 1930s, after observing Adolf Hitler and other totalitarian leaders of Europe skillfully manipulate words and symbols to seize and maintain political control, he began working on a book that he hoped would explain this deliberate misuse of language to students as well as to a general audience. Based on the theories of Alfred Korzybski, considered the founder of general semantics (the study of how people evaluate words and how that evaluation in turn influences their behavior), Hayakawa's Language in Action (entitled Language in Thought and Action in subsequent editions) was published in 1941. With its blend of humor and clear explanations of a difficult yet fascinating subject, it became a bestseller and has remained a staple in many high school and college courses.

Hayakawa soon was recognized as one of the leading experts in the field and went on to establish the International Society for General Semantics and serve for nearly thirty years as editor of its quarterly journal, ETC. He later wrote a total of seven other books on language and communication, including Language, Meaning and Maturity (1954), Our Language and Our World (1959), Symbol, Status and Personality (1963), and Through the Communication Barrier (1979). All were written in a way that was understandable to a popular audience, an approach that led some in the academic community to reject Hayakawa as not "scholarly" enough. He shrugged off the criticism and continued to do as he pleased, which was to find ways of enhancing appreciation for his teachings by relating them to situations people might encounter in everyday life.

In 1955, after a five-year stint as an instructor in semantics at the University of Chicago, Hayakawa joined the faculty of San Francisco State College (later University) on a part-time basis, which allowed him the freedom to lecture elsewhere (which he did frequently) and write. He was still there when growing student unrest at San Francisco State thrust him into the unexpected role of college president near the end of 1968.

Hayakawa's sudden promotion came after an especially turbulent year on campuses across the nation. Demonstrations, sit-ins, and strikes had become popular means of protest by students as well as faculty members at many institutions, and San Francisco State was no exception. There, a relatively small group of radical students demanded that the school eliminate the ROTC program, relax admission standards to make it possible for more members of minority groups to enroll, establish a separate black studies department, and reinstate a suspended black instructor. When officials refused to agree to these "non-negotiable" demands, some students proceeded to disrupt classes, vandalize buildings, and launch a strike. Local police were called in to restore order, but the turmoil continued for weeks throughout 1968 and led to the resignations of two San Francisco State presidents within seven months.

In 1973, Hayakawa retired from the presidency of San Francisco State, switched his official party affiliation from Democrat to Republican, and announced his intention to seek a seat in the U.S. Senate. Under California law, however, he turned out to be ineligible to run because he did not change parties at least 12 months before becoming a candidate. Undaunted, Hayakawa tried again in 1976 and won on a platform that emphasized conservative measures such as decentralized government, lower taxes, and fewer regulations on business.

Although he preferred to describe himself as a "Republican unpredictable," Hayakawa quickly revealed himself to be one of the most conservative members of the Senate. He opposed busing to achieve racial integration in public schools, tried to withhold public funds from universities with affirmative action programs, supported reducing the minimum wage for younger workers, and proposed a constitutional amendment making English the country's official language. He also was known for his eccentricities, among them his habit of nodding off during Senate proceedings—a practice that earned him the nickname "Sleepin' Sam." (He claimed that he only fell asleep when a speaker took twenty minutes to say something that could have been said in two.) What was not generally known, however, was that Hayakawa suffered from the sleeping disorder narcolepsy, which quite suddenly plunges its victims into brief periods of deep sleep.

By the time he was up for re-election in 1982, Hayakawa had lost the backing of wealthy California conservatives, so he quickly withdrew from the race. But he did not completely desert politics or abandon the spotlight. From 1983 until 1990, for example, he served as special advisor to the U.S. Secretary of State for East Asian and Pacific Affairs. He also caused an uproar in the Japanese American community during the 1980s when he opposed efforts to seek redress for those who had been uprooted from their homes and sent to internment camps during World War II because they were perceived as a threat to national security. (Hayakawa was a Canadian citizen at the time and living in Chicago, so he was spared the fate of many West Coast Japanese Americans.) He argued that it was a reasonable course of action for the U.S. government to take given the bombing of Pearl Harbor and the well-known ferocity of Japanese soldiers and that he was "embarrassed" by the "ridiculous" attempts of some to seek an apology and compensation for their imprisonment.

Because Hayakawa himself had experienced racial prejudice—he was denied citizenship until the mid-1950s on account of his race, and his longtime marriage to a white woman was not considered legal in many states—many people, especially other Japanese Americans, found his conservative stance on such issues puzzling if not infuriating. Although he later reversed his position on the redress question, he created a yet another stir with his outspoken opposition to making the United States a bilingual society, declaring that "the most rapid way of getting out of the ghetto is to speak good English."

In an expression of support for this cause, Hayakawa helped establish and then served as honorary chairman of U.S. English, a private lobbying organization based in Washington, D.C., that is dedicated to making English the country's official language and abolishing bilingual education programs in public schools. He also founded the California English Campaign, which in 1986 succeeded in persuading voters to have English declared the official language of that particular state. (Several other states—mostly those with large Hispanic populations—have since followed suit.)

On April 23, 1982, in an appearance in the nation's capital before the Subcommittee on Education, Arts and Humanities of the Senate Committee on Labor and Human Resources, Hayakawa (who was then still a member of the Senate) outlined the reasons behind his opposition to fostering bilingualism in the United States. He also used the occasion to urge support for his proposed constitutional amendment as well as for a pending bilingual education bill.

BILINGUAL EDUCATION IMPROVEMENT ACT: A COMMON BASIS FOR COMMUNICATION

Thank you, Mr. Chairman. I am honored to follow the testimony of my good friend Secretary Terrel Bell of the Department of Education. He has described in detail the Bilingual Education Improvement Act, S. 2412, which I introduced in the Senate this past Wednesday. I am pleased to work with Secretary Bell on this issue, as we are both committed to giving school districts more flexibility in their teaching methods while targeting the immigrant population in greatest need of English instruction.

"All too often, bilingual education programs have strayed from their original intent of teaching English."

Today I would like to address bilingual education as it relates to a much broader issue: the question of what language will be used in the United States. As most of you know I have proposed a constitutional amendment, Senate Joint Resolution 72, which declares as the law of the land what is already a social and political reality: that English is the official language of the United States. This amendment is needed to clarify the confusing signals we have given in recent years to immigrant groups. For example the requirements for naturalization as a U.S. citizen say you must be able to "read, write and speak words in ordinary usage in

the English language." And though you must be a citizen to vote, some recent legislation has required bilingual ballots in certain locations. This amendment would end that contradictory, logically conflicting situation.

Our immigration laws already require English for citizenship. The role of bilingual education is then to equip immigrants with the necessary English language skills to qualify them for this requirement. The problem is that all too often, bilingual education programs have strayed from their original intent of teaching English. A related issue is the full scale of interpretations for the term "bilingual education." Chances are that when one asks five people for a definition, five very different answers will be given. According to one interpretation, it simply means the teaching of English to non-English-speakers. This is the method I prefer and is usually called English-as-a-Second-Language or ESL. On the opposite side of the scale bilingual education is a more or less permanent two-track education system involving the maintenance of a second culture and an emphasis on ethnic heritage. This method is called transitional bilingual education and involves teaching academic subjects to immigrants in their own language coupled with English language instruction. This is the definition used to determine eligibility for Title VII funding.

We all grew up with the concept of the American melting pot, that is the merging of a multitude of foreign cultures into one. This melting pot has succeeded in creating a vibrant new culture among peoples of many different cultural backgrounds largely because of the widespread use of a common language, English. In this world of national strife, it is a unique concept. I believe every member of this committee will agree that it had a fundamental impact on our nation's greatness. In light of the growing emphasis on maintaining a second culture and instruction in the native languages, I ask myself what are we trying to do? Where do we want to go? Demographic research tells us that in some of our states, ten or twenty years from now there will be a majority of individuals with Spanish background. It seems to me that we are preparing the ground for permanently and officially bilingual states. From here to separatist movements à la Québec would be the final step. Is this the development which we want to promote?

I believe that my constitutional amendment as well as my Title VII amendments will prevent a crisis similar to the separatist movement of French Canadians. That confused state of affairs is a result of controversy about which language shall be the official one used in Canada. I want to avoid a similar situation here in America where use of another language is encouraged to the point that it could become an official language alongside English. This would perpetuate differences between English-speaking and non-English-speaking citizens and isolate one group from the other. There can be no doubt that recent immigrants love this country and want to fully participate in its society. But well-intentioned transitional bilingual education programs have often inhibited their command of English and retarded their full citizenship.

Congress recognized the importance of teaching English to immigrants in 1968 when it passed Title VII of the Elementary and Secondary Education Act. This Act permitted the development of pilot projects to teach English to underprivileged immigrant children. In 1978 Congress expanded the bilingual education program, dropped the poverty qualification and required appreciation for the cultural heritage of the students served by federal funds. These amendments also introduced the option of providing academic instruction in the native languages of the students, coupled with English classes. This method of instruction, transitional bilingual education, has been interpreted by Title VII regulations as the only acceptable method of instruction for bilingual education. The unfortunate result of Congress' 1978 action was to deprive local schools of their flexibility to determine the

S. I. Hayakawa

best method of instruction for their particular non-English-speaking students.

I agree wholeheartedly that we need to do all we can to teach the English language to non-English-speaking students. However, I cannot support a rigid mandate prescribing a single method of instruction. I believe that given the flexibility to choose their own program, local schools will emphasize English instruction. Without the expensive requirement of a full academic curriculum in foreign languages, schools will be able to teach more non-English-speaking students for the same cost. I have met with many school boards who are struggling to maintain high quality education in the midst of reduced budgets. Through my personal communications studies, I have observed that the more academic instruction children get in their immigrant parents' language, the less quickly they learn English. I personally believe that ESL and immersion techniques allow non-English-speaking students to master our language so they can join the mainstream of society more quickly than through transitional bilingual education. My legislation broadens the range of instructional approaches for serving children of limited English proficiency. I expect school boards to welcome this opportunity to provide more efficient and cost effective instruction to their immigrant students while maintaining their eligibility for Title VII funds.

What the learning of a new language requires, as is well known in U.S. military language schools, is total immersion in the new language, or as close to total immersion as possible. Though I personally support intensive methods of English instruction, I must point out that even my proposed constitutional amendment does not prohibit the use of minority languages to assist non-English-speaking students. On the contrary, it specifically states that it "shall not prohibit educational instruction in a language other than English as required as a transitional method of making students who use a language other than English proficient in English." My bilingual education proposal follows the same line of reasoning by allowing local schools the freedom to choose the teaching method that will best serve their immigrant population and maintain their eligibility for federal bilingual education funds.

Some immigrant groups argue that transitional bilingual education is necessary to preserve equal educational rights for non-English-speaking students while they are learning English. I believe that this requirement can actually result in discrimination in the administration of Title VII programs. The cost of providing academic subjects in a language other than English can exclude many of our recent immigrant groups such as the Indochinese who speak a variety of languages. Many local districts educating these students simply cannot afford to provide academic instruction in the many Indochinese languages which are often represented in one school. Imagine the cost of providing academic instruction in Cambodian, Hmong, Laotian, and Vietnamese in several grades. These students are no more fluent in English than the traditional immigrant groups funded under Title VII. However, because local schools often use intensive English instruction for Indochinese students, they will not qualify for Title VII money. Section 2, subsection 2 of the Bilingual Education Improvement Act would correct this by allowing funding for projects which use a variety of methods for teaching children with limited English proficiency including but not limited to transitional bilingual education, ESL, or immersion. Section 2, subsection B insures educational quality for students served by requiring applicant schools to show that they have selected instruction methods that will complement the special needs and characteristics of the Title VII students.

The acquisition of a new language is far easier for children than for adults. Children at the ages of four to six are at the height of their language-learning powers. In families where the father speaks to the children in one language, the mother in another, and the maid in a third, the children grow up trilingual with no difficulty. From the age of six onward, there is a gradual decline in a child's language-learning powers, so that learning a new language as an adolescent is a more difficult and self-

conscious process than it is for a child. For anyone over twenty, it is a much more difficult process, involving conceptualization, like learning rules of grammar. A child picks up unfamiliar grammar without conscious effort. Because of these differences in the rates and methods of language learning among different age groups, school children, especially under the age of ten, should be exposed to English constantly through contact with English-speaking classmates and playmates. They will learn English effortlessly, without the sense of undergoing a difficult experience.

The second provision of the Bilingual Education Improvement Act would give priority funding to Title VII projects which serve children who are both of limited English proficiency and whose usual language is not English. In our current period of limited federal resources in education, both Secretary Bell and I agree that it is imperative to target Title VII funds to this particular group of immigrant children. It is clear that the proposed Fiscal Year 1983 budget of $94.5 million cannot serve the approximately 3.6 million students who are technically eligible for Title VII aid. This provision of my legislation will target those who are most limited in their ability to speak English without tampering with the current definition of eligibility for Title VII funding. During our discussions, Secretary Bell and I have agreed that this effort to channel Title VII funds to the students who are least proficient in English is not to be interpreted as a federal mandate which will intrude in the local schools' determinations about their immigrant students. It is an incentive to local school officials to set priorities for using limited federal bilingual education funds. We agree that this new provision will be immensely helpful in clarifying a target population of students who are the *most* limited in their ability to speak English.

The third provision in this legislation would authorize several programs under Title VII which were previously under the Vocational Education Act. Vocational training for immigrant adults and out-of-school youth, training funds for teachers of immigrant students, and bilingual materials development have all proved to be small but effective programs. This provision would remove the set-aside for each program required under the Vocational Education Act and would allow the Department of Education to set priorities for the use of these funds. The focus of this funding will be for demonstration projects which will identify successful teaching methods rather than service projects which merely maintain the status quo. I am very encouraged by Secretary Bell's interest in using these programs as catalysts of research and development which will encourage state and local education agencies to share in the formulation of new training methods.

Another small, but extremely important provision of my legislation would require English proficiency for instructors in bilingual education programs. I was shocked to learn that Title VII currently places greater importance on its teachers knowing the native language of their students than on knowing English. My legislation will amend Section 721 (B) of the 1978 Act to fund programs "including only those teachers who are proficient in English, and, to the extent possible, in any other language used to provide instruction." The emphasis is reversed from knowledge of the immigrant language to English, which Secretary Bell and I agree reflects the true intent of federally-funded bilingual education.

The issue of English as our official language and bilingual education for immigrants is especially timely in light of the Census Bureau figures released this past Tuesday. The 1980 census found that 23 million people in the United States aged 5 or older speak a language other than English at home. We as Americans must reassess our commitment to the preservation of English as our common language. Learning English has been the primary task of every immigrant group for two centuries. Participation in the common language has rapidly made the political and economic benefits of American society available to each new group. Those who have mastered English have overcome the major hurdle to participation in our democracy. Passage of my English language amendment, as well as my bilingual education proposal, will insure that we maintain a common basis for communicating and sharing ideas.

Source:

Vital Speeches of the Day, "Bilingual Education Improvement Act: A Common Basis for Communication," June 15, 1982, pp. 521-523.

Yuri Kochiyama *is a Harlem-based Asian American activist who has worked for civil rights, international liberation struggles in Africa and third world countries, and improving life in the Harlem community. In the following memoir of her early life, which Kochiyama has said was apolitical, she tells of her father's arrest after Japan's bombing of Pearl Harbor, Hawaii, her internment in the "swamp lands" of Jerome, Arkansas, her release, and her career as a waitress, which was cut short by racial discrimination.*

Kochiyama says, "I was so red, white, and blue.... I'm a totally different person now than I was back then. I was naive about so many things. The more I think about it, the more I realize how little you learn about American history." A key influence on Kochiyama was Malcolm X (1925-1965), who told her that she must know the people's history in order to know what direction to go.

THEN CAME THE WAR

by Yuri Kochiyama

"I was red, white and blue when I was growing up. I taught Sunday school, and was very, very American. But I was also very provincial. We were just kids rooting for our high school.

"My father owned a fish market. Terminal Island was nearby, and that was where many Japanese families lived. It was a fishing town. My family lived in the city proper. San Pedro was very mixed, predominately white, but there were blacks also.

"I was nineteen at the time of the evacuation. I had just finished junior college. I was looking for a job, and didn't realize how different the school world was from the work world. In the school world, I never felt racism. But when you got into the work world, it was very difficult. This was 1941, just before the war. I finally did get a job at a department store. But for us back then, it was a big thing, because I don't think they had ever hired an Asian in a department store before. I tried, because I saw a Mexican friend who got a job there. Even then they didn't hire me on a regular basis, just on Saturdays, summer vacation, Easter vacation, and Christmas vacation. Other than that, I was working like the others—at a vegetable stand, or doing part-time domestic work. Back then, I only knew of two Japanese American girl friends who got jobs as secretaries—but these were in Japanese companies. But generally you almost never saw a Japanese American working in a white place. It was hard for Asians. Even for Japanese, the best jobs they felt they could get were in Chinatowns, such as in Los Angeles. Most Japanese were either in some aspect of fishing, such as in the canneries, or went right from school to work on the farms. That was what it was like in the town of San Pedro. I loved working in the department store, because it was a small town, and you got to know and see everyone. The town itself was wonderful. People were very friendly. I didn't see my job as work—it was like a community job.

"Everything changed for me on the day Pearl Harbor was bombed. On that very day—December 7, the FBI came and they took my father. He had just come home from the hospital the day before. For several days we didn't know where they had taken him. Then we found out that he was taken to the federal prison at Terminal Island. Overnight, things changed for us. They took all men who lived near the Pacific waters, and had anything to do with fishing. A month later, they took every fisherman from Terminal Island, sixteen and over, to places—not the regular concentration camps—but to detention centers in places like South Dakota, Montana, and New Mexico. They said that all Japanese who had given money to any kind of Japanese organization would have to be taken away. At that time, many people were giving to the Japanese Red Cross. The first group was thirteen hundred Isseis—my parent's generation. They took those who were leaders of the community, or Japanese school teachers, or were teaching martial arts, or who were Buddhist priests. Those categories which would make them very 'Japanesey', were picked up. This really made a tremendous impact on our lives. My twin brother was going to the University at Berkeley. He came rushing back. All of our classmates were joining up, so he volunteered to go into the service. And it seemed strange that here they had my father in prison, and there the draft board okayed my brother. He went right into the army. My other brother, who was two years older, was trying to run my father's fish market. But business was already going down, so he had to close it. He had finished college at the University of California a couple of years before.

"They took my father on December 7th. The day before, he had just come home from the hospital. He had surgery for an ulcer. We only saw him once on December 13. On December 20th they said he could come home. By the time they brought him back, he couldn't talk. He made gutteral sounds and we didn't know if he could hear. He was home for twelve hours. He was dying. The next morning, when we got up, they told us he was gone. He was very sick. And I think the interrogation was very rough. My mother kept begging the authorities to let him go to the hospital until he was well, then put him back in the prison. They did finally put him there, a week or so later. But they put him in a hospital where they were bringing back all these American Merchant Marines who were hit on Wake Island. So he was the only Japanese in that hospital, so they hung a sheet around him that said, Prisoner of War. The feeling where he was was very bad.

"You could see the hysteria of war. There was a sense that war could actually come to American shores. Everybody was yelling to get the 'Japs' out of California. In Congress, people were speaking out. Organizations such as the Sons and Daughters of

Many early Japanese immigrants, like this mother and daughter, were agricultural workers.

the Golden West were screaming 'Get the "Japs" out.' So were the real estate people, who wanted to get the land from the Japanese farmers. The war had whipped up such a hysteria that if there was anyone for the Japanese, you didn't hear about it. I'm sure they were afraid to speak out, because they would be considered not only just 'Jap' lovers, but unpatriotic.

"Just the fact that my father was taken made us suspect to people. But on the whole, the neighbors were quite nice, especially the ones adjacent to us. There was already a six AM to six PM curfew and a five mile limit on where we could go from our homes. So they offered to do our shopping for us, if we needed.

"Most Japanese Americans had to give up their jobs, whatever they did, and were told they had to leave. The edict for 9066—President Roosevelt's edict for evacuation—was in February 1942. We were moved to a detention center that April. By then the Japanese on Terminal Island were just hel-

ter skelter, looking for anywhere they could go. They opened up the Japanese school and Buddhist churches, and families just crowded in. Even farmers brought along their chickens and chicken coops. They just opened up the places for people to stay until they could figure out what to do. Some people left for Colorado and Utah. Those who had relatives could do so. The idea was to evacuate all the Japanese from the coast. But all the money was frozen, so even if you knew where you wanted to go, it wasn't that simple. By then, people knew they would be going into camps, so they were selling what they could, even though they got next to nothing for it.

"We were fortunate, in that our neighbors, who were white, were kind enough to look after our house, and they said they would find people to rent it, and look after it till we got back. But these neighbors were very, very unusual.

"We were sent to an assembly center in Arcadia, California, in April. It was the largest assembly center on the West Coast having nearly twenty thousand people. There were some smaller centers with about six hundred people. All along the West Coast—Washington, Oregon, California—there were many, many assembly centers, but ours was the largest. Most of the assembly centers were either fairgrounds, or race tracks. So many of us lived in stables and they said you could take what you could carry. We were there until October.

"Even though we stayed in a horse stable, everything was well organized. Every unit would hold four to six people. So in some cases, families had to split up, or join others. We slept on army cots, and for mattresses they gave us muslin bags, and told us to fill them with straw. And for chairs, everybody scrounged around for carton boxes, because they could serve as chairs. You could put two together and it could be a little table. So it was just makeshift. But I was amazed how, in a few months, some of those units really looked nice. Japanese women fixed them up. Some people had the foresight to bring material and needles and thread. But they didn't let us bring anything that could be used as weapons. They let us have spoons, but no knives. For those who had small children or babies, it was rough. They said you could take what you could carry. Well, they could only take their babies in their arms, and maybe the little children could carry something, but it was pretty limited.

"I was so red, white and blue, I couldn't believe this was happening to us. America would never do a thing like this to us. This is the greatest country in the world. So I thought this is only going to be for a short while, maybe a few weeks or something, and they will let us go back. At the beginning no one realized how long this would go on. I didn't feel the anger that much because I thought maybe this was the way we could show our love for our country, and we should not make too much fuss or noise, we should abide by what they asked of us. I'm a totally different person now than I was back then. I was naive about so many things. The more I think about, the more I realize how little you learn about American history. It's just what they want you to know.

"At the beginning, we didn't have any idea how temporary or permanent the situation was. We thought we would be able to leave shortly. But after several months they told us this was just temporary quarters, and they were building more permanent quarters elsewhere in the United States. All this was so unbelievable. A year before we would never have thought anything like this could have happened to us—not in this country. As time went by, the sense of frustration grew. Many families were already divided. The fathers, the heads of the households, were taken to other camps. In the beginning, there was no way for the sons to get in touch with their families. Before our group left for the detention camp, we were saying goodbye almost every day to other groups who were going to places like Arizona and Utah. Here we finally had made so many new friends—people who we met, lived with, shared the time, and gotten to know. So it was even sad on that note and the goodbyes were difficult. Here we had gotten close to these people, and now we had to separate again. I don't think we even thought about where they were going to take us, or how long we would have to stay there. When we got on the trains to leave for the camps, we didn't know where we were going. None of the groups knew. It was later on that we learned so and so ended up in Arizona, or Colorado, or some other place. We were all at these assembly centers for about seven months. Once they started pushing people out, it was done very quickly. By October, our group headed out for Jerome, Arkansas, which is on the Tex-Arkana corner.

"We were on the train for five days. The blinds were down, so we couldn't look out, and other people couldn't look in to see who was in the train. We stopped in Nebraska, and everybody pulled the blinds to see what Nebraska looked like. The interesting thing was, there was a troop train stopped at the station too. These American soldiers looked out, and saw all these Asians, and they wondered what we were doing on the train. So the Japanese raised the windows, and so did the soldiers. It wasn't a bad feeling at all. There was none of that you 'Japs' kind of thing. The women were about the same age as the soldiers—eighteen to twenty-five, and we had the same thing on our minds. In camps, there wasn't much to do, so the fun thing was to receive letters, so on our train, all the girls who were my age, were yelling to the guys, 'Hey, give us your address where you're going, we'll write you.' And they said, 'Are you sure you're going to write?' We exchanged addresses and for a long time I wrote to some of those soldiers. On the other side of the train, I'll never forget there was this old guy, about sixty, who came to our window and said, 'We have some Japanese living here. This is Omaha, Nebraska.' This guy was very nice, and didn't seem to have any ill feelings for Japanese. He had calling cards, and he said 'Will any of you people write to me?' We said, 'sure', so he threw in a bunch of calling cards, and I got one, and I wrote to him for years. I wrote to him about what camp was like, because he said, 'Let me know what it's like wherever you end up.' And he wrote back, and told me what was happening in Omaha, Nebraska. There were many, many interesting experiences too. Our mail were generally not censored, but all the mail from the soldiers was. Letters meant everything.

"When we got to Jerome, Arkansas, we were shocked because we had never seen an area like it. There was forest all around us. And they told us to wait till the rains hit. This would not only turn into mud, but Arkansas swamp lands. That's where they put us—in swamp lands, surrounded by forests. It was nothing like California.

"I'm speaking as a person of twenty who had good health. Up until then, I had lived a fairly comfortable life. But there were many others who didn't see the whole experience the same way. Especially those who were older and in poor health and had experienced racism. One more thing like this could break them. I was at an age where transitions were not hard; the point where anything new could even be considered exciting. But for people in poor health, it was hell.

"There were army-type barracks, with two hundred to two hundred and five people to each block and every block had its own mess hall, facility for washing clothes, showering. It was all surrounded by barbed wire, and armed soldiers. I think they said only seven people were killed in total, though thirty were shot, because they went too close to the fence. Where we were, nobody thought of escaping because you'd be more scared of the swamps—the poisonous snakes, the bayous. Climatic conditions were very harsh. Although Arkansas is in the South, the winters were very, very cold. We had a pot bellied stove in every room and we burned wood. Everything was very organized. We got there in October, and were warned to prepare ourselves. So on our block, for instance, males eighteen and over could go out in the forest to chop down trees for wood for the winter. The men would bring back the trees, and the women sawed the trees. Everybody worked. The children would pile up the wood for each unit.

"They told us when it rained, it would be very wet, so we would have to build our own drainage system. One of the barracks was to hold meetings, so block heads would call meetings. There was a block council to represent the people from different areas.

"When we first arrived, there were some things that weren't completely fixed. For instance, the roofers would come by, and everyone would hunger for information from the outside world. We wanted to know what was happening with the war. We weren't allowed to bring radios; that was contraband. And there were no televisions then. So we would ask the workers to bring us back some papers, and they would give us papers from Texas or Arkansas, so for the first time we would find out about news from the outside.

"Just before we went in to the camps, we saw that being a Japanese wasn't such a good thing, because everybody was turning against the Japanese, thinking we were saboteurs, or linking us with Pearl Harbor. But when I saw the kind of work they did at camp, I felt so proud of the Japanese, and proud to be Japanese, and wondered why I was so white, white when I was outside, because I was always with white folks. Many people had brothers or sons who were in the military and Japanese American servicemen would come into the camp to visit the families, and we felt so proud of them when they came in their uniforms. We knew that it would only be a matter of time before they would be shipped overseas. Also what made us feel proud was the forming of the 442 unit.

"I was one of these real American patriots then. I've changed now. But back then, I was all American. Growing up, my mother would say we're Japanese. But I'd say 'No, I'm American.' I think a lot of Japanese grew up that way. People would say to them, 'You're Japanese,' and they would say, 'No, we're Americans.' I don't even think they used the hyphenated term 'Japanese-American' back then. At the time, I was ashamed of being Japanese. I think many Japanese Americans felt the same way. Pearl Harbor was a shameful act, and being Japanese Americans, even though we had nothing to do with it, we still somehow felt we were blamed for it. I hated Japan at that point. So I saw myself at that part of my history as an American, and not as a Japanese, or Japanese American. That sort of changed while I was in the camp.

"I hated the war, because it wasn't just between the governments. It went down to the people, and it nurtured hate. What was happening during the war were many things I didn't like. I hoped that one day when the war was over there could be a way that people could come together in their relationships.

"Now I can relate to Japan in a more mature way, where I see its faults and its very, very negative history. But I also see its potential. Scientifically and technologically it has really gone far. But I'm disappointed that when it comes to human rights she hasn't grown. The Japan of today—I feel there are still things lacking. For instance, I don't think the students have the opportunity to have more leeway in developing their lives.

"We always called the camps 'relocation centers' while we were there. Now we feel it is apropos to call them concentration camps. It is not the same as the concentration camps of Europe; those we feel were death camps. Concentration camps were a concentration of people placed in an area, and disempowered and disenfranchised. So it is apropos to call what I was in a concentration camp. After two years in the camp, I was released."

After the War: "Going home wasn't much of a problem for us because our neighbors had looked after our place. But for most of our Japanese friends, starting over again was very difficult after the war.

"I returned in October of 1945. It was very hard to find work, at least for me. I wasn't expecting to find anything good, just something to tie me over until my boyfriend came back from New York. The only thing I was looking for was to work in a restaurant as a waitress. But I couldn't find anything. I would walk from one end of the town to the other, and down every main avenue. But as soon as they found out I was Japanese, they would say no. Or they would ask me if I was in the union, and of course I couldn't be in the union because I had just gotten there. Anyway, no Japanese could be in the union, so if the answer was no I'm not in the union, they would say no. So finally what I did was go into the rough area of San Pedro—there's a strip near the wharf—and I went down there. I was determined to keep the jobs as long as I could. But for a while, I could last maybe two hours, and somebody would say 'Is that a "Jap?"' And as soon as someone would ask that, the boss would say, 'sorry, you gotta go. We don't want trouble here.' The strip wasn't that big, so after I'd go the whole length of it, I'd have to keep coming back to the same restaurants, an say, 'Gee, will you give me another chance,' I figure, all these service men were coming back and the restaurants didn't have enough waitresses to come in and take these jobs. And so they'd say 'Okay. But soon as somebody asks who you are, or if you're a "Jap," or any problem about being a "Jap," you go.' So I said, 'Okay, sure. How about keeping me until that happens?' So sometimes I'd last a night, sometimes a couple of nights that no one would say anything. Sometimes people threw cups at me or hot coffee. At first they didn't know what I was. They thought I was Chinese. Then someone would say, 'I bet she's a Jap.' And I wasn't going to say I wasn't. So as soon as I said 'Yeah,' then it was like an uproar. Rather than have them say, 'Get out,' I just walked out. I mean, there was no point in fighting it. If you just walked out, there was less chance of getting hurt. But one place I lasted two weeks. These owners didn't want to have to let me go. But they didn't want to have problems with the people.

"And so I did this until I left for New York which was about three months later. I would work

the dinner shift, from six at night to three in the morning. When you are young you tend not to take things as strongly. Everything is like an adventure. Looking back, I felt the people who were the kindest to me were those who went out and fought, those who just got back from Japan or the Far East. I think the worst ones were the ones who stayed here and worked in defense plants, who felt they had to be so patriotic. On the West Coast, there wasn't hysteria anymore, but there were hostile feelings towards the Japanese, because they were coming back. It took a while, but my mother said that things were getting back to normal, and that the Japanese were slowly being accepted again. At the time, I didn't go through the bitterness that many others went through, cause it's not just what they went through, but it is also what they experienced before that. I mean, I happened to have a much more comfortable life before, so you sort of see things in a different light. You see that there are all kinds of Americans, and that they're not all people who hate Japs. You know too that it was hysteria that had a lot to do with it.

"All Japanese, before they left camp, were told not to congregate among Japanese, and not to speak Japanese. They were told by the authorities. There was even a piece of paper that gave you instructions. But then people who went on to places like Chicago where there were churches, so they did congregate in churches. But they did ask people not to. I think psychologically the Japanese, having gone through a period where they were so hated by everyone, didn't even want to admit they were Japanese, or accept the fact that they were Japanese. Of course, they would say they were Japanese Americans. But I think the psychological damage of the war time period, and of racism itself, has left its mark. There is a stigma being Japanese. I think that is why such a large number of Japanese, in particular, Japanese American women, have married out of the race. On the West Coast I've heard people say that sixty to seventy percent of the Japanese women have married, I guess, mostly whites. Japanese men are doing it too, but not to that degree. I guess Japanese Americans just didn't want to have that Japanese identity, or that Japanese part. There is definitely some self hate and part of that has to do with the racism that's so deeply a part of this society.

"Historically, Americans have always been putting people behind walls. First there were the American Indians who were put on reservations, Africans in slavery, their lives on the plantations, Chicanos doing migratory work, and the kinds of camps they lived in, and even too, the Chinese when they worked on the railroad camps where they were almost isolated, dispossessed people—disempowered. And I feel those are the things we should fight against so they won't happen again. It wasn't so long ago—in 1979—that the feeling against the Iranians was so strong because of the takeover of the U.S. embassy in Iran, where they wanted to deport Iranian students. And that is when a group called Concerned Japanese Americans organized, and that was the first issue we took up, and then we connected it with what the Japanese had gone through. This whole period of what the Japanese went through is important. If we can see the connections of how often this happens in history, we can stem the tide of these things happening again by speaking out against them.

"Most Japanese Americans who worked years and years for redress never thought it would happen the way it did. The papers have been signed, we will be given reparation, and there was an apology from the government. I think the redress movement itself was very good because it was a learning experience for the Japanese people; we could get out into our communities and speak about what happened to us and link it with experiences of other people. In that sense, though, it wasn't done as much as it should have been. Some Japanese Americans didn't even learn that part. They just started the movement as a reaction to the bad experience they had. They don't even see other ethnic groups who have gone through it. It showed us, too, how vulnerable everybody is. It showed us that even though there is a constitution, that constitutional rights could be taken away very easily."

Source:

Joann Faung Jean Lee. *Asian American Experiences in the United States: Oral Histories of First to Fourth Generation Americans from China, the Philippines, Japan, India, the Pacific Islands, Vietnam and Cambodia.* Jefferson, NC: McFarland & Co., 1991. pp. 10-18.

A hero of World War II and the first Japanese American to serve in the U.S. Congress, Daniel K. Inouye (1924-) has served the people of Hawaii since their island home became the fiftieth state in 1959. Initially a member of the House of Representatives, he was elected to the Senate in 1962, and there he has wielded considerable power and influence for the Democrats in a characteristically low-key fashion that emphasizes compromise over confrontation. It is an approach that has brought Inouye the respect of his colleagues within the government and the support of his constituents, who have re-elected him to national office a total of seven times.

Inouye is a member of the generation known by the Japanese term nisei, which describes the U.S.-born children of parents who immigrated from Japan. His father was just a young boy when he arrived in Hawaii with his own parents. Later, as an adult, he worked in Honolulu as a file clerk to support his family, earning just enough for him, his wife, and four children to live in a state of genteel poverty. But as his son Dan later recalled, his childhood was a happy one, and he grew up with the feeling that a better future awaited him if he were willing to work for it.

By the time he had reached his senior year of high school, Inouye's dream was to become a surgeon. But those plans changed forever on the morning of December 7, 1941, as he and his family were getting ready to go to church. Over the radio came news of the Japanese air raid then in progress at Pearl Harbor. Inouye, who had been teaching first aid at the local Red Cross station, rushed there to help and stayed on duty for nearly a week. He ended up spending much of the rest of his senior year attending classes during the day and working a 12-hour shift for the Red Cross at night—a manic schedule he felt compelled to observe out of guilt over the fact that the attack had been carried out by the Japanese. Meanwhile, in the streets of Honolulu, he and other Hawaiians of Japanese descent endured taunts, insults, and sometimes outright hatred from whites.

In the fall of 1942, Inouye enrolled in the pre-med program at the University of Hawaii. He also added his voice to those of many other young nisei men who were petitioning the U.S. government to allow them to serve in the armed forces and thus demonstrate their loyalty to the country. Finally, in January of 1943, the War Department announced that it would accept fifteen hundred nisei volunteers for a new unit, the 442nd Regimental Combat Team. Inouye quit school and immediately joined up.

The 442nd went on to become the most decorated unit in U.S. military history; its four thousand members—who adopted "Go for Broke!" as their motto— received more than 18,000 medals for bravery. Inouye earned 15 of them himself as one of the 442nd's most heroic leaders. Fighting in Italy during the last few months of the war, he was critically wounded while directing a difficult uphill assault against a heavily-fortified German position on a high ridge. He spent the next two years in the hospital recovering from multiple bullet wounds to his abdomen and leg and the amputation of his right arm.

Upon returning home in 1947, Inouye resumed his education at the University of Hawaii. No longer able or interested in pursuing a career in medicine, he opted instead to study law with an eye toward one day entering public life. So, after receiving his bachelor's degree in 1950, he headed to Washington, D.C., where he attended George Washington University Law School. Following his 1952 graduation, he returned to Honolulu and became involved in politics as a Democrat, winning election to the Territorial House in 1954 and serving two terms as majority leader. In 1958, his bid for a seat in the Territorial Senate met with success, and there, too, he assumed the role of majority leader.

By the time Hawaii was admitted to the union as the fiftieth state in 1959, Inouye was so popular with his fellow islanders that he easily captured the new state's first seat in the U.S. House of Representatives. Three years later, he decided to run for the U.S. Senate seat being vacated by one of Hawaii's first senators and ended up beating his Republican opponent by more than a two-to-one margin.

From the very beginning of his congressional career, Inouye has tended to hold a liberal opinion on social issues but a more moderate or even conservative one on economic and defense issues. He has, for example, consistently supported civil rights legislation through the years, including the landmark Civil Rights Act of 1964, and also backed the "Great Society" social welfare programs of President Lyndon Johnson. As a loyal Democrat, he sided with the president on the conduct of the Vietnam War but aligned himself with the forces in his party calling for peace once Republican Richard Nixon took office.

Inouye's loyalty was rewarded during the 1960s with his appointment to a number of high-ranking positions in the party, including assistant majority whip and vice-chairman of the Democratic Senatorial Campaign Committee. He was also mentioned several times as a possible vice-presidential candidate, particularly after he delivered the following keynote address to delegates attending the Democratic National Convention in Chicago on August 29, 1968. At the time, the country was in turmoil—race riots had exploded in many major cities over several previous summers, shock waves still reverberated from the recent assassinations of Martin Luther King, Jr., and Robert F. Kennedy, and antiwar demonstrations were erupting on university and college campuses across the nation (and even right outside the convention hall). Inouye won widespread acclaim for a stirring speech in which he criticized the forces threatening to tear apart the United States and urged concerned citizens to take positive rather than negative action to correct political and social ills.

During the administrations of presidents Richard Nixon, Gerald Ford, Jimmy Carter, Ronald Reagan, George Bush, and Bill Clinton, Inouye continued to favor liberal causes such as abortion rights, gun control, organized labor, and consumer protection laws while voting to support some Cold War-era military measures, including funding for development of a neutron bomb. He has also been a longtime champion of Israel.

Inouye's influence in a number of these areas has been considerable thanks to the high-ranking positions he has held on key Senate committees—assignments that have occasionally put him in the national spotlight. In 1973, for example, Inouye served as a member of the Senate Watergate Committee, a role in which he won over many fans for his patient yet tenacious questioning of less-than-cooperative witnesses. He again found himself in the public eye in 1987, when he chaired the Iran-Contra hearings.

But Inouye's most significant and enduring work has probably been carried out behind the scenes. In 1976, for instance, he served as chairman of the Senate Select Committee on Intelligence, which drafted rules governing the covert operations of U.S. intelligence organizations at home and abroad in an effort to curb some of their more flagrant abuses of power. As a longtime member of the Senate Appropriations Committee and former chairman of its Foreign Operations Subcommittee, Inouye has wielded a great deal of clout in foreign policy matters by determining which countries will receive aid and how much they will receive. More recently, he played an important role in overseeing developments in cable television, telephone communications, and the "Information Superhighway" as former chairman of the Science, and Transportation Subcommittee on Communications of the Senate Commerce Committee.

Because of his own experience with racial prejudice during World War II, Inouye has always been especially sensitive to discrimination against minorities. Of particular interest to him through the years have been the concerns of Native Americans, and as chairman of the Senate Committee on Indian Affairs he earned their trust and respect for his strong support of tribal sovereignty and self-determination. On December 2, 1991, Inouye addressed some of the major issues facing Native Americans and his Senate Committee in a speech he delivered at the annual convention of the National Congress of American Indians, held that year in San Francisco.

Another subject of intense personal interest for Inouye is his wartime service and the strong bond he has maintained through the years with his fellow members of the 442nd Regimental Combat Team. In March of 1993, hundreds of survivors met in Honolulu to mark the fiftieth anniversary of the founding of their unit, the bravery they displayed overseas, and their triumph over bigotry at home. One of the two featured speakers at the reunion was Inouye, who delivered a poignant keynote address on March 24. The senator supplied a copy of his speech.

DANIEL INOUYE'S KEYNOTE ADDRESS TO THE 442ND REGIMENTAL COMBAT TEAM

This gathering is an important one—it will be a gathering of nostalgia. . .a gathering of sad memories. . .a gathering of laughter and fun. . .a gathering of goodbyes, for this may be our last roll call of the regiment.

We have travelled vast distances—from every state and from many foreign lands—to be together in Honolulu. We have traveled a lifetime together for this meeting in Honolulu. When did this journey to Honolulu begin?

Although this is our 50th reunion, our journey began before that date. Our fate was decided 52 years, 3 months and 2 weeks ago on that tragic Sunday in December. Our journey began on December 7, 1941.

> "*Their only crime, if any, was that they were born of Japanese parents and for that crime, they were incarcerated in internment camps.. .*"

Soon after that tragic Sunday morning, we who were of Japanese ancestry were considered by our nation to be citizens without a country. I am certain all of us remember that the Selective Service system of our country designated us to be unfit for military service because we were "enemy aliens." Soon after that, on February 19, 1942, the White House issued an extraordinary Executive Order—Executive Order 9066. This dreaded Executive Order forcibly uprooted our mainland brothers and their families and their loved ones from their homes with only those possessions that they were able to carry themselves and were granted forty-eight hours to carry out this order.

Our mainland brothers were not charged or indicted or convicted for the commission of any crime—because no crime was committed. Their only crime, if any, was that they were born of Japanese parents and for that crime, they were incarcerated in internment camps surrounded by barbed-wire fences, guarded by machine-gun towers. They were sent to strange places with strange names—Manzanar, Tule Lake, Rohwer, Gila, Topaz. Although a few members of Hawaii's Japanese community were interned in Honouliuli (a rather well-kept secret), very few, if any of us in Hawaii, were aware of the mass internment of our mainland brothers and their families.

Although we were separated by a vast ocean and mountain ranges, we from the mainland and Hawaii shared one deep-seated desire—to rid ourselves of that insulting and degrading designation, "enemy alien." We wanted to serve our country. We wanted to demonstrate our love for our country.

After many months of petitions and letters, another Executive Order was issued with the declaration that ". . .Americanism is a matter of mind and heart; Americanism is not, and never was, a matter of race or ancestry." By this Executive Order, the formation of the special combat team made up of Japanese Americans was authorized.

More than the anticipated numbers volunteered; in fact, in Hawaii, about eighty-five percent of the eligible men of Japanese Americans volunteered. Those who were selected assembled in Schofield Barracks to prepare for our departure from Hawaii. That was fifty years ago. In early April, we boarded railway flatbeds in Wahiawa and rode to Iwilei. There we got off the trains with our heavy duffel bags to march to Pier 7. But keep in mind that most of us had less than two weeks of military training and many of us were yet to be toughened and hardened. And so we found ourselves struggling with those heavy bags on a march of over a mile. This was the farewell parade of the 442nd. For many parents this was the last sight of their sons. I cannot understand why the Army did not place those duffel bags in trucks and permit us to march heads up and tall as we said goodbye to Hawaii. For many, the last look of their sons must have been a rather sad one because we looked like a ragtag formation of prisoners of war. I will never forget our sad departure from Hawaii.

But after several weeks, we from Hawaii and the mainland gathered in Camp Shelby in Hattiesburg, Mississippi, the home of chiggers and ticks, sweat and dirt.

All of us were of the same ancestry, but somehow our first encounter was an unhappy one. In a few days, violent arguments and fights erupted within our area and these fights became commonplace. The men of the regiment found themselves segregated into two camps, one from Hawaii and the other from the mainland. This relationship was so bad that senior Army officers seriously considered disbanding the regiment.

Many projects were initiated and many lectures were delivered to bring about unity, but all failed except the Rohwer experiment. Our regimental records will not disclose the name of the author of this experiment, but history will show that we owe much to him.

Whoever he was, [he] suggested that the internees of Rohwer send an invitation to the regiment inviting young enlisted men from Hawaii to join them for a weekend of fun and festivities in the camp. As I recall, each company selected ten enlisted men. I was fortunate to be one of those selected by E Company. On the appointed day, these men from Hawaii, all cleanly showered, smelling of after-shave lotion, with their guitars and ukuleles, boarded trucks for this journey to Rohwer. Rohwer was an internment camp in Arkansas.

From the time we left Shelby in the early morning hours, this special convoy was a convoy of laughter and music. All were anticipating happy times with the young ladies of Rohwer.

Suddenly, this fantasy was shattered. We came in sight of the Rohwer internment camp. In the distance, we could see rows of barracks surrounded by high barbed-wire fences with machine-gun towers. The music stopped and there was no laughter.

Keep in mind that very few, if any of us, were aware of these camps. Our mainland brothers never spoke of them, never complained, and so we did not know.

When we finally came to the gate, we were ordered to get off the trucks. We were in uniform and were confronted by men in similar uniforms but they had rifles with bayonets. For a moment, I thought that there would be a tragic encounter, but fortunately nothing happened as we were escorted through the gate. There we were greeted by the people of Rohwer who were all persons of Japanese ancestry—grandparents, parents, children, grandchildren. Although a dance was held that evening, I doubt if any of us really enjoyed ourselves. But it was an unforgettable evening.

When we left Rohwer the following morning, the singing and the laughter and music that filled our trucks when we left Camp Shelby was replaced by grim silence. The atmosphere was grim and quiet, and I believe that all of us, as we reflected upon that strange visit, asked ourselves the question, "Would I have volunteered from a camp like

Daniel K. Inouye

Rohwer?" To this day, I cannot give an answer because I really do not know if I would have volunteered to serve our nation if I had been interned in one of those camps.

So suddenly, our respect, admiration, and love for our Kotonk brothers rose to phenomenal heights. They suddenly became our blood brothers and overnight a new, tough, tightly united military fighting machine was formed. It was a regiment made up of blood brothers and we were ready to live up to our motto, "Go for Broke." And thus the 442nd Infantry Regimental Combat Team was formed.

There are too many battles to recall—from Belvedere to Bruyeres, from Hill 140 to the Po Valley. But there is one we will never forget and one hopefully that our nation will always remember—the Battle of the Lost Battalion.

This battle began during the last week of October, 1944. The members of the First Battalion of the 141st Infantry Regiment of the 36th Texas Division found themselves surrounded by a large number of enemy troops. This "lost battalion" was ordered to fight its way back, but could not do so. The Second and Third Battalions of the Texas Regiment were ordered to break through but they were thrown back, and so on October 26, the 442nd was ordered to go into the lines to rescue the "lost battalion." On November 15, the rescue was successfully concluded.

Two days later, we were ordered to assemble in formal retreat parade formation to personally receive the commendation of the 36th Division from the commanding general of the Texas unit. The men of the regiment assembled in a vast field of a French farm. I can still hear the company commanders making their reports—A Company, all present and accounted for; B Company, all present and accounted for; E Company, all present and accounted for. It was an eerie scene. It has been reported that General Dahlquist, who had ordered this formation, was at first angered by the small attendance and reprimanded our commander, who in reply is reported to have said, "Sir, this *is* the regiment." As a result of the Battle of the Lost Battalion, two thousand men were in hospitals and over three hundred had died. The price was heavy. Although we did not whimper or complain, we were sensitive to the fact that the rescuers of the Texas Battalion were not members of the Texas Division. They were Japanese Americans from Hawaii and from mainland internment camps. They were "enemy aliens."

I can still hear the proud and defiant voices of the company commanders as they made their reports. I can still see the company commander of E Company making his report. E Company had forty-two men, and though we were less than a quarter of the authorized company strength, E Company was the largest company at that retreat parade. K Company was led by a staff sergeant. K Company was made up of twelve men. When I heard the last commander shout out his report, "All present and accounted for," like many of you, I could almost feel the insulting and degrading designation that was placed on our shoulders long ago in December, 1941—the designation of "enemy alien"—fall crashing to the ground in that faraway French farm. And we knew that from that moment on, no one could ever, ever, question our loyalty and our love for our country. The insulting stigma was finally taken away.

Years later, the United States Army called upon a special commission of military historians, analysts and strategists to select the ten most important battles of the U.S. Army Infantry from the Revolutionary War to the Korean War. The Battle of the Lost Battalion was selected as one of the honored ten. Our battle is listed together with our nation's most glorious and historic battles, such as the Battle of Vicksburg during the Civil War, the Battle at Meuse-Argonne in France during World War I, and the Battle of Leyte in the Philippines during World War II. Today, specially commissioned paintings of these ten most important battles are proudly displayed in the Pentagon.

Over the years, many have asked us—"Why?" "Why did you fight and serve so well?" My son, like your sons and daughters, has asked the same question—"Why?" "Why were you willing and ready to give your life?" We have tried to provide answers to these questions and I hope that my answer to my son made sense.

I told my son it was a matter of honor. I told him about my father's farewell message when I left home to put on the uniform of my country. My father was not a man of eloquence but he said, "Whatever you do, do not dishonor the family and do not dishonor the country." I told my son that for many of us, to have done any less than what we had done in battle would have dishonored our families and our country.

Second, I told my son that there is an often-used Japanese phrase—*Kodomo no tame ni*. Though most of us who went into battle were young and single, we wanted to leave a legacy of honor and pride and the promise of a good life for our yet-to-be-born children and their children.

My brothers, I believe we can assure ourselves that we did succeed in upholding our honor and that of our families and our nation. And I respectfully and humbly believe that our service and the sacrifices of those who gave their all on the battlefield assure a better life for our children and their children.

Yes, I believe we can stand tall this evening in knowing that our journey together, a journey that began on that tragic Sunday morning, was not in vain. And so tonight, let us embrace with our hearts and minds the memory of those brothers who are not with us this evening and let us do so with all of our affection and gratitude. Let us embrace with deep love our loved ones for having stood with us and walked with us on our journey. Let us embrace with everlasting gratitude and Aloha the many friends and neighbors who supported us throughout our journey. Let us embrace with everlasting love our great nation.

And finally, let us embrace our sons and daughters with full pride and with the restful assurance that the story of our journey of honor will live on for generations to come.

And so, my brothers, let us this evening, in the spirit of our regiment, stand tall with pride, have fun, and let's "Go for Broke."

Source:

Transcript of speech delivered March 24, 1993, before survivors of the 442nd Regimental Combat Team in Honolulu, HI.

JEWISH AMERICANS

Anti-Semitism and persecution have existed for Jews throughout their history, and in all of the countries in which they have settled. In the 1400s, Jews in Spain were persecuted and banished; many took refuge in the United States and the Ottoman Empire. Though Jews have been in America since before colonial times (some Jews made the passage with Christopher Columbus), it was during the early 1800s that European Jews began coming to America in waves, primarily to escape economic troubles and anti-Semitism in their homelands. Many came from Germany and settled in towns and cities, or became itinerant peddlers. The next wave came from Russia. A series of pogroms (persecutions) in 1881 and the passing of the May Laws of 1882 which restricted the rights of Russian Jews sent another group of immigrants to American shores. Russian Jews came to the United States in droves until Congress restricted immigration in 1924. By 1920, the American Jewish population was at approximately four million.

Uriah P. Levy was a Captain in the United States Navy. Because he was Jewish, Levy was the target of much anti-Semitic sympathy: he was court martialed six times and, in 1855, was dismissed "to improve the efficiency of the navy." The general public protested this decision, and Levy's case was the subject of a Court of Inquiry that reinstated him in 1858. He finished his naval career as the commander of a squadron in the Mediterranean.

This document, which highlights the prejudice that Jews found in America in the late 1800s, is Levy's defense to the Court of Inquiry. In it, Levy describes the measures taken to block his success in the Navy, from attempting to block his passage on a particular ship to the attempt to block his nomination for the position of Captain. He calls for the officials of the court to remember that America is a colony based on the premise of freedom of religious belief, stating that, "What is my case to-day, if you yield to this injustice, may to-morrow be that of the Roman Catholic or the Unitarian; the Episcopalian or the Methodist; the Presbyterian or the Baptist." Levy points out that prejudice based on religious faith has no place in the military judicial system.

BEING OF JEWISH PERSUASION

by Uriah P. Levy

My parents were Israelites, and I was nurtured in the faith of my ancestors. In deciding to adhere to it, I have but exercised a right, guaranteed to me by the constitution of my native State, and of the United States—a right given to all men by their Maker—a right more precious to each of us than life itself. But, while claiming and exercising this freedom of conscience, I have never failed to acknowledge and respect the like freedom of others. I might safely defy the citation of a single act, in the whole course of my official career, injurious to the religious rights of any other person. Remembering always that the great mass of my fellow-citizens were Christians; profoundly grateful to the Christian founders of our republic, for their justice and liberality to my long persecuted race; I have earnestly endeavored, in all places and circumstances, to act up to the wise and tolerant spirit of our political institutions, I have therefore been careful to treat every Christian, and especially every Christian under my command, with exemplary justice and ungrudging liberality. Of this, you have had clear proof so far as my command of the Vandalia is concerned, from the lips of Lieutenants (Edmund) Lanier and (John N.) Maffit. They testify to the observance, on board that ship, under the standing rules and regulations prescribed by me, of the Christian Sabbath, and to the scrupulous regard paid by me on all occasions, to the religious rights and feelings of the officers and men.

I have to complain—more in sorrow than in anger do I say it—that in my official experience I have met with little to encourage, though with much to frustrate, these conciliatory efforts. At an early day, and especially from the time when it became known to the officers of may age and grade, that I aspired to a lieutenancy, and still more, after I had gained it, I was forced to encounter a large share of the prejudice and hostility by which, for so many ages, the Jew has been pursued. I need not speak to you of the incompatibility of these sentiments with the genius of Christianity, or the precepts of its author. You should know this far better than I; but I may ask you to unite with the wisest and best men of our own country and of Europe, in denouncing them, not merely as injurious to the peace and welfare of the community, but as repugnant to every dictate of reason, humanity and justice.

In February, 1818, I was transferred, by Commodore (Charles) Stewart, from his ship, the Franklin, 74, to the frigate United States, under the command of Captain (William M.) Crane. Under the influence of the double prejudice to which I have alluded, a conspiracy was formed among certain officers of this frigate to prevent my reception in her. Commodore (T.A.C.) Jones, in answer to the eight interrogatory on my part, gives a full account of it. He says:

"Lieutenant Levy, for several months, was fourth, and I first lieutenant, of the frigate United States, where he discharged his duty satisfactorily to the captain as well as to the first lieutenant, notwithstanding his advent into our ship was attend with such novel and discouraging circumstances as, in justice to captain Levy, renders it necessary here to record them.

"On the arrival of the Franklin, of 74 guns, at Syracuse, in 1818, bearing the broad pennant of commodore Charles Stewart, to relive commodore (John S.) Chauncey, then in command of the Mediterranean squadron, it was understood that lieutenant Levy, a supernumerary on board of the Franklin, was to be ordered to the frigate United States, then short of her complement of lieutenants. Whereupon, the *ward-room mess*, without consulting me, determined to remonstrate against Levy's coming aboard. I was called on by a member of the mess to communicate their wishes to Captain Crane and ask his interference.

"Astonished at such a proposition, I required as to the cause, when I was answered, that he was a Jew, and not an agreeable person, and they did not want to be brought in contact with him in our then very pleasant and harmonious mess of some eight or nine persons; and, moreover, that he was an interloper, having entered the navy as *master*, to the prejudice of the older midshipmen, &c. &c. Such was the reply, in substance, to my inquiry. I then asked the relator if he, or any member of our mess, knew anything of his own knowledge, derogatory to lieutenant Levy, as an officer and as a gentleman. The answer was *no*, but they had heard thus and so, &c., &c. I endeavored to point out the difficulties that might result from a procedure so much at variance with military subordination, and the justice due to a brother officer, against whom they had nothing but vague and ill-defined rumors; but my counsel then did not prevail. The remonstrance was made directly to captain Crane, and by captain

Crane to Commodore Stewart. Levy soon after reported on board the frigate United States, for duty. When Lieutenant Levy came on board, he asked a private interview with me, wishing my advice as the procedures he ought to pursue under such embarrassing circumstances. I gave it freely and simply, to the effect, vis.: do your duty as an officer and a gentleman, be civil to all, however reserved you may choose to be to any, and the first man who observed a different course towards you, call him to a strict and prompt account. Our mess-mates were gentlemen, and having perceived their error before lieutenant Levy got on board, had, in accordance with my previous advice, determined to receive lieutenant Levy as a gentleman and a brother officer, and to respect and treat him as such, till by his conduct he should prove himself unworthy. I continued a few months longer on board the frigate United States, as her first lieu-tenant, during the whole of which time Lieutenant Levy's conduct and deportment was altogether unexceptionable, and I know that, perhaps with a single exception, those who opposed his joining our mess, not only relented, but deeply regretted the false step they had incautiously taken."

During the few months that Commodore Jones remained in the ship United States, his wise and just counsels had the effect he describes. After he left her, I am sorry to be obliged to say, the old prejudices revived in the breasts of too may of my associates.

In December, 1824, a conspiracy of the same kind was formed among the junior offices of the ward-room mess, on board the North Carolina. She was about to sail for the Mediterranean to join the squadron in that sea; and I was ordered to take pas-sage in her, and to report myself to Commodore Creighton, the commander-in-chief of the squadron. Commodore Issac Mayo, one of the wit-nesses produced by me, gives a full account of this cabal, and of his refusal to join it. His testimony will be referred to hereafter, in another connexion.. . .

In 1844, the President (John Tyler) nominated me to the Senate for promotion as a captain. This nomination was confirmed on the (31st) day of May, 1844,—my appointment to take rank from the 29th March, 1844. The circumstances attending this appointment were of peculiar interest to me; and it is most important that they should be fully understood by the Court. Attempts were made, out-side the Senate by certain officers of the Navy, to induce that body to reject my nomination. The naval Committee of the Senate, to whom the nomi-nation had been referred, were approached by offi-cers hostile to or prejudiced against me; and such objections were made to my appointment, that the

committee felt it proper to call on the Secretary of the Navy for all papers on file relating to my official conduct. The archives of the Department were ran-sacked; charges preferred against me during my ser-vice as sailing-master, lieutenant and commander, growing (with a single exception) out of those petty altercations and personal quarrels unfortunately too common in our profession, were raked up; and the records of all courts martial before which, in the course of thirty years, I had been brought, were laid before the committee. These documents having been thoroughly examined by them, they reported in favor of the nomination; and on their report it was unanimously confirmed.

There is but one safeguard; and this is to be found in an honest, whole-hearted, inflexible support of the wise, the just, the impartial guaranteed of the Constitution. I have the fullest confidence that you will faithfully adhere to this guarantee; and, therefore, with like confidence, I leave my destiny in your hands.

When, in 1855, I complained to the Secretary (of the Navy, James C.) Dobbin of "some unseen influence" seeking "through unmerited prejudice to injure me with the Department," and to prevent it from according to me my just rights, I stated that I then fully believed, and what I had long before sus-pected to be the fact, I was driven to this conclusion by the persistent refusal of the several secretaries to employ me, in the face of all proofs of my fitness, in the records of the Department, and of the recom-mendations and support of so many distinguished men, in support of my applications. I could draw, from the circumstances, no other inference; nor do I think that any other can be drawn by you. But the fact is not now left to inference merely. You have, in the deposition of the Secretary, Mr. (George) Ban-croft, direct evidence of the fact. In answer to the ninth interrogatory on my part, he says:

"When Secretary of the Navy, I never had cause to doubt, and never doubted, Captain Levy's competence to serve the United States in the grade of captain. I did not find myself able to give a com-mand, for three reasons:

1st. The excessive number of officers of his grade made it impossible to employ all of them who were fit.

2d. The good of the service, moreover, seemed to require bringing forward officers less advanced in years than most of the captains, and the law sanc-tioned that course.

3d. I perceived a strong prejudice in the service against Captain Levy, which seemed to me, in a considerable part, attributable to his being of the Jewish persuasion; and while I, as an executive officer, had the same liberal views which guided the President and Senate in commissioning him as a captain, I always endeavored in fitting out ships to have some reference to that harmonious co-operation which is essential to the highest effectiveness.

To the first of these reasons no exception can be taken. The second is founded on a favorite theory of Mr. Bancroft, while Secretary, to which, were it impartially carried out, I should be as little disposed to object as any other officer of my rank and age.

The third reason assigned by Mr. Bancroft, though last in order, is not least in importance.

The fact that it is assigned by him as one of the reasons for not giving me a command, justified the inference that the first two reasons would not have been sufficient to produce that result without the addition of the third.

From what source and in what manner, Mr. Bancroft perceived the strong prejudice in the service against me, of which he speaks, he does not state. But it is easy to trace it to its origin. He had never been officially connected with the Navy until he came to Washington in 1845, as head of the Department. He was then brought into intercourse with such officers of the Navy as were enable, by their rank, their connection with bureaux, or their social position to cultivate the acquaintance, and get the ear of the secretary. It was only by means of such intercourse, that it was possible for him to become acquainted with the prejudices which existed in the service against any of its members. It was only in this way that he could learn that any such prejudice existed against me. Among the officers of the Navy to whom the secretary was this peculiarly accessible, there were some who were friendly to me; but there were others who were not only unfriendly, but also active and bitter in their hostility against me. How else than through intercourse with those who had the motive, and took the pains, to force it upon him, was it possible for Mr. Bancroft to know that any prejudice existed against me in the Navy; and how could he form any estimate as to its strength, except from the frequency and rancor with which it was obtruded upon his notice?

From the same source which informed him of the prejudice, he learned its nature and grounds— the chief, if not the sole ground, being peculiar religious faith— my "being of the Jewish persuasion." Doubtless, those who could make such a fact the pretext for a prejudice against a brother officer, so inveterate and unyielding, as to compel the head of

the department reluctantly to recognize and admit as—to some extent as least—an element of his official action, would not scruple to disparage and traduce, in other respects, the object of their aversion. But even their efforts failed to awaken, for a moment, in the mind of the secretary, a solitary doubt as to my *competence*. This he tells us in the most emphatic terms.

In the satisfaction which this avowal gives me—in the gratitude I owe, and shall ever cherish, to one who, in spite of such efforts, retained towards me an opinion so favorable—I could almost pass over, without remark, the injury done me—most unwittingly, I am sure—by his allowing to such an objection any weight whatever. Had it then come to my knowledge, I could have shown him, just as I have now shown to you, form the records of the department, that during my year's command of the Vandalia, my religious faith never impaired the efficiency of my ship; that I never permitted it to interfere with the rights, or to wound the feelings, of my Christian officers and men; and that I did what I could, and all that they desired, to respect and satisfy those rights and feelings. I might have shown to him, as I have shown to you, by the evidence of the many officers, who, in this investigation, have testified in my behalf, that the prejudice to which he was constrained to give such serious effect against me, was far from being so general or so strong as he led to believe;—that officers, more in number than my traducers, and far better qualified to judge, were untainted by it—treated it with contempt, and denounced it as inconsistent with the spirit of our institutions—unworthy of the present age, and degrading to the honor of the naval service. And I might thus, perhaps, have afforded him the opportunity, which, I doubt not, he would gladly have seized, not only from a sense of justice to myself, but in accordance with his own liberal and enlightened convictions, of setting his face, like a flint, against t double-headed hydra of personal prejudice and religious bigotry, and of driving it forever from the councils of his department. The benefit of such an act to myself would have been insignificant, in comparison with the vindication it would have furnished of the dignity and justice of our Government, and its faithful conservation of the most sacred of our public and private rights.. . .

Mr. President and Gentlemen of the Court:

My defence, so far as it depends on the examination of the evidence, is before you; and here, perhaps, I ought to stop. But the peculiarities of my case—the importance and far-reaching interest of the principles it involves—requires, what I hope you will allow me, a few additional remarks.

That the allegation of unfitness for the naval service, made against me by the Government, was wholly unsupported by evidence; and that I have made out a complete defense against the attempt to justify my dismissal, and an affirmative title to restoration, by the proofs on my part; these I regard as undeniable propositions. And yet there are those connected with the navy, who, notwithstanding all the proofs I have produces, are hostile to my restoration. This, it would be vain to deny to others, or to conceal from myself. Should any one of these dare to obtrude upon you the opinion or the wish, that I should not be restored; or, being restored, should not be placed upon the active list; you have only to refer him to the oath which you have take, to silence and rebuke him. Permit me— not that I suppose you have forgotten its terms, but because of their peculiar pertinency to my case—to quote the closing words of this oath. It not only requires you, as before remarked "well and truly to examine and inquire, according to the evidence, into the matter now before you; "but, to do this, "without partiality or prejudice. "This oath, although exceedingly brief, is exceedingly comprehensive and precise. The lawmakers who framed it well know the special dangers to which Courts of Inquiry are exposed—partiality towards influential prosecutors and accusers, and prejudice against the accused. Against these, the oath solemnly warns you; and if ever there was a case in which such a warning was right and seasonable, this is that case.

The Government, with its vase power and influence, is, in name at least, my prosecutor. Men in high places, who have once done me grievous wrong, are interested to prevent the remedying of that wrong. There are others, not without their influence, who, by their activity in support of the wrong, and in opposition to the remedy, have a common interest with my prosecutors.

Never, on the other hand, was there a man, in the ranks of our profession, against whom, in the breasts of certain members of that profession, prejudices so unjust and yet so strong, have so long and so incessantly rankled. Such, too, are the origin and character of these prejudices, as to make them, of all others, the most inveterate and unyielding. The prejudice felt by men of little minds, who think themselves, by the accidental circumstances of wealth or ancestry, better than the less favored of their fellows; the prejudice of *caste*, which looks down on the man who, by honest toil, is the maker of his own fortunes; this prejudice is stubborn as well as bitter, and of this I have has, as you have seen the proofs, my full share. But this is placable and transient compared with that generated and nourished by religious intolerance and bigotry.

The first article of the amendments to the Constitution of the United States, specially declares, in its first clause, that "Congress shall make no law respecting an establishment of religion, or prohibiting the free exercise thereof; "this showing by its place, no less than by its language, how highly freedom of conscience was valued by the founders of our Republic. In the constitutions of the several States, now in force, the like provision is contained. Our liberality and justice, in this regard, have been honored by the friends of liberty and human rights throughout the world. An eminent British writer, about thirty years ago, in the ablest of their reviews, used, in reference to this point, the following language:

"They have fairly and completely, and probably forever, extinguished that spirit of religious persecution which has been the employment and the curse of mankind, for four or five centuries; not only that persecution which imprisons and scourges for religious opinions, but the tyranny of incapacitation, which by disqualifying from civil offices, and cutting a man off from the lawful objects of ambition, endeavors to strangle religious freedom in silence, and to enjoy all the advantages, without the blood, and noise, and fire of the persecution.********** In this particular, the Americans are at the head of all the nations of the world."

Little did the author of this generous tribute to our country suspect, that even while he was penning it, there were those in the American navy, with whom it was a question whether a Jew should be tolerated in the service? Still less did the dream, that at the very moment when, in his own country, a representative of the illustrious house of RUSSELL, eminent by his services in the cause of freedom, of education, and of justice, is about giving himself, with the full assent of his government, to the work of Jewish emancipation, a spectacle like the present should be witnessed in this land of equality and freedom. For with those who would now deny to me, because of my religious faith, the restoration, to which, by half a century of witnesses, I have proved myself entitled, what is it but an attempt to place the professors of this faith under the ban of incapacitation?

This is the case before you; and, in this view, its importance cannot be overrated. It is the case of every Israelite in the Union. I need not speak to you of their number. They are unsurpassed by any portion of our people in loyalty to the Constitution and to the Union; in their quiet obedience to the laws; and in the cheerfulness with which they contribute to the public burthens. Many of them have been distinguished by their liberal donations to the general interests of education and of charity; in some cases, too—of which the name of JUDAH TOURO will remind you—to charities controlled by Christians. And of all my brethren in this land—as well those of foreign birth as of American descent—how rarely does any one of them become a charge on your State or municipal treasuries! How largely do they all contribute to the activities of trade; to the interests of commerce; to the stock of public wealth! Are all these to be prescribed? And is this to be done while we retain in our Constitution the language I have quoted? Is this language to be spoken to the ear, but broken to the hope, of my race? Are the thousands of Judah and the ten thousands of Israel, in their dispersions throughout the earth, who look to America, as a land bright which promise—are they now to learn, to their sorrow and dismay, that we, too, have sunk into the mire of religious intolerance and bigotry? And are American Christians now to begin the persecution of the Jews? Of the Jews, who stand among them the representatives of the patriarchs and prophets,—the Jews, to whom were committed the oracles of God,—the Jews, from whom these oracles have been received, and who are the living witnesses of their truth;—the Jews, from whom came the founder of Christianity;—the Jews, to whom, as Christians themselves believe, have been made promises of greatness and of glory, in whose fulfilment are bound up the hopes, not merely of remnant of Israel, but of all the races of men? And think not, if you once enter on this career, that it can be limited to the Jew. What is my case to-day, if you yield to this injustice, may to-morrow be that of the Roman Catholic or the Unitarian; the Episcopalian or the Methodist; the Presbyterian or the Baptist. There is but one safeguard; and this is to be found in an honest, whole-hearted, inflexible support of the wise, the just, the impartial guaranteed of the Constitution. I have the fullest confidence that you will faithfully adhere to this guarantee; and, therefore, with like confidence, I leave my destiny in your hands.

Source:

The Jews in America, 1621-1970: A Chronology & Fact Book. Compiled and edited by Irving J. Sloan. Dobbs Ferry, NY: Oceana Publications, 1971.

On November 9 and 10, 1862, Major General Ulysses S. Grant issued what became known as "Grant's Jew Order." At that time, Grant was in command of the Department of Tennessee, which included North Mississippi, Parts of Kentucky, and West Tennessee. The order was: "The Jews, as a class, violating every regulation of trade established by the Treasury Department, and also Department orders, are hereby expelled by the Treasury Department." The order seemed so out of character for General Grant, that upon being told such an order had been issued, the Secretary of War Edwin Stanton dismissed it as impossible. According to Rabbi Wise, "neither the former (General Halleck) nor the latter (Secretary Stanton) believed that Grant could have issued an order so absurd and ridiculous."

General Grant was compelled to make the order as frustration mounted over cotton trade and commerce that continued serving the civilian market behind Confederate lines. Both Confederate and Union governments had banned trade with the enemy, but it continued nonetheless. Southerners complained bitterly about growers who failed to burn their cotton, but instead sold it to Yankees on the sly. The blockade imposed by the Union on the Southern shoreline prevented commerce with European nations, so Confederates resorted to secret direct trade with the North. Much of the smuggled goods came down South through Kentucky. The trickle became a deluge during 1862 when the union conquered the Mississippi Valley. Nashville, New Orleans and Memphis became centers of illegal trade. In an effort to regulate and control the trade, the Union issued permits that made exchanges legitimate. However, bribes and illegal trading continued.

Generals Sherman and Grant had tried unsuccessfully to stop the cotton trade through Memphis and western Tennessee using the system of permits and requiring payment for cotton to be made in U.S. greenbacks (instead of gold that could be melted and used by the Confederates). Some of the highly visible traders who defied these efforts were Jews. Grant's own father is said to have brought three Jewish merchants to Memphis to seek permits, and this family involvement pushed Grant to issue the order to exclude Jews. In this newspaper editorial, Rabbi Wise gives his perspective on this issue and describes how General Halleck and President Lincoln revoked Grant's order. Rabbi Isaac Meyer Wise was a member of the delegation sent to meet with the President concerning discrimination against the Jews in the United States.

RABBI ISAAC MAYER WISE AND ORDER NO. 11

The history of General Grant's order and its revocation forms quite an interesting chapter in the annals of the day. Gentlemen from Paducah, Ky., telegraphed to the President, who informed General Halleck instantly; we wrote immediately to Secretary (of War) Stanton; but neither former nor the latter believed that Gen. Grant could have issued an order so absurd and ridiculous, and, therefore, did not do anything in the matter. When Mr. Kaskel came to Washington, January 3, and was introduced to the President, by Mr. Gurley of Cincinnati, the President at once gave order to Gen. Halleck to revoke said order. General Halleck would not believe in the existence of such order, till Mr. Kaskel showed him the official copy. General Halleck instantly and peremptorily revoked the order and telegraphed to Gen. Grant to inform all post commanders instantly, of the will of the government in this matter. The Cincinnati and Louisville delegation came too late.—The order was rescinded. Still we thought it proper to see the President and express our thanks for his promptness in this matter.—Mark, however, how democratic things look in Washington. We arrived from Baltimore about 5 P.M. on Wednesday (January 6), arrived in the hotel without changing clothes. Rev. Dr. Lilienthal inquired and was informed that Mr. Gurley was in the same house, but was not in at present. Meanwhile, Mr. Bijur and myself went to Mr. Pendleton of Cincinnati and talked half an hour to him.

On returning to our hotel we met Mr. Gurley, who without bestowing any consideration on our traveling garbs, went with us to the White House and before 8 P.M. we were introduced to the President, who being all alone, received us with that frank cordiality, which, though usually neglected, becomes men high in office so well. Having expressed our thanks for the promptness and dispatch in revoking Gen. Grant's order, the President gave utterance to his surprise that Gen. Grant should have issued so ridiculous an order, and added—"to condemn a class is, to say the least, to wrong the good with the bad. I do not like to hear a class or nationality condemned on account of a few sinners." The President, we must confess, fully illustrated to us and convinced us that he knows no distinction between Jew and Gentile, that he feels no prejudice against any nationality, and that he by no means will allow that a citizen in any wise be wronged on account of his place of birth or religious confession. He illustrated this point to us in a very happy manner, of which we can only give the substance at present, and promise to give particulars on another occasion. Now then, in our traveling habiliment, we spoke about half an hour to the President of the U.S. in an open and frank manner, and were dismissed in the same simple style.

Sorry we are to say the Congress did not think proper to be as just as the President is. Congress is not now the people's legislative body, it belongs to a party. Senator Powel (1) of Kentucky, as noted elsewhere, introduced a resolution condemning the unjust order of Gen. Grant, to inform others that orders of this kind must not be issued; but the resolution was tabled to be killed, when called up again. Mr. Pendleton of Cincinnati, attempted in vain on Monday and Tuesday to bring the following resolution before the House. He finally succeeded on Wednesday (yesterday) to propose the following:

Mr. Pendleton offered a preamble setting forth that Major-General Grant, on the 17th of December, as the commander of the Department of the Tennessee, did issue an order stating that the Jews, as a class, had violated ever regulation of trade established in that department, and for this were to be expelled from the department within twenty-four hours, &c., and as in the pursuance of the order General Grant caused many peaceful citizens to be expelled within twenty-four hours without allegation of misconduct, and with no other proof than that they were members of a certain religious denomination; and whereas said sweeping order makes no discrimination between the innocent and the guilty, and it is illegal, unjust, tyrannical and cruel, therefore

Resolved, That the said order deserves the sternest condemnation of the House and of the President of the United States as Commander-in-Chief of the Army and Navy.

Mr. PENDLETON moved the previous question on the passage of this proposition.

Mr. WASHBURNE (R) moved that it be laid upon the table; and this was agreed to—yeas 56, nays 53.

On motion of Mr. Washburne, the everlasting Mr. Washburne, the resolution was tabled by a vote of 56 yeas to 53 nays. If the Hebrew citizens of the United States were "gentlemen of color," Mr. Washburne would certainly have made a brilliant effort to vindicate their rights and expose a general who committed a gross outrage on them. But being only white men, it would not pay. Partisan legislation, that is all we have to expect of this congress. Mr. Pendleton said Washburne's motive was that of friendship for Grant, whom to defend in congress he had several times taken upon himself; but Republican members openly says, it is a rule of the House to vote down everything coming from the other side, viz: the democratic. How do you like this remarkable impartiality?

Having to see a good many things to-day, we must conclude this, to say more to-morrow.

THE EDITOR.
(Isaac Mayer Wise)

Source:

The Jews in America, 1621-1970: A Chronology & Fact Book. Compiled and edited by Irving J. Sloan. Dobbs Ferry, NY: Oceana Publications, 1971. pp. 111-113.

In the late nineteenth and early twentieth centuries, millions of immigrants traveled to the "promised land" of America from eastern Europe. In the space of 50 years, from 1877 to 1927, the number of Jews in the United States skyrocketed from less than 250,000 to more than 4 million, and the Jewish-American population grew faster than that of the nation as a whole. This created a backlash of anti-Semitism, which found expression in, among other things, interest in the notorious Protocols of the Elders of Zion, *a forgery that purported to describe a widespread Jewish plot to destroy modern civilization and build a universal Jewish state in its place. The hostility resembled that met by Irish Catholics when they began to immigrate in large numbers in the mid-nineteenth century and inspired fears of a "popeish" conspiracy to bring the new, overwhelmingly Protestant nation to its knees.*

But Jews were accustomed to anti-Semitism. There was far more of it, including more violence, in the homelands they had left than in the United States. More troubling for most was the common immigrants' ordeal of adjusting to a new and strange culture. In Russia, the homeland of some 95 percent of Jewish immigrants, they had lived a constricted and insulated life in small rural towns, where they had worked as shopkeepers, peddlers, and marketers of farm goods, and where women had seldom ventured further than to the synagogue to pray. In America, many were caught in "culture shock"—completely perplexed by the complexity, pace, and variety of daily life in a pluralistic and urban society. Yiddish-speaking Jewish immi-

grants often turned to the Jewish Daily Forward, *a working-class newspaper written in Yiddish, for advice and counsel.*

In 1906 the paper started a feature called "A Bintel Brief" (meaning "A Bundle of Letters"), in which the editors answered letters from their readers on a wide range of subjects. Here is a sampling of three letters from Jewish women immigrants, and the paper's answers, from 1907-1910.

LETTERS TO THE *JEWISH DAILY FORWARD*

Dear Editor,

I am one of those unfortunate girls thrown by fate into a dark and dismal shop, and I need your counsel.

Along with my parents, sisters and brothers, I came from Russian Poland where I had been well educated. But because of the terrible things going on in Russia we were forced to emigrate to America. I am now seventeen years old, but I look younger and they say I am attractive.

A relative talked us into moving to Vineland, New Jersey, and here in this small town I went to work in a shop. In this shop there is a foreman who is an exploiter, and he sets prices on the work. He figures it out so that the wages are very low, he insults and reviles the workers, he fires them and then takes them back. And worse than all of this, in spite of the fact that he has a wife and several children, he often allows himself to "have fun" with some of the working girls. It was my bad luck to be one of the girls that he tried to make advances to. And woe to any girl who doesn't willingly accept them.

Though my few hard-earned dollars mean a lot to my family of eight souls, I didn't want to accept the foreman's vulgar advances. He started to pick on me, said my work was no good, and when I proved to him he was wrong, he started to shout at me in the vilest language. He insulted me in Yiddish and then in English, so the American workers could understand too. Then, as if the Devil were after me, I ran home.

I am left without a job. Can you imagine my circumstances and that of my parents who depend on my earnings? The girls in the shop were very upset over the foreman's vulgarity but they don't want him to throw them out, so they are afraid to be witnesses against him. What can be done about this? I beg you to answer me.

Respectfully,
A Shopgirl

Answer:

Such a scoundrel should be taught a lesson that could be an example to others. The girl is advised to bring out into the open the whole story about the foreman, because there in the small town it shouldn't be difficult to have him thrown out of the shop and for her to get her job back.

1909

Dear Editor,

Please print my letter and give me an answer. You might possibly save my life with it. I have no peace, neither day nor night, and I am afraid I will go mad because of my dreams.

I came to America three years ago from a small town in Lithuania, and I was twenty years old at that time. Besides me, my parents had five more unmarried daughters. My father was a Hebrew teacher. We used to help out by plucking chickens, making cigarettes, washing clothes for people, and we lived in poverty. The house was like a Gehenna. There was always yelling, cursing, and even beating of each other. It was bitter for me till a cousin of mine took pity on me. He sent a steamship ticket and money. He wrote that I should come to America and he would marry me.

I didn't know him, because he was a little boy when he left our town, but my delight knew no bounds. When I came to him, I found he was a sick man, and a few weeks later he died.

Then I began to work on ladies' waists. The "pleasant" life of a girl in the dreary shop must certainly be familiar to you. I toiled, and like all shopgirls, I hoped and waited for deliverance through a good match.

Landsleit and matchmakers were busy. I met plenty of prospective bridegrooms, but though I was attractive and well built, no one grabbed me. Thus a year passed. Then I met a woman who told me she was a matchmaker and had many suitors "in stock." I spilled out all my heartaches to her. First she talked me out of marrying a work-worn operator with whom I would have to live in poverty, then she told me that pretty girls could wallow in pleasure if they made the right friends. She made such a connection for me. But I had not imagined what that meant.

What I lived through afterwards is impossible for me to describe. The woman handed me over to bandits, and when I wanted to run away from them they locked me in a room without windows and beat me savagely.

Time passed and I got used to the horrible life. Later I even had an opportunity to escape, because they used to send me out on the streets, but life had become meaningless for me anyway, and nothing mattered any more. I lived this way for six months, degraded and dejected, until I got sick and they drove me out of that house.

I appealed for admission into several hospitals, but they didn't want to take me in. I had no money, because the rogues had taken everything from me. I tried to appeal to landsleit for help, but since they already knew all about me, they chased me away. I had decided to throw myself into the river, but wandering around on the streets, I met a richly dressed man who was quite drunk. I took over six hundred dollars from him and spent the money on doctors, who cured me.

Then I got a job as a maid for fine people who knew nothing about my past, and I have been working for them for quite a while. I am devoted and diligent, they like me, and everything is fine.

A short time ago the woman of the house died, but I continued to work there. In time, her husband proposed that I marry him. The children, who are not yet grown up, also want me to be their "mother." I know it would be good for them and for me to remain there. The man is honest and good; but my heart won't allow me to deceive him and conceal my past. What shall I do now?

Miserable

Answer:

Such letters from victims of "white slavery" come to our attention quite often, but we do not publish them. We are disgusted by this plague on society, and dislike bringing it to the attention of our readers. But as we read this letter we felt we dare not discard it, because it can serve as a warning for other girls. They must, in their dreary lives, attempt to withstand these temptations and guard themselves from going astray.

This letter writer, who comes to us with her bitter and earnest tears, asking advice, has sufficient reason to fear that if the man finds out about her past he will send her away. But it is hard to conceal something that many people know. Such a thing cannot be kept secret forever. When the man finds out about it from someone else, he would feel that she had betrayed him and it would be worse.

Therefore, "Honesty is the best policy." She should tell him the truth, and whatever will be, will be.

1910

Worthy Editor,

My husband, ———— deserted me and our three small children, leaving us in desperate need. I was left without a bit of bread for the children, with debts in the grocery store and the butcher's, and last month's rent unpaid.

I am not complaining so much about his abandoning me as about the grief and suffering of our little children, who beg for food, which I cannot give them. I am young and healthy, I am able and willing to work in order to support my children, but unfortunately I am tied down because my baby is only six months old. I looked for an institution which would take care of my baby, but my friends advise against it.

The local Jewish Welfare Agencies are allowing me and my children to die of hunger, and this is because my "faithful" husband brought me over from Canada just four months ago and therefore I do not yet deserve to eat their bread.

It breaks my heart but I have come to the conclusion that in order to save my innocent children from hunger and cold I have to give them away.

I will sell my beautiful children to people who will give them a home. I will sell them, not for money, but for bread, for a secure home where they will have enough food and warm clothing for the winter.

I, the unhappy young mother, am willing to sign a contract, with my heart's blood, stating that the children belong to the good people who will treat them tenderly. Those who are willing and able to give my children a good home can apply to me.

Respectfully,
Mrs. P
Chicago

Answer:

What kind of society are we living in that forces a mother to such desperate straits that there is no other way out than to sell her three children for a piece of bread? Isn't this enough to kindle a hellish fire of hatred in every human heart for such a system?

The first to be damned is the heartless father, but who knows what's wrong with him? Perhaps he, too, is unhappy. We hope, though, that this letter will reach him and he will return to aid them.

We also ask our friends and readers to take an interest in this unfortunate woman and to help her so that she herself can be a mother to her children.

Source:
Jewish Daily Forward (newspaper). 1907-1910.

The Hebrew word Pesach means "pass over" and refers to the eight days beginning on the fifteenth day of Nisan, the seventh month of the lunar year. It alludes to the story in Exodus about the angel of death who killed the first-born children of the Egyptians, but "passed over" the houses of the children of Israel which had been marked, by God's command, with the blood of a lamb slaughtered in preparation for their redemption from slavery. On the anniversary of this date, the Israelites were required to slaughter a lamb, and in the days of the temple at Jerusalem, pour its blood on the altar and eat its flesh. Later, a ceremonial meal known as the Seder assumed ritualistic primacy. During this meal, the Haggadah, a book containing the liturgy and the story of deliverance, was read and symbolic food served. This food includes meat of the paschal lamb; matzo or unleavened bread, unfermented and sun-baked because of the hasty departure from Egypt; bitter herbs recalling the harsh life of slavery and wine symbolizing the fruitfulness of the earth. Seder means "order" or "narration," and suggests the order of the service and the ordering effect of ceremonially narrating the biblical story through the generations. Passover absorbed an older Semitic festival of spring renewal. Today it is essentially a household holiday—a reaffirmation of familial, religious, historic, and seasonal traditions that have continuing significance. It is ongoing also in another sense, for its culmination is seen as the presentation of the Ten Commandments and the Covenant between God and Israel at Mount Sinai.

KNAIDLACH (MATZO BALLS) AND CHICKEN SOUP

Ingredients for matzo balls:

2 tbsp soft butter

2 eggs

½ cup matzo meal

½ tsp salt

2 tbsp hot water

2 quarts simmering salted water.

Whisk the butter and eggs together in a small bowl with a fork. Gradually stir in the salt and matzo meal. Refrigerate the mixture for 30 minutes or until batter is thick enough to make balls. With wet hands, shape the batter into small balls. Drop the balls gently into 2 quarts of simmering salted water. Cover and continue simmering for 25 minutes. Remove with a slotted spoon and add balls to chicken soup (see below). Simmer in soup for another 15 minutes.

Ingredients for chicken soup:

1 4-5 lb chicken, quartered

3 quarts cold water

1 cup carrots, peeled and cut into chunks

The central feature of the Seder is the gathering of family and friends with room for the "unexpected guest."

2 celery stalks
1 large onion, peeled and chopped into chunks
2 cloves, whole
2 peppercorns
1 bayleaf
salt, to taste
a few sprigs of fresh dill
Rinse chicken. Place chicken in large pot and cover with water and bring to a boil. Reduce to simmer and remove scum that rises to top. Cover and sim-

mer for another half hour. Add chopped vegetables and seasonings. Simmer for 2 hours. Chicken should be tender. Remove chicken and vegetables and strain the soup. Cool and refrigerate soup until fat can be skimmed off. Bring the soup to a simmer again and add matzo balls. Season to taste.

Source:
Anonymous.

*P*urim is a feast day celebrated on the fourteenth day of Adar, the sixth month of
the Jewish calendar. It commemorates the escape of the Persian Jews from a massacre planned by Haman, minister of the king, Ahasuerus, through the intercession
of Esther, the queen. This story is recounted in the Old Testament Book of Esther.
Haman's anger had been provoked by a Jewish leader, Mordecai, who, for religious
reasons, refused to bow in homage to him. Haman persuaded the king that the Jews
were disobedient and seditious, and obtained a decree permitting their destruction.
Lots were cast to determine when this should take place. Unknown to the king or
Haman, Esther was the cousin of Mordecai, and she revealed Haman's machinations and Mordecai's past services to Ahasuerus. The king could not legally alter his
decree, but he granted the Jews the right to defend themselves, thus forestalling an
attack, and had Haman hanged. Purim, also called the Feast of Lots, is characterized by frivolity—feasting, dancing, masquerade, playacting based on the story of
Esther saving her people from Haman, and in more recent times, beauty contests
for the selection of a "Queen Esther" who reigns over this Jewish carnival.

HAMANTASHEN
(HAMAN'S POCKETS)

These triangular pastries are traditionally filled with
poppy seeds, although other fillings, such as prunes,
can be used. One reason given for the shape of the
pastries is that it is reminiscent of the tri-cornered
hat worn by Haman and other officials in Persia.
Also, the tasty "surprise" in hamantashen reflects
how God's will was also hidden during Purim.

Ingredients for Dough

1¼ cup sugar
2¼ cup flour
2½ tsp baking powder
1 tsp salt
½ cup butter
¾ cup milk
2 large eggs
1 egg, beaten, for glaze

For Filling: If a can of poppy seeds is available, you
can make traditional hamantashen. If not, prune or
apricot jam can be substituted.

Melt butter and blend with sugar. Add eggs and
milk. Mix in dry ingredients thoroughly and knead
well. Roll into a ball and refrigerate for one hour.
Roll out the dough to ¼ inch thickness and using a
cutter or glass, cut into four-inch circles. Place a
tablespoon of filling in the center of each circle.
Pull up three sides of the dough and pinch in to create sides of triangle. Glaze the pastry by brushing tri-
angles with beaten egg. Place on greased cookie
sheets and bake in oven at 350° Fahrenheit. Bake
for approximately 20 minutes or until brown.

Source:
Anonymous.

A teacher at the Ramaz Hebrew Day School in New York directs the preparation of Purim baskets. The baskets are being filled with apples, lollipops, and hamantashen, a triangular filled pastry.

*L*etty Cottin Pogrebin is a well known journalist and author writing on issues pertinent to Jewish feminism and life in the United States. She was a founding editor of Ms. Magazine, and has been published in national magazines and journals. Her article, "Different Kinds of Survival," highlights the tensions between African Americans and Jews, both minority populations in the United States. Black history and Jewish history are strikingly different: blacks were brought to America to be sold into slavery while Jews came to America to pursue the promise of a better life. Pogrebin suggests that while Jews and blacks have developed a divisive relationship in America, they have much in common. Most notably, she argues, their common struggle for survival, as blacks struggle to improve their living conditions and Jews struggle to preserve their history. Pogrebin suggests that though the survival needs of blacks and Jews differ, both minorities in America express their needs with an intensity that is remarkable, and these two groups are the only minorities who ". . .take each other seriously, the only minority groups who still seem to believe that our destinies are interwoven." She then suggests that African-Americans are looking for Jews to use their power and success in America to help them improve their living conditions, as only one minority group can help another. What is more, Pogrebin believes that this is the Jews' responsibility.

DIFFERENT KINDS OF SURVIVAL

Letty Cottin Pogrebin

According to a Yankelovich poll, in the last quarter-century anti-Semitism has declined among whites but increased among blacks. Today blacks are twice as likely as whites to hold significant anti-Semitic attitudes and, even more alarming, it is younger and better-educated blacks who tend to be the most bigoted. By the same token, although a 1990 poll done by the National Opinion Research Center found that Jews have more positive attitudes toward blacks and a greater commitment to equal opportunity than do other white Americans, the poll also found that a majority of Jews do not favor government help or government spending to benefit blacks. Worse still, a Harris poll found that Jews are more likely than other whites to be upset if blacks move into their neighborhood; and 20 percent of Jews said they did not want their children to attend school with blacks, as compared with only 14 percent of other whites.

In light of the recent controversy over Professor Leonard Jeffries's views and the continuing confrontation between African-Americans and Hasidic Jews in Brooklyn's Crown Heights section, it's fair to say that black-Jewish relations are at one of their periodic flashpoints. No longer can blacks and Jews be drawn together simply because other Americans hate us both. No longer can we expect each other to agree on what constitutes racism, anti-Semitism or institutional barriers to equal opportunity. No longer can a single speech or slogan move us to march together. Now we often march in opposite directions or face each other across an abyss. Now our two communities clash regularly over issues of power, priorities, competitive oppression and conflicting self-interest. Now it takes arguing, negotiating and struggling to find common ground within our changed circumstances and new suspicions. Now I know that black-Jewish coalition building takes work and leaves scars.

During the 1984 presidential campaign, when Jesse Jackson was excoriated for his "Hymietown" statement and full-page ads appeared from an organization called "Jews Against Jackson." the growing enmity between our two communities reached a boiling point. In response, several black-Jewish dialogues were started. One of them was a consciousness-raising-type group composed of three blacks and three Jews, founded by Harriet Michel, then president of the New York Urban League, and myself That group is still meeting regularly. Also in 1984, I helped to form a thirty-member black-Jewish women's group whose purpose was to prepare our two communities to play a constructive role at the Nairobi United Nations Conference on Women. Although it continued meeting after the conference was over, this group petered out within two years. At first, I attributed its failure to waning black interest.

"Why do you think so many black women stopped coming to our dialogue meetings even though we started out with an equal representation?" I asked a black friend who had been part of the group.

"You Jews have to stop acting like God's chosen people." she barked, her eyes hard and angry. "The world doesn't revolve around you. Relations with Jews are not a priority for most African-Americans; our main concern is survival."

To blacks, America is the nation that enslaved them and continues to deny them opportunities. To Jews, it is a promised land that made good on its promises.

The differences between blacks and Jews are rarely more obvious than when each group speaks about its own "survival." a word that both use frequently but with quite dissimilar meanings. For blacks, survival means actual physical endurance, staying alive in the face of violent crime, drugs, hunger, homelessness, and infant mortality rates that are more than triple those of whites; it means surviving as a viable community when 30 percent of the adults and 75 percent of the young live in poverty, when 44 percent of black 17-year-olds are functionally illiterate and black unemployment is twice the white rate. For Jews, survival means keeping a minority culture and a religion alive against all odds, guarding against anti-Semitism and the slippery slope that could lead from hate speech to the gas chambers, and helping to guarantee the security of Israel.

In other words, blacks worry about their actual conditions and fear for the present; Jews worry about their history and fear for the future. Black survival is threatened by poverty; Jewish survival is threatened by affluence (with its temptation of intermarriage with the more privileged majority), assimilation and moral corruption. Racism is a bacterium, potentially curable but now deadly; anti-Semitism is a virus, potentially deadly but currently contained.

"In America, though permitted to be rich, Jews are not permitted to be comfortable." asserts writer Leonard Fein. When those who make us uncomfortable are black—for instance, Spike Lee, whose film Mo' Better Blues included the gratuitously stereotyped nightclub owners Joe and Josh Flatbush; or the rap group Public Enemy, whose best-selling record called Jews "Christ killers" and whose "Minister of Information," Professor Griff, said, "Jews are responsible for the majority of wickedness that goes on across the globe'; or talk-show host Oprah Winfrey, who benignly accepted the claim of a guest that Jews murder children for religious ritual; or Nobel laureate Bishop Desmond Tutu, who lectured Jews on forgiving the Nazis for the murder of the Six Million—we Jews somehow feel more threatened and betrayed, expecting better from our former allies. The color of the perpetrator does not determine the degree of our safety, only the degree of our surprise.

A totally assimilated Jewish friend of mine says he can never relax as long as a swastika is painted on even one wall in America. I have a recurrent dream in which my children and I are being herded into cattle cars en route to Auschwitz. Every Jew remembers that our people were powerful and well-off in the 1930s in Berlin and Prague and Warsaw, but their prosperity didn't save them. We remember how quickly Jews and Israel were scapegoated in the United States during the gas shortages of the 1970s and the farm crisis of the 1980s. We notice that no matter how few we are, Jews are blamed for the slightest economic reversal in the Soviet Union, Eastern Europe and France. In 1991, we heard whispers that the war in the Persian Gulf was the fault of the Jews. So, regardless of what we have accomplished in life we continue to fear the swastika and smell the smoke. In fact, the more we flourish, the surer we are that the anti-Semites are out there begrudging our success. As the old joke would have it, paranoids have enemies too.

My cattle-car dream takes me unawares every few years, like a dormant parasite that eats away at the intestines with no apparent provocation. I have toured the Dachau concentration camp near Munich, but that was long before I had children. I lost relatives to the Nazis, but my own immediate family, spawned in the 1960s, has never been in danger. Still, I dream that dream. I tell this to my black friend with the angry eyes. I want her to remember that in her lifetime and mine, one out of every three Jews in the world was slaughtered.

"Even if never personally threatened, you would need constant reassurance if one-third of your relatives had been murdered'" I tell her.

My friend listens but she still doesn't get it. She grew up in a neighborhood where Jews collected the rent, ran the shops, employed black domestic workers, checked up on welfare clients and taught black children. She works now in New York City, where every Jew she sees is thriving. She points out that 30 million American blacks have only twenty-six Congressional representatives and no black senators, while 6 million American Jews have thirty-three Jewish members of the House and eight Jewish senators. Through her eyes I see how it might seem unbelievable that a people so affluent, powerful and white could possibly be quaking at the summit.

How very differently our two out-groups view the world. To blacks, America is the nation that enslaved them and continues to deny them opportunities. To Jews, it is a promised land that made good on its promises. Blacks worry that their (bad) situation will never improve—therefore their issues are fundamental issues like affordable housing, better education and affirmative action. Jews worry that our (good) situation will not last—therefore our issues are safety issues like freedom of religion (separation of church and state), freedom of immigration (Soviet Jews, Ethiopian Jews) and a secure Israel. To summarize these complex differences in an oversimplified statement, African-Americans need relief in the form of practical economic assistance; Jews need relief in the form of normalized group and individual acceptance.

Assistance. Acceptance. Clearly these needs are not comparable, but they can be experienced with comparable intensity and they can lead people to the same place. Thus, blacks enter into dialogue in the hope it will result in action to address their needs, while for Jews, dialogue is the need: If blacks are still talking to us, we think, maybe the liberal alliance is not dead, maybe we don't have to stand alone, maybe we can feel a little safer in America.

Dialogue has taught me that each group inaccurately perceives the negative power of the other. Blacks are not really in a position to hurt Jews, but because of their superior numbers and a few high-profile anti-Semites, Jews fear them. Jews are not really in a position to hurt blacks, but blacks believe we are determined to keep them down. African-Americans are saying, If we're supposed to be brothers and sisters, how come you're doing so well and we're in the streets? Jews are saying, If we're supposed to be friends, how come you keep picking on us?

Maybe Jews and blacks lock horns more than other groups because we are the only ones who take each other seriously, the only minority groups who still seem to believe that our destinies are interwoven. (There are innumerable Jewish-black dialogues, but where are the Italian-black or Irish-black conclaves?) Or maybe we are encouraged to fight in public as surrogate combatants for the bigots in the dominant culture. As the media magnify every black-Jewish clash, other Americans can let off steam vicariously while avoiding the anger that might otherwise be directed at them. Meanwhile, blacks and Jews get hooked on the oldest scam in the world: divide and conquer.

I refuse to let that happen. While I had been hurt by my friend's angry words, talking with her clarified that I was the one who had not understood. I had suggested that there was something wrong with African-Americans for dropping out of the dialogue, when in fact there was something wrong with the dialogue for failing to serve the needs of its black participants. Because the Jewish agenda—creating alliances—was being fulfilled, Jews kept showing up at the meetings. But the black agenda—cooperative activism—had stalled, so some black women had stopped coming. It was as simple as that. Beneath her fury, my friend was really saying, "Stop complaining. Your needs are being met and mine are not." She saw Jews getting what they craved (acceptance), while what blacks craved (assistance) wasn't forthcoming.

Given their survival emergencies, the African-Americans in many of these dialogue groups have become impatient with the Jewish need for feel-good talk about the old civil rights alliance. Our African-American dialogue partners want to be seen as equals. They want to focus on today's realities. They want us to regard the underclass as a human problem, not a black problem, and black advancement as a moral imperative, not a quid pro quo for black-Jewish friendship. They want us to stop telling them what we have in common and to start listening to black assessments of our differences. They want us to use our political and economic power to get some action.

Blacks are asking Jews to go beyond tension reduction into practical, nitty-gritty activism and advocacy work. They want biracial teams to organize and lobby for economic and social programs in the areas of affordable housing, child care, health, dropout prevention, education and drug treatment. They want us to mount joint press conferences, petition campaigns, conferences, demonstrations, vigils and fact-finding trips. They want public education projects, guest columns in each other's newspapers, pulpit exchanges in each other's churches and synagogues, black-Jewish pairs speaking in the schools, Jewish intellectuals promoting books by and about African-Americans, career internships for black students. They expect us to work together monitoring police prejudice, hate crimes, media distortions, vandalism, harassment. They want Jews to "interrupt" racism whenever we see or hear it. And they want financial support for black self-reliance projects—they want white resources put into programs that African-Americans control.

African-Americans may not realize it, but what they are asking Jews to do, in my opinion, is to act Jewish. How we each practice religious Judaism is a private matter, but the practice of moral Judaism is something I believe most Jews must express publicly through our commitments.

To be morally Jewish requires doing tzedakah (the Hebrew word meaning charity, caring and "right action," whose linguistic root, tzedek, means justice) and gemilut hesed (acts of loving-kindness). These are actions, not just talk. The pursuit of justice is one definition of activism. It is also, as I've said, what makes and keeps us Jews. If we lose our purpose, we lose our peoplehood and become no more than an odd collection of folks with common ancestors, unique religious laws and an uncanny potential for victimization. That's not Jewish enough for me.

Letty Cottin Pogrebin is a founding editor of Ms. This article is adapted from her new book, *Deborah, Golda, and Me: Being Female and Jewish in America* (Crown).

Source:
The Nation, Sept 23, 1991, vol. 253, no. 9, pp. 332 (4).

KOREAN AMERICANS

George Jones's review about Koreans in Hawaii in 1906 paints a tranquil picture of Koreans that contrasts with the Korean experience in the United States at that time. Hawaii was annexed by the United States in 1898, but did not share the anti-Asian sentiment of the U.S. mainland. In 1910, the U.S. Census reported that 4,533 Koreans remained in Hawaii and 461 were living in the United States. Violent discrimination against Koreans was practiced in San Francisco, where restaurants refused to seat Asian customers. In fact, California laws supported anti-Asian behaviors; for instance, the Webb-Heney Land Law made it illegal for Asians to own property. The anti-Asian bias across the United States resulted in the Oriental Exclusion Act of 1924, which banned all Asian immigration to the United States for 30 years.

Koreans do not have a long history of immigration. Rather, the nation's policy for centuries has been one of isolation. First, under Chinese rule in the seventeenth century, Korea was nicknamed the Hermit Kingdom because so few Koreans ventured out of the country. For three hundred years Korea was a tributary state of China. In 1876, the Japanese negotiated a treaty that gave them authority over Korea. Korea did not become a Japanese protectorate, however, until China was defeated in 1895 in the Sino-Japanese War. By that time, a negative stereotype was developing in the United States press, in part because of the American writer Jack London. London covered the Russian-Japanese conflict of 1904 and included derogatory comments about Koreans.

The U.S. Census records show that between 1903 and 1905, about 7,200 Koreans immigrated to Hawaii to work for the Hawaiian Sugar Planter's Association. Immigration ceased in 1905 when Japan dismantled the Korean emigration office and prohibited Koreans from leaving the country. Koreans in Hawaii developed a close-knit community. Jones comments that "in Hawaii the Korean is at his best." The availability of medical assistance, the steady wage, and the opportunity for education are cited as benefits, though Jones makes clear his religious interest in the Koreans. In fact, between 1890 and 1905, 64 Korean students came to the United States for further education at the urging of American missionaries. Jones was not the only missionary urging Koreans to immigrate. Horace N. Allen, a former Presbyterian missionary in Korea, was appointed to a diplomatic post in Korea, where he sought to counter Japanese influence. Allen encouraged immigration to Hawaii and helped set up the opportunity for Koreans to work on the sugar plantations. He is said to have used both legal and illegal means to accomplish his objective.

THE KOREANS IN HAWAII

Hawaii, one of the beautiful portions of the earth's surface, presents one of the most vividly interesting yet tragic chapters of history to be found in human annals. For centuries the home of a generous, proud Island race, its original owners are fast vanishing away and other races have entered upon their inheritance. One is impressed with this as he moves about the Islands. Instead of the brown Kanaka, sturdy of physique and generous and happy-go-lucky in character, Japanese, Chinese and Koreans alternating with Portuguese and Puerto Ricans meet the eye everywhere. The population is highly cosmopolitan in character, with the Asiatic in the lead.

From January 1903 to December 1905, 7,394 Koreans found their was to the Islands, of whom 755 were women and 447 were children under 14 years of age. The emigration ceasing about this time very few have gone there since. The departures have been very small in number so that probably eighty per cent or about 5,700 Koreans must be still residing in the Islands. Of those who have left the Islands, three-fourths have gone on the Mainland where they may be found in large cities like San Francisco, Oakland, Los Angeles, and Pasadena working as house servants; or in the country districts of California as laborers on the fruit farms; they are on the cattle ranches in Wyoming, for the Korean abroad takes naturally to horses and owns one for himself as soon as possible. They are down in the corn belt, and may be found working as track hands along the Union Pacific and Southern Pacific Railroads.

It is in Hawaii the Korean is at his best. At first he had some difficulty in adjusting himself to his surroundings. Everything was new and strange and he had to learn how to handle himself. He did not know how to live, but it did not take him long to learn how to do so. He had to learn what to wear and where to get it, what to eat, where to buy it, and how to cook it; how to work and how to take care of himself. The Korean, when placed in favorable circumstances, is wonderfully quick to learn and in a marvelously short length of time, he learned his lessons and today the universal testimony is that the Korean is a very desirable plantation hand.

To understand the circumstances surrounding the Korean in Hawaii, it is necessary to understand one thing—sugar. The Korean's whole experience is wrapped up in that one word. Sugar is the keynote to everything in Hawaii, Nature has so ordained it. "Directly or indirectly all industries in Hawaii are ultimately dependent upon the sugar industry—the social, economic and political structure of the Islands alike are built upon a foundation of sugar." The total value of exports from Hawaii for the year ending June 30, 1905 was $35,123,867 and of this amount, sugar represented $35,113,409.

Hawaii is a land of surprising limitations. From the above, it will be seen that it is a land of practically one crop, the entire population being dependent virtually on this one industry. The superficial land area of the Islands is only about 6,000 square miles and of this, it is estimated that only one-tenth is arable, giving us only about 600 square miles to provide sustenance for the entire population of these islands. This area is divided into a few great plantations, some of them containing thousands of acres stretching for miles along the coast employing a small army of laborers and producing as high as 45,000 tons of sugar on a single plantation.

Employed in producing this great crop are 48,229—divided according to the following percentage (1905).

Japanese	65.80
Chinese	9.14
Korean	9.71
Portuguese	6.23
Hawaiian	3.01
Puerto Rican	3.95
Caucasian	2.09
Negro, South Sea	.07
	100.00

From this it will be seen that the Koreans rank second in numbers on the sugar plantations, and play no small part in the production of Hawaii's great crop It is further interesting to note the distribution of Koreans on the Plantations according to occupations.

Administration	10
Cultivation	4,384
Irrigation	1
Manufacture	19
Superintendence	4
Transportation	248
Unclassified	17
	4,683

By administration is meant clerks, interpreters and the like. Only one Korean is down as working at irrigation. This is one of the most expert forms of farm labor and through more Koreans are at work now at it, for I personally knew of a gang of twenty of them who were doing fine, yet it is doubtful if they will ever play a large part in this as irrigation is done largely by Japanese who are regarded as unexcelled at it. In the work of manufacture, an increasing number of Koreans are being taken into the mills, while some, a very few, have been taken into the engine room of certain mills and started out as firemen and machinists. Very few have been employed as lunas or bosses though I met several of whom their bosses spoke very highly, but most of the Koreans work under white or Hawaiian bosses, either in gangs by themselves or in mixed gangs alongside Japanese, Puerto Ricans and Portuguese.

From this, it will be seen that about seventy-five percent of the Koreans are at work on the plantations. The balance is made up of the women—for as a rule the Korean women are not compelled by their husbands to work in the fields; the children who are compelled to go to school; the store keepers and inn keepers; the students and the floating population in Honolulu.

The Korean field hand receives $18 a month in U.S. gold for twenty-six days of labor. No Sunday labor is required, everything being shut down on the plantations on the Sabbath. If he has a family he is given a house to himself with a little garden patch. Fresh clean water and fuel are supplied gratis, and the hospital with a trained resident physician is always open to him. Schools conveniently located, with American teachers, furnish education in English for his children. In the larger settlements like Ewa, a school in Korean, taught by a Korean schoolmaster, is maintained by the Koreans themselves.

If the Korean is unmarried, he is assigned to a dormitory with other Koreans, the number being strictly limited by law to the cubic contents of the house. Sanitary inspection is both frequent and rigid and the Korean has learned to understand its value. Actual living expenses vary from $5.00 to $9.00 a month. This diet usually consists of rice with vegetable salad, meat, soup, and bread and butter. The Koreans eat much fruit, especially the papaya and the pineapple and more recently, have taken to American tinned provisions. In visiting their camps, I had many a meal with Koreans which though homely, was well cooked and as good as any man might wish. As a rule, the Koreans live well. They wear American clothing, eat American food, and act as much like Americans as they can.

The Korean gets his breakfast about four o'clock in the morning and by five o'clock he is in the field at work. If it is some distance to his field, he is carried on the plantation railroad back and forth. Quite a number of the Koreans own their own horses and ride back and forth. This is true of the bosses, interpreters and Korean business men. A little incident will illustrate this.

I arrived at Mokuleea earlier than was expected so there was no one to meet me. My Korean companion told me there was a Korean store kept by a Christian a little distance away and we could get a horse there. On arriving at this store, what was my surprise to find a young man and his family whom I had baptized and taken into the church in Korea some years before, running this store and happy and prosperous. After the surprise and pleasure of the meeting, he quickly hitched up his horse and wagon, drove me to the camp two miles away, hastened back for his wife and baby born a few months before on American soil, and thus a future American citizen, and that night in the little chapel erected by the Koreans themselves I baptized the baby with several adult Koreans.

The Korean's day in the field is ten hours. He takes his lunch with him and eats it in the field. He gets back to camp about 4:30 P.M., usually takes a hot bath, puts on clean clothes, and is ready for supper and the evening.

One third of all the Koreans in Hawaii are professing Christians. They dominate the life in the camps on the Islands of Oahu, Kauai and Maui where they are stamping out gambling and intoxication. The Sugar Planter's Association is composed of gentlemen of the highest character and integrity, genuinely interested in the welfare of their hands and ready to cooperate in every sensible measure that promises better things for their men. There is a total absence of the "Jim Crow" spirit in Hawaii and the good nature with which the various races mix there is wonderful. On the railroads and steamers, they crowd and jostle each other but no one ever complains and all nationalities stand an equal show. A Chinese or a Korean, if he puts up the money, can travel first class and receive as much attention as any other nationality. There is a kind-hearted, gentle and generous spirit in everything in Hawaii that is delightful.

Under such conditions the Korean grows and develops very rapidly. Hawaii is the land of great possibilities for him. Being a farm laborer, he gets the very training he needs to fit himself for usefulness in his native land. Hawaii becomes to him a vast School of Agriculture where he learns something of the character and treatment of different soils; methods of irrigation and fertilization; care and system in the handling of the crops. He learns how to work according to system, and also the value and obligation of law and regulation. If a thousand selected Koreans a year could be permitted to emigrate to Hawaii in a few years, they would return and develop the natural resources of Korea, adding many fold to the value and financial resources.

Source:

George Heber Jones, "The Koreans in Hawaii." In *Korea Review*, VI, 11, November 1906, pp. 401-406.

In 1907, the governments of Japan and the United States entered into an accord known as the "Gentlemen's Agreement," concerned primarily with the immigration of Japanese workers to the United States. The agreement provided the basis for an Executive Order issued in 1907 by President Theodore Roosevelt (1858-1919; President 1901-1909) controlling immigration both of Japanese and of Koreans, whose nation was controlled by Japan.

Years of isolation had earned Korea the nickname of the "Hermit Kingdom" until, beginning in the 1830s, it was forcibly opened to the outside world. A number of countries fought over control of the Korean peninsula, and though the United States and Britain had their interests, the contest was primarily between the three major powers in the region: Japan, China, and Russia. Japan followed its victory over China in the Sino—Japanese War (1894-95) with the invasion of Korea.

Under Japanese domination, Koreans managed to learn about democracy in American schools; but when they looked for outside help in breaking Japanese control over their country, it was to Russia they turned. Japan's victory in the Russo—Japanese War (1904-1905) was the first notable case of a non-European power defeating a European one, and it signified the rise of Japan among world nations. Roosevelt won a Nobel Peace Prize by helping to secure a treaty between the Russians and Japanese in Portsmouth, New Hampshire, but he was well aware of Japan's growing influence.

American concerns over Korean immigration rose with an influx of Koreans to the newly acquired Hawaiian Islands in 1903. Up until the mid-1800s, Hawaiians had primarily worked their islands' vast sugar plantations, but rising labor demands and a decrease in the Hawaiian population had led to the introduction of Chinese labor in 1852. In 1882, the United States passed a law excluding Chinese immigration, and when Hawaii officially became a U.S. territory in 1900, the law was extended to the islands as well. Thus Hawaiian plantation owners turned to Korean labor.

In 1902, a representative of the plantation owners met in San Francisco with Horace Allen, U.S. ambassador to Korea. With the help of businessman David William Deshler and promoters such as the Reverend George Heber Jones, he recruited what became a group of 102 Korean immigrants in 1903. Some seven thousand Koreans had arrived in Hawaii by 1905, when Japan—which would officially annex Korea in 1910—put an end to Korean immigration for fear that too many workers many would flee the country.

Meanwhile, anti-Japanese sentiment on the West Coast was growing, fueled both by old-fashioned racism and by fears that Japanese workers would undercut the wages paid to American labor. When the San Francisco school board in 1906 ordered the segregation of Japanese students, this angered the government of Japan, *which called on Roosevelt to take action. As tensions in California mounted, Roosevelt in 1907 invited San Francisco school officials and California legislators to meet with him in Washington. The result was an agreement to allow most Japanese students to attend public schools; in return, Roosevelt promised to take steps to stem the tide of Japanese immigration.*

Roosevelt then turned to the Japanese, entering into negotiations which led to the "Gentlemen's Agreement." According to the terms of the latter, Japan promised that it would not issue passports to laborers, and that it would recognize the power of the U.S. government to keep out Japanese immigrants with passports from other countries. In return, America permitted Japanese who had already been to the United States to come back, and allowed the immigration of immediate family members of Japanese workers already in the United States.

These rules applied to Koreans as well, and for the latter they actually led to an increase, rather than a decrease, in immigration. The reason for this was the loophole regarding immediate family members. Up to that point, the vast majority of Korean immigrants had been single men, and there followed a massive effort, orchestrated by parents and village matchmakers, to pair those bachelors up with brides.

EXECUTIVE ORDER KNOWN AS THE "GENTLEMEN'S AGREEMENT"

Whereas, by the act entitled "An Act to regulate the immigration of aliens into the United States," approved February 20, 1907, whenever the President is satisfied that passports issued by any foreign government to its citizens to go to any country other than the United States or to any insular possession of the United States or to the Canal Zone, are being used for the purpose of enabling the holders to come to the continental territory of the United States to the detriment of labor conditions therein, it is made the duty of the President to refuse to permit such citizens of the country issuing such passports to enter the continental territory of the United States from such country or from such insular possession or from the Canal Zone;

And whereas, upon sufficient evidence produced before me by the Department of Commerce and Labor, I am satisfied that passports issued by the Government of Japan to citizens of that country or Korea and who are laborers, skilled or unskilled, to go to Mexico, to Canada and to Hawaii, are being used for the purpose of enabling the holders thereof to come to the continental territory of the United States to the detriment of labor conditions therein;

I hereby order that such citizens of Japan or Korea, to-wit: Japanese or Korean laborers, skilled and unskilled, who have received passports to go to Mexico, Canada or Hawaii, and come therefrom, be refused permission to enter the continental territory of the United States.

It is further ordered that the Secretary of Commerce and Labor be, and he hereby is, directed to take, thru Bureau and Immigration and Naturalization, such measures and to make and enforce such rules and regulations as may be necessary to carry this order into effect.

Theodore Roosevelt
The White House,
March 14, 1907
No. 589

Source:
Executive Order No. 589, issued by President Theodore Roosevelt on March 14, 1907.

Cathy Song, who grew up in Hawaii, deals in her poetry with the intricacies of familial relationships and the experiences of her immigrant ancestors. In Picture Bride, a collection of her poems, she explores her immigrant grandmother's life as a type of mail-order bride. The collection won the prestigious Yale Series of Younger Poets Award in 1982.

Picture brides were a result of the Gentlemen's Agreement of 1907, under which Japanese and Korean women could immigrate to Hawaii only if they were relatives of laborers already there. Japanese and Korean men who wanted to settle and start families in Hawaii asked relatives in Asia to look for prospective brides. Marriages were arranged by the exchange of short biographies and photographs — hence the phrase "picture bride." If a suitable match was found, the bride would set off by ship to meet her groom for the first time.

In "Picture Bride," the title poem of her collection, Song poses a series of questions about her grandmother, who left Korea at the age of 23 to marry a 39-year-old stranger. "What things did my grandmother / take with her?" Song asks. "Did she simply close / the door of her father's house / and walk away?"

PICTURE BRIDE
by Cathy Song

She was a year younger
than I,
twenty-three when she left Korea.
Did she simply close
the door of her father's house
and walk away? And
was it a long way
through the tailor shops of Pusan
to the wharf where the boat
waited to take her to an island
whose name she had
only recently learned,
on whose shore
a man waited,
turning her photograph
to the light when the lanterns
in the camp outside
Waialua Sugar Mill were lit
and the inside of his room

grew luminous
from the wings of moths
migrating out of the cane stalks?
What things did my grandmother
take with her? And when
she arrived to look
into the face of the stranger
who was her husband,
thirteen years older than she,
did she politely untie
the silk bow of her jacket,
her tent-shaped dress
filling with the dry wind
that blew from the surrounding fields
where the men were burning the cane?

Source:
Picture Bride. New Haven: Yale UP, 1983. pp. 3-4.

Picture Brides, a type of mail-order bride, were a result of the Gentleman's Agreement of 1907.

C*harles Ryu is a minister who tells first-generation Koreans to claim America as their land so subsequent generations can inherit America too. Ryu relates the significance of church in Korean-American life as a social, educational, and linguistic meeting place. Ryu says that the church is deeply entwined in Korean Americans' lives and that "almost seventy to eighty percent of Korean Americans belong to church."*

Ryu also discusses what it means to be a Korean Christian or Korean American Christian in the face of Western imperialism: "For instance, when they [missionaries] came to Korea, every family had a little shrine to their ancestors. The missionaries asked them to destroy it, so my grandparents destroyed it. But my family kept that remembrance part, and made it into a Christian memorial service. . . The annual ceremonies for our grandparents are a blending of Christianity and Confucianism."

KOREANS AND CHURCH

by Charles Ryu

"As a minister for first generation Koreans, I tell people they should be ready for their death, in the sense that unless they die and are buried here, Koreans cannot claim the land. I think that is very Asian. Where your ancestors are buried is your home. And if the first generation who have been here twenty years are still in the mode of 'making it' when they reach their sixties and seventies, the second generation and 1.5 generation will be forever lost. If the first generation says I will make my home here—this is where I will live, where I will be buried, and I will let my children inherit the land and be responsible citizens of the U.S. and of the world with Korean heritage—that would be wonderful. So in a way, I sort of push that, here and there.

"In America, whatever the reason, the church has become a major and central anchoring institution for Korean immigrant society. Whereas no other institution supported the Korean immigrants, the church played the role of anything and everything—from social service, to education, to learning the Korean language; a place to gather, to meet other people, for social gratification, you name it. The way we think of church is more than in a religious connotation, as a place to go and pray, have worship service, to learn of God and comfort. Your identify is tied so closely to the church you go to. I think almost seventy to eighty percent of Korean Americans belong to church. And it becomes social evangelism. If those who had never considered themselves to be Christian want to be Korean, they go to church. They just go there for social reasons. You are acclimated into the gospel, and you say, I want to be baptized. Your life revolves around the church. It could also become a ghetto in the sense of a Chinatown or a Korea-town. But at the same time, it can be a place, if done properly, where the bruised identity can be healed and affirmed, because living in American society as a minority is a very difficult thing. You are nobody out there, but when you come to church, you are a somebody. The role of the black church in the civil rights era was the same thing.

"Probably American churches have become specifically religious. I have my love life, my civil life, my professional life, and I have this church, religious life. But the Korean churches provide a new community of some sort that permeates the social matrix. It is such a solid, close knit community, because everyone feels in a sense alienated outside, so there is this centripetal force. At the same time, most who come are well established or potentially well established.

"A lot of people who belong to the English language service (which I am a part of), come here and say this is the only place they feel is home. I mean, they are executives in big corporations, or they might work at Time magazine or Morgan Stanley. And they do very well, yet feel America is like a wilderness. They come here and feel affirmed. They say, 'I don't have to prove anything. 'When I am with Koreans, I have to prove I am Korean. When I am with others, I feel I have to prove I am American. You gather all these English speaking Koreans in one place, in the religious context of God loves you as you are, and the sense of community, and the whole being is affirmed. I see that need, and civic organizations don't provide that. They may take care of one or two needs, whereas church can provide holistic needs."

Religion and Korea: "There have been so many dissertations written on why Koreans are so into church and religion, but no one seems to know why.

"Korean culture has been a very religious culture from the beginning. It is fraught with religious symbolism. Koreans tend to use foreign religions to express their religiosity. First Buddhism was introduced to Korea. It ultimately became a state religion. Buddhist religious language became the medium for Korean religiosity. Then Confucianism came, and then Christianity. And somehow Christianity made sense to Korean people because it is a very powerful or attractive religion. Even now, after one century, over twenty-five percent of the Korean population claim to be of the Christian religion. So whether you belong to an organized religion or not, Koreans always saw their lives in somewhat religious terms. Christianity is a universal religion, but Christians are still very racist, sexist, and parochial—including Koreans. So this open brotherhood and sisterhood is more of an ideal to be reached than the reality.

"American white missionaries who went to Korea are of fundamentalist sorts. They somehow confused the kingdom of God with American culture. To become Christian meant destroying Korean culture, which is part of the painful history of Korean Christians. So from the early on, the way we understood the Korean culture matrix was always in

Churches provide a sense of community among Korean Americans.

terms of Western Christianity. So I am struggling very hard today to understand what it means to be a Korean-Christian, or a Korean American-Christian.

"For instance, when they [missionaries] came to Korea, every family had a little shrine to their ancestors. The missionaries asked them to destroy it, so my grandparents destroyed it. But my family kept that remembrance part, and made it into a Christian memorial service, which is very interesting. We still have the memorial service in L.A. (where my parents are). We still remember in Korean. The annual ceremonies for our grandparents are a blending of Christianity and Confucianism which is very similar to the veneration of saints in Catholic Christianity. The stories and oral histories of our families we share are still very much a part of our lives. The first week

of January is when people gather to remember my father's father—where he was born, where he was educated. Three or four years ago, my father started making maps in English so that the second generation, now being born, can understand. But in terms of understanding our ancestors, that's very Confucianistic. We learned that from Confucianism. Confucianism was the state religion for five centuries."

Source:

Joann Faung Jean Lee. *Asian American Experiences in the United States: Oral Histories of First to Fourth Generation Americans from China, the Philippines, Japan, India, the Pacific Islands, Vietnam and Cambodia*. Jefferson, NC: McFarland & Co., 1991. pp. 161-163.

In the United States, ethnic foods gained popular attention in the 1990s as Americans, in their quest for a healthy diet while eating out, looked beyond hamburgers and fries, to sample new dishes. While Chinese and Japanese cuisine have been a part of the American dining experience for decades, it was only in the 1990s that Tibetan, Nelapese, and Korean food also became available in large cities where such specialty menus could reach a diverse market. Popular interest in Korean food is growing with the opening of restaurants in Atlanta, Chicago, St. Petersburg, Denver, Los Angeles, Boston, Seattle, Washington, Louisville, Kentucky, and of course, New York. Some cities offer ethnic celebrations where Korean food can be sampled, such as the Chicago Korean street festival sponsored by area restaurants and the Korean American Restaurant Association of the Midwest.

Americans are surprised to discover that when they order food at a Korean restaurant, they are not ordering the main dish because the main dish is rice and pickles and it is served at no extra cost. The steamed rice, called pap, is the main dish for all three meals of the day. It's bland taste makes it the perfect backdrop for an endless variety of dishes. What's ordered are the side dishes that are meant to flavor the rice, and many restaurants offer as many as 70 choices. All of the food is placed on the table at the same time and not served in courses. Everything is served hot. Additionally, the same dishes are served for breakfast, lunch, and dinner. Some of the better known side dishes include barbecue beef ribs (kal bi), barbecue beef (bulgogi), teriyaki chicken, vegetable pancakes with green onions (boo cin gae), bean sprout salad, a dried persimmon desert, dumplings stuffed with beef, pork and tofu, sautéed Korean chilies with garlic greens, and soup (kuk) such as taenjang kuk that's made of soybean paste, tofu, and an assortment of vegetables.

Korean seasonings are a pleasant experience to the American's taste buds. Korean cuisine is spicy hot, salty, and sour, and these three flavors are derived from fermented bean paste (dejan), spicy chili paste (gochu Jang), and soy sauce. Yet Americans and Korean are alike in their fervent love of barbecue and beef. Korean barbecue is cooked in a hot pit called a sinsulo, and it is flavored with hot red peppers, soy sauce, and sesame oil. Whereas other Asians major on fish, Koreans eat more beef. Seafood dishes are still an important part of Korean diet. Squid braised with a red pepper sauce (Mul Ojing-o) and poached clams (dae hapjo gae) can be found in most Korean restaurants and homes.

Koreans use the pickling process to increase the variety of the foods available. Koreans grow more vegetables than other Asian countries, and pickle them to create the signature Korean dish, Kimchi. Cabbage is harvested just before winter, seasoned with salt water for a few hours, then mixed with hot peppers and spices and stored in a clay jar that is buried. During the winter this jar is dug up and portions removed as needed. Kimchi, pap, and kuk are the basic dishes of a typical Korean meal.

The lack of popularity of Korean food could be attributed to the fact that there were few Korean immigrants prior to World War II. Japan had closed Korea's emigration office in 1905 and did not allow Koreans to leave. The United States had laws totally excluding Koreans from immigration. After Japan surrendered at the close of World War II, Korean immigration to the United States was permitted, and it increased during the U.S. occupation of Korea and the Korean War (1950-1953). A significant community of Korean Americans did not develop, however, until after the new immigration regulations of 1965 dropped the old restrictions. About 8,000 Koreans immigrated from 1952 to 1960, compared with 13,000 who came from 1965 to 1970. By the late 1970s immigration officials estimated that *there were between 250,000 and 300,000 Koreans in the United States. The U.S. Census Bureau reports that 338,800 Koreans immigrated between 1981 and 1996.*

WHERE KOREAN FOOD IS JUST WAITING TO BE DISCOVERED

In a city that emphatically embraces Thai, Japanese and Indian food, as well as Chinese dishes from a dizzying number of regions, there is still one major Asian cuisine so unknown to many New Yorkers that it's as if it were meant to be a secret.

And it almost is. Korean food—bold, healthful, a treasure for the adventurous—has almost been reserved for Koreans, whose restaurants have made little effort to reach beyond their traditional clientele.

Koreans often ask themselves why Americans haven't discovered their cooking, said Namji Steinmann, the vice president for education of the Asia Society. "The main reason is that the food is not marketed to non-Koreans," she said. And the neighborhoods where it can be found are few. Mostly, they are near the garment district and in Flushing, Queens.

But that is slowly changing.

Some wonderful dishes are emerging from their cloisters: delicious fried dumplings, crisp potato and scallion pancakes, hearty noodle soups and barbecued beef, sweetly charred along the edges. There is kimchi, the fiery condiment made from salted and fermented vegetables, which enlivens so many dishes. And then there's bibimbop, the colorful, satisfying bowl of rice and vegetables topped with meat or fish.

One way to discover them is to go directly to one of the traditional enclaves like Korea-town, the bustling West 30's between Fifth Avenue, and Broadway, where meats barbecued on tabletop grills are a mainstay.

But unlike Chinese restaurants or even Italian restaurants, which have long accommodated American tastes by serving the soup first, or by accepting the notion that pasta can be a main course, these Korean restaurants serve strictly Korean style: no matter what you order, it's all put on the table at once. And often, with little or no explanation.

"They expect you'll eat and scoot out, not linger," Ms. Steinmann said.

But as a new, more expensive generation of Korean-Americans comes to the forefront, new ways to experience their cuisine are emerging.

Jenny Kwak was 19 six years ago, when she opened Dok Suni's with her mother, Myeng Ja Kwak. It was the first of the hip little downtown places, and Ms. Kwak stressed setting and service. "For Americans, Koreatown's food is good, but the atmosphere is not there," she said. "I grew up in the Village, so I wanted a place that was cozier and darker and where people might go on a date."

At Dok Suni's and at a new Korean restaurant, Clay, also downtown, the menu is fairly limited and organized to be easily understood by Westerners. The food is served course by course. "We've been criticized by Koreans for how we serve." Ms. Kwak said.

When Anita Lo started cooking at Mirezi, a Korean-influenced Asian restaurant in Greenwich Village that was well received but that closed last fall, she said she was not afraid to prepare traditional dishes, but the menu had to be simplified and divided into appetizers, main courses and desserts.

"The problem is Americans do not know how to navigate the cuisine, how to put a meal together," said Brad Kelley, the owner of Bop, which opened on the Bowery last year. "Korean food seems foreign until you break it down. Koreatown can be pretty intimidating to Americans, and it's often their first association with Korean food."

Bop, which started as a tiny experiment in SoHo before moving to its present site, also has a limited selection of classic and updated dishes, including stir-fried glass noodles and clams steamed with ginger, garlic and sake. Some more challenging dishes served in Koreatown, like beef tripe broiled at the table or cold tofu with Spam and cucumber, have been edited out.

Even though the dishes on the menus at most of the Koreatown restaurants come with an English translation, and may be put into categories like "starters," "hot pots" and "chef's specialties," Americans often do not know what to expect, especially when there are 50 or more choices. Korean waiters who do not speak English are unable to communicate well, while Westerners do not want to appear foolish about not understanding the food and how it's meant to be eaten. It's an unfortunate standoff.

One exception is Hangawi, a serene Buddhist vegetarian restaurant on East 32d Street, where the servers go out of their way to explain the menu, which is offered entirely in English, and to make suggestions about the food, which is served on fine pottery in a succession of courses. The food, including grilled codonopsis (mountain root with ginger soy sauce) and acorn noodles with fresh vegetables, seems more exotic and refined than what is served in the barbecue places down the block.

In general, however, Korean is not a subtle cuisine. It is bold, rustic and often vibrantly spiced. There is great variety, but chili and garlic are the dominant flavors. Herbs like cilantro, common in other Asian cuisines, are rare. The pickles and vinegar add a cleansing note. The delicate artistry of the Japanese table or of some Chinese cuisines, especially Cantonese, is not easy to find in Korean restaurants. But if anything, the robust and forthright seasonings should add to its attraction for Americans.

Rocco DiSpirito, who serves Asian-influenced food at Union Pacific in the Flatiron district, called it the "Southern Italian cooking of Asia."

"It's rich and garlicky," he said. "Peasant fare. When I want to use an Asian treatment for meat, I look to Korea." He prepares Kobe beef marinated Korean style in soy and ginger. He has also served cod seasoned with Kimchi, the ubiquitous pickled cabbage.

This pickle, the soul of Korean food, may be familiar to New Yorkers from salad bars. But there are hundreds of versions, made with everything from radishes to cucumbers and fermented fish to fresh pears. It is also used as an ingredient, to season soups, pancakes, dumplings, rice, noodle dishes and stir-fries. Koreans even eat it for breakfast.

Aside from spicy kimchi, Korean food has other appeals, including crowd pleasers like jap chae (stir-fried noodles with vegetables and beef) and mandoo gui (fried dumplings). Though there is little or no chicken on Korean menus, the cuisine is long on vegetables. Even the ubiquitous beef barbecue is not eaten plain but is piled with scallions and other vegetable condiments and wrapped in frilly lettuce leaves.

In most Korean restaurants, dishes like beef grilled in the center of the table are meant to be shared, a concept that Americans have embraced when they dine on Chinese, Indian and Thai food (to say nothing of desserts served at a table for four in a place like Le Cirque 2000).

"Koreans like to sample a lot of tastes, not fill up on one thing," Ms. Kwak of Dok Suni's said.

In fact, Namhee Kong, the librarian at the Korean Cultural Service in Manhattan, said that what elevates a Korean restaurant meal from an everyday bowl of soup and dish of rice at home is not the number of courses but the array and elaborateness of the kimchi and other spicy, tangy and soothing like side dishes. There might be three or four accompaniments at home, but 20 or 30 could cover the table for a banquet.

That's an extreme, but having given some New Yorkers a brief sampling of Korean food, Ms. Kwak and hen mother now have a broader menu in mind. Come summer, they plan to open Do Hwa, a larger, more elaborate restaurant than Dok Suni's, on Carmine Street in Greenwich Village.

"I don't want to lose the new things I've done, but I also want to show more of the traditions," Ms. Kwak said. "I think Americans might be ready."

How to Order Hot Pot, Dumpling or Stir-Fry

Here are some of the classic dishes of Korean cuisine. Keep in mind that there are no standard transliterations, so spelling varies from menu to menu.

BIBIMBOP The paella of Korea. A casserole of vegetables and seaweed slivers over sticky rice, often with meat or fish and a fried egg on top. "Bibim" means "mixture" and "bop" means "rice," and it's meant to be eaten all mixed together.

BULGOGI Marinated paper-thin slices of boneless rib-eye steak, which diners barbecue at the table. Forget medium rare; let the meat become darkly seared on the edges for a hint of caramelized sweetness. Then dip it into a soy-based sauce and wrap it in a lettuce leaf with scallion salad.

HAE MOOL JUNGOL Seafood hot pot fueled with chili and garlic, which is cooked on a table burner. Jungol means hot pot, and hae mool is seafood. Definitely main-course material.

JAP CHAE A stir-fry of vermicelli, usually with carrots, onions, peppers, spinach and beef in a rich soy-based sauce. An excellent introduction to Korean cuisines. It is often listed as a starter but should be shared. Otherwise, consider it a main dish. Otherwise, consider it a main dish. Rice and kimchi are essential alongside.

KALBI Beef short ribs. Thin, cross-cut slices, including the bone, marinated and barbecued at the table. Kalbi tang is a soup with meltingly tender short ribs.

KIMCHI The ubiquitous condiment of fermented pickles laced with chilies, which sparks the appetite. Any dish with kimchi as part of its name will be aglow with it.

MANDOO Half-circle dumplings, filled with pork and vegetables, or just vegetables. They are fried (mandoo gui), steamed (mandoo jhim) or served in soup (mandoo gook), and they come with a soy and vinegar dipping sauce.

NAJ-JI BOK-GUM Octopus stir-fried with vegetables and noodles in a moderately fiery sauce. Bok-gum dishes are stir-fried or sautéed, and served in heaping platters to be eaten with rice.

NYENG MYUN A refreshing casserole of cold buckwheat vermicelli in a light beef broth with sliced beef and a hard-cooked egg. It is eaten with rice and can take additional seasoning, like mustard powder. Dishes called myun are noodle-based.

PA JUN A crispy rice-flour pancake often made with seafood and scallions. It may be the size of a dinner plate and enough to feed four as an appetizer.

PANCHAN Four or more little dishes offered free at the beginning of a meal as nibbles and condiments. In the new-wave places, they are optional, and cost extra.

SOON DOO-BOO JI-GAE A casserole with tofu, often spicy. Doo-boo means tofu, and ji-gae is a casserole.

SUL LONG TANG A bland, milky looking broth of long-simmered beef and bones, with rice, noodles and pieces of brisket. A meal in itself. Add scallions and salt and pepper.

Source:

"Where Korean Food is Just Waiting to be Discovered," by Florence Fabricant. In *New York Times*, Wednesday, April 7, 1999.

LAOTIAN AMERICANS

John Tenhula's interview with Ge Lor, a Hmong highland dweller in Laos who immigrated to the United States with his wife and two sons in the early 1980s, shows the struggles that many immigrants grapple with in adjusting to a new profession in a different culture. Ge Lor explains that American farming was different than the farming that he was used to in Laos. The Hmong were simple farmers who used hand tools and slash and burn agricultural techniques. Lor explains that, even though he benefitted from a training program, learning the business aspects of American farming was as difficult as learning how to plant cash crops and how to use pesticides.

Laotians have not, in general, been in the United States for a long time. In 1975, Hmong refugees from Laos began to flee to Thailand and to other countries, including the United States. As Laos was taken over by Communist insurgents, Laotians fled, fearing persecution by the new government, military conscription, and arbitrary arrest of anyone suspected of political crimes or disloyalty. The Hmong, one ethnic group in the Laotian community, which also includes the Mien and Khmu groups, as well as several other smaller groups, were targeted as enemies of the new government because they had worked with the United States Central Intelligence Agency during the Vietnam War. In the 1990 census, the Lao immigrants numbered 250,000, with an estimated 90,000 Hmong.

Laotian immigrants were originally dispersed throughout the United States, but they quickly settled in a few specific areas, with about 45 percent of the Laotian population residing in California in 1990. There were also large communities in Wisconsin, Minnesota, Texas, Washington and Massachusetts. Many Laotian immigrants work in high technology or light industry assembly plants, and some run small grocery or video stores. Few Lao immigrants have been able to succeed in American farming. Instead, they establish themselves as truck farmers, growing vegetables and selling them at Asian-American markets and farmers' markets. Ge Lor points out that even this kind of farming has its difficulties, especially in providing the necessary vehicles for transporting vegetables to market. Ge Lor's story relates how the Hmong in the area have carved out a niche in farming by establishing family-run cooperatives, and gives examples of mistakes as well as of a successful cooperative.

AN INTERVIEW WITH GE LOR ABOUT LEARNING AMERICAN FARMING

He has enormous hands and a big smile. He tries very hard to make me comfortable in his modest house decorated with Early American furniture. He speaks in Lao.

We were highland people in Laos. I had worked for an American company and left Laos for Thailand in 1979. After one year of living in Kansas, my family—a wife and two sons—moved to Fresno, California. We moved mostly because there were no other Laotian [Hmong] people in Kansas. When we arrived, we met other Laotian people from Providence and Minnesota. They came to California for the same reasons. There are now about 23,000 Laotians in Fresno County. The one thing that we could do that everyone else was doing in Fresno was farming. But this was a different kind of farming. We are talking about hi-tech farming, not the hand-tool farming we were used to in Laos. It's not so simple as turning the soil and planting seeds. Farming here is very modern, and to compete, we had to learn about these new techniques.

I was part of a program that helped train thirty-five new farmers in hi-tech farming skills in 1981. The program lasted almost one year. It was about all aspects of farming from technical fieldwork to using pesticides. The program was from the federal government, and we were supposed to eventually teach other refugees about farming.

Our idea was to get involved in planting cash crops that we could work on as a community. It would be crops that the large farmers didn't want to grow. For many Laotians, farming is a good job because it doesn't require English and all of the family can work on it at the same time. Laotians have large families so this could be a good thing for business. Other ideas were that it meant the families could be together, not separated, and that it was good to work in the sunshine.

What did you learn?

What I learned most was the technical-mechanical things about farming as a big business. How to rent and lease land, to hope for some venture capital to buy land. How to guess when and what crops might bring a profit. I never thought of farming as such a serious business. What I learned was more business than agriculture.

We had the idea of forming Laotian cooperative gardening that would be able to use the Laotian people in cash-crop ventures that would be long-term profitable for the people—not just to supplement incomes, but that would be their main source of income. We made many mistakes. What we learned was that there is a lot of competition in the United States, especially from Mexico, for bringing in these crops. You must really understand marketing and distribution ideas about getting your fruits and vegetables out when they are ready.

Tell me about the farm cooperative effort.

Well, in 1982, with the land leased because we had no venture capital available through any of the banks, about twenty of us started a cooperative farm that would, we hoped, bring in about a hundred families total. But this never worked. We were very new at this and we had no marketing experience or knowledge of selling things and we did not see our competition. What happened was our first crop was cherry tomatoes. They had brought in a good price the year before. They are a good crop to grow and we looked at all of those aspects. The market price for tomatoes is usually top price, but what we did not know was that all other farmers would plant cherry tomatoes. What happened was that the market was flooded and by then Mexico was sending tomatoes at even a lower price. Most important, these tomatoes all came ripe at once and we had not planned for the transportation of them. To rent vehicles at that time was almost impossible. We had no way to move them and they were rotting in the fields. It was a disaster.

What did you learn?

From that disaster we learned a great amount of information. We are looking for our place in the agriculture business. For example, the Koreans have the poultry business and the Japanese have oranges—we are looking to the small gardens for the Laotians.

I hope the Laotian people make it as farmers. I am part of a cooperative now that is hoping for a government contract for vegetables and fruits for Merced Air Force Base and possibly a base in Texas. This would be a big deal—$4 million contract a year and would employ one hundred refugees, but this is not yet a firm offer. We have the workers but what we need is the ability to buy and improve the transport system. We need a Laotian trucking association with coolers. Then we need heavy farm equipment. I think it will come in time but it takes so long.

We have our successful program here. Not far from here is a family cooperative of twenty acres. They own the land now. The father has three sons and all of them are married with children. They all live at the farm, so about twenty people work on

the farm and the expenses are low. They have a very good business this year in eggplant—very few people grew eggplant and the prices were very high. In their third year, they are going to buy machinery and a big refrigerated truck to ship the produce.

Source:

Voices from Southeast Asia: The Refugee Experience in the United States, compiled by John Tenhula. New York: Holmes & Meier, 1991.

*I*mmigrants have traditionally worked in jobs that other members of American society are unwilling to do. In major cities such as New York, these menial jobs are usually within the service industry as hotel housekeeping and restaurant clean-up workers. These low-wage jobs rarely provide medical benefits and are usually done in poor and even dangerous working conditions. Immigrants of previous centuries worked in mines, on the docks, on the railroad, and in factories. In the Midwest, the 1990s job for immigrants is with the meatpacking industry. Workers are typically uneducated and impoverished Laotians and Mexicans. "The Heartland's Raw Deal: How Meatpacking Is Creating a New Immigrant Underclass" describes the lives of these workers. Moreover, it examines the need for this type of workforce, one willing to work for low wages and in hazardous conditions, and how a specific industry recruited these immigrants in order to compete and survive.

According to the 1990 U.S. census there were about 150,000 Laotian Americans living in the United States. About 58,058 indicated they lived in California, with 7,750 in Fresno, 6,261 in San Diego, 4,885 in Sacramento, and 4,045 in Stockton. The second largest group lived in Texas, and the third and fourth largest groups lived in Minnesota and Washington. The meatpacking communities mentioned in this article are located from the Dakotas through Minnesota, Nebraska, Iowa, Kansas and Texas. Many of these communities attracted Laotian Americans after the 1990 census was taken. The 2000 census will likely show additional immigrant population shifts.

Laotian Americans did not begin to come to America in large numbers until 1976. Laos, along with Vietnam and Cambodia, was once known as French Indochina. Laos was a French protectorate from 1893 until the end of World War II. After Vietnam fell to the Communists in 1975, Laos entered a time of internal political conflict that caused thousands of Laotians to flee. In 1975, only 800 Laotian refugees were admitted to the United States. U.S. officials viewed Laotian refugees who fled to Thailand as economic migrants rather than refugees fleeing political oppression. However, the plight of Laotian refugees in Thailand and Cambodia gained international attention. The Indochina Migration and Refugee Assistant Act of 1975 provided money for resettlement in four camps in the United States located in California, Florida, Arkansas and Pennsylvania. In 1976 the United States admitted 10,200 Laotian refugees who had fled to Thailand and were living in refugee detention camps. The family reunification plan allowed refugees already in the United States to sponsor the entry of their relatives, so that from 1979 until

1981, 105,000 Laotians came to the United States. Each refugee was processed while in the resettlement camp, and then was allowed to choose from one of nine sponsoring private social service agencies who became responsible for the welfare and settlement of the refugee. Theses agencies, including the United States Catholic Conference, the International Rescue Committee, the Lutheran Immigration and Refugee Service, the Church World Service, the American Council for Nationalities Service, the Tolstoy Foundation, the American Fund for Czechoslovak Refugees, and the Travelers Aid International Social Service of America, found jobs and places to live for the Laotians. Many refugees, however, moved again in a second migration to urban areas to form Laotian American communities.

According to the U.S. Census Bureau, between 1981 and 1990, 145,600 Laotians immigrated to the United States. Many of the Laotian immigrants of the 1990s have come under the provision of family reunification immigration. According to the Bureau of the Census, 37,700 Laotians immigrated from 1991 to 1996. The aggressive recruitment of Laotians by some of the meatpacking companies included paying family members in the United States bonuses for recruiting family members to immigrate. The meatpacking plant in Storm Lake, Iowa employed 1,500 Laotians.

THE HEARTLAND'S RAW DEAL: HOW MEATPACKING IS CREATING A NEW IMMIGRANT UNDERCLASS

STORM LAKE, IOWA

Thirty-year-old Lauro Ibarro left his wife and daughter behind in Reynosa, Mexico, and dodged the traps of U.S. Immigration to make a better life for them all by slaughtering pigs in the mammoth plant that defines life in this northwest Iowa town of 10,000 Instead, a few days before Christmas, he met a horrible death. Awakened in the middle of the night by flames and smoke inside the small uninsulated trailer that he shared with his sister and her family, Lauro ran instinctively out into the foot of snow piled on the ground. Realizing that his two nieces, 5-year-old Karen Luna and 3-year-old Crystal Luna, were still inside, Lauro dove back into the blaze to rescue them. But neither he nor the two little girls escaped. A police report identified a malfunctioning kerosene space heater as the culprit-the same device that so many Latino working families have here as their only feeble defense against Iowa's five long months of winter.

At the wake the next evening, dusted by snow and dressed in jeans, parkas and workboots, some 200 or more of Lauro Ibarro's neighbors—all Latinos overflowed the Sliefert Mortuary in a rare exercise of public, collective grief. Sometimes only a tragedy of such proportions is sufficient to overcome the inertia imposed by the routine disappointments of everyday life lived out so far from what was once home.

The death of these three was a reminder of the precarious, undignified life shared not only by the mourners at the wake but by the 600 or more Mexican and Central American workers and their families who have come to live here in Storm Lake. Alongside 1,500 Laotians, these immigrant workers are now the majority of the work force at the world's second-largest pork factory, operated by Iowa Beef Processors (I.B.P.). And it's not just here in Storm Lake. In a sweeping regional arc from the Dakotas through Minnesota, Nebraska and Iowa, and down through Kansas into northern Texas and the foothills of the Missouri Ozarks, dozens of once lily-white heartland meatpacking communities have become the new homes to tens of thousands of impoverished Third World workers.

Putting the lie to the conventional wisdom undergirding our immigration policy, the arrival of these workers en masse is neither serendipitous nor the product of cunning smugglers. Rather, it is the direct result of a conscious survival strategy undertaken by a key U.S. industry, a plan developed and fully implemented only in the past few years.

Beef, pork and poultry packers have been aggressively recruiting the most vulnerable of foreign workers to relocate to the U.S. plains in exchange for $6-an-hour jobs in the country's most dangerous industry. Since permanence is hardly a requirement for these jobs, the concepts of promotion and significant salary increase have as much as disappeared. That as many as half of these new immigrants lack legal residence seems no obstacle to an industry now thriving on a docile, disempowered work force with an astronomical turnover.

Staggering illness and injury rates—36 per 100 workers in meat—and stress caused by difficult, repetitive work often means employment for just a few months before a worker quits or the company forces him/her off the job. (Government safety inspections have dropped 43 percent overall since 1994, because of budget cuts and an increasingly pro-business slant at the Occupational Safety and Health Administration.) When disabled workers and their families remain in their new homes, the social cost of their survival is then passed by the company to the public.

Moreover, this radical restructuring of food processing could be carried out only with the acquiescence of local and state governments, which have showered the meatpacking giants with millions in tax rebates and subsidies, and only with the hypocrisy of our immigration policy-makers, who abhor illegal aliens except when they're desperate enough to accept underpaid jobs under the most adverse conditions. "The entire debate over whether or not immigrants are of economic benefit is disingenuous," says University of Northern Iowa anthropologist Mark Grey, an expert on the restructured packing industry. "No one wants to state the truth—that food processing in America today would collapse were it not for immigrant labor."

As an added insult, these new immigrants are being left even more vulnerable by the Clinton Administration's new welfare and immigration reforms, which have a direct and devastating impact on their already fragile existence. Taken together, these economic and political factors have converged in the heartland to lay the foundations for a new rural underclass. Welcome to Mexico on the Missouri.

Bringing the War Back Home

Twenty-five years ago, when the population of this town—which bills itself as The City Beautiful—was sitting at 8,400, the government counted twenty-two minority residents, mostly students at the small Buena Vista University. Today, nearly half of Storm Lake's kindergarten class is nonwhite. With nearly everyone in town working at either I.B.P. or at Sara Lee's Bil-Mar turkey plant, unemployment here is about 2 percent. But the prevailing low wage insured that one in four families was the recipient of some sort of public or private charity this past year. Over the past decade the county hospital has seen its unpaid costs zoom from $129,000 a year to $3 million. In 1996 three cases of full-blown TB, the classic disease of poverty, were reported, and another 380 residents were treated for TB infection.

"Living here is like living on the moon," says the Rev. Tom Lo Van, a pudgy 34-year-old Laotian Lutheran with an infectious laugh. "Our people don't know the law, their rights or where to go when they are sick. We work, we pay taxes and we have problems like everyone else. But there isn't a single person in the government who speaks our language."

"**N**o one wants to state the truth—that food processing in America today would collapse were it not for immigrant labor."—University of Northern Iowa anthropologist Mark Grey.

Reverend Tom is about as unlikely a candidate for social agitator as you could find. He was born in the U.S. Embassy in Laos, and his father was the U.S. mission's cook after serving fifteen years with the C.I.A.'s favorite cut-out, Air America. The only professional-class Laotian in town, the Reverend is his community's most forceful—some would say lone—public advocate.

In the mid-seventies Iowa Republican politicians seeded Storm Lake with twenty-four Laotian refugee families, most of them headed by veterans of the Royal Laotian Army, allies of the U.S. forces in Vietnam. A half-dozen years later, when I.B.P. came to town, it hired some of the local Laotians and offered them $150 bounties to recruit relatives to come to Storm Lake. The company itself sent out head-hunting teams to other Laotian settlements in the United States, causing the Laotian population to swell to 1,500 or more—almost all of them of the Taiwan ethnic minority.

Reverend Tom takes me on a daylong tour of his flock, an itinerary with no geographical or community anchor. Despite their strong presence, the Lao have no newspaper or radio in town, no Lao "district" per se. On the edge of town two Lao-run convenience markets selling sticky rice and magazines imported from Thailand serve as the unofficial gathering and gossip point. "No one wants to rent to us," says the Reverend. "We get what nobody else will take."

Less than fifty yards from I.B.P.'s shipping depot, we visit Lao women living in a series of railroad shacks in conditions so bad that they remind me of the scavengers I once saw living in wooden huts in Seoul. Their small rooms are overwhelmed with the medicinal reek of Ben-Gay and Tiger Balm, used in industrial quantities to quench the fire in fingers and elbows pushed to their limit by work on the slaughterhouse floor.

This human conveyor belt is powered by the grueling work regimen, which generates an astonishing worker turnover rate of more than 80 percent a year-a rate common to the entire industry.

In a walk-up apartment with a surplus army cot for a bed and discarded patio lounge as a couch, one male worker, Symery, greets us with what seems to be a permanently crooked wrist. After being recruited by friends in 1992 to work at I.B.P., he took a job cutting the meat off backbones. In his fifth month on the job, thirty days before the company begins granting its limited health care package, he slashed his palm open. He paid for the medical care himself, with the company discounting his weekly check. A second accident this past July left him disabled, he says. But I.B.P. recognizes only the reports of its own contract doctors, and they certified Symery as fit to work. The result: He has had no income since the summer. "I.B.P. isn't humane," he says. "No one worked like I did. No one could do boning like me."

Another Lao worker, who prides himself on having worked with U.S. troops to block the Ho Chi Minh trail, is now in the same sort of predicament. Injured and out of work, with two rooms full of kids to support, he finally got his first $352 Supplemental Security Income disability check on December 1. "He has gotten it just in time to lose it again," says Reverend Tom, referring to the Clinton welfare bill provision that cuts off S.S.I. to legal resident aliens. "When the face of the poor was white, America didn't have the stomach to cut welfare. Now if you want to help, you are called a wimp, a fool. The only hope these people have is to become U.S. citizens. We're doing what we can. But many

only have a third-grade education. How are they going to learn enough English?"

But Tom's greatest lament is reserved for the Laotian youth. He sees little evidence that the current plight of his people is just the newest chapter in the U.S. immigration story, where the first generation suffers but its children prosper. "This new generation is worse off," he says. "Our kids have no self-identity, no sense of belonging. They see no way out only picking up at I.B.P. when their parents leave off. No role models. Eighty percent of our kids drop out of high school."

Life Underground

At least the Storm Lake Lao have Reverend Tom. The more transient Latino community, bunkered mostly into two dilapidated trailer parks known as Little Mexico, has produced no visible community leaders. The handful of clergy and social workers who are this group's only advocates insist on remaining anonymous and low profile. This is, after all, a company town, and paranoia runs deep.

And rightfully so. Unlike the Lao, who are all legal residents, something like half the Latino workers and their families here are undocumented. Several workers tell me that valid Social Security cards—that belong to others—can be purchased for $300 to $500 and that the company does no checking. Other workers contend that I.B.P. management personnel moonlight in document-trafficking. That's a story the company denies.

I.B.P. openly admits that many of these Latinos-legal residents and otherwise-have come here recruited by the company, which has consistently used labor brokers to comb the border areas in south Texas and California to shuttle up new recruits at as much as $300 a head. A cursory look at a birth certificate or Social Security card was enough to satisfy the broker and the personnel department that the labor draftees were legal.

"The company loves to work with illegals," says 45-year-old Heriberto from inside his trailer, a few yards away from the scene of the December fire. "When you are illegal you can't talk back," he adds. Heriberto brings home $300 for a six-day, forty-eight-hour week. One paycheck goes for trailer rent. Another is sent back to relatives in Mexico. "You keep your head down and follow orders. We say you can't do nothing." Switching to Spanish, he says, "Dices nada porque la planta es del gobierno" (You say nothing because the plant is the government). Indeed. Though Latinos make up about a quarter of the I.B.P. work force and have the most dangerous jobs, Latino surnames show up on less than 5 percent of the worker comp claims filed between 1987 and 1995.

But as inhospitable as work is at Storm Lake, the average wage of about $7 an hour still trumps Mexico's $4-a-day minimum wage. Now that a migrant trail is firmly in place, the company has been able to scale back but not eliminate its overt recruitment and rely on word of mouth. As many as 150 Mexican workers in Storm Lake, for example, come from the same small village of Santa Rita in the state of Jalisco. There's a constant commerce of workers, relatives and friends between Storm Lake and Santa Rita. This human conveyor belt is powered by the grueling work regimen, which generates an astonishing worker turnover rate of more than 80 percent a year-a rate common to the entire industry. "Perfect for the company," says Heriberto. "Most workers leave before six months is up and the company has to start paying health insurance."

Meanwhile, in 1995 I.B.P. stripped off a juicy $257 million in profits on sales of $12 billion. Its C.E.O., Robert Peterson, made $1 million in salary and $5.2 million in bonuses that year. Storm Lake shows none of the blight that metastasized through the region after the eighties farm collapse. Its small and tidy downtown has no board-ups or vacancies. Four locally owned banks are thriving. The housing market is corset-tight. "You can't even rent," says Mayor Sandra Madsen. "We have two big payrolls, a stable downtown. Five years from now I think this town will realize we are all better off for the change we have gone through."

Perhaps. But for the moment, the dominant atmosphere is one of apartheid. "Race determines everything here," says an outreach worker to the Latino community. "Where you live, where you work, how much you earn, where you worship, even where you shop." Latinos and Laos simply steer clear of the all-white downtown area "that even I don't feel welcome in," says Reverend Tom. The immigrant workers restrict their shopping to the more anonymous Wal-Mart and the cavernous Hy-Vee supermarket on the town outskirts. When I stop to make a phone call from the local Conoco station, two locals overhear me speaking in Spanish. "Fuckin' Mexican should learn English," one says loudly to the other. The editor of the forward-looking Storm Lake Times, which has been a "pro-diversity" voice, jokes that the local good old boys like to call his paper "The Gook Times."

A lot of the local xenophobes had their big moment last May, when on a Friday afternoon seventeen armed Border Patrol officers-backed by agents from the Immigration and Naturalization Service, units from local law enforcement and surveil-lance planes circling over the I.B.P. plant-staged an almost tragicomic raid on Storm Lake. In what amounted to a military occupation, agents spent two days going door to door in Little Mexico, setting up roadblocks and rousting suspects off the street in a sweep for illegals. A publicity-seeking U.S. Attorney even showed up to take credit for an operation he had little to do with. Prodded into action by the local police chief, who along with the I.N.S. had built up a database of some 600 suspected illegal aliens in town, the federal agents eventually arrested and deported a total of seventy-eight Latinos.

But when hundreds of other fearful workers-likely all undocumented or with false ID-failed to show up for work the next Monday and the pork began to spoil, I.B.P. management panicked. In a story corroborated by several sources, executives started calling community workers who have the confidence of their Latino clients. "I.B.P. told us to tell everyone to come back to work that afternoon," says a social worker. "It was O.K. now. The I.N.S. was gone and nobody was going to check anything."

Within a few weeks, say several workers, even some of those deported to Mexico were back on the job. "They just got some new ID," says one worker. "And the same gringos who turned them in hired them back like nothing had happened." After the raid was over an I.N.S. official met with the press and said I.B.P. had cooperated in the raid and would face no employer sanctions or fines.

'Your Tired, Your Poor. . .'

I.B.P. doesn't like chatting with the press. But Roberto Trevino, the 29-year-old personnel director at the Heartland Company, a turkey processing plant, gave me a gracious tour of his facility a few hours up the road in Marshall, Minnesota. Five hundred workers-70 percent of them Latinos and Asians, and some Somalis, all in white smocks and caps and under the stress of constantly clanging machinery and chilly temperatures-slaughter, carve, trim and package 32,000 gobblers a day and then ship them throughout America under more than sixty different brand names, including Manor House and Janet Lee.

The college-educated son of Chicano farm workers, Trevino sees his work at least in part as philanthropic. "This is about the whole American immigrant experience. We are providing a stepping stone," he says. "We go to areas of unemployment to recruit. To South Texas: Eagle Pass, El Paso, Brownsville. If you are new in this country you are not going to be a doctor. Instead you take the jobs Americans don't want and you may not get ahead. But you do it for your kids." Yet even Trevino indirectly admits that in the restructured, low-pay workplace, there is little of the stability that we have come to associate with earlier waves of immigration. His turnover hovers at 100 percent. One of five workers is a "re-hire."

"With our workers coming from Texas and Mexico we realize this is not home," he says, contradicting his earlier notion of facilitating assimilation. "This is where you work."

That's not true for the 150 or so Somalis who live and work in Marshall. They can't go back. Some were in a Kenyan refugee camp on a Friday only to find themselves by the next Monday resettled in Minnesota and slashing away at turkeys. In the early nineties other Somalis had poured into Marshall from San Diego, where work had become scarce. But that inflow has now slowed. "A few years back there was a misunderstanding in our plant over rest periods and there was a Somali strike," says Trevino with a chuckle. "The first in the U.S. We fired them all. About eighty workers. Let me tell you, the word got out on the Somali grapevine fast. And now when they come to work here they understand what American work standards are. No labor trouble since then."

Trevino's hard-line attitude is emblematic of an industry that has reinvented itself over the past fifteen years. The bitter strike at Hormel's Austin, Minnesota, plant in 1985-86 (the subject of Barbara Kopple's Academy Award-winning documentary, American Dream) was the signal event in a labor counterrevolution that has convulsed and redrawn the face of U.S. meatpacking. And if you could boil that counterrevolution down into one slogan it would be: Death to Middle-Class Meatpackers!

Prior to the Reagan era, that's exactly what the meatpackers in Storm Lake were. The space now occupied by I.B.P. was the old Hygrade plant. The work force, unionized and virtually all white, was averaging $30,000 a year or more—some $51,000 in today's dollars. Refusing to reach agreement with its unions, Hygrade closed down in 1981.

After being enticed with $10 million in local tax subsidies, I.B.P. re-opened the plant a year later, offering $6 an hour. The pattern of de-unionization and ruralization was regional. One after another, meatpacking plants moved from the big cities, where they were close to labor, into the countryside, where they were near the animals and could save on transport costs. As supermarkets took on more specialty butchers, the processing plants needed more, but less-skilled, workers. Unions became anathema. The industry's hourly pay, including benefits, peaked at $19 in 1980. By 1992 it was below sixties levels at $12 an hour, and it has

continued to fall. By 1995 unionization was half of what it was in 1963.

Where the new plants opened, labor was in relatively short supply. And even in Storm Lake, where hundreds of former Hygrade workers re-applied for the new jobs, I.B.P. hired back only thirty. "The company wanted to bar union-experienced workers from the shop floor," says Mark Grey. With just a few companies—I.B.P., Cargill, Con-Agra—dominating the field, competition was, no pun intended, cutthroat. Production lines were sped up; injury rates climbed. What was once a stable work force became frenetically mobile.

And so it has been primarily over the past five to eight years that the industry has implemented a strategy of targeted recruitment and begun to employ methods of labor control that one group of researchers says "recall systems of peonage."

"The best hope these new communities have is that they become unionized someday," says Joe Amato, director of regional studies at Southwest State University in Marshall. "But how? How can transitory, invisible communities articulate what they want, let alone achieve it?"

With a Wink and a Handcuff

Since 1992 the I.N.S. has arrested more than 1,000 meatpacking workers in the Midwest. This past summer, as part of a six-week regional sweep ordered by the Clinton Administration, 209 undocumented workers were detained in Iowa. The average pay for those arrested was $6.02 an hour. Now the four biggest meatpackers, including I.B.P. and Swift, have agreed to participate in an I.N.S. program that will use computers to check IDs.

Local Latino workers laugh it all off. "Everyone knows the company and the I.N.S. are in together on all this. They never make the company pay a fine, do they?" says Javier, an I.B.P. worker in Storm Lake who works under the ID he purchased in the name of a legal resident. "Everyone knows they are never going to arrest all of us. Who would do this shitty work for them? We know that every now and then the migra will come in and take a few away to keep the politicians happy. And then we won't see them again for another two years. That's how it works."

For more than a century now there's been a pattern of U.S. industries—one after another—actively recruiting Mexican labor while the rest of society turned a blind eye, says Fred Krissman, anthropologist at Washington State University. "You can go back to the 1920s and find all sorts of academic research in that period referring to Mexicans who could be brought here to work and then sent back home like homing pigeons to procreate." And there's always been that cognitive dissonance between the reality and the policy. "In 1954 during what was called Operation Wetback, a million Mexicans were randomly rounded up in the United States and deported," says Krissman. "At the same time we were bringing in 300,000 Mexicans in the Bracero program. We had trains running both ways on public money!"

The solution, he argues, is to dump current immigration policy and opt for the model of the European Union. When you have a system that frees the flow of capital across borders, you should move toward a transnationalization of labor, too. If you work in the United States you should have legal papers in the United States, and all such workers should be protected by serious enforcement of health and safety regulations on the books. This doesn't mean immigrant workers would suddenly make middle class wages, but it would be the first step toward eliminating the employer abuses rained down on people with no legal standing. Most important, it would be a radical leap toward stabilizing these now-underground communities. At best, unions would have a better shot at organizing; at a minimum, individual workers would stand a better chance of raising their wages.

This is not a likely option when politicians from both parties struggle to outdo each other in cracking down on illegal aliens. Here in Iowa, where a steady stream of Mexican workers is keeping his state's industries humming, the very liberal Senator Tom Harkin has been barnstorming—even after the election—promising he will bring more I.N.S. agents into the state.

There's that great line in the movie *Burn* when Marlon Brando, portraying a rogue Marxist in the employ of the fictitious Royal Sugar Company as a counter insurgency adviser and warning the local plantation's overseers of trouble ahead, says something like: In times of great social crisis, the contradictions of an entire century can come to bear in a single week.

And apparently, so can social consciousness expand when put under enough stress. That's the

thought that keeps running through my mind as I sit and talk with Mark Prosser, the beefy, blond, self-described "very conservative" police chief Storm Lake. I ask him how, if at all, he's changed since the influx of immigrants. "We are all prejudiced" he says, "but I really had to face and confront my biases. I don't think the people I used to work with in East St. Louis where I worked on the [police] force would even recognize me today."

Prosser proceeds to tell me that it was only because of his persistent prodding over more than a year's time that the Border Patrol finally staged its Storm Lake raid last May. With so many local residents with so much false ID it was becoming impossible to carry out even routine policing. "But you know," the chief continues, "the problem wasn't solved by the raid. In retrospect, I don't think the taxpayers' money was well spent, given the number of illegals who were here."

"You don't think enough were arrested?" I ask.

"No, that's not it," the chief answers. "I've come to a conclusion. The emphasis has to be on legalization, not arrests. There's just got to be a better way. We have to get these people into the system and get them legalized. You know, I really admire these people. Really. I doubt seriously I would ever invite a federal agency to come in again."

I leave Chief Prosser's office and pick up the paper on the corner. A headline says that the day before, in nearby Omaha, I.N.S. agents raided a city-contracted garbage hauler and arrested more than seventy illegals—about half the company work force. One shot was fired at an escaping alien.

Marc Cooper is host and executive producer of *RadioNation*. He wishes to thank Professor Mark Grey of the University of Northern Iowa for sharing his invaluable research.

Source:
Marc Cooper. In *The Nation*, Feb 3, 1997. Vol. 264, no. 4. pp. 11(6).

LEBANESE AMERICANS

*L*ebanese immigration, by both Christians and Muslims, to the United States began in 1878. By the late 1800s, immigration from Lebanon began in earnest. The country, which had been conquered by the Ottoman Empire in the mid-1800s, suffered severe economic and political struggles. In addition, World War I brought famine to the area, and many Lebanese left their native country to find a more stable and prosperous life in the United States. The peak immigration period was between 1913 and 1914, when 9,000 Lebanese arrived in America. "Where the Twain Shall Meet—Lebanese in Cortland County" provides historical background on Lebanese immigrants who came to the United States and settled in Cortland County in upstate New York. There, first generation Lebanese immigrants primarily worked as farmers and as peddlers. Peddling was the primary means of earning a living for many new Lebanese immigrants. Lebanese immigrants were, in general, entrepreneurs and also ran small shops or made goods for peddlers to sell.

The family and community was largely responsible for maintaining the traditions of Lebanese immigrants. Families often helped incoming immigrants, who they termed "cousins," even though they were not a part of the family. The church also played an important part in maintaining tradition for Lebanese Christians, as was the mosque for Lebanese Muslims. Traditions in music, dance, food and ceremony were passed from the first generation to the next. The article provides excellent examples of celebrations, including descriptions of foods, songs and activities that are traditionally Lebanese.

The success of the first generation, however, brought changes for the second generation. As the first generation moved quickly into the middle-class, they lost their ties with tradition and assimilated more easily into main-stream American culture. The article points out that Lebanese who gained an education often broke family ties that were traditionally very strong, and which held communities together. Second generation Lebanese developed new cultural patterns, participating more fully in the political and social lives of their American communities.

WHERE THE TWAIN SHALL MEET— LEBANESE IN CORTLAND COUNTY

Joseph Abdallah was 20 when he and his 18-year-old sister, Mime Jaber, ventured into Solon, in Cortland County, in 1898. Within a few years, their brother Isaac, then 16, and a 17-year-old friend, Michael Nauseef, joined them. Two years later, Mike sent for his wife, Selma, and his daughter, Mary. This small group of young people marked the start of a stream of immigrants from Lebanon that enriched Cortland County with a colorful variety of folkways.

No one knows now whether these newcomers arrived in Cortland County by chance or purpose. But we do know that people left Lebanon for a variety of reasons. Some were self-imposed exiles who sought to escape the economic and political struggles between Moslems and Christians or to flee the hated rule of their most recent conquerors, the Ottoman Turks. The turn of the century rivalry in the Middle East between England and France drove other Lebanese to seek freedom in new lands.

Some were lured from their homeland by the excitement of adventure in a new part of the world. American and French missionaries had established schools in that ancient crossroads and were inspiring the student to seek their fortune elsewhere. Others sought new lands for strictly economic reasons. Where families were large and property did not suffice to support all the members, younger sons departed in search of better opportunities. With poor land and low incomes, the reasons for seeking another life were obvious. Some, who were comfortable, even departed from the religious, political and economic turmoil in Lebanon merely to insure a better life for their children.

Like most immigrant groups, these Lebanese knew little or no English when they first arrived in the United States. A system had to be devised to make certain they would be directed safely across the Atlantic and to their destinations. On the boat, the ship's personnel advised them. In New York, immigration officials saw the newcomers to their train. Conductors put on them tags to indicate their destination and to make certain they made the correct changes. It was by such arrangements that most Lebanese in the early twentieth century traveled from Beirut to Cortland, not knowing which route to follow and not knowing how to ask directions.

The story is told of one man who realized that the tag indicating his destination was similar to that used in his native land to mark convicts. Fearful of being jailed or of being mistaken for a convict, he complicated his situation by hiding his tag.

The language difference was not the only problem the Lebanese encountered in their new surroundings. At the time when these first arrivals reached Cortland County, Lebanon did not exist as an independent nation but was a part of a larger Syria, then under Turkish rule. Lebanon did not become independent until 1920. Therefore, both immigrants and Americans were often confused about the nativity of the Lebanese. The 1905 census for Cortland County lists the native origins of the first Lebanese as "Asi-Turkey," and the 1915 census placed their birth in "Assyria." In 1925, the census credited them to Syria, but later immigrants listed their origins as Lebanon. This confusion has caused a joking feud among the immigrants who came at different times. Although many came from the same villages, some call themselves Syrians while others insist that they are Lebanese.

Another native custom created additional difficulties over the names of individuals. With the Lebanese concern for family and genealogy, a man whose eldest son is Alfred is called *Boo Alfred*, or "father of Alfred;" his wife is *Imm Alfred*, or "mother of Alfred;" and the son, if his father's name is, for example, Salem, is called *Ibn Salem*, or "son of Salem." When asked for their names in making out their passports, many would reply, "*Ibn*—." In this way, several Lebanese took their father's first name as their last, and in Cortland such Arabic first names as Abdallah, Joseph, Ferris, Ossit, Calale and Nauseef are all used as last names.

Language difficulties, however, did not prevent the arrivals from Lebanon from becoming American citizens, inasmuch as citizenship was easily obtained in the early years of the present man, according to a local tradition, had carefully prepared his answers. When asked, "Who was the first President of the United States?" He quickly replied, "George Wash-a-clothes."

In general, the Lebanese who arrived in Cortland County could be divided into three groups: a group of farmers in Solon; a group of peddlers, mainly residents of Homer; and a group of city workers (laborers and small businessmen) in Cortland.

Most of the Lebanese who came to Cortland County had been property-owners in their native land. They were, however, able to bring with them only a little money as they usually had transferred their land to other members of the family. But whether they had money, or not, in Lebanon they had, at least, been self-employed. Thus they experienced a change in status when they moved to their new homeland. Those who wanted to continue making a living on the land first had to earn money to buy it, either as peddlers or as farm laborers.

Syrian Hill

Joseph Abdallah had set this pattern: after earning money by peddling, he bought a farm on an isolated hill in Solon. His presence there with his family attracted other Lebanese. Soon there developed a colony of Lebanese farmers and farm laborers in the place which is now called Syrian Hill. Many of these farm workers earned enough money to rent a farm until eventually they were able to buy their own land.

These determined peddlers traveled throughout the area, selling what they could, eating if food were offered and sleeping where they found a bed. On Saturday, they returned to Homer with the $10 or $15 each averaged for their week's toil.

Mrs. Mary Ossite, who was born in Lebanon and who came to Solon in 1904 at a young age, has told of a typical day on Syrian Hill in the years after 1910. The activities did not differ greatly from those of other rural New Yorkers of the time. The men arose at four in the morning to milk the cows while the women prepared breakfast which was served between five and six. After breakfast, Mike Nauseef, Mary's father, loaded the milk on a wagon and headed for Maybury's Mill where the local farmers sold their milk. He returned within an hour or an hour and a half to spend the rest of the day doing the seasonal chores—plowing, planting, weeding, reaping, mending fences and taking care of the other duties that a farm required. When time allowed, men lumbered for their own profit. Two men could cut, split, and pile four cords of wood a day. A cord of wood sold for 25 cents so they could each make 50 cents for a day's work.

In the meantime, the women cooked, canned, sewed, washed, worked in the garden—doing whatever had to be done that they could fit into their busy day. Some even went out to peddle in order to help their husbands earn money to pay for renting or purchasing a farm. The women also cut, washed, fluffed and flattened sheep's wool to make quilts. They salted the sheep hide for days, washed it in a stream and then dried it to make a rug for the floor. The women helped each other with these time-consuming tasks. If one were going to town, she made the rounds to see if her neighbors needed anything. If someone were sick, the women would help with the cooking, washing and sewing; or the men would help with the farm chores.

When not needed for chores around the farm, the children attended the predominantly Lebanese primary school on Syrian Hill. A typical one-room school of the time, it had an adjacent shed for wood and an outside toilet. Inside were a round, barrel-like "church" stove, a tank with a spigot for water and rows of desks of different sizes. The Syrian Hill children often missed school in the winter as it was a strenuous hike through woods and snow over the wind-swept hill.

Evenings and Sundays were times for family gatherings. And a Lebanese family included everyone from parents to distant cousins. Mr. Joseph Yaman, born in Lebanon in 1893, has described this Lebanese characteristic, "If I love a man, then he's my relative." So all Lebanese became cousins but, for the record, "distant cousins."

In the evenings, families visited with neighbors. Sunday, however, was the big day. Mother and fathers, sisters and brothers, aunts and uncles, nieces and nephews, cousins and "distant cousins" would gather on Syrian Hill. Those from the city often arrived Saturday night, perhaps catching a ride part of the way and walking the rest of the distance. On Sunday, they assembled in an opening in the woods. After killing a young lamb to roast on a spit they set about to prepare a feast of traditional Lebanese dishes. They wee certain to serve *shish-ka-bob*, the Arabic dish that has become best known in the United States, and which is actually a Turkish name for what the Lebanese call *Lahim mishwa*. It consists of small pieces of meat arranged alternately with onions on a skewer. If there is a national Lebanese dish, it is probably *kibbee*, raw lamb meat ground and mixed in a ratio of two to one with wheat germ which has been soaked in water and then has had most of the water squeezed from it. The meat and wheat germ are spiced with ground onions, salt, pepper, cinnamon, and ground basil. *Kibbee* can also be made into patties and fried or can be filled with a meat layer, such as finely cut lamb cooked with pine seeds and spices, and then roasted in an oven.

These meat dishes were accompanied by *hummoose, lubee, coosa, batata* and *tabulee*. Hummoose can be used as and appetizer or eaten with the meal. For *hummoose*, chic peas are boiled until they are well cooked and are then finely ground and mixed with *tahini* (ground, hulled sesame seed), oil, lemon juice and salt and water. *Lubee* consists of string beans cooked in a tomato sauce. The beans may also be made into a salad, after having been cooked and allowed to cool and seasoned with oil, lemon juice and salt. *Coosa* is squash and is often made into *mihshe coosa* in which the insides of the squash are removed. The squash is filled with a stuffing of finely cut or ground meat, rice, tomato paste and spices and then cooked in tomato sauce. *Batata*, or potatoes, were prepared in many ways. One of the best loved *batata* dishes is *yahkne*, peeled potatoes cooked in a tomato sauce with, perhaps, lamb meat or chicken cooked in the same sauce. *Tabulee* is a favorite summer salad and was sure to be served at these outings. It is prepared from finely cut tomatoes, onions, parsley and mint mixed with wheat germ which has been soaked in water and then has had the water squeezed out. This mixture is spiced with salt, pepper, oil, lemon juice and cinnamon.

When bread was served, it consisted of large round and very thin loaves, similar to, but thinner than, the crust of *pizza*. The dough could be simply rolled and baked in an oven, but to be made correctly it should be spun in the air, tossing the dough in and out of the hands in order to make it as thin as possible.

At these Sunday gatherings there was certain to be sufficient *arak* to satisfy the thirstiest Lebanese. *Arak*, the national wine, is a white wine similar to anisette. Undiluted, it resembles water but is too potent in this form. It is usually drunk mixed with water. The addition of water gives *arak* a milk-like appearance.

Wherever they went, Lebanese carried with them their *derbakke*, as small drum held under the arm and played with the finger tips. To the beat of the *derbakke* and the music from their voices, they danced traditional circle and handkerchief dances. With stomachs full and muscles aching from dancing, the party settled down to an evening of singing, story-telling and joking. One of the best-loved and most challenging forms of Lebanese singing is *achäd w' räd*, or "give and take." This musical form is a single song with an almost infinite number of verses. One person begins by singing a verse, composed on the spot and often directed to someone in the group. Depending on what has been sung, that person may or may not reply with his own improvised verse, always to the same melody. The *achäd w' räd* continues as long as wit and imagination last. Everyone participates in the singing, since, after one person sings a verse, the whole group repeats it. One conspicuous musical characteristic is the "Ohff," in which the vocalist sings a series of notes for as long as possible with a single breath without going off tune. The effect is beautiful but very difficult to do properly and may sound unusual to listeners who are accustomed to the musical styles of western Europe.

Tall Al Qamar, one of the ancient folksongs, has many different sets of words. In one of these, which follows, the setting is a beautiful autumn night with Lebanon's majestic mountains in the background. A man and woman, who love each other but dare not show their emotions, open their hearts before the full moon.

Tall Al Qamar

Woman:
The moon shone over the mountain, and in its
     light I saw my love.
With his finger I saw him pointing at my shadow.
I ventured slowly toward him to see him,
But he sensed me nearing, and he turned and fled
     from me.

Chorus:
But he sensed me nearing, and he turned and fled
     from me.

Man:
Ohff.. . .
I sent the dove to say goodbye to you, but my heart
     would not say goodbye.
And my heart said to me, "Please yourself, but your
     heart is returning to its home."
I started to go, but my heart jumped from me and
     cried, "I won't go with you, return home and
     take me with you."

Chorus:
I won't go with you, return home and take me with
     you.

Woman:
Oh, dove, tell me who has named you a dove.
I prayed by the church that you are keeping my
     love safe for me.
Go now and on your wings bring back something
     that I may have, even the fragrance from my
     love.

Chorus:
Go now and on your wings bring back something
     that I may have, even the fragrance from my
     love.

Man:

Ohff.. . . .

Oh dove of God bring me news of happiness.

Even if you are weary, love will cast off your weariness.

Put me between your wings and take me with you, my body is lighter for you to carry than my words of greeting.

Chorus:

My body is lighter for you to carry than my words of greeting.

They sang other songs expressing their sadness at leaving their country.

One person sings:

Lebanon um wadeeak demhee ala chdoodee
Ough dot rouheet ma'ak nabit ana joudee.
Ruh oud ha marta'ak Mish nakir ahoudee
W' bikeem al nabi'ak ellfine sahreeya.

Then another adds:

Babooree ma atalak mashee ala miya
W' l'youm ruh bihmilak a demooh einy-ya.

1st person:

Lebanon, I'm saying goodbye with tears on my cheeks,

And I'm leaving my soul with you as a reminder of me.

I've not stopped hoping I'm returning to you

And I'll celebrate at your springs two thousand evenings.

2nd person:

My boat, how heavy you are moving through the waters,

And today I can carry you in the tears from my eyes.

Some immigrants after arriving in America still missed their native country but indicated in the following song an optimism about their new life.

Telehna be ross baboor w' atalina,
W' eyoun el weldee nazeer alina.
Nehna baladna hermeet alina
W' be New York rubina seehob.

We climbed to the top of the boat and we ascended,

And the eyes of the mother went with us

As for us, we'll never see our country again

And in New York we'll make new friends.

Peddling Days

These festive occasions were the same for most of the Cortland County Lebanese. Daily life, however, differed somewhat for those who did not seek or could not find farm jobs. Those who lived in the more populous communities clustered first in Homer. There Akil Calale had opened a general store and employed fellow Lebanese as peddlers. As local farmers could not often take time to journey to town, peddlers were usually welcome at the farm.

Mr. Yaman recalled that when he came to Cortland in 1908 there were about 25 or 30 Lebanese; of these about 10 to 15 were peddlers. On weekends, sleeping as many as three to five in one bed, they would all stay in Akil's house behind his store. On Monday morning, the peddlers, both men and women, filled their packs with dry goods and notions (thread, pins, needles and the like) and set out on foot, traveling until nightfall. They sold their goods for cash if they could, but if not, they were willing to barter. They ate only when someone offered them food. They slept if someone offered them the hospitality of a home; or they might take shelter surreptitiously in a barn. Sometimes they walked all night.

Mr. Yaman's description of his ordeals during his first day as a peddler when he was 17 reveals many of the hardships experienced by these immigrants:

> The first day I went with a friend. I thought he could speak English—he had been here six months. We went on a street car from Homer to Preble. This was in February, and it was cold. We peddled all day and sold only 20 cents worth

> At night (we hadn't eaten all day), we walked through Solvay. Five o'clock, I told my partner that we should stay at the next house. I thought it was like the old country where hospitality is never refused. We knocked from house to house from five to eight—people were afraid to let two [strangers] stay overnight. We were cold, and our stomachs were empty. Finally, an old couple named Sherman let us stay. They asked us if we had any supper, and my partner thought she said do you want any supper, so he said yes.

> We went to bed without any supper. The man led us up some steep stairs to the upstairs. The lady was fat so she probably didn't go upstairs much. The bed had no sheets, no pillows. The next day I told my partner to go his way, and I'd go mine.

> I peddled all day, and around four I started to look for a place to stay. I thought I'd better start early. The first place I asked said yes. The people had a daughter who was a school teacher. She tried to talk to me, but I said that I didn't understand English. She got a book and tried to teach me. It made me feel good.

These determined peddlers traveled throughout the area, selling what they could, eating if food were offered and sleeping where they found a bed. On Saturday, they returned to Homer with the $10 or $15 each averaged for their week's toil.

By 1915, Cortland was developing into an industrial community. New jobs were available, and the Lebanese peddlers gave up their former occupation to take advantage of the opportunities. They did not all go to work in the factories. Those who were endowed with a Lebanese quality that has been described as a "traditionally shrewd sense of good bargain" formed their own businesses, such as barber shops, grocery stores, general stores and shoemaker shops; some became milk dealers or gardeners.

The new developments in the economy of the county are reflected in the census records for three decades. In 1905, six Lebanese were listed in Cortland County. All of them lived in Solon, and the three employed men were farmers. In the 1915 census, the Lebanese population was located as follows. 28 in Solon (all but one were farmers); 18 in Cortland (all city workers); 11 in McGraw; 9 in Homer; and 3 in Cortlandville. By 1925 the shift to the city was evident, and the population was distributed among the following communities: Cortland 41, Solon 18, Homer 18, McGraw 12 and Cortlandville 4. No longer were all the Lebanese in Solon farmers, and the number of peddlers in Homer had shrunk to one. At the present time, only a few still live on farms as most now reside in the city of Cortland.

From the time of their first arrival, the Lebanese immigrants always lived together. The farmers occupied Syrian Hill, and peddlers lived near other peddlers. Even the city workers lived in the same neighborhood. In 1915, all of the Lebanese in the city of Cortland lived on the intersecting streets of Winter Street and South Avenue. In 1925, all but one lived on South Main Street, South Avenue and Owego Streets. (South Avenue connects South Main to Owego).

All the occupants of a boarding house might be Lebanese, especially if the owner were also a fellow native. This arrangement was especially advantageous during the years of the depression. Mr. Yaman recalled that "we could take care of each other. None of the Lebanese were out of jobs during the depression, but we didn't make much money. Living together, we had low overhead."

By staying together, the first Lebanese did not often have associations with other people. Even those who worked in factories found that they could easily manage with a small knowledge of English. They made little effort to learn the language and to adopt any more of the new culture than was necessary. Moreover, their fellow workers were themselves recent immigrants and maintained their own customs, thereby encouraging the Lebanese to preserve theirs.

One of the reasons for this adherence to their native folkways undoubtedly stemmed from the deep love that the Lebanese expresses for his *watun*, or country. This intense loyalty, a sort of nationalism away from home, is a stirring emotion that is manifest in the expression *Ibn Arab* (Son of Arab). Many kept close contact with the mother country through newspapers, periodicals and patriotic organizations. The emphasis on hospitality was another cohesive force. Custom and tradition demand that Lebanese be warm and cordial to guests, and any stranger who might reveal that he, too, was Lebanese would be invited to have a meal or spend the night at the home of his new-found fellow countryman.

Recent Changes

But, again, economic forces were at work on old traditions. The self-employed businessman did not preserve close ties with the old folkways. These persons were in contact with the new culture and felt more strongly the pressure to conform to new surroundings. They assimilated the new culture more readily than did the laborers and farmers. These differences produced a subtle cleavage in the once homogeneous population. Whereas the first generation of Lebanese in Cortland County was and is very close, their descendants drew apart and are continuing to draw farther apart.

One of the chief divisive forces at work in the community is education. Those who acquire a college education are likely to move away from Cortland or to associate almost exclusively with those Lebanese who are professionals or businessmen. Those who have not received higher education tend to remain in Cortland, and, although they are identified as being part of the Lebanese population, they usually stay within their own group. As has already been observed, Lebanese place considerable emphasis on family relationships and were accustomed to having close family ties. In modern America, however, occupations no longer depend on the family's ownership of property. Lebanese descendants who attend college, and even some of those who do not, often move away from the family, breaking the intricacy of the large family circle. Thus the primary family, rather than the extended family, as had been conspicuous in Lebanese traditions, is becoming the center of activity. Another indication of the breakdown in what had been

Lebanese homogeneity is the sharp decline during the past decade in the number of marriages taking place between male and female members of the Lebanese community.

A slight but significant religious difference also exerted influence on the Lebanese population in Cortland. Christians in Lebanon are, mainly, either Greek Orthodox or Maronite Catholics. Since they did not find their own churches and did not have sufficient numbers to organize them, they joined the existing religious bodies. The Greek Orthodox became Episcopalians while the Maronites joined the Roman Catholic Church.

Those who assimilated the new culture, along with those who did not, tried to pass on to their children as much of the Lebanese heritage as they could. A vitalizing influence, up to a few years ago, of a slow but steady migration of Lebanese into Cortland had been influential in preserving the old culture and the new Western culture at the same time became neither the heirs to the East nor to the West but to a combination of both. Succeeding generations have become increasingly absorbed with their new environment and participate prominently in the political and social as well as the economic life of Cortland.

One colorful, festive attempt at maintaining Lebanese culture is through the *Hafflie*, or *Mahrajhan*, which are combined social and fund-raising affairs. News of a *Hafflie* is usually spread by word of mouth although some printed announcements may be distributed among the local Lebanese. Tickets are priced at $2 to $5 or even more, depending on whether the tickets include the cost of food. The menu is completely Lebanese as is the singing, dancing and music. Professional dancers may supply entertainment, but there is always an opportunity to dance the popular *debke*, or circle dance. The *Hafflie* raises money for a church and is a social event where *Ibn Arab* and *Bint Arab* (the son and daughter of an Arab) can meet; but, more important, the *Hafflie* is an attempt to keep alive many of the qualities of the old culture.

Now, 66 years after the coming of the first Lebanese into Cortland County, few "old timers" remain. Those who are still living have assessed the effect of the Lebanese on Cortland and agree that their influence has been slight, especially compared to that from the number of Italians who came to the county. Their greatest importance has been in economic affairs. Some own grocery, dry-goods, five and ten cent and liquor stores, ice cream parlors, garages and taxicabs. Others are teachers, tailors, photographers, beauticians, bank clerks and secretaries. Some continue to work as farmers and laborers. The son of the first Lebanese immigrant founded Cortland's largest diary. The son of the man who began peddling at the age of 17 Cortland's largest real estate agency.

Politically, the older generation of Lebanese did not make itself felt for it remained apart from the rest of the community. But the younger generations have worked actively within the existing political parties.

In the social life of the community, the same characteristics prevailed. The first Lebanese remained apart. However, their children and their children's children have become involved in most of the affairs of the community: P.T.A., Heart Fund, Cancer and church drives; they have become Masons, Elks, Moose, Odd Fellows, Rebekahs and members of other organizations.

It is much more apparent, however, that Cortland and American culture affected the Lebanese. The Lebanese had to adjust to a change in status. Once self-employed, with sufficient leisure time essential to the enjoyment of their cultural patterns in their new surroundings, some, temporarily, and others, permanently, became employees with a resulting reduction in leisure and the cultural activities that had occupied that leisure. They suffered a break in family relations as the primary family became the new focus. And with each succeeding generation, they lost the protocol and formalities that had been central to Lebanese customs.

The surviving old-timers agree: some sought adventure and found it, some sought political and religious freedom and found that, some sought economic opportunity and found that, too. They admit that some used what they found to better advantage than others. They agree that neither birth nor breed prevented them from achieving their aims. They stayed and found that in a land with a flexible and liberal atmosphere, they, too, had to be flexible and liberal.

Source:
Suad Joseph. In *New York Folklore Quarterly*, vol. XX, no. 3 (September 1964). pp. 175-191.

LITHUANIAN AMERICANS

The Jungle, *a 1906 novel by Upton Sinclair (1878-1968), was one of the most important works in the history of American literature. Its impact spread far beyond the world of letters: with its scathing portrayal of Chicago meat-packers, it led to public outcries against the scandalous practices of that industry, and this resulted in the passage of the Pure Food and Drug Act in the same year as the novel's publication.*

So well-known is the political impact of The Jungle *that its effect as a work of literature is not as frequently discussed. Nonetheless, Sinclair's lyrical portrait of a Lithuanian wedding celebration—occurring as it does against the grim industrial backdrop that ties the novel together—is a compelling one. It is a mark of his artistry that Sinclair, who was not a Lithuanian himself and therefore must have gathered his facts through research, does not bring in more detail than the reader needs, simply as a way of showing off all he had learned. Instead, he chooses his elements carefully.*

Through skillful imagery, Sinclair weaves a tapestry made up of the men and women—primarily men—in the immigrant community. There is Dede Antanas, a revered figure steeped in a powerful oral tradition from the homeland, whose speech of glad tidings brings his listeners to tears. There is the portly Jokubas Szedvilas, who, trying to lift people's spirits after Dede's mournful speech, hastily makes a few off-color jokes. And there is the violinist Tamoszius Kuzleika, who leads the two other members of his band in a "dreamy" but nimble waltz.

Tamoszius drinks not from a glass or a mug, but a pot of beer, and it is easy to guess that Jokubas's upbeat mood, if not Dede's somber one, has something to do with the alcohol that flows freely at the celebration. The Lithuanian wedding feast, as portrayed by Sinclair, is not an affair for the faint of heart: it is an old-fashioned, Old Country event, with plenty of drinking and dancing.

The wedding party, of course, brings together all age groups, a common occurrence in Europe even if it is not so typical in the United States. Sinclair's paragraph about the different steps danced by the participants is a gorgeous microcosm of immigrant life, showing various stages of assimilation within the American mainstream.

The youngsters prefer the "two-step," a western-style dance with English or Scotch-Irish roots—in other words, something tied to the Anglo-Saxon mainstream of the New World rather than to the Old Country. By contrast, "The older people have dances from home, strange and complicated steps which they execute with grave solemnity." Despite the fact that the band is playing the waltz, a dance commonly associated with eastern Europe, no one present seems to know how to dance it. Many of them join in like true Americans, not worrying much about rules but rather "allow[ing] the undisciplined joy of motion to express itself with their feet . . ."

Sinclair's portrait is every bit as vivid as the one committed to film 85 years later by Swedish filmmaker Lasse Hallstrom, whose Once Around (1991) depicts a Lithuanian wedding celebration. The latter portrays the frenzy of the dance—what Sinclair, using a term to designate particularly fast music, refers to as "a furious prestissimo"—but the power of Sinclair's written words provide a richness that even film cannot capture.

As the evening culminates in a single, monumental event—an event lasting as long as four hours—so the author's narrative builds up to the acziavimas. The latter is a ritual imbued with the culture of an eastern European traditional society, a world almost completely foreign to an Anglo-Saxon accustomed to conducting their affairs with restraint, always preserving their personal space. In the acziavimas, there is no personal space, at least not for the bride or for any of the men present.

The great circular dance, in which each man takes his turn in the center with the bride, is full of symbolism. It is as though each man in the group in turn pledges himself to the bride, another force to protect her from outsiders; and when he has finished the dance, he makes good his pledge with a gift of money to the bride and groom, which he dumps in a hat proffered by the matron Teta Elzbieta. Here Sinclair comes down from the heights of poetry to the realities of economic life by noting that the collective gifts gathered in the hat by night's end, some three hundred dollars, exceeds an immigrant worker's wages for a year.

"A LITHUANIAN WEDDING"
in Upton's Sinclair's *The Jungle*

. . .When the song is over, it is time for the speech, and old Dede Antanas rises to his feet.. . .

Generally it is the custom for the speech at a *veselija* to be taken out of one of the books and learned by heart, but in his youthful days Dede Antanas used to be a scholar, and really made up all the love letters of his friends. Now it is understood that he has composed an original speech of congratulation and benediction, and this is one of the events of the day. Even the boys, who are romping about the room, draw near and listen, and some of the women sob and wipe their aprons in their eyes. It is very solemn, for Antanas Rudkus has become possessed of the idea that he has not much longer to stay with his children. His speech leaves them all so tearful that one of the guests, Jokubas Szedvillas, who keeps a delicatessen store on Halsted Street, and is fat and hearty, is moved to rise and say things may not be as bad as that, and then to go on and make a little speech of his own, in which he showers congratulations and prophecies of happiness upon the bride and groom, proceeding to particulars which greatly delight the young men, but which cause *Ona* to blush more furiously than ever. Jokubas possesses what his wife complacently describes as *poetiszka vaidintuve*—a poetical imagination.

Now a good many of the guests have finished, and, since there is no pretense of ceremony, the banquet begins to break up. Some of the men gather about the bar; some wander about, laughing and singing; but here and there will be a little group, chanting merrily, and in sublime indifference to the others and to the orchestra as well. Everybody is more of less restless—one would guess that something is on their minds. And so it proves. The last tardy diners are scarcely given time to finish, before the tables and debris are shoved into the corner, and the chairs and the babies piled out of the way, and the real celebration of the evening begins. Then Tamoszius Kuszleika, after replenishing himself with a pot of beer, returns to his platform, and, standing up, reviews the scene; he taps authoritatively upon the side of his violin, then tucks it carefully under his chin, then waves his bow in an elaborate flourish, and finally smites the sounding strings and closes his eyes, and floats away in spirit upon the wings of a dreamy waltz. His companion follows, but with his eyes open, watching where he treads, so to speak; and finally Valentinavyczia, after waiting for a little and beating with his foot to get the time, casts up his eyes to the ceiling and begins to say—"Broom! Broom! Broom!"

The company pairs off quickly, and the whole room is in motion. Apparently nobody knows how to waltz, but that is nothing of any consequence—there is music, and they dance, each as he pleases, just as before they sang. Most of them prefer the "two-step," especially the young, with whom it is in fashion. The older people have dances from home, strange and complicated steps which they execute with grave solemnity. Some do not dance anything at all, but simply hold each other's hands and allow the undisciplined joy of motion to express itself with their feet. . .

When Tamoszius and his companions stop for a rest, as perforce they must, now and then, the dancers halt where they are and wait patiently. They never seem to tire, and there is no place for them to sit down if they did. It is only for a minute, anyway, for the leader starts up again, in spite of all the protests of the other two. This time it is another sort of dance, a Lithuanian dance. Those who prefer to, go on with the two-step, but the majority go through an intricate series of motions, resembling more fancy skating than a dance. The climax of it is a furious prestissimo, at which the couples seize hands and begin a mad whirling. This is quite irresistible, and everyone in the room joins in, until the place becomes a maze of flying skirts and bodies, quite dazzling to look upon. . .

After this there is beer for every one, the musicians included, and the revelers take a long breath and prepare for the great event of the evening, which is the *acziavimas*. The *acziavimas* is a ceremony which, once begun, will continue for three or four hours, and it involves one uninterrupted dance. The guests form a great ring, locking hands, and, when the music starts up, begin to move around in a circle. In the centre stands the bride, and one by one, the men step into the enclosure and dance with her. Each dances for several minutes—as long as he pleases; it is a very merry proceeding, with laughter and singing, and when the guest has finished, he finds himself face to face with Teta Elzbieta, who holds the hat. Into it he drops a sum of money—a dollar, or perhaps five dollars, according to his power, and his estimate of the value of the privilege. The guests are expected to pay for this entertainment; if they be proper guests, they will see that there is a neat sum left over for the bride and groom to start life upon.

Most fearful they are to contemplate, the expenses of this entertainment. They will certainly be over two hundred dollars, and may be three hundred; and three hundred dollars is more than the year's income of many a person in this room

Source:

The Jungle, by Upton Sinclair. New York: Doubleday, Page & Company, 1906.

*I*n the late nineteenth and early twentieth centuries, many Lithuanian immigrants were unskilled laborers and came to the United States seeking employment in the packing houses of Chicago. By 1930 almost 200,000 Lithuanians lived in the United States. Chicago continued to be one of several U.S. cities experiencing large increases in their Lithuanian American population. Many faced substantial discrimination.

Estelle Zabritzki's story as told in a 1939 interview typifies the experiences of second generation Lithuanian Americans. Born in Chicago around 1916, like most Lithuanian Americans there she grew up in a devout Roman Catholic home near the industrial yards on the South Side. When illness struck her family, Estelle dropped out of high school to support the family.

Though hoping to find work in the Chicago business district away from the livestock yards, she eventually settled for work at a packinghouse gutting pigs. Although working conditions were difficult, Estelle nevertheless described them with a spunky pride. For example, she related that one could tell if a women worked in the packinghouse because,

> . . .mostly their finger nails are cracked and broken from always being in that pickle water; it has some kind of acid in it and it eats away the nails. . .(They) put me to work in Dry Casings, you might think it's dry there but it isn't, they just call it that to distinguish it from Wet Casings dept., which is where they do the first

cleaning out of pig guts. The workers call it the 'Gut Shanty' and the smell of that place could knock you off your feet.

Estelle married a Lithuanian also employed at the packinghouse. Like other second and third generation Lithuanian Americans, they steadily assimilated into American society, slowly losing their Lithuanian identity. The two incomes enabled them to move into a neat four-room house with new furniture in a nice workers' residential area. However, occupational hazards were a harsh reality for immigrants and Estelle's husband fell ill from unregulated exposure to caustic materials in the packinghouse. He was eventually forced to find work elsewhere.

Lithuanian Americans are noted for their active participation in the rise of union activities in the United States. Estelle was no exception in joining the movement by striving to support her fellow female workers seeking to improve their working conditions and pay.

LITHUANIAN—ESTELLE ZABRITZKI

FORM A

State: Illinois
Name of Worker: Betty Burke
Address: 1339 South Troy Street
Date: May 4, 1939
Subject: Packinghouse worker

1. Date and time of interview: May 1, May 3, evenings

2. Place of interview: 3658 South Hoyne Avenue

3. Name and address of informant: Estelle Zabritzki 3658 South Hoyne Street

4. Name and address of person, if any, who put you in touch with informant: None

5. Name and address of person, if any, accompanying you: None

6. Description of room, house, surroundings, etc.: Four Room house, 2nd floor back, stove heat, very neat and homey. Being married about two years and both working steady, they have all new and good furniture. They live in a cleaner, fairly well-to-do workers' residential section. By 'well-to-do' workers is meant the kind who have skilled jobs in the yards, foremen, small time office executives (from the yards). Three large Catholic churches dominate the social and community life of this small section. Plenty of saloons but all situated on the business streets, not, as in the real yards slums, eight blocks south, scattered thickly on every street, business or 'residential'.

FORM B

Personal History of Informant

1. Ancestry Lithuanian, American born

2. Place and date of birth Chicago, 23 years old

3. Family Married, Husband Lithuanian, American born 6 months old baby girl

4. Places lived in, with dates: South side of Chicago and back of yards

5. Education, with dates: Grammar school, two years of High at Englewood High

6. Occupations and accomplishments, with dates: Never did anything but work in the yards

7. Special skills and interests: Her baby and her husband and her home are the most important things in her life. Union work comes next, but since the baby came she hasn't done much except attend its social affairs.

8. Community and religious activities: Attends a YWCA center recently established in the yards area. Lauds it for its progressive ideas and stimulus to stockyard women workers. Raised a Catholic, but not very religious. Seldom goes to church.

9. Description of informant: A beauty, mild, smiling ways. Says she gets along very well at the yards because they think she's beautiful and dumb. The foremen would come and cry on her shoulders all the time about the union and she would have to be so solicitous and sympathetic and indignant about it all, with a CIO button stowed away in her purse since the first day the union came to the plant.

FORM C: Text of Interview (Unedited)

I'll tell you how I got to working in the yards. I wanted to finish high school but we had a lot of sickness and trouble in my family just then; my father got t.b. and they couldn't afford to send me any more. Oh, I guess if I had begged and coaxed for money to go they would have managed but I was too proud to do that. I thought I'd get a job downtown in an office or department store and then maybe make enough to go back to school. Me and my girl friend used to look for work downtown every day. We lived right near the yards but we wouldn't think of working in that smelly place for anything. But we never got anything in office work and a year went by that way so one time we took a walk and just for fun we walked into Armour's where they hire the girls, you know. We were laughing and hoping they wouldn't give us applications, lots of times they send new girls away because there's so many laid off girls waiting to get back, and we really thought working in the yards was awful. Lots of girls do even now, and even some of them will have the nerve to tell people they don't work in the yards. They'll meet other girls who work there, at a dance or some wedding and they'll say they don't.

But you can always know they're lying, because mostly their finger nails are cracked and broken from always being in that pickle water; it has some kind of acid in it and it eats away the nails.

Well, in walks Miss McCann and she looks over everybody and what did she do but point at me and call me over to her desk. I guess she just liked my looks or something. She put me to work in Dry Casings, you might think it's dry there but it isn't, they just call it that to distinguish it from Wet Casings dept., which is where they do the first cleaning out of pig guts. The workers call it the 'Gut Shanty' and the smell of that place could knock you off your feet. Dry Casings isn't that bad but they don't take visitors through, unless it's some real important person who makes a point of it and wants to see. Lots of those ritzy ladies can't take it, they tighten up their faces at the entrance and think they're ready for anything, but before they're halfway through the place they're green as grass and vomiting like they never did before. The pickle water on the floors gets them all slopped up, just ruins their shoes and silk hose. And are they glad to get out! They bump into each other and fall all over themselves, just like cockroaches, they're so anxious to get away and get cleaned up. We feel sorry for them, they look so uncomfortable.

I operated a power machine in Dry Casings. It's better where I am because the casings are clean and almost dry by the time they come to the machine and I sew them at one end. Mine is a semi-skilled job and I get good pay, piece work, of course. On an average of from $23 to $27 a week. In my dept. there aren't so many layoffs like in the other places. We work about eight months a year, but I was lucky, I only got it three times in the five years I was there. I think they sort of like me, Miss McCann and some of them.

But the first week I was there, you should have seen my hands, all puffed and swollen. I wasn't on sewing then, I was on a stretching machine. That's to see if the casing isn't damaged after the cleaning processes it goes through.

Me and my girl friend used to look for work downtown every day. We lived right near the yards but we wouldn't think of working in that smelly place for anything.

You know that pickle water causes salt ulcers and they're very hard to cure, nearly impossible if you have to keep working in the wet. The acids and salt just rot away a person's skin and bone if he just gets the smallest scratch or cut at work. Most of the girls in casings have to wear wooden shoes and rubber aprons. The company doesn't furnish them. They pay three dollars for the shoes and about one fifty for the aprons.

My husband got the hog's itch from working there. He can't go near the yards now but what he gets it back again. He used to have his hands and arms wrapped up in bandages clear up to his elbows, it was so bad. The company paid his doctor bills for a while till it got a little better but they broke up his seniority. They transferred him to another dept. after he had worked 3 1/2 years in one place, and then after a couple months they laid him off because they said he was 'new' in that department. They just wanted to get rid of him now that he was sick and they had to keep paying doctors to cure him. Finally he got a job outside the yards so he said 'to hell with them'.

Source:

Library of Congress. *American Life Histories: Manuscripts from the Federal Writers' Project, 1936-1940* from the American Memory website (http://memory.loc.gov/ammem/wpaintro/wpa-home.html).

MACEDONIAN AMERICANS

After 1945, most Macedonian immigrants arrived from Yugoslavia and Greece. Earlier immigrants came from the western region of the Balkan peninsular. The identification of immigrants as is confusing, because immigrants prior to World War II identified themselves Bulgarians or Macedonian Bulgarians. The confusion reflects several changes of the geographic boundaries of Macedonia, a country in the former Yugoslavia that was originally the ancient kingdom of Philip and Alexander the Great. Macedonia is generally defined as the region bounded on the south by the Aegean Sea, Mount Olympus, the Viatritsa River and the Pindud Mountains; on the north by the Sar, Osogovske, and Rila Dagh mountains; on the east by the Rhodope Mountains and the Mesta River: and on the west by Lake Ohrid, the Drin River and the Korab Mountains.

Macedonian Americans settled in the industrial center of the north, such as Ft. Wayne, Indiana, where the wedding of "Immigrant Macedonian Wedding" takes place. Other industrial centers with significant Macedonian populations include New York, Michigan, Ohio, Illinois, Pennsylvania, Wisconsin, Washington and Missouri. Some Macedonian Americans also settled in California. Cities such as Detroit, Chicago, Cleveland, Cincinnati and Syracuse have established communities of Macedonian Americans. Since the 1950s, immigrants from Yugoslavia's Socialist Republic of Macedonia sought to maintain their cultural identity by forming organizations such as the United Macedonians and many local Macedonian-American clubs. These organizations sponsor folk ensembles, theater troupes, and ethnic festivals. Many Macedonian church facilities are the site of vecherinks (an evening party usually with dancing) on holidays and Sundays.

Macedonian Americans have a Slavic heritage. Over 90 percent of Macedonians belong to the Eastern Orthodox Church, which is also the Church of the Greeks. Macedonian customs are very similar to Greek customs, though at times in their history, Macedonians joined with Bulgarians to resist Greek influence. In the United States, the Eastern Orthodox churches are responsible to local boards and provide a community center where social events such as weddings take place. The wedding customs described in this document reflect influences from Greece, Turkey and Bulgaria, which are all countries that at one time or another exerted political control over Macedonia. The mixture of customs sometimes causes friction, as is mentioned in "Immigrant Macedonian Wedding"; for instance, the use of a Greek-style altar-table cloth upset the Bulgarian priest performing the wedding ceremony.

Ethnic identity among Macedonian Americans is still strong because many marriages are between partners of the same faith. The length of engagement among Macedonian American couples is longer than the typical two-month period that characterizes engagements among couples in Macedonia. The American wedding is also more elaborate and expensive. Traditional Macedonian costumes are not used in American wedding ceremonies. However, some traditions are maintained, as this description of the wedding ritual shows.

IMMIGRANT MACEDONIAN WEDDING

Introduction

The Macedonian community in Ft. Wayne, has approximately two-hundred families of Slavic background. Although the first Macedonians settled there at the time of World War I, an Orthodox church was not consecrated until 1948. At present time, however, St. Nicholas Macedono-Bulgarian Orthodox Church serves as one of the major focal points for the community at large. In addition to the Church, certain political organizations, and a national newspaper, (*The Macedonian Tribune,* a bilingual paper published weekly in Indianapolis), the Macedonian community maintains its identity through the continued celebration of certain family rituals. The most important of these, the ritual set apart from any other because of its significance to the whole community, is that of the marriage.

Some customs within the wedding ritual which were practiced assiduously in the Old Country (presently Greece, Bulgaria, Yugoslavia, and Albania) are no longer found in Ft. Wayne. Practicality, the desire to conform to the American way of life, and the direct influence of American wedding customs are the three most logical explanations for these losses. However, it is dangerous to assume that rituals of this type simply decline in importance and frequency of practice, the longer a minority group remains in a foreign environment. Today, children in the second and third generations are expressing a desire to maintain the old customs, even if they have been absent for an entire generation. In addition, within the Ft. Wayne Macedonian community these revivals are constantly bolstered by the fact that new emigrants continue to arrive.

The following materials will give a composite picture of a more or less typical immigrant Macedonian wedding in Ft. Wayne. Additional materials will give comparative views of the Macedonian wedding ritual as it was practiced in the Old Country. Supplementary notes are either from the personal observation of the compiler, or from interview materials which were not tape recorded. Interview materials are from three sources and are so noted.

Two specific weddings are catalogued: the first occurred in June, 1963, and SA is the principal narrator. The second took place in May, 1969, and ES and LS supply the information. ES and LS were *Nunko* and *Nunka* for this wedding. Finally, RN speaks of his uncle's wedding in Yugoslav Macedonia, which took place in 1920.

Parenthetical remarks are made by the compiler. Initials in place of names have been used to prevent jeopardizing future fieldwork with other immigrants, as well as to protect the anonymity of the informants.

I. General Remarks Concerning the Wedding Ritual

The wedding is a ritual of such importance to the Macedonian immigrant community that it is never treated lightly. All of those who have participated in weddings in the past are acutely aware of the ritual's significance. Each informant, in addition to specific information concerning the wedding ritual, supplied a certain number of general comments.

ES: The customs here are somewhat related although we have something different from what they have. Here in the States we don't quite do the same things we did in the Old Country. The reason for that is we're trying to blend, sort of, with the Americans as well. We have omitted some and we have added quite a few. That is, we have added the American customs, blended them together with the Macedonian, and we have omitted a few of the Macedonian part of it. Such as getting the bride and groom ready on the day of the wedding.

One of the first customs to be lost in this country, and indeed, a custom which lost favor some years ago in Macedonia, is the arranged marriage.

RN: Of course the weddings [in the Old Country] are not as elaborate as they are here. There they invite your relatives and your friends to dinner. These weddings usually start on a Thursday night. For the family, that's the time when everybody comes and donates something for the wedding on the bride's side or the groom's side. But it's a very important event, the wedding. The whole village, or at least your group is affected. In our. . .[present day Yugoslav Macedonia] it was the tradition to start on a Thursday. They thought Wednesday was a little, you know, too far in advance. But the whole ritual, not only the service, might go on until the next Wednesday. There's more to it, you know, than just the actual service.

SA: From the Monday before, here at least in Ft. Wayne, our people expect big displays of the gifts. And you have to pin up their telegrams and their cards. And even though now they got the modern thing of the stores delivering the gift to the house, they didn't have that at one time here; they still come. The major relatives still come and bring their gifts personally. We all think that the personal visit is important. And other people still know that even though the stores sent out the gift, they tell the store, 'Now, I want it there by Tuesday because we're going over to visit Tuesday night.' And generally when they come, they'll bring a pastry. Sometimes it's store-bought, but 75 to 80 percent of the time it's homemade. It's a Macedonian or Bulgarian pastry. And then, of course, you have to extend yourself. They expect the groom to be here. This is every night the whole week. And the tempo just starts building up from there. On Thursdays, then, the family ladies, the grandmothers, the aunts, and the cousins who are beyond the generation of the bride and groom will come in. And that's when they start even here. They start making the bread and making the pastries.

II. The Arrangement of the Marriage

One of the first customs to be lost in this country, and indeed, a custom which lost favor some years ago in Macedonia, is the arranged marriage. Matchmakers (Macedonia: *posturnitsi*; Bulgarian: *svatovnitsi*), usually older women, were contacted by one of the sets of parents and it was she and she alone who completed the necessary negotiations. The bride and groom-to-be were simply not consulted.

RN: Well, there were cases when the parents decided this, but it cannot be said that the parents always decided without the previous consent of the boy and girl. But once the parents decided, it had to be done. There was no change of mind. You had to go through the same traditional routine of getting married. Which was that you don't go to the girl's house and give her a ring and tell her that from this day on you were engaged. Your family had to send a matchmaker to the girl's house. And they, of course, using all the professional know-how, because they had done this years and years, you know, in a row. They told the family of the girl what advantages it would be for the girl to marry the boy, because he is of very good stock and the family had very good prospects of acquiring land.

The girl has nothing to do with it. She was in another room. 'Course she knew what the matchmakers were doing, you know, but she was not present when all this was done. But when I asked my mother one time, and my father, what was the deciding factor in this matchmaking business, I mean what was the arrangement. . .what persuaded the parents of the girl and of the boy to agree to this kind of marriage, he said the stock from which the girl and the boy came was the main factor. If the boy was of good stock, but I mean stock of people who were morally preserved and things like that, I don't mean just of healthy stock, people who were truthful to their words, then all right.

LS: Well, just about before the end of the ceremony, they lift the veil, and then the groom is supposed to actually see the bride for the first time. Like, see, years ago they used to make the marriage between the families. And a lot of times there were two families from two different villages and the groom and the bride had never seen each other. They just walk in the church and that's it. He's married to her, no matter what she looked like. That was years ago.

In the most recent Macedonian wedding in Ft. Wayne, the groom's parents were still in Greek Macedonia when the couple decided to marry. It was the general consensus of opinion that, although some modern weddings still *seem* to be arranged, knowledge and consent is always assumed by all parties before arrangements are begun.

III. The Engagement

In what is present-day Yugoslav Macedonia, the engagement was a specific and important event. The engagement was the first official meeting of the two families involved. Both sets of parents met the matchmaker in their respective house as many times as was necessary. Following these meetings, the family of the groom went to the bride's house and the bargain was sealed. The matchmaking and engagement meetings all took place on Sundays, the traditional days for any major part of the wedding ritual.

RN: And all I know that two Sundays after this [the completion of the matchmaking], all of us got dressed in our best outfits—Easter outfits what you call in the United States—and at the head of the priest, we went to the girl's house. There were about fifteen or twenty of us. The closest relatives of our immediate family. And when we went to this house, we found the closest relatives of their family. We were met very charmingly, you know, in a very gentlemanly way and my father acted as the father of my uncle because my grandfather had passed away. So, according to custom, her father had to shake hands with my father first and then with my mother.

And everybody sits down, and the priest started the conversation. And he said to the father of the girl, "Well, you know why we have come here. We have come here to ask for the hand of your daughter. We have talked it over. We have thought that this was going to be a very good match for both of us. But it is understood that she is going to marry K and live in K's house." [In rare circumstances, if one family has all daughters and another all sons, a boy can go to live in the girl's house and even take her name. This phenomenon is called *domozo* {Tr. 'house groom'}.]

Then they called the girl to come into the room. And the father of the girl said, "These people from the K and N family have come to ask for your hand. Are you willing to accept K for a husband? Do you want to be engaged to him?"

And then she said she had heard a lot of good things about K and that she knows the N family and she be very happy to accept the offer. And then the father said, "In that case you kiss the hand of the priest." And she did, and then she kissed the hand of my father because he had acted as the father of K. Then she hugged and kissed my mother and then, of course, the rest of us. And her aunt, whose name I forgot, came out with *Podargus*—presents. She had something different already made. I mean, she did not do them [at] this time. But every girl must be prepared for this emergency or this contingency or this particular moment of her life. So she gave my uncle an embroidered shirt, you know. And my mother got a blouse; my father, two pair of hand-made stockings, you know, *choragi*. And they gave me something, I don't know, I forgot. But they gave every one of us something.

As with arranged marriages, the official meaning and use of the engagement have largely been lost in the New World. In most cases, either the parents had already been acquainted for some years, or, because of geographic location, they would meet only on the day of the wedding, if even that were possible. In the 1969 wedding, about which ES and L.S. speak, the engagement was marked by a small American-style party. The groom's parents were still in Macedonia and met the bride and bride's parents only the day before the actual ceremony. This case seems to be typical of almost all contemporary New World Macedonian weddings.

Regarding the length of the engagements RN remarks concerning the Old Country:

RN: Not more than two months. After two months, they got to get married. There is no such engagements like here, two, three years. Because nobody can wait that long. And they see no reason for waiting since everybody who has a daughter and a son to get marries, they're prepared, more or less, you know, halfway prepared to have a wedding at any time. And when a boy is eighteen and a girl is sixteen or seventeen, the father, the parents of the

two, you know, should be ready for any emergency, because they may decide to get married and they have to be ready.

Engagements in Ft. Wayne, however, Old Country traditions to the contrary, seem to vary in length in the same way as any traditional American engagement. The couple in the 1969 wedding, for example, were engaged officially for five months. They felt that at least this much time was necessary in order to make suitable arrangements.

IV. The Nunko and Nunka

The members of the wedding party (*svadbari*) in an immigrant Macedonian wedding are principally the same as in a traditional American wedding with the exception of godparents. In the case of the 1969 wedding in Ft. Wayne, the bride was from that city, sixteen years old, and did not intend to finish High School. She had been in America for five years. The groom, twenty-six years old, was from Ontario and had been in Canada for three years. He worked there as a mechanic. Both were from Greek Macedonia originally, but they had not known one another in the Old Country.

Each had a series of ushers and bridesmaid (*pobratini* and *posestrimi*), numbering five and seven respectively. Children involved in the actual ceremony numbered three: a flower girl (cousin of the bride), a ring bearer, and a candle bearer (both sons of the *Nunko* and *Nunka*, "Godfather" and "Godmother"). All of these individuals were traditional Macedonian participants.

Only two members of the wedding party are not found in the traditional American ceremony. The *Nunko* and *Nunka* are, beside the groom and the bride, the most important participants. Roughly equivalent to the Best Man, the *Nunko* supervises the wedding arrangements, may have the power to decide where and when the wedding is to be, and in the past, decided on the names of the betrothed couple's children. In addition, the *Nunko* must be responsible for children in the event of the death of the parents. Finally, the *Nunko* is expected to help the bride's father with the cost of the wedding (usually $1000 and up) and to give the largest present.

The *Nunko* and *Nunka*, therefore, act as sponsors for the young couple, and their authority during the entire wedding ritual is unchallenged. In the past, the *Nunko*, or his direct descendent, was also the sponsor at one's baptism.

RN: The *Kum* [Bulgarian word for Macedonian *Nunko*] is already known because he is the man who is already baptizing or christening the boy; he or his son or his daughter is going to be the *Kum*. You know, there is no question about the *Kum*.

That's traditional. There are *kumove* [plural form] who have been *kumove* to a family two hundred years.. . .It's a tradition to keep, it's like a throne you inherit, you know. Whether you like him or not, you have to invite him to be your *kum*. But then, it's inevitable. It's part of the tradition.

Among immigrants, however, inviting someone to be the *Nunko* is more voluntary:

ES: Well, usually they choose the closest friend. Actually the groom is the one who chooses the *Nunko*. Usually they don't ask relatives, but stick to friends.

Interviewer: Is the *Nunka* automatically his wife?

ES: Yes, automatically, if he is married. If he is not married, then they choose one from the bride's side. But usually they try to get someone who is married.

V. Saturday: The Day Before the Wedding

The two most important events on the day of the wedding in Ft. Wayne are the rehearsal at the church and the rehearsal dinner, usually given at the bride's house. Ordinarily, as was the case at the 1969 wedding, the morning is taken up by the preparation of the food both for the party that night and for the festivities the next day unless the wedding dinner should be catered. Normally, the *koluk*, the traditional wedding cake, is made on Saturday morning. This is a large, sweet, bread-like, yeast cake, about two feet in diameter and made from a recipe similar to the Easter bread or *kosunak*. Small candies are implanted in the top of the *koluk*. Traditionally, this cake is made by the *Nunka*, but in the case of the 1969 wedding, the grandmother of the bride made it because she knew the recipe, thus freeing the *Nunka* from this extra duty. There was, in addition, a traditional white American-style wedding cake at the reception, bought by the *Nunko*.

SA describes the Saturday festivities on the day before his wedding in 1963:

SA: Saturday, then, we still have the custom of holding the bridal, the rehearsal dinners within the home. We don't go out. We don't go to a hall. The rehearsal dinners are held her and of course it's ,—everybody comes here after the rehearsal and they cook off the lambs and the beef and the chicken and whatever. And the pastries and the rices and the salads and everything. And that basically really kicks off the wedding.

Interviewer: What kind of Macedonian dishes?

SA: Just the typical stuff we always eat. The bake lamb, always the festive dish. The rices [*pilaf*], the *piti* [a flaky pastry, usually served with white goat cheese filling], *banitsa* the Bulgarians call it. The salads, the normal Macedonian desserts of various kinds. That's when the groom exchanges his gift with the bride and that's also when the bride gives her, she *darvi's* [Tr. to give a gift.' During the engagement meeting in the Old Country, we noted that the bride gave a handmade gift to all the important relatives on the groom's side. In America, then, this custom is delayed until the day before the wedding.] her relatives and the groom's relatives. She gives them ties and neckties and shirts and different things.

Interviewer: Does she place it [the gift] over their shoulders according to the custom in Macedonia?

SA: No. Here we have modified that tradition by having them very nicely gift wrapped. Generally they carry out the color theme of the wedding. By Saturday night everybody know whether it's going to be a white wedding, a red wedding or a pink wedding or a blue wedding.

In the past, Saturday was also the traditional day on which the guests were invited to the wedding

RN: Some of them, if they're close relatives, they get invited with the music, you know. But others are told by the *mladi-pobratim* [Tr. 'Junior ushers'] day—sometimes more, but usually day ahead of time—they go and say Mr. So-and-So, *na edi-koe-si data da se zhenili koe-si, vie ste pokanili da doidete na vechera,* you know [Tr. On such and such a date, So-and-So will be married, and you are invited to come for the evening.'] But if he doesn't say you are invited *vaccaria* [Tr. 'Evening'], which means they are *pokanite* [Tr. 'invited'] only to come to the church wedding. And after the church wedding, they might as well go home, you know. Or they can go for the dance in the yard, but nothing else. So in this way in the villages, small villages everybody goes to the wedding because the villages are composed of 50, 60, 70 houses, you know, and it's easy to prepare enough for all. But in a town like [mine], where you have six or seven thousand people, you cannot invite everybody. Because in the first place you don't have enough room. Sometimes you may leave some of your relatives and close friends out because there is no more room, you know to sit them down.. . .But now on Saturday, the *Nunko* and the priest, they sit on the most honorable place. The priest says the *molitva*, you know, the prayer, and then the *Nunko* gets up and he also gives blessing. He mentions everybody of the groom. Then they sit down. And nobody takes a bite of the food that is already on the table before the *Nunko* takes his fork on his plate and starts eating. And then everybody else.

Even the priest waits, because the *Nunko* is all-powerful. The *Nunko*, even the priest, then everybody [can begin].

Important guests, such as the close relatives of the bride and groom, are "invited with the music." In these cases, the Macedonian band, which is to play at the reception, accompanies one or several of the ushers and the important persons are invited in a formal style. Ordinarily, the person is offered wine from a traditional wooden bottle, the *buklitsa*, and perhaps one traditional circle dance, a *horo*, is performed. Less important guests are simply invited by one of the junior ushers, without benefit of music. In Ft. Wayne, and only in some cases, it is the *Nunko* alone who is officially "invited with the music." This event takes place on Sunday, immediately before the ceremony. Other invitations are simply sent by mail.

In the 1969 wedding in Ft. Wayne, the rehearsal began in the church at 4 P.M. Only the individuals actually involved in the service attended. The ceremony was run through twice, and each person was shown where to stand and told what duties he or she had to perform. The rehearsal dinner began in the bride's house at seven P.M. Cocktails were served first, all being referred to as *rakiya*, or Macedonian plum brandy. The most common drink was Seagram's #7 Crown mixed with 7-Up. A long table was set up in the basement of the bride's home at which twelve people could sit on a side. In typical Macedonian style, soft drinks, beer, white cheese, bread, pickled peppers, olives, and plates of sliced tomatoes were left on the table at all times. These are all considered both in the Old Country and in America to be the traditional "hors d'oeuvres" to be eaten with any strong alcoholic drink. The groom, the *Nunko*, and two or three of the groom's special friends sat at the middle of one side of the table. Drinking was constant and heavy. During this time, the bride remained upstairs with various other guests.

The rest of the house was also full of guests. The bride's mother estimated that there were "a couple hundred" guests in all. The basement was decorated with colored paper streamers. Food was served continuously. A small buffet table at one end of the basement held platters of bake lamb, rice pilaf, a large salad bowl, white cheese, four different types of pastries, ripe olives, bread, raw celery, baked chicken, *pita* and paper plates and silverware. All of these platters were replenished constantly and guests were urged to eat and drink as much as possible.

By ten o'clock, the groom's close friends had become mellow enough to begin singing. Most were love songs, sung in the Macedonian dialect of their region and the groom was always indicated as the subject of the songs. After the singing began, the bride came downstairs and joined the groom and was also included as the subject of the songs. No musical instruments were played, although the singers who began most of the songs were to play in the band the next day. Singing was always in unison with men and women joining equally. Coffee was served at eleven o'clock and drinks consumed continuously. The party ended approximately 4:30 A.M.

VI. Sunday, the Day of the Wedding

1. *Shaving the Groom*

In Macedonia, on the morning of the wedding, one of the *Nunko's* duties was to shave the groom. The purpose of this custom was two-fold. First, the young groom was thought to be too nervous to perform the act himself.

ES: So after this [the inviting of the *Nunko*], we go to the groom's house. And the tradition there is where the band is playing, the best man [the *Nunko*] shaves the groom.

LS: The groom is supposed to be so nervous that they don't want him to cut himself.

ES: He should be shaved by the best man. This is the tradition. How it arrived, we don't know. We just follow it. There is also some singing that goes along with it. This is all omitted here [in the United States].

In Macedonia, on the morning of the wedding, one of the *Nunko's* duties was to shave the groom. The purpose of this custom was two-fold. First, the young groom was thought to be too nervous to perform the act himself.

Second, this was the last opportunity the groom had to be with his male friends in his bachelor state. Thus many of the songs traditionally sung at this time were very ribald, all using the groom as the butt of jokes and emphasizing the difficulties of married life. This custom has been lost in the New World, although everyone knows of it. At the rehearsal for the 1969 wedding, the priest made elaborate jokes about the shaving ceremony to the great amusement of the participants.

2. *The Costumes*

None of the traditional Macedonian costumes are used in wedding ceremonies in the United States. Many families have their mother's or their grandmother's wedding dresses, but *LS* told me, for example, "We use it for Hallowe'en costumes around here. I've won a few door prizes with it." In Ft. Wayne, the bride invariably wears the traditional American style white gown and carries a small bouquet. Referring to the men in the 1969 wedding the *Nunko* said:

LS: No, the men will have the Tux. Rented Tux. They can have long tails, or no tails, or just the evening jacket. In this case they'll have white jackets with black Tux pants, and they have cummerbunds with bow ties and white shirts.

SA remarked that at his wedding in 1963 in Ft. Wayne, all the men wore "strollers," or Morning Clothes. In addition to the cutaway coat, the costume included gray top hats. His bride wore traditional white dress with a long veil.

Bridesmaids generally wear the same model dress in the same color, although the *Nunko's* dress is slightly different in order to set her apart.

3. Inviting the Nunko

This custom seems to be retained in about half of the Macedonian weddings in Ft. Wayne, and its retention seems directly proportional to the length of time the couple to be married have been in the United States.

The Old Country tradition:

RN: On Friday before the dinner, the *star-probratim* [Tr. 'the chief usher'], the *mlad-probratim* [Tr. 'the junior usher'], the *zed*, which is the groom, and a few of the relatives go to invite the *Nunko* to come to the wedding. The *Nunko* does not come unless all these go accompanied by the music, the musicians. They go by the *Nunko*, and the *Nunko* waits in his house. They say,-the *star-probratim*-"We have come here to invite you to do the honor of being the *Nunko* to Mr. So-and-So who is getting married tomorrow. And we come here to invite you to come to the groom's house.' And he replies that he has been waiting may years for this honor, because he Christened the boy, you know, when he was a little boy, and this is one of the happiest moments of his life. Whether he means it or not, this is the procedure.

In the Old Country, both the invitation and the reply are very stylized, and the answers are always given as expected, whether they are sincere or not. In the 1963 Ft. Wayne wedding, the *Nunko* was not formally invited. The groom had privately asked the *Nunko* some time previously and he had accepted. In the 1969 wedding, the *Nunko* was formally invited by the groom, his ushers, and a five piece Macedonian band. This group came to the *Nunko's* house at about 11:30 A.M. on Sunday. Traditional greetings were exchanged (*"Da se kerdose!"* tr. 'may it be a happy bondage!'), and the band began to play. Several circle dances were completed and the Nunko paid the band members liberally.

This is always done in traditional style with the Nunko pressing a bill ($20 and several $1 bills in this case) onto the perspiring forehead of the lead player, in this case a clarinetist, The bill stuck there for all to see. After the dances were over, the whole company adjourned to the garage where a light snack had been laid out on a long trestle table. The snack consisted of baked lamb, white cheese, olives, bread, champagne, and other assorted cocktails. At 12:15 P.M. the whole group went to the bride's house in a convoy, blowing their car horns along the entire route.

4. The Bride Leaves Her Mother's House for the Last Time

In almost all Slavic cultures, the event of the new bride leaving her mother's house is a time of great sadness. The mother, and at times other close female relatives, wail and lament in somewhat the same stylized manner as they would at a funeral. In the United States the mother of the bride might cry unashamedly as her daughter left, but she would not chant the traditional words of farewell as she would in the Old Country.

ES: Some of the ladies, the older ones, the immediate family would sing a song and the mother, naturally, would start crying as the daughter departs from her life.

Interviewer: Is this similar to *Oplakvane* [Tr. 'funeral laments']?

ES: *Oplakvane*, yes.

LS: They don't sing it here, but generally the mother does cry because that is the last time the daughter would be in that house, because usually the young couple would take up an apartment or housekeeping of their own.

ES: This is being done away with more and more. The ones who are brought up here do not.

As the bride leaves the house, there is one other custom which again is followed in about half the Macedonian ceremonies. Just before the bride comes down the steps of her house, her mother pours a glass of water on the steps. This symbolic act represents two things as it was explained by the participants. First, in stepping over the water, the bride irrevocably separates her old life as a daughter from her new life as a wife. Second, there is an implicit wish in the act of throwing water that the bride's life flow as smoothly as the water flows over the stones of the steps.

In Bulgaria the same ritual takes place, but in this case it is performed after the wedding. As the bride approaches her new home, her mother-in-law places a bucket of water in her paths. Before she enters the house, she must kick over the bucket.

5. From the Bride's House to the Church

In Macedonia, all brides and grooms went to the church by making a series of turns to the right. In many cultures, the right hand is considered good luck. Among the Slavs, the left hand can be considered in certain situations an instrument of the Devil. In Ft. Wayne, this custom seems to be followed about half the time. From the description of the 1963 wedding:

SA: We have another custom then in going to the church. It's a paganism and I don't know why, but we follow it very strictly because my mother is superstitious. That in going to the church, it could only be done by making a series of right turns. And, of course, this makes a roundabout way of getting there because my wife dressed a half a block from the church. Since she didn't have a family here, she dressed at my sister's home.. . .My sister lives half a block from the church but it took them seven blocks to get to the church because of a series right turns.

However, from the *Nunko's* description of the May 1970 wedding:

Interviewer: How about the question of turning right? Is that still done?

ES: I don't think so, no. No, because what we're going to do at this wedding, as soon as they get finished inviting the *Nunko* officially to the wedding, I'm going to jump in the car and go over to the bride's house. And in the meantime, they'll get there, the men. Then we come out of the bride's house, get in the car and go straight to the church. [In fact, this trip involved two left turns.]

There is one further custom which was followed in the Old Country but which has been dropped in immigrant weddings.

ES: While the bride and the party go to the church, they stop occasionally, usually three times, and the bride makes a cross. Very slowly. And *natanie*, bows. So, this omitted here [in the United States].

In over twenty interviews, this is the only description of such a custom.

6. The Service

It would not be worthwhile in this paper to describe every aspect of the church wedding service. The Ft. Wayne Macedono-Bulgarian Orthodox Church follows the general Orthodox liturgy. The couple to be married choose only in which language they wish the service, Church Slavonic or English. In the case of the 1963 wedding, the service was conducted entirely in Slavonic. For the 1969 wedding, the couple chose English. However, due to a misunderstanding, the priest gave part of the service in Slavonic.

Because the Macedonian community is composed of several nationalities who happen to speak a common language, there is always a certain amount of friction between the various groups. In this case, the priest, a Bulgarian, was upset at the fact that a Greek-style altar-table cloth was used without his knowledge or consent. Failure to ask his approval before the service, therefore, resulted in his giving the service largely in Church Slavonic. Since something was done against his wishes, he felt that he should do something against the wishes of the couple to be married. Although a very minor occurrence, it demonstrates the tensions within the community very well.

Despite the fact that the Orthodox service is normally the same, there are, however, several folk customs which also appear. These customs, depending on the attitudes of the individual parish priest, are neither sanctioned officially by the church, nor are they officially condemned. They are accepted, simply, as "Old Country traditions."

a). *The Platno*. During the service, a piece of cloth, usually bought by the *Nunko*, is draped over the shoulders of the young couple. From the description of the 1969 wedding:

LS: That's not required. That's not even part of the ceremony, but it's just something that's always done. It's approximately two and a half yards of material and the priest just adds that to the ceremony. And they put the material around the groom and the bride to bind them together, you know. For a few minutes. And then they take the material off, and then she's supposed to take that material and make her first dress out of it.

ES: The material is still on while the dance, the traditional dance in the church, is being performed. Three times around the table. They don't dance it here, they just walk around. The tradition is that this is happiness as the Church provides.

A similar statement from 1963:

SA: For our service we insisted really that the *Nunko* buy the *platno* which was the same material that my wife's dress was made out of, and that we be shrouded with that. We had that on us before we were crowned and we kept it on all the time we did the three circles around the altar table.

In LS's statement, it was noted that the bride's first dress was to be made from the *platno*. SA stated, however, that the bride's wedding dress was already made from the same material as the *platno*.

The tradition, although still used, has begun to lose some of its original meaning.

In further interviews with several other informants, it was said that many couples buy the *platno*, but instead of being draped with it, they use it as a covering for the altar table.

b). *Candy on the Altar Table*. This tradition, quite common in Macedonia, is used more and more rarely in the United States. The candy did not appear in the May 1970 wedding. SA relates, however, that in 1963:

SA: We still bring the candy, and set the candy on the altar table with the wine. And, of course, it's supposed to be symbolic of the bitter and the sweet which our priest doesn't serve—doesn't give to us, but we use it..

c). *The Receiving Line*. After the service is completed, the wedding party lines up outside the church door and greets the guests. At this time, many guests give the bride and groom money. In various interviews, sums as large as $200 have been mentioned.

SA: We form up the line and the relatives are all expected to pass us a bill when they go through. Everybody follows that custom. They pass it on to you very shyly, you know, and you have to look at it and remember what it is because you have to thank them. And they still do that. That's one custom that even people who want to do away with all customs don't want to do away with that one.

In his final sentence, SA demonstrates clearly his desire that Old Country customs be maintained. He is obviously conscious of the fact that there are those within the Macedonian community who would simply neglect all these customs. However, on the subject of receiving money, SA ironically implies that even those who wish to become completely divorced from their Macedonian heritage still maintain a custom if it brings in money.

After all the guests have greeted the bride and groom, rice is usually thrown. In the Old Country, *zhito* (wheat), was generally thrown. To this mixture were added pennies and sweet candy. The symbolism of the three items is clear: wheat for fertility; pennies to insure spiritual and material abundance; and candy to guarantee that the couple's future life be sweet. In the United States, several informants have said that at their weddings, a mixture of pennies, candy, and rice was thrown over them.

At the 1969 wedding, however, all the principals in the wedding party neglected to buy rice or to have a mixture ready. Thus the bride and groom waited patiently until one of the ushers could find a store and bring back a package of rice. At this point, all the women in the wedding party made

sure that some of the rice got down the front of the bride's gown. Again the fertility symbolism needs no explanation.

7. *The Wedding Dinner*

A large sit-down dinner for the relatives and friends of the bride and groom is held after the service, usually in a restaurant hall. Seats were provided at the 1969 wedding dinner for approximately 350 people in a Kentucky Fried Chicken restaurant. The principals sat at a head table. Several times during the meal, the other diners began banging rhythmically on their plates with their forks. After a few moments of this the bride and groom stood, kissed each other, and sat down. The meal took about an hour and a half, and this kissing ritual was repeated six times. This is thought to be a purely American-developed custom. Many Macedonian immigrants stated that this same thing happened at their weddings, but only in America. Thus, although originally an American custom, this performance has evidently become a part of the Macedonian immigrant wedding.

Although a minor tradition, this practice is a very interesting development. The Macedonians have adopted a custom which never occurred in Macedonia, and have claimed it as their own: that is, they have adopted a non-Macedonian custom to reinforce their ethnic identity. Everyone knows, for example, that the white bridal gown is a modern innovation, and not part of the old peasant tradition. The banging of the forks, however, and the response of the bride and groom, is thought to be a new *Macedonian* custom. This new custom, therefore, represents a subconscious effort to incorporate a new immigrant Macedonian tradition.

8. *The Reception*

The last major event of the wedding day is the reception. A large hall is rented, often the Macedonian Hall in Ft. Wayne which is situated near the church. The reception generally starts in the early evening, several hours following the afternoon wedding dinner. Two main features characterize the reception. First, the *Nunko* performs the dance with the *koluk*, the special wedding bread. Holding the bread over his head, the *Nunko* leads one traditional *hero*, or circle dance. Then the *Nunko* stands in one position, still holding the bread high in the air, and the bride and groom dance under it. Shortly after this, principal male relatives and the ushers also dance with the bread.

The second feature of the reception is the leadership of the dances. All the main relatives of both the bride and the groom must lead at least one *hobo*. The bride and the groom lead the first two, followed by the *Nunko, Nunko,* parents, and assorted relatives. There seems to be a subtle pecking order in this ritual. Everyone knows instinctively whose turn it is to lead the dance, and no one dares take over the lead out of turn. If a relative were omitted, he would have a perfect right to be highly offended.

In the 1963 wedding, the dance with the bread came first and the relatives leading the succeeding *Hera* came second:

SA: And then at night, of course, we still go through the traditional rituals. The band starts playing. Nobody from the general public starts leading the dance or even participating in the dance until the families have their complete swing of it.. . .Nothing starts at the reception until the dance is done with the bread. That starts the whole chain of command, sort of starts working. The parents of the bride and groom; brothers and sisters of the bride and groom, aunts and uncles of the bride and groom lead the dance. Bridesmaids and ushers and all, they all have to get a chance at it. Some of it's only half-circle. Then the public gets in on it and it goes from there.

In 1969 wedding, however, the bride and groom were detained with the photographer for some time after the dinner. Therefore the band and many of the guests were ready to start the reception before the principals arrived. Dancing proceeded from six o'clock until seven without the bride and groom. Upon their arrival, the relatives began to lead the dances and it was not until all the relatives had led their particular *hero* and that the *Nunko* performed the dance with the bread. Before the 1969 wedding, the *Nunko* stated:

ES: To my opinion, they serve the same purpose. The *koluk* serves the same purpose as the cake that we have here. Because the *koluk*, the whole ceremony of the wedding is surrounded around the *koluk*. They have an emphasis around the *koluk*. Now after the reception is started, around the middle of the reception, they will take the *koluk* and they'll dance with it. The *Nunko* starts it. He holds it over his head like this. [ES stands with arms over head.] Now, at the same time he goes and he passes it over the heads of those who are participating on the dance itself. And the *kolubchii* take over, which would be the ushers [Bulgarian tr. '*po-bratimi*']. Then they dance with it. Then after that's done, the *koluk* is cut up, divided, and given to the people, like the cake.. . . The bread, being grain, could represent fertility, I don't know. It's just an old custom.

9. *Following the Reception*

SA: And we have had a tradition in our family, the old tradition probably carries over from the Old Country, and each one of us has followed, that even though the bride and groom go out of the house for the wedding night, the honeymoon night, invariably every one of us—my brother, my sister, me and my wife—have returned to the house and had coffee and pastry with the women who are still extending the wedding custom and tradition. Although instead of dancing to live music, they're singing and helping the mother clean her house and scrape the pots and pans they did all the cooking with.

VII. Peripheral Customs

1. *Music in the Church*

Ordinarily, instrumental music is never allowed in Orthodox churches. St. Nicholas Macedono-Bulgarian Orthodox Church in Ft. Wayne, however, has, as one informant put it, "bowed to custom" (meaning American custom) and has installed an organ. For the 1963 wedding, the couple insisted on organ arrangements of Orthodox choral music. In the 1969 wedding, however, the organist (also the accordionist in the Macedonian band) played selections such as *Bless This House* before the service began and the *Mendelssohn Wedding March* as the bride moved toward the altar table. As far as could be determined, couples rarely use standard pieces and no real musical tradition has been established.

2. *The Sanduk*

The *sanduk* is the Macedonian equivalent of the American Hope Chest. Traditionally in Macedonia, every young girl below marriageable age prepared certain household items to take with her to her new home. RN describes the process in the Old Country:

RN: They had two, three *sandutsi* [plural form, tr. 'chests'] sometimes. First she had to bring a big, two, three sheets for the bed, you know. Then she had to bring a bedspread, handmade by her or her mother. Then she had to bring pillows, you know, pillow cases, things like that. She also brings a rug for the bedroom, handmade, big. Some of those rugs last a lifetime. Because they got material, you know, last a lifetime. But all of these things, if they go to a village, they bring three, four extra horses, you know. For the load. If it is [within one town], only like three, four blocks, they usually have a wagon drawn by horses. The wagon follows the wedding processions. They go, they load the wagon first, hah! With all the dowry that she has. And then the bride comes out and the bride is taken. Without the dowry, in the wagon, the bride. . .no go, hah! They were very practical Macedonians, you know. They wanted to see the reality first.

The tradition of the *sanduk* remains only to a small extent in Ft. Wayne. Only occasional immigrant brides prepare one. One informant related that a bride's mother tried to make the *Nunko* pay several hundred dollars for her daughter's *sanduk* when the *Nunko* came to take the bride to the church. The *Nunko* was so outraged that he threatened to call off the wedding, and traditionally, it was within his power to do so. The *sanduk* went along quietly.

SA remarks concerning his 1963 wedding:

SA: We didn't have the *sanduk* because like I say my wife's folks were from [another city] and it wasn't convenient.

Interviewer: Is it usually done still?

SA: It's still done with the people of our traditions. I mean now we're still the first generation.. . .I think we're the last of that breed.. . .Now the kids getting married are second generation, born in this country, and I don't think they're still following that custom because their parents didn't.

3. *The Dowry*

In Macedonia, in addition to the *sanduk*, it was also customary for the father of the bride to give a sum of money to the groom's family. However, this custom apparently died out in Macedonia some years ago because greedy fathers-in-law were asking for impossible sums of money. This custom is not and has not been practiced among immigrants, except perhaps, in a very token way. Neither the 1963 nor the 1969 wedding contained this custom. Other informants told of having paid a silver dollar to the father of the groom as a token dowry.

4. *Traditional Wedding Greetings*

During the week before the wedding, when two people meet who are in some way connected with the wedding party they exchange formulalized greetings. Some of these traditions are still used in Ft. Wayne.

A person bringing a present to the bride, for example would say:

ES: '*Da se kerdose!*' It's a little more than 'I wish you happiness.' More like 'Happy bondage,' or 'may everything go well.' You say this to the bride and the groom and to the relatives, the immediate family.

LS: Like if you go to a wedding and two people meet each other, two women, let's say they meet each other—they're at the wedding now—and the one would say to the other, which ever it is the first, would say, '*Da se kerdose!*' meaning 'Happiness for the one who got married.' And then the one that received that would turn around and say, '*I na tvoite!*,'

meaning 'You may have the same happiness for your children.' [Literally translated: 'And on yours.'] Or if you don't have children, or it happens that one is married and one is single [meaning one of the two women greeting each other], you turn around and say '*Na tvoiya glava!*' [Literally, 'on your head!']. That means 'may we dance at your wedding?'

ES: Now suppose that you are married and you have no children. We say '*Surdse!*' [Tr. 'heart.'] That means may you have the blessing of having a child. This goes then if you go to a grandmother. She has no kids. Her kids are grown up, and you say '*I na vnutsi!*', means 'your grandchildren,' you see. It depends on the person you're actually talking to.. . .Now if you are single and I come to you and I say, '*Da se kerdose, I na glave!*', that is, 'Happy bondage to the ones who are getting married, and may it return on your head.' And you say, *I na tvoi detsa!*' [Tr. 'children']. You see what I mean because I have *detsa*.

5. *Proof of the Bride's Virginity*

In the Old Country, great emphasis was put on the fact that every bride was expected to be pure. The morning after the wedding night, usually on a Tuesday, even though the service was completed on Sunday, the groom was required to show tangible evidence of his wife's purity.

RN: Now the next morning, early in the morning, the relatives of the groom would come and they wait. They wait to see by the white shirt that she's been wearing on the evening she went to bed and had her first contact with her husband if there was any blood on her shirt. The *svekurva* [mother-in-law] and the *posestrima*, and if the groom has a sister, those are the women who check, and the *kumitsa* [Tr. Macedonian '*Nunko*']. She has to be there. And they have to discover at least a drop of blood. They have to find out that she has really been a virgin. And if she is a virgin, they take the *riza* [Tr. 'nightgown' or 'shirt'], she puts on another one, they wrap it up beautifully. And the *pobratimi*, the *Nunko* and the *svekur* [father-in-law], they go to the bride's house. They lay this *riza* in front of the father and the mother of the bride and tell them that everything is OK.. . .And then they have the last meal of the wedding and they drink *blaga rakiya*. [Tr. 'plum brandy sweetened with burnt sugar.' This drink is symbolic of the fact that the bride was indeed pure.]

This custom, according to many informants, has been discontinued even in Macedonia, but nevertheless all are aware that the custom existed. *Blaga rakiya* is now used in some weddings in Bulgaria when a person is invited to the wedding. The sweet drink in this case is the same symbolic meaning as the use of candy on the altar table or candy thrown over the young couple as the emerge from the church.

Proof of the bride's virginity is not practiced in the Macedonian community in Ft. Wayne. However, part of the custom may have been retained without the participants being aware of it. From the description of the 1963 wedding:

SA: And then we still have Tuesday. I wasn't here my wedding [sic], but when my sister and my brother got married, we still had a group of relatives come over Tuesday night for the last slug [drink], and then it was ended.

In the 1969 wedding, this practice was not observed. Perhaps the hypothesis that this is a carry-over from the old custom is somewhat rarefied, but in each case, both the Old Country custom and the Ft. Wayne custom, the event took place on Tuesday. Something was offered to drink, only the close relatives were invited, and this was the last event in the entire marriage ritual.

VIII. Concluding Remarks

The preceding transcriptions or taped interviews and personal observations give a clear, if somewhat brief, idea of the present-day immigrant Macedonian wedding Ft. Wayne. It is not necessary to point out that the Macedonian-American ritual differs sharply in some ways from its traditional peasant counterpart in the Old Country. Certain customs are obviously lost due to impracticality and a desire for, or the pressure of conformity. However, it is necessary to say that although the ritual has changed, the significance has not. The wedding is still the focal point of the Macedonian folk ritual complex. No other ritual underlines the community's Slavic heritage in the same manner. Church practices and folkways are blended into a single unit, and this unit, albeit practiced irregularly, affirms the value and power of the Macedonian heritage.

Every informant was remarkably proud of his background. The Macedonian community in Ft. Wayne contains exceptionally few people who attempt to deny that they are immigrants. Indeed, they always make it a point to state that they are Macedonians, whether first, second, or even third generation. Their own views of the weddings are that if it is a practice which supplies cohesion to the very fabric of the Macedonian community, something which neither Church, nor folk customs could accomplish alone.

Indiana University
Bloomington, Indiana

Informants

ES, 42, was born in Greek Macedonia and came to the United States in 1948. A tavern owner by occupation, he lives in Ft. Wayne and was *Nunko* in the 1969 wedding. ES was interviewed by the author on May 1, 1969.

RN, 58, was born in Yugoslav Macedonia and came to the United States in 1923. A businessman, he resides in Ft. Wayne. He was interviewed by the author February 20, 1970.

SA, 35, was born in the United States of Greek Macedonian parents. A restauranteur, he was the groom in the 1963 wedding and presently lives in Ft. Wayne. SA was interviewed by the author on November 15, 1969.

LS, 36, was born in Southern Bulgaria and came to the United States in 1951. A housewife and mother of two, she is married to ES. LS was *Nunko* in the 1969 wedding. She now resides in Ft. Wayne and was interviewed by the author on May 1, 1969.

Source:

Philip V. R. Tilney. In *Indiana Folklore*, vol. III, no. 1, 1970. pp. 3-34.

MEXICAN AMERICANS

When Luis Valdéz's play Zoot Suit opened in Los Angeles, California, in 1978, a local newspaper trumpeted the event by proclaiming, "On July 30, 1978, the Second Zoot Suit Riot begins." Less than one year later, Zoot Suit opened on Broadway, thus becoming the first play written by a Chicano to appear on New York City's Great White Way. The New York run was only four weeks, but the play proved to be a long-running hit in Los Angeles. In 1981, Valdéz directed a movie version, which featured Edward James Olmos.

Valdéz's play, which is excerpted here, focuses on the events leading up to and following the Sleepy Lagoon murder trial of 1942. That year, white newspapers in Los Angeles began reporting that Mexican American teenagers increasingly posed a threat to public safety. Although the reports were unfounded, a sort of siege mentality took hold of the Anglo population.

In retrospect, the wave of generalized fear was probably due to the increased visibility of Chicano youths as a result of a conspicuous new fashion. Many of these youths had taken to wearing zoot suits—baggy pants with long, padded-shoulder jackets—and carrying gold watch chains. The Chicanos had adopted the suits, sometimes also called drape shapes, from east coast African Americans and movie stars. (The brightly colored outfit worn by the actor Denzel Washington early on in Spike Lee's movie Malcolm X is an example of a zoot suit.) The Chicanos made the style their own, and it soon became a statement of ethnic pride.

On August 2, 1942, a young man was found dead near Sleepy Lagoon, a reservoir where local teens hung out. The death could well have been accidental, but the Los Angeles police and the press grasped onto the idea that they had discovered evidence of the crime wave they had been positing. With little or no evidence, the police arrested about two dozen young Chicanos, all of them wearers of zoot suits and supposedly members of what the police called the 38th Street Gang. The youths were charged with murder. (An additional 300 or so Chicanos were detained as a result of the case.)

A series of clashes followed between authorities and Chicanos ("zoot-suiters"). In June 1943, a group of U.S. Navy sailors on shore leave claimed they had been attacked by zooters. When the police failed to respond swiftly and forcefully to the alleged attack, hundreds of sailors and other servicemen cruised the streets of Los Angeles in taxis, looking for Chicanos. They beat up anyone wearing a zoot suit, as well as many African Americans and Asian Americans.

The attacks on these minority groups have been attributed in part to the personal anxiety the servicemen may have felt about their immediate future. These events occurred at the height of U.S. involvement in World War II (1941-1945); most of the sailors were about to be sent into a war zone, and they were probably drunk as they caroused the streets of Los Angeles. Their singling out of Asian Americans, for instance, was probably a generalized reaction against the Japanese, even though all of the Japanese Americans on the west coast had already been *placed in internment camps for the duration of the war, and the Asian Americans targeted by the servicemen were likely Chinese, whose original homeland was an ally of the United States.*

As for African Americans, the racial bias then permeating the United States often produced such racially motivated rioting. The servicemen may have thought they were at greater risk than the Chicanos and African American civilians they saw on the streets of Los Angeles. The reality, however, was something else. Because the U.S. armed forces was still segregated, African Americans in the U.S. Army were often put in the most dangerous and least glamorous positions (driving trucks at the front lines, for example); similarly, the Army and Navy often relied on black civilians as well as military personnel to handle ammunition, as was demonstrated when a dock full of ammunition blew up in San Francisco, California, during the war, killing mostly black workers.

Perhaps the greatest irony in this incident was not revealed until after the war, when it was shown that Mexican Americans had earned more Medals of Honor in the war than any other minority group in the United States.

Valdéz based his play on the events of the rioting. He created a memorable narrator, El Pachuco, who functions as a one-man Greek chorus. The excerpt included here is the play's dazzling prologue. Valdéz's character emerges on stage by using a switchblade—a weapon long stereotypically associated with pachucos—to slice through a Los Angeles Herald headline mistakenly claiming that soldiers and sailors were "called in" to put down zooters. El Pachuco then addresses the audience, at first in pachuco slang, then in English. His speech is a fiery, provocative statement about pachuco identity.

PROLOGUE FROM *ZOOT SUIT*
by Luis Valdéz

Setting

The giant facsimile of a newspaper front page serves as a drop curtain.

The huge masthead reads: *Los Angeles Herald Express* Thursday, June 3, 1943.

A headline cries out: Zoot-Suiter Hordes Invade Los Angeles. US Navy and Marines are called in.

Behind this are black drapes creating a place of haunting shadows larger than life. The somber shapes and outlines of pachuco images hang subtly, black on black, against a back-ground of heavy fabric evoking memories and feelings like an old suit hanging forgotten in the depths of a closet somewhere, sometime. . .Below this is a sweeping, curving place of levels and rounded corners with the hard, ingrained brilliance of countless spit shines, like the memory of a dance hall.

Act One

Prologue

A switchblade plunges through the newspaper. It slowly cuts a rip to the bottom of the drop. To the sounds of "Perdido" by Duke Ellington, El Pachuco emerges from the slit. He adjusts his clothing, meticulously fussing with his collar, suspenders, cuffs. He tends to his hair, combing back every strand into a long luxurious ducktail, with infinite loving pains. Then He reaches into the slit and pulls out his coat and hat. He dons them. His fantastic costume is complete. It is a zoot suit. He is transformed into the very image of the pachuco myth, from his pork-pie hat to the tip of his four-foot watch chain. Now He turns to the audience. His three-soled shoes with metal taps click-clack as He proudly, slovenly, defiantly makes his way downstage. He stops and assumes a pachuco stance.

Luis Valdéz

Pachuco:

¿Que le watcha a mis trapos, ese?
¿Sabe que, carnal?
Estas garras me las plante porque
Vamos a dejarnos caer un play, ¿sabe?

(He crosses to center stage, models his clothes.)

Watcha mi tacuche, ese. Alivianese con mis calcos,
tando,
lisa, tramos, y carlango, ese.
  (Pause.)

Nel, sabe que, usted esta muy verdolaga. Como se me
  hace
que es puro square.

  (El Pachuco breaks character and addresses the
audience in perfect English.)

Ladies and gentlemen
the play you are about to see
is a construct of fact and fantasy.
The Pachuco Style was an act in Life
and his language a new creation.
His will to be was an awesome force
eluding all documentation. . .
A mythical, quizzical, frightening being
precursor of revolution
Or a piteous, hideous heroic joke
deserving of absolution?
I speak as an actor on the stage.
The Pachuco was existential
for he was an Actor in the streets
both profane and reverential.
It was the secret fantasy of every bato
in or out of the Chicanada
to put on a Zoot Suit and play the Myth
mas chucote que la chingada.
  (Puts hat back on and turns.)

Pos orale!
  (Music. The newspaper drop flies. El Pachuco
begins his chuco stroll upstage, swinging his watch
chain.)

Source:
Luis Valdéz, *Zoot Suit and Other Plays*. Houston,
  Texas: Arte Público Press, 1992.

The memoirs of Juan N. Seguín constitute one of the most revealing documentations of the anti-Mexican racist backlash in Texas during the 1840s. Seguín, promoted to colonel in the Texas army by General Sam Houston (1793-1863) himself, was a veteran of the 1835 siege of Bexar, Texas, raised forces for the defense of the Alamo (which he survived only because he was acting as a courier at the time), and led a Mexican-Texan (Tejano) troop at the Battle of the San Jacinto (1836). After the war ended and Texas won its independence from Mexico, he was elected as the San Antonio representative to the first and second congresses of the Republic of Texas. In 1842, he was elected mayor of San Antonio.

But his fortunes fell when he was falsely accused of having pro-Mexican political leanings. As ridiculous as such an accusation was against so ardent a Texas patriot, Seguín and his family were severely harassed. Finally, Seguín, his family, and some 1,000 other Tejanos were forced to flee for their lives in the late 1840s, leaving behind most of their property.

It will be noted that other prominent Tejanos, such as Lorenzo de Zavala, Judge J. M. Rodriguez, and Antonio Menchaca, were not forced to flee, nor did they apparently suffer from much racial harassment. There could be several reasons for this radically different treatment. One is that all three of these men claimed to be of pure Spanish bloodlines; another may be that their children married Anglos; a third is that they were wealthy men with considerable political power.

The Seguíns owned a good-sized ranch, but were not considered wealthy, and Juan Seguín's political position, as the mayor of an increasingly rowdy frontier town, was guaranteed to make more enemies than friends. As for the hundreds of other Tejanos who fled Texas during the 1840s, most were simply poor farmers and ranchers whose land could be had by anyone who could drive them off it. Tejanos whose skills were regarded as necessary—saddle and boot makers, blacksmiths, and other craftspeople, for example—seem not to have suffered as severely as local landowners.

PERSONAL MEMOIRS OF JUAN N. SEGUÍN, FROM THE YEAR 1844 TO THE RETREAT OF GENERAL WOLL FROM THE CITY OF SAN ANTONIO

Preface

A native of the City of San Antonio de Bexar, I embraced the cause of Texas at the report of the first cannon which foretold her liberty; filled an honorable situation in the ranks of the conquerors of San Jacinto, and was a member of the legislative body of the Republic. I now find myself, in the very land, which in other times bestowed on me such bright and repeated evidences of trust and esteem, exposed to the attacks of scribblers and personal enemies, who, to serve political purposes, and engender strife, falsify historical facts, which they are but imperfectly acquainted. I owe it to myself, my children and friends, to answer them with a short, but true exposition of my acts, from the beginning of my public career, to the time of the return of General Woll from the Rio Grande, with the Mexican forces, amongst which I was then serving.

Juan Nepomuceno Seguín

I address myself to the American people; to that people impetuous, as the whirlwind, when aroused by the hypocritical clamors of designing men, but just, impartial and composed, whenever men and facts are submitted to their judgment.

I have been the object of the hatred and passionate attacks of some few disorganisers, who, for a time, ruled, as masters, over the poor and oppressed population of San Antonio. Harpy-like, ready to pounce on every thing that attracted the notice of their rapacious avarice, I was an obstacle to the execution of their vile designs. They, therefore, leagued together to exasperate and ruin me; spread against me malignant calumnies, and made use of odious machinations to sully my honor, and tarnish my well earned reputation.

A victim to the wickedness of a few men, whose imposture was favored by their origin, and recent domination over the country; a foreigner in my native land; could I be expected stoically to endure their outrages and insults? Crushed by sorrow, convinced that my death alone would satisfy my enemies, I sought for a shelter amongst those against whom I had fought; I separated from my country, parents, family, relatives and friends, and what was more, from the institutions, on behalf of which I had drawn my sword, with an earnest wish to see Texas free and happy.

In that involuntary exile, my only ambition was to devote my time, far from the tumult of war, to the support of my family, who shared in my sad condition.

Fate, however, had not exhausted its cup of bitterness. Thrown into a prison, in a foreign country, I had no alternative left, but, to linger in a loathsome confinement, or to accept military service. On one hand, my wife and children, reduced to beggary, and separated from me; on the other hand, to turn my arms against my own country. The alternative was sad, the struggle of feelings violent; at last the father triumphed over the citizen; I seized a sword that galled my hand. (Who amongst my readers will not understand my situation?) I served Mexico; I served her loyally and faithfully; I was compelled to fight my own countrymen, but I was never guilty of the barbarous and unworthy deeds of which I am accused by my enemies.

Ere the tomb closes over me and my cotemporaries [sic], I wish to lay open to publicity this stormy period of my life; I do it for friends as well as for my enemies, I challenge the latter to contest, with facts, the statements I am about to make, and I leave the decision unhesitatingly to the witnesses of the events.

Memoirs, &c.

In October 1834, I was Political Chief of the Department of Behar. Dissatisfied with the reactionary designs of General Santa Anna, who was at that time President of the Republic of Mexico, and endeavored to overthrow the Federal system, I issued a circular, in which I urged every Municipality in Texas to appoint delegates to a convention that was to meet at San Antonio, for the purpose of taking into consideration the impending dangers, and for devising the means to avert them.

All the Municipalities appointed their delegates, but the convention never met, the General Government having ordered Col. Jose Maria Mendoza to march with his forces from Matamoras to San Antonio, and prevent the meeting of the delegates. The proofs of the above facts exist in the archives of the Country of Bejar.

In April 1835, the Governor of Coahuila and Texas called for assistance from the various Departments, to resist the aggressions of Santa Anna against that State. I volunteered my services, and received from the Political Chief, Don Angel Navarro, the command of a party of National Guards, sent from San Antonio to Monclova. In our encounters with the troops of Santa Anna, I was efficiently assisted by Col. B. R. Milam and Maj. John R. Allen. On our withdrawal from Monclova, disgusted with the weakness of the Executive, who had given up the struggle, we pledged ourselves to use all our influence to rouse Texas against the tyrannical government of Santa Anna.

We returned to San Antonio in the beginning of June. The Military Commander, Col. Domingo Ugartchea, considering me opposed to the existing government, ordered two officers to watch secretly my motions. This, however, did not prevent me from working diligently to prepare for the intended movement.

We had agreed that the movement should begin in the center of Texas, but, not hearing from that quarter, I determined to send an agent to Brazoria, Juan A. Zambrano, with directions to sound the disposition of the people. On the return of the agent, we were apprized that there was a great deal of talk about a revolution, in public meetings, but that the moment for an armed movement was still remote. Our agent was sent to Victoria, and he there called a meeting of the citizens, but the Military Commander of Goliad sent down a detachment of troops to prevent the assembly and arrest the promoters.

We were despairing of a successful issue, when the Military Commander of Texas, informed of the revolutionary feelings which were spreading over the colonies, determined upon removing from the town of Gonzales a piece of artillery, lent to that Corporation by the Political Chief Saucedo. This was at the time a delicate undertaking. A lieutenant was detailed to carry it into execution, with orders to use force if necessary. On the same day that the military detachment started for Gonzales, I went to the lower ranchos on the San Antonio River; at Salvador Flores I held a meeting of the neighbors, and induced several to take up arms, well satisfied that the beginning of the revolution was close at hand. The officer sent to Gonzales met some resistance at the "Perra," and thought it prudent to beat a hasty retreat. Col. Ugartchea was making preparations to proceed in person towards Gonzales, with a respectable force, when he received orders from Gen. Cos to await his arrival.

A few days after the entry of Gen. Cos into San Antonio, Major Collinsworth, surprising the garrison of Goliad, took possession of that place. So soon as I was informed of that circumstance, I marched with my company to reinforce the Major, but, at the "Conquista" crossing on the San Antonio River, I was overtaken by an express from General Stephen F. Austin, who informed me that he was marching on San Antonio, and requested me to join him, in order to attack General Cos. I retraced my steps, after having requested Captain Manuel Flores to go and meet General Austin and inform him of my readiness to comply with his wishes, and that I would take with me all the men I could possibly enlist on my route.

On the 13th of October, I met Austin on the Salado, at the crossing of the Gonzales road, and joined my forces with his small army. Upon this occasion I had the honor to become acquainted with General Sam Houston, who accompanied Austin. On the same day we had a slight encounter with the forces under Cos, who retired into San Antonio. Austin, as Commander-in-Chief of the army, gave me the appointment of Captain.

I was commanded to accompany Col. Bowie to the Mission of San Jose, with my company, with orders to approach the city as nearly as possible, following the banks of the river. We arrived, on the evening of the 21st of November, at the Mission of Concepcion, and noticing that we had been observed by the scouts of Gen. Cos, passed the night in making preparations to resist an attack which we considered imminent. We were not deceived; on the morning of the 22d a force was seen moving along the road from San Antonio to the Mission. A few men, sent by Bowie to reconnoitre, made such a rash charge, that they were cut off from their line of retreat, and had to shut themselves up in the steeple of the church, where they remained during the action. The day was soon ours; the enemy retreating, with the loss of one piece of artillery.

I was detailed to forage for the army, and was successful in doing so, returning to the camp with a liberal supply of provisions. Our camp was shortly moved to within one mile of the Alamo, whence we proceeded to the "Molino Blanco," and established headquarters. On the 11th of December we entered the city, and after having taken possession of the houses of the Curate Garza, Veramendi, Garza, Flores, and others, we obliged the enemy to capitulate [sic] and withdraw towards Laredo.

After the capture of San Antonio, Captain Travis' company and mine were detailed to go in pursuit of the Mexican forces, and capture from them a cavallado which they had in the Parrita, Laredo road; we succeeded, taking nearly one hundred head of horses, which were sent to San Felipe de Austin, for the benefit of the public service. I was afterwards detailed to the ranchos on the San Antonio river, to see if I could find more horses belonging to the Mexican troops.

On the 2d of January, 1836, I received from the Provisional Government the commission of Captain of Regular Cavalry, with orders to report to Lieutenant-Colonel Travis in San Antonio.

On the 22d of February, at 2 o'clock P.M., General Santa Anna took possession of the city, with over 4000 men, and in the mean time we fell back on the Alamo.

On the 28th, the enemy commenced the bombardment, meanwhile we met in a Council of War, and taking into consideration our perilous situation, it was resolved by a majority of the council, that I should leave the fort, and proceed with a communication to Colonel Fannin, requesting him to come to our assistance. I left the Alamo on the night of the council; on the following day I met, at the Ranch of San Bartolo, on the Cibolo, Captain Desac, who, by orders of Fannin, had foraged on my ranch, carrying off a great number of beeves, corn, &c. Desac informed me that Fannin could not delay more than two days his arrival at the Cibolo, on his way to render assistance to the defenders of the Alamo. I therefore determined to wait for him. I sent Fannin, by express, the communication from Travis, informing him at the same time of the critical position of the defenders of the Alamo. Fannin answered me, through Lieutenant Finley, that he had advanced as far as "Rancho Nuevo," but, being informed of the movements of General Urrea, lie had countermarched to Goliad, to defend that place; adding, that lie could not respond to Travis' call, their respective commands being separate, and depending upon General Houston, then at Gonzales, with whom he advised me to communicate. I lost no time in repairing to Gonzales, and reported myself to the General, informing him of the purport of my mission. He commanded me to wait at Gonzales for further orders. General Houston ordered Captain Salvador Flores with 25 men of my company to the lower ranchos on the San Antonio river, to protect the inhabitants from the depredations of the Indians.

Afterwards, I was ordered to take possession, with the balance of my company, of the "Perra," distant about four miles on the road to San Antonio, with instructions to report every evening at head-quarters. Thus my company was forming the vanguard of the Texan army, on the road to San Antonio.

On the 6th of March, I received orders to go to San Antonio with my company and a party of American citizens, carrying, on the horses, provisions for the defenders of the Alamo.

Arrived at the Cibolo, and not hearing the signal gun which was to be discharged every fifteen minutes, as long as the place held out, we retraced our steps to convey to the General-in-Chief the sad tidings. A new party was sent out, which soon came back, having met with Anselmo Vergara and Andres Barcena, both soldiers of my company, whom I had left for purposes of observation in the vicinity of San Antonio; they brought the intelligence of the fall of the Alamo. Their report was so circumstantial as to preclude any doubts about that disastrous event.

The Texan army began its retreat towards the centre of the country. I was put in command of the rear-guard, with orders not to leave any families behind. I continued covering the rear-guard, until we had crossed the Arenoso creek, near the Brazos, where I was, by orders of the General, detached with Captain Mosley Baker, to the town of San Felipe de Austin, to cut off the enemy from the passage of the river. We remained in that position, and within sight of the Brigade of General Ramirez, who occupied San Felipe. I was subsequently ordered to occupy with my company Gross' house, farther up the river. Our main army was then encamped in the bottom of the Paloma or Molino Creek, on the Western bank of the Brazos River, where it remained until information was received that the enemy had crossed the river at Fort Bend, and was marching towards Harrisburg. Our army began at once to cross the river, on board the steamer Yellow Stone, and when the whole force had crossed, took up the march, with the intention of harassing the enemy's rear-guard.

The army was taking its noon rest, near Buffalo Bayou, when two soldiers of my company, who had gone out to water horses, reported that they had seen three Mexicans riding at full speed over the prairie. Without delay, I advised the General, who immediately sent Captains Karnes and ____ in pursuit. These officers returned shortly, bringing as prisoners a captain, a citizen, and an express bearer of despatches from Mexico to the enemy.

We were apprised by the prisoners that Santa Anna was at Harrisburg with 800 men; and a perusal of their papers made us acquainted with the fact that Cos was to bring him reinforcements. To prevent the concentration of forces, General Sam Houston gave the order to resume the march. The army, artillery, and train, crossed over Buffalo Bayou on rafts, during which operation, General Rusk, then Secretary of War, did not spare his personal labor. It was dark when the crossing was effected. In the course of the night we passed through Harrisburg, the ruins of which were still smoking, having been set on fire by the enemy. We continued our march all night. At daybreak a man was taken prisoner, who, or discovering us, had attempted to escape. He was a printer belonging to San Felipe, and informed us that the enemy were at a distance of about 8 miles, on the way back to Harrisburg. Our scouts came in soon with the information that the enemy were countermarching towards Buffalo Bayou.

Conscious of the starving condition of the troops, who had not eaten for twenty-four hours, General Houston resolved on camping, in a small motte, contiguous to the San Jacinto River.

We were beginning to cook our meal, when the enemy showed themselves close to us. We rushed to arms, and formed in line of battle. On their nearer approach we were ordered to lay down on the ground, thus concealing ourselves in the grass. A height, adjacent to our position, was soon occupied by the enemy, upon which, the General ordered the band to strike up "Will you come to the bower." The enemy answered with its artillery, and we joined the chorus with a brisk musketry. We were soon charged by a skirmishing party on foot, detached from the right wing of the enemy; they were quickly driven back by a party of our cavalry, supported by the artillery. The enemy kept up their fire until they had selected a camping ground, distant about 400 steps from ours, and protected by two mottes. Both armies ceased firing; we resumed the cooking of our meal, composed of meat only, but had the good fortune to capture a boat loaded with provisions, which afforded some seasoning to a repast that otherwise would have been rather scanty.

On the same evening General Lamar went out with a party of Cavalry, to draw the enemy into a fight; the result was a slight skirmish, ending in the wounding of two or three on each side.

On the morning of the 21st of April, General Houston, for the purpose of cutting off the communication of General Cos' forces with those of Santa Anna, ordered deaf Smith to burn the bridge over the river, but, on reaching it, he saw that the had come too late, the enemy's reinforcements had already crossed. However, the bridge was destroyed, and Smith returned to our camp at the very moment when Cos united with Santa Anna.

At noon, General Rusk came to partake of dinner in my tent. When he had done eating, he asked me if the Mexicans were not in the habit of taking a siesta at that hour. I answered in the affirmative, adding, moreover, that in such cases they kept under arms their main and advanced guards, and a line of sentinels. General Rusk observed that he thought so; however, the moment seemed to him favorable to attack the enemy, and he further said: "Do you feel like fighting?" I answered that I was always ready and willing to fight, upon which the General rose, saying: "Well, let us go!" I made at once my dispositions; the General proceeded along the line, speaking to the Captains, and our force was soon under arms. Generals Houston and Rusk delivered short addresses, and we formed into line of battle in front of the enemy. My company was in the

left wing, under Colonel Sherman. We marched onward on the prairie, and were met by a column of infantry, which we drove back briskly. Before falling in with that column, we had dispersed an ambuscade that had opened their fire against us within pistol shot. The whole enemy's line, panic struck, took to flight. We were already on the bank of the river, in pursuit of the fugitives, when my attention was called to a Mexican officer, who, emerging from the river where lie had kept himself concealed, gave himself up and requested me to spare his life. Being sheltered by weeds and grass, he seemed afraid to leave his retreat, owing to the fire which was kept up against the fugitives. I ordered those who were close to me to cease firing, which order was extended along the line to a considerable distance. Then, the officer who had addressed me came out, followed by Colonels Bringas, Almonte, Dias, and quite a number of other officers.

On my way to the camp with the prisoners, an officer, named Sanchez, conducted me to a place where $25,000 had been concealed. I reached the camp at dark, presented my prisoners to the General, who congratulated me, and I reported to him the discovery of the money. Colonel Forbes was at once detailed to go and bring it in.

On this great and glorious day my company was conspicuous for efficiency and gallantry; however, we did not lose one single man, to the surprise of those who had witnessed our honorable and perilous situation.

Two days after the capture of Santa Anna, and four days after the battle, Captain Karnes and myself were detailed with our companies to observe the retreat of the remains of the Mexican army. We overtook their rearguard at the "Contrabando" marsh, where some of their wagons had broken down. As soon as the escort saw us they took to flight, leaving the whole property in our possession.

Gen. Ampudia sent me a communication requesting me to attend to the sick and wounded whom he had left behind.

We crossed the Colorado at the heels of the enemy, and after proceeding a short distance, we met General Woll, who was bearer of a safe conduct. We camped every night on the ground abandoned each morning by the enemy, until we reached Victoria, which had been already evacuated by them. Shortly afterwards Colonel Sherman arrived, in command of the vanguard of our army, and subsequently General Rusk, then Commander-in-Chief, who established his headquarters in that town.

On the 30th of May, I received from the General-in-Chief my promotion to the rank of Lieutenant-Colonel of the Texan army, and was ordered to take possession of San Antonio. I left Victoria on the 1st of June, and, on the Cabeza creek, met General Andrade, who was retreating towards Matamoras.

Agreeably to my instructions, I sent to that General a communication, informing him that my orders were to take possession of San Antonio. His answer was that the place was occupied by Captain Castaneda, who was instructed to surrender it to the first Texan officer who should come to demand it.

I took possession of San Antonio on the 4th of June; on the 10th, Colonel Smith came to occupy it with the regiment of Mississippi Mounted Volunteers; on the 24th I received orders to fall back with my command to head-quarters at Victoria, information having been received that the Mexican army was marching from Matamoras to Texas.

When we were convinced of the falseness of that report, I applied to the General for leave to go to Nacogdoches on a visit to my family, then in that town on their return from the Sabine, where they had sought a refuge from the Mexican army. My application was favorably received, and leave of absence for twenty-two days granted to me.

I found all the members of my family sick with fever, and the disease did not spare me, but compelled me to exceed the term of my leave. General Houston, who was then at Nacogdoches, getting cured of the wounds he received at San Jacinto, gave me a certificate stating the causes of my delay in returning to my post. I left Nacogdoches on the 20th of August, and on my passage through Columbus I received, from tile Secretary of War, orders to report myself to the President for instructions.

I arrived at Velasco on the 10th of September; on the next day the President handed to me my commission of Lieutenant-Colonel, appointing me to the command of the City of San Antonio, with orders to proceed to my destination without delay.

I arrived at head-quarters, at Lavaca, on the 15th of the same month, and reported to General Rusk, who ordered me to begin recruiting my regiment in that town.

On the 11th of October I left headquarters, with my regiment dismounted, and with instructions to procure horses in San Antonio, where I arrived on the 17th.

1837. In March, being in command of San Antonio, I received orders from General Felix Houston to destroy that city and transfer its inhabitants to the east bank of the Brazos. At the same time, Lieutenant-Colonel Switzer of the Volunteers came, with instructions to assist me in carrying out

the order. Considering the measure premature and unjust, I took upon myself the responsibility of disobeying the order, until I had referred the matter to the President, with whom I made use of all my influence to have the order rescinded. The President prevailed upon General Houston to desist; I thus averted the impending destruction of San Antonio, but, in consequence, made Gen. F. Houston my bitter enemy.

As I had received neither funds nor stores for the subsistence of my command, I was compelled to make requisitions upon the citizens for corn and beeves. At this time, Don Jose Antonio Navarro delivered to me, for that object, goods to over the amount of $3000.

In April, I received orders to seize upon the horses of the citizens of San Antonio, to mount my command. I was instructed to act with "discernment" in the discharge of this duty, but, however prudent I might be, I could not avoid creating a good deal of dissatisfaction, and several complaints were transmitted to the Government.

1838. In March, on obtaining a leave of absence for three months, to go to New Orleans, I turned over the command of San Antonio to Colonel Karnes. On my return, I was apprized that my fellow-citizens had done me the honor to elect me as Senator to Congress. During my term, I was appointed as Chairman of the Committee on Military Affairs. At the expiration of my term as Senator, I was elected Mayor of the City of Sail Antonio.

Here I must digress from my narrative, to call attention to the situation of my family in those times that tried the stoutest hearts.

No sooner was General Cos informed that I had taken an active part in the revolution, than he removed my father from the office of Postmaster, which he had filled for several years. He forced him to leave San Antonio at once, and he had consequently to walk the thirty-three miles which separated him from his rancho, where my family was living. Such was the hurry with which he was compelled to depart, that he was obliged to leave his family, who remained exposed to our fire during the whole siege.

When we received intelligence from our spies on the Rio Grande, that Santa Anna was preparing to invade Texas, my father, with his, my own, and several other families, removed toward the centre of the country.

My family took with them above three thousand head of sheep. They had reached Gonzales when Santa Anna took possession of San Antonio, and as soon as some other families joined them, they proceeded towards the Colorado, via Columbus. On their arrival at San Felipe de Austin, the citizens of that place, terror struck at the sight of the hurried flight of such a number of families, endeavored to take the advance. The confusion and delay caused oil the road by that immense straggling column of fugitives were such, that when my family were beginning to cross the Colorado with their cattle, the enemy was at their heels. General Ramirez y Lesma did not fail to take hold of that rich booty, and the shepherds only escaped by swimming over the river. The loss to three of the families was very severe, nay, irretrievable. They did not stop on their flight, until they reached the town of San Augustine, cast of Nacogdoches. When the families received the welcome tidings of the victory of San Jacinto, they went to Nacogdoches. There, all the members of my family, without excepting a single person, were attacked by fever. Thus, prostrated on their couches, deprived of all resources, they had to struggle in the midst of their sufferings, to assist one another. Want of money compelled them to part, little by little, with their valuables and articles of clothing. A son, an uncle, and several more remote relatives of mine fell victims to the disease. Seeing that the fever did not abate, the families determined upon moving towards the interior.

The train presented a spectacle which beggars description. Old men and children were lying in the wagons, and for several days, Captain Menchaca, who was the only person able to stand up, had to drive the whole train, as well as attend to the sick.

The families reached San Antonio at last. There was not one of them who had not to lament the loss of a relative, and to crown their misfortunes, they found their houses in ruins, their fields laid waste, and their cattle destroyed or dispersed.

I, myself, found my ranch despoiled; what little was spared by the retreating enemy, had been wasted by our own army; ruin and misery met me on my return to my unpretending home.

But let me draw a veil over those past and sorrowful days, and resume my narrative.

The tokens of esteem, and evidences of trust and confidence, repeatedly bestowed upon me by the Supreme Magistrate, General Rusk, and other dignitaries of the Republic, could not fail to arouse against me much invidious and malignant feeling. The jealousy evinced against me by several officers of the companies recently arrived at San Antonio, from the United States, soon spread amongst the American straggling adventurers, who were already beginning to work their dark intrigues against the native families, whose only crime was, that they owned large tracts of land and desirable property.

John W. Smith, a bitter enemy of several of the richest families of San Antonio, by whom be had been covered with favors, joined the conspiracy which was organized to ruin me.

I will also point out the origin of another enmity which, on several occasions, endangered my life. In those evil days, San Antonio was swarming with adventurers from every quarter of the globe. Many a noble heart grasped the sword in the defense of tile liberty of Texas, cheerfully pouring out their blood for our cause, and to them everlasting public gratitude is due; but there were also many bad men, fugitives from their country, who found in this land an open field for their criminal designs.

San Antonio claimed then, as it claims now, to be the first city of Texas; it was also the receptacle of the scum of society. My political and social situation brought me into continual contact with that class of people. At every hour of the day and night, my countrymen ran to me for protection against the assaults or exactions of those adventurers. Some times, by persuasion, I prevailed on them to desist; some times, also, force had to be resorted to. How could I have done otherwise? Were not the victims my own count men, friends and associates'? Could leave them defenceless, exposed to the assaults of foreigners, who, on the pretext that they were Mexicans, treated them worse than brutes. Sound reason and the dictates of humanity would have precluded a different conduct on my part.

In 1840, General Canales, who was at the head of a movement in favor of the federation, in the States of Tamaulipas, Nueva Leon and Coahuila, after having been routed by the Mexican forces, sought refuge in San Antonio. There he endeavored to raise companies of volunteers, to renew the struggle, and requested me to join him in the enterprise. I promised him my co-operation, provided I could procure the consent of General Lamar, then President of the Republic. Canales proceeded to the Capital and Galveston, and succeeded in raising some companies, with which we went to Mexico to carry out his designs. In the meantime, I had an interview with the President, who not only authorized me to raise volunteers, but, ordered that I should be supplied with arms from the armories of Texas. General Lamar yielded to my request with evident satisfaction, as he thought and declared that any movement against the tyrannical government then existing in Mexico would be promotive of the independence of Texas.

I recruited my men and marched to Mexico, but on reaching the frontier, I heard that Canales was in treaty with Arista, thus putting an end to the revolutionary attempt. One of the articles of the treaty, stated that Mexico should pay for the services rendered by the volunteers. At the request of the officers and men of my brigade, I went to Monterey to receive the money due them. But on my arrival at Monterey, Arista refused to pay me, alleging that he had to take advice in the city of Mexico.

Fully aware that his only object was to seek for a pretext to reject our claims, and withhold payment, I determined to return to Texas.

Immediately after my return, I went to the capital to report to the President the result of the expedition.

In the same year, Don Rafael Uribe, of Guerrero, passed through San Antonio, on his way to the capital, as bearer of a secret communication from General Arista to the President of Texas. Senior Uribe requested me to accompany him. I attended at several interviews between that gentleman and the President, and found out that Arista's intention was to have an understanding with the Executive of Texas, to the effect of pursuing the Indians, who committed depredations on both frontiers.

In fitting out my expedition to assist the Federalists, I contracted some money obligations which it was necessary to comply with. Availing myself of offers made by Senor Uribe, I entered with him into a smuggling operation. For this object, Messrs. Ogden and Howard gave me a credit of $3000, on a mortgage on part of my property.

The President having appointed Messrs. Van Ness and Morris to treat upon the subject of Uribe's mission, in their company, and that of Messrs. Blo, Davis, Murphy, Ogden, and Chevallie, I proceeded on a trip to Mexico. When Arista was apprised of our arrival at Guerrero, he made a good deal of fuss to exculpate himself in the eyes of his government. He ordered his forces to march from Matamoras to San Fernando, and issued orders to the effect that all the Americans at Guerrero should proceed to Monterey, but that I should remain at Guerrero. Chevallie, who was sick of the fever, had to remain with me until the return of our associates.

Arista having ordered us to leave the country without delay, I was compelled to leave my goods on consignment to be disposed of. When I heard that they had been sold, I sent Chevallie with some men of San Antonio to the place appointed by my agent, to receive the proceeds of the sale, but the agent not having shown himself, Chevallie returned to San Antonio empty handed. Shortly afterwards, an American, who came from Mexico, informed me that a certain Calvillo, who was on the look out for smugglers, had seized upon my money.

1842. After the retreat of the Mexican army under Santa Anna, until Vasquez' invasion in 1842, the war between Texas and Mexico ceased to be carried on actively. Although open commercial intercourse did not exist, it was carried on by smuggling, at which the Mexican authorities used to wink, provided it was not carried on too openly, so as to oblige them to notice it, or so extensively as to arouse their avarice.

In the beginning of this year, I was elected Mayor of San Antonio. Two years previously a gunsmith, named Goodman, had taken possession of certain houses situated on the Military Plaza, which were the property of the city. He used to shoe the horses of the volunteers who passed through San Antonio, and thus accumulated a debt against the Republic, for the payment of which he applied to the President to give him possession of the buildings referred to, which had always been known as city property.

The board of Aldermen passed a resolution to the effect, that Goodman should be compelled to leave the premises; Goodman resisted, alleging that the houses had been given to him by the President, in payment for public services. The Board could not, of course, acknowledge in the President any power to dispose of the city property, and consequently directed me to carry the resolution into effect. My compliance with the instructions of the Board caused Goodman to become my most bitter and inveterate enemy in the city.

The term for the mortgage that Messrs. Ogden and Howard held on my property, had run out. In order to raise money and comply with my engagements, I determined to go to Mexico for a drove of sheep. But fearful that this new trip would prove as fatal as the one already alluded to, I wrote to General Vasquez, who was then in command of the Mexican frontier, requesting him to give me a pass. The tenor of Vasquez' answer caused me to apprehend that an expedition was preparing against Texas, for the following month of March.

I called a session of the Board of Aldermen, (of which the Hon. S. A. Maverick was a member,) and laid before them the communication of General Vasquez, stating, that according to my construction of the letter we might soon expect the approach of the Mexicans.

A few days afterwards, Don Jose Maria Garcia, of Laredo, came to San Antonio; his report was so circumstantial, as to preclude all possible doubts as to the near approach of Vasquez to San Antonio.

Notice was immediately sent to the Government of the impending danger. In the various meetings held to devise means of defence, I expressed my candid opinion as to the impossibility of defending San Antonio. I observed, that for myself, I was going to the town of Seguín, and advised every one to do the same.

On leaving the city, I passed through a street where some men were making breast-works; I stated to them that I was going to my ranch, and thence to Seguín, in case the Mexican forces should take possession of San Antonio.

From the Nueces River, Vasquez forwarded a proclamation by Arista, to the inhabitants of Texas. I received at my ranch, a bundle of those proclamations, which I transmitted at once to the Corporation of San Antonio.

As soon as Vasquez entered the city, those who had determined upon defending the place, withdrew to Seguín. Amongst them were Dunn and Chevallie, who had succeeded in escaping from the hands of the Mexicans, into which they had fallen while on a reconnoitering expedition on the Medina.

The latter told me that Vasquez and his officers stated that I was in favor of the Mexicans; and Chevallie further added, that, one day as he was talking with Vasquez, a man, named Sanchez, came within sight, whereupon the General observed: "You see that man! Well, Colonel Seguín sent him to me, when he was at Rio Grande, Seguín is with us." He then drew a letter from his pocket, stating that it was from me. Chevallie asked to be allowed to see it, as he knew my handwriting, but the General refused and cut short the interview.

On my return to San Antonio, several persons told me that the Mexican officers had declared that I was in their favor. This rumor, and some threats uttered against me by Goodman, left me but little doubt that my enemies would try to ruin me.

Some of the citizens of San Antonio had taken up arms in favor of the enemy. Judge Hemphill advised me to have them arrested and tried, but as I started out with the party who went in pursuit of the Mexicans I could not follow his advice.

Having observed that Vasquez gained ground on us, we fell back on the Nueces river. When we came back to San Antonio, reports were widely spreading about my pretended treason. Captain Manuel Flores, Lieutenant Ambrosio Rodriguez, Matias Curbier, and five or six other Mexicans, dismounted with me to find out the origin of the imposture. I went out with several friends, leaving Curbier in my house. I had reached the Main Plaza, when several persons came running to inform me, that some Americans were murdering Curbier. We ran back to the house, where we found poor Curbier covered with blood. On being asked who assaulted him, be answered, that the gunsmith Goodman, in company with several Americans, had struck him with a rifle. A few minutes afterwards, Goodman returned to my house, with about thirty volunteers, but, observing that we were prepared to meet him, they did not attempt to attack us. We went out of the house and then to Mr. Guilbeau's, who offered me his protection. He went out into the street, pistol in hand, and succeeded in dispersing the mob, which had formed in front of my house. Mr. John Twohig offered me a shelter for that night; on the next morning, I went under disguise to Mr. Van Ness' house; Twohig, who recognised me in the street, warned me to "open my eyes." I remained one day at Mr. Van Ness'; next day General Burleson arrived at San Antonio, commanding a respectable force of volunteers. I presented myself to him, asking for a Court of Inquiry; he answered, that there were no grounds for such proceedings. In tile evening I went to the camp, and, jointly with Colonel Patton, received a commission to forage for provisions in the lower ranchos. I complied with this trust.

I remained, hiding from rancho to rancho, for over fifteen days. Every party of volunteers en route to San Antonio, declared, "they want to kill Seguín. "I could no longer go from farm to farm, and determined to go to my own farm and raise fortification, &c.

Several of my relatives and friends joined me. Hardly a day elapsed without receiving notice that a party was preparing to attack me; we were constantly kept under arms. Several parties came in sight, but, probably seeing that we were prepared to receive them, refrained from attacking. On the 30th of April, a friend from San Antonio sent me word that Captain Scott, and his company, were coming down by the river, burning the ranchos on their way. The inhabitants of the lower ranchos called on us for aid against Scott. With those in my house, and others to the number of about 100, I started to lend them aid. I proceeded, observing the movements of Scott, from the junction of the Medina to Pajaritos. At that place we dispersed and I returned to my wretched life. In those days I could not go to San Antonio without peril of my life.

Matters being in this state, I saw that it was necessary to take some step which would place me in security, and save my family from constant wretchedness. I had to leave Texas, abandon all, for which I had fought and spent my fortune, to become a wanderer. The ingratitude of those, who had assumed to themselves the fight of convicting me; their credulity in declaring me a traitor, on mere rumors, when I had to plead in my favor the loyal patriotism with which I had always served Texas, wounded me deeply.

But, before leaving my country, perhaps forever, I determined to consult with all those interested in my welfare. I held a family council. All were in favor of my removing for some time to the interior of Texas. But, to accomplish this, there were some unavoidable obstacles. I could not take one step, from my ranch towards the Brazos, without being exposed to the rifle of the first person who might meet me, for, through the whole country, credit had been given to the rumors against me. To emigrate with my family was impossible, as I was a ruined man, from the time of the invasion of Santa Anna and our flight to Nacogdoches; furthermore, the country of the Brazos was unhealthier than that of Nacogdoches, and what might we not expect to suffer from disease in a new country, and without friends or means.

Seeing that all these plans were impracticable, I resolved to seek a refuge amongst my enemies, braving all dangers. But before taking this step, I sent in my resignation to the Corporation of San Antonio, as Mayor of the city, stating to them, that, unable any longer to suffer the persecutions of some ungrateful Americans, who strove to murder me, I had determined to free my family and friends from their continual misery on my account, and go and live peaceably in Mexico. That for the reasons I resigned my office, with all the privileges and honors as a Texan.

I left Bexar without any engagements towards Texas; my services paid by persecutions, exiled and deprived of my privileges as a Texan citizen, I was in this country a being out of the pale of society, and when she could not protect the rights of her citizens, they were privileged to seek protection elsewhere. I had been tried by a rabble, condemned without a bearing, and consequently was at liberty to provide for my own safety.

I arrived at Laredo, and the Military Commander of that place put me in prison, stating, that he could not do otherwise, until he bad consulted with General Arista, whom he advised of my arrest. Arista ordered that I should be sent to Monterey. I arrived in that city, and earnestly prayed the General to allow me to retire to Saltillo, where I had several relatives who could aid me. General Arista answered, that, as he had informed Santa Anna of my imprisonment, he could not comply with my request. Santa Anna directed, that I should be sent to the City of Mexico, but Arista, feeling for my unfortunate position, interceded with him in my behalf, to have the order revoked. The latter complied, but on condition, that I should return to Texas, with a company of explorers, to attack its citizens, and, by spilling my blood, vindicate myself.

By orders of General Arista, I proceeded to Rio Grande, to join General Woll, who told me, that Santa Anna, by his request, had allowed me to go with him, in his expedition to Texas, but, I should receive no command until my services proved if I were worthy.

I started with the expedition of General Woll. In the vicinity of San Antonio, on the 10th of September, I received an order to take a company of Cavalry, and keep the outlets of the city. By this order the city was blockaded, and consequently it was difficult for any person to escape. When I returned from complying with this order, at dawn of day, the General determined to enter the city with the Infantry and Artillery. I was sent to the vanguard, with orders to take possession of the Military Square at all hazards. I entered the Square without opposition, and shortly afterwards the firing commenced on the Main Square. John Hernandez came out of Goodman's shop, with a message from him to the effect, that, if I would pardon him for what he had done against me, he would leave his place of concealment and deliver himself tip. I sent him word, that I had no rancor against him, he delivered himself tip, and I placed him under tile special charge of Captain Lexal. Those who had made some show of resistance in the Main Square Surrendered, and the whole city was in the possession of General Woll.

Next day, I was ordered, with 200 men, to take the Gonzales road, and go near that town. On the Cibolo I divided my forces, sending a portion up the creek, another down the creek, and with the main body proceeded on the Gonzales road. Next day, these parties joined the main body. Lieutenant Carvajal, who commanded one of the parties, reported, that lie had killed, in the Azufrosa, three Texans, who would not surrender.

I returned to San Antonio. A party of Texans appeared by the Garita road, and the troops were put under arms. The General took one hundred Infantry, the Cavalry under Montero, and one piece of artillery, and proceeded towards the Salado. The General ordered 100 Presidiales to attack. The commander of those forces sent word that the enemy were in an advantageous position and that lie required reinforcements. The answer of the General was, to send me with orders "to attack at all hazards." I obeyed; on the first charge, I lost 3 killed and 8 wounded, on the second, 7 killed and 15 wounded; I was preparing for a third charge, when Colonel Carrasco came to relieve me from my command. I returned to the side of the General, made my report, whereupon he ordered the hiring to cease.

A new attack was preparing, when tile attention of the General was called to some troops on our rear-guard. The aids reported them to be enemies, and near at hand. Colonel Montero was ordered, with his cavalry, to attack them. He called on them, to surrender to the Mexican Government, they answered with scoffing and bantering, Montero formed his dragoons, the Texans commenced firing, killing two soldiers; Montero dismounted his troops, also began firing, and sent for more ammunition. The General angrily sent him a message, asking, whether his dragoons had no sabres or lances. Before Montero received this answer, had charged, sabre in hand, ending the engagement in a few minutes; only some ten or fifteen Texans survived. During this time, I remained by the side of General Woll, and was there when Montero made his report and brought in the prisoners.

At dusk, the troops received orders to return to San Antonio. In accordance with his orders, not to remain over a month on this side of the Rio Grande, General Woll begun his retreat by the road he came.

The families, who left San Antonio, were put under my charge, and, consequently, I was not in the affair of "Arroyo Hondo."

Remarks

After the expedition of General Woll, I did not return to Texas till the treaty of Guadalupe Hidalgo. During my absence nothing appeared that could stamp me as a traitor. My enemies had accomplished their object; they had killed me politically in Texas, and the less they spoke of me, the less risk they incurred of being exposed in the infamous means they had used to accomplish my ruin.

As to my reputed treason with Vasquez, when we consider that Don Antonio Navarro and I were the only Mexicans of note, in Western Texas, who had taken a prominent part in the war, the interest the Mexican General had in causing us to be distrusted, will be seen. Mr. Navarro was then a prisoner; I alone remained; and if they were able to make the Texans distrust me, they gained a point. This is proved by the fact, that, since I withdrew from the service, there was never seen a regiment of Mexico-Texans. The rumor, that I was a traitor, was seized with avidity by my enemies in San Antonio.

Some envied my military position, as held by a Mexican; others found in me an obstacle to the accomplishment of their villainous plans. The number of land suits which still encumbers the docket of Bexar county, would indicate the nature of these plans, and any one, who has listened to the evidence elicited in cases of this description, will readily discover the base means adopted to deprive rightful owners of their property.

But, returning again to the charge of treason, if I had sold myself to Mexico, the bargain would have been naturally with the Government; it would have been the interest of Mexico to keep the secret, and not allow inferior officers to know it. Whilst I enjoyed the confidence of the Texans, I might have been useful in imparting secrets, &c., but as soon as my fellow-citizens distrusted me, I was absolutely useless. And is it not strange that the Mexican officers should have been so anxious to inform the Texans of my treason? General Vasquez merely took out a paper from his pocket, and observed to Chevallie that that was from me; and when the latter desired to see the letter, Vasquez refused to shew [sic] it to him.

But I take the expedition of Vasquez to be my best defence. What did Vasquez accomplish in that expedition? The coming into and going out of San Antonio, without taking any further steps. Undoubtedly, if I had been confederated with him, I would have tried to make his expedition something more than a mere military promenade. Far from doing this, however, I presented the letter, which I received from Vasquez, to the corporation of San Antonio; I predicted the expedition, and counselled such steps as I thought should be taken.

And, why, if my treason were so clear, did the patriotic and brave Burleson refuse to subject me to a Court of Enquiry? Undoubtedly, he knew it to be his duty to put me on trial, if the slightest suspicion existed as to my character. He refused; and this proved that Burleson and the superior officers were convinced of the shallowness of the charges against me.

During the electoral campaign, of August, 1855, I was frequently attacked in newspapers, and was styled in some "the murderer of the Salado." As for some time previously I had proposed to publish my memoirs, I thought it useless to enter into a newspaper war, more particularly as the attacks against me were anonymous, and were directed with a venom which made me conclude that I owed them to the malevolence of a personal enemy.

I have related my participation in Woll's expedition and have only to say, that neither I nor any of my posterity will ever have reason to blush for it.

During my military career, I can proudly assert, that I never deviated from the line of duty; that I never shed, or caused to be shed, human blood unnecessarily; that I never insulted, by word or deed, a prisoner; and that, in the fulfilment of my duty, I always drew a distinction between my obligations, as a soldier on the battle-field, and, as a civilized man after it.

I have finished my memoirs; I neither have the capacity nor the desire to adorn my acts with literary phrases. I have attempted a short and clear narrative of my public life, in relation to Texas. I give it publicity, without omitting or suppressing anything that I thought of the least interest, and confidently I submit to the public verdict.

Several of those who witnessed the facts which I have related, are still alive and amongst us; they can state whether I have in any way falsified the record.

Source:

Documentary Archives: Multicultural America CD-ROM. Woodbridge, CT: Primary Source Media, 1997.

The Supreme Court case, Hernandez v. Texas (1954), provided the first major victory for Mexican Americans seeking to address ethnic discrimination through legal channels. It was also the first U.S. Supreme Court case to be briefed and argued by Mexican American attorneys. In this case, the Supreme Court held that the Texas court could not "limit the scope of the equal protection clause to the white and Negro classes." Chief Justice Earl Warren spoke for the court when he said that the Fourteenth Amendment of the U.S. Constitution must be applied to Mexican Americans. The Fourteenth Amendment guarantees due process of law and equal protection for all citizens born or naturalized and prohibits states from creating laws that abridge the privileges and immunities of citizens. The Supreme Court held that the state of Texas had excluded Mexican Americans from jury duty, making it impossible for a Mexican American being tried in a Texas court to be judged by a jury of his peers.

The value of a Supreme Court decision cannot be overstated. This decision became the basis for many cases attacking discrimination against Mexican Americans in all areas of American life, though real social changes did not occur until after the 1960s. By the mid-1960s, with the passage of the National Civil Rights Act of 1964, the civil rights of all minorities came to national attention. Yet, by 1970, the U.S. Commission on Civil Rights reported that Mexican Americans were still being denied equal treatment by the judicial and legal systems. Nonetheless, this Supreme Court case in 1954 laid the groundwork for legally-mandated social changes throughout the twentieth century, and would have an impact on millions of people. The 1990 Census Bureau reported that approximately 12 million people of Mexican ancestry live in the United States. In addition, the non-Hispanic white population declined in 16 states during the 1980s. Three-quarters of the nation's 22.4 million Hispanics (a term including Mexican Americans) live in California, Texas, New York, Florida, or Illinois.

HERNANDEZ V. TEXAS

347 U.S. 475

Certiorari to the Court of Criminal Appeals of Texas. No. 406.

Argued January 11, 1954.
Decided May 3, 1954.

The systematic exclusion of persons of Mexican descent from service as jury commissioners, grand jurors, and petit jurors in the Texas county in which petitioner was indicted and tried for murder, although there were a substantial number of such persons in the county fully qualified to serve, deprived petitioner, a person of Mexican descent, of the equal protection of the laws guaranteed by the Fourteenth Amendment, and his conviction in a state court is reversed. pp. 476-482.

(a) The constitutional guarantee of equal protection of the laws is not directed solely against discrimination between whites and Negroes. pp. 477-478.

(b) When the existence of a distinct class is demonstrated, and it is shown that the laws, as written or as applied, single out that class for different treatment not based on some reasonable classification, the guarantees of the Constitution have been violated. p. 478.

(c) The exclusion of otherwise eligible persons from jury service solely because of their ancestry or national origin is discrimination prohibited by the Fourteenth Amendment. pp. 478-479.

(d) The evidence in this case was sufficient to prove that, in the county in question, persons of Mexican descent constitute a separate class, distinct from "whites." pp. 479-480.

(e) A prima facie case of denial of the equal protection of the laws was established in this case by evidence that there were in the county a substantial number of persons of Mexican descent with the qualifications required for jury service but that none of them had served on a jury commission, grand jury or petit jury for 25 years. pp. 480-481.

(f) The testimony of five jury commissioners that they had not discriminated against persons of Mexican descent in selecting jurors, and that their only objective had been to select those whom they thought best qualified, was not enough to overcome petitioner's prima facie case of denial of the equal protection of the laws. pp. 481-482.

(g) Petitioner had the constitutional right to be indicted and tried by juries from which all members of his class were not systematically excluded. p. 482.

___ Tex. Cr. R. ___, 251 S. W. 2d 531, reversed. [347 U.S. 475, 476]

Carlos C. Cadena and Gus C. Garcia argued the cause for petitioner. With them on the brief were Maury Maverick, Sr. and John J. Herrera.

Horace Wimberly, Assistant Attorney General of Texas, argued the cause for respondent. With him on the brief were John Ben Shepperd, Attorney General, and Rudy G. Rice, Milton Richardson and Wayne L. Hartman, Assistant Attorneys General, for respondent.

MR. CHIEF JUSTICE WARREN delivered the opinion of the Court.

The petitioner, Pete Hernandez, was indicted for the murder of one Joe Espinosa by a grand jury in Jackson County, Texas. He was convicted and sentenced to life imprisonment. The Texas Court of Criminal Appeals affirmed the judgment of the trial court. ___ Tex. Cr. R. ___, 251 S. W. 2d 531. Prior to the trial, the petitioner, by his counsel, offered timely motions to quash the indictment and the jury panel. He alleged that persons of Mexican descent were systematically excluded from service as jury commissioners, [Footnote 1] grand jurors, and petit jurors, although there were such persons fully [347 U.S. 475, 477] qualified to serve residing in Jackson County. The petitioner asserted that exclusion of this class deprived him, as a member of the class, of the equal protection of the laws guaranteed by the Fourteenth Amendment of the Constitution. After a hearing, the trial court denied the motions. At the trial, the motions were renewed, further evidence taken, and the motions again denied. An allegation that the trial court erred in denying the motions was the sole basis of petitioner's appeal. In affirming the judgment of the trial court, the Texas Court of Criminal Appeals considered and passed upon the substantial federal question raised by the petitioner. We granted a writ of certiorari to review that decision. 346 U.S. 811.

In numerous decisions, this Court has held that it is a denial of the equal protection of the laws to try a defendant of a particular race or color under an indictment issued by a grand jury, or before a petit jury, from which all persons of his race or color have, solely because of that race or color, been excluded by the State, whether acting through its legislature, its courts, or its executive or administrative officers. [Footnote 2] Although the Court has had little occasion to rule on the question directly, it has been recognized since *Strauder v. West Virginia*, 100 U.S. 303, that the exclusion of a class of persons from jury service on grounds other than race or color may also deprive a defendant who is a member of that class of the constitutional guarantee of equal protection of the laws. [Footnote 3] The State of Texas would have us hold that there are only two classes—white and Negro—within the contemplation of the Fourteenth Amendment. The decisions of this Court [347 U.S. 475, 478] do not support that view. [Footnote 4] And, except where the question presented involves the exclusion of persons of Mexican descent from juries, [Footnote 5] Texas courts have taken a broader view of the scope of the equal protection clause. [Footnote 6]

The Fourteenth Amendment is not directed solely against discrimination due to a "two-class theory"—that is, based upon differences between "white" and Negro.

Throughout our history differences in race and color have defined easily identifiable groups which have at times required the aid of the courts in securing equal treatment under the laws. But community prejudices are not static, and from time to time other differences from the community norm may define other groups which need the same protection. Whether such a group exists within a community is a question of fact. When the existence of a distinct class is demonstrated, and it is further shown that the laws, as written or as applied, single out that class for different treatment not based on some reasonable classification, the guarantees of the Constitution have been violated. The Fourteenth Amendment is not directed solely against discrimination due to a "two-class theory"—that is, based upon differences between "white" and Negro.

As the petitioner acknowledges, the Texas system of selecting grand and petit jurors by the use of jury commissions is fair on its face and capable of being utilized [347 U.S. 475, 479] without discrimination. [Footnote 7] But as this Court has held, the system is susceptible to abuse and can be employed in a discriminatory manner. [Footnote 8] The exclusion of otherwise eligible persons from jury service solely because of their ancestry or national origin is discrimination prohibited by the Fourteenth Amendment. The Texas statute makes no such discrimination, but the petitioner alleges that those administering the law do.

The petitioner's initial burden in substantiating his charge of group discrimination was to prove that persons of Mexican descent constitute a separate class in Jackson County, distinct from "whites." [Footnote 9] One method by which this may be demonstrated is by showing the attitude of the community. Here the testimony of responsible officials and citizens contained the admission that residents of the community distinguished between "white" and "Mexican." The participation of persons of Mexican descent in business and community groups was shown to be slight. Until very recent times, children of Mexican descent were required to attend a segregated school for the first four grades. [Footnote 10] At least one restaurant in town prominently displayed a sign announcing "No Mexicans Served." On the courthouse grounds at the time of the [347 U.S. 475, 480] hearing, there were two men's toilets, one unmarked, and the other marked "Colored Men" and "Hombres Aqui" ("Men Here"). No substantial evidence was offered to rebut the logical inference to be drawn from these facts, and it must be concluded that petitioner succeeded in his proof.

Having established the existence of a class, petitioner was then charged with the burden of proving discrimination. To do so, he relied on the pattern of proof established by *Norris v. Alabama*, 294 U.S. 587. In that case, proof that Negroes constituted a substantial segment of the population of the jurisdiction, that some Negroes were qualified to serve as jurors, and that none had been called for jury service over an extended period of time, was held to constitute prima facie proof of the systematic exclusion of Negroes from jury service. This holding, sometimes called the "rule of exclusion," has been applied in other cases, [Footnote 11] and it is available in supplying proof of discrimination against any delineated class.

The petitioner established that 14% of the population of Jackson County were persons with Mexican or Latin-American surnames, and that 11% of the males over 21 bore such names. [Footnote 12] The County Tax Assessor testified [347 U.S. 475, 481] that 6 or 7 percent of the freeholders on the tax rolls of the County were persons of Mexican descent. The State of Texas stipulated that "for the last twenty-five years there is no record of any person with a Mexican or Latin American name having served on a jury commission, grand jury or petit jury in Jackson County." [Footnote 13] The parties also stipulated that "there are some male persons of Mexican or Latin

American descent in Jackson County who, by virtue of being citizens, householders, or freeholders, and having all other legal prerequisites to jury service, are eligible to serve as members of a jury commission, grand jury and/or petit jury." [Footnote 14]

The petitioner met the burden of proof imposed in *Norris v. Alabama, supra.* To rebut the strong prima facie case of the denial of the equal protection of the laws guaranteed by the Constitution thus established, the State offered the testimony of five jury commissioners that they had not discriminated against persons of Mexican or Latin-American descent in selecting jurors. They stated that their only objective had been to select those whom they thought were best qualified. This testimony is not enough to overcome the petitioner's case. As the Court said in *Norris v. Alabama:*

> "That showing as to the long-continued exclusion of negroes from jury service, and as to the many negroes qualified for that service, could not be met by mere generalities. If, in the presence of such testimony as defendant adduced, the mere general assertions by officials of their performance of duty were to be accepted as an adequate justification for [347 U.S. 475, 482] the complete exclusion of negroes from jury service, the constitutional provision. . . would be but a vain and illusory requirement." [Footnote 15]

The same reasoning is applicable to these facts.

Circumstances or chance may well dictate that no persons in a certain class will serve on a particular jury or during some particular period. But it taxes our credulity to say that mere chance resulted in there being no members of this class among the over six thousand jurors called in the past 25 years. The result bespeaks discrimination, whether or not it was a conscious decision on the part of any individual jury commissioner. The judgment of conviction must be reversed.

To say that this decision revives the rejected contention that the Fourteenth Amendment requires proportional representation of all the component ethnic groups of the community on every jury [Footnote 16] ignores the facts. The petitioner did not seek proportional representation, nor did he claim a right to have persons of Mexican descent sit on the particular juries which he faced. [Footnote 17] His only claim is the right to be indicted and tried by juries from which all members of his class are not systematically excluded—juries selected from among all qualified persons regardless of national origin or descent. To this much, he is entitled by the Constitution.

Reversed.

Footnotes

[Footnote 1] Texas law provides that at each term of court, the judge shall appoint three to five jury commissioners. The judge instructs these commissioners as to their duties. After taking an oath that they will not knowingly select a grand juror they believe unfit or unqualified, the commissioners retire to a room in the courthouse where they select from the county assessment roll the names of 16 grand jurors from different parts of the county. These names are placed in a sealed envelope and delivered to the clerk. Thirty days before court meets, the clerk delivers a copy of the list to the sheriff who summons the jurors. Vernon's Tex. Code Crim. Proc., 1948, Arts. 333-350. The general jury panel is also selected by the jury commission. Vernon's Tex. Rev. Civ. Stat., 1948, Art. 2107. In capital cases, a special venire may be selected from the list furnished by the commissioners. Vernon's Tex. Code Crim. Proc., 1948, Art. 592.

[Footnote 2] See *Carter v. Texas,* 177 U.S. 442, 447.

[Footnote 3] "Nor if a law should be passed excluding all naturalized Celtic Irishmen [from jury service], would there be any doubt of its inconsistency with the spirit of the amendment." 100 U.S., at 308. Cf. *American Sugar Refining Co. v. Louisiana,* 179 U.S. 89, 92.

[Footnote 4] See *Truax v. Raich,* 239 U.S. 33; *Takahashi v. Fish & Game Commission,* 334 U.S. 410. Cf. *Hirabayashi v. United States,* 320 U.S. 81, 100: "Distinctions between citizens solely because of their ancestry are by their very nature odious to a free people whose institutions are founded upon the doctrine of equality."

[Footnote 5] *Sanchez v. State,* 147 Tex. Cr. R. 436, 181 S. W. 2d 87; *Salazar v. State,* 149 Tex. Cr. R. 260, 193 S. W. 2d 211; *Sanchez v. State,* 243 S. W. 2d 700.

[Footnote 6] In *Juarez v. State,* 102 Tex. Cr. R. 297, 277 S. W. 1091, the Texas court held that the systematic exclusion of Roman Catholics from juries was barred by the Fourteenth Amendment. In *Clifton v. Puente,* 218 S. W. 2d 272, the Texas court ruled that restrictive covenants prohibiting the sale of land to persons of Mexican descent were unenforceable.

[Footnote 7] *Smith v. Texas,* 311 U.S. 128, 130.

[Footnote 8] *Smith v. Texas, supra,* note 7; *Hill v. Texas,* 316 U.S. 400; *Cassell v. Texas,* 339 U.S. 282; *Ross v. Texas,* 341 U.S. 918.

[Footnote 9] We do not have before us the question whether or not the Court might take judicial notice that persons of Mexican descent are there considered as a separate class. See Marden, Minorities in American Society; McDonagh & Richards, Ethnic Relations in the United States.

[Footnote 10] The reason given by the school superintendent for this segregation was that these children needed special help in learning English. In this special school, however, each teacher taught two grades, while in the regular school each taught only one in most instances. Most of the children of Mexican descent left school by the fifth or sixth grade.

[Footnote 11] See note 8, supra.

[Footnote 12] The 1950 census report shows that of the 12,916 residents of Jackson County, 1,865, or about 14%, had Mexican or Latin-American surnames. U.S. Census of Population, 1950, Vol. II, pt. 43, p. 180; id., Vol. IV, pt. 3, c. C, p. 45. Of these 1,865, 1,738 were native-born American citizens and 65 were naturalized citizens. Id., Vol. IV, pt. 3, c. C, p. 45. Of the 3,754 males over 21 years of age in the County, 408, or about 11%, had Spanish surnames. Id., Vol. II, pt. 43, p. 180; id., Vol. IV, pt. 3, c. C, p. 67. The State

challenges any reliance on names as showing the descent of persons in the County. However, just as persons of a different race are distinguished by color, these Spanish names provide ready identification of the members of this class. In selecting jurors, the jury commissioners work from a list of names.

[Footnote 13] R. 34.

[Footnote 14] R. 55. The parties also stipulated that there were no persons of Mexican or Latin-American descent on the list of talesmen. R. 83. Each item of each stipulation was amply supported by the testimony adduced at the hearing.

[Footnote 15] 294 U.S., at 598.

[Footnote 16] See *Akins v. Texas*, 325 U.S. 398, 403; *Cassell v. Texas*, 339 U.S. 282, 286-287.

[Footnote 17] See *Akins v. Texas*, supra, note 16, at 403. [347 U.S. 475, 483]

Source:

Hernandez v. Texas 347 U.S. 475 (1954). Obtained June 7, 1999, from FindLaw.com website.

*B*eginning in the early twentieth century, Mexican immigrants came to the United States in large numbers. However, many Mexican-Americans in the Southwest have roots in the United States that date as far back as the late 1500s. In the early 1900s, Mexican immigrants were a source of labor for coal and copper mines and in agricultural work. In 1911, the Dillingham commission exempted Mexicans from the head tax for immigrants that had been established earlier in 1903 and 1907. Between 1900 and 1929, one million Mexicans immigrated to the United States, largely due to a tremendous increase in population in Mexico, but also because of the Mexican Revolution, which lasted from 1910 to 1926. The ease with which they found jobs encouraged chain migration, as relatives followed these immigrants to the United States, sometimes bringing entire families.

Mexican immigrants brought their culture with them, and sought to preserve family traditions in their lives in America. One of their important traditions was the celebration of festivals, and these often included traditional dances. The description of the matachines dance in this document is drawn according to the observations of anthropologists and dates from the early to mid-twentieth century. In it, the matachines dance is described in thorough detail, including costume (and varying costumes between differing tribes), music and portions of the dance. The matachines dance is derived from European ritual dances and is generally staged by small groups of men, some of whom dress the part of women. This dance is not only found in Mexico, but in New Mexico as well, forming a link between the Pueblo tribes to Mexican Sonora tribes. The men performing the dance are vowed to membership in a society that performs this dance, and the dance is a ritual part of the celebration.

MATACHINES DANCE

There exist a surprising number of firsthand observations of the New World matachines dances as observed between 1902 and 1955 in various places in Old and New Mexico. The best of these are the painstaking observations of the anthropologists, Bennett and Zingg, Hawley, Spicer, and Parsons, but all of them seem to be accurate descriptions. There are two striking omissions. There appears to be no professional description of the choreography (as might have been done with the new methods of dance notation), and there are no transcriptions or adequate discussions of the music in any of these accounts, although Frances Toor has transcribed the music of other dances. The present article will supply a number of transcriptions. While the various accounts reveal local differences, it is possible to see a remarkable degree of uniformity in the dance, even though danced at isolated villages, far removed from one another.

In general, at all these places, the dances share the following characteristics:

I. The matachines dancers are a group dedicated to the service, through dancing, of the Virgin of Guadalupe.

II. There is a leader, known usually as *el Monarca.*

III. There is a girl (or, in Mexico, a boy dressed as a girl) known as *la Malinche.*

IV. There are two lines of dancers, each ranging in number from six to twelve or even larger numbers.

V. There is a character known as *el Toro.*

VI. There is a clownish character, often masked, known as *el Abuelo* ("the grandfather") who speaks in falsetto.

VII. The dancers usually dance on December 12, the feast day of the Virgin of Guadalupe, and on other special occasions.

VIII. They usually dance to the music of fiddle and guitar.

IX. They wear tall, mitre-like, decorative headdresses, have their faces partially covered by fringes or handkerchiefs, and wear bright colored ribbons and aprons.

X. They carry in one hand a gourd rattle with which they keep the rhythm of the dance steps and in the other a wooden trident, often gaily painted.

XI. The dance often terminates with the figurative killing of the bull.

XII. They dance in front of, or inside, the Catholic church of the village.

The dance of the Aztecas in Tortugas, New Mexico, the dance of the Indios in Saltillo, Mexico, and the dance of the Negritos in Papantla, Mexico, so closely resemble the description above that it seems reasonable to conclude that they are related. The chief difference between these dances and the matachines seems to be in the matter of costuming. The New Mexico Indian corn dances in ways resemble the matachines dance—the dancers form two lines, there are comic characters like *el Abuelo*, gourd rattles are carried—but the costumes, the music, and the manner of dancing are all strikingly different.

That the dances of the Aztecas and Indicos are indeed related to the matachines dance seems to be confirmed by the similarity of the names given to certain of the dances by the different groups, even when performed at villages remote from one another. For instance, at San Antonio, Tortugas and Tierra Amarilla, all far removed from one another, one of the matachines dances is called "*la Malinche.*" The same title is used for one of the dances by the Aztecas of Tortugas.

Both the matachines at Tierra Amarilla and the Aztecas dance a dance called "*la Cruz*" (the cross).

Both the Aztecas of Tortugas and the Indios of Saltillo dance another called "*el Redoblado.*"

The musical selections which I have chosen and which are transcribed below bear for purposes of identification the serial numbers used in the catalog of the author's collection of recordings, texts, and transcriptions. The matachines dances are numbered 1143 to 1154 inclusive and are performed by a solo fiddler. They are of particular interest as the fiddler was intelligent and articulate and was able to ascribe a definite title to, and give some information about, each dance. These twelve dances, he said constitute one complete set of the dances done each year on December 12, the feast day of Our Lady of Guadalupe, at Tortugas. They are repeated on Christmas Day and New Year's.

The fiddler, Pete Maese, himself danced with other dancers from 1928 to 1941 and these are the tunes which he learned from his predecessor, whom he knew as an old man. When the old man died

Christmas Day Matachines dancers at San Juan Pueblo.

Maese was elected as fiddler. The dancers at Tortugas are known as "matachines" or *"Danzantes."* The group are of mixed blood—Indian, Spanish, American. Some fifteen of them, including Maese, have been sworn in as slaves of the Virgin and dance in fulfillment of their vows.

The ceremonies commence with *la Entrada* ("the entry"), a danced procession that terminates in front of the main entrance of the Catholic church where the other dances take place. The dancers consist of a leader known as *el Monarca*, six to eight little pre-adolescent girls in white communion dresses who alternate in the part of *la Malinche* (*la Malinche* was the Indian mistress of Hernando Cortes), the matachines dancers (twelve in number), *el Polverero* ("powder man") who carries a shotgun and fires it precisely on the final note of each dance. This is intended as a salute to the Virgin. There are also two additional characters—*el Toro* and *el Abuelo* who act as clowns.

The titles of the dances furnish a clue as to the nature of the dance formations.

"La Batalla" ("The Battle") is self-explanatory. In *"la Mudanza"* ("The Cross") dancers exchange places in a crisscross movement. *"La Ese"* (the letter S) is a description of the pattern by which the dancers move from one position to the next. *"Guajes"* ("Gourds") is the name given to a gourd filled with dried beans or other noisemaking particles which is carried by each of the *danzantes*. These add a percussive rhythm to the dance. *"Los Panos"* ("The Handkerchiefs") employs large handkerchiefs. In *"El Son de la Malinche"* several of the little malinches dance, the one in the lead escorted by *el Monarca*. *"La Entre Rejida"* ("The Weaving Entrance") is distinguished by a dance pattern which is supposed to stimulate the weaving of cloth. *"La Transa"* ("The Braids") is a Maypole dance. *"La Procession"* ("The Procession") is what its name indicates. The dance known as *"el Toro"* ("The Bull") is characterized by a simulated combat

between *el Monarca* and *el Toro*, who is dressed to resemble a bull. *El Monarca* eventually kills the bull after the dancers make a circle like a bull ring. This is regarded as a humorous dance, the bull acting as a clown. The bull charges and before being killed is supposed to kill *el Abuelo*. Actually, this is supposed to end the dances but these are not always taken in the proper sequence. In *"la Escondida"* ("The Hid-

den One") one of the malinches is symbolically hidden by *el Monarca* and the *danzantes*, presumably from pursuit by *el Toro*.

Source:

"The Matachines Dance—A Ritual Folk Dance" by J.D. Robb. In *Western Folklore*, XX (1961), pp. 94-101.

*I*n her role as president and general counsel of the Mexican American Legal Defense and Educational Fund (MALDEF), a national organization devoted to protecting the civil rights of Latinos, Antonia Hernández is one of the country's most prominent activists. Monitoring the impact of laws and public policy on Hispanic Americans and challenging inequities through the courts have formed the basis of MALDEF's mission, and these same concerns have been of paramount importance to Hernández since she took over the reins of the organization in 1985. Of particular interest to her are immigration issues, perhaps because she herself is a native of Mexico and is therefore well acquainted with the problems many newcomers face.

Hernández was born in the town of Torreón in the state of Coahuila, in the north central part of Mexico. When she was eight years old, her family settled in predominantly Hispanic East Los Angeles. There she and her five brothers and sisters grew up poor while their parents urged all of their children to seek higher education and find ways to make their lives meaningful in service to others. With that goal in mind, young Antonia pursued a career in education at the University of California in Los Angeles (UCLA), earning a bachelor's degree in 1970 and a teaching certificate in 1971.

While teaching, Hernández realized that she might be able to do more to help her community if she worked for change through the court system. So Hernández enrolled in UCLA's law school and earned her law degree in 1974.

After graduation, Hernández was hired on as a staff attorney with the Los Angeles Center for Law and Justice and three years later, she became directing attorney of a Los Angeles-area Legal Aid office, working on civil and criminal cases as well as fighting for bills in the state legislature. Hernández left there in 1979 for a job in Washington, D.C., as staff counsel to the U.S. Senate Committee on the Judiciary, which required her to keep committee members informed on issues involving human rights and immigration.

Hernández lost her job after Senate control shifted from the Democrats to the Republicans following the 1980 election, but it was not long before MALDEF approached her about becoming a staff attorney in the group's Washington office. Hernández was offered the top post in 1985. At MALDEF, Hernández directs all litigation and advocacy programs and plans the organization's long-range goals and objectives. She has been instrumental in a number of MALDEF's major initiatives, such as defeating a bill in Congress that would have required Latinos to carry identification cards, promoting affirmative action in both the public and private employment sectors, and challenging questionable school and voting district boundaries.

Hernández is often called upon to articulate MALDEF's view on issues of particular importance to Latinos, among them discrimination, bilingual education, voting rights, and even U.S. Census Bureau policies and statistics. Immigration remains a major concern, too, especially in the wake of recent trends that indicate more and more Americans are ready to deal with the problem of illegal immigrants in ways that some people view as unduly harsh and punitive.

In elections held during the fall of 1994, for example, Californians were asked to vote on Proposition 187, a controversial measure that would have barred illegal immigrants from attending public schools and receiving welfare and non-emergency health-care services, among other things. Proposition 187 sparked intense debate throughout the nation but was naturally a much hotter issue in California, where the rhetoric reached a fever pitch in the weeks before the election. On several occasions that fall, Hernández was asked to explain Proposition 187 and its implications to groups of interested voters. One such instance was on October 5, 1994, when she spoke at Temple Isaiah in Los Angeles.

Proposition 187 was approved by California voters in November of 1994, but opponents immediately launched various court challenges that have prevented its provisions from going into effect. Her remarks that evening are reprinted here from a copy of her speech provided by MALDEF. It should be noted that in September of 1999, a federal judge approved an agreement between civil rights groups and state officials dropping Proposition 187.

ARE WE COMPASSION FATIGUED?
a speech by Antonia Hernández

I want to thank Mr. Levine for inviting me to speak to you this evening. I commend both Mr. Levine and Rabbi Gann for their concern over Proposition 187.

Immigration—legal and illegal—is an inherently difficult and complex issue that defies simplistic and reactionary solutions like 187.

On the one hand, I know all too well that it is easier to "crack down" on the undocumented worker, easier to punish the children of undocumented immigrants, easier to assume that aggressive posture than to deal with the root economic causes of the migration north.

There is no question that the influx has changed the dynamics of cities like Los Angeles, and its impact has been felt in Washington as surely as Sacramento.

We cannot ignore that fact.

Yet, despite all the rhetoric about undocumented immigrants living off the system, the fact is that they come to work and build a better life for themselves and their children, not to take advantage of our educational, medical, and public services. They come to share in our great American work ethic.

We know that many immigrants come from the lowest socioeconomic strata of Mexico and Central America. We know that the immigrant is no longer a male looking to work seasonally and then return to his native country. Entire families are migrating north and settling permanently.

It is therefore critical that we approach undocumented immigration with the facts.

In 1993, only 1.5 percent of immigrants received Social Security.

In 1992 the INS [Immigration and Naturalization Service] reported that 0.5 percent of undocumented immigrants received food stamps or AFDC and about half had private health insurance while only 21 percent used any government health services.

According to the Urban Institute, when all levels of government are considered together, immigrants contribute more in taxes paid than in services received.

Yet in the past few years, public discourse over immigration policy, shaped by misinformation, has shifted dangerously toward extremism. The by-product of that movement has created a rise in xenophobia and the scapegoating of immigrants.

Indeed, in the past several months, we have seen the federal government approve such proposals as banning emergency aid to undocumented immigrants who were victims of the earthquake in Los Angeles, funding the unemployment benefits extension program by cutting off benefits to legal permanent residents, and consider cutting off educational benefits to undocumented children in the public schools.

So taken by the effort to deny aid to undocumented immigrants who had been victimized by the earthquake, Secretary of Housing and Urban Development Henry Cisneros was compelled to say: "It is sad that the circumstances of a disaster would result in making these kinds of distinctions about human suffering."

In California, the Department of Motor Vehicles on March 1 began requiring proof of citizenship or legal status in order to obtain a driver's license or identification card. And now, California faces an extremist immigration policy under Proposition 187, one that could cost California taxpayers $15 billion and do nothing to address any immigration concerns.

All of these efforts are extreme and retrograde and speak to the virulence of the anti-immigrant sentiment that has gripped the state and nation.

I will tell you that I have always been averse to extremism and no less so when it comes to immigration policy.

For me, the answer lies in compassion, moderation and—above all—reason.

While we all have legitimate concerns about illegal immigration, the truth is that Proposition 187 is intended to save money and solve problems but will only make the situation worse and create a host of new problems—expensive ones.

Proposition 187 does nothing to enforce the laws we already have, nor does it beef up enforcement at the borders.

Recklessly drafted, 187 violates federal laws that control federal funding to our schools and hospitals. The independent analysis of 187 in the voter pamphlet shows passage of the proposition could cost our schools and hospitals $15 billion in lost federal funds.

Let's put that staggering amount in a context that every Californian can understand. Replacing

Antonia Hernández

that money would necessitate a $1,600 annual tax increase for the average California family.

Proponents of the proposition claim that the state will save hundreds of millions of dollars by denying "nonemergency" medical care to the undocumented. First of all, the estimated undocumented immigrant use of the medical services that 187 would prohibit is very low, just a fraction of one percent of California's budget.

"I will tell you that I have always been averse to extremism and no less so when it comes to immigration policy."

Also, refusal to provide fundamental health care is a severe danger to public interest. If 187 is successful in denying these basic services, undocumented persons will not be treated even if their medical problems are serious, even if they have communicable diseases, even if a low-cost dose of preventive medicine or an immunization could keep them from ending up in county emergency rooms with far more serious ailments that will cost the state even more to treat.

In this country, we long ago recognized that health is a community concern. Volumes of treatises on public health recognized the danger to all of society if certain diseases and injuries are left untreated. The trend toward health care reform shows above all that we believe illnesses are not confined solely to one segment of our population.

Yet, under this provision, children would not be immunized and persons in desperate need of medical attention will not seek such care for fear of being reported to the INS. This constitutes not just a threat to the individual but a threat to our public health. As a society, we are best protected by treating the disease, not by turning away the individual in need of care.

By imposing yet another bureaucratic procedure in providing services, the provision will increase escalating costs of publicly-funded health services. Moreover, requiring verification and denying benefits or services on the basis of suspicion could cause unnecessary, and potentially life-endangering, delays and denials of care to citizens and legal residents who are otherwise entitled to medical assistance.

Finally, requiring health providers to notify the INS of their suspicion that someone may be undocumented compromises the patient-doctor confidentiality privilege. And, to the extent that the undocumented participate in drug abuse programs, the proposition may violate federal law that prohibits such providers from issuing information regarding the identity, diagnosis or treatment of any patient.

When you get beyond all the misinformation, you realize that undocumented immigrants are already ineligible for the vast majority of public social services such as state welfare or food stamps. One-eighty-seven's provision to deny such services to the undocumented merely creates a costly, enormous and unnecessary bureaucratic burden. Because existing federal verification procedures already prevent and discourage the undocumented from applying for public social services, the administrative costs of implementing this provision would offset, and most likely exceed any potential savings.

One-eighty-seven's public services provision also violates federal privacy protections for applicants under the Systematic Alien Verification of Eligibility (SAVE) system that already requires computerized verification of eligibility for such services but prohibits the use of immigration status information for enforcement purposes.

Additionally, the proposition violates federal law which prohibits the state from denying or delaying eligibility for benefits until the applicant has been given the opportunity to rebut any determination by the agency that he or she is undocumented. The proposition lacks the due process protections Congress created when it recognized that the INS verification system is not only time-consuming, but often inaccurate, and therefore could result in wrongful denial of services to United States citizens and legal residents.

One-eighty-seven is opposed by the California PTA and the entire education community because it will cost our schools more than it could ever save them. Even the U.S. Secretary of Education has informed state officials that 187 would violate federal laws and will force a cutoff of federal funds to California schools. At a time when California is working to improve educational quality, Proposition 187 would reduce the educational opportunities for all California children.

The provision to deny an education to undocumented children violates the United States Constitution under *Plyler v. Doe*, a 1982 United States Supreme Court case which recognized the right of all children to public education. [In *Plyler v. Doe*, the Supreme Court ruled that the state of Texas could not bar the children of illegal immigrants from attending public school.] It would also violate the state constitution's right to education.

Requiring schools to report to the INS any pupil or parent suspected of being undocumented violates the federal Family Educational Rights and Privacy Act (FERPA), which prohibits the release of information about public school students except in the most limited circumstances. FERPA is enforced by the federal government through the denial of federal funding. Thus, the proposition puts at serious risk the federal money that supports the education of all California children. Federal monies may also be denied to California colleges, and universities that violate FERPA.

Moreover, this provision would officially establish our public schools as agencies of family investigation and arms of government law enforcement. School officials, teachers, and other school employees would become immigration officials, responding to rumors and suspicions instead of educating our children. Fear of being reported to the INS may also cause undocumented parents to withdraw their United States citizen children from school—creating an underclass of uneducated United States citizens.

Finally, the cost to implement such a verification system could exceed tens of millions of dollars annually. Exclusion of undocumented students from California colleges and universities would result in loss of revenue and would take those students who may be the best and brightest of our communities and relegate them, perhaps permanently, to the underclass.

One-eighty-seven will mean more crime, not less, because it will kick an estimated three hundred thousand kids out of school and onto our streets, with no supervision. For this reason, LA County Sheriff Sherman Block and the state's largest law enforcement association of rank and file police officers and deputy sheriffs, the Peace Officers Research Association of California (PORAC), have spoken out against 187.

Additionally, 187s law enforcement provisions duplicate current law which encourages, and in some cases requires, local law enforcement to notify the INS of certain arrestees' immigration status. In fact, through a computerized booking system, police in several counties—including Los Angeles County—effectively report all suspected undocumented arrestees to the INS. These counties have established a booking system that allows the INS access to information regarding all foreign-born criminal arrestees.

Aside from duplicating already-existing practices, these provisions of the proposition would severely endanger the public safety. An increased distrust of the police would develop in many communities, leading to reduced cooperation with law enforcement agencies, increased criminal behavior because many witnesses and victims would not report crime for fear of being reported to the INS, and the undermining of efforts to implement community policing and other models of police-community cooperation.

There are additional disturbing questions about 187 that have been documented in recent press accounts. The people behind 187 are bankrolled by the Pioneer Fund, which is a secretive group that funds white supremacy research.

Alan Nelson, coauthor of 187, wrote the proposition while he was a paid lobbyist for the Federation for American Immigration Reform (FAIR). FAIR has received one million dollars from the Pioneer Fund, one of the longest and most consistent financial supporters of Nelson's FAIR. FAIR has also been the recipient of some of the Pioneer Fund's largest contributions in recent years. The Internal Revenue Service reports a long-standing financial relationship between the two groups.

FAIR has even admitted to the relationship. On March 30 of this year, FAIR's executive director Dan Stein admitted in the *San Francisco Chronicle*: "I think they support our work because the [Pioneer] trustees agree with what we're doing."

Despite Nelson's attempts to publicly distance himself from FAIR by starting a new organization this past May, the fact remains that he was FAIR's lobbyist when he authored 187.

Incorporated in 1937 by strict immigration, eugenics and sterilization advocates who saw selective breeding as a means of improving the quality of race, the Pioneer Fund remains an active, but secretive organization based in New York. In addition to

FAIR, the Pioneer Fund supports a number of controversial research projects and organizational efforts. Among them are the much-criticized works of Dr. William Shockley, who called for the sterilization of individuals with lower than average IQs; the well-known Minnesota Twins Study; researchers claiming to prove the inferiority of blacks with the use of gonad and cranium size studies; organizations promoting the notion that the "purity" of the white race is endangered by "inferior genetic stock"; and the editor of the neo-Nazi "mouthpiece" *Mankind Quarterly*, with its close ties to the mentor of Joseph Mengele of Auschwitz.

The ties of Nelson to these white supremacist supporters raise some very serious and fundamental concerns about 187 and sheds a whole new light on the "SUSPECT" reporting requirements of the proposition. I urge voters to read the 187 provisions which require that authorities report to the INS and the attorney general ANYONE they MERELY "SUSPECT" to be here illegally—in other words, anyone with "foreign" features, an accent or ethnic last name.

And 187 provides no protections for citizens or legal residents, particularly those with such attributes, against false accusations. Unlike current law, the proposition eliminates the required due process by not requiring an arrest to be lawful or that "suspicion" of undocumented status be "reasonable." The absence of "reasonableness" means there is little to protect immigrant witnesses and victims of crime from being falsely arrested and turned over to the INS. In effect, the provision turns police officers into INS agents, with all of the attendant fear that such status generates in immigrants, both legal residents and undocumented persons.

In summary:

One-eighty-seven punishes innocent children by denying them health care and education.

According to the state legislative analyst's offices, 187 will cost California taxpayers in excess of fifteen billion dollars in lost federal funds and in the development and administration of elaborate verification and notifications systems, and training of all state and local agencies.

One-eighty-seven will severely endanger the public safety by kicking three hundred thousand unsupervised kids out of school.

One-eighty-seven jeopardizes the privacy of Californians—forcing government employees, teachers, doctors, and other health care providers to act as INS agents, responding to rumors and suspicions instead of doing their jobs.

The people behind one 187 have close ties to a white supremacist group. By requiring all "suspects" to be reported to the authorities 187 would create a police-state mentality.

One-eighty-seven is unconstitutional, blatantly violating a clear ruling of the United States Supreme Court, and will force a cut in federal funds for our schools.

Finally, 187 does nothing to curb unlawful immigration into the state.

As a nation, we have been too apt to forget the benefits immigrants bring. We have also been given the opportunity to heed the lessons of our immigration history, and to this day we have squandered that opportunity. Instead, we have found ourselves in a desultory discourse that appeals to our worst nature as Americans, that plays to our darkest fears of "the foreigner."

Perhaps the saddest part of it all is that in so doing we have victimized not only voiceless immigrants but ourselves. For as I look upon this room and all the many faces, I am reminded again of this nation's great good fortune—that blessing—to be inheritor of such wealth, a true common wealth.

William Saroyan once wrote: "This is America, and the only foreigners here are those who forget it is America."

There has been all too much forgetting and not enough acknowledgment of our own immigrant stories, and the debate over immigration policy must be refracted through such a multicolored prism.

For if we are unable to bring some reason and decency to this debate, what is at stake is nothing less than who we are as a people, and how we define ourselves as a nation.

In the end, however, I remain optimistic that we will find our way to dealing compassionately and thoughtfully with immigrants. We will begin to move beyond the rhetoric and misinformation and posit the solutions to an issue that defies simplistic and reactionary approaches. I am optimistic because it is not our nature as Americans to turn our backs on those in need in the wake of a disaster—undocumented immigrants or not. It is not our nature to punish children and blame the ills of a nation on a small sector of our society. It is not our nature to turn away from issues that must be dealt with.

We will find our way to a reasoned and dignified policy by adhering to the sense of humanity that has made this country great, and acknowledges the role of the government controlling our borders. I know that we are a good and decent people—that is our nature and our franchise as Americans.

Thank you.

Source:

Mexican American Legal Defense and Educational Fund, 634 South Spring Street, Eleventh Floor, Los Angeles, CA 90014. (213) 629-2512.

MORMONS

In 1827, an American named Joseph Smith discovered golden plates buried in a hill in rural New York. Smith said that an angel named Moroni had appeared to him and given him the collection of golden tablets written in ancient Egyptian hieroglyphs, and two "seer's stones" that made translations of the tablets possible. Smith sat behind a curtain and dictated a translation of the sacred tablets, and the translations became known as the Book of Mormon. It was first published in 1830, along with the testimonies of 11 people who declared that they had also seen the tablets before the angel Moroni came to take them back. Thus was born the Church of Jesus Christ of Latter-day Saints. The book attracted a following shortly after publication. The 1830 edition contained 590 pages and was later revised and corrected by Smith. Later editions were divided into chapters and verses, and it has been published in more than 40 languages.

Smith believed that this book was a religious record of ancient inhabitants of North America. The book records the history of ancient emigrants from Jerusalem to America. Led by the prophet Lehi about 600 B.C., they settled in America and established a civilized society that eventually fought a series of internal wars. After his crucifixion, Jesus appeared to these people of the New World. In 421 A.D. the dark-skinned Lamanites wiped out the Nephites. The Lamanites were ancestors of the Native Americans.

Proponents of the new religion described it as the culmination of Christianity. Smith continued to have visions. He and his followers moved to Illinois and founded a self-sufficient community. After a schism in the community surrounding plural marriage, a mob lynched him along with one of his followers. Brigham Young stepped forward to lead the movement and they fled to Utah, where they again established an autonomous state until the United States expanded into the area in 1850.

From its earliest days, the Mormons have been embroiled in controversy. The authenticity of the Book of Mormon is contested by claims that a clergyman named Solomon Spaulding wrote it. The disappearance of the original texts into the hands of an angel is dismissed by opponents as a convenient cover for the fake discovery of the tablets. In 1993 and 1994 the church excommunicated intellectuals who questioned the historicity of the Book of Mormon. Nevertheless, the Church of Jesus Christ of Latter-day Saints has grown to be more than an American religious denomination. In 1991, of its 8,000,000 members, only half lived in the United States. The state if Utah is 77 percent Mormon, but only one-eighth of the church members live there.

THE BOOK OF MORMON

An Account Written by The Hand of Mormon Upon Plates *Taken From the Plates of Nephi*

Wherefore, it is an abridgement of the record of the people of Nephi, and also of the Lamanites—Written to the Lamanites, who are a remnant of the house of Israel; and also to the Jew and Gentile—Written by way of commandment, and also by the spirit of prophecy and of revelation—Written and sealed up, and hid up unto the Lord, that they might not be destroyed—To come forth by the gift and power of God unto the interpretation thereof—Sealed by the hand of Moroni, and hid up unto the Lord, to come forth in due time by way of the Gentile—The interpretation by the gift of God.

An abridgement taken from the Book of Ether also, which is a record of the people of Jared, who were scattered at the time the Lord confounded the language of the people, when they were building a tower to get to heaven—Which is to show unto the remnant of the House of Israel what great things the Lord hath done for their fathers; and that they may know the covenants of the Lord hath done for their fathers; and that they may know the covenants of the Lord, that they are not cast off forever—And also to the convincing of the Jew and Gentile that Jesus is the Christ, the Eternal God, manifesting himself unto all nations—and now, if there are faults they are mistakes of men; wherefore, condemn not the things of God, that ye may be found spotless at the judgement-seat of Christ.

TRANSLATED BY JOSEPH SMITH, Jun.

**PUBLISHED BY
The Church of Jesus Christ of
Latter-day Saints**
SALT LAKE CITY, UTAH, U.S.A.

**BRIEF ANALYSIS
OF THE
BOOK OF MORMON**

Three classes of Record Plates are indicated on the title-pages of The Book of Mormon, namely:

1. *The Plates of Nephi*, which as the text of the Book makes clear, were of two kinds—(a) the Larger Plates; (b) the Smaller Plates. The former were more particularly devoted to the secular history of the peoples concerned, while the latter were occupied mostly by sacred records.

2. *The Plates of Mormon*, containing an abridgment from the Plates of Nephi, made by Mormon, with many commentaries and a continuation of the history by himself, and with further additions by Moroni, son of Mormon.

3. *The Plates of Ether*, containing an history of the Jaredites, which account was abridged by Moroni, who inserted comments of his own, and incorporated the record with the general history under the title, Book of Ether.

To these may be added another set of plates, which are of frequent mention in the Book of Mormon, namely:

4. *The Brass Plates of Laban*, brought by the people of Lehi from Jeruslaem, and containing Hebrew Scriptures and genealogies, many extracts from which appear in the Nephite records.

The Book of Mormon comprises fifteen main parts or divisions, known, with one exception, as books, each designated by the name of its principal author. Of these, the first six books, namely, First Nephi, Second Nephi, Jacob, Enos, Jarom, and Omni, are translations from the corresponding sections of the Smaller Plates of Nephi. Between the books of Omni and Mosiah, we find *The Words of Mormon*, connecting the record of Nephi, as engraved on the Smaller Plates, with Mormon's abridgement of the Larger Plates for the periods following. *The Words of Mormon* constitute a brief explanation of the preceding portions of the record, and a preface to the parts following.

The body of the Book, from Mosiah to Mormon, chapter 7, inclusive, is the translation of Mormon's abridgement of the Plates of Nephi. The latter part of the Book of Mormon, from the beginning of Mormon, chapter 8, to the end of the volume, was engraved my Mormon's son, Moroni, who proceeded to finish the record, as the Book of Ether. Later he added the parts known to us as the Book of Moroni.

The period covered by Book of Mormon annals extends from B.C. 600 to A.D. 421. In or about the latter year, Moroni, the last of the Nephite historians, sealed the sacred record and hit it up unto the Lord, to be brought forth in the latter days, as predicted by the voice of God through his ancient prophets. In A.D. 1827, this same Moroni, then a resurrected personage, delivered the engraved plates to Joseph Smith.

ORIGIN OF THE BOOK OF MORMON

Joseph Smith, through whom, by the gift and power of God, the ancient Scripture, known as THE BOOK OF MORMON, has been brought forth and translated into the English tongue, made personal and circumstantial record of the matter. He affirmed that during the night of September 21, 1823, he sought the Lord in fervent prayer, having previously received a Divine manifestation of transcendent import. His account follows:

"While I was thus in the act of calling upon God, I discovered a light appearing in my room, which continued to increase until the room was lighter than at noonday, when immediately a personage appeared at my bedside, standing in the air, for his feet did not touch the floor.

"He had on a loose robe of most exquisite whiteness. It was a whiteness beyond anything earthly thing could be made to appear so exceedingly white and brilliant. His hands were naked, and his arms also, a little above the ankles. His head and neck were also bare. I could discover that he had no other clothing on but this robe, as it was open, so that I could see into his bosom.

"Not only was his robe exceedingly white, but his whole person was glorious beyond description, and his countenance truly like lightning. The room was exceedingly light, but not so very bright as immediately around his person. When I first looked upon him, I was afraid; but the fear soon left me.

"He called me by name, and said unto me that he was a messenger sent from the presence of God to me, and that his name of Moroni; that God had a work for me to do; and that my name should be had for good and evil among all nations, kindreds, and tongues, or that it should be both good and evil spoken of among all people.

"He said there was a book deposited , written upon gold plates, giving an account of the former inhabitants of this continent, and the source from whence they sprang. He also said that the fulness of the everlasting Gospel was contained in it, as delivered by the Savior to the ancient inhabitants;

"Also that there were two stones in silver bows—and these stones, fastened to a breastplate, constituted what is called the Urim and Thummim—deposited with the plates; and the possession and use of these stones were what constituted *Seers* in ancient or former times; and that God had prepared them for the purpose of translating the book.

"Again he told me, that when I got those plates of which he had spoken—for the time that they should be obtained was not yet fulfilled—I should not show them to any person; neither the breastplate with the Urim and Thummim; only to those to whom I should be commanded to show them; if I did I should be destroyed. While he was conversing with me about the plates, the vision was opened to my mind that I could see the place where the plates were deposited, and that so clearly and distinctly that I knew the place again when I visited it.

"After this communication, I saw the light in the room begin to gather immediately around the person of him who had been speaking to me, and it continued to do so, until the room was again left dark, except just around him, when instantly I saw, as it were, a conduit open right up into heaven, and he ascended until he entirely discovered that my room was again beginning to get lighted, and in an instant, as it were, the same heavenly messenger was again by my bedside.

"I lay musing on the singularity of the scene, and marveling greatly at what had been told to me by this extraordinary messenger; when, in the midst of my meditation, I suddenly discovered that my room was again beginning to get lighted, and in an instant, as it were, the same heavenly messenger was again by my bedside.

"He commenced, and again related the very same things which he had done at his first visit, without the least variation; which having done, he informed me of great judgements which were coming upon the earth, with great desolations by famine, sword, and pestilence; and that these grievous judgements would come on the earth in this generation. Having related these things, he again ascended as he had done before.

"By this time, so deep were the impressions made on my mind, that sleep had fled from my eyes, and I lay overwhelmed in astonishment at what I had both seen and heard. But what was my surprise when again I beheld the same messenger at my bedside, and heard him rehearse or repeat over again to me the same things as before; and added a caution to me, telling me that Satan would try to tempt me (in consequence of the indigent circumstances of my father's family), to get the plates for the purpose of getting rich. This he forbade me, saying that I must have no other object in view in getting the plates but to glorify God, and must not be influenced by any other motive than that of building His kingdom; otherwise I could not get them.

"After this third visit, he again ascended into heaven as before, and I was again left to ponder on the strangeness of what I had just experienced; when almost immediately after the heavenly messenger had ascended from me the third time, the cock crowed, and I found that day was approaching, so that our interviews must have occupied the whole of that night.

"I shortly after arose from my bed, and, as usual, went to the necessary labors of the day; but, in attempting to work as at other time, I found my strength so exhausted as to render me entirely unable. My father, who was laboring along with me, discovered something to be wrong with me, and told me to go home. I started with the intention of going to the house; but, in attempting to cross the fence out of the field where we were, my strength entirely failed me, and I fell helpless on the ground, and for a times was quite unconscious of anything.

"The first thing that I can recollect was a voice speaking unto me, calling me by my name. I looked up, and beheld the same messenger standing over my head, surrounded by light as before. He then again related unto me all that he had related to me the previous night, and commanded me to go to my father and tell him of the vision and commandments which I had received.

"I obeyed; I returned to my father in the field, and rehearsed the whole matter to him. He replied to me that it was of God, and told me to go and do as commanded by the messenger. I left the field, and went to the place where the messenger. I left the field, and went to the place where the messenger had told me the plates were deposited; and owing to the distinctness of the vision which I had concerning it, I knew the place the instant that I arrived there.

"Convenient to the village of Manchester, Ontario county, New York, stands a hill of considerable size, and the most elevated of any in the neighborhood. On the west side of this hill, not far from the top, under a stone of considerable size, lay the plates deposited in a stone box. This stone was thick and rounding in the middle on the upper side, and thinner towards the edge, so that the middle part of it was visible above the ground, but the edges, so that the middle part of it was visible above the ground, but the edge all around was covered with earth.

"Having removed the earth, I obtained a lever, which I got fixed under the edge of the stone, and with a little exertion raised it up. I looked in, and there indeed did I behold the plates, the Urim and Thummim, and the breastplate, as stated by the messenger. The box in which they lay was formed by laying stones crossways of the box, and on these stones lay the plates and the other things with them.

"I made an attempt to take them out, but was forbidden by the messenger, and was again informed that the time for bringing them fourth had not yet arrived, neither would it, until four years from that time; but he told me that I should come to that place precisely in one year from that time, and that he would be there meet with me, and that I should continue to do so until the time should come for obtaining the plates.

"Accordingly, as I had been commanded I went at the end of each year, and at each time I found the same messenger there, and received instruction and intelligence from him at each of our interviews, respecting what the Lord was going to do, and how and in what manner His kingdom was to be conducted in the last days.

"At length the time arrived for obtaining the plates, the Urim and Thummim, and the breastplate. On the twenty-second day of September, one thousand eight hundred and twenty-seven, having gone as usual at the end of another year to the place where they were deposited, the same heavenly messenger delivered them up to me with this charge: That I should be responsible for them; that if I should let them go carelessly, or through any neglect of mine, I should be cut off; but that if I would use all my endeavors to preserve them, until he, the messenger, should call for them, they should be protected.

"I soon found out the reason why I had received such strict charges to keep them safe, and why it was that the messenger had said that when I had done what was required at my hand, he would call for them. For no sooner was it known that I had them from me. Every stratagem that could be invented were resorted to for that purpose. The persecution became more bitter and severe than before, and multitudes were on the alert continually to get them from me if possible. But by the wisdom of God, they remained safe in my hands, until I had accomplished by them what was required at my hand. When, according to arrangements, the messenger called for them, I delivered them up to him; and he has them in his charge until this day, being the second day of May, one thousand eight hundred and thirty-eight."

For the complete record, see *Pearl of Great Price*, pages 81-101, and *History of the Church of Jesus Christ of Latter-day Saints*, volume 1, chapters 1 to 6 inclusive.

The ancient record, thus bought forth from the earth, as the voice of a people speaking from the dust, and translated into modern speech by the gift and power of God as attested by Divine affirmation, was first published to the world in the year 1830 as THE BOOK OF MORMON.

The Testimony of Three Witnesses

BE IT KNOWN unto all nations, kindreds, tongues, and people, unto whom this work shall come: That we, through the grace of God the Father, and our Lord Jesus Christ, have seen the plates which contain this record, which is a record of the people of Nephi, and also of the Lamanites, their brethern, and also of the people of Jared, who came from the tower of which hath been spoken. And we also know that they have been translated by the gift and power of God, and not of man. And we declare with words of soberness, that an angel of God came down from heaven, and he brought and laid before our eyes, that we beheld and saw the plates, and the engravings thereon; and we know that it is by the grace of God the Father, and our Lord Jesus Christ, that we beheld and bear record that these things are true. And it is marvelous in our eyes. Nevertheless, the voice of the Lord commanded us that we should bear record of it; wherefore, to be obedient unto the commandments of God, we bear testimony of these things. And we know that if we are faithful in Christ, we shall rid our garments of the blood of all men, and be found spotless before the judgement-seat of Christ, and shall dwell with him eternally in the heavens. And the honor be to the father, and to the Son, and the Holy Ghost, which is one God. Amen.

Oliver Cowdery
David Whitmer
Martin Harris

And Also
The Testimony of Eight Witnesses

BE IT KNOWN unto all nations, kindreds, tongues, and people, unto whom this work shall come: That Joseph Smith, Jun, the translator of this work, has shown unto us the plates of which hath been spoken, which have the appearance of gold; and as many of the leaves as the said Smith has translated we did handle with our hands; and we also saw the engravings thereon, all of which has the appearance of ancient work, and of curious workmanship. And this we bear record with words of soberness, that the said Smith has shown unto us, for we have seen and hefted, and know of a surety that he said Smith has got the plates of which we have spoken. And we give our names unto the world, to witness unto the world that which we have seen. And we lie not, God bearing witness of it.

Christian Whitmer / Hiram Paige
Jacob Whitmer / Joseph Smith, Sen.
Peter Whitmer, Jun. / Hyrum Smith
John Whitmer / Samuel H. Smith

Source:

The Book of Mormon. Salt Lake City, UT: The Church of Jesus Christ of Latter-day Saints, 1920 [first edition with double-column pages, chapter headings, chronological data, revised foot-note references, pronouncing vocabulary, and index].

Mormonism started in 1827, when its prophet, Joseph Smith Jr. received a visit from an angel. A native of Vermont, Smith was living in New York at the time. The angel Moroni told him it was his task to translate an ancient book, dating back to the fourth century when a people called the Nephites lived in the Americas. Mormon was the leader of the Nephites; Moroni, his son. After finding the gold-plated book near his Palmyra, New York home, Smith received a further visitation from the beyond—in the person of John the Baptist—who ordained him to start a religion that would restore the true church and the true gospel to the earth. Smith completed and published his translation in 1830, and Mormonism was born.

The Book of Mormon *purported to cover the period from 600* B.C. *to the fifth century* A.D. *It concerned the progress of an ancient Hebrew tribe from Jerusalem to America, where it split into two groups, the Lamanites and the Nephites. The former became American Indians, while the latter preserved their Jewish faith. Jesus appeared to the Nephites, whose prophet, Mormon, wrote his teachings upon golden plates. Ultimately, the Lamanites defeated the Nephites, and the plates remained lost until Smith found them. Critics took this as a conflation of Biblical legend and Smith's imagination. Mormons regard it as divine truth.*

*Mormonism had a rough early history in the United States. Although it attract-
ed followers, the faith, following another divine message to Smith, soon began promoting the practice of polygamy— or plural marriage of a man to multiple wives.
Smith himself is believed to have had 27. Polygamy had been illegal under English
common law, and mid-nineteenth century America reacted with repulsion, as
newspaper editors, novelists, and politicians railed until Congress passed anti-
polygamy laws aimed at the Mormons. At one point, federal lawmakers even
repealed the legal incorporation of the church and moved to seize its assets. As a
result, the church had to revert to monogamy in the 1890s.*

*This article examines the Mormon Pioneer Day celebrations from the mid-to-
late 1800s as documented in the* Desert News, *the Salt Lake City newspaper. Pioneer Day commemorated the entrance of the community in 1847 into Salt Lake
Valley, where it had fled from persecution in other states. Beginning in 1849 when
the Mormons were still a struggling pioneer community, these colorful annual
parades demonstrated and reaffirmed their convictions. By 1874, the community
was thriving, and the much larger scale of the celebration reflected this fact. The
1880 celebration marked a half-century of Mormonism. No longer a fledgling faith
scrabbling on the frontier, Mormons could point to their successes and to heroes
such as Brigham Young, a shrewd businessman and the father of 56 children who
was Utah's governor from 1850 to 1857.*

MORMON PIONEER DAY

For festive purposes the day that came to be the
annual Mormon celebration par excellence was
July 24, the official day of entry into the Salt Lake
Valley in1847. Long enough after July 4, Pioneer
Day was still in the summer and seemed to be a
time after sowing and before harvest when a day of
celebration could be afforded. The day was not celebrated in 1848 due to the harsh conditions, but in
1849 an elaborate celebration was held. Included in
the procession, for example, were:

Twelve bishops, bearing banners of their wards.

Twenty-four young ladies, dressed in white,
with white scarfs on their right shoulders, and a
wreath of white roses on their heads, each carrying
the Bible and Book of Mormon; and one bearing a
banner, "Hail to our Chieftain."

Twelve more bishops, carrying flags of their
wards.

Twenty-four silver greys [older men], each having a staff, painted red on the upper part, and a
branch of white ribbons fastened at the top, one of
them carrying the flag.

After parading to the tune of band music, the
people settled down to a round of addresses, poems,
toasts, and more speeches. It was quite an extrava-
ganza for a young, precariously established frontier
community.

Besides the annual celebration, longer inter-
vals seem to have lent themselves to commemorative purposes. On July 24, 1874, for example, a
jubilee was held celebrating the twenty-seventh
anniversary of the arrival of the Saints in the valley. The Sunday School prepared a program held in
the Tabernacle, featuring bands, a special hymn
entitled "O Lord Accept Our Jubilee," prayers, and
sermons. Participating in the "grand Sunday School
jubilee" were some eight or ten thousand children.

Celebrations were also held in the individual
settlements throughout Mormon country. In 1874,
for example, there was a celebration in Bloomington, Idaho:

At sunrise this morning silence was broken by
a volley of twenty-four guns.

The people assembled at the schoolhouse at
nine o'clock A.M., formed a procession and
marched to martial music through the principal
streets then back to the schoolhouse in the following manner—twelve fathers of Israel, twelve mothers of Israel, twelve daughters of Zion dressed in
white, and twelve sons of Zion, the citizens and
Sunday School children following in line.

A log cabin typical of those used by Mormon settlers in the mid-eighteenth century. The Mormons settled in the unchartered Utah wilderness to escape religious persecution in the East.

The services consisted of an oration by James H. Hart, George Osmond read an address in behalf of the daughters of Zion, John Walker sons of Zion, Sister Jarvis in behalf of the mothers of Israel. A number of toasts were given.

At two o'clock all were seated at table, spread with viands, including strawberries, sugar, and cream.

At four o'clock the dance opened for the small children, and in the evening for larger children and parents.

All was joy, peace, and unity. The whole was gotten up under the auspices of the Relief Society.

Even more than the usual annual celebration or that of the twenty-fifth anniversary, the fiftieth anniversary was emphasized. There was then a sense of historical distance. While a few of the original members and leaders remained, a new generation had come to the fore. Besides, the celebration of fifty years had Old Testament precedent as a time of jubilee. Such an opportunity presented itself in 1880, fifty years from the organization of the church. Coinciding with General Conference, this date was mentioned by many of the speakers, including especially church historian Franklin D. Richards, who reviewed the history of the church during the preceding decades. He mentioned Stephen A. Douglas, Sen. Thomas Hart Benton and the Mormon Battalion, the coming of Johnston's Army, and the fate of government officials.

"In all these things we recognized the hand of the Lord," he said, "and we should reflect on His providences and be stirred up to individual righteousness, and to battle against the drunkenness and whoredoms and various forms of evil now being introduced by our enemies for our overthrow." Other sermons followed the same theme, as did the great prayer of Apostle Orson Pratt.

In July 1880 the jubilee was continued in a mammoth celebration. In the parade or procession were the following:

The surviving Pioneers of 1847 in five wagons. Portrait of Brigham Young on both sides of the first wagon with the inscriptions "Gone Before Us" and "Absent But Not Forgotten." Above them was the "old pioneer banner," on which were the names of all the pioneers and a picture of Joseph Smith blowing a trumpet. Also the U.S. flag.

Surviving members of Zion's Camp.

Surviving members of the Mormon Battalion and wagon with "Women of the Mormon Battalion."

The "minute Men."

Wagon with representatives of various countries of the earth. On the side were various mottoes.

24 couples. "The ladies looked lovely in cream-colored riding habits, with white silk caps and white feathers, and the young men presented a fine appearance in black dress suits, white neckties, and white gloves."

Education, History, Geography, Science, and Art.

The parade continued with representation of different church auxiliaries, school children, and industry of Utah. The whole procession extended over three miles. During part of this 1880 celebration Wilford Woodruff told of Brigham Young's "this-is-the-place" statement that has since become a standard feature of pioneer celebrations.

Source:
Davis Bitton, "The Revitalization of Mormon History." In *Utah Historical Quarterly*, vol. 43, 1975.

NAVAJOS

During the 1970s, federal policy toward Native Americans shifted away from disastrous attempts to terminate Indian governments, the policy of the 1950s and 1960s, and toward a more constructive attitude of fostering self-determination. This movement led to the passage, in 1975, of the Indian Self-Determination and Education Assistance Act. Title VII of the Act provided for self-education of Native Americans, and it was under this provision that a group of researchers set about interviewing Navajos such as Jane Begay regarding their ancestors' memories of the "Long Walk."

The latter describes the Navajos' removal from their homeland by federal troops, who in 1863 marched them some three hundred miles southeast to Fort Sumner. The fort, on the Pecos River in the Bosque Redondo Valley, lies in an extremely dry and barren part of what is now east central New Mexico. One day the outlaw William Bonney, better known as Billy the Kid (1859?-1881), would be buried at Fort Sumner, but much earlier, it became home to a temporary population that included between six and nine thousand Navajos.

In 1850, two years after its defeat of Mexico, the federal government declared the Territory of New Mexico part of the United States. For more than a decade, this fact had little effect on the Navajos, though changes were evident: the territory had a governor, James Calhoun, along with a new military post called Fort Defiance, commanded by a Colonel Sumner.

Fort Defiance was built on Navajo lands, a signal of what was to come; but before the federal government could begin removing the Native Americans from their lands, the Civil War intervened. Suddenly most military personnel were needed back east, to fight the Confederacy. To take their place, the federal government passed the Homestead Act, which encouraged settlement, in 1862.

In March of 1862, Union troops defeated Confederate sympathizers at Glorieta Pass, a battle Alvin M. Josephy, Jr., in The Civil War in the American West, called "the Gettysburg of the West." With the rebels effectively subdued for the remainder of the war, Brigadier General James H. Carleton, who arrived in New Mexico later that year with a troop of California volunteers, could focus his attention on subduing the Indians. Around that time, the federal government established the new post of Fort Sumner, named for the Fort Defiance commander of an earlier era.

Carleton had long been friends with Christopher "Kit" Carson (1809-1868), then a colonel in command of the 1st New Mexico Volunteers. Originally Carson had disagreed with the government's strict policies toward the Indians, but over the course of a campaign that lasted nearly a year, he was vigorous in his efforts against the Native Americans.

Carson dealt first with the Apaches, placing some 400 of them in a reservation attached to Fort Sumner by the end of March, 1863. Then he turned his attention to *the Navajos, a much larger force. Carson's message to the Navajos was as ominous as it was terse: "Go to Bosque Redondo, or we will pursue and destroy you. We will not make peace with you on any terms." Having destroyed the Indians' crops, livestock, and orchards, by the spring of 1864, Carson's forces had secured their surrender.*

The movement to Bosque Redondo took nearly three months, and by the fall, there were eight or nine thousand people—the overwhelming majority of them Navajos—at Fort Sumner's Bosque Redondo Reservation. What followed were some extremely hard years: efforts at farming failed because the land was not suited to it, and the government was compelled to provide rations to the Navajos and others interned at the reservation. Approximately three thousand people died of malnutrition, exposure, and sickness during the months and years that followed.

Change did not come until 1867, two years after the conclusion of fighting in the east. In that year, newly promoted Lieutenant General William T. Sherman (1820-1891), famous for the Atlanta campaign that helped bring about the end of the war, arrived at Fort Sumner. Officials in Washington had realized that their Navajo policy had proven a disaster, costly not only in dollars but in good will—not to mention human lives. Sherman, whose mission it was to determine what should be done with the reservation, decided that it should be abandoned and the Navajos allowed to return to their own lands.

Therefore the Navajos were released from Fort Sumner on June 1, 1868. Their lands had in the meantime been much reduced, and by then consisted of only about one hundred square miles. They were ordered not to conduct raiding activities beyond their territories. In the years that followed, the Navajo Nation enjoyed a renewal as its lands and population grew once again, and its crops and livestock flourished.

JANE BEGAY'S STORY: THE LONG WALK

Jane Begay is from the Lake Valley area. She is of the Tsénahabilhii (Sleep Rock People) clan and is fifty-three years old. Her maternal grandmother told her the story of the Long Walk. Her maternal grandmother had two names; one was Tom Chischilly's Mother, and the other was Kinánibaá, her given name in Navajo. This is the story of Jane Begay's great-grandmother as told to her daughter, Jane Begay's grandmother.

My mother gave birth to several girls, but only one son. They were fleeing from the enemy when the son was born, and they had very little food. The baby was fed plant seeds, but he did not survive. He died from lack of mutton. (It was believed by the Navajos that a person can die from not eating mutton.) They never had enough mutton to eat because they were always on the move, fleeing from the enemies.

They did have a have a herd of horses, and they would butcher one once in a while. The soldiers had already taken away the sheep.

At one time, the Navajos traded with the Mexicans. The people would make about three pairs of moccasins and trade them for sheep. When opportunity came, they would also take small Mexican boys back with them to herd the sheep. There were some Navajos who lived peacefully, but soon raiding began to appeal to more people. The women would say among themselves, "I am going to the Mexicans to get some white sheep and a Mexican baby."

Later the Mexicans came and took back their sheep from the Navajos. They also took sheep that originally belonged to the Navajos, who were constantly moving around trying to avoid the enemies.

When the Mexicans raided the Navajos, they even destroyed their eating utensils, such as grinding stones. Their food was also destroyed. Flour was scattered to the wind, and corn was thrown into the fire to burn. Sometimes all the Navajos' material possessions were burned by the enemy. These events often looked like the second night of the squaw dance. The only thing the People could do was grieve for their losses. My grandmother was one of the People who material possession were burned.

The Navajos lost many of their people during that time. Many young girls were captured. Because the men were the ones who did most of the raiding, the Mexicans killed many of the boys. Sometimes they would cut a baby's throat right in the cradleboard.

One time when the People were running from their enemies and they had traveled some distance, my grandmother realized that she had forgotten her beads which she had hung on a branch near their camp. She said, "I went back on a horse because I knew I could depend upon the horse." Along the way, somebody told her that she was going into enemy territory and that she might be killed. It was either her maternal uncle or her cousin who went back with her.

When they got to the place where she had left her beads, they noticed tracks of a large herd of sheep and hoof prints of horses wearing metal horseshoes. My grandmother looked for her beads and found them still hanging on the branch. She put them around her neck and took off on the horse.

Moving to Fort Defiance

From there they kept moving toward the mountains and eventually arrived at a shelter. There a Navajo woman and man on horseback told them that the People were taking shelter at Fort Defiance. They were told that it was becoming impossible to find a safe place to hide. Many of the People had been killed. All different Indian tribes, the Pueblos, and other Indians had united and were in the warpath against the Navajos. This was the message that the People were passing to each other. The People all moved toward Fort Defiance. If they were found along the way, they were killed. The People thought of the darkness as their mother, because as soon as darkness came, they felt protected. In the daytime the People were full of fear.

Their food supply was eventually diminished so that they had to depend upon plant seeds which they prepared with grinding stones. Today you still see grinding stones at many locations, such as on hillsides. It is said that they had belonged to the Anáasází, but some of these grinders actually belonged to the Navajos. Food was cooked in clay pots over a fire. In this way, the People had at least one meal a day.

My grandmother's mother had a brother-in-law who went to Fort Defiance ahead of the other people. This group included the extended family. Anytime someone in the family left the group for some reason and returned, the family would cry and greet each other. It was a very emotional time the Navajos.

The People finally arrived at Fort Defiance under the protection of the soldiers. They received food, but they did not understand the language that was spoken. The People thought that coffee was like other beans, so they prepared it like regular beans. Some of the People died from food that was not prepared properly.

Several Navajo men became leaders during that time. One was a Navajo man named K'aa'ke'e-he (Wounded One), and another was Hastiin' Ch'il' Haajiní (Manuelito). These leaders would make speeches to the People at Fort Defiance. They also interpreted for the people who only spoke the Navajo language.

While at Fort Defiance under the protection of the soldiers, different tribes of Indians were still attacking the Navajos. It was decided that the Navajos would be sent to Fort Sumner. The journey began with a wagon train. The wagons were pulled by oxen and left deep ruts in the ground. The people would alternate riding on the wagon and walking. The journey took past Mount Taylor.

Events along the trail

Along the trail somewhere, the horse that my grandmother's mother loved most developed an iltih (lump) in the leg. My great-grandmother and great-grandfather were instructed to stay with the horse until it died. The rest of the People moved on to Fort Sumner.

While my great-grandparents were waiting for the horse to die, a Navajo family came by some children. They asked what my grandparents were going to do with the horse. They told the people that they were waiting for the animal to die.

The Navajo family had some copper bracelets, a corn pollen bag, and some other valuables that they wanted to trade for the horse. My great-grandparents took the jewelry and then killed the horse for the Navajo family.

The family began to butcher the horse. They built a fire and sang a song around the horse that said, "This is mine." Parts of the muscles of the horse were draining with matter, but they continued to butcher. The family was just beginning to cook the meat when my great-grandparents told the people, "We are going now," and they left.

My great-grandfather ran on foot a great distance while my great-grandmother rode a big mule. In this way, they traveled to catch up with the rest of the party who were on their way to Fort Sumner. They followed the deep ruts cut by the wagon train. The grass and plants had all been trampled down by the travelers. The trail looked like it had made a big curve.

My great-grandmother suggested that they follow the trail of the others, but my great-grandfather wanted to take a straighter shortcut. My great-grandfather would run ahead, and my and my great-grandmother would ride the mule and catch up with him. Along the trail they saw fresh tracks of horses with metal horseshoes and fresh manure. These tracks led in the opposite direction from which the Navajos had traveled. My great-grandparents then took a different trail. The relatives told them that they regretted having them left them with the dying horse.

Charlie Jim, who was from the Beautiful Rock area, had a father-in-law who was born at Fort Sumner just about the time the people were ready to leave. His name was Hastiin Chala Bídaghaa'. Two weaving-batten-sticks were tied together, and some wool was placed on a donkey for his mother because it gave a smooth ride. By the time they started their journey back from Fort Sumner, most

of the people had already left. His father was told that he was crazy for lingering on at Fort Sumner when everybody else had gone.

Some of the people were fortunate to still have a small flock of sheep and a few horses when they returned to their land. My great-grandmother had a few horses left that had not been taken from her on the journey.

Other memories

There was a story of the Long Walk told by my maternal grandfather's side of the family. The story was about struggling to take care of a chronically sick wife. There was also a story of a white man who went among the Navajos asking to be given a woman for his wife, but the people refused the request.

Another story was about a group of people playing with a black ball that was sewn together. Upon closer observation, it was found that the ball was made of wool. The ball was taken apart, and the wool was woven into rugs which were sold for money.

Source:

Oral History Stories of the Long Walk, by the Diné of the Eastern Region of the Navajo Reservation. Collected and recorded by the Title VII Bilingual Staff. Crownpoint, NM: Lake Valley Navajo School, 1991. pp. 17-20.

Native Americans inhabited North America long before English settlers colonized the New World. Archaeologists estimate that aboriginal groups who were later called Indians by English settlers either migrated to the Western Hemisphere through what is now the Bering Strait c.26,000 B.C. or evolved in the region. Although Native Americans had indigenous rights to the land, by the nineteenth century nearly all Native American Indian tribes were driven off their land and placed on reservations. Through the Indian Removal Act of 1830 many of the Native American Indian tribes such as the Chickasaw, Choctaw, Creek, Seminole and the Cherokee in the east were driven west. The campaign to drive the Indians west, which resulted in the death of thousands was dubbed the "Trail of Tears and Death." In 1871 the U.S. government stopped recognizing Indian territories as independent nations. The Dawes Act of 1887 broke up tribal land into individual grants and robbed American Indians of 86 million acres of land.

A series of wars between English settlers and later the U.S. government and American Indians resulted in their inevitable submission to the white man. In the early seventeenth century the Powhatan and Pequot tribes were massacred by the

English settlers. When the American colonists needed the assistance of Native Americans during the Revolutionary War, trade and land rights agreements were established. However, after the war the agreements were ignored. In 1886 the Apache chief Geronimo surrendered to U.S. military forces. The Great Plains Indians including the Apache, Sioux, and Cheyenne won a significant victory at the battle of Little Bighorn, but were eventually defeated. The defeat of the Plains Indians was symbolized by the surrender of Crazy Horse in 1877 who was the inspiration behind the defeat of General Custer's forces at Little Bighorn. Of the treatment of Native Americans by the U.S. government throughout history Moquin and Van Doren contend that "it can be asserted without qualification that no other ethnic group has been so consistently treated with such malevolence over so long a period of time."

Of the remaining tribal groups in existence today the Navajo are the largest. The Navajo migrated from the North and settled in Arizona and New Mexico around 1000 A.D. the Navajo are known for their agricultural development, weaving, and sand painting which they learned from the Pueblos. The Navajo are also pastoralists, or sheep herders, which they learned from the Spanish in the 1600s. The tribe fought diligently against the Spanish and American settlers in the nineteenth century to protect their land rights, however were finally defeated by Kit Carson at Fort Sumner in 1864. The tribe was subsequently relocated to a reservation in 1868. A Navajo chief named Manuelito recorded some of his experiences with the white man which undoubtedly captured the sentiments of Native Americans toward whites. Manuelito said, "[t]he American Nation is too powerful for us to fight." However, in the end, Manuelito was grateful that the white man helped the Navajo relocate to their homeland in Arizona and western New Mexico. Having land of their own was essentially all the American Indians wanted from the white man. The injustices suffered by Native Americans, who had indigenous rights to North American land, is undoubtedly one of the most regrettable chapters in American history.

THE AMERICAN NATION IS TOO POWERFUL FOR US TO FIGHT

Manuelito is the head chief of the east side of the reservation, and Ganada-Mucho is head chief of the western side. You have already heard some of the history of the tribe. When our fathers lived they heard that the Americans were coming across the great river westward. Now we are settling among the powerful people. We heard of the guns and powder and lead—first flint locks, then percussion caps, and now repeating rifles. We first saw the Americans at Cottonwood Wash. We had wars with the Mexicans and Pueblos. We captured mules from the Mexicans, and had many mules. The Americans came to trade with us. When the Americans first came we had a big dance, and they danced with our women. We also traded. The Americans went back to Santa Fe, which the Mexi-cans then held. Afterwards we heard that the Mexicans had reached Santa Fe, and that the Mexicans had disarmed them and made them prisoners. This is how the Mexican war began. Had the Mexicans let the Americans alone they would not have been defeated by the Americans. Then there were many soldiers at Santa Fe, and the Mexican governor was driven away. They did not kill the governor. Therefore we like the Americans. The Americans fight fair, and we like them. Then the soldiers built the fort here, and gave us an agent who advised us to behave well. He told us to live peaceably with the whites; to keep our promises. They wrote down promises, and so always remember them. From that on we had sheep and horses. We had lots of horses, and felt good; we had a fight with the Americans, and were whipped. At that time we thought we hade a big country, extending over a great deal of land. We fought for that country because we did not want to lose it, but we made a mistake. We lost nearly everything, but we had some beads left, and with them we thought we were rich. I have always advised the young men to avoid war. I am ashamed for having gone to war. The American nation is too powerful for us to fight. When we had a fight for a few days we felt fresh, but in a short time we were worn out, and the soldiers starved us out. Then the Americans gave us something to eat, and we came in from the mountains and went to Texas. We were there for a few years; many of our people died from the climate. Then we became good friends with the white people. The Comanches wanted us to fight, but we would not join them. One day the soldiers went after the Comanches. I and the soldiers charged on the Comanches, but the Comanches drove us back, and I was left alone to fight them; so the white men came in twelve days to talk with us, as our people were dying off. People from Washington held a council with us. He explained how the whites punished those who disobeyed the law. We promised to obey the laws if we were permitted to get back to our own country. We promised to keep the treaty you read to us to-day. We promised to obey four times to do so. We all said "yes" to the treaty, and he gave us good advice. He was General Sherman. We told him we would try to remember what he said. He said: "I want all you people to look at me." He stood up for us to see him. He said if we would do right we could look people in the face. Then he said: "My children, I will send you back to your homes." The nights and days were long before it came time for us to go to our homes. The day before we were to start we went a little way towards home, because we were so anxious to start. We came back and the Americans gave us a little stock to start with and we thanked them for that. We told the drivers to whip the mules, we were in such a hurry. When we saw the top of the mountain from Albuquerque we wondered if it was our mountain, and we felt like talking to the ground, we loved it so, and some of the old men and women cried with joy when they reached their homes. The agent told us here how large our reservation was to be. A small piece of land was surveyed off to us, but we think we ought to have had more. Then we began to talk about more land, and we went to Washington to see about our land. Some backed out of going for fear of strange animals and from bad water, but I thought I might as well die there as here. I thought I could do something at Washington about the land. I had a short talk with the Commissioner. We were to talk with him the next day, but the agent brought us back without giving us a chance to say what we wanted. I saw a man whom I called my younger brother; he was short and fat; and we came back on foot. So Ganada-Mucho thought he would go on to Washington and fix things up, and he got sick and couldn't stand it, and came back without seeing the Commissioner. I tell these things in order that you might know what troubles we have had, and how little satisfaction we got. Therefore we have told you that the reservation was not large enough for our sheep and horses; what the others have told you is true. It is true about the snow on the mountains in the center of the reservation. It is nice there in the summer, but we have to move away in the winter. But we like to be at the mountains in the summer because there is good water and grass there, but in the winter we always move our camps. We like the southern part of the country because the land is richer. We can have farms there. We want the reservation to be extended below the railroad on the south, and also in an easterly direction.

We all appreciate the goods issued to us by the Government. At first we did not understand, now we know how to use plows and scrapers. We have good use for these things and wagons. We can then make new farms and raise crops. We are thankful for what the Government sends. We give nothing back to the whites. When we make blankets our women sell them. They look well in white men's rooms on the beds or walls. If I had a good house I would keep the blankets myself. When my man comes from the East we tell him our troubles. There are some bad men, both whites and Indians, whom we cannot keep from doing mischief. The whites control them by laws, and we talk ours into being good. I am glad the young men have freed their minds; now we old men have our say.

Source:
House Executive Document No. 263, 49th Congress, 1st Session, pp. 14-15.

*T*he Navajo is the largest of all Indian tribes in the United States, numbering about 170,000. Though dating their arrival is difficult, anthropologists place the Navajo in the southwest between 900 and 1200 A.D., when they migrated from the Athabascan tribes in Canada. The Navajo were influenced by other southwestern tribes, specifically the Pueblos. The Pueblos were refugees of Spanish oppression in the seventeenth century. In the eighteenth century, Hopi refugees came to Navajo land, settling primarily in Canyon de Chelly, in northeastern Arizona. These contacts influenced Navajo artistic traditions, such as pottery making and weaving, and also affected Navajo agriculture. In the nineteenth century, the Navajo were influenced by Mexican immigrants, who taught them silversmithing.

Deescheeny Nez Tracy is a Navajo and retired stone mason who lives on the Navajo Reservation, a tract of land more than 24,000 square miles, spanning the four corners area and including parts of Utah, Arizona, and New Mexico. In this oral history interview, Tracy talks about the traditional Navajo way of life that revolved primarily around farming and herding sheep and cattle. Traditional Navajo culture centered around the family and the clan, and the author gives a brief description of clan relationships. Clan relationships determined how people were related to one another and governed rules of conduct between people and groups.

The author discusses the attempted destruction of the Navajo nation in 1863, when Colonel Kit Carson was ordered by the government to subdue the Navajo. Carson destroyed the Navajo's crops and herds and in 1864, forced some 8,000 captured Navajo to make what is known as "the Long Walk" to Bosque Redondo, an arid patch of 21 acres of land 180 miles south of Santa Fe. Manuelito, a Navajo chief, strongly opposed the forced relocation and led a group of 4,000 Navajo in a two year guerrilla war against Carson. In 1866, starvation forced him to surrender and he and his people were taken to Bosque Redondo. In 1868, however, he was given permission to travel to Washington D.C. to argue for the return of the Navajo homeland to the Navajo people. He was successful, and the Navajo returned that same year. Four years later, the Navajo Reservation was established.

The author, who says he was born in 1900, states that he has seen tremendous change in the way of life on the reservation. Once prosperous farmers and shepherds, the Navajo have seen an increase in unemployment as land for farming and grazing became scarce. Thousands of Navajo have left the reservation to work as transient workers, or have moved to cities such as Los Angeles or Kansas City, to seek employment. Unemployment on the reservation has been the driving force behind increases in social problems like alcoholism and crime. To promote understanding of the Navajo, the author promotes balance in Navajo education, stressing both an education in traditional tribal ways and in contemporary matters. He says that people need to be aware of what if happening and in order to do that, the Navajo must work to preserve their traditional beliefs and ways of life into the future.

DEESCHEENY NEZ TRACY

MY CLAN IS A LARGE ONE whose members live here and there from west of Tuba City, Arizona, across hundreds of miles to the eastern part of the Reservation in New Mexico. It is the Start of the Red Streak People (*Deeshchii'nii*).

When the four original clans began to migrate they separated into new clans. The first grandmother from whom I am descended was the Black Streak Wood People (*Tsi'naajinii*). Those people lived at the foot of Blanca Peak (*Sis Naajiní*) at a place called Dark Rain Rays Descend.

In a legend two girl children were taken from a family, one of them to a place called Slumber Rock; and she became the beginning of the clan of Sleep Rock People (*Tsénhabiłnii*). The other maiden came to a place called Red Cliff Gorge. She became the first Start of the Red Streak People. Thus, people just stopped at locations where they chose to make their settlements, and clans were named according to the description of the location. The three clans were group related. Many Navajos who belong to these clans do not know the relationships, especially the young people. They have little knowledge of clan ties. In fact, some do not know what a clan really is.

In hot weather one should run up a high hill without stopping. He cannot find wealth at the foot of the hill or halfway up. Success is waiting for him at the top.

Later, a young girl came to Red Bottom Rock, and she became the first of the Red Bottom People (*Tłááshchí'i*). This added another related clan, making four. Their adopted clan is the Red House People (*Kinłichí' nii*), who really came from the Pueblo Indians. They migrated into the Red Streak People who adopted them. The Many Goats People (*Tł'ízí łání*) also make a related clan. All are scattered to various points of the Reservation now. All of them are one group that are related from the Black Streak Wood People clan. These clans should have respect for one another. They should not intermarry, but, today, such group relationships are not rightfully observed and followed. It may be because the Navajo Nation now is very much over-populated. However, we who are in our elderly age still respect our relationships. The tribal census count now shows that there are 150,000 or more Navajos.

I was born FOR the Bitter Water Clan (*Tódích'íí'nii*), on my father's side. It is one of the original clans, known as Children of Changing Woman.

My mother's name was Start of Red Streak Woman, and she died of old age. She was born for Near the Water People (*Tó'áhaní*). It also is an original clan which Changing woman created long ago.

My visitor (interviewer) says he is of the Towering House clan (*Kinyaa' áa nii*). It is slightly related to me; so I greeted the man as my paternal grandson. Before we met today we did not know one another. By introduction we recognized our clans and realized we are related. [The interviewer was Hoke Denetsosie, who wrote a chapter in this book and was one of its artists—EDITOR'S NOTE.]

We elders want the young people to learn to respect their clans, as we did years ago. We think it is important, and we do not want it to be forgotten. Today, projects and programs are working on the problem in order to help the young people find themselves. At Navajo Community College I have spoken to the students on clan relationships several times. I did not go into great detail. It always was in a class where the students were Navajos, other Indians and Anglos. That made it complicated, and I know that some did not understand what I was saying or my real meanings. I spoke in Navajo. I could tell that those were not really interested.

I have made many public speeches, but I still have a difficult time organizing a talk to make it interesting and understandable. Speaking before an audience of different tribes and Anglos is hard because of saying a few words at a time and then waiting until they are translated. A person may forget what he has just said and repeat himself, which bores his listeners. Probably recording this way is better because then only Navajos can listen to the tape, and they will understand what it is all about. Anglos and others will read my account after it is translated and printed.

I was born at Ganado, Arizona, where the local chapter house stands now. There were landmarks from the remains of our shade shack posts until the chapter house was built there recently. I have seen those posts, and I know I was born there in 1900 in the middle of July, during the full moon.

I am not a medicine man, and I have little knowledge of the rituals. My family was poor and my mother had to support us. She wove rugs and sold them in order to buy what we needed. Now, in some schools girls are learning the art of weaving. They work with wool, and the trade is one of the sources of income that our people depend upon. During shearing time the women select the best wool to work with. It is processed by carding, spinning it to the right size for the loom, dyeing and then weaving. The spun wool is made various colors. Vegetable dyes are used a lot by many women because buyers prefer such rugs. They gather the plants, roots and barks that are needed for dyeing. When we see various types of real Navajo rugs in stores or at the Arts and Crafts Guild we admire them. They are made beautifully. Some designs are so attractive that it is hard to believe they were done by hand. Truly, they are a result of traditional education, the young ladies learning the art at home.

Another art is silversmithing. The first workers made copper and brass conchos and buttons. After silver was introduced they began to make numerous other things. Today there are many silversmiths, making squash blossom necklaces, rings, bracelets and other beautiful jewelry with turquoise and other valued stones. Some are made with gold. Young people are learning to be silversmiths because it is a good money-making art. The white man is credited with bringing the tools and other equipment used in modern silversmithing. Tools of long ago are no loner in use today. We are aware of the white man's knowledge, inventions and discoveries, and that is what makes our world progress. Science is a wonderful thing.

It has been more than a hundred years since our Navajo fore-fathers were released from their confinement at Fort Sumner. They made a compromise with the white men; and one promise, before getting freedom, was to allow the children to attend school. So, today, most of the schools on the Reservation are full to capacity. I grew as a boy during times of hardship. There was very little food or clothing. The few trading posts that existed were not equipped with much merchandise or food like today. Young people now are fortunate to have their parents buy for them what they need. My family had only a few head of sheep when I was a child.

I was told that my mother and grandmother were alone when I was born at the break of dawn. My mother had a hard time delivering me, and she later said that I almost killed her. I also was told that I took my first step when I was 12 months old, which is about the right time for a child to begin walking.

I shall tell you briefly a story pertaining to Navajo history-mythology. The legend is carried on by our elders and medicine men.

Long ago, Changing Woman (also known as White Shell Woman) bore two boys—twins—on the summit of Gobernador Knob (Ch'óol'í'í). It took place during the monster era. The man-eating creatures were a great menace to the People. (Ruins of ancient people are all over the Reservation and other places close by.) The Holy People gathered in a council discussing what should be done to get rid of the monsters. That was why Changing woman was born—so that she would bring forth two great warriors who could destroy the monsters. She reared her sons in a little hogan in an underground dugout, concealed by a huge flat rock, in order to keep them safe. That is why we have dugouts cellars to preserve our perishable belongings and harvested crops. Changing Woman was pregnant nine months before the twins were born. Thus, when the surface people came into existence it was said the women should be pregnant nine months before babies would be born. She kept her baby boys underground in the hogan; and, on the twelfth day, their mother came to feed them, they were walking. Today it is 12 months before a child begins to walk, but the figure "12" still is true.

The twins grew up strong and healthy. They were the children of the Sun. Stories say that he was the father. Later, the twins took a long journey to their father's home on the western ocean. They went on the journey for a special purpose—to get weapons to save the people. They did destroy the evil monsters, and the people began to grow in numbers and to live at peace again.

I have said that I am not a medicine man, but I feel that I am a competent consultant. We have a saying that as long as one has hands to work with, a mind to think with, eyes to see with, ears to hear with and legs to stand on, he has his life to live—as long the Great Spirit allows. And, if one is a capable person, he can think back to the past and forward to the future. That is how life goes on.

Talking about rug-making again, it really is hard work. A woman can spend many days, or weeks—even months—weaving a rug. It is a very tiresome job; but, when it finally is completed, she and her family rejoice because they will have money to buy some of the things they want.

Grinding corn also used to be a hard job for the women, and it still is when they do it. The corn flour is used to prepare many types of corn bread, gruels, mush or puddings. The women long ago knew how to prepare such native foods. Candy and other delicacies were unheard of. Very seldom did sugar, coffee and commercial flour appear on trading post shelves.

Native foods are very nutritious and give plenty of energy for long periods of time. Eating lots of such food keeps a person's teeth clean and makes them last longer. Children in times past had few cavities and seldom had to have teeth pulled.

The people planted corn, squash and beans. Fruit trees, melons and other vegetables were introduced by Anglos or by other Indian tribes.

When I was six years old I began to understand my surroundings. I remember that we ate a lot of corn, prepared in various ways. I was eight years old when I was told I had to prepare myself for manhood. I had to rise very early in the mornings. I was not allowed to sleep past sunrise. In the winter, when it snowed, I was forced to take snow baths. Also, all year long I ran a long distance very early each morning if I did not have to fetch the horses. My mother was very strict, and she lectured to me far into the nights about good living. In the winter, when the snow was knee deep, my mother would build a good fire in the hogan. Then, at dawn, she chased me outside into the deep snow without my clothes. If I hesitated, she threw me into the snow and then warmed me by the fire. She did it because she loved me and wanted me to become a "man." It was done so that my body could endure the cold weather and make me strong and healthy. There was no such thing as catching a cold. The wise man would say, "If you come face to face with an obstacle you can overcome it easily. You develop quick and strong legs, strong lungs, strong resistance and a strong voice. By doing that you are prepared for cold or hot weather, hunger or thirst, even sickness." That is why my mother taught me how to be ready for these emergencies. Yelling as loud as a person can while running either in cold or hot weather makes the voice strong, also the lungs and legs.

Twisting the body while running develops strong muscles and limbers them up. Exercising by wrestling with a tree stump will make your arms strong and develop muscles generally. Then, when one is healthy and strong he or she is almost immune to sickness and will reach an old age. If one is lazy and sleeps late, he or she will be weak and shiftless; sickness and poverty will be at the door.

That person may spend a lot of money on healing ceremonies to keep going because he or she never developed the body; and the mind will be weak. There will be problems all the time. All of this teaching was part of my traditional education, and I remember it well. For example, after my mother had thrown me into the snow a few times I realized I had to do it; so I jumped right in.

I remember breaking ice eight inches thick in the pond which was almost a mile from home. At dawn I raced to the pond. Then, when I had broken a hole large enough for me, I took a plunge into the icy water—naked. I ran home with my body covered with frost and my hair hanging down in icicles. I had to take either a snow bath or an ice water plunge.

My mother once said, "When you take a plunge into the water there are many good things beneath the ice, and you must jump in to get them. When you do, you will be covered with those things, and you will bring them home as gifts you have earned. Wealth and health are shut in under the ice; so it is up to the individual to get them. The ones who have ambition and energy are those who are capable of getting the good things. The ones who are lazy and won't help themselves never will have a chance to sit on a good fat horse or own fat sheep."

These are words of wisdom to the young people from the old-time elders. Racing at early dawn also holds good fortune for a person. One who rises early and races will be gifted and blessed, even if he or she comes from a poor family. Success eventually will come to the individual who earns it. A person with a good sound mind is dependable. A man who is a failure has many problems, especially after he gets married and begins having children. He will possess little with which he can keep his family. His children will be hungry, and he may have to depend on his relatives to feed them. The welfare of his children is the number one priority a man must prepare himself for, if he is to be ready to support a family.

In hot weather one should run up a high hill without stopping. He cannot find wealth at the foot of the hill or halfway up. Success is waiting for him at the top. All traditional education refers to good horses and fat sheep, and they are at the top of the hill. It takes a lot of sweat and thirst, but it is very rewarding. I did all that my mother taught me. At first I thought there were no horses waiting on the hill-top or riches under the ice, but I understood what she meant after I began to have my own livestock. I treasure what I have worked so hard for all my life. My mother was right; and she raised me herself. My father was not with us.

In the year 1918, soon after the first World War, the great influenza epidemic hit our country. Many Navajos died from the horrible sickness because we did not have hospitals or medicines. It was the same year that the Ganado Lake dam went under construction, and I first began working. John (Don) Lorenzo Hubbell and his two sons had their trading post at Ganado. It now is a National historical site. Ganado Lake is a Navajo recreation area. The Hubbells were great friends to the Navajo people. They helped many of them. Old Don Lorenzo was half Spanish through his mother, and the

Navajos called him Old Mexican (*Naakaii Sani*). He had opened the trading post back about 1878. He had married a Spanish woman, and they had four children—two boys and two girls. One boy was Ramon; the other Lorenzo, Jr. the girls were Barbara and Adele. The family owned a number of trading posts. The old man died about 1930.

Ramon made the suggestion for the lake project, and he took a delegation to Washington to get approval. His interest and promotion paid off. The bureau of Reclamation approved the idea. The Hubbells provided the mule teams that were used to pull the dirt scoops. Ramon hired me to work with the teams and as a caretaker for the mules. He was like a father to me. He taught me how to manage the animals. He was Spanish-American and I a Navajo, but he treated me like his own son, and I loved him for it.

I worked on the dam construction all summer and part of that fall. In October the flu epidemic hit the construction crew; so work was shut down. We had been paid $1.25 a day. It was my first earned money; and I had no complaints, although we worked very hard—sometimes for 10 hours a day.

I supported my mother because she had worked hard to bring me up. I thought I should repay my debts to her. I was glad that she had made me a strong and healthy man with the early exercises she had forced on me. She also had taught me how to farm, to work hard at it and not let the weeds get out of control in the cornfields.

A farm is very special and cannot be neglected because it provides food. Five things that are very valuable and require a lot of attention are the corn, horses, cattle, sheep and goats. For many generations they were our sources of survival.

At an early age Navajo children used to be taught to care for those things. The girls also had their lessons, working with wool and learning to cook traditional foods. They, too, exercised by racing and by grinding corn to develop strong arms and backs. Nowadays, many young people fail to listen to their parents. As I have mentioned, I did listen, and you see me at the age of 76—still strong and healthy. My life has been filled with good things. My horses and cattle are fat and beautiful, and my sheep are well taken care of. Not one horse has a sore back or is over-ridden. Navajos still judge by the appearance of farm and livestock.

Back in the 1930s everything changed suddenly when livestock reduction was forced upon the Navajos. They blamed John Collier, the Indian Commissioner, when they lost their stock. Many thousands of sheep, goats and horses were taken away or were destroyed before their eyes.

We are grateful to our leaders of more than 100 years ago who signed the Treaty of 1868 that promised education for our children. Education is wonderful. Among other things, Navajos learned to improve their living conditions and now can maintain nice clean houses. Many have modern facilities, like electricity and gas to cook and to heat their homes, as well as running hot and cold water and bathrooms. These all make life easier. Many of us don't have to haul or chop firewood now, or haul drinking water. I moved into my new house a little over two years ago, and all I do is press a button or turn a knob, and I get all the conveniences of a nice comfortable home. At first, it seemed strange and uncomfortable to me, but I got accustomed to it. It took a while before I realized that it was not a dream. I am uneducated, but my children all have their educations, and they taught me all that I needed to know about the home.

When I was a child my mother said she needed me at home; and she refused to let me attend school. So, I had no knowledge in the English language until my children taught me a few words.

Navajos should honor and respect all who are related. It will help in living a long life, with prosperity.

When I speak to people at meetings or talk to students, I traditionally greet my audience with "My friends," "My grandchildren," "My children" or whatever relates to brotherhood. Being friendly and respectful to everyone can prolong a person's life, while jealousy and hate are evil and lead only to loneliness, ill health and tragedy. We must learn to avoid unpleasantness as much as possible. As parents we want to have happy homes so that our children can enjoy life and live comfortably.

Regarding religion, I regret to say that many Navajo people now are careless about their beliefs; and some ceremonies are forgotten or have become extinct because nobody has relearned the chants. Now, we want to keep all that are left.

Today, many of our people have chosen the Anglo religions and have turned against their own. Many churches are on the Reservation now, and the missionaries have converted numerous Navajos to Christian beliefs. The churches are well organized, and each has its own president or head man, which make for strong organization. We do not have such an organization like this in our religion to keep us together. That is one reason it gradually is fading away. We see some of our most sacred ceremonies used as social gatherings. Some people have little respect for our sacred religion, but others still have faith and depend on our healing ceremonies when they are in need.

Large tents are set up for revival camp meetings, and many of our people fill them. This helps to make them turn away from the Navajo religion; even some of our medicine men cast their healing paraphernalia aside to join the Christians, and most young people have little interest in the long and tedious task of learning ceremonies. They do not ask questions or inquire about the legends pertaining to the ceremonies.

As I said before, we must learn our clan relationships. Our young people we do not know who they are because no one has told them. When you ask, "What clan are you?" they often reply, "I don't know." Some who do know are reluctant to tell because they are afraid that boyfriends or girlfriends may be related to them. That is one reason persons should ask before they begin going together or getting married. Until not long ago, our people lived up to the rule of clan relatives not marrying, even though there possibly was no real blood relationship. The elders strongly lectured to the young people about their relatives. They forbade their children to intermarry. Navajos should honor and respect all who are related. It will help in living a long life, with prosperity. That is a part of traditional education.

Anglo education is important, too, of course. Our children go to school to learn that culture and the English language. They return home during the summers, and some of the girls practice what they learned in being good housekeepers and good cooks. The boys try to find employment to keep themselves busy. They teach their parents at home about improvements in living conditions, and that is what I mean by education being important. My main regret is that I never had a chance to be educated.

The white man is very generous. He shares his knowledge by teaching our children what they need to know. A big problem is that our children are taught the Anglo culture, and, then, when they return home, some are uncomfortable. They do not want too live in primitive dwelling places. They are unhappy; and some leave their homes or do not want to go there after school is out. They are accustomed to soft beds, clean clothes, plenty of water, electricity, etc.

As I have said, I am not educated, except in the traditional way, but I respect education, especially in the Navajo way; and I have some knowledge of our history and mythology. I have faith in our culture. Learning to be a good medicine man,

whom the people can rely on, takes at least four or five years (perhaps 10 or 12) of studying and listening. It is something like going to a university; and the time put into the training is tiresome. The lessons mostly are given at night, with the instructor constantly at hand. Prolonged sitting without sleep is strenuous. To become a Christian takes only a short time—a few lessons and prayers, and you are converted. To be a priest or preacher requires a lot of study. Prayers in our ceremonies are very long; and some are said four times, eight times, even 12 times. Twenty-four is the limit; so you see what I mean by "long." Some say they can be repeated up to 40 times.

The prayers were granted to the Navajos by the Holy People long ago. I don't know if any medicine men still carry their prayers to that extent. I heard that one from the Black Mountain area still does. Long, long ago there were songs about sheep being created. They were called the sheep songs. Also, horses had their songs. Those songs told that they were all made from vegetation in places that were to provide their food and their medicine. Sadly, this mostly is forgotten now. Only a few still are known and used. Many of the sacred songs that were known to produce rain clouds are either forgotten or the people have become careless with them. They have little respect for them now. That is why much of our land is barren. There is no moisture for the vegetation to grow. Long ago the medicine men performed rain rituals requesting rain, and they had knowledge in the Rain Way. They used special offerings of pollen and placement of the variegated sacred stones. They had much faith in the ritual, and it actually brought dark clouds and rain. That great gift was granted to the people by the Holy Divinities. In churches, the ministers or priests pray for goodness for the people. I often have asked them why they do not pray for rain, and I get the reply, "We try to," Why is it we have little rain?

There is another religion which some people adopted not long ago. It is the peyote ritual. I don't know whether they pray for rain. I have no part in this cult and not much with other churches. My belief remains with the Navajo religion. I do not make comparisons to other churches, saying which is the best. I just stick to my own native beliefs. I believe in freedom of religion, though. Everyone can be what he wants. As for me, I have successfully lived my 76 years in good health. So far, I haven't had a single ceremony performed in my behalf, thanks to my mother for bringing me up as she did.

Long ago the people had rituals for "good health and long life." There were songs and prayers, also herb medicines. Much of that knowledge, too, is forgotten and lost. It was so important that I don't know why the people didn't keep it. And that is why we must preserve all that we have left today. Gathering all of the information that is vital and keeping it on records or tapes, or printing it in books, can be our Bible, like the white man has. We must continue using our healing ceremonies. Medicine men must be trained to make it possible. We need their services for our sick people. Many have requested that I tell the ceremonial legends, but I am telling the truth when I say that I have no great knowledge of them.

After the people were taken in exile to Fort Sumner (Bosque Redondo or *Hwééldi*) the most noted medicine men were asked to perform special ceremonies so the people could gain their freedom and return to their homeland safely. That was done according to what the Holy People had instructed at the beginning of our history. There may be some medicine men left who have knowledge of the ceremonies which brought our people back to begin new lives for themselves. As we all know, the Navajos have increased tremendously from the handful who survived the hardships and sufferings, or who had escaped being rounded up on the Reservation, from maybe 12,000 to about 150,000.

All was going well, and the people had increased their livestock very rapidly, when along came John Collier and stomped his big foot on our sheep, goats and horses—and crushed them before our eyes. We believe that is when the rain went with the sheep. If it hadn't happened we would have rain and green ranges with sheep grazing all over. Now we have only small units to our permits, and the sandstorms erase a herd's hoof prints in seconds. When there once stood large sheepfolds, now there are little ones, or nothing. Dust blows in those places. That is how it is at Ganado. We try to fill our permits, but many folds are left empty. The people are partly at fault by some of them ceasing in care for sheep. They have forgotten the songs and prayers which produce more livestock. Many are hungry for mutton, but they buy their meat supplies from the grocery stores when they can afford to do so. Those who are fortunate still have mutton on their tables. In our area there once grew abundant vegetation for grazing, but it is gone and only harmful weeds grow heavily, which kill our sheep when they eat too many of them. There are the locoweeds (*Ch'il'aghání*) and owl's foot. They have yellow flowers and look pretty, but they don't smell good. They can be poisonous to livestock. They are enemies, like the evil monsters of long ago. These plants can survive without much moisture because they are evil plants and grow abundantly on the ranges. Good grazing areas are hard to find, and the people

lose many sheep because of bad plants. I know because I herded sheep until just recently. I began to get tired; so my children forbade me to herd. I was a good farmer, too. I worked on three farms, and they produced abundant crops. Now there is hardly any rain, and I'm tired. I do not do heavy work anymore. My farms are idle. Sand dunes are all one sees there now. Years back, when we had more rain, the people depended on their farms. Today, many are lazy, and few plant corn or squash. Some lucky people have irrigated farms and use them.

Without so much farming, unemployment is high on the Reservation. Many of the yong people cannot find jobs, and the No. 1 problem is drinking. Many who are unemployed turn to drink because they have nothing else to do. Some who are working spend much of their earnings for liquor, and they end up in jail. Some lose their jobs. On paydays we see t hem swarm into surrounding towns like Gallup, Holbrook, Winslow, Flagstaff and Farmington to get drunk, and some don't return.

The Great Spirit gave us a limited time to live, and we should not take our lives for granted or spoil them.

A majority of our people do not know how to save their money. As soon as they are paid they spend every cent and find themselves penniless the next day. When one of them wants to buy a car he goes to a second-hand car lot, probably off the Reservation. He purchases an automobile which he thinks looks neat, but he fails to check the real condition of the car. He is proud and happy about it, and he drives away, anxious to show off; but, before he gets back home, the car stalls on a hill, and he walks the rest of the way. There are many crooked car dealers who cheat the Indians because they know that many are ignorant and not aware of what makes a good buy. They only want the money. A car is wonderful to have, and it gets a person where he wants to go faster, but he must realize the expense, and he must KNOW the dealer.

I understand a little about the white men. From their beginning they were gifted with wisdom—knowledge, inventions and great discoveries. They have scientific minds and have done wonders in this world in the fields of medicine, science, manufacturing, commerce and all others, including machinery devices. They even got to the moon. Who knows where else they will go!

It was predicted long ago that the Holy People would be angered if in any way we tried to bother the moon or the sun. At the beginning the moon and the sun were lifted upward by the Wind People and placed in their respective locations, where they are now. Maybe the Wind People are angry, because we have more windstorms and hurricanes on the earth. Is it the wrath of the Wind People because the white men tromped on the moon? The world is changing. It seems like conditions are worse today. Even here on the Reservation our tribal government has it controversies. More problems develop, and our children are right in the midst of it all. Things may get better, however, if we all have faith in the Great Spirit and ask him to guide us back into the road of the pollen. If we turn against out religion and mock our ceremonies, using the ceremonial sites for social affairs, then someday we will suffer the consequences. More and more people will weaken and go crazy. The use of drugs and bad smoking and drinking habits will produce even more addicts and alcoholics, most of whom will end in disaster. As I see it, people have no willpower. They weaken at the sight of a bottle of wine. They gulp it all down in a few swallows, to the last drop. Most do not know how to drink socially. Those who have money to spend run to the nearest liquor establishment, not thinking first of family needs. Later, when they find themselves in jail, they remember their families and ask help to get out. Their money is gone, and they are hungry. I have seen many who have gone to workshops or to rehabilitation centers fall back upon drinking again.

As I record this story of my life and thoughts about Navajo history and traditional culture I think of how people these days have telephones, telegrams, television and radio systems to communicate to the far ends of the world. And I believe that in some way radios, tape recorders, etc. have corrupted many minds. Our young people spend their money on those things to occupy more of their time at home. They do not listen to their parents or other elders, and they do not care to work. From the silly music they compose their own songs which they sing and giggle about at the squaw dances and other ceremonial affairs. They have lost respect for, and faith in, our sacred ceremonies. The squaw dance is a healing ceremony, NOT a Navajo social dance, as some call it, where people drink and make up stupid songs to amuse themselves with. It is ridiculous and shameful, but it is how many of our sacred healing ceremonies go today. The young people see all of those bad things on television, and learn and copy all they see—drinking parties, sex, prostitutes, addicts and narcotics rings, murder and all kinds of violence. They are enemies to the human body. I do not drink or smoke or do evil, and that is why I am very critical. I never wasted my money on such things. I take care of myself, and that is the reason I have lived so long without a single "sing" (healing ceremony)

done for me. A person who comes in contact with a lot of sick people with contagious ailments will pick up the germs and become sick later. The same idea applies to coming in contact with the evils of television and today's life.

I seldom go anywhere now. I stay close to my home, unless it is necessary to go out. I am using myself and my good health as an example because I hope some people may realize how precious a human life is. The Great Spirit gave us a limited time to live, and we should not take our lives for granted or spoil them. Until fairly recent years our cornfields were our life-givers. Corn was the main source of food. In fact, the farm was where most of our food came from—food that made us strong and healthy. But today we have all kinds of useless foods; some are just imitations; many are harmful sweets and candies, pastries, sodas, and so on. That is where people get different kinds of ailments—toothaches, stomach aches, colds, blood disease, high blood preasure, heart attacks and more. In the homes the refrigerators are full of pop and Kool-Aid. Our children sit in front of the TV and consume gallons of pop into all hours of the nights. When morning comes they want to sleep until noon. That is life to them. We seldom hear about a person running at dawn yelling at the top of his voice, or the screams that come from taking an ice-cold plunge or rolling in the snow. We hear only the screaming of the radios and stereo players. Who is to blame? The white man made the inventions.

Another problem I want to mention is that the young do not speak their native tongue as they used to do. I have a bunch of grandchildren, both boys and girls, who do not know how to speak Navajo. It is hard for me to communicate with them because I do not understand them, and they do not understand me. All they yell is "Grandpa," and I say "What." They laugh and shake their heads when I speak to them. Parents should speak to their children in Navajo while they still are very young. We must not let our native tongue or our culture become extinct, and practice in speaking Navajo will help keep them.

People should be aware of what is happening today. Money earned is worth less than the cost of living, and that cost keeps right on rising. What about the future? The Navajos may have to go back to their native foods to survive. The Navajos may have to go back to their native foods to survive. That would mean working our farms again and gathering native foods, like seeds, berries and roots. It is difficult to raise crops now, with the lack of moisture. Also, the price of wool is low, and the trading posts do not buy mutton from us anymore.

All the meat the consumers buy comes from the packing companies. We do not know how old the meat is because it is kept frozen. Meat and other things we buy may be three or four months old, maybe much older, and that may be the cause of the children having upset stomachs. The outpatient clinics are packed full all the time in the hospitals and elsewhere. There is more sickness and misery among the people today. Many women are plump and short, and the men are pot-bellied and short, too.

Years ago, the men were slim, tall, brawny and healthy. There were hardly any fat men or women because they kept themselves busy all the time. Modern conveniences give more leisure time today, and the people have become lazy.

Now, for my final part of this recording, I want to tell about my main job—my work experience. Just how I learned to be good at my trade may sound unbelievable because, in a way, I don't understand how I did it. I have told you I am an uneducated man. Nevertheless, although I have no knowledge of the English language and cannot write, I learned a fine trade.

In 1922, at the Ganado Mission, a white man (he was an Italian) was supervising the construction of the stone buildings for the school there. He had a crew of the same nationality who were professional stone masons. There was one particular man, an elderly one, that I worked with. The foreman of the crew hired me to lift the heavy stones for that man and to keep him well supplied with concrete, mud or cement. We were working on the powerhouse. A Presbyterian white minister was the first superintendent of the mission school. His name was Mr. Mitchell, but the Navajos called him Slim Missionary. He worked very hard to establish that mission school for the Navajos. He could speak Navajo fluently. He was a good man, and he helped me to get employment with the construction crew. Each mason had a Navajo helper. I watched the elderly man chisel the stones into rectangular or square shaped blocks. I did not know at first how it was done. He used a small sledge hammer and a chisel to cut the stones. When the man was busy working at something else I wold pick up his tools and to do what he did. I practiced every chance I got. When I first watched him it looked real easy to do, and I wanted to learn. I was just a young man then, but my eagerness persuaded me to learn fast. The man was happy that I took an interest in the trade.

Not long afterward he let me do a little work until I got the hang of it. We worked together real well. In about a month's time we completed the walls of the building, and the carpenter crew took over. That was the beginning of my first job as a stone mason; and I went on to help construct other stone buildings in that area. Every year one more building was added to the mission school. I was well on the way to becoming a real good stone mason. We constructed the buildings that had to be done, and, after that, I naturally was laid off.

A few years later the government provided a special project for the people, and I worked with it. I don't remember what year it was, but I believe it was during the livestock reduction period. The people were told to build houses for themselves; so a crew of men moved from one location to another, building homes on a voluntary basis. No one got paid for the work. The men only helped one another. No one got paid for the work. The men only helped one another. Food was furnished by the family whose house we were working on.

I have told you about the Hubbells—old Don Lorenzo and his sons, Ramon and Lorenzo, Jr.—who had the first trading post at Ganado. Later, they hired a crew of stone masons to construct a building adjacent to the trading post. I was one of those masons. Our foreman was a Navajo man named James. He had gone to school and had vocational training in stone masonry. The other hired men knew little about it, and we had a hard time getting the work done. My experience of a few years before helped me, though. I was the only one who could cut the stones and block them because I remembered how ti was done. We completed the building in about three months. The roof was made from narrow ponderosa pine logs, and the building still stands in the same way we built it.

Several years later construction was started on the Window Rock headquarters (the Navajo capital) of the most Bureau of Indian Affairs. When the government took away most of our livestock it had promised employment for the people so they could earn money to support themselves. I worked at Window Rock on the construction of those buildings. After that, I was well recognized for my ability as a stone mason. For example, a man who owned sheep gave me 60 head to build him a stone house a few miles west of Ganado. Another man also hired me to build a house in the same area, but he gave me only 50 head of sheep for the work. Those stone houses still stand, but they now are abandoned and wind-beaten.

It was in midwinter when I heard that more construction was in progress at Window Rock. There were not many automobiles then. We traveled mostly by horses and wagons. The place where I lived was called Bitter Water. It is where I live now.

After I had completed the stone houses near Ganado I decided to find employment at Window Rock again; so I packed my horse with all the necessary tools, bedding and some food supplies. When I arrived there, construction was progressing slowly. The stones were being hauled in from the rock quarry to where the men were working on the foundations. I looked at what they were doing, and it did not look good to me. I supposed that most of them were inexperienced and were just learning. I went to the employment office and was hired. When I reported for work the foreman gave me some instructions on how it was done. I knew all of that; so I got my tools out and began cutting the stones into perfect shapes, and I laid them evenly. After the foreman saw my work he assigned me to the more difficult job of blocking in the corners of the walls. Our construction superintendent was a white man. The stone mason foreman was James Salt, a Navajo. He kept himself busy running from one section to the other where the masons were working. Some were cutting the stones and blocking them, while others laid them. I did my own cutting of the stones—the way I wanted—and laid the cornerstones for the walls. Most of the men were earning a four-dollar-a-day rate. My wage, though, was eight dollars a day because I was well experienced and my qualifications were good.

That was how I was employed, even though I had no education. I had learned by experience. It is just a matter of setting your mind on what you really want to do and getting involved in it. I worked at Window Rock the rest of the winter, until April. By that time some of the men had become good stone masons because I had taught them how it was done. The administration building was completed, and construction closed down temporarily. I left Window Rock and went home because I had a lot of work to do in planting; besides, it was lambing time and sheep shearing time.

The next fall, construction began again at Window Rock. That time it was the power plant. After we had finished building the walls, the men who were working on the huge chimney were afraid to go any higher than 25 feet; so three of us offered to finish the job. The chimney was 130 feet tall after its completion. We did it in about a month. Just recently that chimney was torn down and the whole plant was remodeled because it does not burn coal anymore. The furnaces are gone, replaced with huge generators for a heating system.

After the powerhouse was completed we constructed the Navajo Council chambers. That is where the laws and regulations are made and where the Navajo government is planned for the people. I again did the difficult work of laying the cornerstones for the walls. I shaped the stones that were rounded into curves, and I blocked the long stones for the windows. Curving the stones is hard work. We also had done it when we built the big chimney for the powerhouse.

Next, we constructed other buildings—the employees' buildings—the employees' buildings, the houses in the residential section on the hillside, apartments, etc. When all the houses were completed I began working at Fort Defiance on the new hospital. We had a government inspector from Washington who checked our work at the end of each day. He approved mine and always complimented me. He said I did an excellent job and accomplished more than the other men. I got far ahead of all the professional stone masons; and, for that reason, they did not like me and rarely spoke to me. (Some of those men lost their jobs because of mistakes they made and for other reasons), but I did my best and stayed on the job. There always will be jealousy. That was the way it was against me, but I paid no attention to it. When we had finished all the walls no one wanted the job of stacking the tall chimney; and another Navajo mason and I constructed it, and it still stands. The man I worked with was a good mason, too, I knew him only as Yellow Horse's nephew.

I left my job before the chimney was completed; we only had about three feet to go. It was spring, and I had to do much planting and other work at home. The white man who supervised the construction rate me as one of the best stone masons he had known.

Later, I helped build the new powerhouse at Fort Defiance. It was different there because I had to work with a hard crew. The men were Anglos—tough and ill-tempered. I managed to work with them, but I tried to keep out of their way. After the building was completed, they built the chimney themselves. I left in the late fall. Later, I helped construct more houses at Fort Defiance and other places where I was recommended.

In recent years concrete blocks have been used instead of native stone for building houses. They are cheaper to work with and lighter to handle than stones. When they were new I did not know how to lay them until I watched and saw how it was done. Then I began working them as the other masons did.

When the government school a t Thoreau, New Mexico, was under construction I got word to work there. They needed some good brick and concrete block layers. The BIA area office sent a letter asking me to report for work. Some men had been laid off because of lack of experience. Only a few were on the job when I got there, and the work they were doing was slow. When I reached Gallup, a man named Carl Todacheene, of Shiprock, took me to Thoreau where I was to begin work. He introduced me to the construction supervisor, a black man.

"This man is a skillful block layer," said Carl. The man looked me over and laughed. "Him?" he replied. "Naw! Not him." He told us he had to lay off many men who said they could work, and he had his doubts about me, too. He wanted to test me first. He handed me a trowel and gave me five minutes to fill in a section that had been left open. First, I got the concrete blocks and stood them up where I needed them. Then, I slapped some cement on the trowel and quickly spread it on the tops of the blocks that were already set. Next, I placed the blocks real evenly, first putting cement on each one as I layed it in. After that I scraped off all the excess cement, cleaned and smoothed each one.

The supervisor watched as I finished, in less than five minutes, the job he had told me to do. He laughed again and said, "You're hired." I reported for work the following day at 8 o'clock. Again, though, I had to leave in the spring. My family, as usual, needed me at home for the spring planting, the lambing and the shearing.

We thought we got a good wage rate back then, when masons generally earned about $3.25 an hour. Today, however, a stone mason's pay is several times that amount.

I had a good career to look forward to when I was classified as a professional stone mason and bricklayer. I received offers and worked at various places in the country. They included Phoenix, Arizona; Barstow, California; Stewart, Nevada, and Carson, Nevada. I became a member of the union; so, wherever I was needed, I would go. I turned down some jobs because I had farms to work on and livestock to tend.

In all the places I worked not once did I sign my name. I used only my thumb prints when I had to sign applications or a paycheck. After my long years of successful work experience many do not believe that I cannot write or speak English. But, even with that handicap, I learned an excellent trade, and I worked hard to be a good stone mason. I am proud of myself. All the supervisors I have

worked for have given me good ratings. I also am a qualified bricklayer. I added that trade by experience and determination.

I have supervised construction projects on the Reservation. Some men who had school training in stone masonry and bricklaying worked under me, even though I am a non-educated man. One of the construction jobs I supervised was the tribal jail building at Lupton, Arizona, a few years ago. Mr. Henry Whipple, who was our construction superintendent at Window Rock, knew my skills as a cinder-block layer and placed me in that position. I had constructed cinder-block (or concrete block) houses here and there on the Reservation. I also had supervised the construction of the jail building at Navajo Springs near Navajo Mountain and at Chinle, Arizona. I also helped construct the large Civic Center at Window Rock. I laid the rock tiles in the washrooms of the Civic Center.

Then, while I was working with the construction crew on the new police and judicial building at Window Rock, I received a notice of retirement. I had earned it, and my social security benefit is my income now. I do not depend on any livestock. My children take care of what is left of the livestock after the reduction program.

I have described my work experiences and how I became an expert stone mason. I am using myself as an example of how one can become a good, skillful worker in any trade he likes; and I hope that many young people will think carefully about my story so that someday they, too, will be successful and become good workers.

I am glad that I have taught some men to be fine stone masons. I feel that I have done my share, especially now that my thoughts and the story of my life have been recorded for publishing in a book by the Navajo Community College Press. Finally, I am happy that this material—along with accounts by a number of other elderly Navajos—will be used in the College's curriculum and will be read by Indians and non-Indians all over the country. Perhaps it will contribute to a better understanding of my people.

Source:

Stories of Traditional Navajo Life and Culture, edited by Broderick H. Johnson. Tsaile, AZ: Navajo Community College Press, 1977. pp. 149-172.

Historically, the contributions of women to social development in the United States have been underappreciated. Among the Navajo tribe, however, women play a central role in the community and are revered for their contribution. The Navajo migrated from the North and settled in Arizona and New Mexico around 1000 A.D. The Navajo are known for their agricultural development, weaving, and sand painting which they learned from the Pueblos. The Navajo are also pastoralists, or sheep herders, which they learned from the Spanish in the 1600s. The tribe fought diligently against the Spanish and American settlers in the nineteenth century to protect their land rights, however were overcome by Kit Carson at Fort Sumner in 1864. The tribe was subsequently relocated to a reservation in 1868.

One of the most widely celebrated forms of expression among the Navajo is painting, which was originally used to convey their elaborate mythology and folklore. Emmi Whitehorse, a painter from the Navajo reservation near Chaco Canyon, New Mexico, carries on the tradition with her postmodern art. Postmodernism often emphasizes the disunity of the self and the primacy of cultural diversity in its expression. One of the themes that Emmi Whitehorse incorporates in her art is the power, strength, and beauty of the feminine. She also privileges ambiguity in her work, leaving its interpretation to the beholder, which is another common theme of postmodern art. Whitehorse tends to feature imposing images of women in her paintings and the men are always depicted as small and marginal figures. This is somewhat of an extension of Navajo culture which celebrates the primacy of the female. For example, the Navajo hold a celebration for females when they reach puberty and the mother picks or recommends a spouse for her daughters.

Traditionally, when a man and woman were joined in marriage the man would move in with his wife's family and become a workhorse for her family. The matriarchal tendency of Navajo society was eventually undermined by western notions of male domination and leadership but the Navajo still hold females in high regard. Respect for women is reflected in one of the creation stories passed on in Navajo folklore. The myth holds that a the first women, called "Changing Woman," gave birth to two twin boys, who, upon growing up, wished to meet their father. Their father, the Sun, did not want children, and would kill his sons upon learning of their existence. Before setting the boys on their journey to meet their father, Changing Woman furnished weapons for the boys with which to protect themselves and warned them of their father's intention. The boys ultimately outwitted their father which earned his respect and he decided not to kill them. One of the principles of the creation myth is that the female passes on the wisdom and strength with which to survive in the world. Moreover, according to Whitehorse, the mother liberated her people by defying the wishes of the Sun by having the twins. Whitehorse represented the story in one of her paintings.

IN MY FAMILY, WOMEN RAN EVERYTHING

The Santa Fe studio of painter Emmi Whitehorse is a comfortable place. The patio is home to plants, two cats, and a large black rabbit. Inside the converted warehouse, a skylight illuminates Whitehorse's treasures—an abstract "chief's blanket," Navajo fetishes standing like sentinels beside hand-woven baskets, Pueblo pots, and high-tech stereo speakers. The walls are alive with her canvases, which blend European influences with her personal visual language. Figures from her childhood on the Navajo Reservation float in seas of color. Emmi Whitehorse took me on a tour of her work, then we drank tea and she reflected on her passage from shepherdess to "postmodern painter."

My work isn't something mystical that has to be pondered. See this funny little bird? Birds represent different things in different cultures, so when I first showed the painting, everybody thought it was an allusion to some Native American ritual. I said, "Well, if that's what you want to believe, fine. But I just saw it on a beer label, and I'm painting it." [Laughs.]

I incorporate common, everyday things in my work. I play with images. In these canvases, there are childlike forms. There's a comb, like the one we used to use to beat down the wool and tighten the weaving. I like the shape. There's a little house and an upside-down fork floating in space over denuded trees.

There are female body parts in the works, but they're ambiguous. This big figure started out looking like a bowling pin—you know, elongated head and long body. Then the head disappeared, and the bust came in. In this other painting, there's a woman with a head, but she's armless. [Laughs.] You can see the hips and waist, she has this big strapless ruffly dress on, the kind girls wear to the prom. This upside-down thing here, that's the same female form—I flipped it around—only she doesn't have the ruffly dress on; she's become a chalice.

I don't want to be too literal in the work. I'm ambiguous. I'm interested in the presence of the woman. I'm intrigued by the femininity of the female form.

In my family, the female owned everything, the women ran everything. They owned the land and the sheep. They nurtured and carried the family. The woman was responsible for the survival of the people. So in my work, the female is always very big, she is imposing, she is like this big Goliath in the work. The male image is tiny.

In this other canvas, there's a woman shaped like a vase, like the older Navajo women. Even in old age, I think the women still retain a grace that is unequaled.

My grandmother is like that. She's very giving, and she instilled a lot of traditional values in us without having to preach. She was a weaver. She learned how to weave from her mother. Her work is elegant. She is very finicky, very concerned with what she wears in public. She won't go out on a short trip to the store without putting on her best clothes: a traditional Navajo velveteen top and three-tiered cotton skirt down to her ankles. She used to make her clothes, but now she has trouble seeing, so she has someone make them to her specifications. She's eighty-two, and she's pretty healthy, except for arthritis.

Our system worked well until the missionaries came and said that we were "living in sin." How can living with nature be a sin?

I was born in 1957. I lived with my family in a hogan in a place called Whitehorse Lake on the edge of the Navajo Reservation. It's near Chaco Canyon, New Mexico. Each family lives on a plot of land divided into sections or squares so that each of the relatives can have a section for his or her family. There was my grandmother (I never saw my grandfather), my parents, and five children. Most of the family is still living there.

In olden times, Navajo women would scheme to arrange a marriage for their children to someone from a wealthy family. Wealth meant having cows and horses, or a car. A lot of tribal people were material-oriented, and still are. The mother and grandmother would pick the mate for a girl, but they wouldn't force you. They'd ask you if it was okay first. Our tradition was that the man came to live with his wife's family.

What if a woman was unhappy with her husband? In earlier times, it was easy. She just picked up all his stuff and put it outside the door of the hogan, and that was it. He couldn't contest it. He had to go.

The man joined his wife's family basically to ensure the survival of that family. In other words, he sort of became the work-horse. He would haul the wood, and chop the firewood; he'd take care of the sheep too. He'd make sure there was water for the animals. Older men and medicine men were highly regarded. But that was back then.

Our system worked well until the missionaries came and said that we were "living in sin." How can living with nature be a sin? They said that men are supposed to run everything. That threw everything asunder. My generation of young men was greatly affected by the fact that they had to constantly straddle the fence between traditional teachings and western ideals. Unfortunately, many turned to alcohol and destroyed their well-being.

My father worked in California for Amtrak when I was very young, so we children became the caretakers of our animals. We had over two hundred head of sheep. We had to take them out every day to graze. Every spring, Grandmother marked the ears—it was the same as branding. We would help castrate lambs. When little ones were abandoned, we had to bottle-feed them, to be mother to al those motherless lambs. We'd shear the sheep in the spring. We had to use huge shears, and cut each sheep's wool by hand. This would take days. Afterwards, we'd take the wool to market, about fifteen to twenty tremendous burlap sacks. We'd get something like five dollars per pound totaling around five thousand dollars, a substantial amount of money that we would live on for a year. Grandmother also had goats that produced mohair which she used for her weaving.

We'd help Grandmother card the wool after it had been washed. It was a nasty business because wool from the sheep is very dirty and oily. We'd sit and pick all the burrs and twigs out. Using a flat wooden brushlike comb, we'd comb it clean and make little long, flat bundles of wool. While we worked, my grandmother told us creation stories like this one, but only in the wintertime.

Changing Woman was the first woman, born through a sort of immaculate conception. She gave birth to twin boys; the Sun was their father. But because the Sun didn't want children, Changing Woman had to hide their birth, and she raised them in secrecy. When they grew up, they asked who their father was. When Changing Woman could no longer put them off, she told them it was the Sun, and they wanted to go and see him. Changing Woman prepared the boys for the journey. She plucked stars and lightning bolts out of which she fashioned a bow and arrow for each boy. She warned them that their father would try to kill them.

Along their journey, the boys met a gopher who befriended them, and offered to help them outsmart the sun. When they arrived at the home of the Sun, they announced, "We are the sons of Changing Woman. We know you are our father." The Sun was very angry, and decided to do away with the boys right away. He prepared a sweat for them; he put oversize rocks inside so it would overheat. But the gopher was wise to the Sun; he went inside without being seen, he dug a large tunnel in the middle of the floor that led deep down and to the outside. When the Sun turned up the heat, the boys crawled into this tunnel. Each time the Sun turned up the heat, he would call out to the boys, "How are you doing?" Each time they would answer, "Fine." This went on until the Sun was tired out, and finally the Sun called out to the boys to come out. They emerged unhurt, and the Sun gave in and accepted the boys as his sons.

I asked Emmi Whitehorse if her story affirms her image of woman as a positive force.

Yes. By defying the Sun and having the Twins, Changing Woman liberated her people who had been suppressed by the greedy Sun. She released her people from the underworld where the Sun wanted them to stay; she moved them forward. At one point, I incorporated that story into my painting. See these two figures? They are the Twins.

I was the baby of the family. My siblings had gone off to school, not by their own choice. I wanted to be with them, so I begged my mom to let me go to school. I thought I would play on the swings and merry-go-round all day. She said, "Fine." She enrolled me the very next day! (My mother and my grandmother don't speak English. They never went to school.)

So at a very early age, I went to a Bureau of Indian Affairs boarding school near my home in Whitehorse Lake. I hated it. We were marched around like little cadets: girls were herded around in one area, boys in another. It was a very lonely. In the dining room, we were required to sit boy-girl, and that was torture. [Laughs.] All you could do was numb yourself to the whole ordeal.

I wasn't interested in any of the subjects, except art. When we had drawing time, I came alive. That was the only thing I excelled in. That kept me going.

Some of the teachers were very demeaning and made us feel ashamed of our culture. We were forced to wear uncomfortable dresses and hose, with a tight girdle. Boy did we hate it! We couldn't wear our hair loose; it had to be curled, or braided, or piled up on top of our heads to fulfill the school's idea of the "ideal girl."

At Christmas, if we got lucky, we would get gifts, and one year, we all got Barbie dolls. Barbie had a size D bust and a nine-teen-inch waist, long legs and blond hair. We all thought we were supposed to look like her. Well, we found out that no matter how we manipulated our bodies, we could never look like Barbie. We had tanned skin and dark hair. When I got older, I realized we had wasted so much time agonizing over something that could never be, and that didn't need changing! I started drawing the female figure with this pinched-in waist and a big top—I was poking fun at the "ideal figure."

We were only allowed to go home in the summer. At home, mother never pushed us hard; she never made important decisions for us. She never encouraged us to be lawyers or physicians. She let us do what we wanted to do.

During the summer months, I got to participate in some ceremonies. We had a Blessing ceremony when we finished our new home. Once when my mother was sick, she hired a medicine man to come and sing over her, but the medicine man considered us too young to witness it, and sent us away. Did she get well? She must have. [Laughs.]

I didn't have a puberty ceremony because I was away at school, and also I was uncomfortable with the idea of having one. This was the sixties. I thought it was too old-fashioned. Miniskirts were in, puberty rites were not! Now, I think it's such a wonderful ceremony, I should have had it. If I have a daughter I will want her to have one.

In this painting there's a long bundle of sticks used in the girl's puberty ceremony. Your grandmother gives them to you; you use them to stir the blue cornmeal during the ceremony, and you keep them for the rest of your life.

I went to a puberty ceremony when I was around eight years old. The girl who was being initiated into womanhood was about twelve or thirteen. We camped out at the girl's home for a week with all our relatives, men, women and children. Now, I guess you'd drive over every day. With the girl, we spent a whole day grinding the blue corn for the "Navajo cake." When there was enough corn piled up, they would pour it into a big metal container, pour in hot water, add raisins, sweeten it with sprouted wheat (a natural sugar), and it was like a thick pudding. The men would do their part by hauling in water and firewood.

Every morning before sunup, the girl would race out toward the East. We would all line up behind her, grandmothers, mothers and children, as if we were going to run the New York Marathon. Someone would say "Go" and she'd race off. You'd never overtake her, even if you were the fastest runner, because the saying was if you ran past her, you would age quicker than she would. [Laughs.] She would race as far as she could to the East, then she would turn around and run back. It was just a wonderful event.

For the ceremony, the girl was decked out in her best traditional dress and jewelry. Her hair was done up and wrapped with yarn, and a piece of parrot feather with turquoise was tied to her hair.

There was specific songs. I remember the medicine man singing and conducting the ceremony. He was sitting in front of us in the hogan with his legs crossed. My sister and I noticed that he had a hole in the toe of his moccasin. We started giggling hysterically, and my grandmother got angry and chased us out of the hogan. We were put to work gathering firewood and grinding corn. We weren't allowed back in, so we never heard the rest of the ceremony.

Recently, my sister's daughter got married in a traditional ceremony at my mother's home. We all went to help with the wedding preparations. We prepared food for the feast. We butchered a sheep and made mutton stew soup. We cooked various other dishes and of course fried bread.

The bride and groom were dressed in their traditional clothes. He wore a velveteen shirt and blue jeans. The bride wore a purple velveteen blouse and a purple satin skirt with see-through white lace overlayed on the skirt. She had her hair done up Navajo fashion. The couple both wore moccasins.

The bride and groom sat in a corner of the hogan on blankets. The groom's family sat on one side of the hogan, the bride's family on the other side. The groom's mother was a medicine woman, so she conducted the ceremony and said the prayers. It was wonderful to have a woman do that.

The medicine woman poured water over the couple's hands—they had to wash before starting the ceremony. A little basket of corn mush was brought in; the couple dipped into the mush with their fingers, marking the four corners as they worked around the lip of the basket, then they ate some.

Next, they opened the floor so that anyone could talk. It all had to do with maintaining a good home and family relationships. Elders counseled the couple on how to be diplomatic. The girl's grandmother told her how to be caring, the boy's father told him how to be giving, financially and emotionally, to his wife. This went on for hours, it seemed, until everybody had run out of things to say and was out of breath.

Finally the food was brought in. The lamb's ribs were given to the groom's family—these are considered a delicacy. The rest of us got to eat mutton stew and fry bread. Everyone ate in a circle around the food.

After the meal, it shifted gears to modern life. Someone from my family had ordered this wonderful three-tiered cake decorated with the plastic image of a couple—standing on the very top. [Laughs.] They cut it and passed it out to the guests. There were gifts: a roaster, glasses, a Cuisinart. You didn't get that in the old days. It was bizarre because the first part of the ceremony had been so traditional. But they were young, in fact, they played their favorite music at the end—heavy metal! It was accepted. Everyone went away happy.

After the guests had all left, the bridge gathered all the gifts and carried them out to a 1992 Ford Escort, and we watched them drive off.

I thought, well, if I ever decide to get married, I'll have a traditional wedding at night, on my grandmother's land.

In high school, I entered an art contest with a small abstract painting; it won an award, and I got a small scholarship to the University of New Mexico in Albuquerque. The school was male-dominated, and I was very disappointed. When I arrived at my first art history class, I didn't know who Picasso was, I had no idea what modern art was about. I took all the art classes I could, and became a bit more comfortable. I took courses in modern dance, music history and creative writing. I was fascinated. I started showing my work while I was an undergraduate.

I was so happy the day I got my master's degree in fine arts. I sent invitations to all my family and relatives, but my dad was the only one who showed up for the graduation. My sisters were in town, but

guess where they went instead. [Laughs.] To a Jimmy Swaggert revival meeting! After the graduation ceremony was over, they came and congratulated me and we all went out for dinner. It was sad that they weren't interested in what I had done, but later I forgave them. The evangelist meeting was more important to them at that time in their lives.

At one point in my life, I suffered from low self-esteem pretty badly. I was trying very hard not to look ethnic. I thought my nose was too big. I guess I was trying to eliminate every trace of who I was. Then a close friend said, "Look at all the things the Navajo are famous for: the weavings, the silversmithing, baskets. These are just as valid as what the Europeans have come up with." It dawned on me that there was this wealth of aesthetic objects my people were creating. Why not be proud of it?

I began looking at the stories my grandmother told me when I was a child, and started incorporating the images into my work. The work became more centered. In some of the paintings you'll see the arc from the bottom of the Navajo wedding basket, or the shape of the cradle board my mother made for me using boards from an orange crate. In another painting, there is a brush made out of dried grass, which Navajo women used to use to brush their hair.

Everything my grandmother stood for I now hold scared: her love for animals, her limitless compassion for humanity. I would like to be like her when I get older. I will probably trade in my LizWear for a velveteen blouse and a traditional long skirt when I'm sixty years old. [Laughs.]

From an interview with the author,
July 15, 1992.

Source:
Emmi Whitehorse. In *Messengers of the Wind*, edited by Jane Katz. New York: Ballantine Books, 1995. pp. 55-65.

NEPALESE
AMERICANS

Nepal is a landlocked country of over 23.6 million people living between the Tibet Autonomous Region of the People's Republic of China to the north and India to the south. Eighty-three percent of Nepal's total land area is high mountains and hills, with over 1,300 peaks, including the world's highest mountain. According to the 1990 U.S. Census there were 2,616 Americans with Nepalese ancestry, a small ethnic group that is slowly growing. In 1998, 226 Nepalese were winners of the government's diversity lottery which makes 50,000 permanent visas available to people from countries with low rates of immigration to the United States.

While not all Nepalese are Sherpas, Sherpas are the best known ethnic group of the Himalayan country of Nepal, from an American perspective. Adventure travel was a $220 billion industry in 1997, expanding at a rate of nine percent each year, and the idea of climbing Everest focused many Americans' attention on Sherpas, who serve as climbing guides for most expeditions into the mountains. Sherpas are only eight percent of the population, with Rai being the major ethnic group, making up 64 percent of the population, and with Singsawa accounting for 18 percent, with Brahmin and Chhetri accounting for four percent, and other caste groups comprising six percent. Nepal has 60 ethnic groups who speak 11 languages and over 70 dialects. All Sherpas speak Tibet-Burmese language.

Sherpas claim the eastern Nepal Himalayan region as home. The lifestyle is difficult and a day's work revolves around basic issues of food preparation and care of livestock. Nepal in the 1990s was predominantly a rural-agricultural society where more than 90 percent of the population lives in rural areas. Sherpa culture originates from the Kham region of Tibet known as Salmogang. Conflicts forced Sherpas to leave Tibet around 1480 and settle in Nepal. The Sherpas of this area follow a sect of Buddhism known as Nyingmapa. The beliefs of the Sherpa include the use of the hanging prayer flags, prayer wheels, monastic and nunnery life, and visits to pilgrimage sites. Sherpas believe in reincarnation and prayer to offset evil spirits.

Many Sherpas immigrated to the United States hoping to make money and then eventually return to Nepal, where 9 million live below the international poverty line, and 73 percent of the population is illiterate. Life expectancy is only 55 years. Sherpas who immigrate to the United States usually settle in urban areas such as New York City, Denver, Boston, Chicago, Dallas, Portland, Gainsville and St. Paul. They usually live in close communities, so a new immigrant typically moves in with a Sherpa already settled in a city. Acclimation is still very difficult because in Nepal there are interdependent relationships among people that do not exist in American culture, where individualism is stressed.

LOOKING FOR A SHERPA IN NEPAL? TRY NEW YORK

Immigrants Very Much in Vogue, With a Little Help From a New Everest Boom

The Sherpas are bemused.

When they began settling in New York City, the famously trustworthy mountain people for Nepal who have hefted supplies (and not a few Western climbers) to the summit of Everest fully expected the immigrant's struggle of hard work and homesickness.

But they never expected to be cool.

"Thanks to the new Everest boom, the Sherpas are very much in vogue," said Dr. Vincanne Adams, Princeton University anthropology professor who has been studying them since 1982. "After all the books and movies, there is kind of celebrity aspect to being a Sherpa."

This has provoked no little astonishment and a measure of delight among nearly 500 Sherpas living in New York City, the largest settlement in the United States. Until now, the city's newest microcommunity had grown so quietly that it was off the scope of most demographers.

But in recent weeks, Sherpas have loomed large in the glow of The Movie, as they call it: the Imax film "Everest," which chronicles an expedition to the 29,028-foot summit of the world's tallest mountain. The film has racked up the highest per screen attendance gross—$54,099, according to Variety—of any film playing in the country.

The film is just the latest manifestation of Everestmania. There is also the book "Into Thin Air," by Jon Krakauer, which chronicles the May 1996 blizzard that killed eight climbers. It has been on the best-seller list of The New York Times for 47 weeks. And the National Geographic Society's $35 coffee-table book on the Imax expedition, "Everest: Mountain Without Mercy," has sold 150,000 copies since October.

"The Imax film is a very big event for us," said Dhamey Norgay, a Sherpa who works in Manhattan as a program coordinator at Philip Morris. "It was very moving for so many of us to see our mountains again, and our culture portrayed on the big screen."

The 28-year-old Mr. Norgay is the youngest son of the most illustrious Sherpa, the late Tenzing Norgay, who made the first ascent of Everest with Edmund Hillary on May 29, 1953. The younger Norgay remembers the cold and the wind of Everest more than 20 years later, when he hiked there at age 9 with his father up to the 130,000-foot level. "We've lost a lot of family members on that mountain," he said. All told, 53 Sherpas have died on Everest.

Paradoxically, most of the city's Sherpas have no Everest experience. "When people hear that I'm a Sherpa, they asked how many times I've climbed Everest," said Zing Sherpa Lama, president of the United Sherpa Association in New York. "They're disappointed when I tell them that I've seen Mount Everest—from a very long distance."

Mr. Norgay and Mr. Sherpa Lama spoke on a recent evening in a rented banquet room at St. Vartan's Armenian Cathedral in Manhattan. They and 600 other Sherpas from across the land—nearly all the current population in America—had gathered to celebrate Lhosar, the Sherpa equivalent of the Chinese New Year. A red, yellow and green banner proclaimed "Happy Lhosar 1998, Year of the Earth Tiger 2125." Standing before it was Ang Babu Lama, a Buddhist monk, who chanted Tibetan prayers. "I came for a short visit last month and the Sherpas won't let me go," Mr. Babu Lama said after the ceremony.

In New York, there are no monks to perform birth-and-death services, and the nearest Buddhist monasteries are hours away in the Hudson Valley.

"When I came to New York, I was the only Sherpa in the phone book," said Lakhpa Thundup Sherpa, who arrived in 1979. By 1982, "there were only four Sherpas in New York, and perhaps 15 in all the country," said Mr. Sherpa Lama, the association president, who arrived that year as a student. "The community began growing dramatically only after 1990."

"These days the joke is that if you're looking for a Sherpa in Nepal, you'll find him in New York," said Sonam Sherpa, who has been here for 13 years and works as a treasury analyst at Metro North.

Surrounded by Buddhist artifacts, Gelmu Sherpa—part of a dramatic increase in the U.S. population of Sherpas—rubs a "singing bowl," which resonates with a soft hum in her shop in New York.

Sherpas are scattered throughout the boroughs, though there are concentrations in Queens and Brooklyn, and for some it can be a lonely life. As they work in the United States to save money to buy land or businesses back in Nepal, they are separated from spouses and children.

"Many Sherpas here miss their families at home," said Lakpha Sherpa Pinasha, a computer-science student at Hunter College who has been in the United States for the last year and a half. "I certainly do. After I graduate, I intend to return to look for a job."

As in Nepal and in Darjeeling (where there is a large Sherpa community), "the Sherpas in New York tend to stick together," said David Breashears, the veteran Everest climber who directed the Imax film. "Pretty much literally, since they often cluster five or so to an apartment."

Amid the struggling economy of Nepal, "the image of America is of a place where you can pick money off the sidewalk," said Jangbu Sherpa, 26, who helped carry the Breashears team's cameras and film up through the final 3,000 feet, the "death zone" to the Everest summit. "I think more Sherpas would like to move here."

But many work for a while and leave. "I lived in the United States for nine years," said Jamling Tenzing Norgay, "but I decided to go back to my homeland because I missed people."

Mr. Norgay, at 33 the second-oldest son of Tenzing Norgay, is a focal point of the Imax film as he assaults the Everest summit to honor his father, who died in 1986. Now Mr. Norgay runs an adventure-travel business in Nepal, and visits the United States three times each year.

Sherpa means "Easterner," and refers to an ethnic group that began migrating to the Everest region of Nepal from eastern Tibet nearly 500 years ago.

As a group, New York City's Sherpas are accomplished polyglots: in addition to Sherpa, they know Nepalese, English and Hindi, and even French and Japanese if they worked in international tourism back home.

Required to take the name Sherpa on Nepalese passports, many have used the designation here on drivers' licenses and credit cards. But all Sherpas have other clan, village and family names.

Many Sherpas have clustered in the health-food store business and city construction work; some drive taxis and do domestic work and others toil here in the trekking business.

Mr. Sherpa Lama got his first job at a health food store in 1982 by offering to work free for two weeks.

"After the second week," he said, "the owner began paying me and then asked if I knew any other Sherpas so he could hire them." He did and the owner did. Now Mr. Sherpa Lama is the manager of Healthy Pleasures, believed to be the largest health food store in the city.

Although Sherpas' mountain upbringing stresses humble generosity, many express a pride that "we do things that others cannot do," as several Sherpas put it.

Their culture and Tibetan Buddhist religion have long attracted intense interest in the United States. "I think Americans have always been interested in the Tibetan peoples—you know, the land of Shangri-La," said Dawa Tsering, the United States representatives of the Dalai Lama. "But the

'Everest' film and the recent books, and movies like 'Kundun' and 'sevens Year in Tibet,' have created a new wave of interest in the culture and traditions."

Those traditions are up for grabs here and in Tibet, where "the Sherpas and Tibetans share commons danger that their culture is being assimilated," Mr. Tsering said.

This hardly seemed an issue at the Lhosar party in the Armenian Cathedral. Volunteers passed around plates of khapsey, sweet little New Year's cakes fried in butter. And hundreds of Sherpas imbibed chaang, a rice wine similar to sake.

Married women wore intricately colored pangden, traditional aprons of lamb's wool, and many women wore coral and agate "dze beads," necklaces passed from generation to generation, some of them worth tens of thousands of dollars.

Soon, three dozen revelers joined in a rendition of "Happiness and Prosperity."

Their admirers wish them both. "You cannot but have a sense of awe about these indomitable mountain people who have been the backbone and engine of every Everest expedition since the 1920's," Mr. Breashears said. He employed 24 Sherpas during his ascent to the summit of Everest, and he was instrumental in organizing rescue efforts after the 1996 tragedy.

"I would trust them with my life," he said, "and have."

Source:
New York Times, April 3, 1998.

NEZ PERCÉS

Among the most poignant stories of Indian resistance against the westward migration of white settlers was that of Chief Joseph and his tribe, a small group known as the Nez Percé. (French explorers gave them that name, which means "pierced nose," after observing their custom of wearing nose rings.) Their ancestral home was a large tract of land that stretched across what is now southeastern Washington, northeastern Oregon, and central Idaho. For the most part, they lived peacefully with neighboring tribes and the few white farmers and trappers they encountered while hunting and fishing. When the Pacific Northwest came under U.S. control in 1848, however, a surge in the number of white settlers attracted to the area led to tensions that eventually destroyed the Nez Percé way of life.

Joseph, who was born around 1840 in Oregon's Wallowa Valley, grew up during this troubled time as the son of a chief who repeatedly cautioned his people to be careful in their dealings with whites. In 1855, however, some of the Nez Percés signed a treaty giving up most of their land; in return, U.S. government officials assured them that the Wallowa Valley could serve as their reservation. Eight years later, even this land was ceded to the whites in a treaty not sanctioned by all the Nez Percés, including the band led by Joseph's father.

By the time Joseph assumed the title of chief from his father around 1871, his band of Nez Percés were waging a war of passive resistance against further white encroachment and attempts to move them to a reservation in Lapwai, Idaho. But before long, the discovery of gold in the Wallowa Valley increased pressure on U.S. authorities to make the Indians leave the area. Finally, in the spring of 1877, General Oliver O. Howard issued an ultimatum: either the Nez Percés agreed to give up all of their lands and relocate to Lapwai within 30 days, or the army would see to it that they did.

Chief Joseph was not a warrior and had no desire to do battle with the whites. Viewing himself primarily as a protector of the aged, the weak, and the helpless among his people, he advised them to obey General Howard's order. His plea for patience and peace did not find favor with everyone, however; while the Nez Percés were in the process of making their way to their new home, several young male members of the tribe who bitterly resented the way they were being treated attacked and killed some white settlers over the course of several days in mid-June, 1877. The incident touched off a series of skirmishes between the Nez Percés and the U.S. Army in which the Indians defeated the better-equipped and more numerous federal troops. Yet Chief Joseph knew that he could not continue to do so indefinitely (more soldiers were already on the way from other Western outposts), so he made a fateful decision: he and his people would try to escape into Canada.

Over the next eleven weeks, Chief Joseph led a band of several hundred Nez Percé men, women, and children on a retreat of well over a thousand miles through the rugged terrain of the Pacific Northwest, hoping to evade the U.S. government forces and enemy Indians on their trail. On at least a dozen occasions, they directly *engaged their pursuers in battle and in most cases defeated them or fought to a stale-mate. Throughout the well-documented campaign, Chief Joseph never failed to impress his opponents with his courage and his steady determination. They were also impressed with the fact that he did not harm the white settlers his band encountered along the way.*

By late September, the Nez Percés at last found themselves within about 30 miles of the Canadian border at place in Montana known as Eagle Creek. The price they had paid to get that far was a steep one; in addition to those who had fallen in battle, there were many others who died from exhaustion, hunger, and disease. For all who had managed to survive, the coming winter promised severe weather and probable starvation. Surrounded and vastly outnumbered by a well-armed contingent of U.S. troops, Chief Joseph finally surrendered on October 5, 1877. His brief remarks to General Howard and General Nelson A. Miles are among the best-known and most heart-wrenching words ever spoken by a Native American.

CHIEF JOSEPH'S SURRENDER

Tell General Howard I know his heart. What he told me before, I have in my heart. I am tired of fighting. Our chiefs are killed. Looking Glass is dead. Toohoolhoolzote is dead. The old men are all dead. It is the young men who say yes and no. He [Ollokot, Joseph's own brother] who led on the young men is dead. It is cold and we have no blankets. The little children are freezing to death. My people, some of them, have run away to the hills and have no blankets, no food; no one knows where they are—perhaps freezing to death. I want to have time to look for my children and see how many I can find. Maybe I shall find them among the dead. Hear me, my chiefs. I am tired; my heart is sick and sad. From where the sun now stands I will fight no more forever.

Source:

Indian Oratory: Famous Speeches by Noted Indian Chieftains, by W. C. Vanderwerth. Norman: University of Oklahoma Press, 1971.

*I*n the spring of 1877, General Oliver O. Howard issued an ultimatum to the Nez Percés: either the Nez Percés agreed to give up all of their lands and relocate to Lapwai within 30 days, or the U.S. army would see to it that they did. After evading the army for almost three months, and his people cold and facing starvation, Chief Joseph finally surrendered on October 5, 1877. While some of the Nez Percés managed to slip away to Canada, Chief Joseph and his followers were sent to live in Indian Territory in what is now Oklahoma. There they still faced tremendous hardship; many of them (including five of Chief Joseph's children) succumbed to illness. Chief Joseph did his best to bring their desperate condition to the attention of authorities. In 1879, for example, he was allowed to go to Washington, D.C., where on January 14 he testified before a special gathering of cabinet members, congressmen, and other government officials.*

Chief Joseph and his people were never allowed to return to their home in the Wallowa Valley. Instead, they were moved to the Colville Reservation in northern

Washington during the mid-1880s, and it is there that Chief Joseph died in 1904. His eloquent description of how the Nez Percés came to be at odds with the whites is reprinted here from W.C. Vanderwerth's Indian Oratory.

CHIEF JOSEPH'S SPEECH TO THE U.S. GOVERNMENT

My friends, I have been asked to show you my heart. I am glad to have a chance to do so. I want the white people to understand my people. Some of you think an Indian is like a wild animal. This is a great mistake. I will tell you all about our people, and then you can judge whether an Indian is a man or not. I believe much trouble and blood would be saved if we opened our hearts more. I will tell you in my way how the Indian sees things. The white man has more words to tell you how they look to him, but it does not require many words to speak the truth. What I have to say will come from my heart, and I will speak with a straight tongue. Ah-cum-kin-i-ma-me-hut [the Great Spirit] is looking at me, and will hear me.

My name is In-mut-too-yah-lat-lat [Thunder Traveling Over the Mountains]. I am chief of the Wal-lam-wat-kin band of Chute-pa-lu, or Nez Percés. I was born in eastern Oregon, thirty-eight winters ago. My father was chief before me. When a young man, he was called Joseph by Mr. [Henry H.] Spaulding, a missionary. He died a few years ago. He left a good name on earth. He advised me well for my people.

Our fathers gave us many laws, which they had learned from their fathers. These laws were good. They told us to treat all men as they treated us; that we should never be the first to break a bargain; that it was a disgrace to tell a lie; that we should speak only the truth; that it was a shame for one man to take from another his wife, or his property without paying for it. We were taught to believe that the Great Spirit sees and hears everything, and that he never forgets; that hereafter he will give every man a spirit-home according to his desserts: if he has been a good man, he will have a good home; if he has been a bad man, he will have a bad home. This I believe, and all my people believe the same.

We did not know there were other people besides the Indian until about one hundred winters ago, when some men with white faces came to our country. They brought many things with them to trade for furs and skins. They brought tobacco, which was new to us. They brought guns with flint stones on them, which frightened our women and children. Our people could not talk with these white-faced men, but they used signs which all people understand. These men were Frenchmen, and they called our people "Nez Percés," because they wore rings in their noses for ornaments. Although very few of our people wear them now, we are still called by the same name. These French trappers said a great many things to our fathers, which have been planted in our hearts. Some were good for us, but some were bad. Our people were divided in opinion about these men. Some thought they taught more bad than good. An Indian respects a brave man, but he despises a coward. He loves a straight tongue, but he hates a forked tongue. The French trappers told us some truths and some lies.

The first white men of your people who came to our country were named [Meriwether] Lewis and [William] Clark. They also brought many things that our people had never seen. They talked straight, and our people gave them a great feast, as a proof that their hearts were friendly. These men were very kind. They made presents to our chiefs and our people made presents to them. We had a great many horses, of which we gave them what they needed, and they gave us guns and tobacco in return. All the Nez Percés made friends with Lewis and Clark, and agreed to let them pass through their country, and never to make war on white men. This promise the Nez Percés have never broken. No white man can accuse them of bad faith, and speak with a straight tongue. It has always been the pride of the Nez Percés that they were the friends of the white men.

When my father was a young man there came to our country a white man [Spaulding] who talked spirit law. He won the affections of our people because he spoke good things to them. At first he did not say anything about white men wanting to settle on our lands. Nothing was said about that until about twenty winters ago, when a number of white people came into our country and built houses and made farms. At first our people made no complaint. They thought there was room enough

Chief Joseph the Younger

for all to live in peace, and they were learning many things from the white men that seemed to be good. But we soon found that the white men were growing rich very fast, and were greedy to possess everything the Indian had. My father was the first to see through the schemes of the white men, and he warned his tribe to be careful about trading with them. He had suspicion of men who seemed anxious to make money. I was a boy then, but I remember well my father's caution. He had sharper eyes than the rest of our people.

Next there came a white officer [Governor Isaac I. Stevens of the Washington Territory], who invited all the Nez Percés to a treaty council [in 1855]. After the council was opened he made known his heart. He said there were a great many white people in our country, and many more would come; that he wanted the land marked out so that the Indians and white men could be separated. If they were to live in peace it was necessary, he said, that the Indians should have a country set apart for them, and in that country they must stay. My father, who represented his band, refused to have anything to do with the council, because he wished to be a free man. He claimed that no man owned any part of the earth, and a man could not sell what he did not own.

Mr. Spaulding took hold of my father's arm and said, "Come and sign the treaty." My father pushed him away, and said: "Why do you ask me to sign away my country? It is your business to talk to us about spirit matters and not to talk to us about parting with our land." Governor Stevens urged my father to sign his treaty, but he refused. "I will not sign your paper," he said; "you go where you please, so do I; you are not a child, I am no child; I can think for myself. No man can think for me. I have no other home than this. I will not give it up to any man. My people would have no home. Take away your paper. I will not touch it with my hand."

My father left the council. Some of the chiefs of the other bands of the Nez Percés signed the treaty, and then Governor Stevens gave them presents of blankets. My father cautioned his people to take no presents, for "after a while," he said, "they will claim that you have accepted pay for your country." Since that time four bands of the Nez Percés have received annuities from the United States. My father was invited to many councils, and they tried hard to make him sign the treaty, but he was firm as the rock, and would not sign away his home. His refusal caused a difference among the Nez Percés.

Eight years later [1863] was the next treaty council. A chief called Lawyer, because he was a great talker, took the lead in this council, and sold nearly all the Nez Percés country. My father was not there. He said to me: "When you go into council with the white man, always remember your country. Do not give it away. The white man will cheat you out of your home. I have taken no pay from the United States. I have never sold our land." In this treaty Lawyer acted without authority from our band. He had no right to sell the Wallowa [winding water] country. That had always belonged to my father's own people, and the other bands had never disputed our right to it. No other Indians ever claimed Wallowa.

In order to have all people understand how much land we owned, my father planted poles around it and said: "Inside is the home of my people—the white man may take the land outside. Inside this boundary all our people were born. It circles around the graves of our fathers, and we will never give up these graves to any man."

The United States claimed they had bought all the Nez Percés country outside the Lapwai Reservation, from Lawyer and other chiefs, but we continued to live on this land in peace until eight years ago, when white men began to come inside the bounds my father had set. We warned them against this great wrong, but they would not leave our land, and some bad blood was raised. The white men represented that we were going upon the warpath. They reported many things that were false.

The United States government again asked for a treaty council. My father had become blind and feeble. He could no longer speak for his people. It was then that I took my father's place as chief. In this council I made my first speech to white men. I said to the agent who held the council: "I did not want to come to this council, but I came hoping that we could save blood. The white man has no right to come here and take our country. We have never accepted any presents from the government. Neither Lawyer nor any other chief had authority to sell this land. It has always belonged to my people. It came unclouded to them from our fathers, and we will defend this land as long as a drop of Indian blood warms the hearts of our men."

The agent said he had orders, from the Great White Chief at Washington, for us to go upon the Lapwai Reservation, and that if we obeyed he would help us in many ways. "You must move to the agency," he said. I answered him: "I will not. I do not need your help; we have plenty, and we are contented and happy if the white man will let us alone. The reservation is too small for so many people with all their stock. You can keep your presents; we can go to your towns and pay for all we need; we have plenty of horses and cattle to sell, and we won't have any help from you; we are free now; we can go where we please. Our fathers were born here. Here they lived, here they died, here are their graves. We will never leave them." The agent went away, and we had peace for a little while.

Soon after this my father sent for me. I saw he was dying. I took his hand in mine. He said: "My son, my body is returning to my mother earth, and my spirit is going very soon to see the Great Spirit Chief. When I am gone, think of your country. You are the chief of these people. They look to you to guide them. Always remember that your father never sold this country. You must stop your ears whenever you are asked to sign a treaty selling your home. A few years more, and white men will be all around you. They have their eyes on this land. My son, never forget my dying words. This country holds your father's body. Never sell the bones of your father and your mother." I pressed my father's hand and told him I would protect his grave with my life. My father smiled and passed away to the spirit land.

I buried him in that beautiful valley of winding waters. I love that land more than all the rest of the world. A man who would not love his father's grave is worse than a wild animal.

For a short time we lived quietly. But this could not last. White men had found gold in the mountains around the land of winding water. They stole many horses from us, and we could not get them back because we were Indians. The white men told lies for each other. They drove off a great many of our cattle. Some white men branded our young cattle so they could claim them. We had no friend who would plead our cause before the law councils. It seemed to me that some of the white men in Wallowa were doing these things on purpose to get up a war. They knew that we were not strong enough to fight them. I labored hard to avoid trouble and bloodshed. We gave up some of our country to the white men, thinking that then we could have peace. We were mistaken. The white man would not let us alone. We could have avenged our wrongs many times, but we did not. Whenever the government has asked us to help them against other Indians, we have never refused. When the white men were few and we were strong we could have killed them all off, but the Nez Percés wished to live at peace.

If we have not done so, we have not been to blame. I believe that the old treaty has never been correctly reported. If we ever owned the land we own it still, for we never sold it. In the treaty councils the commissioners have claimed that our country had been sold to the government. Suppose a white man should come to me and say, "Joseph, I like your horses, and I want to buy them." I say to him, "No, my horses suit me, I will not sell them." Then he goes to my neighbor, and says to him: "Joseph has some good horses. I want to buy them, but he refuses to sell." My neighbor answers, "Pay me the money, and I will sell you Joseph's horses." The white man returns to me, and says, "Joseph, I have bought your horses, and you must let me have them." If we sold our lands to the government, this is the way they were bought.

On account of the treaty made by the other bands of the Nez Percés, the white men claimed my lands. We were troubled greatly by white men crowding over the line. Some of these were good men, and we lived on peaceful terms with them, but they were not all good.

Nearly every year the agent came over from Lapwai and ordered us on to the reservation. We always replied that we were satisfied to live in Wallowa. We were careful to refuse presents or annuities which he offered.

Through all the years since the white men came to Wallowa we have been threatened and taunted by them and the treaty Nez Percés. They have given us no rest. We have had a few good friends among white men, and they have always advised my people to bear these taunts without fighting. Our young men were quick-tempered, and I have had great trouble in keeping them from doing rash things. I have carried a heavy load on my back ever since I was a boy. I learned then that we were but few, while the white men were many, and that we could not hold our own with them. We were like deer. They were like grizzly bears. We had a small country. Their country was large. We were contented to let things remain as the Great Spirit Chief made them. They were not; and would change the rivers and mountains if they did not suit them.

Year after year we have been threatened, but no war was made upon my people until General Howard came to our country two years ago and told us he was the white war-chief of all that country. He said: "I have a great many soldiers at my back. I am going to bring them up here, and then I will talk to you again. I will not let white men laugh at me the next time I come. The country belongs to the government, and I intend to make you go upon the reservation."

I remonstrated with him against bringing more soldiers to the Nez Percés country. He had one house full of troops all the time at Fort Lapwai.

The next spring the agent at Umatilla agency sent an Indian runner to tell me to meet General Howard at Walla Walla. I could not go myself, but I sent my brother and five other head men to meet him, and they had a long talk.

> **"We were contented to let things remain as the Great Spirit Chief made them. [White men] were not; and would change the rivers and mountains if they did not suit them."**

General Howard said: "You have talked straight, and it is all right. You can stay in Wallowa." He insisted that my brother should go with him to Fort Lapwai. When the party arrived there General Howard sent out runners and called all the Indians in to a grand council. I was in that council. I said to General Howard, "We are ready to listen." He answered that he would not talk then, but would hold a council next day, when he would talk plainly. I said to General Howard: "I am ready to talk today. I have been in a great many councils, but I am no wiser. We are all sprung from a woman, although we are unlike in many things. We can not be made over again. You are as you were made, and as you were made you can remain. We are just as we were made by the Great Spirit, and you can not change us; then why should children of one mother and one father quarrel—why should one try to cheat the other? I do not believe that the Great Spirit Chief gave one kind of men the right to tell another kind of men what they must do."

General Howard replied: "You deny my authority, do you? You want to dictate to me, do you?"

Then one of my chiefs—Too-hool-hool-suit—rose in the council and said to General Howard: "The Great Spirit Chief made the world as it is, and as he wanted it, and he made a part of it for us to live upon. I do not see where you get authority to say that we shall not live where he placed us."

General Howard lost his temper and said: "Shut up! I don't want to hear any more of such talk. The law [the treaty] says you shall go upon the reservation to live, and I want you to do so, but you persist in disobeying the law. If you do not move, I will take the matter into my own hand, and make you suffer for your disobedience."

Too-hool-hool-suit answered: "Who are you, that you ask us to talk, and then tell me I sha'n't talk? Are you the Great Spirit? Did you make the world? Did you make the sun? Did you make the rivers to run for us to drink? Did you make the grass to grow? Did you make all these things, that you talk to us as though we were boys? If you did, then you have the right to talk as you do."

General Howard replied, "You are an impudent fellow, and I will put you in the guard house," and then ordered a soldier to arrest him.

Too-hool-hool-suit made no resistance. He asked General Howard: "Is that your order? I don't care. I have expressed my heart to you. I have nothing to take back. I have spoken for my country. You can arrest me, but you can not change me or make me take back what I have said."

The soldiers came forward and seized my friend and took him to the guard house. My men whispered among themselves whether they should let this thing be done. I counseled them to submit. I knew if we resisted that all the white men present, including General Howard, would be killed in a moment, and we would be blamed. If I had said nothing, General Howard would never have given another unjust order against my men. I saw the danger, and, while they dragged Too-hool-hool-suit to prison, I arose and said: "I am going to talk now. I don't care whether you arrest me or not." I turned to my people and said: "The arrest of Too-hool-hool-suit was wrong, but we will not resent the insult. We were invited to this council to express our hearts, and we have done so." Too-hool-hool-suit was prisoner for five days before he was released.

The council broke up for that day. On the next morning General Howard came to my lodge, and invited me to go with him and White-Bird and Looking-Glass, to look for land for my people. As we rode along we came to some good land that was already occupied by Indians and white people. General Howard, pointing to this land, said: "If you will come on to the reservation, I will give you these lands and move these people off."

I replied: "No. It would be wrong to disturb these people. I have no right to take their homes. I have never taken what did not belong to me. I will not now."

We rode all day upon the reservation, and found no good land unoccupied. I have been informed by men who do not lie that General Howard sent a letter that night, telling the soldiers at Walla Walla to go to Wallowa Valley, and drive us out upon our return home.

In the council, next day, General Howard informed me, in a haughty spirit, that he would give my people thirty days to go back home, collect all their stock, and move on to the reservation, saying, "If you are not here in that time, I shall consider that you want to fight, and will send my soldiers to drive you on."

I said: "War can be avoided, and it ought to be avoided. I want no war. My people have always been the friends of the white man. Why are you in such a hurry? I can not get ready to move in thirty days. Our stock is scattered, and Snake River is very high. Let us wait until fall, then the river will be low. We want time to hunt up our stock and gather supplies for winter."

General Howard replied: "If you let the time run over one day, the soldiers will be there to drive you on to the reservation, and all your cattle and horses outside of the reservation at that time will fall into the hands of the white men."

I knew I had never sold my country, and that I had no land in Lapwai; but I did not want bloodshed. I did not want my people killed. I did not want anybody killed. Some of my people had been murdered by white men, and the white murderers were never punished for it. I told General Howard about this, and again said I wanted no war. I wanted the people who lived upon the lands I was to occupy at Lapwai to have time to gather their harvest.

I said in my heart that, rather than have war, I would give up my country. I would give up my father's grave. I would give up everything rather than have the blood of white men upon the hands of my people.

General Howard refused to allow me more than thirty days to move my people and their stock. I am sure that he began to prepare for war at once.

When I returned to Wallowa I found my people very much excited upon discovering that the soldiers were already in the Wallowa Valley. We held a council and decided to move immediately, to avoid bloodshed.

Too-hool-hool-suit, who felt outraged by his imprisonment, talked for war, and made many of my young men willing to fight rather than be driven like dogs from the land where they were born. He declared that blood alone would wash out the disgrace General Howard had put upon him. It required a strong heart to stand up against such talk, but I urged my people to be quiet, and not to begin a war.

We gathered all the stock we could find, and made an attempt to move. We left many of our horses and cattle in Wallowa, and we lost several hundred in crossing the river. All of my people succeeded in getting across in safety. Many of the Nez Percés came together in Rocky Canyon to hold a grand council. I went with all my people. This council lasted ten days. There was a great deal of war talk, and a great deal of excitement. There was one young brave present whose father had been killed by a white man five years before. This man's blood was bad against white men, and he left the council calling for revenge.

Again I counseled peace, and I thought the danger was past. We had not complied with General Howard's order because we could not, but we intended to do so as soon as possible. I was leaving the council to kill beef for my family, when news came that the young man whose father has been killed had gone out with several other hot-blooded young braves and killed four white men. He rode up to the council and shouted: "Why do you sit here like women? The war has begun already."

I was deeply grieved. All the lodges were moved except my brother's and my own. I saw clearly that the war was upon us when I learned that my young men had been secretly buying ammunition. I heard then that Too-hool-hool-suit, who had been imprisoned by General Howard, had succeeded in organizing a war party. I knew that their acts would involve all my people. I saw that the war could not be prevented. The time had passed. I counseled peace from the beginning. I knew that we were too weak to fight the United States. We had many grievances, but I knew that war would bring more. We had good white friends, who advised us against taking the war path. My friend and brother, Mr. [Arthur I.] Chapman, who has been with us since the surrender, told us just how the war would end. Mr. Chapman took sides against us, and helped General Howard. I do not blame him for doing so. He tried hard to prevent bloodshed. We hoped the white settlers would not join the soldiers. Before the war commenced we had discussed this matter all over, and many of my people were in favor of warning them that if they took no part against us they should not be molested in the event of war being begun by General Howard. This plan was voted down in the war council.

There were bad men among my people who had quarreled with white men, and they talked of their wrongs until they roused all the bad hearts in the council. Still I could not believe that they would begin the war. I know that my young men did a great wrong, but I ask, who was first to blame? They had been insulted a thousand times; their fathers and brothers had been killed; their mothers and wives had been disgraced; they had been driven to madness by whisky sold to them by white men; they had been told by General Howard that all their horses and cattle which they had been unable to drive out of Wallowa were to fall into the hands of white men; and, added to all this, they were homeless and desperate.

I would have given my own life if I could have undone the killing of white men by my people. I blame my young men and I blame the white men. I blame General Howard for not giving my people time to get their stock away from Wallowa. I do not acknowledge that he had the right to order me to leave Wallowa at any time. I deny that either my father or myself ever sold that land. It is still our land. It may never again be our home, but my father sleeps there, and I love it as I love my mother. I left there, hoping to avoid bloodshed.

If General Howard had given me plenty of time to gather up my stock, and treated Too-hool-hool-suit as a man should be treated, there would have been no war.

My friends among white men have blamed me for the war. I am not to blame. When my young men began the killing, my heart was hurt. Although I did not justify them, I remembered all the insults I had endured, and my blood was on fire. Still I would have taken my people to the buffalo country without fighting, if possible.

I could see no other way to avoid a war. We moved over to White Bird Creek, sixteen miles away, and there encamped, intending to collect our stock before leaving; but the soldiers attacked us, and the first battle was fought. We numbered in that battle sixty men, and the soldiers a hundred. The fight lasted but a few minutes, when the soldiers retreated before us for twelve miles. They lost thirty-three killed, and had seven wounded. When an Indian fights, he only shoots to kill; but soldiers shoot at random. None of the soldiers were scalped. We do not believe in scalping, nor in killing wounded men. Soldiers do not kill many Indians unless they are wounded and left upon the battlefield. Then they kill Indians.

Seven days after the first battle, General Howard arrived in the Nez Percés country, bringing seven hundred more soldiers. It was now war in earnest. We crossed the Salmon River, hoping General Howard would follow. We were not disappointed. He did follow us, and we got back between him and his supplies, and cut him off for three days. He sent out two companies to open the way. We attacked them, killing one officer, two guides, and ten men.

We withdrew, hoping the soldiers would follow, but they had got fighting enough for that day. They entrenched themselves, and next day we attacked them again. The battle lasted all day, and was renewed next morning. We killed four and wounded seven or eight.

About this time General Howard found out that we were in his rear. Five days later he attacked us with three hundred and fifty soldiers and settlers. We had two hundred and fifty warriors. The fight lasted twenty-seven hours. We lost four killed and several wounded. General Howard's loss was twenty-nine men killed and sixty wounded.

The following day the soldiers charged upon us, and we retreated with our families and stock a few miles, leaving eighty lodges to fall into General Howard's hands.

Finding that we were outnumbered, we retreated to Bitter Root Valley. Here another body of soldiers came upon us and demanded our surrender. We refused. They said, "You can not get by us." We answered, "We are going by you without fighting if you will let us, but we are going by you anyhow." We then made a treaty with these soldiers. We agreed not to molest any one, and they agreed that we might pass through the Bitter Root country in peace. We bought provisions and traded stock with white men there.

We understood that there was to be no more war. We intended to go peaceably to the buffalo country, and leave the question of returning to our country to be settled afterward.

With this understanding we traveled on for four days, and, thinking that the trouble was all over, we stopped and prepared tent poles to take with us. We started again, and at the end of two days we saw three white men passing our camp. Thinking that peace had been made, we did not molest them. We could have killed them or taken them prisoners, but we did not suspect them of being spies, which they were.

That night the soldiers surrounded our camp. About daybreak one of my men went out to look after his horses. The soldiers saw him and shot him down like a coyote. I have since learned that these soldiers were not those we had left behind. They had come upon us from another direction. The new white war-chief's name was [General John] Gibbon. He charged upon us while some of my people were still asleep. We had a hard fight. Some of my men crept around and attacked the soldiers from the rear. In this battle we lost nearly all our lodges, but we finally drove General Gibbon back.

Finding that he was not able to capture us, he sent to his camp a few miles away for his big guns [cannons], but my men had captured them and all the ammunition. We damaged the big guns all we could, and carried away the powder and lead. In the fight with General Gibbon we lost fifty women and children and thirty fighting men. We remained long enough to bury our dead. The Nez Percés never make war on women and children; we could have killed a great many women and children while the war lasted, but we would feel ashamed to do so cowardly an act.

We never scalp our enemies, but when General Howard came up and joined General Gibbon, their Indian scouts dug up our dead and scalped them. I have been told that General Howard did not order this great shame to be done.

We retreated as rapidly as we could toward the buffalo country. After six days General Howard came close to us, and we went out and attacked him, and captured nearly all his horses and mules (about two hundred and fifty head). We then marched on to the Yellowstone Basin.

On the way we captured one white man and two white women. We released them at the end of three days. They were treated kindly. The women were not insulted. Can the white soldiers tell me of one time when Indian women were taken prisoners, and held three days and then released without being insulted? Were the Nez Percés women who fell into the hands of General Howard's soldiers treated with as much respect? I deny that a Nez Percé was ever guilty of such a crime.

A few days later we captured two more white men. One of them stole a horse and escaped. We gave the other a poor horse and told him he was free.

Nine days' march brought us to the mouth of Clarke's Fork of the Yellowstone. We did not know what had become of General Howard, but we supposed that he had sent for more horses and mules. He did not come up, but another new war chief [General Samuel D. Sturgis] attacked us. We held

him in check while we moved all our women and children and stock out of danger, leaving a few men to cover our retreat.

Several days passed, and we heard nothing of General Howard, or Gibbon, or Sturgis. We had repulsed each in turn, and began to feel secure, when another army, under General Miles, struck us. This was the fourth army, each of which outnumbered our fighting force, that we had encountered within sixty days.

We had no knowledge of General Miles' army until a short time before he made a charge upon us, cutting our camp in two, and capturing nearly all of our horses. About seventy men, myself among them, were cut off. My little daughter, twelve years old, was with me. I gave her a rope, and told her to catch a horse and join the others who were cut off from the camp. I have not seen her since, but I have learned that she is alive and well.

"The Nez Percés never make war on women and children;. . .we would feel ashamed to do so cowardly an act."

I thought of my wife and children, who were now surrounded by soldiers, and I resolved to go to them or die. With a prayer in my mouth to the Great Spirit Chief who rules above, I dashed unarmed through the line of soldiers. It seemed to me that there were guns on every side, before and behind me. My clothes were cut to pieces and my horse was wounded, but I was unhurt. As I reached the door of my lodge, my wife handed me my rifle, saying: "Here's your gun. Fight!"

The soldiers kept up a continuous fire. Six of my men were killed in one spot near me. Ten or twelve soldiers charged into our camp and got possession of two lodges, killing three Nez Percés and losing three of their men, who fell inside our lines. I called my men to drive them back. We fought at close range, not more than twenty steps apart, and drove the soldiers back upon their main line, leaving their dead in our hands. We secured their arms and ammunition. We lost, the first day and night, eighteen men and three women. General Miles lost twenty-six killed and forty wounded. The following day General Miles sent a messenger into my camp under protection of a white flag. I sent my friend Yellow Bull to meet him.

Yellow Bull understood the messenger to say that General Miles wished me to consider the situation; that he did not want to kill my people unnecessarily. Yellow Bull understood this to be a demand for me to surrender and save blood. Upon reporting this message to me, Yellow Bull said he wondered whether General Miles was in earnest. I sent him back with my answer, that I had made up my mind, but would think about it and send word soon. A little later he sent some Cheyenne scouts with another message. I went out to meet them. They said they believed that General Miles was sincere and really wanted peace. I walked on to General Miles' tent. He met me and we shook hands. He said, "Come, let us sit down by the fire and talk this matter over." I remained with him all night; next morning Yellow Bull came over to see if I was alive, and why I did not return.

General Miles would not let me leave the tent to see my friend alone.

Yellow Bull said to me: "They have got you in their power, and I am afraid they will never let you go again. I have an officer in our camp, and I will hold him until they let you go free."

I said: "I do not know what they mean to do with me, but if they kill me you must not kill the officer. It will do no good to avenge my death by killing him."

Yellow Bull returned to my camp. I did not make any agreement that day with General Miles. The battle was renewed while I was with him. I was very anxious about my people. I knew that we were near Sitting Bull's camp in King George's land, and I thought maybe the Nez Percés who had escaped would return with assistance. No great damage was done to either party during the night.

On the following morning I returned to my camp by agreement, meeting the officer who had been held a prisoner in my camp at the flag of truce. My people were divided about surrendering. We could have escaped from Bear Paw Mountain if we had left our wounded, old women, and children behind. We were unwilling to do this. We had never heard of a wounded Indian recovering while in the hands of white men.

On the evening of the fourth day General Howard came in with a small escort, together with my friend Chapman. We could now talk understandingly. General Miles said to me in plain words, "If you will come out and give up your arms, I will spare your lives and send you to your reservation." I do not know what passed between General Miles and General Howard.

I could not bear to see my wounded men and women suffer any longer; we had lost enough already. General Miles had promised that we might return to our own country with what stock we had left. I thought we could start again. I believed General Miles, or I never would have surrendered. I have heard that he has been censured for making the promise to return us to Lapwai. He could not

have made any other terms with me at that time. I would have held him in check until my friends came to my assistance, and then neither of the generals nor their soldiers would have ever left Bear Paw Mountain alive.

On the fifth day I went to General Miles and gave up my gun, and said, "From where the sun now stands I will fight no more." My people needed rest—we wanted peace.

I was told we could go with General Miles to Tongue River and stay there until spring, when we would be sent back to our country. Finally it was decided that we were to be taken to Tongue River. We had nothing to say about it. After our arrival at Tongue River, General Miles received orders to take us to Bismarck. The reason given was, that subsistence would be cheaper there.

General Miles was opposed to this order. He said: "You must not blame me. I have endeavored to keep my word, but the chief who is over me has given the order, and I must obey it or resign. That would do you no good. Some other officer would carry out the order."

I believe General Miles would have kept his word if he could have done so. I do not blame him for what we have suffered since the surrender. I do not know who is to blame. We gave up all our horses—over eleven hundred—and all our saddles—over one hundred—and we have not heard from them since. Somebody has got our horses.

General Miles turned my people over to another soldier, and we were taken to Bismarck. Captain Johnson, who now had charge of us, received an order to take us to Fort Leavenworth. At Leavenworth we were placed on a low river bottom, with no water except river water to drink and cook with. We had always lived in a healthy country, where the mountains were high and the water was cold and clear. Many of my people sickened and died, and we buried them in this strange land. I cannot tell how much my heart suffered for my people while at Leavenworth. The Great Spirit Chief who rules above seemed to be looking some other way, and did not see what was being done to my people.

During the hot days [July, 1878] we received notice that we were to be moved farther away from our own country. We were not asked if we were willing to go. We were ordered to get into railroad cars. Three of my people died on the way to Baxter Springs [Kansas]. It was worse to die there than to die fighting in the mountains.

We were moved from Baxter Springs to the Indian Territory, and set down without our lodges.

We had but little medicine, and we were nearly all sick. Seventy of my people have died since we moved there.

We have had a great many visitors who have talked many ways. Some of the chiefs [General Fish and Colonel William Stickney] from Washington came to see us, and selected land for us to live upon. We have not moved to that land, for it is not a good place to live.

The Commissioner Chief [E.A. Hayt, the Commissioner of Indian Affairs] came to see us. I told him, as I told everyone, that I expected General Miles' word would be carried out. He said it "could not be done; that white men now lived in my country and all the land was taken up; that, if I returned to Wallowa, I could not live in peace; that law-papers were out against my young men who began the war, and that the government could not protect my people." This talk fell like a heavy stone upon my heart. I saw that I could not gain anything by talking to him. Other law chiefs [members of a congressional committee] came to see me and said they would help me to get a healthy country. I did not know who to believe. The white people have too many chiefs. They do not understand each other. They do not all talk alike.

The Commissioner Chief [Hayt] invited me to go with him and hunt for a better home than we have now. I like the land we found [west of the Osage Reservation] better than any place I have seen in that country; but it is not a healthy land. There are no mountains and rivers. The water is warm. It is not a good country for stock. I do not believe my people can live there. I am afraid they will all die. The Indians who occupy that country are dying off. I promised Chief Hayt to go there, and do the best I could until the government got ready to make good General Miles' word. I was not satisfied, but I could not help myself.

Then the Inspector Chief [General John O'Neil] came to my camp and we had a long talk. He said I ought to have a home in the mountain country north, and that he would write a letter to the Great Chief at Washington. Again the hope of seeing the mountains of Idaho and Oregon grew up in my heart.

At last I was granted permission to come to Washington and bring my friend Yellow Bull and our interpreter with me. I am glad we came. I have shaken hands with a great many friends, but there are some things I want to know which no one seems able to explain. I cannot understand how the government sends a man out to fight us, as it did General Miles, and then breaks his word. Such a government has something wrong about it. I cannot

understand why so many chiefs are allowed to talk so many different ways, and promise so many different things. I have seen the Great Father Chief [President Rutherford B. Hayes], the next Great Chief [Secretary of the Interior Carl Schurz], the Commissioner Chief [Hayt], the Law Chief [General Butler], and many other law chiefs [congressmen], and they all say they are my friends, and that I shall have justice, but while their mouths all talk right I do not understand why nothing is done for my people. I have heard talk and talk, but nothing is done.

Good words do not last long unless they amount to something. Words do not pay for my dead people. They do not pay for my country, now overrun by white men. They do not protect my father's grave. They do not pay for all my horses and cattle. Good words will not give me back my children. Good words will not make good the promise of your War Chief General Miles. Good words will not give my people good health and stop them from dying. Good words will not get my people a home where they can live in peace and take care of themselves. I am tired of talk that comes to nothing. It makes my heart sick when I remember all the good words and all the broken promises. There has been too much talking by men who had no right to talk. Too many misrepresentations have been made, too many misunderstandings have come up between the white men about the Indians.

> **"I** am tired of talk that comes to nothing. It makes my heart sick when I remember all the good words and all the broken promises."

If the white man wants to live in peace with the Indian he can live in peace. There need be no trouble. Treat all men alike. Give them the same law. Give them all an even chance to live and grow. All men were made by the same Great Spirit Chief. They are all brothers. The earth is the mother of all people, and all people should have equal rights upon it. You might as well expect the rivers to run backward as that any man who was born a free man should be contented when penned up and denied liberty to go where he pleases. If you tie a horse to a stake, do you expect he will grow fat? If you pen an Indian up on a small spot of earth, and compel him to stay there, he will not be contented, nor will he grow and prosper. I have asked some of the great white chiefs where they get their authority to say to the Indian that he shall stay in one place, while he sees white men going where they please. They cannot tell me.

I only ask of the government to be treated as all other men are treated. If I cannot go to my own home, let me have a home in some country where my people will not die so fast. I would like to go to Bitter Root Valley. There my people would be healthy; where they are now they are dying. Three have died since I left my camp to come to Washington.

When I think of our condition my heart is heavy. I see men of my race treated as outlaws and driven from country to country, or shot down like animals.

I know that my race must change. We can not hold our own with the white men as we are. We only ask an even chance to live as other men live. We ask to be recognized as men. We ask that the same law shall work alike on all men. If the Indian breaks the law, punish him by the law. If the white man breaks the law, punish him also.

Let me be a free man—free to travel, free to stop, free to work, free to trade where I choose, free to choose my own teachers, free to follow the religion of my fathers, free to think and talk and act for myself—and I will obey every law, or submit to the penalty.

Whenever the white man treats an Indian as they treat each other, then we will have no more wars. We shall all be alike—brothers of one father and one mother, with one sky above us and one country around us, and one government for all. Then the Great Spirit Chief who rules above will smile upon this land, and send rain to wash out the bloody spots made by brothers' hands from the face of the earth. For this time the Indian race are waiting and praying. I hope that no more groans of wounded men and women will ever go to the ear of the Great Spirit Chief above, and that all people may be one people. In-mut-too-yah-lat-lat has spoken for his people.

Source:

Indian Oratory: Famous Speeches by Noted Indian Chieftains, by W. C. Vanderwerth. Norman: University of Oklahoma Press, 1971.

NICARAGUAN AMERICANS

In 1986, the United States government amended the Immigration and Nationality Act in an effort to reduce the flow of illegal immigration through border enforcement and sanctions against employers hiring illegally-entered workers. The new law granted legal status to 2.6 million illegal immigrants already here. Then when America's businesses needed more high-tech immigrants, the law changed again in the Immigration Act of 1990, which increased the levels of immigration for highly skilled professionals. However, special admission categories for refugees allow political refugees to legally slip around quotas and gain admission.

Immigration in the latter half of the twentieth century does not equal immigration of the turn of the century, when foreign-born population composed 15 percent of the population. By comparison, immigrants in the late 1990s constitute ten percent of the total population. Still, the Christian Science Monitor reported in May of 1999 that economists called before the House Immigration Subcommittee hearing warned that the greatest influx of immigrants in United States history was underway in 1999. Two-thirds of U.S. population growth stems from immigration. The foreign-born population has grown from 8.6 million in 1965, 4.4 percent of the total, to 27 million in 1999, or 9.7 percent. These figures do not include six million undocumented immigrants. The results are that one in eight workers are foreign-born. The economists urged the house subcommittee to reduce the annual number of immigrants to 555,000, the level suggested in 1995 by the U.S. Commission on Immigration Reform. In 1999, the annual number of immigrants permitted is 900,000, and 80 percent of these enter under family reunification provisions.

"Just Being With Them Makes Me Happy" adds a Nicaraguan voice to the voices of numerous immigrants who have come to the United States in search of a better life. Prepared over a ten-year relationship with a scholar intent on documenting the illegal immigrant experience, it tells the particular story of Nicaragua. The political instability of Nicaragua and the hopes and efforts of the Nicaraguans to rescue their beloved country, are described, as well as how immigration to the United States became a necessary step for some Nicaraguans. Yet at the same time this is the story of every immigrant, regardless of time and nationality. The personal feelings and life cycles of the newly arrived foreign born person are the common thread across groups. The time of arrival, the place of settlement, and the condition of the former country, while influencing the assimilation experience, are not as significant in the writings of immigrants as is the sense of being captured by America.

"Just Being With Them Makes Me Happy" speaks of the experiences of the undocumented immigrant population, which by 1994 was between 3.2 and 3.8 million people. Like Yamileth, the Nicaraguan, anywhere between 1.2 and 1.7 of these immigrants live in California, a state staggering under the load of immigrant social services and public education. New York, Texas, Florida, Illinois, and Arizona also bear similar loads. Californians have responded with anti-immigrant legislation. But, this response is nothing new. The first U.S. immigration law in 1882 *contained a restriction designed to hinder Chinese immigration. An act in 1924 excluded all Asians.*

"Just Being With Them Makes Me Happy"

"I used to feel so empty, especially last fall when I was pregnant, but now I don't. I give infinite thanks to God and tot he help that I've received from Marisa, from Manuel, and from everyone around me. One way or another, they've supported me. They love Diana, and just being with her makes me happy.

"I do have problems with my son, who's jealous. He says that everyone brings Diana presents but not him. 'marisa gives presents to the baby and not to me,' he complains, 'and Manuel picks her up and plays with her.' I grab my son and I tease both of them, Diana and Miguel. 'Ay, my two little balck ones, mis negritos,' [*Negrito,* as Yamileth uses it, is a term of endearment. Her neighbors in Estelí had often called her*Negrita,* and she in turn uses the name with her children. When she referred to African Americans, she usually chose the word *moreno,* which means brown.] I tell them, 'it's so beautiful to have my two black ones.' I try to distribute the love evenly, but even Nora is jealous and says contemptuously about Diana, 'Now they don't love me, only her.'

Work satisfies me a lot. I love it, especially since I'd be doing what I love to do, but the pay is too little.

"Miguel loves to squeeze Diana and wants her to be big enough to walk. She still has to be treated delicately, but they don't do that. No one in the house treats her with tenderness. Instead, they act as if she's a child of two years. It frightens me, but, at the same time, I can't say no because I could lose those who love me. I worry, though, when she's sleeping here with me on the couch. I almost never sleep. I worry because on television they say many children die. They don't know the cause, but they turn up dead. So I lie there all night making sure she breathes. Leticia laughs because she wonder how I sleep without falling off the couch. I put Diana on the inside and I take the outside. The reason I don't fall is that I lie on the edge, awake and worrying about her. It's an L-shaped couch, and Miguel sleeps on the other end. Our feet cross. Sometimes we start playing at night and he tickles

me. He often wants the three of us to sleep on one side, but I tell him, 'that's impossible. Why don't we sleep on the floor instead?' One night we tried it, but Diana didn't like it.

"But no, I no longer have that emptiness. I'm happy. I have a strong commitment to Marisa, more than anyone, because it's she who has to take care of the food. If Diana has an appointment one day, Marisa doesn't go to work or tells Manuel that he has to get up early to take me to the clinic. When the family hears Diana cry, they're concerned, attentive, so I have much to be thankful for. So I try to keep the house clean, to help them with many things, to have food for them when I can. In that way I can pay back what they're doing, not just for my daughter but for my son and for me, too.

"I tell Marisa that we need to buy beans and rice—that's what's most necessary—and, when we have some extra money, we buy meat or chicken, but always we have Nicaraguan rice and beans, *gallo pinto.* Morning, noon, afternoon, or night, someone is always here wanting to eat it.

"For myself, I have no money to spend. Anyhow, I don't go out in the street, partly because I'm afraid if I go with my daughter that they might take her from me or something will happen. I don't know, there are so many things in my mind that I, instead of maturing, have become more childlike for fear of something happening to my daughter. So I don't go. I prefer to call Marisa and say, 'marisa, if you have money, bring such and such a thing, *chiltomá* [a sweet green pepper and a medicinal herb, possibly for tea] or mint.' Whatever spices I might need, she gets when she can.

"Some days are more difficult than others, but I have faith that God will help Marisa and that Manuel will find a job because those two don't want me to look for work and take the child. There's no one around here to leave her with. They're all African Americans, and African Americans don't have confidence in anyone besides themselves.

"One day I went shopping on Miguel's bike, and I rode fast because I had left Diana with him. On the corner I met up with a man who wanted me to get off the bike and give it to him. I understood what he wanted but I said, 'No speaking English.' He tried to take it from me, but I pushed him away. He followed me to the store, but I asked the clerk if he would let me put my bike in the store. At every moment you have to be ready because they'll take your shoes right off you.

"I've always had the idea of returning to Nicaragua but not right now, not tomorrow, nor the morning after. A reason to stay in the United States was to have had my daughter here. They took good care of me and gave both my daughter and me good medical care without it costing a cent. They told me that I'd have to pay it back, little by little. I'm sure that if I find a good job, I'll do it, especially with a conscience like mine. All medicines are available here, and everything is easier.

"Miguel is supposed to be going to Belmont High School, but I'm frightened to let him go. He left Canoga Park School because he though that the gangs would catch him and make him do something by force. He left, not out of fear, but out of terror. I know that it's important for him to go to school, but I'm afraid of losing him. In one month, four children have died in Los Angeles from stray bullets. That kind of tension makes you nervous. Maybe I feel it more than others because I've seen so much in Los Angeles and in my country. Having seen so many things . . . it's another tension, maybe a little different, but with the same fear of losing a loved one. The tension never ends. People say they're not safe at home, not at work, and not in the streets. It's just best not to go out.

"It's gotten even more dangerous in our old neighborhood on Bonnie Brae [just north of Pico Boulevard]. There still are barricades in the streets, but it's more closed, not possible for anything to enter, no cars. It's sealed off with permanent posts put in the ground. It's the most secure measure. No longer do cars enter, and the people who come into the neighborhood have criminal records and are known to be buying and distributing drugs. Only people enter, no cars.

"My visa has expired now. People tell me I can get false documents, but I've been afraid to do that because la migra can catch me. They say I can deceive the government, though, but what I can't do is deceive myself. My conscience tells me not to. Besides, they'd find out and that would make me more ashamed. I don't want anyone in Nicaragua to say that we did anything dishonest. It's better to stay quietly undocumented, quietly looking for work, and not doing things we shouldn't.

"Alejandra called [in September] to ask how I was. She realized that I had the baby and she want-ed to talk with me. I had no idea that David was at her side when she called. She asked, 'How's the baby? Well?'

"'Yes, of course. I sent you some photos. Did you get them?'

"'Yes, I did,' she said, and then added, 'Listen, someone you know was killed in an ambush.'

"'david?'

"'Yes, David.'

"'I don't believe you.'

"'It's true, and you know who he was with? All those friends who hand around with him.'

"I didn't believe her.

"Suddenly she burst into laughter. 'Yes, I'm lying! Don't believe me! Do you want to talk with him?' And she put him on the line.

"**B**oth of them, David and Alejandra, want me to return. I would like to go back, I would, but the problem is that I have to consider my children, especially Diana."

"He told me that he was fine and asked when I was going to return. We talked for a long time—fifteen minutes—and he told me he was no longer in the military because there had been another cut back with the new president. He was planting rice on his land—he has quite a bit—with his mother and brothers in Jalapa. He's also working for the Farm Workers Association [Asociación de Trabajadores del Campo] by organizing the workers in the field, just like a good Sandinista. That makes me happy because I told him that in spite of what happens, he shouldn't let anything take away the ideas we fought for. I was chatting with him, talking politically, and he explained to me that we need to give the Sandinista Front the strength to rise up again and return to power. It will be difficult, he said, but we had to figure out how to do it.

"Both of them, David and Alejandra, want me to return. I would like to go back, I would, but the problem is that I have to consider my children, especially Diana. She's young, and I worry about her food. They're offering me work, again related to the women's association, but they couldn't promise that I'd make a nice salary, or even enough to pay the water bill, the electricity, and buy food for Diana. Work satisfies me a lot. I love it, especially since I'd be doing what I love to do, but the pay is too little. I just don't think it would be enough. If I went back, though, I'd live in Estelí so we wouldn't see each other every day. But when we'd meet, it would go on for a week!

"The situation in Nicaragua is like it is everywhere. There's food, but you need to buy it. Here in the United States there are so many things to buy, but how can you buy them without money? Here I feel more tension, so much so that it makes me want to cry, and I feel a desperateness because I'm not doing anything. I mean, even though I'm doing a lot—I clean the house and cook after I come home from working in the beauty salon. I wash people's hair, comb it out, and spray it so that it's ready for Marisa to work on. Some people come for permanents and need a treatment. Marisa says, 'Look, *Tía*, put the treatment on that woman, and put this woman under the dryer for so many minutes,' and I do it. Sometimes, we have only two clients a day; but last Saturday, six people came at eight o'clock in the morning to get ready for the *quinceñera*, the celebration [of a teenage girl] for being fifteen years old. The other day, though, no one came. So we have ups and downs her, too, just as in Nicaragua.

"Yes, I used to think that by being with David, I was doing something that hurt the other woman, that damaged women throughout the world. But now I don't know. Being there, looking at things to see if it's the same or isn't . . . I mean, I have those feelings, but not when I'm there! When I'm there, I don't know if that's true. Look, I know it's not right to share him or to make life impossible for her because then neither one of us will feel secure about what we have. I, for example, have never had the idea that he would be with me for all of my life. I have lived with the idea that I'll have him with me when I can, and he'll be with me when he can, and I feel good about that. But then, again, I don't know. The only problem is if she realizes that he wants to see me. I would try not to go there, but if I have to work there, I have to go, but I don't want to cause problems with her, nor cause problems for the work I'd be doing. The Farm Workers Association has regional meetings there every couple of weeks, depending on what we're planning. I'd have to go—maybe to take care of something personally! But no, I don't feel sure of him. No, no.

"David found out about Diana because I sen him some photographs through Alejandra. I didn't know that she had been elected to be AMNLAE's regional director and thought she was still working in a school. She wrote to me about her operation and that she might lose her job, but four months later she wrote to me about her new position and asked me when I wanted to come. Before that, I had sent her a letter with the photos and she took them to Jalapa. That's how David found out. I had written just a few words to him on a sheet, all stapled shut, because I wasn't sure if it would get to him or if Alejandra was going to be able to see him. I thought she was still teaching and had to spend all week in the school, which would leave her with no pretext to visit Jalapa. But, as it turns out, with her new job she travels throughout the region.

"Yes, he was happy. He could hear Diana, so I put her on the phone so he could talk with her and hear her. It made him happy, and her, too.

"The family still doesn't know about David. All they know is that I brought Diana from Nicaragua—and they don't even believe that! That I do not like, but it's their problem, not mine."

Source:

Chapter 8 of *Undocumented in L.A.: An Immigrant's Story*, by Dianne Walta Hart. Wilmington, DE: Scholarly Resources Inc., 1997. pp. 93-98.

NIGERIAN AMERICANS

*T*hrough an interview, Tunde Ayobami shared an early Nigerian immigrant story of coming to America in search of a higher education. Tunde was born in the late 1940s while Nigeria was in the latter years of British rule. In its quest for independence, Nigeria suffered from prolonged violent political turmoil and marked economic disruption. Under such conditions, Tunde was raised by his father, a government employee, who lived in a shack.

Tunde attended Baptist missionary high school where he not only learned English, the official language of Nigeria, but also gained familiarity with western culture from the school's American teachers. At the time, Nigerian students commonly sought college educations abroad, usually either in the United States or Russia.

Preferring America's capitalist society and taking advantage of ties with a white American friend in Bristol, Rhode Island, Tunde came to the United States in 1969 at 21 years of age. Initially living with his friend's family, he worked for their small construction business and also as a gardener for a wealthy woman. Pursuing his quest for higher education, Tunde entered Bristol Community College while first working in a textile mill operating dye machines and later at a bakery. Tunde's initial impression was not what he anticipated, "I was disappointed for the fact that the money wasn't easy to get. Judging from the Hollywood pictures and how people were smashing cars and everybody walk leisurely on the street, I thought I was going to a paradise, you don't have to earn money."

Tunde expressed great pleasure with living in New England rather than the more common Nigerian immigrant choices of New York City or other large Eastern cities. Being the first Nigerian to reside in the area, Tunde became a local celebrity of sorts.

With a growing robust oil economy in Nigeria in the 1970s, many more Nigerians traveled to the United States to study. For those arriving in Rhode Island, Tunde proudly assisted them with finding jobs and schools. Tunde graduated from Southeastern Massachusetts University in medical technology. Unlike many Nigerians coming to the United States for school and then returning home, Tunde chose to stay. Soon, tiring of medical laboratory work, Tunde became a successful black salesmen operating in a large five state area from Pennsylvania to Wisconsin.

TUNDE AYOBAMI

When I was going to high school, my parents separated, and my mother couldn't take all the children. My twin sisters were about six months old, and one stayed with my father. I was taking care of her. You know, the custom is putting the babies in a pouch on the back and tying them. At first I was a little bit shy, being a boy, and it was something meant for a woman to do. It's not like staying in the house. I'm talking about going out, walking about a mile and back, and the baby on my back. You know, like going out on errands, going to market. And people just look at me when I go in the store, and they start laughing. A lot of the women give me praise, and then I start feeling good, so then I didn't worry about it.

So I was living with my father. He work for the government—shows films, educational films, to tourists. There's no way to describe the house. In fact, I would say it's a shack. Families living in one or two rooms, and everybody shares the same bathroom and the same kitchen.

My parents were Baptists, and I went to a Baptist missionary high school. English was the language in the school, and you have to learn the local language, too—Yoruba. It's my tribal language, and it's the third widely spoken language in the continent.

After I left school I got a job in a broadcasting house. I was involved with overseas transmission— news stories, propaganda, and all the rest of it— during the Nigerian-Biafra war. Not exactly a newscaster, but I had access to everything I want to find out. It was a good job, but it wasn't meant for me.

I wanted to come here for along time, but everybody has an alternative—either coming to the U.S. or going to the USSR. They have a university—they call it Friendship University—in Moscow. And I had the opportunity to go to the USSR to study for free. Like I said before, the easiest one is always the one with no money. In other words, all you have to do is take a taxi to the airport and get into the—what's this Russian airline—Aeroflot. And it takes you to Moscow and they drive you into the college. That's all! But here you got to get all kinds of money and prepare documents and passports. But Africans, in general, they are not so crazy about communism. Africans, as far as I'm concerned, are capitalists. Well, I just didn't like the Russian ideas.

I knew about the U.S. while I was growing up, because I did have a lot of friends. I mean Americans who came to Nigeria to teach, mostly white.

We met and we exchanged addresses, magazines, things like this. This was while I was in the high school. They tell me all the things about America, all good things. So I was keen to come in here.

My father, of course, he didn't want me to go anywhere. Because for one thing, I'm the number one in the family and I'm supposed to take care of everybody. He was thinking of when he dies; who is going to be the head of the family. But, by the same token, he always respect my individual decision. Well, I said I'm going to travel out to the U.S.

I have a friend—then he was about fifteen years old—I'm talking about white American family, from Bristol, Rhode Island. We got in touch through the ham radio operation. Then we started to write each other. And when I was coming here and I didn't have any money, he sent some money to me. It was 1969, and I was about twenty-one. I come with the idea of just going to school and going back; because, for one thing, I didn't know what to expect. I just knew what I was gong to do: Go to school, get my degree, and go back.

Aviation was in my mind when I left, and I got an admission to an aviation training center in Florida. Bur once I went through the Atlantic, I changed my mind [*Laughs*.] That was my first time in a plane. It was scary up there. When I got up there, I couldn't see any houses. I couldn't even see any water. All you see is white clouds. So I said there is no way I was going to do this—a pilot. I decided not to go to Florida.

I landed in JFK and I found my way to Rhode Island, to the family. Oh, they are wonderful. That's my American mother and father. She was a marvelous woman. That's why I call her mom, even up to now. I stayed with them for two months. Within this two months, I was introduced to all kind of people. Everybody want to see our picture together, everything like that. There was a big write-up in the *Bristol Journal*. And I met the reverend of the church, and everything.

The family has a small construction business, and I helped them out. And I was working as a gardener in Mrs. Marjory Carruthers's. She was really rich. I was mowing the lawn with the lawnmower, taking care of the flowers.

I was disappointed for the fact that the money wasn't easy to get. Judging from the Hollywood pictures and how people were smashing cars and everybody walk leisurely on the street, I thought I was going to a paradise; you don't have to earn money. [*Laughs.*]

After a couple of months I found a school, Bristol Community College. I was looking, because I didn't want to go to Florida, like I said. They took me and they give me a first-semester scholarship.

Then I didn't want to be driving from Bristol to the school, because I didn't have a car. The guy I went to talk to in school introduce me to Peter, and Pete told me, "Hey, if you are looking for a place to live, I have an apartment on so-and-so street." I said, "Okay, let's try it." I was so innocent.

It's one of those old houses—two-bedroom apartment with a living room. Yeah, my own bedroom! At first I liked it. It was really different, but it was part of the experience, I feel. During the week, maybe eight people—hippies—stay there. But on the weekend, maybe about twenty. You know, they bring their bags, and three in there and four in here. Oh, they were excellent people. I like them. But you cannot study there, because they always play the music loud and smoke, and they can't open the windows and everything seeps into my bedroom. They didn't get involved with the drugs until later on; and when it was getting bad and they were disturbing the neighbors, the neighbors had to be calling the cops. I found out that just being present where they are using drugs make me one of them, you know. So that was when I decided to leave.

Meanwhile, a guy came—a black American—by the name of John. He was told about me in the school, and so he introduced himself and invited me for some drinks. Then we started talking, and his intention was to come and get a partner for an apartment. So I move into his apartment. We were compatible, and we became very good friends.

I used to go to school eight to three. From three to eleven I go to work. First, I was working in a textile mill. I operate the dyeing machines—real dirty job. Then I went to a cookie place, a bakery, and I started off on the assembly line. Well, the belt was moving, and you got to pack them in the box, the container, with my apron on and my hat. We have to [*claps hands twice, sharply*] pack them in there and we have to do so many things, because everything was rushing. Oh, yeah, it was a tough job. You're standing, you can't go anywhere, everybody is keeping up production. See, you can't talk to machines. If you want to go to the men's room, you have to call the foreman to come and stand in for you. Then I was promoted to the bakery room. That is in the oven room; 120 degrees on a normal day.

I got involved in different things, and I got to meet different people. I was a Sunday School teacher.

It was the Baptist church in Fall River, and I'd go there every Sunday. A wealthy lady, she bought a bike for me, and I went to church on my bike. I was teaching the tenth and twelfth graders. I had a lot of talks, you know—interviews and talk shows—I'd go to the Kiwanis, the deacon's lunch. I talked about Africa and business in Africa and how Americans can come to Africa, and all these kind of things.

I was the first Nigerian in the area. Before I came here, none of us had the idea of going to the suburbs. New York, Boston, Philadelphia—big cities. When I go to visit them, they say, "Where are you, anyway? I never heard of the place. We'll come to see you sometime." So they come and stay over the weekend; and we travel around, I show them places. Most of them didn't know any other place but New York City. But I tell them this place is really peaceful. And when they come to Rhode Island, I try to find jobs for them and find school at the same time. They pay less money for the school, which is an attraction. And I introduced a lot of Nigerians to the church. So everybody come, and most of them have been able to finish school and go to wherever they want to go.

I was disappointed for the fact that the money wasn't easy to get. Judging from the Hollywood pictures and how people were smashing cars and everybody walk leisurely on the street, I thought I was going to a paradise; you don't have to earn money.

When I finished Bristol Community College, I applied to four-year colleges. I got an admission to Southeastern Massachusetts University, and that was where I went. I finished my college program—medical technology. After I finished school, I got interviews from different companies, and this company hired me. I was in the lab, doing hematology. It was a good job. You know, the lab is always interesting. But the moment you are not given an opportunity to do anything—you know, like management changes and everybody has different ideas—and when the company say, "Well, this is the way we're going to stay," it became so boring staying in the lab, because we do the same thing every time. So I decided to leave the lab and get into sales, technical sales.

I went to the boss and I said, "I don't want to be in the lab. I want to get into sales somewhere." He said there was no position, but later I found out it was because he didn't think I would ever make a good salesman. Most people didn't think I would make it. First, because of my accent; they said I would never sell anybody.

So I was waiting for the best time to quit the company. But the management changed, and the new guy, the vice-president, thought it was a good idea to challenge everybody who wants to do something, so I got into the sales field. I'm one of the first black employees in sales in my company. In my division, I'm the first one. In another department there is another one—not African.

Now I'm a technical sales rep, and what I do—besides make money for the company—is to go to some customers. My territory includes Pennsylvania, Illinois, Minnesota, Wisconsin, Indiana. Maybe an average of two days a week I'm not home. But it depends on planning. I like it. I like it very much. The territory was dying before I took it over, and now the sales has been going up, up, up, up, up. Since I've been on the road, my territory has been improved about 200 percent. The vice-president just wrote me a note, congratulating me. He said, "Keep it up."

Why? Well, number one is I work hard on the territory—more than most of the salesmen that are in there. Every day the average salesman makes about three calls and then comes home. I go five, six, seven. I leave home by six and I make many calls—which makes me coming home after everybody. All of them quit by three; I'm still on the road till four-thirty. I quit at five. On my own, because I'm on salary. It's not a commission, so it's no incentive. That's why a lot of them didn't do the job as it should be done. Some of the customers told me they had dropped the business because the salesman hadn't called on them in a year, two years. I check up, I follow up on samples, I try to develop the business.

Well, in sales, you see your contribution. It's not like in the lab where you come out with a product, and before you turn your head, the boss is taking over and saying, "Yeah, I made it. Its my idea." He gets the credit and you do the work. But now you see that when you work hard, the money comes in. This is the contribution. Every month I can say I made a hundred thousand dollars, or sometimes five hundred thousand dollars, for the company—from me! They know *I'm* the one getting the business. I hope for the future. I think I can get into management, which is one of the reasons that I took the job.

Source:

American Mosaic by Joan Morrison and Charlotte Fox Zabusky. New York: E.P. Dutton, 1980. pp. 404-408.

Norwegian Americans

Songs were one of the more entertaining and communal methods of describing the immigrant experience in America. Songs, written by and for immigrants of the same ethnicity, provided not only enjoyment but also information about the conditions of life as a newcomer in the United States. Many of the folk songs contained colorful images of the opportunities and benefits available in America, although some warned of harsh conditions and others spoke tenderly about the people and places left behind in the Old World.

With tongue in cheek, Ditmar Meidell, editor of a humorous journal in Norway, wrote "Oleana" as a satire of those songs. Oleana was a Norwegian settlement in Potter County, Pennsylvania. Contrary to the songs and tales that many people had heard in Norway, residents of Oleana struggled; their lives were characterized by hard work, desolate and unproductive farmland, and frustration, rather than by the great opportunities and fertile soils described in advertisements. Meidell's song ridiculed emigrants' high expectations and contrasted the promise with the reality of life in Oleana. Setting aside Meidell's sarcasm and hyperbole, "Oleana" provides comic appeal as well as insights into immigrants' hopes for freedom, social standing, and economic success in America.

Oleana

En Splinterny Vise Til Oleanas Pris Digtet Af En Oleanafarer

I Oleana der er det godt at vaere,
I Norge vil jeg inte Slavelaenken baere!

Ole—Ole—Ole oh! Oleana!
Ole—Ole—Ole oh! Oleana!

I Oleana der faar jeg Jord for Intet,
af Jorden voxer Kornet,—og det gaar
    gesvint det.

Ole—Ole—Ole oh! Oleana!
Ole—Ole—Ole—oh! etc.

Aa Kornet det taersker sig selv oppaa Laaven,
imens ligger jeg aa hviler mig I Koven.

Ole—Ole—Ole—oh! etc.

Hej Markedsgang! Poteterne skulde Du se, Du.
Der braendes mindst en Pot af hvereneste en Du.
    one of them.

A Brand New Ballad in Praise of Oleana by a Settler There

In Oleana, that's where I'd like to be,
and not drag the chains of slavery in Norway.

Ole—Ole—Ole oh! Oleana!
Ole—Ole—Ole oh! Oleana!

In Oleana they give you land for nothing,
and the grain just pops out of the ground. Golly,
    that's easy.

Ole—Ole—Ole oh! Oleana!
Ole—Ole—Ole—oh! etc.

The grain threshes itself in the granary
while I stretch out at ease in my bunk.

Ole—Ole—Ole—oh! etc.

And the markets! You just ought to see the potatoes!
You can distill at least a quart of whiskey from every

Ole—Ole—Ole—oh! etc.

Ja Bayerol saa godt, som han Ytteborg kan brygge,
det risler I Baekkene til Fattigmandens Hygge.

Ole—Ole—Ole—oh! etc.

Aa Laxene dem springer saa lystig i Baekke,
dem hopper selv i Gryden aa roper: dem ska' daekke!

Ole—Ole—Ole—oh! etc.

Aa brunstegte Griser de loper om saa flinke
aa forespor sig hofligt, om Nogen vil ha' Skinke.

Ole—Ole—Ole—oh! etc.

Aa Kjorene dem melker aa kjaerner aa yster
liksaa naturlig som Else, mi Syster.

Ole—Ole—Ole—oh! etc.

Aa Storstuten sjelve staar inte og haenger,
han banker sine Kalve, fordi de gaar og slaenger.

Ole—Ole—Ole—oh! etc.

Aa Kalvene de slagter sig hurtig og flaar sig
aa stejker sig fortere end man tar en Taar sig!

Ole—Ole—Ole—oh! etc.

Aa Hona vaerper Aeg saa svaere som Stabur,
mens Hanen angir Tiden som et ottedags Slaguhr.

Ole—Ole—Ole—oh! etc.

Fra Skyerne det regner med Kolerakaker.
Aa Gubevare Dere vel for dejlige Saker!

Ole—Ole—Ole—oh! etc.

Aa Sola hu skinner saa trufast hele Natta
saa atte man kan se I Morke liksom Katta!

Ole—Ole—Ole—oh! etc.

Aa Maanen hver Aften er fuld—det er sikkert.
Jeg ligger just aa ser paa'n med Flaska tel Kjikkert.

Ole—Ole—Ole—oh! etc.

Ja to Daler Dagen det faar Du for at svire,
aa er Du rektig doven, saa kanske Du faar fire.
      four.

Ole—Ole—Ole—oh! etc.

Aa Kjaerringa og Unger dem falder paa
      Kommynen.
Betaler dem, ikke, saa faar dem paa Trynen!

Ole—Ole—Ole—oh! etc.

Kronarbejde findes ej—nej det var saa ligt da!
jeg sad nok ikke ellersen saa frisk her aa digta.

Ole—Ole—Ole—oh! etc.

Vi gaar I Flojelsklaeder besat med Solverknapper,
Aa ryker af Merskum, som Kjaerringa stapper.

Ole—Ole—Ole—oh! etc.

And Munchener beer, as sweet as Ytteborg's,
runs in the creeks for the poor man's delectation.

Ole—Ole—Ole—oh! etc.

And the salmon, they leap like mad in the rivers,
and hop into the kettles, and cry out for a cover.

Ole—Ole—Ole—oh! etc.

And little roasted piggies rush about the streets,
politely inquiring if you wish for ham.

Ole—Ole—Ole—oh! etc.

And the cows, they milk and churn and make cheese
just as skillfully as Else, my sister.

Ole—Ole—Ole—oh! etc.

And the bull himself doesn't stand around idle;
he beats his calves for loafing and shirking.

Ole—Ole—Ole—oh! etc.

And the calves, they kill and flay themselves
and turn to veal roast faster than you can take a drink.

Ole—Ole—Ole—oh! etc.

And the hens lay eggs as big as a store-house,
and the cocks strike the hour like an eight-day clock.

Ole—Ole—Ole—oh! etc.

And cakes fairly rain from the skies above you.
Good Lord, what wondrous tidbits!

Ole—Ole—Ole—oh! etc.

The sun shines faithfully all night long,
so that you can see in the dark just like a cat.

Ole—Ole—Ole—oh! etc.

The moon is full every night, that is certain:
I am observing it now with a bottle for telescope.

Ole—Ole—Ole—oh! etc.

You bet, they give you two dollars a day for carousing;
and if you are good and lazy, they'll probably give you

Ole—Ole—Ole—oh! etc.

The old woman and the kids, why, they go
      on the township;
if the authorities don't pay they get it on the snout.

You don't have to work to support your bastards;
if you did, I shouldn't be sitting here spinning verses.

And we all stalk about in velvet suits with silver buttons,
smoking meer-schaum pipes which the old woman
      fills for us.

Ole—Ole—Ole—oh! etc.

Aa Kjaerringa maa brase aa styre aa stelle — aa blir hu sint, saa banker hu sig sjelv—skal jeg fortaelle.	And she has to sweat and toil and struggle; and if she doesn't do it, she gives herself a beating.

Ole—Ole—Ole—oh! etc.

Aa Fiolin det speller vil Allesammen—hejsan! Aa Danser en Polskdans, aa den er'nte lejsan.	And every last one of us plays upon the fiddle, and dances a merry polka; and that's not so bad!

Ole—Ole—Ole—oh! etc.

Ja rejs til Oleana, saa skal Du vel leve, den fattigste Stymper herover er Greve!	Aye, go to Oleana, there you'll begin to live! The poorest wretch in Norway is a count over there.

Ole—Ole—Ole—oh! etc.

I Oleana langt heller vi jeg vaere, end laenger I Norg min Slavelaenke baere!	Oh, I'd much rather live in Oleana than drag the chains of slavery over there in Norway.

Ole—Ole—Ole oh! Oleana!
Ole—Ole—Ole oh! Oleana!

Ole—Ole—Ole oh! Oleana!
Ole—Ole—Ole oh! Oleana!

Ole—Ole—Ole oh! Oleana!
Ole—Ole—Ole oh! Oleana!

Ole—Ole—Ole oh! Oleana!
Ole—Ole—Ole oh! Oleana!

Source:

Ditmar Meidell, "Oleana," 1853. Reprinted in *Norwegian Emigrant Songs and Ballads,* by Theodore Christian Blegen. Minneapolis: University of Minnesota Press, 1936.

*T*he Klondike gold rush of 1897 and 1898 brought thousands of hopeful prospectors, many of them American citizens, into the Yukon Territory, as well as into Alaska, which the United States purchased from Russia in 1867. The most publicized of all the gold rushes, the Klondike gold rush, drew the subject of "The Lure of Gold" to Yukon Territory on the Edmonton trail. This route took him through the Edmonton, Athabasca, and MacKenzie rivers through Yukon Territory, to Dawson, then the capital of the Yukon Territory, just to the east of the Alaska border. The gold rush of 1897 was short-lived. It brought more than 30,000 people to Dawson by 1898, but by 1900 many miners were leaving the territory. The author recalls the hardships of an arduous land and river trek across the wilds of Canada, endured in the search for gold.

Chicago, where the author was living in 1897 before he left for the Yukon, was a major hub for Norwegian immigrants. Immigrants came to the area in their greatest numbers between 1866 and 1872, and again from 1880 to 1893. But by the time of the gold rush, the Midwest no longer presented the ample opportunity for land ownership and employment that it once had. Norwegians began to move into the Pacific Northwest, as well as into British Columbia and Alaska. These areas were promising for fishing, lumber, and ship building. The traditional work ethic that Norwegians brought with them allowed them to easily assimilate into the population, and served adventurers such as the author well. Stoic Norwegians generally valued hard work, conservation of resources, and simplicity. Though the document suggests that the author stayed in Alaska, many Norwegians left America after 1881, with nearly a quarter of all new arrivals to America returning permanently to Norway.

THE LURE OF GOLD

It is hard to believe what me would go through for the lure of gold , but the hardships many of the prospectors went through to reach Alaska in the days of the gold rushes show what men would do for a chance at a lucky strike.

I know because I am one of the three known survivors of the ones who came to Alaska the hard way—by the Edmonton trail. I will tell it as it happened.

One warm Sunday morning in 1897 I opened up the Chicago Tribune (I lived in Chicago then) and read about the rich gold strike at Dawson. A friend, a young fellow named Dietrich, came along riding on a bicycle. He said "I sure would strike out for Dawson if it wasn't for my right hand being crippled." That put the first idea in my head.

A friend of Dietrich named Mohn already was fired with the idea of striking out for Alaska, and said he had arranged to go with another Norwegian named John Sejersted. He invited me to go along with them.

We bought an outfit of 500 pounds of bacon, 500-pounds of hardtack, coffee, tea, dried fruit, etc. We bought eight thoroughbred Scotch collie dogs from Robert Lincoln, Abe's oldest son. While the dogs were high grade. . .[they] were not used to the cold climate, as we later found out.

We planned to go by way of Skagway and Chilcoot pass, but heard of the terrific snow slide at Dyer, so we changed our plans an decided on the Edmonton-Athabasca-MacKenzie River route.

We left Chicago September 15. We built a boat at Edmonton, and hauled it and our supplies by wagon from there to Athabasca landing, where we arrived October 1. We loaded our boat and started down the river that night.

Not being used to river travel, we got stuck on most of the sandbars in that crooked river. That evening we camped on the river bank and crawled into our sleeping bags. We were surprised next morning to find two inches of snow on our sleeping bags. We started down the river again, hitting the sand bars as before. We probably would have had to stay there if the noble hearted Indian river pilot Alex Kennedy had not come along with a large raft and hauled us off the last bar. He piloted us 125 miles to Pelican River, where we camped that winter, hunting, trapping and prospecting.

Prospecting was kind of disappointing, as we expected to find gold on top of the ground. The fact is, we were worried about the price of gold dropping before we got to Dawson. That winter our nearest neighbor was forty miles away.

Shortly after the river froze up Mohn returned home and Sejersted and I remained. The two of us left Pelican River May 28, 1898. From Grand Forks on the Athabasca River we went to Fort McMurray, a distance of 87 miles. There were twelve rapids, some very rough and swift, but we were lucky to have Alex Kennedy as our pilot.

We sailed across Lesser Slave Lake to Slave River, into Great Slave Lake to Fort Resolution, across Great Slave Lake (120 miles) to Fort Providence and down the MacKenzie River to Fort Simpson; where Mr. Camsel was factor for the Hudson Bay Company. On June 28 we started up Liard River, pulling our boat against that swift current. Our toughest spots on that river were Hell's Gate and Devil's Portage.

Sejersted and I had a good outfit but we separated on September 15. I took in John Green, an old Chicago sailor, as my new partner. He had lost his entire outfit when his boat capsized in the river.

We camped at Fort Halkett on October 9, 1898. I spent nearly every day that winter hunting from daybreak to nearly dark. Green didn't feel strong enough to go through to Dawson but decided on going by way of the Stikine River and Wrangell. I put 315 pounds in a hand sled and on March 15, 1899 started off alone; arriving at Dease River Post four days later—a distance of 96 miles.

There I joined three Scotchmen—George Anderson, Forbes, and Johnson. We left on March 26 for Polly Banks. George and I pulled 500 pounds each on a hand sled, traveling ten miles each day. We built a boat at Polly Banks, arriving at Dawson July 8, 1899.

After twenty-two months the only thing I had left in the way of clothing was what I stood in—an old felt hat, flannel shirt, woolen socks, and Indian sash for abelt, and Indian moccasins. I must have been quite a sight, for Mr. Burke, reporter for the "Klondike Nugget," was bound to take my picture.

Twenty-two months travel to find gold—so I know what man will go through for the lure of gold. Today the only two survivors of those who took the Edmonton trail, besides myself, are John S. Mackay, past president of the Yukoners of Vancouver, British Columbia, and Dr. Ralph S. Quimby, an optometrist.

To give you an idea of the ways of the prospectors, take the case of Joe Kaminsky. In March, 1903, no gold had yet been found around Fairbanks. Joe Kaminsky washed out twelve dollars on Gold Stream. No one could believe Joe had washed out the gold there, but I was sure of it, for Joe paid me twelve dollars to go over to the blacksmith's shop and make a plain ring from that particular twelve dollars worth of gold dust. It was worth the money for him to have the souvenir of the first gold washed out in the Fairbanks district.

Source:

Library of Congress. *American Life Histories: Manuscripts from the Federal Writers' Project, 1936-1940* from the American Memory website (http://memory.loc.gov/ammem/wpaintro/wpahome.html).

OJIBWA

The Ojibwa, or Chippewa as they were also known, are numerically the largest Native American tribe in the United States and Canada. A member of the Algonkian language family, they are spread out around the western Northern Great Lakes region, extending from the northern shore of Lake Huron as far west as Montana, southward well into Wisconsin and Minnesota, and northward to Lake Manitoba. The archaeological records show evidence of Indian fishing around 2500 B.C. In those early times, the Ojibwa lived in numerous, widely scattered, small, autonomous bands.

French-Canadian traders bought beaver furs from the Chippewa from 1620 through 1763, until the French were conquered by the British. British trappers, fur traders and Jesuit missionaries (Blackrobes) entered the area and the fishery trade and territorial wars with the Europeans began. In 1783, the Treaty of Paris ended the American Revolution and established the boundary between Canada and the United States, placing the homeland of the Ojibwa in American territory. From the early 1500s to roughly 1840, the North American fur trade brought American Indians and Euro-Americans together in the exchange of goods and furs. Customs were also exchanged, as is documented in this memoir.

Before settlers could legally expand to the northwest into this area, agreements were needed with the Chippewa who occupied the land. The first of two treaties in 1837 was made with the Chippewa on July 29 at a location where the Minnesota and Mississippi Rivers meet. This treaty ceded all lands of the Chippewa between the Mississippi and St. Croix Rivers with the 46th parallel as the northern boundary. The second treaty was signed in Washington, D.C., on September 29th with the Sioux. By the terms of this treaty, all their lands lying east of the Mississippi River were ceded to the United States. With the advent of these treaties, the white settlers began to explore and settle in the newly ceded lands.

Minnesota's historical records include several recollections of Chippewa traditions. In Christmas and New Year on the Frontier, the author mentions a missionary named William T. Boutwell. Boutwell would permanently locate in Stillwater by 1847, and help establish the first Presbyterian Church in 1849. Another religious man mentioned is Bishop Whipple. In 1859, at the age of 37, Henry B. Whipple was elected the first Bishop of Minnesota. The Chippewa in Minnesota called him "Straight Tongue" for his honesty and outspokenness. To others he was known as the Apostle to the Indians. Whipple oversaw the construction of the Zion Episcopal Church building in Rome, New York, that was constructed in 1850 and was still in use in 1999.

The Leech Lake mentioned in the document now is the site of a reservation, located in north central Minnesota in the counties of Beltrami, Cass, Hubbard, and Itasca, with tribal headquarters in Cass Lake, Minnesota. The reservation was established by treaty with the U.S. government in 1855. The Leech Lake Reservation has 14,069 tribally owned acres and 12,693 allotted acres. Most of the reser-

vation land is located within the boundaries of the Chippewa National Forest. In 1999, a trading post had been reconstructed on its original Leech Lake 1804 site.

The Red Lake mentioned is also the site of a reservation, located in the northern Minnesota counties of Beltrami and Clearwater, approximately 27 miles north of Bemidji. Unique among the Ojibwa reservations, Red Lake never ceded land by treaty to the United States and is not part of the Minnesota Chippewa Tribe. The Red Lake Band was the first group to organize in Minnesota under a written constitution in 1918, when a General Council was established as the governing body. Unlike the other Chippewa bands, the Red Lake Band did not accept the Indian Reorganization Act of 1934. Red Lake is a closed reservation and, therefore, was not open to homestead entries and the land has not been allotted to individual natives. All land is held in common by the members of the Band. The tribe lives on 636,954 acres of aboriginal land. The band owns scattered tracts of land extending up to the Canadian border and including most of the Northwest Angle. It amounts to an additional 156,690 acres for a total of 825,654 acres, larger than the state of Rhode Island. All land is held communally by the Red Lake Band. Red Lake is America's largest fresh water lake wholly contained within one state.

OJIBWA KISSING DAY

When missionaries began to work among the Minnesota Indians, particularly among the Chippewa of the North, they found that the natives made much of New Year's Day. They celebrated the holiday, which they called "Kissing day," after the manner of the French-Canadian traders and voyageurs. The puritanical religious leaders often were obliged, much against their wishes, to observe the day in the native manner. William T. Boutwell, who went to Leech Lake in 1833, found that the Indians there were in the habit of visiting the resident trader on January 1 to receive presents, "when all, male and female, old and young, must give and receive a kiss, a cake, or something else." They seemed to expect similar treatment from Boutwell, for on the first day of 1834 they caused the pious missionary considerable annoyance by appearing at his cabin at breakfast time. He relates the story as follows:

> Open came our door, and in came 5 or 6 women and as many children. An old squaw, with clean face, for once, came up and saluted me with, "bon jour," giving her hand at the same time, which I received, returning her compliment, "bon jour." But this was not all. She had been too long among Canadians not to learn some of their New Year Customs. She approached—approached so near, to give and receive a kiss, that I was obliged to give her a slip, and dodge! This vexed the old lady and provoked her to say, that I thought her too dirty. But pleased, or displeased, I was determined to give no

countenance to a custom which I hated more than dirt.

At Red Lake twelve years later a band of missionaries planned a New Year's celebration which seemed to please the natives, who "honored" them "with a salute of two guns." The missionaries at this place recognized the Indian custom and took part in the celebration. According to Lucy M. Lewis, the wife of one of the missionaries, all the mission workers gathered at early dawn at the house of their leader, "the most convenient place to meet the Indians who assemble to give the greeting and receive a cake or two & a draught of sweetened water. It is the custom through the country to make calls & receive cakes." But instead of offering kisses, these Indians sang a "New Year's hymn learned in school for the occasion." The Red Lake missionaries marked New Year's Eve by assembling the pupils of the mission school and giving them presents. In 1845 the gifts consisted of flannel shirts for the boys and "short gowns" for the girls. The Indian children "came with cleaner faces & hands than usual," writes Mrs. Lewis, "as a little soap had previously been distributed." The custom of giving the Indians presents during the holiday season was continued by later missionaries, and it doubtless had an influence in creating good will. In 1881 Bishop Whipple, "with his usual kindness, sent an abundant supply of Christmas candy to all the Indian churches and stations" of Episcopal church in northern Minnesota. A hundred pounds was sent to White Earth, and fifty pounds each to several other stations, including those at Red and Leech lakes. This, according to one writer, "was enough to sweeten the whole Ojibway nation and gave many an Indian boy and girl and man and woman the only taste of candy they have during the year. It made a great many people happy."

While missionaries were introducing the white man's customs in northern Minnesota, settlement was progressing in the southern part of the territory, and a few well-defined communities that were to become cities were established. They were peopled by newcomers, many of whom came from New England or other parts of the East, bringing with them the social customs of their old homes. By 1850 the gay and often crude Christmas celebration of the voyageur and the Indian had been replaced in Minnesota by a more conventional and refined holiday. The observance was, however, far from puritanical. People went to church on Christmas, but they also attended balls or other parties "gotten up with as much elegance and taste as can be displayed in any of the great cities," they arranged for amateur theatricals and community Christmas trees, and they enjoyed elaborate dinners. In St. Paul, according to a statement in a local newspaper, the Christmas season of 1850 was "rich in social entertainments and interesting religious exercises."

Source:

Bertha L. Heilbron. "Christmas and New Year's on the Frontier." In *Minnesota History*, vol. XVI, no. 4. pp. 375-377.

*I*nspired by the notion of preserving their rich cultural heritage, the Native American community has developed a university system. The Native American Educational Service (NAES) based in Chicago, is an accredited university system founded in 1974. According to its co-founder, Faith Smith, NAES college is designed to help Native Americans bridge the gap between tribe and community. Many Native Americans have grown detached from their cultural roots and feel alienated from American culture. The university system helps Native Americans reacquaint themselves with their roots and, at the same time, nurture a sense of belonging to the larger community in which they reside. The NAES system primarily offers Bachelor of Arts degrees in community studies.

Between 1955 and 1970 a large number of Native Americans moved to Chicago. Although the Bureau of Indian Affairs helped those who experienced difficulties finding gainful employment, there were only resources enough to provide for six months. Welfare was an option that some participated in after the six month period, however, the majority of Native Americans denied such assistance. The Chicago Indian Center provided the more than 13,000 Native Americans with enough resources and support to foster a sense of independence. The Chicago Indian Center provided food, child care, emotional support, and held powwows and weddings for the budding Native American community. Perhaps more importantly, the center offered Native Americans a voice in their decision making process.

According to Faith Smith, part of the problem with the development of the Native American community today is a feeling of displacement. While affirmative action programs presented Native Americans with an opportunity to earn college degrees, after being filtered through the American college system many found that they had lost their ties to the tribes from which they came and were unable or unwilling to assimilate into American culture. The Native American Educational Service was developed with this sense of detachment in mind. The system began as a community health network that taught the art of self-healing, a common charac-

teristic among Native American tribes. The organization secured a small grant and began to expand into a learning institution.

The college emphasizes the human side of education, encouraging students to share their own experiences in the classroom. Among the subjects dealt with at the university is racism which most Native Americans have had to deal with in one fashion or another. The university provides a forum for changing negative self-images that many Native Americans develop at an early age. Smith explains that, "people of color have to work hard to break through the barriers of poverty and racism. And they are doing it."

Not only is the university system enabling the Native American community to connect with their roots and develop a sense of belonging, it is also providing them with the necessary strength to assert their "own voice." Smith explains that different governments and legal bodies have always spoken for the Native American community. The NAES system is encouraging more Native Americans to define their own needs and helping them develop the strength to articulate those needs both inside and outside the community.

I SEE AN INCREDIBLE FORCE WITHIN NATIVE PEOPLE

An elderly woman listens to Dakota language tapes while her daughter programs a computer. A class analyzes river water samples for a course in ecology. They are all involved in lifelong learning at NAES College in Chicago, which began as a small grassroots operation and has evolved into NAES, a national Indian-oriented college system.

An estimated seventeen thousand Native Americans live in the Chicago area. I went there to meet Faith Smith, the woman Chicago Indians refer to as "our college president." She has been a delegate to the White House Conference on Indian Education and serves on a variety of boards, including the Ms. Foundation, the Funding Exchange, and Common Cause. She prods "the system" to respond to the special needs of Indians. Faith Smith is dignified, soft-spoken, direct. She believes in people power. In her office in the small gray and white building that NAES headquarters, she told me: "A recent fire destroyed much of our college building, but so many people came in to help us clean up, they came with their shovels and bags of food, they shared our struggle, and we rebuilt."

My family moved to Chicago from our reservation in Wisconsin, and after college, I became a caseworker at the Indian Center. Over thirteen thousand Native American families had been relocated to Chicago from 1955 to 1970. I met Indians from Little Alaskan villages, from California rancheros and New Mexican pueblos. The trust status of some of their tribes had been terminated. The Bureau of Indian Affairs usually helped them for six months, then they were on their own. Jobs were hard to get. Most didn't feel comfortable going to welfare—they'd rather do without.

Two or three Native families would live in one apartment. Landlords would raise the rent if the bureau was paying. There were cockroaches. The people didn't know about subways or elevators, they didn't know that the streets were dangerous at night. I remember, there was this man from Arizona who had just been in the city a few months—they found him dead in an alley, with all his teeth knocked out. The police told us it was an accident, they said he had run into a wall.

Some Indians came apart. Some went home in a box. Some of them went back to their home communities—I'd have to make the arrangements for them. Those who stayed often came to the Chicago Indian Center because they needed bus fare or a ride to the doctor. We treated them with the same respect we showed members of the board of directors. No matter how somebody was dressed, no matter what their lifestyle was, we wanted them to know they belonged there.

People came to the Indian Center to obtain child care. They'd come to eat fry bread, attend a powwow, a wedding, a ceremony after a death—the things that bind people together. Over the years, they obtained schooling, they prospered and became part of stable communities, but they still came back to the Indian Center to work with youth and elders.

The Chicago Indian Center was the first in the country to involve urban Indians in decision making. It was exciting. Still, as a woman you have to deal with the stress of working, continuing your education, going home and making dinner for the family. The challenges and the failures force you to stand back and take a look at what is really important. That helps you keep your sanity.

In 1971, I found myself in the midst of a terrible political battle. Some staff members wanted to back away from social service. Some of us felt our job was to provide social service, and we spoke out. We were attacked in the Indian community and in the papers. I had seen that happen to others. In Indian communities, you grow up being political.

Most of our students come from families where nobody has a college degree, so when you see them working for several years to meet all the requirements, then graduating and taking what they've learned back to their communities, it's thrilling.

I went to Purdue University in the 1960s. Because of affirmative action, colleges were vacuuming Indian communities across the country, finding the brightest Indians, but after college, a lot of them couldn't take the transition back home. They had changed. Their communities had changed. They didn't fit in anymore. I know a lot of people today in my age group who are really lost. They've lost their relationship to tribe and community. They don't fit into white society.

I majored in education, and looked at the education of Native people. There were Indian kids who wouldn't question a teacher in a classroom, wouldn't look a teacher in the face, their parents wouldn't come to school. Families were alienated from the classroom and the system, and the children would drop out.

Faith Smith was a cofounder of NAES in 1974. This innovative program gives Native people some grounding in their history and culture while they work toward a Bachelor of Arts degree in community studies. An estimated 70 percent of NAES students graduate, and many go on to further education.

We began NAES in order to make higher education meaningful to Native people. We volunteered a lot of our time; we sold arts and crafts to raise funds. We got some support from an Indian

health project I was working for. We linked for a while with Antioch College which had pioneered the work-study model and nongraded classes.

We began in a small space we shared with another organization. We had eleven students in a class in community health, mostly adults working in the human services field. We looked at programs involving people in their own healing. That concept was new to whites, but it was what Indian people did all the time. We got a grant which enabled us to bring people in from other parts of the country: someone who ran an effective alcohol-abuse treatment program, a Navajo healer. For their ceremonies, Navahoes call singers, notify clan members, get food together, and collect money to pay the healer. He talked about healing as a community process.

People came to our classes. Even if they worked all day and had families, they came to class two nights a week. Once a student disappeared, so some of the students went to find her; she was undergoing a crisis and they gave her support. A few years later, she came back and said, "I left something undone." She completed her degree and now she's in graduate school.

People brought their life experiences into the classroom. My mother had lost most of her Ojibway language in boarding school, but she began volunteering here, and coming to language class. Pretty soon, she was studying traditional child-rearing practices of the Ojibway, and sharing what she remembered. So there's a sense of continuity. What you know is part of the wholeness of who you are.

One of our classes dealt with racism. The students who had grown up on reservations remembered being called "dirty, lazy Indians." It was spring and the fishing rights protest in northern Wisconsin was warming up. Students came into class and said, "We were down at the boat docks, and they called us timber niggers." Well, I grew up with that. It destroys your self-esteem. But in that class, people who had always accepted racism as "the way it is" began to talk about how to change attitudes.

One student was an alcoholic relocated here from South Dakota. He did a research project on the skid-row society that developed among Chicago Indians. Had some non-Indian done that study, it would have dealt with "oppressed peoples," but he wrote and talked not about the people's pathologies but their strengths. He said that when he became involved with Native people at the Indian Center, he stopped drinking. "You know, there were bad things about that life," he said, "but we supported each other." Now he's counseling other alcoholics in a way that allows them to be people. He's over sixty, and he's going to graduate school.

Over the years, we've had students dealing with the issues of chemical dependency, suicide prevention, treaty and land claims issues, child welfare. A student on the Fort Peck campus in Montana did a study of Head Start programs on reservations that influenced federal and state policy.

Most of our students come from families where nobody has a college degree, so when you see them working for several years to meet all the requirement, then graduating and taking what they've learned back to their communities, it's thrilling. We do not all come to the table equally endowed. People of color have to work hard to break through the barriers of poverty and racism. And they are doing it.

It took years to obtain accreditation. We'd go to a meeting of college presidents—mostly white, middle-class men in suits, and we'd have to explain what the baseline knowledge was for our program, and how we would put it into practice. Without a standard curriculum, it was hard to convey in a meeting. We'd say: "We're not isolated from the rest of the world. We're not separate little enclaves preserving our culture. We are acting out who we are at this time. We interact with different peoples and with government. We have to be the ones to define our needs."

It's important for us to verbalize our needs, but non-Indians sometimes wear blinders. I remember sitting in a seminar at the Newberry Library. A white scholar was complaining about an Indian "informant" he had talked to about the history of a tribe. The Indian had told him all kinds of crazy stories about what went on on the reservation. I'm sure that Indian man thought it was a stitch to put on this white man who sat there with his notebook and tape recorder. The scholar was angry—he'd used up an eight-month fellowship—but the Indians in the audience knew that the scholar would organize a theoretical construct about tribal life that might have nothing to with reality. We knew that whatever he wrote, our lives would be the same.

Over the last two hundred years, our own governments and the legal system have been defined for us. Indian voices have rarely been heard, women's voices have rarely been defined for us. Indian voices have rarely been heard, women's voices have rarely been heard. Many of these systems have not worked.

I'm impatient for things to change. I'm probably the orneriest person in the city. [Laughs.] That allows you to survive. I know that progress will come only when Indian people decide to change. There's incredible strength within our communities. Women are gaining power.

I joined Common Cause because I feel we need to have impact on institutions which influence public policy. Without access to power, Indian people will continue to remain at the bottom of the economic ladder. While Indian people have developed individual entrepreneurial skills, community-based economic development is needed to impact on the lives of Native people as a whole.

I'm a single parent with a twenty-one-year-old son. I want to make sure he will feel part of and contribute to Indian communities. I took him back to my reservation in Hayward, Wisconsin. We went into a restaurant, and all the white people got up and left. We went into a store, and the woman wouldn't put our groceries in a bag. She shoved them at me. We saw other Indians just put their food in their arms and walk out of the store, but I insisted that she put the food in the bag.

I told my son, "You can walk out, you can stand there and scream, or you can find a way to deal with it head-on." Anger is a compelling force that makes you take on issues directly. You just can't view "the others" as powerful. Recently people on our reservation boycotted that store.

My son's generation has had to face racism, but not the same barriers I faced growing up, so the young people are more positive. They know who they are. Part of that comes from the longtime existence of Indian organizations in Chicago. They've grown up with Indian canoe clubs, girls' cheerleaders, baseball teams, powwows, activities which recreate a sense of tribe and community.

In 1990, a fellowship enabled me to travel, and I went to Africa to see firsthand the struggles of other indigenous peoples trying to break colonial ties. In Zimbabwe, although they won independence from Britain in 1980, school tests are still sent to Cambridge to be graded. I attended a celebration in Namibia, which finally won its independence from South Africa, but only after thousands of Native people were killed. I went to New Zealand where the Maori women are seeking recognition of their cultural traditions and a national voice, just as we are.

We need to form coalitions, to cross boundaries, to understand how the same issues impact on communities of poor people, and on women all over the world. There are common concerns that transcend race and national boundaries.

I see an incredible force that exists within tribal people across the world, and within Native peoples here in this country, which allows us to flourish in our tribalness, in the face of tremendous adversity.

From an interview with the author, August 26, 1991.

Source:

Faith Smith. In *Messengers of the Wind: Native American Women Tell Their Life Stories*, edited by Jane Katz. New York: Ballantine Books, 1995. pp. 123-129.

ONEIDAS

*T*he Oneida reservation in northeast Wisconsin is a thriving community today. The economy is fueled by a tobacco industry and a tourist center with lavish hotels and energized casinos. The community's self-sufficiency, however, did not come easy. The Oneida peoples have been inhabitants of North America for approximately 10,000 years. They were the smallest of the five nations of the Iroquois Confederacy. The other nations were the Mohawk, Cayuga, Onondaga, and the Seneca. The Iroquois Confederacy was founded in the sixteenth century and dissolved around the Revolutionary War. The Confederacy divided over the war with the Oneida and Tuscarora (later admitted into the confederacy) fighting on the side the colonists while the remaining nations sided with the British. The Oneidas were alienated from the confederacy because of their participation in the war. The United States, however, vowed to support the nation in exchange for their help during the revolution.

The promise was later sealed in a treaty, the 1794 Treaty of Canandaigua. However, New York state did not honor the treaty by failing to protect and preserve the Oneida's ancestral lands. The Oneidas saw their six million acres of land disintegrate to a mere 32 acres. It was at this time, around the 1830s, that many members of the Oneida nation began to migrate north and westward, to Canada and Wisconsin. In 1973 and 1985, in large part because of the persistence of Mary Cornelius Winder, the Supreme Court ruled that the treaties the Oneida entered into with New York state were illegal. The Oneida, however, decided not to wait for state and federal authorities to resolve the matter. The nation began an entertainment center in Verona, NY which has grown into a multi-million dollar tourist center. The entertainment center, called the Turning Stone Casino Resort, features New York's only casino, retail shops, and a championship golf course.

The Oneida nation is a matrilineal society which means tribal clans and membership are passed along through the mother. Females are held in the highest esteem among the Oneidas; the majority of the members of the administrative body within the Oneida community are women today. According to Roberta Hill Whiteman the Oneida community is organic; they grow and care for one another as a single unit. Whiteman, a professor of Native American literature and creative writing at the University of Wisconsin, has close ties to the Oneida nation. She explains that, "[w]hen there's money at Oneida, it doesn't necessarily go to individual tribe members; more often, it goes to the community as a whole."

Whiteman says that life outside the reservation has been just as difficult for Oneidas in the United States. She and her family have faced discrimination getting jobs, buying a home, and racism in public schools because of their dark skin tone. The Oneidas have also faced difficulty securing gaming commissions and have been exploited by developers when valuable resources were found on the reservation. In spite of the adversity the Oneida nation has faced on and off the reservation, they have grown stronger as a community, demonstrating allegiance to the long held belief that the Oneidas are survivors.

LET US SURVIVE

Drive around the progressive Oneida Reservation in northeastern Wisconsin, and you'll see Native people in suits, toting briefcases, going to work in an up-to-date computer center and industrial park. You'll also see Oneidas in jeans tending gardens. The tribe operates a tobacco business, a large hotel and a bustling "activity center" housing several casinos. Revenues from these enterprises have enabled the tribe to create new housing, parks, roads, and cultural and social service programs.

The Oneidas are on the move, but just a generation ago, like other reservation communities, they were suffering from the loss of much of their land base and widespread poverty. For those Oneidas who had college degrees, there were few jobs on the reservation, and the surrounding white society was a hostile environment.

Growing up in the adjoining city of Green Bay, Roberta Hill Whiteman formed close ties to the Oneida community, which she renews on frequent visits to her relatives here. A poet, author of Star Quilt *and* Philadelphia Flowers, *she is a professor of Native American literature and creature writing at the University of Wisconsin. I asked her to comment on the place she considers home.*

When you're oppressed and afraid you may be viewed as "pagan," you don't talk about your ceremonies; you keep it quiet.

My husband always teases me about my family. My sisters and I love to talk and tell stories. One of my cousins has been tribal chairman at Oneida, one is an attorney, another one is a comedian.. So we joke a lot about how much we all love to talk. [Laughs.]

There is a matriarchal tradition at Oneida. Women are prominent. One of our first tribal chairpersons in the 1940s was a woman; currently, Debbie Doxtator is chairwoman of the tribe. In fact, six out of nine council members are women. It seems to me that Oneida men are willing to give women space and a voice in political affairs.

Oneidas see all living things as interconnected. Every individual has to be responsible to every other being in order for life to continue. Oneida is an organic community. By that I mean that people try to keep within their own community the means of staying alive. When there's a good harvest, everyone shares. When I lived there, the tribe had a cooperative garden and a cannery so I could go and help with the process of planting and harvesting and storing. Now, the tribe also has a farm for

raising beef cattle. But Oneida is back to back with a white population that basically wants to take over our land and make us a suburb, and this causes some tensions.

When there's money at Oneida, it doesn't necessarily go to individual tribal members; more often, it goes to the community as a whole. The casino enterprises have been helpful in terms of establishing services. A lot of the money used to develop housing, sewer and water systems, chemical dependency treatment programs, arts and education has come from bingo revenues.

The federal government controls Indian gaming through a federal commission. To support this commission, Indian nations with gaming enterprises are assessed—this is not the case with other federal commissions. The commission is supposed to regulate competition from Las Vegas and other privately owned gaming corporations. But the head of the commission has ties to Las Vegas.

Native nations working to achieve some economic parity with non-Indian communities around them encounter economic restrictions, not free enterprise. The government says: "We want you to have economic development, but this is the wrong kind of money this is bad money, this may even be my money." I think federal supervision is a euphemism for control. Historically reservations were on unwanted land. Then, when resources were found there, these resources were and still are extracted without any concern for the Indian populations whose lives are hampered by so-called "development." Politicians manipulate the competition between Native needs and the demands of their non-Indian constituents, using the tribes as scapegoats to gain influence. They take a moral stance calling for regulation of Indian gaming while creating state-run dog tracks and lotteries.

It's a way of controlling whatever resources Indian people develop. Furthermore, it's one of the ways in which those in power suppress us and keep other Americans at a distance. By calling into question our ethical belief system, they attempt to delegitimize our social philosophy. If white people fully understood the profound social philosophies of Native people, they might question their own consumer society values.

White people look at the images of Indian cultures—the figure of Coyote, for example—they put on a jacket and well it without understanding what Coyote means to the people. This trivializes the power of the symbol and its complex and important meaning. Besides, someone can make a buck in the bargain.

Once our symbols are diminished, it's easier for the government to continue the process of fragmenting Indian communities that began in the first encounter.

Historically, the Oneida have been part of the Iroquois or Longhouse Confederacy in upstate New York. In the 1820s and 1830s, the American government wanted the Longhouse People to move west. A charlatan named Eleazar Williams who spoke the Mohawk language was involved in moving the Oneida to Wisconsin. The Oneida chose to move, coming in several groups: some were converts (Episcopalians and Methodists came first), some were "pagan." In Wisconsin, they established self-sustaining, organic communities.

After the move, some Oneida tried to hold on to their traditions, especially their language. But "Americanization" was government policy, and the old ways were forbidden. When you're oppressed and afraid you may be viewed as "pagan," you don't talk about your ceremonies; you keep it quiet.

Inside a sacred space
Let us survive.

When my father was growing up at Oneida, it was a Christian community. And it was very poor. He went into the army during World War II; then he went to college, and became a math teacher. He moved to Oneida and then to Green Bay hoping to teach high school, but not one school wanted to hire an Indian math teacher. So he found a job teaching math at the Wisconsin State Reformatory, where I'm sure he faced discrimination. Even though we lived in Green Bay, my dad stayed involved in the Oneida reservation community and was treasurer in the 1950s, when the federal government wanted to terminate us.

My parents wanted to buy a house in a middle-class area of Green Bay. My mother found one, and the realtor told her to bring her husband, and to make an offer. My mother was fair, my father was dark; when he appeared, they were told the house was sold.

My mother was part Indian, Choctaw from Louisiana. She died when I was nine so I don't know much about her. My father raised my sisters and me. I found out years later that the place where my mother grew up was called "the Choctaw Strip." I remember she liked to tell us stories while are ate breakfast.

Growing up in Green Bay in the 1950s, I felt alienated. Green Bay is a border town; the people there felt Indians were in the way. In school some of the white kids called us names. When we protested, we were the ones who were suspended. My father took my sisters and me home to Oneida often. We'd visit the "homestead," my grandmother's house. I was alternately fascinated and frightened because she had died, and the house looked forlorn. But the family had a sense of kinship, there were family gatherings where relatives teased and bantered with each other in a familiar yet ironic way so that folks cold be discussing you, and you might not even be aware of the undercurrent of meaning.

When I was in elementary school, I asked my father to take me to someone who would teach me the Oneida language. He said that knowing it would only cause me suffering. Years later, from talking with elders I learned of the suppression of Indian languages in boarding schools. Some Indian people managed to keep their language, and searched out others who spoke it; some of the knowledge of language and culture was hidden within families; some was lost. When my father told us stories about the Oneida about the Iroquois, we knew it was special, it was something for us to hold in our hearts, and to think about in hard times.

In the sixties in high school, I was trying to understand who I was, and how I fit into the world. I realized that in order to really understand the Oneida, I had to go away and see more of the world. After college I traveled, and taught at Sinte Gieske College on the Rosebud Reservation. In graduate school at the University of Montana, I met Indians from all over the country. We went to powwows; I felt less isolated.

After establishing myself as a writer, I went back to Oneida, and started writing an epic poem, "Under These Viaducts," which incorporates Oneida history up to the Revolutionary War. I'm continuing my research into more recent Oneida history. I want the next generation to grow up knowing what their people went through so they will understand why it's so important to recover their traditions and language.

I began writing a biography of my grandmother, Doctor Lillie Minoka-Hill. I used to love going to her house—I'd sit in her lap and listen to her stories and recitation of poems. She died when I was five, but after her death, I heard stories about her. All during the years I was growing up, when we didn't behave, my father would remind us of things Grandmother did and said so we'd follow her example. In a way, she haunted me. I started looking in archives and talking to people about her—each person remembered something—and I began piecing her story together. The people whom we love are not gone—you can find them again in the oral tradition.

Grandmother lived in an amazing period. From 1870 to 1950, so much was happening to change the face of the country. She was told she was Mohawk from Saint Regis. She was adopted by a Quaker obstetrician who put her through school, and she graduated from the Women's Medical College of Philadelphia in 1899. In 1905 she married my Oneida grandfather, they moved to his reservation in Wisconsin, and she became a farm wife. When Grandfather died, because she had no income she started practicing medicine. I think the women came to her with their childbirth problems because she was a woman. She met with some resistance to modern medicine and so she worked with the midwives using herbal remedies, but most often she used drugs because the dosage was more precise. I'm looking at the environment in which my grandmother lived and worked, and at her role in the community during this time of ongoing depression. People were hungry, and often sick; it was difficult just surviving.

The Oneida had their allotted farmland, but the farms were small and didn't support their families. They used to fish and hunt in order to have something toe at. The men worked in the cranberry fields or traveled around trying to find other jobs, and this split up families. People sold acreage to whites just to stay alive, and often were swindled. I've heard stories of Oneidas being driven out of their homes by the police for nonpayment of taxes they didn't know they owed. And there were foreclosures. In the 1950s, we had large acreage in timber, owned by the community. Over the years, the lumber barons used the allotment system to manipulate the Oneida so they could take that land too.

I saw change taking place in the 1960s. Oneidas started trying to reclaim lost land. Realizing that our students were still facing the blatant racism I faced in the public schools, the tribe established its own school. Now, in addition tot he regular curriculum, our students learn the language and traditions of the Longhouse People.

I've witnessed a wonderful change at Oneida: a rebirth of interest in our spiritual way of life. The Oneida seem to be tolerant and understanding of each other. Our elders who speak the Oneida language are Christian. A grandmother may go to a church service in the morning, and a Longhouse ceremony at night. She will be supportive of her grandchildren's interest in the old ways. I don't see any serious religious friction because all of us belong to more than one "group."

Our people have lived with many and varied traditions. The discussion and interest in them is beautifully chaotic. The seeds of ideas fly about in the wind. In time, we'll recognize which ones need to thrive.

Of course, the government may try to do all kinds of things again to divide us. They may try to destroy the economic development that has taken place since the 1960s. But the reality is it's not going to be able to do that.

Changes come slowly to Indian communities. We know how to wait. Within Euramerican culture, waiting has a bad connotation, but in our communities, waiting sometimes means observing, understanding the way things are, grasping the moment. That's been our sense of how to survive. Without it, there might have been more hardship, more Indian people lost.

When the time is right, we advance. Now, all across this continent, Indian women are gaining power. They are supporting each other in constructive ways. They are recovering their heritage.

. . .We need to be purified by fury.
Once more eagles will restore our prayers.
We'll forget the strangeness of your pity.
Some will anoint the graves with pollen.
Some of us may wake unashamed.
Some will rise that clear morning like the swallows.

From an interview with the author, July 29, 1991. Poetry segments from Roberta Hill Whiteman, Star Quilt *(Minneapolis: Holy Cow Press, 1984). Used by permission.*

Source:

Roberta Hill Whiteman, *Messengers of the Wind,* edited by Jane Katz, Ballantine Books, 1995. pp. 194-201.

PAIUTES

Sarah Winnemucca Hopkins, or Thocmetony, was a Northern Paiute Indian who spent most of her life fighting for peace and justice for her people. As a young girl she learned English, and in 1860, following the wishes of her grandfather, she enrolled in a Catholic convent school in California; however, she was forced to withdraw within a few weeks when wealthy parents objected to the admission of an Indian as a student. During the 1860s and 1870s, she served as an interpreter for and mediator between the U.S. Army and her people. In 1880, she began to lecture on the mistreatment of the Paiutes, and in 1882 she toured eastern cities, giving hundreds of speeches arguing for Indian rights. She taught in a school for Paiute children for several years, but died prematurely (in 1891) of tuberculosis.

It was at this time that the Paiute became known for the elaborate rites of the Ghost Dance, which originated in about 1870 thanks to the medicine man Wovoka (1858?-1932), who predicted that white rule would soon end in the West, replaced by a revived and newly strengthened Indian culture. The cult that surrounded Wovoka spread to other tribes, including the Sioux, who performed the rite just prior to being massacred by the hundreds at Wounded Knee, South Dakota, in 1890.

Sarah Winnemucca Hopkins' book Life Among the Piutes, subtitled "Their Wrongs and Claims," was published first in 1883. It is an important early book by a Native American. In this chapter, she discusses child-rearing practices among the Northern Paiutes, and their general moral structures. She also describes traditional puberty customs and courtship rituals, emphasizing proper behavior and the close ties among family members. She goes on to draw a contrast between traditional Indian life as she has known it and what she sees as the selfish and rude behavior of white people.

LIFE AMONG THE PIUTES (EXCERPT)

Domestic and Social Moralities

Our children are very carefully taught to be good. Their parents tell them stories, traditions of old times, even of the first mother of the human race; and love stories, stories of giants, and fables; and when they ask if these last stories are true, they answer, "Oh, it is only coyote," which means that they are make-believe stories. Coyote is the name of a mean, crafty little animal, half wolf, half dog, and stands for everything low. It is the greatest term of reproach one Indian has for another. Indians do not swear—they have no words for swearing till they learn them of white men. The worst they call each is bad or coyote; but they are very sincere with one another, and if they think each other in the wrong they say so.

We are taught to love everybody. We don't need to be taught to love our fathers and mothers. We love them without being told to. Our tenth cousin is as near to us as our first cousin; and we don't marry into our relations. Our young women are not allowed to talk to any young man that is not their cousin, except at the festive dances, when both are dressed in their best clothes, adorned with beads, feathers or shells, and stand alternately in the ring and take hold of

Sarah Winnemucca Hopkins

hands. These are very pleasant occasions to all the young people.

Many years ago, when my people were happier than they are now, they used to celebrate the Festival of Flowers in the spring. I have been to three of them only in the course of my life.

If you make fun of bad persons, you make yourself beneath them. Be kind to all, both poor and rich, and feed all that come to your wigwam, and your name can be spoken of by every one far and near.

Oh, with what eagerness we girls used to watch every spring for the time when we could meet with our hearts' delight, the young men, whom in civilized life you call beaux. We would all go in company to see if the flowers we were named for were yet in bloom, for almost all the girls are named for flowers. We talked about them in our wigwams, as if we were the flowers, saying, " Oh, I saw myself today in full bloom!" We would talk all the evening in this way in our families with such delight, and such beautiful thoughts of the happy day when we should meet with those who admired us and would help us to sing our flower-songs which we made up as we sang. But we were always sorry for those that were not named after some flower, because we knew they could not join in the flower-songs like ourselves, who were named for flowers of all kinds.

At last one evening came a beautiful voice, which made every girl's heart throb with happiness.

It was the chief, and every one hushed to hear what he said today.

"My dear daughters, we are told that you have seen yourselves in the hills and in the valleys, in full bloom. Five days from to-day your festival day will come. I know every young man's heart stops beating while I am talking. I know how it was with me many years ago. I used to wish the Flower Festival would come every day. Dear young men and young women, you are saying, 'Why put it off five days?' But you all know that is our rule. It gives you time to think, and to show your sweetheart your flower."

All the girls who have flower-names dance along together, and those who have not go together also. Our fathers and mothers and grandfathers and grandmothers make a place for us where we can dance. Each one gathers the flower she is named for, and then all weave them into wreaths and crowns and scarfs, and dress up in them.

Some girls are named for rocks and are called rock-girls, and they find some pretty rocks which they carry; each one such a rock as she is named for, or whatever she is named for. If she cannot, she can take a branch of sage-brush, or a bunch of rye-grass, which have no flower.

They all go marching along, each girl in turn singing of herself; but she is not a girl any more,— she is a flower singing. She sings of herself, and her sweetheart, dancing along by her side, helps her sing the song she makes.

I will repeat what we say of ourselves. "I, Sarah Winnemucca, am a shell-flower, such as I wear on my dress. My name is Thocmetony. I am so beautiful! Who will come and dance with me while I am so beautiful? Oh, come and be happy with me! I shall be beautiful while the earth lasts. Somebody will always admire me; and who will come and be happy with me in the Spirit-land? I shall be beautiful forever there. Yes, I shall be more beautiful than my shell-flower, my Thocmetony! Then, come, oh come, and dance and be happy with me!" The young men sing with us as they dance beside us.

Our parents are waiting for us somewhere to welcome us home. And then we praise the sage-brush and the rye-grass that have no flower, and the pretty rocks that some are named for; and then we present our beautiful flowers to these companions who could carry none. And so all are happy; and that closes the beautiful day.

My people have been so unhappy for a long time they wish now to disincrease, instead of multiply. The mothers are afraid to have more children,

Despite extreme poverty, the many Paiute traditions continued to survive on reservations.

for fear they shall have daughters, who are not safe even in their mother's presence.

The grandmothers have the special care of the daughters just before and after they come to womanhood. The girls are not allowed to get married until they have come to womanhood; and that period is recognized as a very sacred thing, and is the subject of a festival, and has peculiar customs. The young woman is set apart under the care of two of her friends, somewhat older, and a little wigwam, called a teepee, just big enough for the three, is made for them, to which they retire. She goes through certain labors which are thought to be strengthening, and these last twenty-five days. Every day, three times a day, she must gather, and pile up as high as she can, five stacks of wood. This makes fifteen stacks a day. At the end of every five days the attendants take her to a river to bathe. She fasts from all flesh-meat during these twenty five days, and continues to do this for five days in every month all her life. At the end of the twenty-five

days she returns to the family lodge, and gives all her clothing to her attendants in payment for their care. Sometimes the wardrobe is quite extensive.

It is thus publicly known that there is another marriageable woman, and any young man interested in her, or wishing to form an alliance, comes forward. But the courting is very different from the courting of the white people. He never speaks to her, or visits the family, but endeavors to attract her attention by showing his horsemanship, etc. As he knows that she sleeps next to her grandmother in the lodge, he enters in full dress after the family has retired for the night, and seats himself at her feet. If she is not awake, her grandmother wakes her. He does not speak to either young woman or grandmother, but when the young woman wishes him to go away, she rises and goes and lies down by the side of her mother. He then leaves as silently as he came in. This goes on sometimes for a year or longer, if the young woman has not made up her mind. She is never forced by her parents to marry against her wishes. When she knows her own mind, she makes a confidant of her grandmother, and then the young man is summoned by the father of the girl, who asks him in her presence, if he really loves his daughter, and reminds him, if he says he does, of all the duties of a husband. He then asks his daughter the same question, and sets before her minutely all her duties. And these duties are not slight. She is to dress the game, prepare the food, clean the buckskins, make his moccasins, dress his hair, bring all the wood,—in short, do all the household work. She promises to "be himself," and she fulfils her promise. Then he is invited to a feast and all his relatives with him. But after the betrothal, a teepee is erected for the presents that pour in from both sides.

At the wedding feast, all the food is prepared in baskets. The young woman sits by the young man, and hands him the basket of food prepared for him with her own hands. He does not take it with his right hand; but seizes her wrist, and takes it with the left hand. This constitutes the marriage ceremony, and the father pronounces them man and wife. They go to a wigwam of their own, where they live till the first child is born. This event also is celebrated. Both father and mother fast from all flesh, and the father goes through the labor of piling the wood for twenty-five days, and assumes all his wife's household work during that time. If he does not do his part in the care of the child, he is considered an outcast. Every five days his child's basket is changed for a new one, and the five are all carefully put away at the end of the days, the last one containing the navel-string, carefully wrapped up, and all are put up into a tree, and the child put into a new and ornamented basket. All this respect shown to the mother and child makes the parents feel their responsibility, and makes the tie between parents and children very strong. The young mothers often get together and exchange their experiences about the attentions of their husbands; and inquire of each other if the fathers did their duty to their children, and were careful of their wives' health. When they are married they give away all the clothing they have ever worn, and dress themselves anew. The poor people have the same ceremonies, but do not make a feast of it, for want of means.

Our boys are introduced to manhood by their hunting of deer and mountain-sheep. Before they are fifteen or sixteen, they hunt only small game, like rabbits, hares, fowls, etc. They never eat what they kill themselves, but only what their father or elder brothers kill. When a boy becomes strong enough to use larger bows made of sinew, and arrows that are ornamented with eagle-feathers, for the first time, he kills game that is large, a deer or an antelope, or a mountain-sheep. Then he brings home the hide, and his father cuts it into a long coil which is wound into a loop, and the boy takes his quiver and throws it on his back as if he was going on a hunt, and takes his bow and arrows in his hand. Then his father throws the loop over him, and he jumps through it. This he does five times. Now for the first time he eats the flesh of the animal he has killed, and from that time he eats whatever he kills but he has always been faithful to his parents' command not to eat what he has killed before. He can now do whatever he likes, for now he is a man, and no longer considered a boy. If there is a war he can go to it; but the Piutes, and other tribes west of the Rocky Mountains, are not fond of going to war. I never saw a war-dance but once. It is always the whites that begin the wars, for their own selfish purposes. The government does not take care to send the good men; there are a plenty who would take pains to see and understand the chiefs and learn their characters, and their good will to the whites. But the whites have not waited to find out how good the Indians were, and what ideas they had of God, just like those of Jesus, who called him Father, just as my people do, and told men to do to others as they would be done by, just as my people teach their children to do. My people teach their children never to make fun of any one, no matter how they look. If you see your brother or sister doing something wrong, look away, or go away from them. If you make fun of bad persons, you make yourself beneath them. Be kind to all, both poor and rich, and feed all that come to your wigwam, and your name can be spoken of by every one far and near. In this way you will make many friends for yourself. Be kind both to bad and good, for you don't know your own heart. This is the way my people teach their children. It was handed down from father to son for many generations. I never in my life saw our children rude as I have seen white children and grown people in the streets.

Source:
Chapter II of *Life Among the Piutes, Their Wrongs and Claims*. Boston, 1883.

By the late 1880s, most once-free and proud Native Americans were defeated, demoralized, and desperate. In response to their severe situation, a spiritual movement developed among the Paiute Indians in the Far West and quickly spread across the Great Plains. Its leader, the medicine man Wovoka (1858?-1932), preached that an Indian Messiah would come and restore the Indians' lands and buffalo, reunite the living with the dead, and inaugurate an era of peace. For this to happen, the people had to dance the Ghost Dance and follow certain rules of behavior. Wovoka and his priestly followers all claimed to have spoken with Christ and been endowed with him by a vision, according to which all whites would be removed from Indian country within two years and Native Americans would be restored to their rightful place as the dominant people of the land.

It was a compelling vision to such peoples as the Southern Cheyenne, who had been dispersed by the Dawes Severalty Act of 1887 onto small plots of land along the banks of several rivers—the North Canadian, South Canadian, and Washita—and weakened further by internal divisiveness. The Ghost Dance provided them with hope and enabled them to reimagine the glorious days of the buffalo hunt.

In this account of his visit to Wovoka, a Cheyenne named Porcupine provides details about the movement in a statement to a U.S. Army officer in June 1890. Particularly revealing of the Indians' difficult cultural situation are the descriptions of the Messiah bridging the white and Indian worlds. Despite its message of brotherhood and nonviolence, the religion and the dance were banned by U.S. authorities. Tensions heightened by the Ghost Dance movement, combined with a desire for revenge by the U.S. Army, would lead to the massacre at Wounded Knee, South Dakota, in December 1890. When the vision failed to become reality, the Ghost Dance lost its prestige, though some tribes continued to enact it.

PORCUPINE'S ACCOUNT OF THE MESSIAH

In November last [1889] I left the reservation with two other Cheyennes. I went through [Fort] Washakie and took the Union Pacific railroad at Rawlins. We got on early in the morning about breakfast, rode all day on the railroad, and about dark reached a fort [Bridger?]. I stayed there two days, and then took a passenger train, and the next morning got to Fort Hall. I found some lodges of Snakes and Bannocks there. I saw the agent here, and he told me I could stay at the agency, but the chief of the Bannocks who was there took me to his camp near by. The Bannocks told me they were glad to see a Cheyenne and that we ought to make a treaty with the Bannocks.

The chief told me he had been to Washington and had seen the President, and that we ought all to be friends with the whites and live at peace with them and with each other. We talked these matters over for ten days. The agent then sent for me and some of the Bannocks and Shoshones, and asked me where I was going. I told him I was just traveling to meet other Indians and see other countries; that my people were at peace with the whites, and I thought I could travel anywhere I wished. He asked me why I did not have a pass. I said because my agent would not give me one. He said he was glad to see me anyhow, and that the whites and Indians were all friends. Then he asked me where I wanted a pass to. I told him I wanted to go further and some Bannocks and Shoshones wanted to go along. He gave passes—five of them—to the chiefs of the three parties. We took the railroad to a little town near by, and then took a narrow-gauge road. We went on this, riding all night at a very fast rate of speed, and came to a town on a big lake [Ogden or Salt Lake City]. We stayed there one day, taking the cars at night, rode all night, and the next morning about 9 oclock saw a settlement of Indians. We traveled south, going on a narrow-gauge road. We

Wovoka

got off at this Indian town. The Indians here were different from any Indians I ever saw. The women and men were dressed in white people's clothes, the women having their hair banged. These Indians had their faces painted white with black spots. We stayed with these people all day. We took the same road at night and kept on. We traveled all night, and about daylight we saw a lot of houses, and they told us there were a lot more Indians there; so we got off, and there is where we saw Indians living in huts of grass. We stopped here and got something to eat. There were whites living near by. We got on the cars again at night, and during the night we got off among some Indians, who were fish-eaters [Paiute]. We stayed among the Fish-eaters till morning, and then got into a wagon with the son of the chief of the Fish-eaters, and we arrived about noon at an agency on a big river. There was also a big lake near the agency.

All the whites and Indians are brothers, I was told there. I never knew this before.

The agent asked us where we were from and said we were a long ways from home, and that he would write to our agent and let him know we were all right. From this agency we went back to the station, and they told us there were some more Indians to the south. One of the chiefs of the Fish-eaters then furnished us with four wagons. We traveled all day, and then came to another railroad.

We left our wagons here and took the railroad, the Fish-eaters telling us there were some more Indians along the railroad who wanted to see us. We took this railroad about 2 o'clock and about sun down got to another agency, where there were more Fish-eaters. [From diagrams drawn and explanations given of them in addition to the foregoing, there seems to be no doubt that the lakes visited are Pyramid and Walker lakes, western Nevada, and the agencies those of the same name.]

They told us they had heard from the Shoshone agency that the people in this country were all bad people, but that they were good people there. All the Indians from the Bannock agency down to where I finally stopped danced this dance [referring to the late religious dances at the Cheyenne agency], the whites often dancing it themselves. [It will be recollected that he traveled constantly through the Mormon country.] I knew nothing about this dance before going. I happened to run across it, that is all. I will tell you about it. [Here all the Indian auditors removed their hats in token that the talk to follow was to be on a religious subject.] I want you all to listen to this, so that there will be no mistake. There is no harm in what I am to say to anyone. I heard this where I met my friends in Nevada. It is a wonder you people never heard this before. In the dance we had there [Nevada] the whites and Indians danced together. I met there a great many kinds of people, but they all seemed to know all about this religion. The people there seemed all to be good. I never saw any drinking or fighting or bad conduct among them. They treated me well on the cars, without pay. They gave me food without charge, and I found that this was a habit among them toward their neighbors. I thought it strange that the people there should have been so good, so different from those here.

What I am going to say is the truth. The two men sitting near me were with me, and will bear witness that I speak the truth. I and my people have been living in ignorance until I went and found out the truth. All the whites and Indians are brothers, I was told there. I never knew this before.

The Fish-eaters near Pyramid lake told me that Christ had appeared on earth again. They said Christ knew he was coming; that eleven of his children were also coming from a far land. It appeared that Christ had sent for me to go there, and that was why unconsciously I took my journey. It had been foreordained. Christ had summoned myself and others from all heathen tribes, from two to three or four from each of fifteen or sixteen different tribes. There were more different languages than I ever heard before and I did not understand

Arapaho ghost dancers.

any of them. They told me when I got there that my great father was there also, but did not know who he was. The people assembled called a council, and the chief's son went to see the Great Father [messiah], who sent word to us to remain fourteen days in that camp and that he would come to see us. He sent me a small package of something white to eat that I did not know the name of. There were a great many people in the council, and this white food was divided among them. The food was a big white nut. Then I went to the agency at Walker lake and they told us Christ would be there in two days. At the end of two days, on the third morning, hundreds of people gathered at this place. They cleared off a place near the agency in the form of a circus ring and we all gathered there. This space was perfectly cleared of grass etc. We waited there till late in the evening anxious to see Christ. Just before sundown I saw a great many people, mostly Indians, coming dressed in white men's clothes. The Christ was with them. They all formed in this ring around it. They put up sheets all around the circle, as they had no tents. Just after dark some of the Indians told me that the Christ [Father] was arrived. I looked around to find him, and finally saw him sitting on one side of the ring. They all started toward him to see him. They made a big fire to throw light on him. I never looked around, but went forward, and when I saw him I bent my head. I had always thought the Great Father was a white man, but this man looked like an Indian. He sat there a long time and nobody went up to speak to him. He sat with his head bowed all the time. After awhile he rose and said he was very glad to see his children. "I have sent for you and am glad to see you. I am going to talk to you after awhile about your relatives who are dead and gone. My children, I want you to listen to all I have to say to you. I will teach you, too, how to dance a dance, and I want you to dance it. Get ready for your dance and then, when the dance is over, I will talk to you." He was dressed in a white coat with stripes. The rest of his dress was a white man's except that he had on a pair of moccasins. Then he commenced our dance, everybody joining in, the Christ singing while we danced. We danced till late in the night, when he told us we had danced enough.

The next morning, after breakfast was over, we went into the circle and spread canvas over it on the ground, the Christ standing in the midst of us. He told us he was going away that day, but would be back that next morning and talk to us.

In the night when I first saw him I thought he was an Indian, but the next day when I could see better he looked different. He was not so dark as an Indian, nor so light as a white man. He had no beard or whiskers, but very heavy eyebrows. He was a good-looking man. We were crowded up very close. We had been told that nobody was to talk, and even if we whispered the Christ would know it. I had heard that Christ had been crucified, and I looked to see, and I saw a scar on his wrist and one on his face, and he seemed to be the man. I could not see his feet. He would talk to us all day.

That evening we all assembled again to see him depart. When we were assembled, he began to sing, and he commenced to tremble all over, violently for a while, and then sat down. We danced all that night, the Christ lying down beside us apparently dead.

The next morning when we went to eat breakfast, the Christ was with us. After breakfast four heralds went around and called out that the Christ was back with us and wanted to talk with us. The circle was prepared again. The people assembled, and Christ came among us and sat down. He said he wanted to talk to us again and for us to listen. He said: "I am the man who made everything you see around you. I am not lying to you, my children. I made this earth and everything on it. I have been to heaven and seen your dead friends and have seen my own father and mother. In the beginning, after God made the earth, they sent me back to teach the people, and when I came back on earth the people were afraid of me and treated me badly. This is what they did to me [showing his scars]. I did not try to defend myself. I found my children were bad, so went back to heaven and left them. I told them that in so many hundred years I would come back to see my children. At the end of this time I was sent back to try to teach them. My father told me the earth was getting old and worn out, and the people getting bad, and that I was to renew everything as it used to be, and make it better."

He told us also that all our dead were to be resurrected; that they were all to come back to earth, and that as the earth was too small for them and us, he would do away with heaven, and make the earth itself large enough to contain us all; that we must tell all the people we meet about these things. He spoke to us about fighting, and said that was bad, and we must keep from it; that the earth was to be all good hereafter, and we must all be friends with one another. He said that in the fall of the year the youth of all the good people would be renewed, so that nobody would be more than 40 years old, and that if they behaved themselves well after this the youth of everyone would be renewed in the spring. He said if we were all good he would send people among us who could heal all our wounds and sickness by mere touch, and that we would live forever. He told us not to quarrel, or fight, nor strike each other, nor shoot one another; that the whites and Indians were to be all one people. He said if any man disobeyed what he ordered, his tribe would be wiped from the face of the earth; that we must believe everything he said, and that we must not doubt him, or say he lied; that if we did, he would know it; that he would know our thoughts and actions, in no matter what part of the world we might be.

When I heard this from the Christ, and came back home to tell it to my people, I thought they would listen. Where I went to there were lots of white people, but I never had one of them say an unkind word to me. I thought all of your people knew all of this I have told you of, but it seems you do not.

Ever since the Christ I speak of talked to me I have thought what he said was good. I see nothing bad in it. When I got back, I knew my people were bad, and had heard nothing of all this, so I got them together and told them of it and warned them to listen to it for their own good. I talked to them for four nights and five days. I told them just what I have told you here today. I told them what I said were the words of God Almighty, who was looking down on them. I wish some of you had been up in our camp here to have heard my words to the Cheyennes. The only bad thing that there has been in it at all was this: I had just told my people that the Christ would visit the sins of any Indian upon the whole tribe, when the recent trouble [killing of Ferguson] occurred. If any one of you think I am not telling the truth, you can go and see this man I speak of for yourselves. I will go with you, and I would like one or two of my people who doubt me to go with me.

The Christ talked to us all in our respective tongues. You can see this man in your sleep any time you want after you have seen him and shaken hands with him once. Through him you can go to heaven and meet your friends. Since my return I have seen him often in my sleep. About the time the soldiers went up the Rosebud I was lying in my lodge asleep, when this man appeared and told me that the Indians had gotten into trouble, and I was frightened. The next night he appeared to me and told me that everything would come out all right.

Source:

The Ghost-Dance Religion and the Sioux Outbreak of 1890, by James Mooney. Lincoln: University of Nebraska Press, 1991. pp. 793-796.

PALESTINIAN AMERICANS

In 1908, the Ottoman Empire, having ruled Palestinians for four centuries, began drafting young Palestinian men into military service in preparation for World War I. Many Palestinians sought to avoid serving the Ottomans. In a 1930s interview, Ibrahim Hassan describes his father's journey to America to avoid the bloodshed of war and subsequent struggles of a Palestinian immigrant family. Ibrahim's father left for the United States in 1913 temporarily leaving his family behind. Many early Palestinian immigrants settled on the East Coast. However, Ibrahim's father settled in Lincoln, Nebraska where he opened a restaurant. With the conclusion of the war and defeat of the Ottoman Empire, Hassan returned to rejoin his family in Palestine in 1920.

In 1923, missing the lifestyle of the United States, Mr. Hassan moved his wife and Ibrahim to America, regretfully leaving behind extended family and friends. Like many Palestinians, Ibrahim adapted quickly to U.S. society while still retaining his ancestral pride. Despite desires to become a lawyer, his father insisted Ibrahim become employed and not spend more money on schooling.

With Palestine historically lying at the ancient crossroads of East and West trade, the peddler occupation had long been common among Muslim Palestinians. Ibrahim chose an occupation conforming with his Palestinian heritage. He became a traveling salesman peddling Oriental rugs and Italian handmade linens. Ibrahim described using his Holy Land association to boost sales,

> This is the first adventure, and I was successful. I had the advantage from several standpoints, you see. Coming from the Holy Land, for one thing, they thought I was holy. And then my youth. I learned how to find the rich people's homes. I learned to ride the taxi in the town and tell him to take me to rich people's street.... All I needed is one, and then the other one will send me to the other.

By 1931 Ibrahim opened a store in Lincoln to sell his wares. Feeling tradition-bound to marry within his own religion and nationality, Ibrahim married an Arabic women in 1933. Like many Palestinian Americans seeking to perpetuate their Palestinian identity while embracing their American citizenship, Ibrahim aspired to sustain his two daughters' respect for their ancestry as well as respect for the multiculturalism they found in the United States. As Ibrahim described, "that's the way I feel about the United States. It's a beautiful garden composed of so many wonderful and delicious fruit trees."

IBRAHIM HASSAN: FROM PALESTINE, 1922

In 1913, or just about that time, the sparks of war started to fly—the First World War—and the Ottoman Empire, under which we were subjects, started to make its move and conscript young men in the army. A good many of these boys can afford to run away, and my father was one of those. He migrated to the United States. He couldn't bring me and my mother with him, because he was running away and he wasn't able financially.

Well, my father was a struggling immigrant, but he started a restaurant in Lincoln, Nebraska, and he succeeded in saving a few dollars. After World War I was over, in 1920, he went back. I was anxious to see a father, because I didn't remember my father very well. And when he came back again, I was happy. He stayed two years and then brought me with my mother here. You see, after you drink the water of this country, honey does not taste good in the wells of Jacob.

I had the emotional feeling, the sad feelings, departing away from my home and my town and my relatives. I think that I never see them again, going across the seven seas. That was a very sad, very sad affair. And I wasn't looking forward to what I'm going to see, because I don't know what was ahead of me. But I know what I was leaving behind.

We landed near the Bowery. It was not like I used to imagine it. Well, you magnify the United States in your mind, you see. If you happen to land in a good area, all right, your dreams are fulfilled. If you happen to land in a bum area, like the Bowery, you have that disappointment, till you wade through it. Until I was taken, after a few days, out in the upper part of Manhattan—then I changed my illusions about this being a dump city and bad and so forth.

After being in New York for two weeks, we came here to Lincoln to live. I was intense; I was very studious all my life. I wanted to study and become somebody. The law was foremost in my mind. There was this man had this dry-goods business, and also he imports from the old country. He said, "What are you going to do with the boy?" My father says, "The boy's going to school." "Oh, what do you want to do that for?" he said. "Now, if you send him to school and he wants to be a lawyer, he has to go through school ten years—college, specialty, and so forth. And during the course of this time, if you put him to work he'll earn two thou-

sand dollars a year at least." I heard that and I hated the man. It sounded logical to my father. So he wanted me to work. What the hell could I do? I couldn't do anything. I was a kid.

I got hold of a map of the United States and I drew with a pencil around from Lincoln a circle like this—not knowing the geography of the country and the means of transportation and so forth. I picked up some small Oriental rugs and some of these fine, handmade linens that were made I Italy. They're expensive—you have to sell them to the rich. And then I traveled.

This is the first adventure, and I was successful. I had the advantage from several standpoints, you see. Coming from the Holy Land, for one thing, they thought I was holy. And then my youth. I learned how to find the rich people's homes. I learned to ride the taxi in the town and tell him to take me to rich people's street. And I look at this house—looks nice, looks very rich. I put the number down and the name of the street, and I'd back to the hotel and I called these people up. All I needed is one, and then the other one will send me to the other.

I came back here in 1931 and I took a store. I displayed those linens in there, plus Oriental rugs. But you didn't do well in there just from the first day. You had it good and you had it bad; but by perseverance—if you give up, you don't succeed, and I wasn't the kind to give up. And it worked.

In 1933 I was married—a girl of Arabic origin.

Would you have considered marrying an American girl?

Well, at that point it was not very advisable. The boy of Asiatic extract, he had to be obedient to his parents, you know. He could not exercise his own thoughts or have his own choosing—unless he became a bad man, a renegade. So the tendency was to marry your own religion and your own nationality, and you lived happier.. . .

My two daughters say to me, "I'm American." Yes, it's wonderful, you are an American. But you have an origin and you should be proud of your origin and the contribution that your origin brought to this United States. This tree, this almond tree—the roots were almond. Yours was apple, and others were orange roots. Now we have these three, four trees in this garden. Each one is different. Each one is useful. Each one is delicious. And that's the way I feel about the United States. It's a beautiful garden composed of so many wonderful and delicious fruit trees.

Source:

American Mosaic compiled by Joan Morrison and Charlotte Fox Zabusky. New York: E.P. Dutton, 1980. pp. 82-84.

PANAMANIAN AMERICANS

Though finding fame in the United States as a major league baseball player, Rennie Stennett poignantly contrasts through an interview stark differences in inter-cultural relationships he found in the United States as compared to the Central American country of Panama. Rennie was born to a devout Roman Catholic, hard working, lower-income family in the town of Colon in 1951. Like thousands of Panamanians who found employment in the Panama Canal Zone since the canal's completion in 1914, Rennie's father was a tugboat operator.

Panamanian Americans normally grew up to work in low wage jobs, but Rennie was one of the fortunate. Gifted in athletic ability he was recruited by major league baseball scouts and came to the United States in 1969 to play professional baseball. In the off-season, Rennie found employment as a dock checker in the canal zone.

In Panama, racial issues had not been part of Rennie's life, but arriving in the United States he was suddenly faced with brazen discrimination. As Stennett recalled,

> *It was really tough at first. First of all, where I grew up. . . black and white lived there, and we go to same church and everything and no problems. We never had the kind of race problem they had here. I knew about it by the newspapers. So when I came here, I didn't even speak to a white person. I don't want them to think they're better than me.. . . Sometimes I used to get hate mail. You know, people call me names and stuff like that.*

Stennett experienced not only racism, but the extraordinary drive in the United States to accumulate wealth. Money appeared to him to be the guiding force in American society. As Stennett commented,

> *All I had the impression is just money. Whenever it come around to money, the American will be the smartest person in the world, and he will do anything, even kill.. . . This is what it projected in Panama. And then it seems like when I come over, I think it's the same way. You know, you got to have money.*

Rennie played in the major leagues for about a decade until 1981. Like most Panamanian Americans he maintained ties with his homeland was always proud to represent his heritage.

RENNIE STENNETT

I used to dream a lot. I'd see myself pitching in the World Series and stuff like that. But I was mainly busy going to school. I played mostly every sport in school. The first thing I did was I was a swimmer. I never did like American football, but I played a lot of soccer. It was a lot of fun, especially playing in the mud and the rain. The ball—nobody can kick it, because you can't keep your foot on it. It was real exciting. And then I was a lot better basketball player than baseball player by far when I was in high school.

I'd be playing in a basketball league and a baseball league, and sometimes both play the same day. The basketball game would be at six and we would play the second game of the baseball game—second game start at nine. So when I finished playing basketball, I'd catch a bus and go up about fifteen minutes to the stadium and play baseball in the same night. Get home at two, get up to go to school in the morning, plus studies and all that stuff. And I used to do it. I had good stamina. I could play all day. I remember swimming all day in the river, and from there I'd go and play basketball. I was just going, going, going, going. They never gave letters like they do here, because I think I would have gotten them all. But I won "best athlete" in high school. My brother won it, and my sister own it, and another brother won it. It seemed like it was in the family.

My mother was always for me going out and play sports. But she never used to pay too much attention to me. She was really busy, because she was a hairdresser. Yeah, she was always busy. When I was in high school, a lot of people started talking and telling her about me, and my name started coming out in the papers. That's when she and my father would come and see me pitch.

My father, he works on the tugboat, like a seaman, on the Panama Canal. You know, when the ships come, they'll stop, and he would go out in this tug and tow it through the canals. That's what he does. We were a lower-income family.

I'm really proud of my father—the way he brought us up, without having anything like money and stuff like that. He's so religious, you know. Our school bus would leave at eight, and he used to have us getting up at five to say the rosary every morning. We had an altar in his room, a small altar, and we would say the rosary. I'm successful in my career, and I think that has a lot to do with it. I'm not saying I'm really religious or anything. I go to

church and believe in God, but I still have a lot to learn about everything.. . .

It [sports] was mainly for fun then. The scouts been coming since I was in eighth grade, trying to get me to finish school in the United States. They always come down, looking for guys, good ballplayers. The club I was going to sign with at first was the Giants, because they used to come every year. The guy would come to my home and talk to my mother and father, take me all over Panama, and stuff like that. They wanted to bring me over here and I think they was going to pay my schooling, plus I play baseball for that team. Of course, I wanted to play, but my dad, he tell me he want me to at least finish high school.

I guess it was about the last four months in school when I started thinking professional. The Pirates came just before I got out of high school, and that was perfect time. And they offered me a little bit more than the other club. So I went with them.

It was really tough at first. First of all, where I grew up there was black and white lived there, and we go to same church and everything and no problems. We never had the kind of race problem they had here. I knew about it by the newspapers. So when I came here, I didn't even speak to a white person. I don't want them to think they're better than me, so they stay over there and I stay in mine. Sometimes I used to get hate mail. You know, people call me names and stuff like that.

My first year I didn't play league. I played in the minor leagues, Class A. I hate riding buses, but I know it was worth it. Well, in the minors you don't have the beautiful ball parks to play in; the lights are not strong, and they're throwing the ball hard—they don't know where it's going. You have those coaches trying to teach you, but you've got to make it on your own. It was tough. You is the one got to make that adjustment and groom yourself. And when they think you're ready, they'll bring you up to the big leagues.

Well, I'd played in the minor league that year, and just after the season—see, the minor league only play four months—I went back there [Panama]. I want to continue my education, to get credits meanwhile, and I went into a junior college. I was going into physical ed, something that I can be good in. And then I had a chance to work, so I decided to do that, too.

They were interviewing different people for a job on the Canal. I was going—you know, regular shirt and pants. My father said, "Well, you're going for a job, you shouldn't go like that. You should have on a tie." I didn't have much, but I put it on and it really worked, because most of the other guys got the jobs lifting up things, and since I was in a tie, they asked me if I ever did any kind of accounting or anything like that. I didn't, but I tell them I could do it. And that's why I got that job, as a checker on the dock. That's the person that check the items that come off the dock, like different foods and radios and different things. I had a list with what's supposed to be on the ships, and I was to check those.. . .

The second year I played with Class A again. The third year I jumped to Triple A. At the half of the season I came to the big leagues. Some guys take about seven and eight years to get to the big leagues, but I was lucky. I did it in two and a half.. . .

Of course, I read so many things about America. All I had the impression is just money. Whenever it come around to money, the American will be the smartest person in the world, and he will do anything, even kill. That's the impression I get by the movies. Every movie, it's the same—if it's a Western or whatever it is, you will see when it come round to getting that money, the American will be the smartest and toughest, even if it kills him to get the money. This is what it projected in Panama. And then it seems like when I come over, I think it's the same way. You know, you got to have money. Over here a lot of people say, "Hey, you're nothing unless you got money."

Nowadays most people like to meet me because of who I am. I make a lot of money. So I have to be a little on my guard all the time, to find out if the person likes me for me or just for what I am or what I have. That's very important to me.

Source:

American Mosaic: The Immigrant Experience in the Words of Those Who Lived It, compiled by Joan Morrison and Charlotte Fox Zabusky. New York: E.P. Dutton, 1980. pp. 408-411.

PERUVIAN AMERICANS

*J*aime Alvarez's story, as told in an interview, is a compelling account of a native Peruvian's attempt to escape desperate poverty and make a new life. In the mid-twentieth century, Peru's poor economic conditions forced substantial population movement from rural to urban areas. Following this pattern, Jaime, born and raised in rural Peru, at 25 married and found a factory job making fish powder into pet food, a common Peruvian industry. Within a few years Jaime had four daughters. But barely earning enough money to live on, their home was in a shanty district at the outskirts of town.

Eager to provide a brighter future for his children and obtain a better paying job, Jaime decided to journey to the United States in 1971. He traveled alone, hoping to become established and eventually bring the family. Like many Peruvian immigrants taking advantage of relatives already living in the United States, Jaime settled in Connecticut where a cousin lived. Learning English, Jaime began working for a high school equivalence education. Working for low wage, Jaime was employed in the housekeeping department of a large hospital. Many Peruvian Americans, particularly at low income levels like Jaime, had pressure to send money back home to support kids and pay family expenses. This demand made building any savings almost impossible. Jaime anguished over seeking a second job at night because of likely interference with his education. Finally, however, he could afford to bring his wife to the States, but left his daughters with his parents in Peru.

Jaime considered the major societal differences between American and Peruvian societies as primarily economic based. As he remarked in his new country,

> People in this country are different. They are calmer. There, in Peru, we were so overwhelmed by money problems that it made us excitable. Every little disagreement led to a fight or a loud argument. Of course, there are differences in culture, too. But I think it is the money difficulties that are at the bottom of it.

Poor economic conditions leading to social desperation coupled with political violence set the tone for Peruvian personal relations.

Many new workers arriving at Jaime's place of employment were from Latin America. With his bilingual abilities and hard work, Jaime was able to rise to a supervisor position. Still, at the time of the interview his daughters remained in Peru, a difficult situation given the Peruvian strong emphasis on family bonds.

JAIME ALVAREZ: FROM PERU, 1971

At twenty-five years old, I got married and I went to work to the factory. They make the fish flour, uh, fish powder, for the dog's meal or cat's meal. And I worked there for about four years.

Then we had one daughter, then two daughters, then three daughters—finally, four daughters. It was too hard to live in the city, so I built us a house on some land that the government rented to poor people on the outskirts of the city.

It was flat land. Not good for nothing. Not like a suburb—more of a flat shanty town. We had electricity, but no running water, no sewers. The streets were not paved. It took me a long time to get to work every day and to get home at night. We had a hard time having enough to feed the children on my job, and I could see that it would not get any better.

Finally I talked it over with my wife, and we decided that I would come to this country, where I could earn more money, and then the family would come over and be with me. I had heard about how much people make in this country. And, beside, I had a cousin in Connecticut. I wrote to him and he sent me some money, and I took my final pay from the fishmeal factory where I was then working, and I got on a plane and I came to Connecticut. My cousin took me in and helped me a little, and I learned a few words of English. But he really had no room for me, and I got a room of my own I another place soon.

Then I went to night school to learn English, and now I've been here five years and I am working on my high-school equivalency.. . .

I thought, at first, that my wife would come over in one year and then, maybe, the children— one by one in the years after. My parents could take care of them while my wife was with me here. First I thought, one year till they come, then two years, then three. Now I see it will take much longer. It's a very expensive trip from Peru—three hundred dollars for each person. And, besides, I have to have a place for them to live here.

Now I'm working in a hospital and I have room and board and my salary. I can't save money very fast because I have to send money every month to my family, for them to live on. And I just got a letter from my wife that she has to pay $250 in taxes for our house outside of Lima, or they cannot stay there. So I have to send some of my savings to her for that, and it will be longer till one of them can come over. And I don't know how long until they are all here.. . . Perhaps I will take a night, part-time job to earn more money, but then I won't be able to get to night school and get my high-school equivalency.. . .

People in this country are different. They are calmer. There, in Peru, we were so overwhelmed by money problems that it made us excitable. Every little disagreement led to a fight or a loud argument. Of course, there are differences in culture, too. But I think it is the money difficulties that are at the bottom of it. We were all so desperate there.

Here, in the hospital, if I have trouble with a co-worker, we talk it over, and if a supervisor gives an order, he doesn't do it in an insulting tone. And personal relations are pleasanter, too, if you aren't always worrying about money or arguing about how to spend what little you have. Of course, I am poor here, too, but I have my necessities and I can save a little and send some home.

And I am rising in my job. I am foreman of the cleaning staff for the whole floor here, now. And I have applied to be assistant to the director of maintenance. He says I have a good chance of getting the position, because I speak both English and Spanish and can talk with the employees who speak very little English. Almost all our new workers here at the hospital are from Latin countries, and they start out knowing nothing—not even the words for broom or soap. Everything must be translated. That's how it was for me, too, four years ago. But I went to school, and now, maybe, I will get a better job because of it. And then my family will come over and our dreams will be true. But I think that by that time my oldest daughter will be grown.

Well, I must have hope and I do have hope. I will see what the future brings.

Source:

American Mosaic: The Immigrant Experience in the Words of Those Who Lived It, compiled by Joan Morrison and Charlotte Fox Zabusky. New York: E.P. Dutton, 1980. pp. 357-358.

POLISH

AMERICANS

Before the media age, when senses were deluged with visual and audio images, traditional folksongs played an important role in the lives of people. Only in the second half of the twentieth century, after the advent of the portable transistor radio, did folksongs cease to play a central role in entertainment and celebration as well as in daily life. Among the Polish, folksongs were passed from generation to generation within a family and a community through daily life and special events. Folksongs differ from ballads in that folksongs are snippets of stories or even nonsense syllables that are put to music. Ballads have a strong story element with a plot and a refrain. Folksong topics could be about anything in the life or thoughts of a Pole.

The typical folksong structure is a four-line stanza, usually in trochaic or dactyllic meter, with frequent spondees (two long syllables) followed by a six-line stanza. Folksongs have no style rules. Singers can change and combine songs to suit moods. Melodies can be borrowed from anywhere, though there are traditional melodies and themes. In every collection you find a wide variety of texts and melodies. Work songs, lullabies, wedding songs, children's songs, songs about religious devotion, and war ditties spread from family to family to take their place in peasant culture. Folksongs took a life of their own as they diffused beyond the source of origin, sometimes carried by traveling minstrels. Translation into English results in some loss of meaning because English does not match the flexibility of the Polish language with its use of diminutives which can be attached to nouns, adjectives, and adverbs to produce shades of meaning. Most twentieth century collections of folksongs include a wide range of Polish songs.

In 1999, folksongs are sung at special events designed to teach modern Americans about Polish culture, but many of these songs are just as foreign to Polish Americans who are four generations removed from the traditions and memories of Poland as they are to non-Polish Americans. Collections of Polish folksongs survive from lore that has been passed at Polish social gatherings. Serious collecting began as late as 1888 with the founding of the American Folklore Society. By that year, there were one million Polish Americans in the United States. Many of these were second and third generation Polish Americans. The wave of immigrants who came from 1800 to 1860 were the intellectuals and dissidents who fled during the partitioning of Poland and insurrections in 1830 and 1863. These immigrants learned English and their children grew up as assimilated Americans, many of who could understand but not read Polish. Between the mid-nineteenth century and World War I, around 2.5 million Poles immigrated to the United States. The first wave of this group were German Poles, who were better educated and more skilled craftsmen than subsequent groups from Russia and Austria.

Polish Americans maintained a strong ethnic identity throughout the twentieth century. Polish folksongs captured elements of the Polish heritage as well as their immigrant experiences. Clans and kinship communities were very important to immigrants. New immigrants settled in established Polish communities where Polish traditions were continued. Celebrations such as Pulaski Day, honoring the Polish

American who was killed in the Battle of Savannah in the Revolutionary War, on October 11 of each year provided the opportunities for parades and singing, and for bringing out traditional costumes and foods. Folk culture was passed vertically from one generation to the next as well as horizontally across communities of Poles from different old world areas of partitioned Poland.

CHOĆBYM JA JEŹDZIŁ WE DNIE I W NOCY

Though I Should Travel All Day and All Night

Choćbym ja jeździł we dnie i w nocy,	Though I should travel all day and all night,
Choćbym wyjeż dził koniowi oczy,	Though I should ride my poor horse unto death,
Przecież ty musisz moją być,	You should know you must be mine, dear,
Moją wolę wypełnić.	And my will you must fulfill.
Przecież ty musisz moją być,	You should know you must be mine, dear,
Moją wolę wypełnić.	And my will you must fulfill.
A ja się stanę drobną ptaszyną	I shall become a bird of the air,
Będę latała gęstą krzewiną.	Flying about the thicket and woodland.
Przecież ja nie chcę twoją być,	Thus you see I will not be yours,
Twoją wolę wypełnić.	And you will I'll not fulfill.
Mają tu cieśle takie przybory	Carpenters have such powerful tools,
Co wycinają lasy i bory.	Forests and woods can be felled at will.
Przecież itd.	You should etc.
A ja się stanę małą rybeczką	I shall become a fish of the sea
Będę pływała bystrą wodeczką.	And swim in yon rapid waters.
Przecież itd.	Thus you etc.
Mają rybacy takie siateczki	Fishermen's nets are of such fine measure,
Co wyłapują małe rybeczki.	The smallest fish can be snared by them.
Przecież itd.	You should etc.
A ja się stanę dzikiem kaczorem,	I shall become a drake of the wilds;
Będę pływała wielkiem jeziorem.	I shall swim over side open lakes.
Przecież itd.	Thus you etc.
Mają tu strzelcy takowe strzelby	But hunters' guns can reach out so far,
Co wypalają kaczorom we łby.	Even wild drakes are shot through the head.
Przecież itd.	You should etc.
A ja się stanę gwiazdą na niebie,	I shall become a star of the heavens,
Będę świeciła ludziom w potrzebie.	And I shall shine on people in need.
Przecież itd.	Thus you etc.
A ja mam litość nad ubogiemi,	I have compassion on needy people;
Sproszę ja gwiazdy z nieba ku ziemi.	I shall strew all the stars at their feet.
Przecież itd.	You should etc.
Już teraz widzę Boskie zarządy,	Now I can see that this is God's plan;
Gdzie się obróce, znajdziesz mnie	Where'er I turn, there find me you will.
Już teraz muszę twoją być, wszędzie.	I know at last I must be yours,
Wolę twoją wypełnić.	All your wishes to fulfill.

Source:

Merrily We Sing: 105 Polish Folksongs, edited by
Harriet M. Pawlowska. Detroit: Wayne State
University Press, 1961. p. 17.

T he idea of organizing Americans to accomplish a goal involving a country outside the United States has happened many times. In 1999, the Dalai Lama sent a
Tibetan monk and nuns to rally U.S. opinion against China's treatment of Tibet.
When Agaton Giller, a Polish exile living in Switzerland after a failed uprising
against Russian rule in 1863, wrote in 1879 urging the development of an organization that could serve to unite new Polish American immigrants, he, too,
acknowledged the power of the American citizen. In Giller's case, his efforts were
successful.

At the time Giller's letter was published in America, Poland did not exist as an
independent country. In 1795, Poland had been partitioned three ways and was ruled
by Austria, Prussia, and Tsarist Russia. In 1815, a kingdom of Poland within the
Russian empire was established by the Congress of Vienna. But in both Russia and
Germany the Polish language was suppressed. An independent Poland did not emerge
until after World War I. When Giller's letter arrived in America there were an estimated 500,000 Polish Americans. Poles numbered among the earliest colonists, with
Polish names appearing in the records of Jamestown. Those earliest Poles were
recruited because they were skilled craftsmen who created products for export.

The first real immigration wave, however, occurred after the partitioning of
Poland from 1800 to 1860. These immigrants were primarily political dissidents
and intellectuals, and numbered about 30,000. A second wave began around
1860 and continued until World War I. Immigrants in the second wave came in
search of a better life and tended to be from the ruling class, called za cheben (for
bread) immigrants. By 1890 the number of Polish Americans grew to 1,000,000
and in 1900 it doubled again. In the 1990 census, over 9.5 million Americans
claimed Polish ancestry.

Polish Americans frequently traveled back and forth between their old country
and America. Poles tended to work until enough money was saved to return to their
native country. Appealing to the Polish Americans to organize their efforts to help
achieve independence for Poland did not require convincing; the desire to help their
native homeland was always present. That desire found a political voice in 1880
when the Polish National Alliance (PNA) was founded in Philadelphia, Pennsylvania. A group of Polish Americans were invited by Julius Andrzejkowicz, the
owner of a chemical company, to form a nationwide organization committed to an
action program to support the independence of their partitioned Polish homeland
and to give humanitarian assistance to Polish people. Several earlier efforts dating
back to 1842 had been made to bring together politically minded Poles to work for
these causes but because of the rapid growth in the size of Polish immigration in the
United States this effort succeeded. The organization served the Polish American
immigrants by facilitating their own advancement into the mainstream of American
society and bettering the conditions of the immigrant population.

In 1881, the PNA established a newspaper, Zgoda (meaning harmony) to promote its objectives to the larger community. In 1885, it established an insurance program for the material benefit of all who wished to join the Alliance. From the early 1890s onward, it created a variety of programs aimed at enlightening the members of the Polish population in the United States about their heritage and their rights and obligations as Americans. To further advance these aims, the PNA established a daily newspaper in Chicago, Dziennik Zwiazkowy, known today as The Polish Daily News. In 1999, The Polish National Alliance of the United States of North America is the largest of all ethnically-based fraternal insurance benefits societies in this country.

Giller died in 1887, but he would have been satisfied to know that the PNA, working with many other organizations, achieved the goal of a free Poland at the end of World War I. During World War II, the PNA worked for Poland's independence, and continued during the years of the country's occupation by the Soviet Union against its people's will until the collapse of the communist dictatorship in 1989. Today Polish Americans still watch over Poland's interests, a habit formed more than a century ago and embodied in a letter from Agaton Giller.

AGATON GILLER'S LETTER TO POLISH AMERICAN WORKERS

Since emigration exists and constitutes a great power—a fact which cannot be denied—it should be the task of a well understood patriotism to make it as useful as possible for the national cause. This can be done only through organization, which will unify the scattered members and control them in such a way that they will not be wasted but will be preserved for the fatherland.. . .

Every Polish peasant, from whatever Polish province he comes, even from one of those which like Upper Silesia or East Prussia have been for a long time separated from the national body, when transferred to a strange soil among foreigners develops a Polish sentiment and a consciousness of his national character. This phenomenon is incomprehensible for those who saw the peasant at home without a consciousness of national duties. And yet it is quite natural. National consciousness originates in him spontaneously in a foreign country in consequence of the feeling of the striking difference between his speech, his customs, his conceptions from those of the people who surround him.. . .

If after the formation of a conception and sentiment of nationality in him there is some one capable of explaining to him the meaning of this national character and of making him understand the duties resulting from this character then this plain man, formerly ignorant and passive for the national cause, will become an individual consciously and actively serving the idea which rests upon nationality.. . . There is, therefore, no doubt that if a national intellectual class is formed in America the numerous masses can and must be changed into an active human group useful for the national cause, and in order to give them the possibility of becoming useful and at the same time surround them with conditions which will prevent them from losing their nationality it is indispensable to unite the isolated individuals into more or less numerous associations and communities and bind these together in such a way that the resulting organization while serving the purposes of Polish cause will be not only useful but indispensable for the private interests of every one of its members.. . .

When the mass of Poles in America is morally and nationally raised by the fact of being unified and is economically prosperous—which should be also one of the tasks of the organization—it will render great services to Poland, even by the mere fact of representing the Polish name well in America. These services can gradually become very considerable when the Poles begin to exercise and influence upon the public life of the United States, when they can spread among Americans adequate conceptions about the Polish cause and information about the history, literature, and art of our nation, when finally they become intermediaries between Poland and the powerful republic so as to foster sympathy with our efforts for liberation and develop it into an enthusiasm which will express itself in action.

Then only can happen that which is most desirable, i.e., the emigrants who have acquired training in practical lines and wealth in America will begin to return to their fatherland to be useful citizens.. . . We do not need to put forward those benefits which

a large organization of Poles in America could bring at the decisive moment when the future of our fatherland will be at stake, for this is easy to see.

Source:

Poles in America, 1608-1972: A Chronology & Fact Book, compiled edited by Frank Renkiewicz. Dobbs Ferry, NY: Oceana Publications, 1973. pp. 64-65.

*S*ome time in September of 1913, a newly arrived Polish immigrant wrote a letter to an investigating commission—probably a group of social workers—in Massachusetts with a request. He had been in America since May 14 of that year, he wrote, and desired to learn English. But he could not learn the language as long as he found himself surrounded by Poles; therefore he requested that the committee help him find lodging in an American home at an affordable rate.

However, the immigrant, who signed his name "F. N.," did not quite say it that way. In fact his letter was as flawed as it was impressive, both for the writer's bravery in confessing his need and for his sincere desire to improve his knowledge of English. Having stated his case in a variety of haphazard ways, one of the last sentences in his letter summed up his difficulties with the English language: "If you can help me, I please you."

At the time of F. N.'s letter, Poland as a country did not exist, having been parceled out to the empires of Russia, Austria (later Austria-Hungary), and the German state of Prussia in the 1770s and 1790s. Most likely F. N. came from Galicia, an eastern Polish possession acquired by Austria. The reasoning behind this guess can be derived with a little historical detective work.

A number of F. N.'s mistakes in grammar, syntax, and usage fall into a certain pattern. For instance, there is his use of the word "please," in place of "thank" in the above-quoted sentence. In German, it is customary to use the word *bitte* both for "please" and "thank you," and a native German speaker is likely to mix up the two when speaking English. F. N. also uses the German word for the fifth month of the year, *Mai.*

More important, his writing shows a tendency—from the perspective of an English speaker—to bunch up words at the end of a sentence, or to place them in the wrong order. Hence his statement "I want go from them away," or his request for someone to "tell me the best way I can fast lern." This, too, is a trait of the German language, in which parts of speech that usually fall near the beginning or middle of an English sentence—in these examples, an adverb and a verb respectively—often come at the end.

It thus seems quite possible that F. N. lived in a part of Poland where German was spoken, and might have found himself naturally lapsing into German as a more familiar "foreign" tongue than English. This would mean he had lived either in

Austrian- or German-occupied Poland, and several factors rule out the likelihood of his coming from the latter.

First there is the date of his arrival: the great mass of German Polish immigrants had entered the United States by about the turn of the century. Second, there is the fact that the German Poles tended to be highly skilled craftsmen or technicians, whereas F. N. indicated that he worked in a shoe shop, and his references to his work and wages suggest that he was not a skilled shoemaker.

All these factors lead one to infer, with limited certainty, that F. N. came from Galicia, the sector of Poland which bordered on the Ukraine, and which was occupied by the empire of Austria-Hungary. Galicians and Russian Poles were typically less educated than their German Polish counterparts, and this led to stereotypes of Poles as ignorant buffoons. From this stereotype, of course, emerged the infamous Polish jokes.

The latter fact lends a touching quality to the occasionally hilarious mistakes in F. N.'s letter. In his request, he makes clear his earnest and obvious desire to learn English at all costs, a particularly poignant fact in light of the discrimination that he and other Poles then faced in America. Often ridiculed and scorned, many found themselves excluded from mainstream U.S. society, longing—as was F. N.—"to live with american people."

Nine months after F. N.'s letter, an ethnic rivalry in the Austro-Hungarian Empire led to World War I. At war's end in 1918, Poland once again emerged as an independent nation for the first time since 1795. By then some 30 percent of the Galician and Russian Poles had returned to their homeland, but the creation of a Polish state did not lead to a mass exodus of Poles from the United States. Most immigrants—F. N., perhaps, among them—liked it in America, despite the problems, and had decided to stay.

I HOPE YOU WILL UNDERSTAND WHATE I MEAN

I'm in this country four months (from 14 Mai 1913 — Noniton Antverpen). I am polish man. I want be american citizen — and took here first paper in 12 June N 625. By my friends are polish people — I must live with them — I work in the shoes-shop with polish people — I stay all the time with them — at home — in the shop — anywhere.

I want to live with american people, but I do not know anybody of american. I go 4 times to teacher and must pay $2 weekly. I wanted take board in english house, but I could not, for I earn only $5 or 6 in a week, and when I pay teacher $2, I have only $4-$3 — and now english board house is too dear for me. Better job to get is very hard for me, because I do not speak well english and I cannot understand what they say to me. The teacher teach me — but when I come home — I must speak polish and in the shop also. In this way I can live in your country many years — like my friends — and never speak — write well english — and never be good american citizen. I know here many persons, they live here 10 or more years, and they are not citizens, they don't speak well english, they don't know geography and history of this country, they don't know constitution of America — nothing. I don't like be like them I wanted they help me in english — they could not — because they knew nothing. I want go from them away. But where? Not in the country, because I want go in the city, free evening schools and lern. I'm looking for help. If somebody could give me another job between american people, help me live with them and lern english — and could tell me the best way how I can fast lern — it would be very, very good for me. Perhaps you have somebody, here he could help me?

If you can help me, I please you.

I wrote this letter myself and I know no good — but I hope you will understand whate I mean.

Excuse me,

F. N.

Source:

The Poles in America, 1608-1972; A Chronology & Fact Book, compiled and edited by Frank Renkiewicz. Dobbs Ferry, NY: Oceana Publications, 1973. p. 78.

∾

*L*ike many Poles of his time, Adam Laboda was part of a rural class seeking a better economic life. An interview with Adam in the late 1930s provides a glimpse at Eastern European immigrant experiences in the United States. Adam was born to a Roman Catholic farming family and, like many rural Poles, grew up working hard on the family farm.

In the early twentieth century, overpopulation and shortage of land was a critical issue affecting many Poles, including the Labodas. Adam's father could foresee that, despite the Polish tradition of giving a son a part of the family farm upon his marriage, they had too many children in the family to parcel land. So, still a youth of twelve, Adam left for Germany to work on a farm for pay and later became a spinner in a textile mill. With Adolf Hitler's rise to power in the 1930s, non-Germans such as Adam were invited to leave, which he did after two years of working in the country.

After leaving Germany, Adam immigrated to the United States where Poles had a long history of involvement since the American Revolution. Most Poles settled in big city industrial centers, but Adam initially found work as a spinner, typically for low pay and long hours, in a New England textile mill. There he boarded in a company house. As Adam described it,

> At first I work in the mill at Gilbertville, Mass. There were about 24 of us in one house. . .It was a company house. In one room about twice the size of this one (20x15) there were three beds and six boys slept there. We bought our own groceries and gave them to the woman who kept the house and she cooked for us.

Adam returned briefly to Poland to find a bride and eventually they had five children. Living in tenements in Massachusetts, the Labodas' home reflected a closeness to their homeland, complete with Polish newspapers and wall hangings of their former country. The home reflected simple Polish pragmatism and a strong patriarchal nuclear family. At work, Adam experienced first-hand the pervasive discrimination against immigrants, particularly Eastern Europeans. With his children becoming textile workers as well, Adam became involved in the U.S. labor issues, like many Polish Americans, combating anti-Polish and anti-immigrant sentiment in the United States.

ADAM LABODA—POLISH TEXTILE WORKER

Our second visit to Adam Laboda, began at the office of the Berkshire Woolen Company in Pittsfield, where he works as an expert spinner.

We invited him to ride with us to his home in a four-tenement block on Onota Street.

"Oh, I have my own car. You follow along and I'll be there," he said with a grin.

He wore rough working clothes, a fur-lined overcoat over them, his neck was grimed and plastered with black dust from the material which he had been handling. With his son, who is also employed at the mill, he got into a modern sedan parked in the mill-yard and drove rapidly home — a distance of less than a half mile.

He met me at the back door of the tenement which he occupies, as the front doors have tight storm-doors over them and are seldom opened in winter. Removing overshoes he invited me in, through the kitchen, where his wife was serving a meal to members of the family. Four of their five children are working, the youngest, a girl of 13, attends the nearby grammar school. Two older daughters are employed as textile workers , also and another son works on the second shift of the same mill where his father is employed.

Escorted into the front room, the radio was turned on by the older son to entertain me while his father washed up. On a stand was a Polish paper, Nova Anglica published in Chicopee, and on the front page large pictures of Thaddeus Kosciusko and Abraham Lincoln, side by side. Over a small desk against the wall hung a rich tapestry in soft browns and black, a woodland scene, with deer drinking at a pool, out over one corner of it hung a gaudy calendar advertising a Polish market. A Springfield Sunday paper lay on a stool, a phone on another and a thermostat near the kitchen door testified to modern heating apparatus.

Mr. Laboda appeared, still in working clothes but with his curly hair newly combed and face beaming. He lighted a cigarette in a holder and sat near the front window in his favorite rocking chair. In the kitchen voices could be heard, speaking Polish; the dark, good-looking wife and mother and an elderly Polish woman visitor with a kerchief over her head. The stairs to the second floor lead off the front room, for the tiny front hall is used as a coat closet. The two older daughters, home from work, soon came in to hang up their wraps. They are sturdy, buxom girls

in their late 'teens or early twenties. Now and then the older son, who had visited Poland with his father, came to listen to his father's descriptions of the visit and reminded him of incidents.

"What we do for amusement when I am a boy in Poland? We played only about the yard or the barn, for we work very hard and long hours on the farm, all of us. There are so many in the family, eleven of us, and the farm is about 25 acres, your size (American). When we play it is mostly to play soldiers; all the boys and girls play soldiers, always, then and talk a great deal about war and battles, for then at that time where I live we are under Austrian rule, for Poland was partitioned to Austria, Russia and Germany. It was partitioned three times, in 1772, in 1777 and in 1779 and did not be free until 1918. We are taught much of the history of Poland, of its wars and its fighters and of the peasant revolts, which my father told of when the peasants armed themselves with — what you call, sy'es (scythes) on long handles and go to fight the high ups. That is all the weapons they have and they are beaten.

"That picture of Kosciusko is with Lincoln's because their birthday is the same day, yesterday (Feb. 12) and they are both patriots much admired by Polacks. Kosciusko came to fight for America you know and when he went home he led a peasant's revolt but was beaten.

"That picture of Kosciusko is with Lincoln's because their birthday is the same day, yesterday (Feb. 12) and they are both patriots much admired by Polacks. Kosciusko came to fight for America you know and when he went home he led a peasant's revolt but was beaten. There was another one in 1846 when the peasants killed about 2000 of the nobility and won the fight but it did not do so much good. We do not care much about our government because it is Austrian, that is really German when I am a boy and although the men vote they do not think it means much to them and they just vote because it is a custom. Yes, we are very proud of our country's history and we are taught it in school. You see, besides going to the grammar school I also took special work three days a week and learned German. I prepare for high school like your junior high school here and when I am twelve I go to Germany. "No, we do not have much time to play, because of school and work. We get up at 5 o'clock in morning and work 'til dark. We have only kerosene lamps, then and we work hard in daylight, all the time. In winter we children must thresh out the wheat and rye and corn in the barn.

"We use a long stick with a short one tied to it with leather string; what you call it? Flail. Yes, that is it, and we hit the wheat and rye and corn on the barn floor with it and thresh it out, beginning in winter and all through it. We are not too poor but we have so big a family that we have to work hard for we raise all that we eat on the farm. Oh, we have plenty to eat of everything, of cabbage, garlic, beets, turnips, potatoes, everything, and every winter just before Christmas we kill a big hog and have meat for the rest of the winter.

"But when I am twelve my father say to me, 'Adam, you must find a job, because we are so many.' It is the custom when a Polack boy is to be married that the father gives him a share of the farm, maybe two or three acres, you see. But if he gave it to all of us he would have nothing and no one would have enough land, although it is rich land and some families live on only two or three of four acres there. Lots of poor people, oh, yes, many very poor people in Poland.

"We have many, many Jews in Poland. They do not work on the farm but they must always be selling things. They will get a big basket and buy a chicken, a duck, some corn and bread and go around from one house to another and sell it to be eaten. It is cooked already to eat and they sell it in small pieces to people. Then they go on to be merchants, always to sell and buy and sell. They do not work much and we do not care much for them but we are friendly. Never will they touch a pig, only other meat and they must be killed by a kosher butcher, too.

"The Germans are many, too and we are friendly with them. The poor people are very nice, the Germans, and so I found them in Germany, where I went. Yes, I went all alone and I got a job with a farmer and I worked for a farmer and then as a spinner in a mill in Nulki[?], a city there. It took me two days and nights to get there by train. I was treated very well by the German people there, poor people. The high man is hard and military and looks down on all and cannot be spoken to except by title and all that and are not nice to get along with. They are harsh and hard.

"We did not like that kind of Germans at all. All the poor ones are good people. The way it happens that the Jews were chased out of Germany is this; Hitler came along and said to a man, 'Your father was born in Poland; you belong there. Get out!' and they tried to go but they are not really cit-izens of Poland. They were born in Germany and we have too many Jews there now and cannot admit more, not too many, so they could not come to Poland and had to camp at the border and wait and many died and all suffered badly. It is too bad. But I say that the poor German people think Hitler is all right because they have work and food.

"I worked for two years in Germany, six months as a spinner and then go home and then we come to America, as I told you.

"The church? Oh yes, it is an important part of our life. We are Roman Catholics, all about where I lived . We have many, many feast days for the church, besides such as Christmas. Our Santa Claus is St. Nicholas but we do not make so much of it there as here.

"It is strange. There we are near the Vistula River, the biggest river, and over across it is Russia and yet we are under Austrian rule.

I used to swim across the river but Russian soldiers were there and we could not stay and had to swim right back.

"I will tell you that in the old days when my father was young the nobility were cruel. They made the poor people work on large farms of 1000 acres or more and if they did not work fast enough they would whip them with long whips until they bled. They were the same as slaves or serfs then. That is why the peasants revolted and fought with sc'yes. In 1846 they killed many of the high men and divided the land among themselves.

"Our schools were public schools; the principals are mostly men but women are also teachers. The government did not use to make you go to school as it does now.

"About my work in America. At first I work in the mill at Gilbertville (Mass.). There were about 24 of us in one house. That house is still standing but has been moved. It was a company house. In one room about twice the size of this one (20x15) there were three beds and six boys slept there. We bought our own groceries and gave them to the woman who kept the house and she cooked for us. She would furnish the salt and pepper and so forth but we bought the rest and paid each $3 a month for room and the cooking; because, you see, we could only earn about $2.64 a week. I was a spinner, there, but when I wanted to get married I did not want to board but to have a tenement of my own and the company houses could not be bought there.

"So I came to Pittsfield where they told me I could get a job with the Berkshire Woolen, but when I got here they told me to go to Pontoosuc (Pontoosuc Woolen Mfg. Co.) as I would get a better job. Well, I could not talk English yet and I worked there one day and then the boss told me I would have to go. I did not know why. He paid me, I think, $1.50 and I went to the Berkshire Woolen. The boss at Pontoosuc was Irish, his name was Pat Fleming. He is dead now. I was a Polack. You see, I did not know why I was fired at first.

Two weeks later I find out. Well, I went to the Berkshire Woolen and saw the boss and asked for a job spinning. At that time, in 1910, Mr. Gilette of Westfield had died and Mr. Savery and Mr. Noonan came to take it over; they sold most of the company houses, soon. Mr. Noonan was then superintendent. He is the owner now. Well, the boss said, 'You were working at Pontoosuc?' and I told him yes and he said 'Why did you not stay; why did you get fired?' and I did not know and he said, 'We have no work now for you but maybe in two weeks on the night shift' but I needed a job then so I went to the office and went to see Mr. Noonan. I had a Polish friend who talked English for me and told Mr. Noonan I wanted a job and he asked me the same question about Pontoosuc but I did not know, but he called the boss in and told him to put me to work at once at night. So I had a job and I stayed on that job.

"As I say, after I am marry I want a tenement of my own so I buy this one from the Jew who had bought the company houses.

"That was after my visit to Poland, where I was married. I found things much changed. Yes, too much changed, but one thing I noticed, that all the boys would tip there hats and bow and I thought it was because I am an American and they know me and then I found that they are teaching them to be polite, now. They did not use to know how to be polite in the old country but they do now. They are polite to everyone and it is good. Now they must all go to school.

"Poland is a democracy, like us. They have a President but it is the, what you call it, Minister who really rules. He is about the same as a dictator and that is because Poland is afraid of war. They are afraid of enemies on all sides. I get letters from my people and at Christmas time they were much afraid of war because of Hitler. They have now military training for those of 18 to 21 but it is not a draft; it is like our own militia, here. The Polacks are great for marching and for drilling and for music such as drum corps and bands, anyway.

"Well, I found out why I am fired at Pontoosuc; it is just because I am Polack and the other, they are mostly Irish and French, do not like me. It is hard to get acquainted, you see, and then, people were cold to me because there are some Polacks who do not know how to behave. When I come here there are only eight or families here and they are new and some of them are what you call bums. Bum weavers and bum spinners — and just bums that drink too much. They are so poor that they never had money in Poland. They raised things on the farm and when they get a couple dollars here they go out to spend it and get drunk. And the Polacks are always strong and like to show how strong they are and they start throwing things and fighting, and in a boarding house a fight would start and they would break the windows and furniture and the police would have to come.

One day Judge White said in the Court that he was tired of seeing so many Polacks always in court on Monday morning and they ought to be sent back to Poland. The Polacks were to blame all right but they couldn't really help it.

"Well, that made me think and I and some others got together and we organized some societies, the Polish National Alliance and the Falcons and a Young Men's Association, but that one did not last, but the Alliance and the Falcons did. It gave the young fellows something to do in spare time. In Poland they did not have much of any spare time but here they got paid on Saturday and wanted to do something. So we gave them something to do. we have a headquarters in the German Hall that is next to Curtin's Hall on Peck's Road at Wahconah Street and then we built the Falcon's Hall that is called Bel-Air Hall, now, and there they have their meetings and their drum corps and things and you do not see many Polacks in court nowadays. So many are here now that there is good, don't you think? So many came to work in the textile mills and then in the G. E. (General Electric) You see, there were many mills, in 1910, five of them, but now only two or three, one small one and the G. E. is down so the Polacks have had to do other things besides, in business.

"Why, at one time at the mill, when there was a night shift on, some of the bums brought in a case of beer, into the mill and drank it.

Mr. Noonan came in at about ten-thirty and only two machines were running, one of them was mine and the rest of the spinners and weavers were sleeping. He said, 'We will shut down this night shift, this is too much' and he did.

"Well, it looked like I was out of a job but I went to see Mr. Noonan and asked for a day job, and he said 'sure,' and gave me a day job.

I have worked mostly on day work since. I worked all the time except one time when things were down, then I worked for six months at the G. E., but I did not get through at the Berkshire Woolen, even then. It was just when things was slack.

"Yes, four of my children are working, only one little one goes to school and we get along. We do not want the wife to work. We do not think it is right when a woman is a mother to go out to work from the home. It is not right for her to work out, then. In Poland the women work the same as the men. Why they will not let the men milk cows on the farm, for instance! They say that a man's hand is too hard and dirty to milk the cows and the women do it there altogether.

"We have the same kind of liquor in Poland as here but the men do not drink as much except in the cities; the farmers and their families do not have it. They cannot get money to spend on it but you see, when they get to America and make money, even only a little, they do not know what to do except to have what they call a good time and get drunk.

"I was in the court when the judge said there was too many Polacks being arrested. I was never arrested myself but I thought about that and that is why we started the societies. I am still in the Polish Alliance but not in the Falcons, that is for younger people. But these societies have helped a great deal. Polacks are better respected now."

Source:

Library of Congress. *American Life Histories: Manuscripts from the Federal Writers' Project, 1936-1940* from the American Memory website (http://memory.loc.gov/ammem/wpaintro/wpa-home.html).

*A*s part of the European emigration, Polish immigrants have had an easier time racially than many other non-European groups in assimilating or blending into the American scene. However, it is often the case that the children of Polish immigrants assimilate much more quickly and easily than adults. This is illustrated in Stella Kanosky's case study about her family and growing up American in a Polish household.

A constant driving-force in Stella's stories about her family is her father. Many aspects of her family life are colored by his reaction to or his opinions of various situations. Stella's father was a proud, hard-working man who strived to make decisions he thought best for his family. For many generations, Polish Americans in general did not value higher education, and Stella's father was no exception. While he wanted to see his children succeed, they didn't see eye-to-eye on how that could be accomplished. Stella, however, had a great passion for knowledge, and went on to be the first in her family to gain both a bachelors and a masters degree from a prestigious university.

CASE STUDY IN FAMILY RELATIONSHIPS

Home Economics 101, August 1941
by Stella Kanosky

The present situation in this family of eleven is: the mother, 50 years old, in fairly good health, happy and contented; the father, 51 years old, now runs a tavern in this town of 1500 and feels quite successful, in fairly good health, quick-tempered, forgets easily. They live in their own home, all modern facilities, with the four youngest children. They have a car which any of them may drive if they care to. Of these four children, Margaret is the baby, 11 years old; Leo, 13; Joe, 15; and Helen, 17, a senior in high school. These four are quite different from the five who have left home. Bernice, 20, has a civil service job; Victoria, 22, is a special nurse; Stella, 24, is a home economics teacher; John, 26, is married but was drafted; Mary, 28, and the oldest, is married and lives in this same town about a mile from her parents. She has 2 children, a girl, 5, and a boy, 3. They are the only grandchildren. Her husband is just a common laborer who works any job he can find. They manage to make both ends meet and seem happy on the little they have although money is their biggest problem.

The parents are both Polish born, coming to this country in 1910, but not together. Neither were able to speak or understand English. They settled with brothers and sisters already here, near a factory district in a Polish community. They married; the father worked in a foundry. Before the World War they became naturalized citizens. Neither had formal education because they were needed by the family as soon as they were able to work—in the fields, tending stock in fenceless pastures, or working in the homes of other farmers. The pay was meager but helped a great deal.

Mary, John, and Stella were born here in this factory town. The family then moved ten miles out to a farm where Victoria and Bernice were born. Mary and John started in the rural school here. Later the father bought a grocery store in the town where they now live. Here Helen, Joe Leo and Margaret were born.

The father owned and managed this grocery store and meat market; which was a great help in feeding this large family. After 10 years, chain stores caused business to be so little that the father at the beginning of the Roosevelt administration turned his store into a tavern and let the grocery line grad-

ually fade out. The children felt a dislike for this because of criticism in the community. To the father this was a legal means of making a livelihood and made his children see it in that light. Supporting nine children was a big job and he felt proud that he could find a way to keep going. His policy was to let 'them' talk—he was in the 'right'. He was a citizen with just as much right to live as anyone.

All the children are in strong health as are both parents, always have been. There has been little or no childhood disease, very little expense for doctor bills. All have different temperaments. The father is quick-tempered, but easily forgets. He dominates the household when he is there. This has influenced the rest. The mother is the meek, submissive type, but only to save the situation when the father takes command. She has learned to be silent and let him rule. He was right, no matter how wrong. Someone else had to prove he was wrong for him to see it. He didn't like to be criticized by his household. The children are just average with no outstanding good or bad features. There are no special talents mainly because none were allowed to develop. All were busy keeping things going—school, household duties, care of the younger children, personal needs, garden, and yard. Because the parents were very practical, things that took unnecessary money were discouraged—"don't need those things to live"—; if it was free, it was all right. It would take money to let them all do as they pleased. The children never had an allowance and soon learned the value of money. They didn't ask unless it was absolutely necessary. The father managed all the money. The mother received rent from a house they owned in another town. This was for her own use, but she saved it instead of spending. She got extra money to run the house and the father many times supplemented this amount by buying large quantities when on sale. The mother never felt she had to stay within this allowance. If more was needed, she could get it for the father realized they had to eat. But he would complain that it went too fast—what were they spending it on? He never kept track of the actual expense so he never missed this money once it was given out. If you had to have it, you had to have it—something else was sacrificed. The children usually got neces-

The Kanosky family in front of their Illinois home.

sary money from the mother and any extra they would talk out of their father. The family did suffer financially during the depression. Money was borrowed on the house and store, insurance policies were dropped, savings were taken out of the children's names and placed under the father's since he gave them the money to save. The father decided to move the store to another town and lost on this transaction so he moved back and tried again, gritting his teeth and trying to get along. This debt is all paid off now and he has purchased the house they live in, paid it in full, and started a new savings account.

Mary, being the oldest was influenced the most by Polish customs—however, this had a great influence on all of them. The household responsibilities fell first on her shoulders. She was the first to bring the effects of outside contacts into the home, starting in an English speaking school. Both parents wanted to preserve the Polish language and customs which was done easily until the children started school because the mother had few if any contacts with the people other than Polish and the father had a few contacts in his work at the factory and in farm transactions so as to pick up gradually a little knowledge to speak and understand English. When the children started to school, the conflict began.

Mary was a large child of which she was conscious, frequently being called "fatty," which affected her growth with others. Her drab, practical clothing also made her stand off from the others. She wasn't able to cope wit this problem satisfactorily and couldn't take it home because it wasn't understood. All the children wore practical, cheap, drab clothing until they were able to earn for themselves or the older ones changed customs by bringing home their ideas. They were taught to think of clothing as conventional necessities where money could be spared. Finery and style weren't essential. Shoes were shoes as long as they kept your feet dry. A shapeless, dark dress was sufficient to cover the body and keep you warm. "Hand-me-downs" were used whenever possible. All this had its effect and mostly on Mary, being the first to encounter an American community—in the rural school and in the town where they now live. Mary, John, and the father contributed here. The father in his business as a grocer and butcher improved his broken English very rapidly. He picked up business technique and so improved his home-made education, being able to read a little, write very poorly, and figure very little. Now his reading, writing, speaking, vocabulary, and mathematics became much better. Here there were no foreigners—no others speaking Polish. The father's outside influence was brought into the home along with that of the children which was gleaned at school and at play. Mary and John had a speaking ability of Polish when they entered school but soon lost it as the need at home was removed. The older children have all retained a few Polish expressions and can understand it even if they can't speak it. These contacts helped the mother to gradually pick up enough English to talk a few words with her neighbors—which she wasn't

able to do when they first came to this town. It was mostly Polish in the home for her for several years. She has never learned to read or write not even to sign her name. She knows the Polish prayers in her Catholic prayer book and can pick out prices and a few words by sounding them out from the Polish alphabet and fitting this to some English word she knows—a very slow and tedious process.

By the end of the third grade, Mary was doing poorly, didn't pass, so was sent to live with relatives and attend a Polish Catholic school, where she wasn't any too happy. When she finally didn't pass the seventh grade she returned home, spent two years in the eighth grade, graduated, and never went on to school, preferring to go to work, and was backed up by the parents who couldn't see the need of an education if you were able to get a job without an education. The parents got by without one.

John was slow in learning but did get through better than Mary. He flunked the fifth grade. He was well liked in school, a contrast to Mary. However, he, too, felt some drawbacks. He resented strongly being called a "Polack" by the neighborhood boys even in fun. One day Stella playfully called him by his Polish name "Yannek" and was severely scolded by him when he was teased. This conditioned her to be conscious of her ancestry, but as a rule it went unnoticed. John was very athletically inclined and was accepted on that point in any group. He was strong and sturdy as were all the children. Stella patterned after him somewhat as a child. She was proud of his outstanding ability. She was strong and athletically inclined, also. However, school was easy for her. She made honor grades. School was hard for John, but sports kept him going. Praise from the teachers kept Stella interested. She was noticed as an individual. Her background wasn't held against her. Her appearance didn't matter. The teachers didn't notice or rather didn't let her drab clothes and awkward actions interfere. Here she was accepted for her worth. When she wasn't playing actively—ball, racing, etc., she was studying or reading. Because her work pleased the teachers she didn't want to lose their praise so never misbehaved for fear of meeting disapproval. This caused her to be timid, slow to make decisions, afraid to do what the others did id it was against adult principles. She in this way seemed to lose the approval of the group. She was a "student"—no interest in fun or cutting up. To overcome this reaction she dug deeper, hid herself in her work. She lost contact socially, would rather read than associate with others. Reading broadened her knowledge; taught her things she was afraid to learn by actual contact. She sensed she didn't have background and training, didn't know what was the correct thing to do. She got no training at home. She didn't want people to see how ignorant she was outside of a book. So she didn't put herself out to get into a situation where she'd be embarrassed. She had no social confidence in herself, was ill-at-ease around people, shy, felt self-conscious of her appearance. Day dreaming resulted. Reading gave her volumes of information. She never tired of reading. To get rid of excess energy, she played hard and strong, nothing gracefully dainty. She'd rather play ball than learn to dance. Athletics were bringing John out of himself and also her. He won fame in football. She won recognition following him up in high school, being a good athlete, also.

John's athletic ability was either to make or break him. He was a star football player in high school. He had difficulty with his studies but always managed to pass so he could play football. The father was very proud of his son. He was gaining recognition. John graduated from high school after four years of heroic football playing. The father never missed a game. His Johnnie was the best player the high school ever had. College coacher were interested in him and after some high colored talking got the father interested in trying to send John to college. He wasn't sold on the idea because it would cost money and to him a college education didn't help you. Many spend hundreds of dollars on a college education and then took jobs they could have had with no education. Others got to the top without going to college. But because publicity caught his ego—people wanted his son—he said he'd try to send him. There was always money when it played up his ego—donations here and there—beggars asking and getting money. He was very tender hearted and anything sympathetic brought results outside the family. He was used to the family.

John started in the [University of Illinois]—joined a fraternity since this was to help him make the necessary contacts and also help him to meet expenses since the fraternity found him a meal job—washing dishes. Of course it took a lot of talking to get the father to do this as he wasn't in favor of spending money "foolishly"—go to college to learn how to spend more money. John earned and saved all he could working during the summer and vacations. He made the freshman team and earned his letter in his second year. In his junior year he had difficulties with the coach. He left for parts unknown in the middle of the term with his roommate. The university notified the father. He was very angry. He had just loaned him $30 for college expenses and evidently on this he leaves without a sign to anyone. After two weeks he sent word he was in Texas working. The father was afraid he'd never finish his college education and all that

money was wasted—never would be paid back. John worked till the beginning of the second semester, returned and entered again. This time to finish. The father had shown his antagonism several times when money pressed him concerning John. John didn't seem to show appreciation for all the father was doing. He took the money too easily to suit the father. John, of course, meant to pay back all this money. He wasn't taking it free. One day by chance he found a record of all the money he had gotten from his father. It was down in the black and white. This hurt John, made him feel the father didn't trust him. He meant to more than pay the actual amount. Here it was all figured down to the cent, held against him, and thrown at him at every money disagreement the father felt. He was seriously worried when John quit. This record stared him in the face. He was tired of working like a dog, loaning the money and getting no gratitude. Give them hard earned money and get no thanks. He had never believed in the college business. It gave them big ideas—spend money without thinking. He was for letting them start at the bottom like he had to . Nobody sent him to school so he didn't have to work. He worked on his own to get to the top. He was proud of the progress he had made. He was getting old. He was going to save his money for his old age, not spend it on ungrateful children who would probably forget you were hungry once they were out on their own. No more spending his money on college. The children are supposed to support the parents when they are old enough to work—that is why they had children—to work for them and help them in their old age. But this family had American ideas—selfish, ungrateful. He'd have to watch out for himself. Nobody would watch out for him. He talked like this many times. The children all knew how he felt. Yet when John, to whom he had lent the money, was around, he never told him his feelings. He blew off his steam and forgot till the next instance. John graduated, secured a teaching position, eventually paid back the debt for nothing has been said lately and got married. His wife has a civil service job which pays more than his job so she kept it and he was drafted and is now in Camp Forrest. The father is proud of him even as a draftee, now. He has queer ways of showing his affection and feelings, but it is there inside. Certain little special considerations come out now and then to show this. He is concerned about his children but in a way hard to understand. The relationship was on business terms there for a while between John and his father—no father and son feeling. The father had antagonized the relationship. But now they are on equal footing, both men of the world—adults. John now had his own responsibilities, would have to shift for himself.

But just as he looks out for Mary, secretly, subtly, he looks out for John. None of the children were trained to recognize and respond because the feeling was so hidden. Now as adults they begin to see the situation. They were always treated more or less as adults and as children didn't understand adult methods.

Stella from the beginning sailed under different conditions, as was said, she was athletic, patterning after John. She had no difficulty with her studies like Mary and John, however. She spoke English from the beginning as Mary and John brought it home. Then, too, she made contacts in the community. So without this type of handicap, she progressed with fine records. However she feels her scholastic record handicapped her socially. None of the other children ever came near her in their grades. This was continually brought up to them and put them under pressure by the teacher. Stella, in trying to keep up this record cut out social activities. She was shy and timid and felt the others held her ability against her. She couldn't mix, partly because she felt her background, drab clothing, and general appearance were held against her. She turned into herself more than ever. She couldn't do the things others did. She had friends, but few of the bosom type. He wants and desires were put forth in imagination from her reading. Here she was the heroine. She wasn't held back because of what the parents thought. She needn't be afraid to do what she felt. She didn't have to do things just to please someone. She was happy and unafraid. She was beautiful. In her athletic ability she felt unhampered. Clothes didn't matter here, nor beauty.

When in high school Stella worked summers to save for winter expenses. She was ambitious as were most of the children. She knew she could get more what she wanted on her own money. She wouldn't feel so restricted. However, the practical side was drilled into her so deeply that she watched how she spent her money to get the most, getting only what was necessary for basic satisfaction. When the money ran out, she felt uneasy asking her parents for money. Being independent financially for a time made her conscious of dependence. This was due to the approach the parents had. Once you were capable of earning money you should manage to always have money to spend for necessities. They were taught to always have enough aside for necessities. So Stella sacrificed and went without rather than be dependent. It was hard to do. Other children spent what they earned and depended on their parents to provide for them as a duty of parents—children weren't supposed to provide for themselves till they were out of high school—18 years old.

In Poland they were on their own when they were old enough to run. Stella, and the others, though they were proud to be able to earn their own money, felt it was asking a little too much. Nevertheless she worked every summer, saving all and spending wisely. The parents never asked their children to contribute to the income. The money was theirs. They paid no board and room. They could pay for extra privileges according to their own conscience. They still did the housework even if they worked. Dishes still had to be done—cleaning, mopping, dusting, care of own bedroom—care of own clothes. They found time to keep the house going or paid the other children to do it for them.

Stella graduated with honors from both grade school and high school. The teachers wanted to see something done of this. They encouraged her to take a competitive scholarship exam. She had no hopes of going to college. John was costing enough. She took the exam and won a four year scholarship in home economics to the [University of Illinois]. She was pleased to have doe it even if she didn't see how she could use it. When she told the father he wasn't the least bit thrilled. She didn't receive any encouragement. He didn't seem honored. It meant nothing to him. He was sending John and couldn't send her. Girls didn't need education anyway—they'd just get married. Why spend money on them? She said she had her scholarship. He said if that paid all her expenses, all right—and laughed knowing it didn't. He wasn't putting himself out. He was afraid she might start on her own and have to call on him for money he couldn't spare. So he told her not to start. She was stubborn enough that this antagonized her. She would show him. He wouldn't have to help her. She didn't want to hinder John anyway. If she could have she would have given him the scholarship. She started in at the University of Illinois with her scholarship, the money she saved during the summer ($125.00), and a board and room job in a private home in Champaign where she started and finished all four years, developing for herself a second home where she is always welcome and treated as a step-daughter. Their genuine interest and encouragement kept her going. They understood her. She got no encouragement from home. They didn't understand her. She felt out of place, in a different world, at home. They didn't see things her way. This bothered her and still does. When away, she forgets the difference, but when at home she is conscious of it and has gradually trained herself to be the one to do the adjusting. Things have changed at home since she has bee away and she has changed. She has broken away from their ideas and formed ideas of her own. If they are in conflict, she must be understanding and abide by home ideas.

She no longer lives there and shouldn't try to change them for the time she is there. That is their way and it is satisfactory to them. Of course, she had to learn by trial and error to come to this conclusion after many disagreements and arguments with brothers sisters and parents. All at home felt the difference. They were on the defense. It was their home. She was happier away where she was understood. But she became mighty homesick and would have to quit anytime if it wasn't that she was determined to show them she could get through. She really didn't have nerve enough to quit and go home to face the music—disappoint her teachers—convince her family she was better off at home. So she gritted her teeth. It was hard to save every cent. She didn't have time to associate wit them—it took spending money and extra clothes. She thought many times was it worth it.

For her senior year she didn't have the necessary summer's earnings—she had been in summer school. She earned $25 which helped. She planned on borrowing from the U. of I. But her mother said she'd lend it, and there'd be no interest to pay, since she only wanted enough for bare necessities. She had averaged $100 a year for general needy expenses. Her whole education of 4 years amounted to less than $500.00 of her own money counting what she had borrowed ($75). After 4 years of keeping up her courage, skimping, sacrificing, all work and very little play, work every summer and save save save , no encouragement from home, she finished, but not without certain disagreeable effects. John was in school during these years. He was causing financial arguments. The facts have been told. The father blamed Stella along with John—they were both at school. The father took his spite out on her when John wasn't around. She hadn't borrowed any from him but that was beside the point. She had big ideas like John. It antagonized her. Why did he say he was spending on her, too? Why blame her? She never asked him for any money. Hel always asked her if she needed any money and he'd give it to her if she did. But she always said she had enough. She wasn't going to obligate herself. He'd giver her the money and then throw it at her as he did John. No, she'd do without. She didn't refuse gifts of money at Christmas time, however. So when her father blamed her for being ungrateful when he was angry with John, she wouldn't put up with it. It was an accusation unjustly made. She'd show him! She made up her mind to pay back every cent of gift money when she finished and got a job. If that is the way he felt, he could have it all back. She didn't need his money. So when she was a senior she borrowed from her mother who had the rent money for her own use. The mother knew it would prove uncomfortable in a trying situation to borrow from the father. She understood him and let him have his way in silence. She seemed submissive and meek—but afterwards guided the children to what was best and why. No back talk to him, no matter how wrong he was. She had learned.

So she counseled with Stella not to borrow from him and not let him know she borrowed from her. He knew Stella didn't have enough for that last year, having gone to summer school. He offered to loan her the money and accidently found out she had borrowed from the mother after refusing his offer. This was a surprise to him and stirred and hurt him. Stella could tell it hurt and that her realized how she felt. This hurt her. He hadn't meant to be mean—and she hadn't meant to be mean. She felt from then on he treated her as an adult. She was supposed to know what she was doing. She graduated and secured a well paid position for the first year teachers. The father was glad and proud, yet seemed on the defense. He had to work hard for his money—his money was worth more. Before her position started, she got into a heated argument with him for quarreling with a younger sister about nothing important—other than that Helen was shirking her duties so the mother had more to do than need be. This gave him a vent to explode his feelings about work—again—he worked hard, nobody helped him. He had to spend his money on the "kids"—then come home and find a houseful of noise—no rest—no gratitude. He fed and kept them from birth till they were out on a job of their own. He was getting nothing back. He was tired of it. This antagonized Stella. She had been trying to help the situation in the home and got finance thrown in her face. She was sick of the whole affair. It would have been different if his children spent their earnings foolishly, were lazy, and didn't help with anything. They all did all they possibly could for themselves. They demanded nothing, accepted what they got, weren't finicky about their food. He didn't appreciate what they had done to help out—trying not to be a burden. He didn't appreciate what his wife did to help—no she did nothing of any worth. Housework was nothing. Only his eighteen hour daily was work. The rest of the family felt this was unnecessary. He had a young man helping him. He didn't have to work all those hours. Actually he was on the job eight hours. But nobody argued—they knew better. Even the mother remained silent. She had learned to let him rave alone and taught the children to do the same. So when that false statement of rearing that whole family alone, without gratitude, came forth, Stella rebelled. She said he didn't rear her on his own from birth till she was 22, and she wouldn't let him think so. They argued in anger and tears, then avoided each other. She would never ask a favor of him. She would pay him back the actual money he had given her since she was eighteen. She felt he was legally bound to feed and keep her till she was that old although she had done much for herself. She of course was angry—he was, too. They were like two children—quarreling—but the quarrel left its mark. He wouldn't take the money she offered when she started teaching. He'd keep his and she could keep hers. Again he felt his money was better because he worked harder. He didn't refuse in a grudging manner, but in a way to reassure everyone he could get along on his own earnings. Since he is the type that forgets easily, little is now thought of this incident. There have been no disturbances of late. She has her money to do with what she wants. She buys gifts whenever there is a gift occasion. This is mentioned because gifts weren't exchanged in this household until lately when the older girls started the practice on their own earnings. The parents always felt you should get what you need when you need it and not wait til Christmas or your birthday. She gets the mother gifts now that she would never buy for herself because they seem extravagant and unnecessary to one with such a practical mind. However, she appreciates them, large or small. She has a habit of putting away the new and using the old until it falls apart, no matter how inefficient it may be. She wants nice things just to say she has tem. Stella enjoys buying her things but wants her to use them—the new iron instead of the old without a regulator—the new gas stove instead of the kerosene stove—the new bed spread even though the father sleeps on it with his dirty shoes. Both are getting a lot of satisfaction out of these gifts and are coming to a better understanding through them.

Victoria has had a life similar to Stella. They are quite close in age and so associated together quite a bit. Victoria had more difficulty with her school work but did above average work. She was pressed quite a bit by the teachers to produce a record as good as Stella's and this affected her. She tried but was continually told about Stella. She didn't hold this against Stella but did develop an inferiority feeling. She built up a stubborn attitude as well as a barrier to keep out these criticisms. She was trying to protect herself. She was really timid and shy. She was hard to understand because of this wall. She wouldn't let you get near her so to speak. She was fighting a battle and no one could help. She progressed and graduated winning an American Legion award for being a good all round citizen. She was well liked in the community. When she

was with someone she felt confident with, she was very sweet. She was less yielding than Stella, who agreed because she was afraid to disagree not only with her parents but friends and teachers.

After graduating from high school she, too went to work to save for a career—nurse's training. About two weeks before entering, she had a money spat with her father and wasn't going to enter because of it. John and Stella were in the University. Now she was embarking on an educational journey. He couldn't help her and didn't want her to start if she couldn't finish without help from him. This mad her antagonistic—if he was so afraid, she wouldn't start. But after a sensible talk with Stella she got over her stubborn spell and entered. It was tough going, sacrificing clothes and a good time as did Stella. Victoria was more inclined socially than Stella and so missed the clothes. She wouldn't go places she wanted to go because she didn't have the right clothes. She rebelled about her fate whereas Stella accepted it—if she had wanted to go badly enough she would have in the clothes she did have. She graduated and is doing special duty now. She doesn't feel hurt by the struggle anymore than Stella does. It was good for both of them. The appreciate life more. They are more understanding, can see things at home with a different light. They are more sympathetic and are trying to improve the situation at home so the rest won't be handicapped by the lackings in the home. What they have gained from worldly contact they bring home trying to create more family atmosphere, affection, emotion, confidence. The family has changed a lot. Many things are done differently with the continuation of contacts. The parents are different and the children are different—in ways good and bad. Much equipment has been added through Stella and Victoria. Life is beginning to pickup?

Bernice has a personality still different from those described. She has a very easy going nature. Nothing seems to bother her. She makes friends very easily. Her work in school was just average, but she enjoyed it. She was talking with more confidence in herself than any of the rest ever expressed. She expected and took more privileges than those before her. Her ideas were more like the neighborhood children. The others had these ideas but were afraid to express themselves. She wasn't She was more spontaneous.

She graduated from high school and entered the commercial field for a while. She was interested in civil service work so saved her money for business school. She passed her state exam and received a position. She now is awaiting a position of more importance, having passed her National. She is the first not to encounter antagonism in attaining her goal. However, she is the first to show babified traits—cries on leaving home—hesitates in making decisions—wants things done for her that she can do. She seems to be the transition child (she is the middle one, 5th in 9). She was the one to start in expressing herself—what she wanted to do. The ones before her wanted to but were afraid of parental disapproval. However, the parents were being changed along with the children so it was easier for her to do these things without difficulty. She seemed to get her way because she took it. However, this wasn't in an objectionable manner. She was still considerate of others.

Helen came in past the middle point and seems to have thrown everything in an uproar. She was more demanding and less considerate. She got what se wanted no matter what the means or effect on someone else's rights. She was the first to be born in an entirely American community. She was always in a household that was being changed by American contacts being brought into the home. In school she is little concerned, does average work. She expects a good time, nice clothes, certain types of meals. She rebels if she doesn't get them. She has had more of a childhood than the rest who had adult responsibilities as mere children and accepted them. Now she is a senior in high school, is working and spends all her money on fancy clothing that is discarded when the pleasure is gone. This of course hurts the practical mother. She can't understand this daughter who demands and commands. The mother said just this summer that she cant fee she is the mother of such a daughter who treats her as a dog, talks uncivilly, shirks her duties, demanding the mother do them for her. She is entirely different from the rest and is setting a pattern for those below her who are quickly making use of it so that the mother is many times at her wit's ends. She doesn't know what to do with her. Her demands are impossible and without thanks. The more you do the more she wants. She expects these things as a child's rights. This is probably an influence from those she associates with. She is under pressure there and is trying to keep up no matter how. She does her work in the home by moods. If you cross her she is impossible. She works the mother for everything. Finally, the mother has quit trying. It is easier on her nerves not to try to reason with her. She knows she has the mother under her thumb and makes use of it. This causes comment when the older children are home. They can't see how such a change got by. They wouldn't think of doing what she does, talking to her parents the way she does—demanding, getting, never giving, shoving duties onto the mother. They feel the mother has grown tired of her job and doesn't care as much. She is older and it is easier on her nerves not to cause objections. Helen will get her way anyway. She'll save her strength and nerves. It doesn't seem to cause so much disturbance because the mother is used to it while the others find it only on coming home. The mother doesn't want them to interfere when they come home. It just causes trouble—so they just keep still as much as possible. They blame the mother, yet know she isn't to blame. Helen won't listen to anyone once she makes up her mind. She has some sense but seems to feel things are against her so is fighting for herself, disregarding everyone. She won't listen to the advice of anyone—if you had the fun of learning, I will too. She does have a pleasant side when she is very agreeable and will listen to constructive criticism, even asking it—mainly of the older girls who seem to know a few of her problems. She is a good worker when in the mood but can't stand criticism—wants to be her own boss. She wants to get out on her own so she can be her own boss. Nurse's training is her ambition.

Joseph did just average work in school. He flunked the third grade but progressed after that. He seems nervously active but is growing up which may account for it. He is happy, unconcerned about life. He will be in high school this next fall, likes athletics, isn't fussy about clothes or food, does things on his own and takes the consequence. He doesn't help at home if he can get out of it, having a habit of looking around to see if he is doing more than Leo. He isn't afraid of work, but doesn't want to be worked unfairly. He did what he thought was his share. He depends pretty much on his own earnings because he knows he spends foolishly—"it is his money—he earned it—he'll spend it"—and therefore he'll hesitate asking for more when his is gone. He has a big bully attitude but this is just to hide his backwardness. He does odd jobs to earn money but won't stick to one job long if it handicaps his carefree attitude of doing just what he wants to. He wants to do it and get it over with. He and Leo chum around quite a bit but have different attitudes on life.

Leo is in the eighth grade, average intelligence, industrious, and thorough. He seems a little babified compared to Joe. He complains and tattles if things go wrong, cries if unjustly handled, but has a more pleasing personality than Joe. Leo is better liked than Joe by the community because he seems so unaffected and "little-boyish". He is friendly and has a sense of humor whereas Joe is nervous and rough if things put him on the spot. He is always busy, around the house and on odd jobs. Joe is home very little except to eat and sleep. Leo putters around house, has a dog of which he is very proud—likes to sit and play with him. Joe and Leo have a bicycle together which gives them a great deal of pleasure and little cause of trouble. He likes to earn his own money and is proud he can save. This point troubles Joe who is always running short. Leo gives his money to his mother to save, but asks for it when he needs it. He has a special delivery job which keeps him on a schedule. He doesn't mind this—always watches his time to meet all the trains. In between trains he has special jobs of working for other people. He has worked this up himself. His personality has won him many favors—yard jobs, errands, etc. His summer is quite full just taking care of yards, cutting lawns and running errands. He has earned enough to buy himself a lawn mower. He is quite a business man and is proud of himself. He likes to fish and swim and he and Joe go together quite a bit. They are two pretty fine lads. They are both proud of their brothers and sisters, Leo showing it much more easily and unaffectedly than Joe. Leo can sulk—he wants his part taken in conflict [so] he'll cry and be quite a baby if taken advantage of. Joe wouldn't cry—if he loses, she charges it to himself.

Margaret is the baby. She will be in the sixth grade—of average intelligence. She has been spoiled a little if any of them have. She cries for her way if she feels slighted. Money means a lot to her and she works hard for it. A few cents constitute a fortune. Many times the value of money gets her in a tight spot. Helen will take advantage of her willingness to earn a penny. When she wants to shirk her work, she'll ask Margaret to do things for her for pay—a penny to do the dishes alone for her. Margaret will consent, later cry because the job was too big for a penny, but keeps on in tears because she agreed and had been paid. She is fair in what she does, is proud of her brothers and sisters. However, as is true of Joe and Leo, she never tried to take advantage of the money making or lending power of the older ones. They don't ask for extra spending money but very frequently offer to do things for them to earn money. They all know the value of money. Helen does bribe now and then to get clothes she "just has to have"—not in a cheating, but shy, way. She pays back if she actually borrowed the money.

Margaret likes to be grown up. Her attitude is very mature on some points. She probably gets this from her playmates who come from smaller families and have more privileges. She feels she should have them, too, many times crying until she gets her way. She likes to talk back and argue with her mother until she does get her way. However, she is ashamed of Helen when she treats everyone so uncivilly so tries not to be like her. She earns much of her own spending money and expects to spend it as she pleases. She is a responsible child. She and Helen get along grand doing the Saturday cleaning if there are no other bosses around. She takes care of the two grandchildren now and then and is quite capable. She earns money running errands for the neighbors by whom she is well liked. She is willing and cooperative. When she isn't in a pouty mood, she'll do anything within reason.

The family thus described seems quite a muddle. To someone looking at it today much of what the family was like wouldn't be noticeable. There is much more content and peace now than before. There is an attempt to be affectionate, considerate, sympathetic. It seems more like a genuine family and less of a stiff business system. There seems to be an understanding. Education and contact have helped the parents to understand the children and the children to understand the parents. The problems were formed because no one understood anyone. Each individual was trying to solve his problems alone. There was no confiding in anyone. Everyone fought his battle alone. There was lack of approach, training, affection, understanding and sympathy. All this caused misunderstanding socially, economically, and emotionally so the entire family was continually under pressure. There was very little family atmosphere. Today the situation is much different and the pressures have been greatly released; some have been removed altogether. The children have come to realize the parents did the best they knew how with their training. They did what they thought was best and right.

Source:

Stella Kanosky McDermott.

*L*ike *other immigrant groups, the Poles preserved much of their cultural heritage after emigrating to America. With deep roots in centuries of Slavic and Catholic tradition, their celebrations, holidays, and feasts continued to have an important role in contemporary life. This memoir by a second-generation Polish American is based on recollections by the author's grandmother. In one sense, it is a measure of how some old traditions have changed, became modernized, or disappeared in the Polish community of New York Mills. With other traditions, the memoir is a testimony to their longevity and resilience. From worship and cooking to courtship and even housecleaning, the author recounts ancient religious and folk practices that helped bind her grandmother's people together—and to some extent, still do the same for her own.*

A potent force in Polish culture for ten centuries, Catholicism shapes a number of these traditions. Each year, the Christmas Eve dinner features the same 12 dishes. The foods themselves—simple fare such as bread, fish and soup—are primarily significant because of their symbolic number: there are 12 dishes, representing Jesus's 12 apostles. Contemporary practice has trimmed away some of the older aspects of the meal, such as covering the table with straw to represent the Nativity Scene and setting an extra place for visitors. And yet this centuries-old menu persists as a means for Catholic Poles to commemorate their savior's birth.

Food also has a symbolic value on another holy day. During the Catholic celebration of Lent, Holy Saturday is observed by Poles by bringing food to church with them. The priests bless the food, each an item of which carries a symbolic meaning. Eggs, for instance, symbolize Christ's rebirth, while bread symbolizes his sacrifice. Less commonly than in the author's grandmother's day, priests also go to their parishioners' homes to bless the food.

A superstitious fear of bad luck formed some of the old traditions. One largely-discarded religious tradition was to have the house blessed on the Feast of the Three Kings, which commemorated the kings who were believed to have brought gifts to the infant Jesus. In her grandmother's day, the author noted, priests visited the home to write the names of the kings over the door and to sprinkle incense on the stoves; thus was the house "protected from damage" and the inhabitants "brought good luck." At other times, the house could be spared being struck by lightening if blessed flowers were kept in the attic.

The folklore recounted by the author described an age when fate was not to be tempted. Her grandmother remembers the terrible cautions that young Polish women faced: how and when the floor was swept could doom a girl to old maidenhood, or even allow the devil into the house. Conversely, as one Lenten song put it, a girl who fasted during the holy period might just stand a chance that "a handsome young man will come [her] way" If that happened, the traditional three-day long wedding feast, with joyous music, singing—capped by the symbolic gift of a new pillow—awaited.

POLISH CUSTOMS IN NEW YORK MILLS, N.Y.

When my grandmother came to this country from Poland, she was sixteen. Even at this age she brought with her holiday customs, proverbs, recipes, games, and other folk material typical of life in Poland. In becoming Americanized there was much that she forgot, but there is much that she remembers. In talking with her recently I learned a great deal about the Polish people, and I can see her influence in many things our family does today. I would like to share with you some of her reminiscences; I have added comments where these customs are still followed in our family.

On Christmas Eve the whole family gathers together for the evening meal, called WILIA, waiting for the first star to appear before beginning the meal. Earlier in the week each family received from the church the communion wafer; if is a large rectangular piece, rather than the small circles, and is called OPATEK. This is passed down the table, each person breaking off a small piece for himself and wishing the person next to him good luck, good health, and a long life. The table is covered with white cloth, over which straw is placed. In the center of the table is a figure of Christ in the crib, and an extra place is set for a stranger. Twelve different types of foods are served, one for each of the apostles. Foods included are fish; PIEROGI, which is a dough filled with cheese, cabbage, potatoes, or fruit; BARSZCZ, a soup made with beets or mushrooms; BABKA, a sweet bread with raisins; and MAZUREK, a cookie with raisins, figs, and dates. (We still gather together for the meal, starting with the OPATEK and having the traditional foods, but straw is no longer placed on the table, nor is an extra place set; the meal begins as soon as everyone arrives.)

New Year's was celebrated with a dance held in a large hall, decorated with fruit hanging from the walls. While the couples were dancing, the lights went out, and attempts were made to steal the fruit before the lights came on again. At the dance were "policemen" to catch the thieves, and a "judge" to fine them a coin or two. (My mother remembers going to dances like these when she was young, but they are no longer held.)

January sixth, or the Feast of the Three Kings, is called Little Christmas. The priest came to the homes and wrote the initials of the three kings (Kaspar, Melchior, and Balthasar) above the door, with crosses between them:

K + M + B 1968

He then sprinkled incense on the stoves, which were wood burning, and soon the whole house smelled like the church on holy days. In addition, the family was to have holy water, blessed candles, and palms in the house. These protected the house from damage and brought good luck to the inhabitants. Children unable to remember the names of the three kings called them:

Kasper: KAPUSTA: Cabbage

Melchior: MARHAF: Carrots

Balthasar: BUROKI: Beets

(In the small town of New York Mills, where my grandparents settled, the priest used to come to the houses; today little packets containing incense and chalk may be picked up in church.)

The day before Ash Wednesday is called PACZKI day. Paczki are jellybuns. This is a day of feasting and merrymaking which precedes lent. (We still have jellybuns on the Tuesday before Ash Wednesday in our family.)

On Holy Saturday food is taken to the churches in baskets to be blessed. Foods included are eggs (both colored and hard-boiled which have been peeled), for they are the symbols of life (as Christ came from the tomb alive, life can come from the egg); bread (usually rye and BABKA), for Christ gave Himself to us as bread; meat (ham and KIELBASA or Polish sausage), which signifies the physical Christ, who was not an angel but God-man; horseradish, which represents the bitter sorrows Christ underwent; vinegar, for Christ was given gall to drink; and a lamb (of sugar or butter, decorated with the Polish flag), representing Christ, the Lamb of God who takes away our sins. Eggs were colored with onion skins and decorated with wax, especially in the shape of stars; this kind of egg is called PISANKI. On the day after Easter boys would squirt water at the girls through a hollow wooden stick, using a wooden rod. (Today food is still taken to the church, and it is even possible to have the priest come to your home to bless the food. Decorating eggs with wax is no longer done by the younger people; neither is the day after Easter game used, in which the boys squirt the girls.)

June twenty-fourth is the feast of Saint John the Baptist. Until this day no one would go swimming in the nearby streams and river. It is said that on this day he blesses the waters, thus making it safe for people to use them. (My mother remembers my grandmother forbidding swimming until this date, but this custom is no longer carried out.)

On August fifteenth children would take bouquets of flowers, an apple and a carrot were included, to the church to be blessed. The bouquets were then dried and placed in the attic to prevent lightning from striking the house. (My grandmother used to place the flowers in the attic, but today after being blessed, the flowers are placed about the house.)

LIPA, a tea made from the blossoms of the linden tree to which rock candy was added, was given as a remedy for coughs. Tea made from mint leaves was given to cure stomach gases. (My grandmother grows mint and has a linden tree in the back yard. Each year she gathers the leaves and blossoms, carefully dries them, and then stores them in jars for winter use.)

My grandmother remembers these proverbs. Always sweep towards the door; if you sweep towards the center of the room you will end up an old maid. To rock your foot back and forth is to rock the devil. What you do New Year's Eve you will do all year. If you sweep the floor after supper, the devil will come and dance all night.

Three ways of predicting the weather are: 1) A red sun at night means the next day will be windy. 2) Sun at seven means rain by eleven. 3) A cat washing himself is a sign of damp weather. My grandmother's father had two ways of making long range predictions involving the coming year, both done on Christmas Eve. He would throw a handful of hay up at the corner of the house. If the hay stayed there, the year ahead would be prosperous; a not so prosperous year would be had if it fell. Another prediction concerned the year's weather. One curved piece of onion was placed on a window sill for each month, and some salt was sprinkled into each one. On the sixth of January they would be looked at and those that were still damp would signify damp months, the dried out ones dry months.

In one of the many children's games, a ring was formed around a child, who then said:

Round and round walks a bird,
Picking up a beakful.
What he picks with his beak he bites,
But I like you—the best of all.

Girls threw wreaths of grasses into a stream. If a boy managed to retrieve the wreath, he then chased the girl who made it. A third game consisted of having a child, who made it. A third game consisted of

having a child, who was blindfolded with a babushka, sing in the center of a ring of children:

Jez Dem Sobie Choo Choo Babka.
Cujne Wkoa, Cujne Wabka.
Po Chiemku Sobie Hoze.
Wapie Tego ca Me Wdroze.
   (translation)

I am a choo choo babka.
Circle to the left, circle to the right
While I try to grab you.
In the dark I am walking,
Grabbing whoever is in my way.

   The older girls would sing this song during lent.

bym piatki, posciabym srody,
i sie trafi jaki chopiec mody.
bym srody, posciabym piatki,
i sie trafi na zielone swiatki.
   (translation)

I'll fast on Friday, and I'll fast on Wednesday,
So a handsome young man will come my way.
I'll fast on Wednesday, and I'll fast on Friday,
So he'll come before Pentecost Sunday.

My grandmother remembers hearing these tales in Poland.

There was a king who placed people he felt were dangerous in a misha, or mouse tower, to be eaten by rats and mice. The people decided to get even and so they placed the king in the tower, where he received his own punishment. (Here is a variant of the mouse tower on the Rhine, surely.)

Once there was a village where the landowners made the field laborers work long hard hours for only a few grains—not enough to live on. To get even the laborers lined up the landowners and killed them, one by one. The priest, who was in with the landowners, tried to escape by removing his religious garments and hiding in a tree. But at the end he, too, was killed.

A youth named Krakow, after killing a dragon, became the first king of Poland. His only child was a girl, named Wanda, so when he died she became queen. A German prince wanted to marry her for the lands she possessed; this caused a battle in which the Germans were defeated. The prince returned to Germany for reenforcements. Wanda didn't want any more blood-shed, so when he returned, she drowned herself. It is said that in her honor girls throw wreaths of flowers into the river.

Older people would scare children by saying they saw people who had returned to earth after death. The children were also told that gypsies would take them if they strayed far from home.

Weddings began in the morning with the ride to church. The bride and maid of honor came first, riding in a wagon, followed by the groom and best man on horseback. Then came the orchestra, relatives, and neighbors, also in wagons. In this way there would be music and singing all the way to church and back. Sometimes there were as many as twenty-five wagons; the horses pulling them were trimmed with sprigs of greens. After church there were breakfast, dancing, lunch, more merrymaking, dinner (for which a whole cow or pig was killed), and more dancing. This could go on for three days. The mother of the bride gave her daughter a pillow to start out the marriage.

Other foods not mentioned above in connection with holidays are GOABKI, stuffed cabbage; KILACZKI, jam filled pastries; *kapusta*, cabbage; *flaczki*, tripe; and CHRUSCIKI, strips of pastry—for which I give my grandmother's recipe.

Chrusciki

5 yolks and 1 whole egg
1 tbsp. whiskey
1 tbsp. sugar
¼ tsp. salt
1 tbsp. cream
2 cups flour, or more

Add salt to eggs and beat. Add sugar, cream, and liquor and beat again. Add flour and knead. Roll out very thin and cut into strips about 1½" x 4". Make a slit in the center of each and pull one end through. Fry in deep hot fat till lightly browned on both sides. Drain on absorbent paper and dust with powdered sugar.

Source:

Robert Maziarz, "Polish Customs in New York Mills, N. Y." In *New York Folklore*, vol XXIV, 1968. pp. 302-307.

PUEBLOS

This Tewa creation myth tells not how the world was made but how the Pueblo way of life and Pueblo values came into being. In the story, Long Sash and his people make a journey from strife and division (in the north) toward harmony with each other in a new home. The very name of this new home suggests balance: the Middle Place. Several versions of this myth are told by the Pueblo people of the Southwest; this particular version comes from the Nambe and San Ildefonso Pueblo.

From the mid-1500s on, Pueblo culture in the Southwest came under attack by Spanish priests intent on replacing traditional sacred practices with Christianity. In some Pueblo communities, traditional religious practices continued to be exercised in secret. In others, they were blended with Christian practice by a process known as "syncresis," which allowed people to maintain a balance between their own values and the new religion in their midst.

THE STARS ABOVE: LONG SASH AND HIS PEOPLE

The bright star that rises in the east soon after autumn sunset is Long Sash, who guided the ancestors of the Pueblos from the north to their present home. He was a famous warrior, and the people followed him because they knew he could lead them in defense against their enemies. Someone was always attacking the villages, and wrecking the fields. The enemies captured women and children for slaves, and killed many of the men, until Long Sash came to the rescue.

"Take us away from here," the people begged him. "Lead us to a new land, where we can live peacefully."

"My children," Long Sash said, "are you sure you want to leave? Life is hard here, I know, but it will not be easy anywhere. There will be dangers on the way if you travel. Some will be sick; many will be hungry and thirsty; perhaps some of you may die. Think, and be sure you want to take that risk."

"We will face any hardships," the people promised him. "Only lead us away from this dark country, to a place where we may have light and life of our own."

So Long Sash started out, and the people followed him. They set their feet on the Endless Trail that stretches like a white band across the sky. This was the road they were going to follow until they found a place of their own.

As the people traveled along the Endless Trail with Long Sash, they began to grow tired and discouraged. Some of them quarreled with one another. They had little clothing and less food. Long Sash had to teach his followers how to hunt for food, and how to make clothing from feathers. At last he led them to a country that was so new that even Long Sash had never been there before.

In this new country there was no darkness, it was daylight all the time. The people walked and walked, and when they were too tired to go on they rested. Children were born and old people died and still they journeyed.

The quarrels grew more bitter, and the people began to fight among themselves, exchanging blows and inflicting wounds. At last Long Sash said to them, "This must stop. You are hurting yourselves worse than your enemies hurt you. If you are to come to the place of your own, there can never be violence among you. Now you must decide. We will stop here and rest. Many of the women are ready to have their babies. We will wait until the children are delivered and the mothers are strong. Then you must make your own decision, whether you will follow me or take another trail."

There where the two very bright stars are north of Long Sash in the sky, the people rested and made up their minds. Those two bright stars became known as the Place of Decision, and people look up to them for help today, when they come to the turning points in their lives. We all have decisions to make as long as we are on the earth: good or bad, forward or backward, kind or unkind. Those stars can tell us what to do.

When the people had rested and felt stronger, they were ready to go ahead with Long Sash. They told him so, and everybody went forward again. Long Sash watched, to be sure that his children traveled with good hearts and love toward each other.

But Long Sash himself was growing tired, and his own heart was empty and doubting. He heard strange voices speaking in his mind, and could not tell who spoke, or what they were trying to say to him. At last he decided to answer the voices. As he spoke to the unseens, his own people gathered around him to listen.

"Show me a sign to tell me who you are, fathers and mothers," Long Sash began. "My people are tired and I am growing old. Give me a word to tell me we are on the right path and will soon reach our home."

Then while his people watched him, frightened, Long Sash appeared to go to sleep. He dropped down where he had been sitting and his eyes were closed. He lay without moving while the people stayed beside him, because they did not know what to do. They grew more and more afraid.

At last Long Sash opened his eyes. He looked at the people who had gathered around him while he slept. "Don't be frightened," Long Sash told them. "I have been given many signs and promises. The worst part of your journey is over, and we will soon reach its end."

"That's good. Thank you," all the people said.

"Many people will reach this Place of Doubt in their lives," Long Sash went on. "When that happens, you should pray to the Above Persons, your fathers and mothers, for help and for guidance. In order to remind you of that, I will leave my headdress here, where people can look up and see it."

He laid his headdress down, and it became a bright, comforting cluster of stars.

And so the people went on traveling, and all the story of their journey is told in the stars above. Where there are three bright stars close together, they represent two young men who made a drag and fastened their load on it. Then, because there were two of them, they could add an old woman's load to the other two, and go on, pulling three loads on the drag. Those stars are a reminder of the helpfulness of the young men, and of their thoughtfulness of other people.

At last the people came to the end of their journey, and to the Middle Place which was to be their home forever.

Source:

By Leonidas Romero de Vigil, Maria Martinez, and Antonio Da. *Documentary Archives: Multicultural America* CD-ROM. Woodbridge, CT: Primary Source Media, 1997.

PUERTO RICAN AMERICANS

Martín Espada (b. 1957) was born and reared in New York City and has worked as a public advocacy lawyer. He is the author of The Immigrant Iceboy's Bolero *(1984),* Trumpets from the Island of Their Eviction *(1987),* Rebellion Is the Circle of a Lover's Hands *(1990), and* The City of Sick and Coughing Radiators *(1993). Espada has spoken of his poetry as documenting the lives of the forgotten and downtrodden, specifically (but not exclusively) his fellow Puerto Ricans. His poetry also serves as vindication of lives too often and too long lived in silence and suffering.*

In his poem "Trumpets from the Island of Their Eviction," Espada establishes the sounds of trumpets from salsa music as counterpoint to the bullying police presence. A biblical resonance here is the trumpets that knocked down the walls of Jericho; maybe the salsa trumpets can knock down the walls of discrimination and neglect. Espada uses the word eviction pointedly, establishing a link between Puerto Ricans being evicted physically by landlords in the United States and spiritually from their island of origin by a colonizing U.S. government. The poem expresses particular outrage at the assumption that those who do not speak English must necessarily have something wrong with them.

Similar tales of individuals disregarded because of linguistic difference abound in multicultural literature. One of the ironies of this is, of course, that the "standard English" often advocated in schools is itself a language chock-full of words from other cultures and an idiom that derives its robustness from its diverse origins.

TRUMPETS FROM THE ISLAND OF THEIR EVICTION
by Martín Espada

At the bar two blocks away,
immigrants with Spanish mouths
hear trumpets
from the islands of their eviction.
The music swarms into the barrio
of a refugee's imagination,
along with predatory squad cars
and bullying handcuffs.

Their eviction:
like Mrs. Alfaro, evicted
when she trapped ten mice,
sealed them in plastic sandwich bags

and gifted them to the landlord;
like Daniel, the boy stockaded
in the back of retarded classrooms
for having no English
to comfort third-grade teachers;
like my father thirty-five years ago,
brown skin darker than the Air Force uniform
that could not save him, seven days county-jailed
for refusing the back of a Mississippi bus;
like the nameless Florida jíbaro
the grocery stores would not feed
in spite of the dollars he showed,
who returned with a machete,

636

collected cans from shelves
and forced the money
into the clerk's reluctant staring hand.

We are the ones identified by case number,
summons in the wrong language,
judgment without stay of execution.

Mrs. Alfaro has thirty days
to bundle the confusion of five children
down claustrophobic stairs
and away from the apartment.

And at the bar two blocks away,
immigrants with Spanish mouths

hear trumpets
from the islands of their eviction.
The sound scares away devils
like tropical fish
darting between the corals.

Source:
Trumpets from the Islands of Their Eviction, by
    Martín Espada. Expanded edition. Tempe, AZ:
    Bilingual Press/Editorial Bilingüe, 1994. pp.
    17-18.

Described by a New York Times *reporter as a man with "the mind of a politician and the soul of a poet," Luis Muñoz-Marín was instrumental in achieving Puerto Rico's current status as a freely associated commonwealth of the United States. His strong and charismatic leadership also helped transform the island colony once dubbed "the poorhouse of the Caribbean" into one of Latin America's few economic and political success stories. While Puerto Ricans are now inching closer to opting for statehood, they have Muñoz-Marín to thank for instilling in them a sense of self-respect and an appreciation for democratic traditions.*

Muñoz-Marín was influenced by his father, Luis Muñoz-Rivera, a journalist and politician fondly known as "the George Washington of Puerto Rico" for his efforts to secure his country's independence, first from Spain and then from the United States. In 1897, Muñoz-Rivera successfully pressured Spain into granting its Caribbean colony some measure of home rule. The island eventually fell under American control and in 1910, he became Puerto Rico's resident commissioner in Washington, D.C., where he held a non-voting seat in the House of Representatives. Although he died in office in 1916, Muñoz-Rivera is also credited with paving the way for Congress to extend U.S. citizenship to Puerto Ricans in 1917.

Luis Muñoz-Marín was born in San Juan just a few months before American troops occupied Puerto Rico. He spent much of his youth in the company of his father, first in New York City and later in Washington. Muñoz-Marín decided to establish himself as a writer and he spent most of the next 15 years in New York, contributing articles to various newspapers and magazines on topics ranging from U.S. foreign policy to the latest Broadway show.

But Muñoz-Marín could not quite turn his back on his heritage; he returned to Puerto Rico several times during this same period and dabbled in politics, embracing a philosophy that was decidedly less conservative than his father's. He worked on behalf of Latin American labor and unity movements, for instance, and was briefly a member of the Socialist party until joining Puerto Rico's newly-formed Liberal party in 1926. In the pages La Democracia, the newspaper his late father had founded, Muñoz-Marín demanded complete independence for his native land and increased attention to the needs of its poorest citizens, the landless peasants known as jibaros.

It was not until he settled permanently in Puerto Rico in 1931, however, that Muñoz-Marín was able to shake the image many had of him as just a dilettante who occasionally played at politics. The country he saw was reeling from the devastating effects of two hurricanes; there was no sugar cane, coffee, or tobacco to harvest, and the jibaros had crowded into the island's few major cities. Poverty, disease, and illiteracy were widespread.

In 1932, Muñoz-Marín ran for and won a seat in the Puerto Rican House of Representatives. Through his Washington connections, he gained favor almost immediately by obtaining some New Deal money for the island from President Franklin Roosevelt. Muñoz-Marín's popularity further increased after he played a key role in the fight to oust an unpopular governor, appointed by the United States and in pushing through legislation that broke up some of the larger sugar plantations and redistributed the land among the peasants.

In 1937, after a falling out with the Liberal party over how best to help the peasants, Muñoz-Marín established a new party of his own, the Popular Democrats. By this time, his political beliefs had undergone a shift as well; he no longer felt Puerto Rico was quite ready politically or economically to stand completely on its own as a state or nation. So armed with the slogan "Bread, Land, and Liberty," he began to campaign vigorously throughout the island's cities and villages against independence and for continued support from the United States to help the island deal with its many problems. In the 1940 elections, the Popular Democrats did surprisingly well, winning control of the Senate, where Muñoz-Marí was elected president, but falling two votes short of actually controlling the House. But due to skillful politicking, Muñoz-Marín was able to form a coalition that essentially gave him control over the House.

Over the next few years, Muñoz-Marín launched some ambitious land reforms and industrial and farm development plans that counted heavily on government supervision and aid. These programs, which his critics referred to as "socialist experiments," often put him at odds with the island's appointed governor and with the U.S. Congress, and some of his fellow legislators. But he charged ahead with the overwhelming support of the Puerto Rican people, who regarded him as their hero. In 1947, the U.S. Congress voted to make the post of governor of Puerto Rico an elected position instead of an appointed one. Muñoz-Marín easily won the position and under his leadership, Puerto Rico enjoyed lower unemployment rates, improved housing, schools and health care. While it did not eradicate poverty, it did improve the overall living standards of Puerto Ricans.

In 1950, the U.S. Congress, with Muñoz-Marín's urging, granted the island limited self-government. Puerto Rico's people were called on to write their own constitution and subject it to popular vote. The measure eventually passed and received the support of Congress, and Puerto Rico became a commonwealth on July 25, 1952.

Muñoz-Marín remained active in politics for the rest of his life, paying particular attention on the shifts of power between those who wanted to continue the island's commonwealth status and those who favored statehood. Muñoz-Marín favored commonwealth status, believing it was the best way to preserve the island's Hispanic culture while taking advantage of the security and economic aid offered by the United States. Muñoz-Marín died in 1980, but the commonwealth versus statehood battle continues in Puerto Rico. In a special referendum held in November, 1993, 48 percent of islanders approved a measure to retain commonwealth status, 46 percent favored statehood and four percent chose independence.

During his political career, both in print and from the podium, Muñoz-Marín took his case directly to the American people in an effort to win their backing as well. One such instance was on May 26, 1945, when he spoke to a national radio audience tuned to the CBS network about the future of Puerto Rico in the post-World War II era and the role of the United States in that future. At the time, he was beginning to advance the notion that perhaps it was time to re-evaluate the relationship between the two—not exactly with an eye toward independence, but certainly toward increased autonomy.

THE FUTURE OF PUERTO RICO

The future peace of the world depends to an important degree on the solution or solutions that may be found to the colonial problem. It also depends, to a still greater degree, on the prestige of the United States among the peoples of the world—on the confidence that the common man everywhere shall continue to have in the human understanding and the democratic sincerity of the American people.

It is of the utmost importance to democracy that the United States shall not cease to be the champion of democratic rights in the minds of men and women everywhere. It is clear that our great ally Russia is making a bid for the confidence and that trust which have been the traditional heritage of the United States. Of course, Russia's attitude in this respect should not be unwelcome. There is no such thing as too much good will, as too much recognition of rights and liberties. The world certainly needs as much of that as it can get from all possible sources. But certainly Russia's attitude should not be allowed to displace and substitute the traditional American attitude, but only to complement it and support it. Russia's developing international liberalism would appear best in its proper place, that is, as a follower of the tradition that the United States has made its own these many years.

In the treatment of colonies and of otherwise dependent peoples, the United States has an eminent field for sustaining, strengthening, and developing its policy for a good, for a confidence inspiring, for a lasting peace under the principles that have reared the national greatness of the American people.

I am proud to say that in this respect my own country, Puerto Rico, which has contributed without stint to the war effort, is now making what is perhaps a still more important contribution to the peace effort. Puerto Rico is a Caribbean island country of two million people which came under the jurisdiction of the United States as a result of the Spanish-American War almost half a century ago. Puerto Rico is a colony of the United States. It is a colony, it is true, that has been administered in a mild, though not always intelligible, way, by the United States government. But it is a colony. It is what each of the original thirteen states were before 1776; basically its government does not derive its powers from the consent of the governed. That is, by the time-honored definition written by Jefferson, what colonialism means to the American mind; and by that definition, Puerto Rico is a colony of the United States. Puerto Rico is also a very poor country in its economic geography. It has but 3,500 square miles of territory. Half of its land is not arable, much of the rest is not of very good quality; there is not much mineral wealth under that land, and two million people, that is 560 persons per square mile, must make their living from the top of that land. In order for so many people to subsist on such a scarcity of resources, the bulk of production must be of intensive cash-crops that can be sold in extensive markets at reasonably good prices.

It is this same people of Puerto Rico, to whom nature has been so harsh, who have reached their political maturity, according to a message of the late President Roosevelt to the Congress. They have given proof of this maturity. Eighty-five percent of the registered voters vote on the basis of universal adult suffrage. Although political passions frequently run high, elections are absolutely peaceful and orderly. Defeated candidates recognize their defeat and the fairness of the electoral process. The buying of votes has been unheard of for quite some time. The people vote on the clear understanding that they are giving a mandate for certain laws to be enacted and certain policies to be carried out insofar as their elected legislators have the legal authority to do so, and they are vigilant as to whether their clear-cut democratic mandates are carried out or not. The Puerto Rican people, in fact, are more than just a politically mature people. I sincerely and proudly believe that in their hinterland of the world they constitute the best rural school of democracy in America today, and that there is profit in looking to its poverty-stricken electorate as an example of sound democratic practice.

It is these people, so politically sound and so economically harassed, that are now contributing to the peace effort, as they are contributing to the war effort. They are now proposing to the Congress and the government of the United States a plan for self-determination. This plan may well serve as a basis for dealing with the colonial problem in many other parts of the world as well as in Puerto Rico. It should also help the United States in clarifying, maintaining, strengthening, and developing that leadership of hard-pressed mankind everywhere which is of such decisive importance to world justice and world peace.

The legislature of Puerto Rico has unanimously proposed to the Congress of the United States a clear-cut, straightforward method of solving the colonial problem, on the basis of self-determination, in democratic terms, and in the fiber of American policy and tradition. The Puerto Rican proposal is as follows:

It is of the utmost importance to democracy that the United States shall not cease to be the champion of democratic rights in the minds of men and women everywhere.

At the request, the unanimous request, of the legislature of Puerto Rico, all political parties concurring, a bill has been introduced in the Senate by United States Senator Millard E. Tydings, of Maryland, and in the United States House of Representatives by Resident Commissioner Pinero, of Puerto Rico. This bill contains four titles and offers three alternative forms of government to the people of Puerto Rico. Title 1 provides that there shall be a referendum in which the people of Puerto Rico shall decide whether they want independence under certain economic conditions necessary for their survival, or statehood, or dominion status similar to that of Australia or Canada in the British Commonwealth of Nations. Title 2 describes independence. Title 3 describes statehood. Title 4 describes dominion status. If a majority of the people of Puerto Rico vote for independence, then Title 2 shall go into effect. If they vote for statehood, then Title 3 shall go into effect. If they vote for dominion status, then Title 4 shall go into effect. In this manner, if the bill is approved, the people of Puerto Rico themselves will choose their own future, on the basis of an offer by the American Congress, and in choosing it they will have before them the fullest possible picture of what they are voting about.

It is worthy of note that the proposal provides that the United States shall have in perpetuity all the military and naval bases and rights that they may need in Puerto Rico for the defense of the United States and the Western Hemisphere. This is of very great importance, as Puerto Rico constitutes one of the chief military protections of the Panama Canal, and has been called by military authorities "the Gibraltar of the Caribbean." Parallel with these perpetual rights of the United States, under any form of government that the people of Puerto Rico may choose, certain minimum economic conditions are established, also under any form of government that the people of Puerto Rico may choose. These minimum economic conditions are considered necessary if the people are to survive in the face of the difficult economic circumstances that confront them. I should call attention to the fact that these minimum economic conditions do not represent any increase in economic facilities. Therefore the granting of them would not in any way increase the commitments of the United States, but would rather decrease them. What is, therefore, proposed is to wipe out political discontent without intolerably increasing economic suffering and discontent. This is of importance, not only as a matter of justice and of American leadership in democracy but also as a means of surrounding important military defenses with the greatest possible democratic good will.

Let us look at what the colonial problem means in broad terms. Obviously, the United States will have need of military and naval establishments in many parts of the world. But just as obviously these establishments are a second line of defense. The need for military establishments is predicated upon the sensible provision that all good-will means of keeping the peace may fail. The first line of defense is the maintenance of peace, the creation of conditions that, so far as human understanding and good sense can make it so, will tend to keep the world at peace with itself. For that reason, the need for military establishments—the second line of defense—should not contradict the need for democratic procedure in the maintenance of world confidence in American leadership. Neither, of course, should the need to maintain this leadership weaken in any way America's maximum ability to defend itself if peace should fail. The Puerto Rican proposal is made in the clear recognition of these two paramount factors.

Military and naval establishments may be needed in two broadly different kinds of places. They may be needed in small places scantily populated, and they may be needed, as they are in Puerto Rico for instance, among large populations with a developed civilization, with a recognized political maturity, and an acute consciousness that the principles of freedom are applicable to them also. The United States is making this distinction clear at the San Francisco Conference. Military and naval bases and establishments, of course, must be where strategy says they must be, whether on small rocks of the sea where the problems of the population are at a minimum or in developed communities where the problems of the people are of great significance and importance with relation to the general democratic principles and policies at stake.

In offering its proposal for self-determination, Puerto Rico is bearing in mind these considerations. The United States, at San Francisco, are standing for self-government to colonies, which may include independence. The Puerto Rican proposal is a specific proposal for self-government on the basis of an alternative offer by Congress of different forms of self-government, which may include independence, and an acceptance by the people of Puerto Rico, in referendum, of one of the forms of self-government offered by Congress.

The proposal that the legislature of Puerto Rico has unanimously presented to the Congress of the United States is a self-determination proposal as embodied in Senate bill 1002 and in House bill 3237. We make this proposal both as a claim of justice for Puerto Rico and as a contribution to American leadership—a leadership so completely necessary for the prevention of future wars—in the minds and hearts of average men and women the world over. For both reasons we hope to receive for our proposal the support of the American people.

Source:

Vital Speeches of the Day, "The Future of Puerto Rico," August 1, 1945, pp. 619-620.

*I*n 1950, the United States passed Public Law Number 600 granting Puerto Rico the right to draft its own constitution. This was an important step because the island became qualified for statehood with the United States. The Puerto Ricans ratified that law in 1951 and assembled a Constitutional Convention of 92 delegates to draft a constitution modeled after the Constitution of the United States. The United States approved the Constitution of Puerto Rico on July 1, 1952, and on July 25, 1952 Puerto Rico entered a unique relationship with the United States. Puerto Rico is an autonomous Commonwealth of the United States. Puerto Ricans describe this arrangement as un estado libre asociado or a "free associate state" of the United States. This association is closer to that of a territorial possession such as Guam and the Virgin Islands, but not the statehood that the statists in Puerto Rico desired. In 1999 the question of statehood was still a contentious issue for the people of Puerto Rico.

Spain ceded Puerto Rico to the United States in the Treaty of Paris after the Spanish American War of 1898. In 1900, the U.S. Congress set up a civil government on the island. Puerto Ricans were granted American citizenship in 1917 by President Woodrow Wilson, and the United States began programs to relieve problems from overpopulation. After World War II, the island became strategically important to the United States, and several navy bases were constructed in Puerto Rico. At the same time, a nationalist movement for independence began. An uprising in 1950 included an attack on the house used as a temporary residence by President Harry Truman, who escaped unharmed, though a Secret Serviceman was killed by gunfire. But nationalism diminished by 1959, the year that Fidel Castro became Premier of Cuba and Hawaii became the fiftieth state of the United States, reflecting two possible choices for Puerto Rico.

Under their newly drafted constitution, Puerto Ricans elected their own bicameral legislature and governor while being subject to the exclusive authority of the United

States. Puerto Ricans are American citizens whether they were born on the island or in the United States. About 3.8 million people live on the island, and 2 million live in the United States. A resident commissioner represents the island in the U.S. House of Representatives. Prior to 1992 the commissioner lacked the right to vote. The debate in Puerto Rico about statehood was put to voters in December of 1998, and Puerto Ricans voted for the third time, having rejected statehood in 1967 and 1993, to remain an autonomous Commonwealth. If a majority had voted for statehood, U.S. Congress would still have decided the issue, and in 1999, a strong opposition against possible statehood for Puerto Rico existed. In fact, Congress had refused to act on a bill the House passed authorizing a Puerto Rico statehood referendum.

The statehood issue has divided Puerto Rican Americans into two camps: nationalists who support full Puerto Rican independence, and statists who advocate becoming the fifty-first state of the United States. In the election of December 1998, the ballot choices included four defined options and a "none of the above" category. The four options were: continuation of the island's commonwealth status; statehood; full independence; and independence with "free association" with the United States. "None of the above" was indicated by 50.2 percent of the voters, while 46.5 percent supported statehood.

Why did many Puerto Ricans reject statehood? One reason is that Puerto Ricans do not pay federal income taxes yet receive federal aid through programs such as welfare and Medicaid, though levels are lower than states receive. In May of 1999, a senator speaking before the Senate Energy Commission and the governor of Puerto Rico accused Puerto Ricans of choosing a "free lunch" rather than joining the union and paying taxes. But non-Puerto Rican advocates of the status quo or of political independence say that Puerto Rica is a Latin American country. Many Puerto Ricans fear that statehood will adversely affect the island's distinctive Hispanic culture. Either way, the statehood issue provokes controversy, and cannot be assumed to be the last step in a process begun with the drafting of a constitution in 1951.

CONSTITUTIONAL CONVENTION OF PUERTO RICO

We, the people of Puerto Rico, in order to organize ourselves politically on a fully democratic basis, to promote the general welfare, and to secure for ourselves and our posterity the complete enjoyment of human rights, placing our trust in Almighty God, do ordain and establish this Constitution for the commonwealth which, in the exercise of our natural rights, we now create within our union with the United States of America.

In so doing, we declare:

The democratic system is fundamental to the life of the Puerto Rican community;

We understand that the democratic system of government is one in which the will of the people is the source of public power, the political order is subordinate to the rights of man, and the free participation of the citizen in collective decisions is assured;

We consider as determining factors in our life our citizenship of the United States of America and our aspiration continually to enrich our democratic heritage in the individual and collective enjoyment of its rights and privileges; our loyalty to the principles of the Federal Constitution; the coexistence in Puerto Rico of the two great cultures of the American Hemisphere; our fervor for education; our faith in justice; our devotion to the courageous, industrious, and peaceful way of life; our fidelity to individual human values above and beyond social position, racial differences, and economic interests; and our hope for a better world based on these principles.

Article I

The Commonwealth

Section 1. The Commonwealth of Puerto Rico is hereby constituted. Its political power emanates from the people and shall be exercised in accordance with their will, within the terms of the compact agreed upon between the people of Puerto Rico and the United States of America.

Section 2. The government of the Commonwealth of Puerto Rico shall be republican in form and its legislative, judicial and executive branches as established by this Constitution shall be equally subordinate to the sovereignty of the people of Puerto Rico.

Section 3. The political authority of the Commonwealth of Puerto Rico shall extend to the Island of Puerto Rico and to the adjacent islands within its jurisdiction.

Section 4. The seat of the government shall be the city of San Juan.

Article II

Bill of Rights

Section 1. The dignity of the human being is inviolable. All men are equal before the law. No discrimination shall be made on account of race, color, sex, birth, social origin or condition, or political or religious ideas. Both the laws and the system of public education shall embody these principles of essential human equality.

Section 2. The laws guarantee the expression of the will of the people by means of equal, direct and secret universal suffrage and shall protect the citizen against any coercion in the exercise of the electoral franchise.

Section 3. No law shall be made respecting an establishment of religion or prohibiting the free exercise thereof. There shall be complete separation of church and state.

Section 4. No law shall be made abridging the freedom of speech or of the press, or the right of the people peaceably to assemble and to petition the government for a redress of grievances.

Section 5. Every person has the right to an education which shall be directed to the full development of the human personality and to the strengthening of respect for human rights and fundamental freedoms. There shall be a system of free and wholly nonsectarian public education. Instruction in the elementary and secondary schools shall be free and shall be compulsory in the elementary schools to the extent permitted by the facilities of the state. No pubic property or public funds shall be used for the support of schools or educational institutions other than those of the state. Nothing contained in this provision shall prevent the state from furnishing to any child non-educational services established by law for the protection or welfare of children. *(Editor's note: By Resolution 34, approved by the Constitutional Convention and ratified in the referendum held on November 4, 1952, Section 5 of Article II was amended, adding to such section the following declaration: "Compulsory attendance at elementary public schools to the extent permitted by the facilities of the state as herein provided shall not be construed as applicable to those who receive elementary education in schools established under non-governmental auspices.")*

Section 6. Persons may join with each other and organize freely for any lawful purpose, except in military or quasi-military organizations.

Section 7. The right to life, liberty and the enjoyment of property is recognized as a fundamental right of man. The death penalty shall not exist. No person shall be deprived of his liberty or property without due process of law. No person in Puerto Rico shall be denied the equal protection of the laws. No laws impairing the obligation of contracts shall be enacted. A minimum amount of property and possessions shall be exempt from attachment as provided by law.

Section 8. Every person has the right to the protection of law against abusive attacks on his honor, reputation and private or family life.

Section 9. Private property shall not be taken or damaged for public use except upon payment of just compensation and in the manner provided by law. No law shall be enacted authorizing condemnation of printing presses, machinery or material devoted to publications of any kind. The buildings in which these objects are located may be condemned only after a judicial finding of public convenience and necessity pursuant to procedure that shall be provided by law, and may be taken before such a judicial finding only when there is placed at the disposition of the publication an adequate site in which it can be installed and continue to operate for a reasonable time.

Section 10. The right of the people to be secure in their persons, houses, papers and effects against unreasonable searches and seizures shall NOT BE VIOLATED.

Wire-tapping is prohibited.

No warrant for arrest or search and seizure shall issue except by judicial authority and only upon probable cause supported by oath or affirmation, and particularly describing the place to be searched and the persons to be arrested or the things to be seized.

Evidence obtained in violation of this section shall be inadmissible in the courts.

Section 11. In all criminal prosecutions, the accused shall enjoy the right to have a speedy and public trial, to be informed of the nature and cause of the accusation and to have a copy thereof, to be confronted with the witnesses against him, to have compulsory process for obtaining witnesses in his favor, to have assistance of counsel, and to be presumed innocent.

In all prosecutions for a felony the accused shall have the right of trial by an impartial jury composed of twelve residents of the district, who may render their verdict by a majority vote which in no case may be less than nine.

No person shall be compelled in any criminal case to be a witness against himself and the failure of the accused to testify may be neither taken into consideration nor commented upon against him.

No person shall be twice put in jeopardy of punishment for the same offense.

Before conviction every accused shall be entitled to be admitted to bail.

Incarceration prior to trial shall not exceed six months nor shall bail or fines be excessive. No person shall be imprisoned for debt.

Section 12. Neither slavery nor involuntary servitude shall exist except in the latter case as a punishment for crime after the accused has been duly convicted. Cruel and unusual punishments shall not be inflicted. Suspension of civil rights including the right to vote shall cease upon service of the term of imprisonment imposed.

No *ex post facto* law or bill of attainder shall be passed.

Section 13. The writ of *habeas corpus* shall be granted without delay and free of costs. The privilege of the writ of *habeas corpus* shall not be suspended, unless the public safety requires it in case of rebellion, insurrection or invasion. Only the Legislative Assembly shall have the power to suspend the privilege of the writ of *habeas corpus* and the laws regulating its issuance. The military authority shall always be subordinate to civil authority.

Section 14. No titles of nobility or other hereditary honors shall be granted. No officer or employee of the Commonwealth shall accept gifts, donations, decorations or offices from any foreign country or officer without prior authorization by the Legislative Assembly.

Section 15. The employment of children less than fourteen years of age in any occupation which is prejudicial to their health or morals or which places them in jeopardy of life or limb is prohibited.

No child less than sixteen years of age shall be kept in custody in a jail or penitentiary.

Section 16. The right of every employee to choose his occupation freely and to resign therefrom is recognized, as is his right to equal pay for equal work, to a reasonable minimum salary, to protection against risks to his health or person in his work or employment, and to an ordinary workday which shall not exceed eight hours. An employee may work in excess of this daily limit only if he is paid extra compensation as provided by law, at a rate never less than one and one-half times the regular rate at which he is employed.

Section 17. Persons employed by private businesses, enterprises and individual employers and by agencies or instrumentalities of the government operating as private businesses or enterprises, shall have the right to organize and to bargain collectively with their employers through representatives of their own free choosing in order to promote their welfare.

Section 18. In order to assure their right to organize the bargain collectively, persons employed by private businesses, enterprises and individual employers and by agencies or instrumentalities of the government operating as private businesses or enterprises, in their direct relations with their own employers shall have the right to strike, to picket and to engage in other legal concerted activities.

Nothing herein contained shall impair the authority of the Legislative Assembly to enact laws to deal with grave emergencies that clearly imperil the public health or safety or essential public services.

Section 19. The foregoing enumeration of rights shall not be construed restrictively nor does it contemplate the exclusion of other rights not specifically mentioned which belong to the people in a democracy. The power of the Legislative Assembly to enact laws for the protection of the life, health and general welfare of the people shall likewise not be construed restrictively.

Section 20. The Commonwealth also recognizes the existence of the following human rights:

The right of every person to receive free elementary and secondary education.

The right of every person to obtain work.

The right of every person to a standard of living adequate for the health and well-being of himself and of his family, and especially to food, clothing, housing and medical care and necessary social services.

The right of every person to social protection in the event of unemployment, sickness, old age or disability.

The right of motherhood and childhood to special care and assistance.

The rights set forth in this section are closely connected with the progressive development of the economy of the Commonwealth and require, for their full effectiveness, sufficient resources and an agricultural and industrial development not yet attained by the Puerto Rican community.

In the light of their duty to achieve the full liberty of the citizen, the people and the government of Puerto Rico shall do everything in their power to promote the greatest possible expansion of the system of production, to assure the fairest distribution of economic output, and to obtain the maximum understanding between individual initiative and collective cooperation. The executive and judicial branches shall bear in mind this duty and shall construe the laws that tend to fulfill it in the most favorable manner possible.

Editor's note: By Resolution 34, approved by the Constitutional Convention and ratified in referendum on November 4, 1962, Section 20 Article II was eliminated.

Article III

The Legislature

Section 1. The legislative power shall be vested in a Legislative Assembly, which shall consist of two houses, the Senate and the House of Representatives whose members shall be elected by direct vote at each general election.

Section 2. The Senate shall be composed of twenty-seven Senators and the House of Representatives of fifty-one Representatives, except at these numbers may be increased in accordance with the provisions of Section 7 of this Article.

Section 3. For the purpose of election members of the Legislative Assembly, Puerto Rico shall be divided into eight senatorial districts and forty representative districts. Each senatorial district shall elect two Senators and each representative district one Representative.

There shall also be eleven Senators and eleven Representatives elected at large. No elector may vote for more than one candidate for Senator at Large or for more than one candidate for Representative at Large.

Section 4. In the first and subsequent elections under this Constitution the division of senatorial and representative districts as provided in Article VIII shall be in effect. After each decennial census beginning with the year 1960, said division shall be revised by a Board composed of the Chief Justice of the Supreme Court as Chairman and of two additional members appointed by the Governor with the advice and consent of the Senate. The two additional members shall not belong to the same political party. Any revision shall maintain the number of senatorial and representative districts here created, which shall be composed of contiguous and compact territory and shall be organized, insofar as practicable, upon the basis of population and means of communication. Each senatorial district shall always include five representative districts.

The decision of the Board shall be made by majority vote and shall take effect in the general elections next following each revision. The Board shall cease to exist after the completion of each revision.

Section 5. No person shall be a member of the Legislative Assembly unless he is able to read and write the Spanish or English language and unless he is a citizen of the United States and of Puerto Rico and has resided in Puerto Rico at least two years immediately prior to the date of his election or appointment. No person shall be a member of the senate who is not over thirty years of age, and no person shall be a member of the House of Representatives who is not over twenty-five years of age.

Section 6. No person shall be eligible to election or appointment as Senator or Representative for a district unless he has resided therein at least one year immediately prior to his election or appointment. When there is more than one representative district in a municipality, residence in the municipality shall satisfy this requirement.

Section 7. If in a general election more than two-thirds of the members of either house are elected from one political party or from a single ticket, as both are defined by law, the number of members shall be increased in the following cases:

(*a*) If the party or ticket which elected more than two-thirds of the members of either or both houses shall have obtained less than two-thirds of the total number of votes cast for the office of Governor, the number of members of the Senate or of the House of Representatives or of both bodies, whichever may be the case, shall be increased by declaring elected a sufficient number of candidates of the minority party or parties to nine in the Senate and to seventeen in the House of Representatives. When there is more than one minority party, said additional members shall be declared elected from among the candidates of each minority party in the proportion that the number of votes cast for the candidate of each of said parties for the office of Governor bears to the total number of votes cast for the candidates of all the minority parties for the office of Governor.

When one or more minority parties shall have obtained representation in a proportion equal to or greater than the proportion of votes received by their respective candidates for Governor, such party or parties shall not be entitled to additional members until the representation established for each of the other minority parties under these provisions shall have been competed.

(b) If the party or ticket which elected more than two-thirds of the members of either or both houses shall have obtained more than two-thirds of the total number of votes cast for the office of Governor, and one or more than two-thirds of the total number of votes cast for the office of Governor,, and one or more minority parties shall not have elected the number of members in the Senate or in the House of Representatives or in both houses, whichever may be the case, which corresponds to the proportion of votes cast by each of them for the office of Governor, such additional number of their candidates shall be declared elected as is necessary in order to complete said proportion as nearly as possible, but the number of Senators of all the minority parties shall never, under this provision, be more than nine or that of Representatives more than seventeen.

In order to select additional members of the Legislative Assembly from a minority party in accordance with these provisions, its candidates at large who have not been elected shall be the first to be declared elected in the order of the votes that they have obtained, and thereafter its district candidates who, not having been elected, have obtained in their respective districts the highest proportion of the total number of votes cast as compared to the proportion of votes cast in favor of other candidates of the same party not elected to an equal office in the other districts.

The additional Senators and Representatives whose election is declared under this section shall be considered for all purposes as Senators at Large or Representatives at Large.

The measures necessary to implement these guarantees, the method of adjudicating fractions that may result from the application of the rules contained in this section, and the minimum umber of votes that a minority party must cast in favor if its candidate for Governor in order to have the right to the representation provided herein shall be determined by the Legislative Assembly.

Section 8. The term of office of Senators and Representatives shall begin on the second day of January immediately following the date of the general election in which they shall have been elected. If, prior to the fifteen months immediately preceding the date of the next general election, a vacancy occurs in the office of Senator or Representative for a district within thirty days following the date on which the vacancy occurs. This election shall be held not later than ninety days after the call, and the person elected shall hold office for the rest of the unexpired term of his predecessor. When said vacancy occurs during a legislative session, or when the Legislative Assembly or the Senate has been called for a date prior to the certification of the results of the special election, the presiding officer of the appropriate house shall fill said vacancy by appointing the person recommended by the central committee of the political party of which his predecessor in office was a member. Such person shall hold the office until certification of the election of the candidate who was elected. When the vacancy occurs within fifteen months prior to a general election, or when it occurs in the office of a Senator at Large or a Representative at Large, the presiding officer of the appropriate house shall fill it, upon the recommendation of the political party of which the previous holder of the office was a member, by appointing a person selected in the same manner as that in which his predecessor was selected. A vacancy in the office of a Senator at Large or a Representative at Large elected as an independent candidate shall be filled by an election in all districts.

Section 9. Each house shall be the sole judge of the election, returns and qualifications of its members; shall choose its own officers; shall adopt rules for its own officers; shall adopt rules for its own proceedings appropriate to legislative bodies; and, with the concurrence of three-fourths of the total number of members for the causes established in Section 21 of this Article, authorizing impeachments. The Senate shall elect a President and the House of Representatives a Speaker from among their respective members.

Section 10. The Legislative Assembly shall be deemed a continuous body during the term for which its members are elected and shall meet in regular session each year commencing on the second Monday in January. The duration of regular sessions and the periods of time for introduction and consideration of bills shall be prescribed by law. When the Governor calls the Legislative Assembly into special session it may consider only those matters specified in the call or in any special message sent to it by him during the session. No special session shall continue longer than twenty calendar days.

Section 11. The sessions of each house shall be open.

Section 12. A majority of the total number of members of which each house is composed shall constitute a quorum, but a smaller number may adjourn from day to day and shall have authority to compel the attendance of absent members.

Section 13. The two houses shall meet in the Capitol of Puerto Rico and neither of them may adjourn for more than three consecutive days without the consent of the other.

Section 14. No member of the Legislative Assembly shall be arrested while the house of which he is a member is in session, or during the fifteen days before or after such session, except for treason,, felony or breach of the peace. The members of the Legislative Assembly shall not be questioned in any other place for any speech, debate or vote in either house or in any committee.

Section 15. No Senator or Representative may, during the term for which he was elected or chosen, be appointed to any civil office in the Government of Puerto Rico, its municipalities or instrumentalities, which shall have been created or the salary of which shall have been increased during said term. No person may hold office in the Government of Puerto Rico, its municipalities or instrumentalities and be a Senator or Representative at the same time. These provisions shall not prevent a member of the Legislative Assembly from being designated to perform functions *ad honorem*.

Section 16. The Legislative Assembly shall have the power to create, consolidate or reorganize executive departments and to define their functions.

Section 17. No bill shall become a law unless it has been printed, read, referred to a committee and returned therefrom with a written report, but either house may discharge a committee from the study and report of any bill and proceed to the consideration thereof. Each house shall keep a journal of its proceedings and of the votes cast for and against bills. The legislative proceedings shall be published in a daily record in the form determined by law. Every bill, except general appropriation bills, shall be confined to one subject, which shall be clearly expressed in its title, and any part of an act whose subject has not been expressed in the title shall be void. The general appropriation act shall contain only appropriations and rules for their disbursement. No bill shall be amended in a manner that changes its original purpose or incorpo-

rates matters extraneous to it. In amending any article or section of a law, said article or section shall be promulgated in its entirely as amended. All bills for raising revenue shall originate in the House of Representatives, but the Senate may propose or concur with amendments as on other bills.

Section 18. The subjects which may be dealt with by means of joint resolution shall be determined by law, but every joint resolution shall follow the same legislative process as that of a bill.

Section 19. Every bill which is approved by a majority of the total number of members of which each house is composed shall be submitted to the Governor and shall become law if he signs it or if he does not return it, with his objections, to the house in which it originated within ten days (Sundays excepted) counting from the date on which he shall have received it.

When the Governor returns a bill, the house that receives it shall enter his objections on its journal and both houses may reconsider it. If approved by two-thirds of the total number of members of which each house is composed, said bill shall become law.

If the Legislative Assembly adjourns *sine die* before the Governor has acted on a bill that has been presented to him less than ten days before, he is relieved of the obligation of returning it with his objections and the bill shall become law only if the Governor signs it within thirty days after receiving it.

Every final passage or reconsideration of a bill shall be by a roll-call vote.

Section 20. In approving any appropriation bill that contains more than one item, the Governor may eliminate one or more of such items or reduce their amounts, at the same time reducing the total amounts involved.

Section 21. The House of Representatives shall have exclusive power to initiate impeachment proceedings and, with the concurrence of two-thirds of the total number of members of which it is composed, to bring an indictment. The Senate shall have exclusive power to try and to decide impeachment cases, and in meeting for such purposes the Senators shall act in the name of the people and under oath or affirmation. No judgment of conviction in an impeachment trial shall be pronounced without the concurrence of three-fourths of the total number of members of which the Senate is composed, and the judgment shall be limited to removal from office. The person impeached, however, may be liable and subject to indictment, trial, judgment and punishment according to law. The causes of impeachment shall be treason, bribery, other felonies, and misdemeanors involving moral turpitude. The Chief Justice of the Supreme Court shall preside at the impeachment trial of the Governor.

The two houses may conduct impeachment proceedings in their regular or special sessions. The presiding officers of the two houses, upon written request of two-thirds of the total number of members of which the House of Representatives is composed, must convene them to deal with such proceedings.

Section 22. The Governor shall appoint a Controller with the advice and consent of a majority of the total number of members of which each house is composed. The Controller shall meet the requirements prescribed by law and shall hold office for a term of ten years and until his successor has been appointed and qualifies. The Controller shall audit all the revenues, accounts and expenditures of the Commonwealth, of its agencies and instrumentalities and of its municipalities, in order to determine whether they have been made in accordance with law. He shall render annual reports and any special reports that may be required of him by the Legislative Assembly or by the Governor.

In the performance of his duties the Controller shall be authorized to administer oaths, take evidence and compel, under pain of contempt, the attendance of witnesses and the production of books, letters, documents, papers, records and all other articles deemed essential to a full understanding of the matter under investigation.

The Controller may be removed for the causes and pursuant to the procedure established in the preceding section.

Article IV

The Executive

Section 1. The executive power shall be vested in a Governor, who shall be elected by direct vote in each general election.

Section 2. The Governor shall hold office for the term of four years from the second day of January of the year following his election and until his successor has been elected and qualifies. He shall reside in Puerto Rico and maintain his office in its capital city.

Section 3. No person shall be Governor unless, on the date of the election, he is at least thirty-five years of age, and is and has been during the preceding five years a citizen of the United States and a citizen and *bona fide* resident of Puerto Rico.

Section 4. The Governor shall execute the laws and cause them to be executed.

He shall call the Legislative Assembly or the Senate into special session when in his judgment the public interest so requires.

He shall appoint, in the manner prescribed by this Constitution or by law, all officers whose appointment he is authorized to make. He shall have the power to make appointments while the Legislative Assembly is not in session. Any such appointments that require the advice and consent of the Senate or of both houses shall expire at the end of the next regular session.

He shall be the commander-in-chief of the militia.

He shall the power to call out the militia and summon the posse comitatus in order to prevent or suppress rebellion, invasion or any serious disturbance of the public peace.

He shall have the power to proclaim martial law when the public safety requires it in case of rebellion or invasion r imminent danger thereof. The Legislative Assembly shall meet forthwith on their own initiative to ratify or revoke the proclamation.

He shall have the power to suspend the execution of sentences in criminal cases and to grant pardons, commutations of punishment, and total or partial remissions of fines and forfeitures for crimes committed in violation of the laws of Puerto Rico. This power shall not extend to cases of impeachment.

He shall approve or disapprove in accordance with this Constitution the joint resolutions and bills passed by the Legislative Assembly.

He shall present to the Legislative Assembly, at the beginning of each regular session, a message concerning the affairs of the Commonwealth and a report concerning the state of the Treasury of Puerto Rico and the proposed expenditures for the ensuing fiscal year. Said report shall contain the information necessary for the formulation of a program of legislation.

He shall exercise the other powers and functions and discharge the other duties assigned to him by this Constitution or by law.

Section 5. For the purpose of exercising executive power, the Governor shall be assisted by Secretaries whom he shall appoint with the advice and consent of the Senate. The appointment of the Senate. The appointment of the Secretary of State shall in addition require the advice and consent of the House of Representatives, and the person appointed shall fulfill the requirements established in Section 3 of this Article. The Secretaries shall collectively constitute the Governor's advisory council, which shall be designated as the Council of Secretaries.

Section 6. Without prejudice to the power of the Legislative Assembly to create, reorganize and consolidate executive departments and to define their functions, the following departments are hereby established: State, Justice, Education Health, Treasury, Labor, Agriculture and Commerce, and Public Works. Each of these executive departments shall be headed by a Secretary.

Section 7. When a vacancy occurs in the office of Governor, caused by death, resignation, removal, total and permanent incapacity, or any other absolute disability, said office shall devolve upon the Secretary of State, who shall hold it for the rest of the term and until a new Governor has been elected and qualifies. In the event that vacancies exist at the same time in both the office of Governor and that of Secretary of State, the law shall provide which of the Secretaries shall serve as Governor.

Section 8. When for any reason the Governor is temporarily unable to perform his functions, the Secretary of State shall substitute for him during the period he is unable to serve. If for any reason the Secretary of State is not available, the Secretary determined by law shall temporarily hold the office of Governor.

Section 9. If the Governor-elect shall not have qualified, or if he has qualified and a permanent vacancy occurs in the office of Governor before he shall have appointed a Secretary of State, or before said Secretary, having been appointed, shall have qualified, the Legislative Assembly just elected, upon convening for its first regular session, shall elect, by a majority of the total number of members of which each house is composed, a Governor who shall hold office until his successor is elected in the next general election and qualifies.

Section 10. The Governor may be removed for the causes and pursuant to the procedure established in Section 21 of Article III of this Constitution.

Article V

The Judiciary

Section 1. The Judicial power of Puerto Rico shall be vested in a Supreme Court, and in such other courts as may be established by law.

Section 2. The courts of Puerto Rico shall constitute a unified judicial system for purposes of jurisdiction, operation and administration. The Legislative Assembly may create and abolish courts, except for the Supreme Court, in a manner not inconsistent with this Constitution, and shall determine the venue and organization of the courts.

Section 3. The Supreme Court shall be the court of last resort in Puerto Rico and shall be composed of a Chief Justice and four Associate Justices. The number of Justices may be changed only by law upon request of the Supreme Court.

Section 4. The Supreme Court shall sit, in accordance with rules adopted by it, as a full court or in divisions. All the decisions of the Supreme Court shall be concurred in by a majority of its members. No law shall be held unconstitutional except by a majority of the total number of Justices of which the Court is composed in accordance with this Constitution or with law. (Editor's note: As amended in general election of November 8, 1960.)

Section 5. The Supreme Court, any of its divisions or any of its Justices may hear in the first instance petitions for *habeas corpus* and any other causes and proceedings as determined by law.

Section 6. The Supreme Court shall adopt for the courts rules of evidence and of civil and criminal procedure which shall not abridge, enlarge or modify the substantive rights of the parties. The rules thus adopted shall be submitted to the Legislative Assembly at the beginning of its next regular session and shall not go in to effect until sixty days after the close of said session, unless disapproved by the Legislative Assembly, which shall have the power both at said session and subsequently to amend, repeal or supplement any of said rules by a specific law to that effect.

Section 7. The Supreme Court shall adopt rules for the administration of the courts. These rules shall be subject to the laws concerning procurement, personnel, audit and appropriation of funds, and other laws which apply generally to all branches of the government. The Chief Justice shall direct the administration of the courts and shall appoint an administrative director who shall hold office at the will of the Chief Justice.

Section 8. Judges shall be appointed by the Governor with the advice and consent of the Senate. Justices of the Supreme Court shall not assume office until after confirmation by the Senate and shall hold their offices during good behavior. The terms of office of the other judges shall be fixed by law and shall not be less than that fixed for the term of office of a judge of the same or equivalent category existing when this Constitution takes effect. The other officials and employees of the courts shall be appointed in the manner provided by law.

Section 9. No person shall be appointed a Justice of the Supreme Court unless he is a citizen of the United States and of Puerto Rico, shall have been admitted to the practice of law in Puerto Rico at least ten years prior to his appointment, and shall have resided in Puerto Rico at least five years immediately prior thereto.

Section 10. The Legislative Assembly shall establish a retirement system for judges. Retirement shall be compulsory at age of seventy years.

Section 11. Justices of the Supreme Court may be removed for the causes and pursuant to the procedure established in Section 21 of Article III of his Constitution. Judges of the other courts may be removed by the Supreme Court for the causes and pursuant to the procedure provided by law.

Section 12. No judge shall make a direct or indirect financial contribution to any political organization or party, or hold any executive office therein, or participate in a political campaign of any kind, or be a candidate for an elective public office unless he has resigned his judicial office at least six months prior to his nomination.

Section 13. In the event that a court or any of its divisions or sections is changed or abolished by law, the person holding a post of judge therein shall continue to hold it during the rest of the term for which he was appointed and shall perform the judicial functions assigned to him by the Chief Justice of the Supreme Court.

Article VI

General Provisions

Section 1. The Legislative Assembly shall have the power to create, abolish, consolidate and reorganize municipalities; to change their territorial limits; to determine their organization and functions; and to authorize them to develop programs for the general welfare and to create any agencies necessary for that purpose.

No law abolishing or consolidating municipalities shall take effect until ratified in a referendum by a majority of the electors voting in said referendum in each of the municipalities to be abolished or consolidated. The referendum shall be in the manner determined by law, which shall include the applicable procedures of the election laws in effect when the referendum law is approved.

Section 2. The power of the Commonwealth of Puerto Rico to impose and collect taxes and to authorize their imposition and collection by municipalities shall be exercised as determined by the Legislative Assembly and shall never be surrendered or suspended. The power of the Commonwealth of Puerto Rico to contract and to authorize the contracting of debts shall be exercised as determined by the Legislative Assembly, but no direct obligations of the Commonwealth for money borrowed directly by the Commonwealth evidenced by bonds or notes for the payment of which the full faith credit and taxing power of the Commonwealth shall be pledged shall be issued by the Commonwealth if the total of (i) the amount of principal and interest on such bonds and notes, together with the amount of principal of and interest on all such bonds and notes theretofore issued by the Commonwealth and then understanding,, payable in any fiscal year and (ii) any amounts paid by the Commonwealth in the fiscal year next preceding the then current fiscal year for principal or interest on account of any outstanding obligations evidenced by bonds or notes guaranteed by the Commonwealth, shall exceed 15 percent of the average of the total amount of the annual revenues raised under the provisions of Commonwealth legislation and covered into the Treasury of Puerto Rico in the two fiscal years next preceding the then current fiscal year; and no such bonds or notes issued by the Commonwealth for any purpose other than housing facilities shall mature later than 30 years from their date and no bonds or notes issued for housing facilities shall mature later than 40 years from their date; and the Commonwealth shall not guarantee any obligations evidenced by bonds or notes if the total of the amount payable in any fiscal year on account of principal of and interest on al the direct obligations referred to above theretofore issued by the Commonwealth and then outstanding and the amounts referred to in item (ii) above shall exceed 15 percent of the average of the total amount of such annual revenues.

The Legislative Assembly shall fix limitations for the issuance of direct obligations by any of the municipalities of Puerto Rico for money borrowed directly by such municipality evidenced by bonds or notes for the payment of such municipality shall be pledged; provided, however, that no such bonds or notes shall be issued by any municipality in an amount which, together with the amount of all such bonds and notes theretofore issued by such municipality and then outstanding, shall exceed the percentage determined by the Legislative Assembly, which shall be not less than five per centum (10 percent) of the aggregate tax valuation of the property within such municipality.

The Secretary of the Treasury may be required to apply the available revenues including surplus to the payment of interest on the public debt and the amortization thereof in any case provided for by Section 8 of this Article VI at the suit of any holder of bonds or notes issued in evidence thereof. (*Editor's note: As amended by the voters in a referendum held December 10, 1961.*)

Section 3. The rule of taxation in Puerto Rico shall be uniform.

Section 4. General elections shall be held every four years on the day of November determined by the Legislative Assembly. In said elections there shall be elected a Governor, the members of the Legislative Assembly, and the other officials whose election on that date is provided for by law.

Every person over twenty-one years of age shall be entitled to vote if he fulfills the other conditions determined by law. No person shall be deprived of the right to vote because he does not know how to read or does not own property.

All matters concerning the electoral process, registration of voters, political parties and candidates shall be determined by law.

Every popularly elected official shall be elected by direct vote and any candidate who receives more votes than any other candidate for the same office shall be declared elected.

Section 5. The laws shall be promulgated in accordance with the procedure prescribed by law and shall specify the terms under which they shall take effect.

Section 6. If at the end of any fiscal year the appropriations necessary for the ordinary operating expenses of the government and for the payment of interest on and amortization of the public debt for the ensuing fiscal year shall not have been made, the several sums appropriated in the last appropriation acts for the objects and purposes therein specified, so far as the same may be applicable, shall continue in effect item by item, and the Governor shall authorize the payments necessary for such purposes until corresponding appropriations are made.

Section 7. The appropriations made for any fiscal year shall not exceed the total revenues, including available surplus, estimated for said fiscal year unless the imposition of taxes sufficient to cover said appropriations is provided by law.

Section 8. In case the available revenues including surplus for any fiscal year are insufficient to meet the appropriations made for that year, interest on the public debt and amortization thereof shall first be paid, and other disbursements shall thereafter be made in accordance with the order of priorities established by law.

Section 9. Public property and funds shall only be disposed of for public purposes, for the support and operation of state institutions, and pursuant to law.

Section 10. No law shall give extra compensation to any public officer, employee, agent or con-

tractor after services shall have been rendered or contract made. No law shall extend the term of any public officer or diminish his salary or emoluments after his election or appointment. No person shall draw a salary for more than one office or position I the government of Puerto Rico.

Section 11. The salaries of the Governor, the Secretaries, the members of the Legislative Assembly, the Controller and Judges shall be fixed by a special law and, except for the salaries of the members of the Legislative Assembly, shall not be decreased during the terms for which they are elected or appointed. The salaries of the Governor and the Controller shall not be increased during said terms. No increase in the salaries of the members of the Legislative Assembly shall take effect until after the expiration of the term of the Legislative Assembly during which it is enacted. Any reduction of the salaries of the members of the Legislative Assembly shall be elective only during the term of the Legislative Assembly which approves it.

Section 12. The Governor shall occupy and use, free of rent, the buildings and properties belonging to the Commonwealth which have been or shall hereafter be used and occupied by him as chief executive.

Section 13. The procedure for granting franchises, rights, privileges and concessions of a public or quasi-public nature shall be determined by law, but every concession of this kind to a person or private entity must be approved by the Governor or by the executive official whom he designates. Every franchise, right, privilege or concession of a public or quasi-public nature shall be subject to amendment, alteration or repeal as determined by law.

Section 14. No corporation shall be authorized to conduct the business of buying and selling real estate or be permitted to hold or own real estate except such as may be reasonably necessary to enable it to carry out the purposes for which it was created, and every corporation authorized to engage in agriculture shall by its charter be restricted to the ownership and control of not to exceed five hundred acres of land; and this provision shall be held to prevent any member of a corporation engaged in agriculture from being in any wise interested in any other corporation engaged in agriculture.

Corporations, however, may loan funds upon real estate security, and purchase real estate when necessary for the collection of loans, but they shall dispose of real estate so obtained within five years after receiving the title.

Corporations not organized in Puerto Rico, but doing business in Puerto Rico, shall be bound by the provisions of this section so far as they are applicable.

These provisions shall not prevent the ownership, possession or management of lands in excess of five hundred acres by the commonwealth, its agencies or instrumentalities.

Section 15. The Legislative Assembly shall determine all matters concerning the flag, the seal and the anthem of the Commonwealth. Once determined, no law changing them shall take effect until one year after the general election next following the date of enactment of said law.

Section 16. All public officials and employees of the Commonwealth, its agencies, instrumentalities and political subdivisions, before entering upon their respective duties, shall take an oath to support the Constitution of the United States and the Constitution and laws of the Commonwealth of Puerto Rico.

Section 17. In case of invasion, rebellion, epidemic or any other event giving rise to a state of emergency, the Governor may call the Legislative Assembly to meet in a place other than the Capitol of Puerto Rico, subject to the approval or disapproval of the Legislative Assembly. Under the same conditions, the Governor may, during the period of emergency, order the government, its agencies and instrumentalities to be moved temporarily to a place other than the seat of the government.

Section 18. All criminal actions in the courts of the Commonwealth shall be conducted in the name and by the authority of "The People of Puerto Rico" until otherwise provided by law.

Section 19. It shall be the public policy of the Commonwealth to conserve, develop and use its natural resources in the most effective manner possible for the general welfare of the community; to conserve and maintain buildings and places declared by the Legislative Assembly to be of historic or artistic value; to regulate its penal institutions in a manner that effectively achieves their purposes and to provide, within the limits of available resources, for adequate treatment of delinquents in order to make possible their moral and social rehabilitation.

Article VII

Amendments to the Constitution

Section 1. The Legislative Assembly may propose amendments to this Constitution by a concurrent resolution approved by not less than two-thirds of the total number of members of which each house is composed. All proposed amendments shall be submitted to the qualified electors in a special referendum, but if the concurrent resolution is approved by not less than three fourths of the total number of members of which each house is composed, the Legislative Assembly may provide that the referendum shall be held at the same time as the next general election. Each proposed amendment shall be voted be voted on separately and not more than three proposed amendments may be submitted at the same referendum. Every proposed amendments may be submitted at the same referendum. Every proposed amendment shall specify the terms under which it shall take effect, and it shall become a part of this Constitution if it is ratified by a majority of the electors voting thereon. Once approved, a proposed amendment must be published at least three months prior to the date of the referendum.

Section 2. The Legislative Assembly, by a concurrent resolution approved by two-thirds of the total number of members of which each house is composed, may submit to the qualified electors at a referendum, held at the same time as a general election, the question of whether a constitutional convention shall be called to revise this Constitution. If a majority of the electors voting on this question vote in favor of the revision,, it shall be made by a Constitutional Convention elected in the manner provided by law. Every revision of this Constitution shall be submitted to the qualified electors at a special referendum for ratification or rejection by a majority of the votes cast at the referendum.

Section 3. No amendment to this Constitution shall alter the republican form of government established by it or abolish its bill of rights.

Editor's note: By Resolution 34, approved by the Constitutional Convention and ratified in the referendum held in November 4, 1952, the following new sentence was added to Section 3 of Article VII: "Any amendment or revision of this constitution of the United States, with the Puerto Rican Federal Relations Act and with Public Law 600, Eighty-first Congress, adopted in the nature of a compact."

Article VIII

Senatorial and Representative Districts

Section 1. The senatorial and representative districts shall be the following:

I. SENATORIAL DISTRICT OF SAN JUAN, which shall be composed of the following Representative Districts: The Capital of Puerto Rico, excluding the present electoral precincts of Santurce and Rio Piedras; 2.—Electoral zone numbers 1 and 2 of the present precinct of Santurce; 3.—Electoral zone number 3 of the present precinct of Santurce; 4.—Electoral zone number 4 of the present precinct of Santurce; and 6.—Wards Hato Rey, Puerto Nuevo and Caparra Heights of the Capital of Puerto Rico.

II. SENATORIAL DISTRICT OF BAYAMON, which shall be composed of the following Representative Districts: 7.—The municipality of Bayamon; 8.—The municipalities of Carolina and Trujillo Alto; 9.—The present electoral precinct of Rio Piedras, excluding wards Hato Rey, Puerto Nuevo and Caparra Heights of the Capital of Puerto Rico; 10.—The municipalities of Catano, Guaynabo and Toa Baja; and 11.—The municipalities of Toa Alta, Corozal and Naranjito.

III. SENATORIAL DISTRICT OF ARECIBO, which shall be composed of the following Representative Districts: The municipalities of Vega Baja, Vega Alta and Dorado; 12.—The municipalities of Manati and Barceloneta; ;13.—The municipalities of Ciales and Morovis; 14.—The municipality of Arecibo; and 15.—The municipality of Utuado.

IV. SENATORIAL DISTRICT OF AGUADILLA, which shall be composed of the following Representative Districts: 16.—The municipalities of Camuy, Hatillo and Quebradillas; 17.—The municipalities of Aguadilla and Isabela; 18. The municipalities of San Sebastian and Moca; 19.—The municipalities of Lares, Las Marias and Maricao; and 20.—The municipalities of Anasco, Aguada and Rincon.

V. SENATORIAL DISTRICT OF MAYAGUEZ, which shall be composed of the following Representative Districts: 21.—The municipality of Mayaguez; 22.—The municipalities of Cago Rojo, Hormigueros and Lajas; 23.—The municipalities of San German and Sabana Grande; 24.—The municipalities of Yauco and Guanica; and 25.—The municipalities of Guayanillan and Penuelas.

VI. SENATORIAL DISTRICT OF PONCE, which shall be composed of the following Representative Districts: 26.—The first, second, third, fourth, fifth and sixth wards and the City Beach of the municipality of Ponce; 27—The municipality of Ponce, except for the first, second, third, fourth, fifth and sixth wards and the City Beach; 28.—The municipalities of Adjuntas and Jayuya; 29.—The municipalities of Juana Diaz, Santa Isabel and Villalba; and 30.—The municipalities of Coamo and Orocovis.

VII. SENATORIAL DISTRICT OF GUAYAMA, which shall be composed of the following Representative Districts: 31.—The municipalities of Aibonito, Barranquitas and Comerio; 32.—The municipalities of Cayey and Cidra; 33.—The municipalities of Caguas and Aguas Buenas; 34.—The municipalities of Guayama and Salinas; and 35.—The municipalities of Patillas, Maunabo and Arroyo.

VII. SENATORIAL DISTRICT OF HUMACAO, which shall be composed of the following Representative Districts: 36.—The municipalities of Humacao and Yabucoa; 37.—The municipalities of Juncos, Gurabo and San Lorenzo; 38.—The municipalities of Naguabo, Ceiba and Las Piedras; 39.—The municipalities of Fajardo and Vieques and the Island of Culebra; and 40.—The municipalities of Rio Grande, Loiza and Luquillo.

Section 2. Electoral zones numbers 1, 2, 3 and 4 included in three representative districts within the senatorial district of San Juan are those presently existing for purposes of electoral organization in the second precinct of San Juan.

Article IX

Transitory Provisions

Section 1. When this Constitution goes into effect all laws not inconsistent therewith shall continue in full force until amended or repealed, or until they expire by their own terms.

Unless otherwise provided by this Constitution, civil and criminal liabilities, rights, franchises, concessions, privileges, claims, actions, causes of action, contracts, and civil, criminal and administrative proceedings shall continue unaffected, notwithstanding the taking effect of this Constitution.

Section 2. All officers who are in office by election or appointment on the date this Constitution takes effect shall continue to hold their offices and to perform the functions thereof in a manner not inconsistent with this Constitution, unless the functions of their offices are abolished or until their successors are selected and qualify in accordance with this Constitution and laws enacted pursuant thereto.

Section 3. Notwithstanding the age limit fixed by this Constitution for compulsory retirement, all the judges of the courts of Puerto Rico who are holding office on the date this Constitution takes effect shall continue to hold their judicial offices until the expiration of the terms for which they were appointed, and in the case of Justices of the Supreme Court during good behavior.

Section 4. The Commonwealth of Puerto Rico shall be the successor of the People of Puerto Rico for all purposes, including without limitation the collection and payment of debts and liabilities in accordance with their terms.

Section 5. When this Constitution goes into effect, the term "citizen of the Commonwealth of Puerto Rico" shall replace the term "citizen of Puerto Rico" as previously used.

Section 6. Political parties shall continue to enjoy all rights recognized by the election law, provided that on the effective date of this Constitution they fulfill the minimum requirements for the registration of new parties contained in said law. Five years after this Constitution shall have taken effect the Legislative Assembly may change these requirements, but any law increasing them shall not go into effect until after the general election next following its enactment.

Section 7. The Legislative Assembly may enact the laws necessary to supplement and make elective these transitory provisions in order to assure the functioning of the government until the officers provided for by this Constitution are elected or appointed and qualify, and until this constitution takes effect in all respects.

Section 8. If the Legislative Assembly creates a Department of Commerce, the Department of Agriculture and Commerce shall thereafter be called the Department of Agriculture.

Section 9. The first election under the provisions of this Constitution shall be held on the date provided by law, but not later than six months after the effective date of this Constitution. The second general election under this Constitution shall be held in the month of November 1956 on a day provided by law.

Section 10. Constitution shall take effect when the Governor so proclaims, but not later than sixty days after its ratification by the Congress of the Untied States.

Done in Convention, at San Juan, Puerto Rico, on the sixth day of February, in the year of Our Lord one thousand nine hundred and fifty-two.

Source:

"Constitution of the Commonwealth of Puerto Rico," in *Documents on the Constitutional History of Puerto Rico* (Washington, D.C.: Office of the Commonwealth of Puerto Rico, June 1964), pp. 168-192.

*T*he people of Puerto Rico represent a mixture of races, cultures, languages and religions. Racial influences include the native Taíno, African slaves brought by the Spanish, and other Caribbean islanders who came to Puerto Rico in search of work. American culture has had a progressive effect upon Puerto Rican culture since 1898. The years following the invasion of Puerto Rico in 1898 were very rich in literary output. An American influence is especially noticeable after the 1940s, when the question of statehood became an issue. In 1998 the people voted again on that issue and barely rejected statehood once, a reflection of the ambivalent nature of Puerto Rico's relationship with the United States.

Folk writings, such as this poem, often describe a common experience of an ethnic group. Such writings are rarely considered literature; their value is that they capture some aspect of ordinary life that is widely experienced. Poetry written by Puerto Ricans is typically emotional, detailing their experiences and how they have struggled and endured here in the United States. Puerto Rico has produced more poets than writers of other genres. The Spanish culture, particularly its Roman Catholicism, can be said to be the greatest influence on the island's literary history.

The title of this poem, "Aguinaldos," is the Spanish word for Christmas gift. In Puerto Rico it was customary to offer gifts to singers during the Christmas season. This simple rhyming poem was written prior to 1951 and shows the influence of the Roman Catholic heritage of its child author. Most Puerto Ricans are Roman Catholic, so these expressions are easily understood. In Puerto Rico during the Christmas season, singers dressed as "The Three Kings" were commonly seen going from house to house asking for aguinaldos. The simple poem contrasts with the body of Puerto Rican literature and poetry of the 1990s that articulates issues of gender, passion, conflict, history, culture, and religion of the Puerto Rican, and explores larger questions about ethnic identity and their place in American society.

AGUINALDOS

Demen mi aguinaldo	Give me my Christmas gift
Si me lo han de dar	If you are going to give it to me
Que la noche es larga	For the night is long
Y tenemos que andar.	And we have to walk
A la media noche	At midnight
El gallo cantó	The rooster sang
Y en su canto dijo	And in its song it said
Ya Cristo nació.	Now Christ is born.
Ama de casa salgase	Mistress of the house
Para afuera	Come out, outside
Y con un cuchillo	And with a knife
Partiendo cazuela.	Cutting the tart.
Por allá bajito	Down over there
Me dijo un embustero	A liar told me
Que en esta casita	That in this little house
Había mucho y bueno.	There was plenty and good.
Y no dijo embuste	And he didn't lie
Que dijo verdad	He told the truth
Con esta risita	With his little laugh
De ja-ja-ja.	Of ha-ha-ha
Del arroz con dulce	From the sweetened rice
Demen el pegao	Give me the crust
Para mi pollito	For my little chicken
Cabeci y pelao.	Who is bald-headed.
Si me dan pasteles	If you give me pasteles
Demenlos calientes	Give them to me hot
Que pasteles fríos	For cold pasteles
Empachen la gente.	Give people indigestion.
Si me dan arroz	If you give me rice
No me den cuchara	Don't give me a spoon
Que mamá me dijo	For my mother told me
Que se lo llevara.	To take it to her.
Se me fué la puerca	My pig ran away
Después de pela	After it was scalded
La cogí por el rabo	I grabbed it by its tail
Y la heché pa' ca.	And pulled it back here.
Juanita se llama mi prenda adorada	Jenny is the name of my adored love
Que bonito nombre, que mucha me agrada	What a pretty name, how I love it
Si ella me aceptara con el corazón	If she would accept me with her heart
Le haría proporción de hacer la feliz	I would do my part to make her happy
Por no verla aquí sufriendo de amor.	So as not to see her here suffering from love.
En el monte Sión fué que consiguieron	It was on Mount Zion that they obtained
El palo de cedro con mala intención	With evil intention the cedar tree
Donde el redentor puso sus espaldas.	Where the Redeemer laid his back.
Allí le llamaban Jesús Nazareno,	There they called him Jesus of Nazareth
Y dándole el barreno,	And when they nailed his body,
La tierra temblaba.	The earth trembled.

Esta casa tiene
Las puertos de acero
El que vive en ella
Es un caballero.

This house has
Its doors of steel
He who lives in it
Is a gentleman.

Dáme mi aguinaldo
Que me ofreciste el año pasado
Y no me lo diste.

Give me my Christmas gift
Which you offered me last year
And did not give to me.

Yo sembré una mata
En un arenal.
Como no se daba,
La mandé a arrancar
Y la mandé a sembrar
En un terreno nuevo
Para que floreciera
En el año nuevo.

I planted a plant
In a sandy ground.
As it did not bloom,
I had it pulled out
And had it planted
In a new ground
So that it would bloom
On the New Year.

Si tú no conoces
Este que ha llegado,
Es un coronado, Rey de la Heraquía

If you do not know
The one who has arrived,
He is the crowned one, King of the Hierarchy

Que en voz decía
Déme mi aguinaldo.

Whose voice is saying
Give me my Christmas gift.

Yo me enamoré de una Terecita
La encontré bonita y la solicité
Poco después me salió traidora.
Por engañadora que son las mujeres.

I fell in love with a little Terese
I found her pretty and I courted her
A little later she turned out to be a traitoress
For women are so deceiving.

Yo quisiera ser
Lo que tu no eres
Ser el mejor rey
Y adorar mis bienes.

I would like to be
That which you are not
To be the best king
And to worship my possessions.

La virgen María
Iba para Belén
Ella va delante
Detrás San José.

The Virgin Mary
Was going to Bethlehem
She goes in front
Behind goes Saint Joseph.

En este bolsillo
Llevo remolachas
Pa' en las Navidades
Conseguir muchachas.

In this pocket
I carry beets
So that at Christmas time
I can get girls.

Llegaron los reyes
Bendito sea Dios
Ellos van y vuelven
Y nosotros no.

The Three Kings arrived
Blessed be God
They go and return
But we do not.

Estas Navidades
Vamos a gozarlas
Pues en dos semanas
Vamos a pasarlas.

This is the Christmas season
Let us enjoy it
Because in two weeks
We will be past them.

Este árbol de Christmas
Tiene muchos adornos
Y el dueño de casa
Tiene mucho romo.

This Christmas tree
Has many ornaments
And the master of the house
Has a lot of rum.

Aquí está ño Pancho
Con su aguinaldito
El día veinte y cuatro
Le dan su regalito.

Here is Señor Pancho
With his little Christmas gift
On the twenty-fourth
He will get his little present.

Source:

"Selections of Vieques, Yauco, and Luquillo, Puerto Rico," by Maxine W. Gordon. *Journal of American Folklore*, LXIV (1951), pp. 59-61.

ROMANIAN AMERICANS

A Jewish immigrant from Romania, M.E. (Marcus Eli) Ravage (1884-1965) wrote An American in the Making in part, according to the book's introduction, as a response to the fact "that Americans have forgotten America." Americans tended to greet immigrants either with hostility or derision, and seemed to have lost sight of "the pathos and romance" behind the story of many immigrants. He longed, as he wrote, to "show you America as we of the oppressed peoples see it!"

Ravage's was a story common to many immigrants from Romania and elsewhere, a story of hopes and sacrifices and odd jobs. He had worked in the Battery, an area along the southern tip of Manhattan, and served as a tap-boy—that is, the operator of a beer tap in a bar room. His places of employment had included a sweatshop, a factory where immigrants toiled for long hours at low wages. He also became involved in political agitation as an anarchist. Anarchism, a movement that appealed to many immigrant intellectuals, called for the tearing down of society's structures, and for a new decentralized social order of local communities instead of nations.

Ravage's early experience in New York calls to mind an old immigrant joke. A man got off the boat in New York City, and as he was walking along the street, happened to see a $20 bill on the sidewalk. He paused, nearly picked it up, then thought better of it and went on his way, saying to himself, "It is my first day in America—I don't have to work."

Such was the immigrant's perception of America, the land of plenty; and for Ravage, arriving as he did at Christmastime, it seemed indeed that every day in America was a feast day. He rapidly overcame this delusion, but still found himself amazed with the richness of the new land when he moved in with his recently Americanized "Cousin Betty."

Betty and her sister were "modish," or fashionable, and Betty proved it by wearing pince-nez, eyeglasses clipped to the nose with a spring—something considered very stylish at the turn of the century. They even lived on an upper floor of their apartment building, a fact that in his hometown of Vaslui, a city in eastern Romania, was a sign of wealth.

In fact living on an upper floor, in America at least, meant that one had less money rather than more. It meant climbing steps in those days without elevators; but to Ravage and other immigrants, an upper floor was a great joy, along with other pleasures most Americans took for granted, such as running water and gas stoves.

With a humorous and lighthearted touch, Ravage paints a picture of his immigrant family's hardships, on the one hand portraying the difficulties of life, and on the other making these seem like pleasures. Throughout it all, as he reports, his family conducted themselves with nobility, maintaining a pretense of elegance.

Thus "During the day my relative kept up the interesting fiction of an apartment with specialized divisions"—a parlor, a dining-room, and so on. "But between nine and ten o'clock in the evening this imposing structure suddenly crum-

bled away in the most amazing fashion," and the whole apartment became a vast boarding-house. Ravage describes the excruciating pains one had to go through if one came home late, not to mention the many noxious smells of a room "hermetically sealed," or airtight, against the outside cold.

Yet the hardships pale beside the joys in Ravage's narrative. Again and again during his early days in America, he showed a typical immigrant's amazement at American abundance: hence he assumed that his relative would use sand, not soap, to scrub the kitchen floor; and that lights and gas were to be turned off at all possible opportunities. Thus he blew out the pilot light, creating a potentially hazardous gas leak.

Ravage makes little reference to the fact that his family was Jewish, except for comparing Mrs. Segal's shopping attire to the type of clothing one would reserve for going to temple. (He also mentions Purim, a Jewish holiday.) Among the items she bought at the store, he reported, was "a yellow fruit which had the shape of a cucumber and the taste of a muskmelon," presumably squash.

With all this plenty, he asked himself "Was I doing Couza an injustice?" This is apparently a reference to Alexander Ion Couza (1820-73), the Prince of Romania and a great national hero; Ravage was asking, in effect, "Was I doing Romania an injustice by leaving?" In the end, he decided not: no one back home, after all "indulged in such luxuries as beer," a glass of which he enjoyed at the end of his second day in America.

An American in the Making (Excerpt)

The Immigrant's America

As I look back over my transition from the alien to the American state I cannot help wondering at the incredible changes of it. I see a curious row of figures, as in a haze, struggling to some uncertain goal, and with a shock it comes upon me that I am all this motley crew. There is the awkward, unkempt, timid youth of sixteen, with the inevitable bundles, dumbly inquiring his way from the Battery to the slums. A little farther on, shivering in the December drizzle with a tray in his gloveless hand, the vender of unsellable candies dreams of Christmas far away by his Rumanian fireside. A tap-boy in an East Side barroom follows next; his hair parted in the middle, his gift-breeches fitting a little snugly on his well-groomed young carcass, he hums to himself over his tub of glassware. Then the sewing-machine operative, now in his sweat-shop assiduously at work, now at his anarchist meeting scheming to reform the world. And then the student in school and college, with his new struggles and problems piled high over the old, old worries about bread and bed. And then—and then the picture gets too near for a good perspective, and anyhow the tale is all but told. The alien is become the self-made American.

What a fortunate thing it was for me that I got to New York just before Christmas! Fortunate, that is, as immigrant's luck goes. If I had got here after Christmas I would, without a doubt, have starved as well as frozen. You know, of course, why I froze—because I did not obey my mother, which is simply saying that it served me right. Mother, it will be remembered, had insisted that I take with me the old overcoat which she had herself recreated out of a garment once worn by my well-to-do uncle Pincus; and I had refused because, to begin with, I already had too much to lug, and because I could see no sense in carrying old clothes to a country where I would at once become rich enough to buy new ones. That I did not starve, in spite of my landing with the proverbial fifteen cents in my pocket, was due not only to the fact that I tumbled right into the midst of the prosperity of the Christmas shopping season, but to a further piece of good fortune.

What I would have done if little Cousin Betty had not had the foresight to bring over her folks, is more than I can tell. To be sure, the family had arrived only about three months before, but three months is a long time in the evolution of Americans. And so there they were, the whole seven of them—mother and son and five daughters—on the tunefully named Rivington Street, already keeping house and talking English, and the oldest young lady receiving callers, and Betty, her next of age, declaring that she would not go without pince-nez glasses when all the fashionables, including her own sister, possessed and wore them. Betty and her modish sister, being old enough to work, did consequently work at men's neckties, while the remaining four children went to school or kindergarten, or danced on the street to the music of the grind-organ, or stayed at home to be rocked in the cradle, according to their varying tastes and years. Yes, there they were quite Americanized, happy in their five rooms, three of which faced on Allen Street and joined their window-sills right on to the beams of the Elevated trestle. They were still happy, because neckwear was a genteel trade that could be worked at in the home until any hour of the night with the whole family lending a hand, and because Cousin Jacob, the father and tyrant of the household, had been left in Rumania "to settle affairs," because the business of cooking with gas and turning a faucet when you wanted water was an exciting novelty and because keeping roomers was a romantic undertaking. They lived on the third floor, which was something to be proud of, since back home in Vaslui none but the rich could afford to live up-stairs; and of course "up-stairs" in Vaslui was only a beggarly second floor.

As I look back over my transition from the alien to the American state I cannot help wondering at the incredible changes of it.

I never contrived to find out just how many people did share those five rooms. During the day my relative kept up the interesting fiction of an apartment with specialized divisions. Here was the parlor with its sofa and mirror and American rocking-chairs; then came the dining-room with another sofa called a lounge, a round table, and innumerable chairs; then the kitchen with its luxurious fittings in porcelain and metal; then the young ladies' room, in which there was a bureau covered with quantities of odoriferous bottles and powder-boxes and other mysteries; and, last of all, Mrs. Segal's and the children's room. I remember how overwhelmed I was with this impressive luxury when I arrived. But between nine and ten o'clock in the evening this imposing structure suddenly crumbled away in the most amazing fashion. The apartment suddenly became a camp. The sofas opened up and revealed their true character. The bureau lengthened out shamelessly, careless of its daylight pretensions. Even the wash-tubs, it turned out, were a miserable sham. The carved dining-room chairs arranged themselves into two rows that faced each other like dancers in a cotillion. So that I began to ask myself whether there was, after all, anything in that whole surprising apartment but beds.

The two young ladies' room was not, I learned, a young ladies' room at all; it was a female dormitory. The sofa in the parlor alone held four sleepers, of whom I was one. We were ranged broadside, with the rocking-chairs at the foot to insure the proper length. And the floor was by no means exempt. I counted no fewer than nine male inmates in that parlor alone one night. Mrs. Segal with one baby slept on the wash-tubs, while the rest of the youngsters held the kitchen floor. The pretended children's room was occupied by a man and his family of four, whom he had recently brought over, although he, with ambitions for a camp of his own, did not remain long.

Getting in late after the others had retired was an enterprise requiring all a man's courage and circumspection, for it involved the rousing of an alarmed, overworked, grumbling landlady to unbolt the door; the exchange in stage whispers of a complicated system of challenges and passwords through the keyhole; the squeezing through cracks in intermediate doors, which were rendered stationary by the presence of beds on both side; much cautious high-stepping over a vast field of sprawling, unconscious bodies; and lastly, the gentle but firm compressing and condensing of one's relaxed bedmates in order to make room for oneself. It was on such occasions as these also that one first became aware of how heavy the air was with the reek of food and strong breath and fermenting perspiration, the windows being, of course, hermetically sealed with putty and a species of padding imported from home which was tacked around all real and imaginary cracks.

In the morning one was awakened by the puffing of steam-engines and the clatter of wheels outside the windows, and then the turmoil of American existence began in real earnest. First, the furniture must be reconstructed and restored to its decorative character, and the scattered disorder of feather-bedding must be cleared from the floors and whisked away into cupboards and trunks. The men-folks had to fly into their clothes before the ladies emerged from their quarters, so that the latter might pass through the parlor on their way to the kitchen. In spite of all the precautions taken the night before, some one invariably missed one portion or another of his costume, which he promptly proceeded to search for with a great deal of wailing and complaining against his own fate in particular and the intolerable anarchy of Columbus's country in general. Then followed a furious scramble for the sink, because the towel had a way of getting unmanageably wet toward the end; and this made it necessary for Mrs. Segal, who slept in the kitchen, to be up before every one else. By the time the camp had once more become an elegant apartment, the coffee was already steaming on the round table in the dining-room, and the whole colony sat down to partake of it before scattering to its various labors, breakfast and laundry being, of course, included in the rent.

The first two days Mrs. Segal would not hear of my going out to look for work. She insisted that I must rest up from the journey, look around a bit, and in general play the guest. "A guest is a guest even in America," she said. "And don't worry," she added; "you'll have time enough to make the money." After which she smiled in a peculiar manner. So I stayed home alone with her, and feeling that I owed her something in return for her hospitality, I tried to make myself useful to her by helping with the housework. The army of roomers had no sooner dispersed than she packed the youngsters off and threw herself into the task with enthusiasm. "Housekeeping," said she, "is wonderfully easy in America."

I had to agree that it was wonderful, but I myself at least could hardly say that I found it easy. It certainly was an extravagant way of doing things. The first thing we were going to do, she told me, was to scrub the kitchen. "Very well," I said "Where do you keep the sand?" "Sand!" she exclaimed. "This is not Vaslui," and proceeded to take the neatly printed wrapper off a cake of soap which back home would have been thought too good to wash clothes with. For the floor she employed a pretty, white powder out of a metal can and a brush with which I had the night before cleaned my clothes. Moreover, she kept the light burning all the time were in the kitchen, which was criminal wastefulness even if the room was a bit dark. She herself would certainly not have done such a thing at home.

About ten o'clock she started off to market. If she had not told me where she was going, and if it had not been a week-day, I would have believed she was on her way to temple. There she stood in her taffeta gown (it was the very one mother had once told me had come from her wedding) and all the

jewelry I used to see on her at the services in Vaslui, and a pair of brand-new patent-leather pumps. As soon as she was out of the house I took the opportunity to blow out the gas in the kitchen, only, however, to be scolded for my pains when she re-entered and to be informed that greenhorns must keep their eyes open and their hand off. I could see nothing wrong in what I had done, but she kept saying over and over again that I had narrowly escaped death or blowing up the building.

The things she brought back from market! Eggplant in midwinter, and tomatoes, and a yellow fruit which had the shape of a cucumber and the taste of a muskmelon. I had never seen such huge eggplants in all my life. And here was another thing which was entirely strange, but which inquiry revealed was cauliflower—an article father had once eaten at the home of my cousin, the doctor, in Bucharest and had never ceased talking about. Could there be anything in it, after all? I repeatedly asked myself during that day. Was I doing Couza an injustice? Oh, if the Lord would only grant that I should turn out to have been mistaken! Yes, but how about the boarders? If the Segals had actually made their million in these three months, why did they share their fine apartment with strangers? Who but the very lowest of people kept roomers in Vaslui? I could not figure it out. America was surely a land of contradictions.

Mrs. Segal and I had meat in the middle of the day, and then about six, when the two girls got home, there was meat again. I remember writing home about it the next day and telling the folks that they might think I was exaggerating, but that it was literally true, all the same, that in New York every night was Friday night and every day was Saturday, as far as food went, anyway. Why, they even had twists instead of plain rye bread, to say nothing of rice-and-raisins (which is properly a Purim dish) and liver paste and black radish. And then about eight in the evening two young gentlemen called on Cousin Rose and capped the climax of the whole day by insisting on bringing in some beer in a pitcher from the corner saloon. There I was! I could say all I wanted to about America being a sham, but no one would believe a word of it until I could prove that Segals and Abners and Schneers indulged in such luxuries as beer at home—a thing which no one could prove because it was not so.

1917

Source:

An American in the Making, Harper & Brothers Publishers, New York, 1917. pp. 69-77.

*T*he author Andrei Codrescu was born in Sibiu, Romania, in 1946. He fled his native land at the age of 20. A member nation of the Soviet Bloc for two decades, the Romanian government had just passed into the hands of Nicolae Ceausescu a year earlier, in 1965. Ceausescu's iron-fisted rule, which made him one of the harshest communist dictators in post-World War II Europe, lasted nearly a quarter of a century until the 1989 revolution. Along with his mother, Codrescu emigrated to the United States, where today he is a novelist, commentator on National Public Radio, and English literature professor at Louisiana State University.

In the article "Notes of an Alien Son: Immigrant Visions," Codrescu considered the different expectations immigrants have of the United States. Although both he and his mother faced oppression as Jews in Romania, they had very different visions of—and reasons for wanting to go to—America. For his shopkeeper mother, America fit a time-honored immigrant ideal of the land of plenty, where hard work is rewarded with comfort, upward mobility and consumer goods. She received the outward physical rewards of a new car and furniture, which would have made her the envy of Romanians. And yet her experience soon turned to one of grief. Missing her home, family, friends, and customs, she found herself culturally and socially bereft, an experience Codrescu compares to death.

But the author's own sense of exile was joyous. In the contentious late 1960s, young people all over the world were rebelling against the values, traditions, and institutions of their parents, and so was Codrescu. Though a Romanian, his cultural heroes were the same as those of the young Americans he now found himself among—musicians such as Bob Dylan, the Beatles and the Rolling Stones. And though he was literally an exile, Americans his age were also in a kind of "metaphorical exile," as he describes it: they were alienated from the world of their elders. For the rebellious Codrescu, "it was a match made in heaven."

Within his family, the disparity in immigrant experience leads Codrescu to offer two visions of America. One typifies the experience of his mother, whom he deems an economic refugee "in quest of Wal-Mart." That quest brought surface rewards but left her spiritually impoverished. He, on the other hand, sought spiritual freedom, and found it in abundance. He concedes that his immigrant experience was atypical, and happened chiefly because of the unusual atmosphere and temper of the era. But he also asserts that his taste of exile gave him a glimpse of the "original vision" of the country—one rich with the possibility of utopia.

NOTES OF AN ALIEN SON: IMMIGRANT VISIONS

by Andrei Codrescu

After having been in America for nearly thirty years, I am only an immigrant when people want me to talk about it. Paradoxically, it was a recent return to Romania, my native country, that caused me to re-evaluate my American experience. Until that time, I considered myself a model American: drank Jim Beam, wore Converse hightops, quit smoking on tax day. Of course, I may have been too perfect.

I went back to Romania in December 1989 to report on the so-called revolution over there, but in truth I went back in order to smell things. I went there to recover my childhood. I touched the stones of the medieval tower under the Liars' Bridge, where I used to lie still like a lizard in the summer. I put my cheek against the tall door of our old house, built in 1650, with its rusty smell of iron. I sniffed at people's windows to see what they were cooking. There were aromas of paprikash and strudel, and the eternal cabbage.

I made my way into the past through my nose, madeleinizing everything. My childhood, which had been kept locked and preserved in the crumbling city of Hermanstadt, was still there, untouched. It had outlasted my emigration. It was a thousand years old.

Considering, then, that childhood lasts for a thousand years, the past thirty years of adulthood in America do not seem like such a big deal. My old Romanian friends, now adults, had metamorphosed in those three decades into—mostly—fat survivors of a miserable and baroque system where material things were the supreme spiritual value. For them, America was the heavenly Wal-Mart. That's what God was during Communism, because God was everything, and everything can be found at Wal-Mart. Forty years of so-called Communism had done no more than polish to perfection my grandmother's maxim, "In America dogs walk around with pretzels on their tails." Loose translation: In America the sidewalks are paved with gold.

I used to fantasize coming back to my country a celebrated author, envied by all the people who made my life hell in high school. But now I wished, more than anything, that I'd come back as a Wal-Mart. If only I were a Wal-Mart, I could have spread my beauteous aisles to the awe-struck of Hermanstadt and fed them senseless with all the bounty of America.

When I returned to the United States, I reeled about for a few days in shock. Everything was so new, so carelessly abundant, so thoughtlessly shiny, so easily taken for granted. The little corner store with its wilted lettuce and spotted apples was a hundred times more substantial than the biggest bare shelf store in Romania.

My mother, ever a practical woman, started investing in furniture when she came to America. Not just any furniture. Sears furniture. Furniture that she kept the plastic on for fifteen years before she had to conclude, sadly, that Sears wasn't such a great investment. In Romania, she would have been the richest woman on the block.

Which brings us to at least one paradox of immigration. Most people come here because they are sick of being poor. They want to eat and they want to show something for their industry. But soon enough it becomes evident to them that these things aren't enough. They have eaten and they are full, but they have eaten alone and there was no one with whom to make toasts and sing songs. They have new furniture with plastic on it but the neighbors aren't coming over to ooh and aah. If American neighbors or less recent immigrants do come over, they smile condescendingly at the poor taste and the pathetic greed. And so, the greenhorns find themselves poor once more: This time they are lacking something more elusive than salami and furniture. They are bereft of a social and cultural milieu.

My mother, who was middle class by Romanian standards, found herself immensely impoverished after her first flush of material well-being. It wasn't just the disappearance of her milieu—that was obvious—but the feeling that she had, somehow, been had. The American supermarket tomatoes didn't taste at all like the rare genuine item back in Romania. American chicken was tasteless. Mass-produced furniture was built to fall apart. Her car, the crowning glory of her achievements in the eyes of folks back home, was only three years old and was already beginning to wheeze and groan. It began to dawn on my mother that she had perhaps made a bad deal: She had traded in her friends and relatives for ersatz tomatoes, fake chicken, phony furniture.

Leaving behind your kin, your friends, your language, your smells, your childhood, is traumatic.

It is a kind of death. You're dead for the home folk and they are dead to you. When you first arrive on these shores you are in mourning. The only consolation are these products, which had been imbued with religious significance back at home. But when these things turn out not to be the real things, you begin to experience a second death, brought about by betrayal. You begin to suspect that the religious significance you had attached to them was only possible back home, where these things did not exist. Here, where they are plentiful, they have no significance whatsoever. They are inanimate fetishes, somebody else's fetishes, no help to you at all. When this realization dawned on my mother, she began to rage against her new country. She deplored its rudeness, its insensitivity, its outright meanness, its indifference, the chase after the almighty buck, the social isolation of most Americans, their inability to partake in warm, genuine fellowship and, above all, their deplorable lack of awe before what they had made.

This was the second stage of grief for her old self. The first, leaving her country, was sharp and immediate, almost tonic in its violence. The second was more prolonged, more damaging, because no hope was attached to it. Certainly not the hope of return.

And here, thinking of return, she began to reflect that perhaps there had been more to this deal than she'd first thought. True, she had left behind a lot that was good, but she had also left behind a vast range of daily humiliations. If she was ordered to move out of town she had to comply. If a party member took a dislike to her she had to go to extraordinary lengths to placate him because she was considered petit-bourgeois and could easily have lost her small photo shop. She lived in fear of being denounced for something she had said. And worst of all, she was a Jew, which meant that she was structurally incapable of obtaining any justice in her native land. She had lived by the grace of an immensely complicated web of human relations, kept in place by a thousand small concessions, betrayals, indignities, bribes, little and big lies.

At this point, the ersatz tomatoes and the faux chicken did not appear all that important. An imponderable had made its appearance, a bracing, heady feeling of liberty. If she took that ersatz tomato and flung it at the head of the Agriculture Secretary of the United States, she would be making a statement about the disastrous effects of pesticides and mechanized farming. Flinging that faux chicken at Barbara Mandrell would be equally dramatic and perhaps even media-worthy. And she'd probably serve only a suspended sentence. What's more, she didn't have to eat those things, because she could buy organic tomatoes and free-range chicken. Of course, it would cost more, but that was one of the paradoxes of America: To eat as well as people in a Third World country eat (when they eat) costs more.

My mother was beginning to learn two things: one, that she had gotten a good deal after all, because in addition to food and furniture they had thrown in freedom; and two, America is a place of paradoxes—one proceeds from paradox to paradox like a chicken from the pot into the fire.

And that's where I come in. My experience was not at all like that of my mother. I came here for freedom, not for food. I came here in the mid-sixties. Young people East and West at that time had a lot more in common with each other than with the older generations. The triple-chinned hogs of the *nomenklatura* who stared down from the walls of Bucharest were equal in our minds to the Dow Chemical pigs who gave us napalm and Vietnam. By the time I left Romania in 1966, the Iron Curtain was gone: A Hair Curtain fell between generations. Prague 1968 and Chicago 1968 were on the same axis. The end of the old world had begun.

Our anthems were the songs of Dylan, the Beatles, the Rolling Stones, all of whom were roundly despised by my mother because she was sure that such tastes would lead to our being thrown out of America. And she wasn't all that wrong: Her old don't-rock-the-boat instinct was an uncannily fine instrument. At that time, being anti-establishment in America could be perilous. But this wasn't Romania. The difference, the massive difference, was the constitutional right to freedom of speech and assembly. True, for a moment or two—and for several long, scary moments since—those constitutional rights were in real danger. And if Americans felt threatened, you can be sure that many niceties of the law simply didn't apply to refugees.

Nonetheless, I was drunk with freedom and I wasn't about to temper my euphoria with the age-old wariness of European Jews. My mother's main pleasure and strategy in those days was to overstuff me whenever I came to visit. She believed that food would keep me safe. Food keeps you from going out at night, it makes you sleepy, makes you think twice about hitchhiking, makes you, generally, less radical. The very things that alienated my mother—the speed, confusion, social unrest, absence of ceremony—exhilarated me. I had arrived here at an ecstatic moment in history and I was determined to make the most of it. And when, thanks to the marketing know-how of the C.I.A., I got to try LSD for the first time, I became convinced that freedom was infinitely vaster than was generally acknowledged. It was not just a right, it was an atmosphere. It was the air one needed to breathe. And one had to stay skinny.

In 1966, my generation welcomed me into its alienated and skinny arms with a generosity born of outsiderness. Young people at that time had become outsiders to America's mainstream. Those who went to Vietnam were way outside, even though, ostensibly, they served the inside. The others were in voluntary exile from the suburbs that immigrants hoped to live in one day. But what mattered is that we were all on the move. I happened to be a literal exile in a world of, mostly, metaphorical exiles. It was a match made in heaven. America was 19 years old and so was I. I lived in a country of exiles, a place that had its own pantheon of elders, exiled geniuses like Einstein and Nabokov, and whole nomad youth armies. Exile was a place in the mid-sixties, an international Idea State, the only anarchist state in working order. It's not the kind of thing that comes around all that often in American immigrant history.

In the 400 years since Europeans first came here, there have been many immigrant visions of America, most of them a variation of *Ubiprctzel ibipatria*; the true, ineffable one was not a pretzel but a pear—Charles Fourier's pear, to be exact. For Fourier, the pear was the perfect fruit. It was to be eaten in Paradise by lovers. This vision of a utopian New World was entirely about freedom. The freedoms granted by the Bill of Rights were only the steps leading to this new state of being.

The prophetic tradition maintains that America is chosen among nations to bring about the end of history. American utopian communities, which flourished here in the nineteenth century, were reborn with a vengeance a hundred years later. The possibility of utopia is an ingrained American belief, one that, it can be argued, has kept America strong, vigorous and young. Walt Whitman's America was done with the niceties of Europe because it was bigger, ruder and had a greater destiny. This America was also a country of immigrants who gave it their raw muscle and imagination. Diversity and industry were its mainstays. Even Allen Ginsberg, a bitter prophet at the end of the 1950s, could say, "America, I put my queer shoulder to the wheel." Despite the irony, Ginsberg, the son of a Russian Jewish immigrant, really believes that his queer shoulder is needed, that America needs not just its bankers but also its queers.

But this sustaining vision of America is, paradoxically again, marginal. It is often confused with another, similar-sounding creed, which is in all the textbooks and is invoked by politicians on the Fourth of July. Immigrants are used as a rhetorical device to support the goals of the nation-state: America right or wrong. This is the official ideology, which, like the party line in Romania, is meant to drive underground the true and dangerous vision. Its faithful will admit to no contradiction between their love of freedom and their hatred of outsiders.

The history of public opinion on immigration shows mainly opposition to it. As the revolutionary ideas of the eighteenth century receded, compassion for the wretched and persecuted of the earth was dictated mainly by the interests of capitalists. Not that this was necessarily bad. Heartless capitalism in its ever-growing demand for cheap labor saved millions of people from the no-exit countries of the world. It was a deal that ended up yielding unexpected benefits: vigor, energy, imagination, the remaking of cities, new culture. Restless capital, restless people, ever-expanding boundaries—the freedom to move, pick up, start again, shed the accursed identities of static native lands. The deal turned out to have the hidden benefit of liberty. The liberty my mother discovered in America was here: It was a byproduct of the anarchic flow of capital, the vastness of the American space, and a struggle in the name of the original utopian vision. Of course, capitalism annexed the resulting moral capital and put on an idealistic face that it never started out with, and that it quickly sheds whenever production is interrupted. Nonetheless, it is this capitalism with a human face that brought most of us here.

But capitalism with a human face is not the same as the original vision of America. The original American dream is religious, socialist and anticapitalist. It was this utopianism—liberty in its pure, unalloyed state—that I experienced in nondenominational, ahistorical, uneconomical, transcendent flashes in the mid-sixties. It's not simple dialectical Manicheism we are talking about here. It's the mystery itself.

If somebody had asked my mother in the mid-sixties if she was a political refugee, she would have said, "Of course." But privately she would have scoffed at the idea. She was an economic refugee, a warrior in quest of Wal-Mart. In Romania she had been trained at battling lines for every necessity. In America, at last, her skills would come in handy. Alas. But if somebody had asked me, I would have said, "I'm a planetary refugee, a professional refugee, a permanent exile." Not on my citizenship application form, of course. That may have been a bit dramatic, but in truth I never felt like a refugee, either political or economic. What I felt was that it was incumbent upon me to manufacture difference, to make myself as distinct and unassimilable as possible. To increase my foreignness, if you will. That was my contribution to America: not the desire to melt in but the desire to embody an instructive difference.

To the question, "Whose woods are these?"—which Robert Frost never asked because he thought he knew the answer—my mother would have said, without hesitation, "Somebody else's." My mother, like most immigrants, knew only too well that these were somebody else's woods. She only hoped that one day she might have a piece of them. My answer to that question would have been, and I think it still is, "Nobody's." These are nobody's woods and that's how they must be kept: open for everybody, owned by nobody. This is, in part at least, how Native Americans thought of them. It was a mistake, of course. Nobody's woods belong to the first marauding party who claims them. A better answer might be: "These woods belong to mystery; this is the forest of paradoxes; *un bosche oscuro*; we belong to them, not they to us."

Source:
Andrei Codrescu, *The Nation*, Dec. 12, 1994.

RUSSIAN AMERICANS

*L*arge-scale emigration from Russia to the United States did not begin until the late nineteenth century. The first immigration wave of 3.2 million immigrants occurred between the 1880s and 1914. These Russians fled religious discrimination and political repression, as well as a lack of economic opportunity. Letters from Russian immigrants in the United States convinced many that it was possible to immigrate, make money, and return to Russia with personal wealth that could never be amassed in their homeland.

Russia was an economically underdeveloped country of peasants and industrial workers. European Russia included the land area of present-day Lithuania, Belarus, Moldova, and a region of Poland that had been partitioned three ways among Germany, Austria, and Russia. This land area was known as the Pale of Settlement and was the only place that Jews were permitted to settle in Russia. Jewish villages like the one made famous in the Broadway play Fiddler On the Roof were typical of the area. Half of the immigrating wave were Jews who feared attacks because of their religious beliefs. The other half of the immigrant group represented about 66 different nationalities who fell under the umbrella term of Russian.

Sokoloff was apparently a Russian Old Believer, and had lived in America for years, and was educated and accustomed to a clean, urban lifestyle. Along with a traveling companion, he decided to visit Cokesburgh and meet his "fellow countrymen." The "Account of Russian Old Believers in Pittsburgh" provides a snapshot of non-Jewish Russian immigrants and their community in America. These traditionalists, including Orthodox Christian Old Believers and the non-Orthodox Molokan Christian sect, arrived during the first large-scale immigration wave. The believers to whom Sokoloff referred in his document are the Orthodox Christian Old Believers.

In Russia in 988 the ruling family converted to Greek Orthodox Christianity. It was the official religion of the western Russian people until the thirteenth century, when the Mongols, under Genghis Khan, invaded. After Constantinople fell to the Ottoman Turks in 1453, Moscow became increasingly metropolitan, with changes to the Russian church. By 1645 the Romanovs ruled Russia and brought about a merging of the western Russian Ukraine with Moscow by dictating religious reforms that were rejected by the non-Moscow church. In 1667, the Moscow church declared that the dissenters, or Raskolniki, were schismatics, and millions of so-called Old Believers found themselves excluded from full participation in Russian life. Two centuries later, many of the Old Believers immigrated to the United States in search of a better economic life as well as religious freedom. The typical immigrant traveled back to Russia as many as three times, and many returned to Russia to stay after making money in the United States. However, in 1885 the imperial Russian government passed a decree prohibiting all emigration except that of Poles and Jews, drastically reducing the non-Jewish immigrant numbers prior to the first World War. The immigrants that Sokoloff visited had been in the United States less than 20 years.

Old Believers settled in large cities such as San Francisco, Los Angeles and Erie, Pennsylvania, as well as the backwoods of Alaska. The Pennsylvania Russians became coal miners who endured very poor working conditions. Sokoloff lamented the dirty and crowded conditions of the immigrant community, where as many as 20 boarders lived in each household. Sokoloff described the exhausting job of the hazda, the woman who worked as keeper of the boarders. Russians Americans of this time continued a hard working, hard drinking lifestyle that was typical of life back in Russia.

Most immigrants continued to speak Russian and maintained a social distance from other immigrants and Americans. In a few rare cases, Russian was taught in public schools. In Sokoloff's document, he noted that the children of the Old Believers had learned English. In this community of about 3,000 Old Believers there was only one church, with a priest who was of Prussian nationality. Sokoloff observed that the immigrants tolerated what they considered temporary conditions because they intended to return to Russia. For this reason they made little effort to assimilate into American culture. Indeed, Sokoloff described a European view of the typical American as shrewd and agile, meaning slippery and inclined toward selfish pursuits. Americans, likewise, had a negative opinion of Russian Americans, particularly after World War II, with the rule of the Communists. Prior to the existence of the Soviet Union, the Russian immigrant's disinterest in assimilating and frequent trips back to Russia caused other Americans to disdain him.

According to the 1990 census, there were 2,953,000 Americans of Russian ancestry. The Old Believers, White Russian aristocrats, and Molokans today are only a small minority of the Russian American community. Many of them live in Chicago, Cleveland, Pittsburgh, and the coal mining towns of eastern Pennsylvania. The Molokans settled in California, where in 1999, a 20,000-member Russian community lived in San Francisco and Los Angeles.

RUSSIAN OLD BELIEVERS IN PITTSBURGH (EXCERPT)

I was soon punished for my fatuity, however, by another snapshot view. I had come with special purpose to make acquaintance with the Old Believers in Cokeburgh, a mining town to all purposes exactly like many others of the Pittsburgh district, but containing an especially large number of Russians. Out of between 400 or 500 miners (almost all foreigners) 300 were my countrymen, about half of them Old Believers.

I reached Cokeburgh on a beautiful early Sunday morning. I was disagreeably struck, on leaving the train, with the sound of what seemed to be drunken brawls sounding from many houses. Such indeed they were. Yesterday had been pay-day, and bearded men were drinking and drunk. Many houses were deserted, the revelers being grouped in a few. An ugly sight! Dirty, disheveled men in filthy kitchens filled with empty bottles, kegs and barrels; everything helter-skelter. Worst of all was the foul language they were using, without any provocation, regardless of the presence of children. I knew they did not use those bad words in the north of Russia. This is the influence of soldiery, so numerous in Poland and on the borderline and so hateful everywhere. But when I rebuked them, in quiet unrestrained expressions, for their foul language, nobody knocked me down; they were ashamed, for a while at least. They felt insulted only when I refused to drink a glass of beer with them, invariably offered without preliminaries. Many were sitting in the room with their hats on—a thing I would not have believed about a Russian peasant.

The women were by themselves elsewhere, untidy, some barefooted, and almost all in weekday clothes. "Why is this so here," I asked myself, "when I remember the streets of Russian villages on Sunday, bright with all the colors of the rainbow in the women's bands, frocks and kerchiefs?" Possibly the answer was to be found in the fact that the nearest church of Old Believers was about forty miles from Cokeburgh, and Russian Sunday adornment is inseparable from church-going. Only girls of marriageable age, or close to it, were displaying quite American apparel and hairdressing, and this without any connection with the length of time they had lived in America. A nice American lady to whom I showed the picture on the preceding page, when she saw the girl standing first from the left said that she must have been in this country most of her life. Yet she had been here only six months. I talked with her and found her fresh, with rustic, awkward bashfulness.

The village "belle" was also a daughter of the Old Believers, but she had been brought up in this country. Refined in feature and of slender figure, she spoke perfect English, yet showed much of the defiant, overbearing lack of kindness one meets so often in the city shop-girl, whose manners she was evidently imitating. I wished her to pose for a picture with her uncle, but she balked at the suggestion of being photographed with such an un-American object. She could not see, as I did, what a majestic head of a boyar her uncle had, so much like Boyar Morosoff, he who refused to sit "below" a man beneath him in rank at the Czar's table, and being ordered to don a buffon's dress so taunted the Czar with bitter truth and insults that he was beheaded for dessert.

The large woman in the middle of the group was possessor of the sole abstinent husband among the Old Believers, a small taciturn man. "They do not like him; they don't like anybody who does not drink with them," explained the woman, "so he stays at home." He proved to have been in America about seventeen years (the longest term in America of any Russian that I met) and six years in Cokeburgh. Nothing in his manner or in the appearance of his house, though it was decent enough (his wife and he had no children, no boarders), showed particularly the influence of America. There was neither the quaintness of the Russian "izba" about their barren room, nor the comfort and neatness of the American home.

Later, in another mining town in the north of Allegheny County—Russeltown, called by the Russians, "Wet Mines"—I vainly tried to find shelter for the night in some Old Believer's house. My companion was a Russian, just beginning in the business of bookselling. Three men at that time were making their livings by selling books, holy images, and crosses, but mainly books, among Russians in and around Pittsburgh. Ready enough were the Old Believers to let us into their houses, but these were crowded beyond belief. The rumor that Wet Mines was about to start up had brought a multitude from other places.

The bather especially likes that taking-the-breath-away sensation. The amount of heat a peasant can stand by being beaten with birch twigs would take the breath away forever from many a more highly organized being! Steam and birch twigs remove dirt very effectively, without the use of soap.

"Say, Beard, do you have a room in your house for tonight?" This to a burly fellow hardly distinguishable for the darkness, yet unmistakably an Old Believer. "But, my 'bratets' (my dear little brother)," he kindly responded (I was ashamed at having apostrophized him so roughly), "I have just moved to the town and have no furniture whatever in my house; it's on the way. If you don't care—welcome." And this welcome comes out of the darkness to a stranger of whom the "Beard" can see only that he is from the city (a bad recommendation indeed) and that he can talk Russian. No asking to which of the sixty-six nationalities in Russia and almost as many religions he belonged, but straight out, "Welcome." True, there was not very much to which the visitors were welcomed—a quite empty house, a bundle of shawls spread upon a pile of straw in one room—all the furnishings they possessed—and nothing at all in the other. An attractive-looking woman was sitting on the floor gazing dreamily into the blazing coals of the fireplace. In answer to my "God help," she made place for me before the fire. In a moment I was sitting beside her talking to her as though we were old acquaintances. Meanwhile, the man was grabbing a big armful of straw from his own pile and preparing a bed for the bookseller and myself in the other room. I cannot help remembering that bunch of straw. It makes the penny dole of a poor fellow equal to the gift of a Rockefeller. Christians, those peasants are by the strongest claim—natural disposition. That oft-repeated cry, "We must Christianize the foreigners," is like breaking into an open door.

To the woman I complained of the disorder and filth I saw everywhere among my people. "Why are all so dirty? Is it the same over in Russia?" She became animated. "Why! And boarders? How can you keep the house clean with twenty men to take care of, and children?" She had had four, one of whom had died, and she was not yet twenty-three.

"Who keeps boarders over in the country? Not to think of such a thing!" It was too obvious to ask her why Russians do it here. It is the only chance they have to accomplish the main purpose of their coming, which is to save money; an amount insignificant in America, perhaps, but large in a Russian village. Boarders and keepers; and for both sides it is bitter. The "hazda" receives $3 per month from each man. For this sum the latter is entitled to a lodging together with some fifteen other men. A neighbor had twenty-eight at one time, said the woman, in four rooms—the half of a company house—for which she paid $8. Each room was about twenty feet square.

The hazda attends to the washing of underwear and bedclothes, supplies cabbage for the soup, and does the cooking. She reaps some profit from the butcher, baker and grocer on the things she purchases for her boarders. Minor features in the unwritten constitution of keeping boarders are peculiar; the hazda herself, but not her man, has the right, free of charge, of taking part in the mess; so have her ungrown children. When the men wash after coming home from work, she is supposed to wash their backs. Arduous task, undoubtedly, that of boarder-keeping. At the highest estimate, it can bring about $60 per month, if based on twenty boarders. With the husband making a little over this sum, I heard of a couple who had managed to amass $6,000 in five years. They had had exceptionally good fortune, no doubt, up to that point—no seasons of non-employment, sickness or other losses. The husband then died, and although almost half of the money was spent on a tremendous drunken "pomin" (that heathenish survival of accompanying a burial with a carouse), and a gaudy monument in the cemetery, the wife returned to Russia a rich, envied widow, sure to find another husband.

"Say, do you have 'banyas' (bathhouses) there in Suvalki as they do in Great Russia?" "Oh, certainly, my father had a nice banya." So it is; even the poor peasant in north and middle Russia has, besides his "izba," a bathhouse, as an American has a bathroom.

It is not a very elaborate affair; a room with a high bench built stepwise and a big water tub; hot stones from the fire-place in the anteroom are thrown into the tub to heat the water; other are besprinkled, producing an enormous amount of steam, which one can take in degrees of heat on the different steps of the bench. Invariably the bath is accompanied by a "birch broom" beating all over your body, this intensifying the heat. The bather especially likes that taking-the-breath-away sensation. The amount of heat a peasant can stand by being beaten with birch twigs would take the breath away forever from many a more highly organized being! Steam and birch twigs remove dirt very effectively, without the use of soap. It is not to be contended that the peasant loves his banya solely for the sake of cleanliness; it is a pleasure to him. The saying that it is only in the third generation that the foreigner in America takes to the bath, is reversed in the case of Great Russians at least. It is the first generation that changes its habits; it stops taking the bath when it comes to America. A Moscow merchant would not see the insulting point if I should read to him what I saw in a Sunday newspaper not long ago, that he goes to bath once a year; why, he might as well be accused of not liking his vodka as of not liking his bath!

"Why don't you make the bath-houses here?" I asked my hostess, and she explained how much of an undertaking it would be. "Does your husband drink as much as the others?" I continued my inquiry. "Once in awhile; he does not spend much on drink." As a matter of fact, none spend much on drink. A keg of beet costs only $1 and that is sufficient for a good spree for five men. Most know when to stop. The expense comes later at the adjustment of the result of drinking; payment for battery and arrests. "Does your husband beat you?" "Doesn't beat, doesn't love," she answers in a Russian saying.

I nearly failed to notice the woman's children—three of them, sitting quietly not far from us, seemingly possessed of that "contemplative spirit of the East." The eldest, about ten years old, attended school, and spoke English as well as Russian. His father had already taught him to read in Russian.

I still had to provide a quilt and a bedcloth for the night on my straw bed. Again going from house to house, chance brought me first to an English-speaking family, where I was given to understand that I was crazy to ask such a thing—stranger as I was. I could not but agree with them, civilized as I had become, and would doubtless have acted as they did. But in an Old Believer's house, I got a quilt was old and dirty, but the home-made linen cloth, fresh and clean, was exquisite.

Searching for my companion, I came across a group of Old Believers outside a house. Through the light which streamed from an open door I discerned standing with them a tall man, not very well shaved, with drooping mustachios, certainly an American. He proved to be a former Texas cowboy, now a farmer living on 12 acres of land in the vicinity of Wet Mines. I wondered that he kept company with my Old Believers and told him so. "Oh, they are as good as gold to me," said he. As I engaged in conversation with him, not as a Russian but just as a "decent-like furriner," his opinion could not have lacked sincerity. I found him, later on, sitting in an Old Believer's house, among a bearded crowd, drinking and jollying with them. For him they embodied the essential traits of a "white man"—no littleness, no stinginess; readiness to fight on provocation, redoubtable, too, in fight; the good-natured, cheerful disposition; and last but not least, the ability to drink like a fish without dying from it. Oh! If there were but common soil of intercourse with Americans for these Russians other than drinking!

I finally found my companion in an empty house surrounded by a crowd of young fellows who were poring over his case of books. Among them were four American boys. Bottles strewn on the floor made it clear that drinking was going on in this house, although with the exception of red-headed fellow they called "Dutchman," who was rather piggish and obscene, I did not notice anybody behaving badly. All were busied with books. A nice-looking Russian youth was translating the inscriptions under the pictures in a book about the Russian-Japanese War to a refined, sympathetic American chap who might have been driven from a good position by bad times out of the city. The Russian youth talked to me with rapture about the joys of reading a book with the long title, Story About How a Lioness Has Reared a King's Son.

I found the Old Believers the most kind-hearted, good-natured lot of people I had ever met, almost childlike, despite their sometimes sullen looks, and I an asset, is it,—this kindness and good-nature, as qualities for a man to depend upon in the struggle for life? Yet, if the golden age should come, more of these qualities will be needed. The Romans could not imagine that any force but brute force counted. Nowadays the world believes that "brains" alone count. I do not wish to say that every casual American observer will find these men of such kindly disposition as I describe. Ignorance is suspicious, stubbornness is difficult to handle. And he is difficult, the Old Believer. Maybe, too, those good qualities of heart belong to men who have had to struggle only with nature, not with men, for their existence. I am told that here, under the ground, it comes often to ugly fights for cars. Through faulty organization in some of the mines, cars are not furnished promptly not in sufficient number for the coal loaders. And Old Believers, it is said, prove more savage then anybody else in the contest to secure them.

In common with all Russians in America, these men are steady workers, despite their love of drink. "Drunkard and wise—two virtues in him." They are apt to say cynically about themselves. Their industry came rather as a surprise to me. We Russians of advanced thought often agree with the reactionaries in one thing, that the "muzhik" is lazy. "If he were not so lazy there would not be famine; a big stick is good enough for him," says the reactionary. "If he were not so lazy, he could throw all that pile of corruption into Hades," say we. Overworked, the Russian peasant of course is not. Imagine in America a scene like this: A huge fellow lying on the ground in the market-place waiting for an employer. He may be asleep; all his concern is to expose the sole of his bare foot, on which is chalked the price he expects for his labor. Woe to the man who shall arouse him for bargaining!

Is there then real ability among them? You ask. Have any achieved success? To be sure, there is no railroad president among their number, but I know a heater-boss on the South Side, who is boss over five furnaces; he can make $130 to $150 per month. Now, to the ordinary reader this may seem of small account. But I know enough of steel making to assert that it is about as easy for an ordinary American college graduate to become a railroad president as for a Russian peasant to become a heater-boss. The work is skilled and the position is next to that of a roller-boss in responsibility.

The Old Believers show a remarkable weakness in their church organization, caused mainly by the ambiguous position of their priests. In the Greek church, ordination is a sacrament and can be performed only by a bishop. Now bishops can be appointed only by an assembly of bishops, and many Old Believers argue that the so-called "Austrian" bishops are not lawful and they recognize only the priests of the Orthodox church who come over to "old belief." Others either wrangle about their priests, or do not recognize any.

Out of the estimated 10,000 Russians in the state of Pennsylvania, in my opinion close to 3,000 are Old Believers. Of these over 1,000 live in Allegheny County and the vicinity. Yet scattered as they are these people have only one prayer house (in Essen), and one priest—a peasant, quite like any member of his flock, without education, although undeniably a good, sober man. He was born a Prussian citizen and served in the Prussian Guards, with whom he was at Sedan in 1870 as a non-commissioned officer. Afterward he became a Russian, and worked as a small boss on government railroads. Now here he is a primus inter pares with the Old Believers. His six-foot-three, or thereabout, looks extremely sound, and no one would think him to be sixty-seven years old. This priest, however, does not seem to be generally accepted, and many marriages await a blessing in the old country. Lack of organization is generally a weak point with Old Believers; indeed, the worst thing I know about them is that they are not strong union men and they are accused of having broken up the longshoremen's union in Erie. I do not know whether or not this charge be true, but I do know that the derisive "ba, ba's" hurled at them must have been no small factor in any estrangement of the Old Believers from the rest of the workingmen.

If to me should be put the question that so persists in the discussion of any group of immigrants: Are they desirable, those long-bearded Russians? I am almost ready to say no. Not because of their drunkenness; this can be cured, and must be cured. Sweden, thirty years ago, was a land of drunkards; not so today. Not because of their crowded, inhuman living; this can be remedied by regulations similar to those that in time of war are posted on every freight box-car in Russia—"Eight horses or 40 men only." But rather because of the fact that so few wish to become American citizens. I cannot see how a group of men can be desirable in any country which they regard as a purgatory, be they ignorant Russians peasants in America, or highly skilled Belgian engineers in Russia.

Together with the rest of the Russians—for the matter of that, with the rest of the Slavs—these Old Believers live as though yet on passage, in steerage, "temporarily," without thought of adapting themselves to the conditions that surround them, still less of improving them. They expect to go back home. Patriotism has nothing to do with their return. It is a matter of personal expediency.

A similar phenomenon exists in Russia. Our small industrial force there is more than half composed of such hybrid contingents—peasants coming to the industrial centers "to make money for taxes," living in conditions as bad, though hardly worse than those in Pittsburgh. But here the parallel ceases, for though a Russian city is by no means a great center of culture, its civilizing influence on the hordes of peasants who flock to it is much more rapid and effective then is the case in America. Here in this great country of freedom and enlightenment the wall that encircles ignorance seems to be higher and more impregnable than that of China.

Still, if I noticed among my people any inclination to stay here, it was among these same Old Believers. Many have made the journey here two, even three times, and have lost attachment to their native soil. Perhaps these would not now become farmers. If when Old Believers first arrive they could be helped to settle in their primordial capacity of husbandmen, the United States would have in them a good agricultural element. Not that I believe my long-bearded countrymen to be human material inferior for whatever purpose to any other people coming into the United States. But undoubtedly it would be a hard task and a long one to turn into Americans, men who for two hundred years have preserved their Russian traits in Poland. Possibly decent, neighborly Americans—not merely reformers and social workers—could conquer Russian ignorance and superstition if they could overcome their own disgust at the "hideous looks and ugly cries" of the foreigners. So Marius conquered the Cymbrians and Teutons by making his soldiers first face the barbarians without fear. Yet, it can hardly be.

It is up to the Russians themselves to convert their unenlightened compatriots to "Americanism," not using the term in the European sense of shrewdness and agility, but as meaning what is good in civic life. There are already Russians in America fitted for such work. The revolution has sent over here many men who in their own country were ready to risk their lives to teach people how to live like human beings. Where are you? Some, as did Garibaldi, may be making candles for a miserable pittance, lost in dreams of returning home to fight. Others, indignant at themselves and at their countrymen for giving themselves up to selfish pursuits when they have known the service to principals, are denouncing America for all kinds of things. Here is a task for you, *Gde vy? Ot-sovis!*

Source:

Russians in America: A Chronology & Fact Book, compiled and edited by Vladimir Wertsman. Dobbs Ferry, NY: Oceana Publications, 1977. pp. 61-66. Originally in *Survey,* vol. 33 (November 7, 1914), pp. 145-151.

SALVADORAN AMERICANS

El Salvador is the smallest Central American republic. It is bordered by Guatamala and Honduras and its eastern coastline meets the Pacific Ocean. El Salvador has been engaged in internal political strife for much of the 20th century which has caused many to migrate to the United States under the U.S. refugee policy as well as illegally. For some South and Central American immigrants coming to the United States can only improve their condition. This is the case for many Salvadoran immigrants whose country has been engaged in a brutal civil war since 1969 during which 40 to 50,000 civilians were murdered and over one million people fled the country. Roughly half of the Salvadorans that fled the conflict came to the United States. Roberto d' Aubuisson, leader of the right wing Nationalist Republic Alliance (ARENA) was largely responsible for the exodus. Aubuisson sent out death squads who killed thousands of people suspected of being leftists. The United States gave economic and military support estimated at $3 billion to Napoleon Duarte in the 1980s but the leader of the Christian Democratic Party was incapable of stopping the bloodshed, in large part because of internal corruption.

Although the severity of the political turmoil in El Salvador was sufficient to warrant political asylum from the United States, Salvadorans had difficulty coming to the United States under U.S. refugee policy. Part of the reason for this was that the peak of internal conflict in El Salvador came in the 1980s which was the same time the United States was reforming its immigration policy. The result of the change in policy was that only 2.7 percent of the Salvador asylum applicants were admitted to the United States between 1984 and 1988. In addition the impression among U.S. government officials, including the Immigration and Naturalization Service, that the plight of Salvadoran refugees was illegitimate. The intentions of the 1980 Refugee Act were honorable, however, they were not judiciously executed. The immigration laws that prevented many Salvadoran refugees from entering the United States were subsequently redressed to help protect Salvadoran refugees from being deported while the severity of the conditions in El Salvador were studied. Many Hispanic American refugees have begun to apply political pressure in the United States in an effort to persuade the United States to change its immigration policy.

A glimpse of the struggle that Salvadoran immigrants have gone through to migrate to the United States is provided in New Kids on the Block, an oral history of the experiences of immigrant teens in the United States. Francia, a teenage Salvadoran girl, was brought to the United States by her parents who had fled to the United States earlier to escape the political and economic chaos in El Salvador. Francia recalls her neighbor, a teacher, being killed by Salvadoran death squads. She was sad to leave her country but excited about being reunited with her parents. Francia's father worked as an asbestos removal laborer in the United States which enabled him to save enough money to have his family transported to the United States. The family is reunited and living happily in California sending all of their extra income to family members in El Salvador. Unfortunately, few Salvadoran families were as fortunate as Francia's during perhaps the most traumatic period of their nation's history.

FRANCIA

*Some people were what we call "disap-
peared." They had been captured and taken
away, maybe by a death squad, gangs of men
that frighten and kill people.*

Francia was born in San Salvador, the capital of the
small Central American country El Salvador. A
Pacific-coast nation, it borders Guatemala and
Honduras. For more than half of her life, the people
of El Salvador have been locked in a grim civil war.
The sides: the U.S.-backed ruling government and
its army with links to extreme right-wing death
squads versus the left-wing guerrillas. In less than a
decade, an estimated 70,000 have died and 500,000
have fled to the United States. Most Salvadorans
enter illegally, including Francia and her family.
This pint-sized ninth-grader talks about her life and
the day she learned she would finally be joining her
parents in America.

I remember that day—always. My brother,
Guillermo—that's William, Willie, in Spanish—
and I were in school. I was doing equations in math
when the principal came into the room. "Francia,"
she said, "your uncle is here. He says you have
something important to do." I went, "Uncle, what's
wrong?!" And he goes, "You're going to have a surprise. You are going to travel in one month to the
United States to live once more with your mother
and father."

Oh my, we were so happy! We were jumping.
We were running. We were doing this and that. My
parents sent money so my uncle could buy us some
new clothes and pay for the man to bring us here.
Many people from my country who travel to America suffer a lot. Some even die. My father and my
mother trusted this man. They told him to take
care of us. They also told him we would travel with
this lady, my uncle's girlfriend. My father was trying
to make a family again, like before.

Getting ready to leave made me remember the
day so long ago, I was only nine then, when my
father told me he was going to America by himself.
He took Willie and me to school. He said we had to
obey our mother and be nice kids. We said good-
bye. It was very sad. He came in illegally, but I
don't know how he did it. He never talks about it.

Many things were happening in my country. I
was very little, though, and couldn't understand it
all. Some people were what they call "disappeared."
They had been captured and taken away, maybe be
a death squad, gangs of men that frighten and kill
people. Everybody thinks that maybe the army and
the police have done that. But the army says it's the
guerrillas that take them to make them fight
against the army.

The man next door taught school. One day
some men came to his family house and told him
and his family to stand in the street in front of it.
The father, you could hear him saying, "Take anything; just please don't hurt us." The men shot the
father. The mother and the children watched.
Then the men took from the house and left. The
next day the neighbors were gone.

With my father, it's not that he got in trouble.
But the police were looking for a man, and they
confused my father with this guy. Because of the situation in my country, my father knew there could
be trouble. They might put him in jail, or worse.
The life was very hard. Prices were higher and
higher. People couldn't find work. My father wanted a better life for all of us.

El Salvador is a wonderful country. I feel sad
for all these problems. My father worked in a place
where they kill the beef—a slaughterhouse. Since
he was a little boy, my grandfather, his father,
taught him how to do that. That was my grandfather's work, too. My mother was a cook.

After my father went to America, my mother
took us to live with her mother. She lived in a little
town. Maybe a thousand people lived there, not as
many as students in this high school. It was hilly
and there were other little towns on the other sides
of the hills. The people who lived in these towns
planted and grew corn and wheat and every kind of
fruit—mangoes, papayas, oranges. When those
foods and fruits were ready to eat, they took [them]
and sold them.

A year after my father left, he wrote to my
mother, "I have saved money from my job. I want
you to come live with me." My mother told me and
Willie she had to go. They would save two times as
much money so we could also travel to the United
States. Again it was sad saying good-bye, this time
to my mother. Each month my mother and father
sent my grandmother money for the food, the
clothes, the books for school. We lived with her in
a big, big, house, and my other uncle and his wife
lived there, too. Out in the yard were the animals,
so many chickens and ducks and turkeys and dogs.
Every week my cousin Myra would come visit; she
was my same age. We used to go in the back where
there were the trees and very big rocks, and along
with Willie, we'd play soldiers there. If we walked a
little, we came to a river where my aunt would go

to wash the clothes. We used to go swimming there. It was such a nice place.

I didn't think to feel frightened. Everything we needed, my grandmother gave us. Sometimes my parents would call. We had no telephone. We had to go to the public place where there were phones. After one year of living without my brother and me, my mother couldn't stand it. She missed us so much. She worked with a lawyer to try to get papers of us, but it was no good. We would have to travel illegally.

At the border, though, we had a problem. The guards said, "You are supposed to be with your parents if you want to come to Honduras. You can't pass."

This man, the one my parents paid money, and my uncle's girlfriend and Willie and me went in a car from my grandmother's house to the town of San Miguel. We stayed there for one day and then we went in a different car to Honduras. That's the country right next to El Salvador. At the border, though, we had a problem. The guards said, "You are supposed to be with your parents if you want to come to Honduras. You can't pass." Willie and I started crying. We cried and cried. The border guards still said no.

We're Christian people; we started praying. God helped us because this man who was helping us talked to the guards and they said, "Okay, fine, you may go." Maybe he gave them a little money when he talked to them, but I think it was God. So we drove and we drove on little dirt roads. They were bumpy and we never seemed to stop.

Willie was sitting on the girlfriend's lap and he kept saying, "I have to go to the bathroom! I have to go to the bathroom." Finally, he couldn't stand it no more and WHOOOSH. He got her all wet. The lady went, "Oh, my dress!" That's when this man stopped the car and said, "Okay, okay, go to the bathroom." Willie said, "What for? It's too late." My brother was so embarrassed. I was eleven by then, but he was only eight.

It felt like forever, but we did get to Tegucigalpa, the capital of Honduras, where the airport was. We stayed in a hotel for the night and the next morning we sere supposed to take the airplane to Mexico, to Tijuana. But there was a problem with the engine. We had to wait one week until the next plane to Tijuana left. Finally, we got to Mexico and into another car to go to a hotel. That night this man's friend came to meet us. We were going to pass by car from Tijuana to the United States in the dark.

I was so scared, I was going, "Oh, oh, oh." At the border, we were supposed to say something in English. I don't remember what it was because I didn't speak any English then. The man told Willie and me and the lady to practice. We kept practicing and practicing while we drove closer to the border. We met a boy. He got in the car, too, to go across with us. And then you know what happened? I fell asleep with my brother and woke up when we were in Los Angeles already! We went, "What? When did we get here? Are we okay?"

They said, "Everything's okay. You're going to stay in this house until you father gets here."

I was frightened and my brother, too. Other people were staying there. They were speaking Spanish, but I don't think they were from El Salvador. I really don't know who they were, maybe church people. Pretty soon we were on another airplane, this time to Dallas, and then I saw my father waiting for us behind a railing. I just ran and hugged him and said, "Oh, Father, I love you!" And I hugged him some more. We got home and my father was so happy he was playing jokes on my mother.

She said, "Where are the children? Where are the children?"

He went, "They didn't come today. They come tomorrow."

"Oh, you're such a liar."

"No, I'm serious," he said.

Then we couldn't stand it. We went, "Ma, Ma!" We were so excited. It had been two years since we had seen my father and one year for my mother.

I'd have to say [my mother] works not because she wants to or because my father wants her to. She works because we need the money to send back to my country for the rest of the family. We are the only people who can help them. In my country, things are even worse than when we left: more expensive but no more jobs.

Today my father has a job taking asbestos out of buildings. It's dangerous, but it pays good. Before that, he'd worked in a factory, then as a janitor. My mother has a job cleaning house. She cleans two houses a day. It's a lot. First she was working for a lady, but that wasn't fair. My mother would clean two houses for fifty dollars each. This lady did nothing but take my mother to these houses. For that she got all the money from the second house. Now my mother is getting the work on her own.

I'd have to say she works not because she wants to or because my father wants her to. She works because we need the money to send back to my country for the rest of the family. We are the only people who can help them. In my country, things are even worse than when we left: more expensive but no more jobs.

We live in a three-room apartment. My father and my mother live in one room. Willie has one and I have the other. I have my little bed in it, blue curtains, a brown rug, and a dresser with a big mirror. I put my perfume on it and my jewelry.

My parents say, "It's not too soon to start to think about the future. You have to decide what you want to do." I like health careers. Since I was a little girl, I want to be a physician's assistant. I talk to my friends about this, too. They're from all different countries: Colombia, Peru, Equador, Mexico, Guatemala. I like them very much, but my parents say, "First you have to think about yourself. You have to study. Try to pass your classes. Don't cut."

There are some friends in school that push me to do some things that I don't want to do. I tell myself, "I don't have to do it, if I don't want to." They go, "Here, do you want to smoke?" I'm not going to smoke because my friends do. I say to myself, "Do what you think is right, not what other people say." I think it's right to study a lot. "If you study a lot," my parents say, "someday you're going to be somebody in this world. It's difficult; everything is difficult. If you do your best, you're going to make it."

My mother and father want me to get a high position. "Now that you have the opportunity," they say, "you have to take it. Maybe it will never be in front of you again." They tell me also I have to take care of myself. They remind me of all these girls that get pregnant so early. "Be careful on that point," they say. "Everybody makes errors. Sometimes people do things without thinking of the consequences. Think first of what you're going to do, why, and what might happen." To make sure, they don't let me date yet. My father says, maybe if I study enough, I can go out in a year or two. What can I do but obey them?

We read the Bible together. We go to the Baptist church on Sundays. We also have meetings on Wednesday night at 7:30 P.M. and on Saturdays; the teenagers have meetings in the church at 4:30. The pastor is from Mexico; his wife is from Nicaragua. Everybody else is from El Salvador. It helps me so I don't feel completely cut off from my country. For my birthday, it was in April, the church gave me a big party. It was my fifteenth birthday. In my country, we celebrate the fifteenth as important, instead of the sixteenth. I got balloons and earrings and this barrette.

Sometimes I think I would like to go back to my country, see my family, my friends. Life is very different here. Before I came, my mother sent me beautiful pictures from the United States. There were flowers and everything. So when I was in my country, I thought everything here must be beautiful and clean. When you are in a foreign country, everybody thinks being here must be like heaven. But that's not what it is. There is something different about this country. It's hard to describe.

One of the things I like about here is that you can get more things. Like Willie wanted a bicycle. In my country he couldn't get it. Here, he did. My mother has eight pairs of shoes. In my country, she only had one. But what I don't like is that it's such a dangerous country. Well, not in all parts, but where I live there are drugs and gangs and stuff. In my country I didn't even know what drugs meant. In my country people are still innocent until they are like fifteen years old. My little brother, he knows so many things and he's only nine. When I was nine years old, I knew almost nothing about life. I just knew how to go to school, how to eat, how to play.

In my country, I think there is more freedom—no, that's not the word I mean. In some ways it is. In some ways it isn't. In El Salvador you may go to this person's house and that person's house and the people are so nice. You know them and they know you. They won't hurt you like they might in this country. In this country you can't trust anybody, because you don't know what this person wants from you. That's some of the difference between this country and that country. I wish both countries could always be safe for the people.

Source:

New Kids on the Block: Oral Histories of Immigrant Teens, compiled by Janet Bode. New York: Franklin Watts, 1989. pp. 29-37.

*I*llegal aliens live a precarious life in the United States. Immigrants often risk everything to come to the United States with only a dream and their determination to sustain them. Often the dream is to earn enough money to return to their home country and construct a better life for themselves and their loved ones. Although there are laws in the United States designed to protect illegal aliens they often live with the constant fear that they are being hunted by the Immigration and Naturalization Service (INS) and risk deportation or incarceration just by virtue of being in the United States. In reality, the INS exerts only a small portion of its resources on apprehending illegal aliens who have made it past border inspections. And, for the most part, the fear of being turned in to INS authorities is unfounded because federal law prevents U.S. citizens (including employers) from turning illegal aliens in to authorities unless they are suspected of criminal activity.

Still, in the minds of Salvadoran refugees the gap between the myth and reality of deportation is inconsequential. Their situation in the United States is somewhat unique. The U.S. government has been reluctant to grant Salvadoran refugees asylum because of insufficient evidence suggesting that they are fleeing from a hostile environment rather than coming to the United States for economic reasons. The position of the U.S. government regarding asylum has historically been that refugees are welcomed into the United States if returning to their home country could endanger their lives. In 1980 civil war broke out in El Salvador between military leaders backed by the United States and leftist guerrillas during which 40,000 to 50,000 civilians were killed. Some civilians were killed in death-squads. As a result of the bloodshed one million Salvadorans fled the region many of whom entered the United States illegally.

The reality of the Salvadoran struggle is becoming more palpable and the U.S. asylum policy has grown more lenient. One of the reasons the legitimacy of their plight has become more apparent is the literary work of Mario Bencastro. Bencastro, a Salvadoran American author, documented the struggle of Salvadoran immigrants during the long period of unrest in El Salvador in acclaimed novels such as Odyessey to the North (1998) and A Shot in the Cathedral (1993). The latter novel describes how Archbishop Oscar Romero was assassinated shortly after making a plea for peace. The books have alerted Americans to the pain and suffering involved in leaving a beloved country in turmoil and starting a new life elsewhere.

Apart from living with the fear of deportation and being exploited by employers in the U.S. Salvadoran refugees face the task of building lives for themselves in a foreign land. A recent fire in a Deer Park, New York apartment building serves as a reminder that all that they are fighting for could be lost in an instant. One of the tenants, Ana Estela Lopez, a Salvadoran refugee who works for $5.50 per hour washing dishes, saw her modest dream of saving enough money to bring back to El Salvador to open a clothing store and build a new home go up in flames. Her life savings of $4800, which she kept in the apartment because she was afraid to open an account at a bank, was lost in the fire. However, Ms. Lopez was thankful that she and her children escaped with their lives. Others were less fortunate. The tragedy is indicative of the long uphill battle Salvadorans face tying to build a better life for themselves in the United States. But for many Salvadorans it is a risk worth taking because in the long run, with hard work and faith in God, they are confident they will persevere.

AFTER FIRE, HARD LIVES GET HARDER

DEER PARK, N.Y., May 2—For 14 months, ever since she swam across the Rio Grande to come to New York, Ana Estela López has lived in fear. Fear that the police may stop her and report her to the immigration authorities because she had come to the country illegally. Fear that she may lose her $5.55-an-hour job in a chocolate factory. Fear that a car may run over her husband, who used to ride his bicycle to work every day before it was stolen.

Any of those events would have shattered Ms. López's version of the American dream: the opportunity to save $40,000 in a few years to return to her country, El Salvador, with enough money to open a clothing store and build a brick house.

"Do you think that's too much?" asked Ms. López, 36. "I don't know. Maybe I dared to dream too much. I get carried away sometimes."

On her list of apprehensions, Ms. López said, it ever occurred to her to include the fear of a raging fire. For in the end it was a fire, roaring through her building before dawn Saturday, that derailed Ms. López's careful plans. The fire, which the authorities suspect was deliberately set, killed 3 of her 33 neighbors, including a 5-year-old girl, injured 16 others and left every surviving tenant in the two-story building homeless.

The Red Cross took the survivors to the Deer Park Motor Inn, where they will sleep tonight and perhaps another night, Red Cross officials said. After that, it is not clear what will happen to the 30 survivors from 28 West Hills Road, many of them undocumented immigrants from El Salvador who worked long hours washing dishes or mowing lawns to make ends meet and send money home.

Yet, except for a few moments of sadness when they remember the dead, the people who are staying in the motel do not seem to despair over their fate. "God will provide" is their mantra. Their experiences—years of poverty, a devastating war in their country and hard work in the United States—has made them resilient and reluctant to complain even after tragedy.

"It is strange," Ms. López said about her apparent lack of emotions, "but I've seen worse."

Ms. López, who lived in apartment No. 2 on the first floor with her husband and a friend, arrived in New York and in February of 1998, bruised and famished. A friend had to nurse her back to health. Her legs and arms were infected, thorns deeply embedded in her skin. Her toenails had been torn during a 49-day trip from El Salvador to Houston, which included a hike through mountains for four days and four nights.

In Santa María Ostuma, her hometown, she left her 21-year-old daughter and a 2-year-old grandson. It is in part for their sake, Ms. López said, that she dared to come to the United States alone. Her husband, Cristobal Vásquez, 37, joined her last August.

Mr. Vásquez works as a dishwasher from 4 P.M. to 2 or 3 A.M. every day to support his own children, ages 14 and 8, and his parents, all of whom remain in El Salvador. Between the two, they send $475 home every month.

Undocumented immigrants like him have little choice but to silently endure the long hours, he said. "When it comes time to punch the clock at work," he said, "those who have papers leave, and those who don't stay and work."

Ms. López and Mr. Vásquez shared the $700 rent for their one bedroom apartment with a friend, 20-year-old Aracely Zelaya. Together, the couple had been able to save $4,800, which Ms. López kept in the pocket of her one pair of good trousers, handing in the closet. The fire destroyed the pants and the money. The couple had not opened a bank account because they do not have a Social Security number or any other paper that identifies them as living and working in the United States.

"I know it doesn't sound like much to most people, but to us it is more than we've ever had," Ms. López said. "It was everything."

Next door to them, in apartment 3, a couple with two children had carved an extra room out of the living room to accommodate four men, relatives and friends, who needed a place to stay after their long days at work. The four men—Reynaldo Giannis, 33; Arcides Bonilla, 17; José Oscar Bonilla, 18, and Irno Acosta, 38—are from the same town in El Salvador, Cantón Ocote, on the border with Honduras, and work as dishwashers or busboys in a Greek restaurant in Huntington Station.

The men shared the $600 rent while the couple, Faustino and Adoración Bonilla, paid for their grocery bills and all the utilities. Everybody sent home large portions of their paychecks.

Seven months after he arrived in New York three and a half years ago, Mr. Giannis was run over by a car while he rode his bicycle to work. He was in a coma for eight days. After 14 months of therapy, he was able to raise his right arm up to his elbow. By now, he proudly reaches his nose.

But the accident left him incapacitated to work too hard and, therefore, unable to send more than $200 a month to his family, a wife and three children, ages 8, 7 and 5.

"I'm thinking of returning home," Mr. Giannis said. "But it is unclear what I will do there."

The return is difficult, Mr. Giannis said, because to pay part of the $5,500 it cost him to come to the United States through the Mexican border, he sold the family's only possession: three cows whose milk supplemented the family's diet of rice, beans and corn. Besides, he said, with a weak arm, it is doubtful that he can ever work the land again.

In the basement lived a family of 11 people—a couple and their six children, one of whom is married and has two little girls of her own, Roxana, 3, and Maritza, 18 months. They had been living in the building for seven years, said Adelaida, the mother, who declined to give her last name. The family was just getting used to life together after 12 years of separation.

Adelaida's husband left El Salvador in 1987. She followed a year later. Together, they started to bring their children, one at a time, as they saved the $4,500 that smugglers charged to guide them from El Salvador to New York. The last child, a 13-year-old boy, arrived two months ago. They paid $865 in rent, which they found especially difficult these days. Adelaida said her husband's factory closed last month and he had not been able to find another job.

When she thinks of complaining, though, she thinks of María Chicas, the 37-year-old women from apartment 5 who died in the fire while trying to rescue her 5-year-old daughter, María Aurora.

Ms. Chicas's brother, Clemente Chicas, tried to save her, he said. He remembers hugging her burning body in the darkened hallway and forcing her to jump off the second floor window. But, at the last minute, she screamed, "Mi niña!!"—my girl!— and ran off to get her. The two died in the fire.

Ms. Chcias's other daughter, 1-year-old Agustina Elizabeth, escaped in the arms of her father, José Pineda. A friend who shared the apartment with the family, Paola Perla, jumped from the window too and survived.

Next door, in apartment 4, a 40-year-old man, Luis Cruz, jumped to his death.

Mr. Chicas, 42, knows he is lucky to have survived. He pats his chest, where it hurts, and raises his shirt to show a big scratch from the fall. But his heart hurts the most, he said, heavy with pain over his sister's death and with worry over his new responsibilities.

Ms. Chicas left behind five children in El Salvador. Because she was their sole provider, she sent them money every month from her job as a cook in a deli. Mr. Chcas, who followed his sister to the United States so that he too could support his family—eight children and a wife—said that his sister's children are now his responsibility.

"I just have to work harder," he said, dry-eyed. "It's what I've always done."

Source:
New York Times, May 3, 1999.

SAMOAN AMERICANS

May Lee Queen, born to a Samoan mother, was raised on a New Mexico farm. Her tale provides a dramatic saga of an immigrant family's search for a new home. Captain John Lee, May's father, was born in Scotland in 1835 but, while still an infant, moved with his family to Connecticut. At the age of 14, John Lee struck out for a life at sea as a trader. Sailing around the world three times, he discovered a small island in the South Pacific and named it Lee's Island.

With Samoa joining the South Pacific trade circuit, Lee began to visit there as well. The increasing agricultural trade along with the arrival of European missionaries led to an intertwining of European and Samoan cultures on the island. May's mother, Mary Purcell, was a daughter of an English missionary and granddaughter of King Mata Afa of Samoa. Reflecting a growing Samoan emphasis on education, she was also an Oxford graduate.

John and Mary met and married in Samoa, acquired a plantation, and had nine children. Desiring an American education for the children, the Lees left for the United States in 1879 well before most Samoan immigration to the United States a century later. They settled on a Richmond, Virginia farm but, for health reasons, moved to the Southwest. They went first to West Texas, then to New Mexico in 1886 with eleven children, five covered wagons, 200 head of cattle, and 60 horses. Catastrophically, the Lees lost most of their livestock en route. As May described,

> I remember waking up one morning and hearing my mother crying. I looked out and it seemed to me that I saw piles and piles of dead stock all around us. The cattle and horses had died from drinking the alkali water. . .My father was very much discouraged and took what was left. . .

They subsequently settled as farmers raising potatoes and later established a dairy ranch in White Oaks.

Samoans held an expansive view of extended family bonds and the Lee family certainly perpetuated the tradition. Their family was so large their residence became known as Leesville. May recounted the many trades John practiced through his long life and how his children grew up with considerable family pride. May Lee Queen married and settled in California as did a sister, predating a large future wave of Samoan immigrants to the state.

PIONEER STORY—MAY LEE QUEEN

Carrizozo, New Mexico

My father, Captain John Lee, was born November 27, 1835 in Edinburgh Scotland. His parents came to the United States when he was eighteen months old and lived in Moodus; Connecticut. When he was fourteen years old, he ran away to sea. He followed the sea for many years and came to own his own sailing vessel. He traded extensively in the South Seas and dealt mostly in copra. He went around the world three times in a sailing vessel, and discovered a small island that was called Lee's Island. When I was a small girl in school at White Oaks, New Mexico this island was shown on the maps of my geography.

My father married Mary Purcell, who was a daughter of an English missionary of the Church of England, and a graduate of Oxford. My mother was the granddaughter of King Mata Afa, who was king of the island of Samoa. My father and mother were married at Apia Samoa. They owned a plantation near Apia and lived there for several years. They had nine children born on this island.

Father decided that he wanted his children educated in the United States, so they left Apia, Samoa on a sailing vessel for the States. They were six months on the sea. They ran into "calms" and were delayed for days and weeks. Their water and food supplies ran short and they were put on short rations. Just before the food was entirely gone they made the port of Honolulu and the vessel was restocked. They landed at San Francisco about the year 1879.

After visiting my father's family in Connecticut and traveling around a good bit they decided to settle in Richmond, Virginia. Father bought a farm near Richmond and lived there for about a year and a half. Mother and the children had chills and fever and were sick so much that they decided to move.

Father had always wanted a cattle ranch, so they moved down to southwest Texas and bought a cattle ranch about twenty miles from Brackettsville, Texas. The family came by train from Virginia to Texas and had been there only a short time when I was born on June 1st, 1882. About two years later my mother had another baby girl, and she and I were the only children born in the United States. While we were living there Father met a man named McBee who had a ranch at White Oaks, New Mexico. He was always telling Father what a great country New Mexico was, so in 1886 my father sold out his place near Brackettsville and started for New Mexico.

Our family consisted of Father, Mother and the eleven children. My two oldest brothers and my oldest sister were married, so they and their families came with us to New Mexico. We were in five covered wagons drawn by horses. Father had about 200 head of cattle and about 60 horses. The boys drove the stock and the ladies did the cooking. I was about four years old at the time but one or two incidents stand out very clearly in my memory. We were very much afraid of the Indians as we had heard of the terrible things that they had done to wagon trains. We were not molested by them at all, tho' we saw them on several occasions.

I remember waking up one morning and hearing my mother crying. I looked out and it seemed to we that I saw piles and piles of dead stock all around us. The cattle and horses had died from drinking the alkali water. This happened where Seven Rivers emptied into the Pecos River. My father was very much discouraged and took what was left of the cattle and horses and went up an the Peñasco in New Mexico. He bought a farm and we lived there for about a year. We raised lots of potatoes that year and the boys sold them. Father decided to go on to White Oaks, New Mexico, to where the McBee's lived so he sold out the farm and what cattle he had left and we moved to White Oaks. My married brothers and my married sister and their families moved back to Texas. We went to the MeBee ranch which was about two miles from White Oaks. We lived on this ranch a year and Father ran a dairy and sold the milk in White Oaks. At the end of the year Father got us a house nearer town, just above the Old Abe Mine pump station. He opened up a meat shop in town. We children went to school and I remember one teacher especially, named Wharton. The geographys that we studied showed Lee's Island on the map and the teacher often told the class that it was our father who had discovered this island.

My brother Bob married and worked in the South Homestake Mine. He drilled into a "dud" [a percussion cap that had not been exploded] and it blew up and killed him. This was about 1892. There was such a big family of us and all the married ones settled around my father and they called our place Leesville. There were about five families of us. Father used to drive the stage to Socorro. I remember once that he did not get home when the stage was due and my mother got very uneasy. The stage was often held up and we were afraid it had been held up and my father killed. He was a night and day late and just about the time my brothers and some friends got their horses saddled to go look for him we saw the stage coming over the hill into White Oaks. They had run into a terrible snow storm and the horses could not pull the stage through the storm. It was very cold and my father and the passengers were almost frozen. He stopped the stage at our house and the passengers came in and got warmed up and drank some coffee before Father took the stage an into the town. Father wore a beard and I remember that it was all covered with ice and snow and you could only see his eyes. I grew up with Edward L. Queen in White Oaks and we were married in the Methodist Church there on January 1st, 1902, by the Reverend Sam Allison, who now lives in El Paso, Texas.

We have three children, two boys and one girl, all married, and one grandson and one granddaughter, who all now live in California. Of my father's family there are only three left, myself, one brother, Jim Lee , who lives in Douglas, Arizona and one sister Mrs. Ray Lemon, who lives in Carrizozo. My father died in Douglas, Arizona in 1920, at the age of eighty-five years. My mother died in Carrizozo at eighty-one years, in 1925.

Mr. Queen and I leave White Oaks some times for years at a time but we always come back. We have our home here. Judge Andrew R. Hudepeth, who owned the property in White Oaks known as Leesville, made me a gift of a deed to this property in 1936. I am very glad to own our old home.

NARRATOR: May Lee Queen, White Oaks, New Mexico, Aged 56 years.

Source:

Library of Congress. *American Life Histories: Manuscripts from the Federal Writers' Project, 1936-1940* from the American Memory website (http://memory.loc.gov/ammem/wpaintro/wpa-home.html).

*E*ni F. H. Faleomavaega (1943-), U.S. Representative from American Samoa, attended the University of Houston and the University of California at Berkeley. He served in the U.S. Army during the Vietnam War, and later worked as Deputy Attorney General and Lieutenant Governor of American Samoa. After a brief term in Congress during the 1970s, Faleomavaega returned to Capitol Hill in 1988, and became a leader among members of Congress opposed to nuclear tests by the French government in the south Pacific. By the late 1990s, he was the sixth ranking Democrat in the House of Representatives.

On May 26, 1992, he made a speech in recognition of Asian Pacific Heritage Month. In the course of his talk, he touched on a number of subjects important to Americans of Asian and Pacific descent, as well as topics relevant to all Americans. He stressed the significance of the Pacific nations in the twenty-first century, which he called "the Pacific Century." Faleomavaega also noted the significant contributions of Asian Americans and those from the Pacific islands, then turned to a vigorous discussion of American relations with the greatest of Pacific economic powers, Japan.

After his opening pleasantries, Faleomavaega questioned Americans' focus on affairs in Europe and the Middle East, to the detriment of the Pacific area. He observed the emergence of the "Pacific Rim" as a focal point of economic activity in the last quarter of the twentieth century, and though Japan is the most recognized powerhouse of Pacific trade, it is closely followed by a number of others. Thus Faleomavaega noted the "Four Tigers" of the Pacific Rim: South Korea, Taiwan, Hong Kong, and the prosperous city-state of Singapore. Furthermore, there were the up-and-coming giants, the "Little Dragons," as he referred to Indonesia, Thailand, and Malaysia. He did not mention China, though by a number of estimates this populous nation was bound to become an economic superpower in coming decades.

Faleomavaega provided a number of statistics regarding the growth of U.S. trade with Pacific Rim nations, then shifted his focus to the contributions of people from the Pacific living in the United States. He noted a variety of prominent figures in science, the arts, and business. In the latter category, he might have also added the Chinese American entrepreneurs William Mow (1936-), founder of apparel maker Bugle Boy, and Charles B. Wang (1944-), CEO of Computer Associates.

Among prominent Asians and Pacific islanders in America, Faleomavaega paid particular attention to sports stars. Some of these were widely known, such as martial arts expert Bruce Lee, whereas others were less familiar to the population as a whole. One, Olympic diver Greg Louganis, had already become such a mainstream superstar that, ironically, people were less likely to know of his Samoan heritage.

Faleomavaega's concentration on sports figures may have resulted from a fact he noted himself in referring to Lee, who "destroy[ed] the stereotype of the passive, quiet Asian male." Certainly Salevaa Atisanoe, a Samoan sumo wrestler who had risen to prominence in Japan, defied such stereotypes, and Faleomavaega indulged in a lengthy digression regarding the quarter-ton athlete, who happened to be his relative.

The subject of Atisanoe, who seemed not to receive as much respect in Japan as native sumo wrestlers, dovetailed with Faleomavaega's next point, the lack of recognition accorded to Japanese American veterans in World War II. The latter had served with distinction, despite the fact that many of their relatives back home were imprisoned in concentration camps out of fear that they might aid the enemy.

The latter topic brought Faleomavaega to the heart of his speech, a discussion of U.S. relations with Japan. With the latter's emergence as a powerful economic force beginning in the 1970s, Americans had become increasingly resentful of Japan, and as Faleomavaega noted, had come to believe in a number of myths. Among these was the idea that trade with Japan was purely one-way, with the Japanese selling and Americans buying—an assertion Faleomavaega counteracted with a number of statistics.

But of course facts and figures, as Faleomavaega noted, are not at the heart of the misunderstanding. For that reason, he recommended an overhaul of the American education system. He also discussed racial relations between whites, blacks, and Asians, particularly in light of the racial violence that had recently swept Los Angeles following the acquittal of four white police officers for the beating of black motorist Rodney King.

With the end of the Cold War and the removal of the Soviet threat to American stability, Faleomavaega observed, Americans were looking for another enemy; rather than pointing fingers across the sea, he suggested, what the people of the United States most needed was to take a searching look at themselves.

Asian Pacific American Heritage Month 1992: Entering into the Pacific Century

Mr. Speaker, I rise today, along with my esteemed colleagues from Hawaii, The Honorable Patsy Mink, and The Honorable Neil Abercrombie, to commemorate the deep and rich legacy of Americans who have come from Asia and the Pacific Islands. Due to prior commitments in their districts, our distinguished colleague from Guam, The Honorable Ben Blaz, and the respected delegation from California, The Honorable Robert Matsui and The Honorable Norman Mineta, were not able to be present. Their thoughts and hearts are with us today, however, and I submit their statements for the record.

This month, as many of you know, is a special month. President Bush has honored and recognized the contributions of our people by proclaiming May as Asian Pacific American heritage month. The president's action is welcome, overdue, and only fitting, as our nation prepares for the twenty-first century, the dawning of the Pacific Century.

It has always bothered me that our presidents visit Europe so often that they qualify for "Frequent Flier" status, yet they have rarely traveled to the Asia-Pacific region. I believe this has sent the wrong message to the countries of the Pacific, that our friends there continue to take a backseat to Europe and the Middle East when it comes to U.S. foreign policy.

It was thus noteworthy to see President Bush make his first trip abroad to our part of the world. As the President declared early after taking office—America, too, is a Pacific nation and we must renew our determination to strengthen ties and relationships with our allies and partners in the Pacific. Since then, the President and Vice-President have attempted to make good on this commitment by coming to the Pacific on four separate occasions.

It's a beginning, yet, still, not enough attention is being paid by our government to the Asia-Pacific region. The evolving events of the world make it imperative that this change.

In this decade and into the next century, the countries of the Pacific shall play a more crucial role in the economic, political, strategic and security needs of the United States and the world. As has been often-stated, the twenty-first century—the Pacific Century—shall truly be an era marked with miraculous economic advancement by this the world's most dynamic and rapidly developing region.

As many of you know, I was born and raised in the Pacific and my love and interest lie in this part of the world. Although I do not claim to be an expert, my years of travel throughout the Pacific, followed by years of service as a member of the house foreign affairs committee and subcommittee on Asian and Pacific affairs, have given me a perspective which I would like to share with you.

The economy of the Asia-Pacific region today is staggering in size and breathtaking in growth.

Last year, according to the U.S. Department of Commerce, our nation did just shy of $325 billion worth of total trade with the region—easily matching U.S. trade with Europe, and throwing in another $135 billion in excess of our trade relationship with Europe.

Since 1981, U.S. trade with the Asia-Pacific region has expanded by 148%, and is expected to increase to $400 billion by the end of this decade.

Almost two-thirds of the world's population resides in Asia and the Pacific, which perhaps accounts for the Pacific basin's production of two-thirds of the world's gross national product.

Japan and America—key trading partners—alone, accounted for 40% of the world's GNP last year.

Also, in 1991, according to Commerce Department figures, the Asia-Pacific countries purchased close to $125 billion worth of U.S. products. It is significant to note that American exports to the region have increased by 130% since 1981.

South Korea, Taiwan, Hong Kong and Singapore—known in Asia as the "Four Tigers" for their astoundingly rapid economic growth, have been joined by a new wave of "Little Dragons," Indonesia, Malaysia and Thailand, as the economic miracle has spread in the Asia-Pacific region. All of these countries have vigorously expanding economies, some up to 11% annually, placing them among the fastest growing in the world.

These facts paint a picture that has many experts in international finance and economics predicting that the Asia-Pacific region will shortly replace the North Atlantic as the center of world trade. My feeling is that this has already occurred. Yes, my friends, the Pacific Century has indeed begun.

And during this month for celebration, it is only fitting that we honor our fellow Americans of Asian Pacific descent—both from the past and the present—that have blessed and enriched our nation. I submit that Asian Pacific Americans have certainly been an asset to our country's development, and it is most appropriate that our President and Congress have proclaimed May as Asian Pacific heritage month.

The people of the Pacific have contributed much to America's development in the sciences and medicine. For example, in 1899 a Japanese immigrant arrived on the shores of this nation. After years of study and work, this man, Dr. Hideyo Noguchi, isolated the syphilis germ, leading to a cure for this deadly, wide spread disease. For decades, Dr. Makio Murayama conducted vital research in the U.S. that laid the groundwork for combating sickle-cell anemia. In 1973, Dr. Leo Esaki, an Asian immigrant to our country, was awarded the Nobel prize in physics for his electron tunneling theories. And, in engineering, few have matched the several architectural masterpieces created by the genius of Chinese American, I. M. Pei.

Major contributions to U.S. business and industry have also been made by Asian Pacific Americans. Wang laboratories, the innovative business enterprise in computer research and development, was founded in 1955 by Chinese American, An Wang. This nation's largest Tungsten refinery was built in 1953 by industrialist K. C. Li and his company, The Wah Chang Corporation. And, in 1964, an immigrant from Shanghai, China, Gerald Tsai, started from scratch an investment firm, The Manhattan Fund, which today has well over $270 million in assets.

In the entertainment and sports fields, Chinese American martial arts expert Bruce Lee entertained the movie audiences of this nation, while destroying the stereotype of the passive, quiet Asian male. World-class conductor Seiji Ozawa has led the San Francisco and Boston symphonies through many brilliant performances over the years.

A native Hawaiian named Duke Kahanamoku shocked the world by winning the Olympic gold medal in swimming seven decades ago followed by Dr. Sammy Lee, a Korean American who won the Olympic gold medal in high diving. Then there was Tommy Kono of Hawaii, also an Olympic gold medalist in weightlifting. And, yes, perhaps the greatest Olympic diver ever known to the world, a Samoan American by the name of Greg Louganis—whose record in gold medals and national championships will be in the books for a long time. This year, Japanese American Kristi Yamaguichi's enthralling gold medal ice-skating performance at the winter Olympics continues the legacy of milestone achievements by Asian Pacific Americans.

In professional sports, of course, we have Michael Chang blazing new paths in tennis, Pacific-Islanders Brian Williams and Michael Jones of world rugby, and the tens of dozens of Asian Pacific Americans who have made their mark as professional football players in the National Football League.

As our nation enters into the Pacific Century, Asian Pacific Americans can hold their heads high, knowing the contributions of our people have ensured America is, despite her problems, the greatest democracy in the world.

We also have an Asian Pacific American who is making his mark on history, not in or country, but in Japan. Samoan American Salevaa Atisanoe is a 578-pound sumo wrestler in Japan who goes by the name of Konishiki. Salevaa, Konishiki, incidentally, also happens to be a relative of mine.

Konishiki is the first foreigner in this centuries-old sport to reach the rarified air of sumo's second-highest rank. More importantly, though, he is on the verge of attaining the exalted status of grand champion or Yokozuna. No foreigner has ever been permitted to fill this position, as the Japanese associate the Yukozuna with the essence of Shinto's guardian spirits. The ascendance to grand champion status goes to the heart of the Japanese religion and culture.

Although Konishiki has defeated the only existing Yokozuna and has an excellent tournament record, a controversy has erupted as to whether he has the necessary "character" to become a grand champion. By merit and skill, it is uncontested that Konishiki qualifies as a Yokozuna. Many commentators speculate it is because he is not Japanese that he is being denied promotion. For the benefit of my cousin and relations between the U.S. and Japan, I hope that this situation does not escalate into a burning issue of racism.

In honoring Asian Pacific American that have served to enrich our country, I would be remiss, as a

Viet-Nam veteran, if I did not honor the memory of the Asian Pacific American who served in the U.S. Army's 100th Battalion and 442nd Infantry Combat Group. History speaks for itself in documenting that none have shed their blood more valiantly for America than the Japanese Americans that served in these units while fighting enemy forces in Europe during World War II.

The records of the 100th Battalion and 442nd Infantry are without equal. These Asian Pacific American units suffered an unprecedented casualty rate, and received over 18,000 individual decorations, many posthumous, for valor in battle. With so much blood spilled warranting the high number of medals given, it is disturbing and unusual that only one medal of honor, 24 distinguished service crosses and 60 silver stars were awarded. The great number of Asian Pacific American lives lost decreed that more of these ultimate symbols of sacrifice should have been awarded. Even so, the 442nd combat group emerged as the most decorated combat unit of its size in the United States Army.

I am proud to say that we can count The Honorable Daniel K. Inouye a recipient of the distinguished service cross, and the late, highly-respected Senator Spark Matsunaga, both from Hawaii, as members from Congress that distinguished themselves in battle as soldiers of The 100th Battalion and 442nd Infantry.

These Japanese Americans paid their dues in blood to protect our nation from its enemies. It is a shameful black mark on the history our country that when the patriotic survivors of The 100th Battalion and 442nd Infantry returned to the U.S., many were reunited with families that were locked up behind barbed-wire fences, living in concentration camps. You might be interested to know, my colleagues on The Hill, Congressmen Robert Matsui and Norman Mineta, were children of the concentration camps.

The wholesale and arbitrary abolishment of the constitutional rights of these brave Americans will forever serve as a reminder and testament that this must never be allowed to occur again. It was outright racism and bigotry in its ugliest form. I pray that this will never happen again in America.

Which brings me to the increasingly volatile and complicated subject of our country's state of relations with the nation of Japan.

With Japan leading the way amongst democratic countries of the Asia-Pacific Region—being the world's greatest creditor nation, the world's largest donor of foreign aid, and America's strongest financial partner and ally in the defense of our strategi-

cally important sea lanes of the Pacific basin—I am concerned with the hostility mounting in the U.S. against our longtime friend and ally.

Many have said that with the recent collapse of the Soviet Union and the end of the cold war, Americans just have to find someone or something to worry about. Numerous polls verify that Japan is the new public enemy number one.

The myth of the voracious Japanese economic machine that plays by unfair rules, consume anything in its path and gives nothing back in return, has been set upon by certain politicians needing a quick public relations fix, corporate America facing sagging sales, and workers running out of unemployment checks. Jumping on the Japan—bashing wagon is fashionable and easy, and a good way to absolve responsibility for the state of our nation's ills. Unfortunately, it does little to improve our situation but set loose a Pandora's box of hysteria, nonsense, and outright bigotry, compounding the already difficult period of development our country faces.

When you look at the fact—the statistics of our own Department of Commerce—Japan is actually one of America's best customers, buying over $48 billion of U.S. goods in 1991. The Japanese buy more U.S. goods than any nation in the world, except for our neighbor, Canada. Since 1987, Japan has increased import from our country by 70%, and in the same period reduced its trade surplus with the U.S. by 30%.

Taking a longer look back over the last decade, Commerce Department figures reveal that U.S. exports to Japan rose by 117%, which is more rapid growth than our exports to the rest of the world over the past ten years.

It is significant to note, also, that the latest figures on Japanese investment in the U.S. show that $130 billion was added to our economy in 1990. The Department of Commerce estimates for 1990 that Japanese investment produced 897,000 jobs for America's labor force. I would be interested to know how many Americans lost their jobs that year as a result of U.S. corporations and companies deciding, for cheaper labor costs, to set up factories and operations in foreign countries.

Rather than mindlessly point the finger of blame at Japan, perhaps we in this country should look inward for the cause of America's economic malaise. Many experts in the field suggest that Americans must address fundamental problem with our society that lead to problems with the economy. In short, we must put our house in order.

The first job is to rigorously renovate our educational system, from kindergarten on up. America's present system is not producing enough skilled workers, managers, and leaders that can compete effectively in the international marketplace.

We must also concentrate on producing engineers and specialists in math and the sciences, vocations that produce actual products and technology. Too many of our brightest minds are diverted to professions that deal with non-productive paper shuffling for profit. As an attorney, I know a little about this.

The second major task is to rid the public and private sectors of the tremendous debt incurred in the 1980s. In the span of one decade, the U.S. went from the world's greatest creditor nation to one of its worst debtors. The American people, on the federal, state, local and personal levels, must resolve to rid ourselves of this heavy anchor, and start saving. Only then can we hope to compete freely and unburdened, with sufficient capital, as a creditor nation.

Returning to the phenomenon of Japan-bashing, this mindless behavior has precipitated all over the U.S. increasingly ugly and sometimes violent action against Americans—our Americans of Asian Pacific descent. Distinction as to ethnicity, let alone nationality, seems not to be evident. Asian features alone have provoked attacks and beatings against Japanese Americans, Chinese Americans, Thai Americans and Korean Americans, where the assailants thought the victims were Japanese nationals.

as the U.S. economy has remained stagnant, documented incidents of racist graffiti, name-calling, verbal threats, fire-bombings and physical assaults have spread like wildfire from California to Colorado to Michigan to North Carolina and to New York. The pattern of Asian American killings, such as Jim Loo's beating death last year in Raleigh, Vincent Chin's clubbing murder in Detroit in 1982, the machine gun massacre of five Indochinese kids in 1989 at Stockton, and the unexplained murder of a Japanese businessman in Ventura county a few months ago, underscore that these are not isolated incidents.

Taken as a whole, this is clearly a crisis of national dimension brewing for our Asian Pacific American communities. Each survivor of the Japanese American concentration camps and WWII hysteria has commented—it is happening all over again.

So, how do we stop the wholesale destruction of our birthrights as U.S. citizens that occurred in the 1940s from becoming the same nightmare for us today?

I believe Stewart Kwoh of the Asian Pacific American Legal Center of Southern California has some good ideas.

He recommends that we not remain complacent about Japan-bashing but that we should take a very active stance. Our Asian Pacific communities must come together for protection, and not remain isolated, fragmented and thus vulnerable.

Our communities must also aggressively articulate a position against scapegoating, and monitor and hold responsible those elements that make inflammatory anti-Asian statements.

Furthermore, the Asian Pacific communities must reach out and establish ties with other ethnic groups. With the shocking experience of the burning of Koreatown during the L. A. riots fresh in our minds, it is clear that we must work harder to further understanding, compassion, and mutual respect between people of the Asia-Pacific and all other races. Another lesson to be learned from the L. A. riots is that during hard economic times, all people of color and low income are in the same predicament. Let us learn not to feed on each other. As Rodney King said, "Can we get along?"

We must also learn to trust and work with law enforcement authorities. Even in the wake of the King beating and legal travesty, and the recent manslaughter mistrial of a Compton, California, police officer who shot down in cold blood two unarmed Samoan Americans, shooting them 19 times with 13 bullets in their backs—the vast majority of our men and women in blue are good, honest people, professionals that ensure the peace and stability of our communities. We must use this resource to protect us by religiously and quickly reporting all incidents of hate crime.

Finally, our Asia-Pacific communities must be prepared to network with other associations in the nation to provide a unified response to combating racial violence and hostility against anyone, regardless of race, color or creed.

In concluding, let me say that although Mr. Kwoh's points for protection of our communities are well-taken, I believe that the repulsive Japan-bashing America has witnessed is a temporary affliction.

Ladies and gentlemen, our nation has the strength of character, the resilience of ingenuity and the depth of resources necessary to resolve any problem before her, including our present economic woes. When you see young, upstart entrepreneurs like Bill Gates create a computer software giant like Microsoft—which, incidentally, is worth more on the market than Honda and Sony combined—you know that the United States has the right stuff. So do Motorola, Intel, Merck, Emerson Electric, IBM, Corning and many other U.S. companies that are thriving in the international marketplace. America has done it before and we will do it again.

Meanwhile, recent events have shown the world that Japan is, as the Wall Street Journal put it, not the invincible economic terminator of our imaginings. In the past several weeks, Japan's stock market has crashed by 50% from its peak two years ago, and her real estate values in financial centers like Tokyo and Osaka have plummeted drastically. With this unprecedented economic instability, a tremendous amount of Japan's wealth—tens of billions of dollars—has amazingly vanished overnight, and she may be facing for the first time—a recession.

With the dismantling of the evil empire, the birth of numerous new democracies from Communist ruins, a victory over a dictator in the Gulf war and a vibrant stock market that portends a strong economic recovery, indeed, the United States is till strong, and remains the most powerful country on the face of this planet.

Against this backdrop, our fellow American citizens of Asian Pacific descent can take pride, especially this month, in being Americans.

As our nation enters into the Pacific Century, Asian Pacific Americans can hold their heads high, knowing the contributions of our people have ensured America is, despite her problems, the greatest democracy in the world.

Source:

Remarks by the Honorable Eni F. H. Faleomavaega, delegate to the U.S. Congress, American Samoa, delivered during Asian Pacific American Heritage Month to the United States House of Representatives in Washington, D.C. on May 26, 1992. Republished in *Asian American Almanac*. Detroit: Gale Research, 1995. pp. 755-758.

SCOTTISH AND SCOTCH-IRISH AMERICANS

Joseph Doddridge (1769-1826), in his Notes on the Settlement and Indian Wars, provided a detailed portrait of the lives of settlers, including Scotch-Irish pioneers, in Pennsylvania during the late 1700s and early 1800s. Particularly notable were his descriptions of clothing and shelter on the frontier.

The settlers' clothing tended to be modeled on that of Native Americans. This was particularly so of men, though their principal item of dress, the hunting shirt, resembled European fashions of the day. It was made of a sturdy material called linsey, a blend of wool and cotton capable of enduring long periods of wear without washing. Covering this was a cape with a pocket useful for holding all manner of items needed by a man on the frontier. Among such items listed by Doddridge were cakes, which resembled cornbread; jerk, or beef jerky; and tow, a piece of yarn of cloth.

A frontiersman's belt, as Doddridge pointed out, "answered"—that is, served—several purposes. In the area of footwear, settlers almost universally followed the example of Indians, adopting moccasins made from animal skins. These were usually sewn together at the top of the foot and the bottom of the heel, and required constant repairing. Most useful for the latter purpose was an awl, a sharp pointed tool used like a needle for patching the moccasin with the skin of a deer.

Needless to say, it was not a very comfortable environment, and given the fact that moccasins were practically useless in wet weather, it is little surprise that women went barefoot when it was warm. The word "toilet," in Doddridge's time, referred to a small dressing table, and by noting that women were busy with the distaff or shuttle—devices for weaving—he indicated the lack of ease that characterized their lives. It was a world in which people had scanty possessions, and therefore hung up the few items of clothing not already on their bodies as a point of pride.

Doddridge went on to describe the typical settlers' fort, which more or less fits modern ideas regarding the sort of place where Daniel Boone and other pioneer heroes were likely to live. Most dwellings had dirt floors, though a few had floors of puncheon, or split logs with the flat side upward. Cabins were not free-standing, but lined up together: thus only the log walls on either side of a family separated them from their neighbors. This created a sturdy structure for the dwellings, further reinforced by fact that the back wall of the cabin rested against the outer walls of the fort.

At the corners of the forts were the turret-like blockhouses which gave them their distinctive appearance. These jutted beyond the outer walls, and had openings *in the floor overlooking the outside of the fort: thus defenders could shoot at an attacker trying to take up a position of safety against the fort's walls. Not all forts had blockhouses, as Doddridge noted; some were equipped merely with bastions, walls over which defenders could fire.*

It is interesting to note that the settlers built these forts without nails, simply because, as Doddridge pointed out, "such things were not to be had." Instead, they hewed out the logs to make them fit together as closely as they could. Certainly the log forts were sufficient, Doddridge noted, given the fact that the Indians did not have artillery, or cannons.

A second document provides a view of a quite different kind of structure—that of the marriage bond, and the layers of faith and community that it represented— among the Scotch Irish of Pennsylvania. The Reverend Samuel Wilson, born in 1754, served as pastor of the Big Spring Church in Cumberland County, Pennsylvania, beginning in 1787. During the marriage ceremony, directly after asking the congregation if anyone saw any reason why the couple should not be married, he gave the bride and groom a stern and frank speech.

The latter consisted of an introduction in which he reminded the couple of the reason for marriage, followed by a short discussion of mutual obligations, of the husband's duties to his wife, and of the wife's duties to her husband. In both the introduction and the section on mutual obligations, he warned against adultery and fornication, and encouraged the couple both in the production of children, and in the spiritual training of their offspring.

Wilson's discussion of the husband's and wive's roles was clearly in line with injunctions given by the Apostle Paul in Ephesians 5:22-33. To this he added a gentle reminder that if the wife disagreed with her husband, she should attempt to reason with him; but if he did not see things her way, she should go along with him.

PENNSYLVANIA—THE SCOTCH-IRISH CENTRE

On Frontier Life

The hunting shirt was universally worn. This was a kind of loose frock, reaching half way down the thighs, with long sleeves, open before, and so wide as to lap over a foot or more when belted. The cape was large and sometimes handsomely fringed with a ravelled piece of cloth of a different color from that of the hunting shirt itself. The bosom of this dress served as a wallet to hold a chunk of bread, cakes, jerk, tow for wiping the barrel of the rifle, or any other necessary for the hunter or warrior. The belt, which was always tied behind, answered several purposes besides that of holding the dress together. In cold weather the mittens, and sometimes the bullet bag, occupied the front part of it. To the right side was suspended the tomahawk, and to the left the scalping knife in its leathern sheath. The hunting shirt was generally made of linsey, sometimes of coarse linen, and a few of dressed deerskins. These last were very cold and uncomfortable in wet weather. The shirt and jacket were of the common fashion. A pair of drawers, or breeches and leggins, were the dress of the thighs and legs; a pair of moccasons answered for the feet much better than shoes. They were made of dressed deerskin. They were mostly made of a single piece with a gathering seam along the top of the foot, and another along the bottom of the heel, without gathers as high as the ankle joint or a little higher. Flaps were left on each side to reach some distance up the legs. These were nicely adapted to the ankles and lower part of the leg by thongs of deerskin, so that no dust, gravel or snow could get within the moccason.

The moccasons in ordinary use cost but a few hours labor to make them. This was done by an instrument denominated a moccason awl, which was made from the back spring of an old clasp knife. This awl with its buck's horn handle was an appendage of every shot pouch strap, together with a roll of buckskin for mending the moccasons. This was the labor of almost every evening. They were sewed together and patched with deerskin thongs, or whangs, as they were commonly called. In cold weather the moccasons were well stuffed with deers' hair or dry leaves, so as to keep the feet comfortably warm; but in wet weather it was usually said that wearing them was "a decent way of going barefooted," and such was the fact, owing to the spongy texture of the leather of which they were made.

The women usually went barefooted in warm weather. Instead of the toilet, they had to handle the distaff or shuttle, the sickle or weeding hoe, contented if they could obtain their linsey clothing and cover their heads with a sunbonnet made of six or seven hundred linen. The coats and bedgowns of the women, as well as the hunting shirts of the men, were hung in full display on wooden pegs round the walls of their cabins, so while they answered in some degree the place of paper hangings or tapestries, they announced to the stranger as well as neighbor, the wealth or poverty of the family in the articles of clothing.

The fort consisted of cabins, block houses and stockades. A range of cabins commonly formed one side at least of the fort. Divisions or partitions of logs separated the cabins from each other. The walls on the outside were ten or twelve feet high, the slope of the roof being turned wholly inward. A very few of these cabins had puncheon floors; the greater part were earthen. The block houses were built at the angles of the fort. They projected about two feet beyond the outer walls of the cabins and stockades. Their upper stories were about eighteen inches every way larger in dimensions than the under one, leaving an opening at the commencement of the second story to prevent the enemy from making a lodgment under the walls. In some forts, instead of block houses, the angles of the fort were furnished with bastions. A large folding gate made of thick slabs, nearest the spring, closed the fort. The stockades, bastions, cabins and blockhouse walls were furnished with portholes at proper heights and distances.... The whole of this work was made without the aid of a single nail or spike of iron, and for this reason—such things were not to be had. In some places less exposed, a single blockhouse, with a cabin or two, constituted the whole fort. Such places of refuge may appear very trifling to those who have been in the habit of seeing the formidable military garrisons of Europe and America; but they answered the purpose, as the Indians had no artillery. They seldom attacked, and scarcely ever took one of them...."

On Marriage

The design of marriage is, that fornication may be avoided, and as our race is more dignified than the lower creations, so then, our passions should be regulated by reason and religion. It is likewise intended for producing a legitimate offspring, and a seed for the church. There are duties incumbent upon those who enter this relation, some of them are equally binding upon both parties, some upon one party, some upon the other.

First, it is equally binding upon you both to love each other's persons, to avoid freedom with all other which formerly might have been excusable, to keep each other's lawful secrets, fidelity to the marriage bed, and if God shall give you an offspring, it will be mutually binding upon you both, to consult their spiritual, as well as their temporal concerns.

Secondly, it will be particularly binding upon you, Sir, who is to be the head of the family, to maintain the authority which God hath given you. In every society there must be a head, and in families, by divine authority, this is given to the man, but as woman was given to man for an helpmeet and a bosom companion, you are not to treat this woman in a tyrannical manner, much less as a slave, but to love and kindly entreat her, as becomes one so nearly allied to you.

Lastly, it is incumbent upon you, Madam, who is to be the wife, to acknowledge the authority of him who is to be your husband, and for this, you have the example of Sarah, who is commended for calling Abraham, Lord. It seems to be your privilege in matters in which you and he cannot agree, that you advise with him, endeavoring in an easy way by persuasion to gain him to your side; but if you cannot in this way gain you point, it is fit and proper that you submit in matters in which conscience is not concerned. It will be your duty in a particular manner, to use good economy in regard to those things which may be placed in your hands. In a word, you are to be industrious in your place and station.

Source:
The Scotch-Irish in America, Henry Jones Ford.
    Reprint. New York: Arno Press and *New York Times,* 1969. pp. 278-281 [frontier life], pp. 286-288 [marriage].

SICILIAN AMERICANS

John Cacciatore's story dramatizes the difficulties of immigrants settling in an unfamiliar new land. John was born in Santa Stefano di Quisquina, Sicily, in 1860 to a farm peasant family. Growing up in his father's footsteps, he worked with his father as a youth on the farm at a time when Sicily became politically united with Italy. At 22 years of age he married and received his own parcel of land to farm.

Economic conditions declined though. With continuing agricultural crises in Sicily and Italy and increasing peasant revolts, the first major wave of Sicilian immigration to the United States began in the 1880s. After suffering the deaths of two infant sons, John and his wife decided to join the exodus and settled in New Orleans, a key destination for Sicilian and Italian immigrants. There, John quickly found work for a produce company handling imported Honduran bananas.

In 1887 at the age of 27, John became enamored with stories of Tampa, Florida. Although he had not actually seen the area, John convinced his wife that they should relocate there. Temporarily leaving his wife behind, he soon left to find a job. Though Tampa was not what he had hoped, John found work as a stripper removing stems from tobacco leaves at a cigar maker. After a couple of years, his wife joined him and also gained employment with the cigar manufacturers.

In an interview, John reflected on the long struggle to save enough money to buy a house. Finally, a key opportunity arose when the factory owner offered houses at reduced costs to employees. As John described,

> I still have this house, although considerably remodeled. I paid $100 cash, and the balance I paid off in monthly terms. I was able to do this with the help of my wife, she worked also at the cigar factory. We worked in several factories, sometimes in West Tampa, and sometimes in Ybor City, wherever working conditions were better. In all, I worked 28 years at the cigar factories.

Cigar manufacturing eventually declined and they subsisted as landlords for several properties.

LIFE HISTORY OF MR. JOHN CACCIATORE

I was born in the town of Santa Stefano di Quisquina, Sicily, on May 12th, 1860, and am now 75 years of age. My father was a farm peasant working the sail for a land owner. Since my early years I toiled at the farm with my father.

I was married at the age of 22 years, and then leased a tract of land which I worked planting wheat, horse feed, potatoes and vegetables. After we had been married a year, my wife gave birth to a child, a baby boy, who died when he was a year old. In the year 1885 my wife again gave birth to another son who died soon after.

In this same year I decided to come to New Orleans where many Italians were living at that time. The trip was long and tedious, lasting 30 days. I was afterwards introduced to Mr. Vaccaro who was the owner of the steamship line in which I had sailed to America with my wife. We soon became fast friends, and he proposed to me that I work for him at his Produce Company in New Orleans. He handled bananas chiefly which he brought from Honduras. There I was employed as foreman, which position I held for some two years.

Several friends described Tampa to me with such glowing colors that I soon became entrused, and decided to come here and try my fortune. Accordingly, in 1887, leaving my wife in New Orleans, I took the train to Mobile. At Mobile I took the boat that brought me here. We[?] disembarked at the Lafayette Street bridge. I was then 27 years of age.

I had expected to see a flourishing city, but my expectations were too high, for what I saw before me almost brought me to tears. There was nothing, what one may truthfully say, nothing. Franklin was a long sandy street. There were very few houses, and those were far apart with tall pine trees surrounding them. The Hillsborough County Court House was a small wooden building. Some men were just beginning to work on the foundation of the Tampa Bay Hotel.

Ybor City was not connected to Tampa as it is today. There was a Wilderness between the two cities, and a distance of more than one mile between the two places. All of Ybor City was not worth one cent to me. In different places of Ybor City a tall species of grass grew, proper of swampy places. This grass grew from 5 to 6 feet high. I was completely disillusioned with what I saw. There was a stagnant water hole where the society of the Centro Espanol (Spanish Club) is today located. A small wooden bridge spanned this pond. I remember that I was afraid to cross the bridge, and especially so at night, because of the alligators that lived there. They would often crawl into the bridge and bask there in the sun all day long.

The factory of Martinez Ybor had some twenty cigar makers; Sanches y Haya had some fifteen; while Yendas had about ten. I worked for a time at the factory of Modesto Monet as stripper, [footnote: stripper in a cigar factory is one who removes the stem from the tobacco leaf.] and made 35¢ for my first day's work. Of course, I was then only learning the cigar business, and could not expect to make more. When I became skilled in my work as stripper, I would make from $1.00 to $1.25 a day.

While still at this work, I gradually began learning the cigarmakers' trade as I saw that they were making a much more comfortable income. When I had become somewhat proficient as a cigarmaker, I was earning from $14.00 to $15.00 a week.

When I had been in Tampa some two or three years I sent for my wife who was still living in New Orleans. When she arrived in Tampa she burst out crying at what she saw: wilderness, swamps, alligators, mosquitoes, and open closets. The only thing she would say when she arrived was: "Why have you brought me to such a place?"

Here we had two more sons, and one died. We had in all four children, of whom three died. We only had one child left whom we were able to raise.

At about this time Mr. Martinez Ybor (the cigar manufacturer) was offering homes for sale at a very low price. I, therefore, went to him and purchased a home at the corner of 18th Street and 8th Avenue for the price of $725. I still have this house, although considerably remodeled. I paid $100 cash, and the balance I paid off in monthly terms. I was able to do this with the help of my wife, she worked also at the cigar factory. We worked in several factories, sometimes in West Tampa, and sometimes in Ybor City, wherever working conditions were better.

In all, I worked 28 years at the cigar factories. At the end of this time my sight became somewhat impaired, and I was, therefore, obliged to discontinue my work.

My son grew up into a young man, married and had two children; both boys. One of my grandsons is married, and the other is still single. My son has now been out of work for the past three years.

I am living at present from what little rent I can collect from the various buildings that I own. There are families that have been living in my houses seven weeks without paying rent, yet should I wish to dislodge them I must go to the Court House and pay them $5.00, and then wait three more weeks before they are finally dislodged.

These properties are mine. I have worked hard in order to have them, yet I cannot do as I deem proper with them. If I cannot pay the taxes these houses will be taken from me. If I cannot collect my rents, I am not able to pay the taxes. I should, therefore, be allowed to dislodge these that cannot pay their rent, and without going through so much trouble. It is not justice to expect taxes to be paid when you cannot collect your rents.

There is not much hope in Ybor City. The cigar factories are on a continuous decline. The factory of Corral & Wediska had 1500 persons working, today it has only some 150 or 200 persons.

The railroad between Tampa and Jacksonville had over 40 men working daily along the tracks, keeping the grass from growing over the rails, seeing that the tires along the tracks were well kept, etc. Today they do not have a single man doing this.

The Trust has also purchased many factories here and have removed them to the Northern cities.

The people of Ybor City are orphans, not only of father and mother, but of everything in life. They cannot find work at the cigar factories because of the machines. If the government would place a tax of $5,000 on each machine, the manufacturers would soon have to discontinue them, and there would be work for those that are still left here.

Under present conditions the people of Ybor City have no other alternative but to leave for New York City. Here they get only 50¢ a week for the maintenance of a whole family, and the single person is not given any relief whatever. In New York City they are given a home, groceries, coal to warm themselves in winter, and electric lights. Here they are not given anything.

There is not an employee of HavaTampa that is from Ybor City. All their employees are women who come from little towns near Tampa. The factory is situated here in Ybor City, yet very few Latins if any, are employed. This factory pays their employees whatever they please.

Source:

Library of Congress. *American Life Histories: Manuscripts from the Federal Writers' Project, 1936-1940* from the American Memory website (http://memory.loc.gov/ammem/wpaintro/wpa-home.html).

Sicilian Americans in the 1940s continued the old world tradition of celebrating a holy day devoted to Saint Joseph. This celebration is described in detail in this article that appeared in the September 1940 Southern Folklore Quarterly. The information was based on interviews with Sicilian Americans who themselves participated in the Catholic tradition of honoring the patron saint of the poor and of orphans, known in Italian as San Giuseppi. The author, Charles Speroni, is an authority on Italian culture, and in 1999 was the Chairman of the Department of Italian at the University of California at Los Angeles.

The original Sicilian custom of celebrating St. Joseph's Day was the community's way of helping its poorest people. The Americanized version, which became more elaborate and expensive, is held in fulfillment of an individual's promise to honor St. Joseph after prayers to this patron saint resulted in the healing of a loved one. The American celebration depends on individual families within a community, and different households choose to participate each year. Households who plan to celebrate tell neighbors in advance.

The festival occurs on March 19, during the religious period of Lent, when many Catholics abstain from eating meats. A festive altar which includes a picture of the Holy Family, Mary, Joseph and the Infant Jesus, is set up on a table in the living room or dining room of the home. A large table is loaded with food and flowers, and includes a cake with "Saint Joseph" written on it. Three places are set at the table for the Holy Family. A priest comes by the home on the evening before St. Joseph's Day to bless the altar and loaded table. From then until the ceremony the following day at noon nothing can be added or removed from the table. The celebration is a community affair. Three children are chosen to represent the Holy Family, and after celebrating Mass at the local church, they enact a ritual of knocking at the home three houses away, where they are refused entry. They then knock at the second house and are again refused. They then arrive at the celebrants house to be admitted and served.

The children eat in a prescribed manner, then the food is offered to anyone who visits. Visitors who go from house to house also are given a plate of spaghetti. Any leftovers are distributed among the poor the following day. The celebration is an expense that a family is allowed to share only among others who had made a pledge to St. Joseph during the previous year. This holiday scene is most prevalent in Sicilian Americans neighborhood clusters, like in San Francisco's North Beach, or "Little Sicily" in Chicago, and "Little Palermo" in New Orleans. Between 1880 and 1930, more than 1.1 million Sicilians Americans joined such communities.

St. Joseph's Day was one of many religious and cultural traditions that continued Sicilian values and lifestyles in the Sicilian American communities. For example, the San Francisco community celebrated the Madonna del Lume (Holy Mother of Light) with a procession down to the Fisherman's Warf for the ancient Blessing of the Fishing Fleet, followed by parties with music and dancing. In the St. Joseph's Day celebration, memorized dialogue kept the tradition in the same form from celebration to celebration, and taught second and third generations about the Sicilian culture of their ancestors.

THE OBSERVANCE OF SAINT JOSEPH'S DAY

Among the sundry customs brought to this country by Sicilians, an important place belongs to the colorful and elaborate celebration of Saint Joseph, the patron saint of the poor and of orphans. Preparations for the festivities of the day of "San Giuseppi", March 19, begin many weeks in advance. Everything must be ready by the eve of the preceding day, when scores, if not hundreds, of friends, neighbors, and curiosity seekers, go visiting the houses where "altars" have been prepared in honor of the saint.

Before describing these altars and the ceremony connected with them, a word must be said about the people who set them up. Contrary to the original custom in Sicily, where festivities are held mainly to help the poorest people of the community, here in Southern California, and probably in all other parts of the United States where Sicilians honor Saint Joseph, the altars are prepared in fulfillment of a promise made to the saint in a moment of need. For instance, a middle-aged Sicilian woman told me that about a year ago her small son was taken very ill with pneumonia. Doctors had almost given up all hope of saving him when the mother prayed very fervently and asked Saint Joseph to help her child, promising that, in return, she would set up an altar in his honor. The boy soon recovered, and when the month of March arrived, his mother did not forget her promise to "San Gisippuzzu". Another woman made an altar because Saint Joseph healed her husband who had been severely hurt in an automobile accident. And in another family, thanks were thus

David Garcia adds cream topping to some of the 15,000 zeppole baked for the Southern Italian holiday of St. Joseph's Day.

rendered to the good carpenter for curing one of its members from cancer.

These festive altars are usually set up on a large table in the living-room or in the dining-room of the house, and very frequently, especially if prepared by people of means, the table is so large that it occupies almost every square foot of the room. The altar is placed against the wall facing the entrance of the room, and is dominated by a large picture of the Holy Family: Mary, Joseph, and the Infant Jesus. If in the prayers other saints have been invoked besides Saint Joseph, their images—frequently statuettes—are placed at the foot of the altar. In some houses the altar is artistically decorated with beautiful lace-work, and the walls of the room are completely covered by rich and brightly-colored religious tapestries. Especially impressive are the scores and scores of choice edibles which make the table groan under their weight. With the exception of meat—Saint Joseph's day, it will be remembered, falls during Lent—everything imaginable can be found on those tables of plenty. All sorts of fruits, fresh and cooked vegetables, fish dishes decorated in various ways, rice, many kinds of cookies, cakes (some made or stuffed with figs), numberless loaves of bread of different shapes, wines, and the very characteristic roasted chick-peas, almonds, and horse-beans (they taste much better than the name might imply!). In addition, each table must always have a large square cake with "Saint Joseph" written on it. This cake is usu-

ally donated by a friend of the family. Another dish that must be on the table is a platter containing a large baked fish beautifully decorated. And the, a maze of flowers; on one table they even had an orchid. This year, since Saint Joseph's day fell just a few days before Easter, I noticed two new items on the table: a little lamb (made with bread-crumb covered with beaten egg white and sprinkled with coconut), and one or more pots of green wheat symbolizing the resurrection of Christ.

At the end of the table facing the altar there are three or more places set for the three members of the Holy Family, and for as many saints as the hostess has decided to have. On the evening of the 18th, the priest visits the various houses where altars have been blessed, no food can be touched or taken away from them until after the ceremony which takes place on the following day.

In the morning the children chosen to represent Jesus, Mary and Joseph, and the other saints, go to church to hear mass. Then, a few minutes before noon, either in their best clothes or, if possible, dressed to resemble the holy persons they represent, they walk to the third house from the one where an altar has been prepared. Saint Joseph knocks at the door and asks to be given shelter:

Simu tri poviri pillirini
[We are three poor pilgrims]
Simu stanchi di caminu

[We are tired of walking]
Vulimu 'nu pocu di risettu
[We want to rest a while]
E 'nu pocu di ristolu.
[And we want a little nourishment.]

The people of the house have been warned beforehand, and they refuse admittance to the Holy Family:

Chista casa nun é locanna
[This house is not an inn]
Itevinni a n'autra banna.
[Go elsewhere.]

Then they proceed to the next house, and Saint Joseph asks Mary to knock:

Tupuliati vui Maria,
[You knock, Mary,]
Chi forsi vi dunano accansu.
[Perhaps they will heed you.]

But the lady of the second house answers with the same words of the lady of the first, and the "saints" continue to the third house, where Mary asks the Infant Jesus to knock:

Tupuliati vui Gesù Bamminu.
[You knock, Infant Jesus.]

When the child knocks he says:

Simu Gesù, Maria, e Giuseppi.
[We are Jesus, Mary, and Joseph.]

and the woman of the house answers:

Site vui Giuseppi, e Maria
[It is you, Joseph and Mary,]
Trasiti tutti in cumpagnia.
[Come in, all of you.]

The ceremony is practically the same in every house; the words accompanying the ceremony, however, are frequently very different. There probably are as many versions of it as there are localities in Sicily where Saint Joseph's day is commemorated. Just to mention another version of the brief ceremony, Saint Joseph goes to the first door and knocks with his symbolic rod. When the door is opened, he says:

C'è locu pu alluggiari tri poviri pillerini?
[Is there room to shelter three poor pilgrims?]
And the lady says:

Nun c' è locu pu vui oggi.
[There is no room for you today.]
Then Saint Joseph says:

Madunnuzza c'avimu a fari?
[Mary dear, what shall we do?]

And Mary answers:

Comu vori Gesù.
[What Jesus wishes.]

At the second door the exact thing is repeated. At the third, the hostess says:

C' è locu pu Gesù, Giuseppi, e Maria
[There is room for Jesus, Joseph, and Mary,]
Chista nun è cchiù a casa mia,
[This is no longer my house,]
È di Gesù, Giuseppi, e Maria.

[It is that of Jesus, Joseph, and Mary.]

Once the Holy Family is within, the master of the house takes from the table some blessed wine and with it washes the right hand of the children representing Jesus, Mary, and Joseph. Then they are seated at the table, and the people who have come tot he ceremony and who are very devout Catholics, kiss the right hand of these "saints." Sometimes they also touch their right foot and then kiss their own hand which has thus become blessed. The washing of the hand and the touching of the foot are not always carried out.

After the "saints" are seated, each one of them is served by an appointed person who sees to it that the saint upon whom he is waiting is not served the same food twice. In some families just the host and the hostess wait on the "saints". Everything is served to them on a clean dish. I was told that they must have three mouthfuls of all they are offered. The first course always consists of an artistically decorated orange: something like an orange salad. This is followed by variously prepared fish, fennels, artichokes, sardines, rice, *pasta ca' muddica* (spaghetti with sauce made of breadcrumbs, celery, and grated cheese), fruit, etc., etc. After about three hours, when the "saints" have finished eating, they are given, to take home, a basketful of the food that is left on the table. Then the food is at the disposal of all visitors who are offered also a dish of spaghetti seasoned with *muddica*. One woman informed me that during the afternoon and evening of Saint Joseph's day she served no less than ninety pounds of spaghetti!

On the following morning, whatever food remains must be distributed among friends or preferable among the poor people of the neighborhood.

I asked several women whether in Sicily they prepared such elaborate and costly tables, and they invariably told me that, because of the much lower standard of living, what they or their parents used to do there hardly compares with what they can afford to do here.

The same family does not necessarily set up an altar just once; it depends entirely on the promise made to Saint Joseph. In one family they have been making altars for over twenty years.

Judging by the humble dwellings inhabited by most of the families devoted to Jesus' foster-father, it must be quite burdensome for them to prepare such sumptuous tables. Many of the poorer people must start saving months ahead of time, and do away with many so-called luxuries of the present age. It is true, however, that friends and neighbors who have addressed their prayers to Saint Joseph are allowed to contribute to the decoration of the table either with money, or, more often, with cakes, candles, and flowers, and this certainly helps to bear the expenses encountered by the more indigent worshipers of the good carpenter.

Source:

J. D. Clark. In *Southern Folklore Quarterly*, vol. IV, Gainesville, Florida, 1940. pp. 135-139.

*S*icilians made up the majority of Italian immigrants who came to America. In the late 1800s, over half of the Italian immigrants who migrated favored the United States as their destination. The emigration was primarily caused by a series of agricultural crises. An excess of wheat depressed Sicilian wheat exports; the United States cut imports of Italian citrus fruits because of increased production in local markets; and wine grapes became diseased. At the same time, Sicily's population was on the rise, tripling between 1800 and 1909. Artisans were also economically disadvantaged when industrialized Western Europe exported inexpensive manufactured goods to Sicily, making their crafts less necessary. Thus, increased immigration to the United States occurred.

Sicilians in America came to many different parts of the country and settled in both urban and rural areas. There were several Sicilian settlements, especially in San Francisco, Birmingham, Milwaukee, Tampa, Chicago and New Orleans, an area with one of the largest concentrations of Sicilians. Anthony Navarra, the author of "Old Tales and New Tongues," is a second generation Sicilian American whose parents came to settle in America, first his father and then his mother. The document only hints at how the family came to America: his grandfather lived long enough "to see all his children, as leaves fall in autumn, depart to seek their fortunes overseas (one as far as Australia where he is today a prosperous merchant in Sydney)."

The author more pointedly describes the work that his mother did in order to keep the family together. Like many Sicilian-American women, she had to help supplement the family income and was engaged in factory work, sewing, and taking in boarders. Sicilian men often arrived in America and earned money to send back to family in Sicily, or saved money to bring people over.

Sicilians traditionally place a very high value on family, and the author describes how his upbringing and position as a storyteller is a direct result of the storytelling of both his grandfather and his mother. The author honors the close ties between generations, and the stories he tells are passed down. By passing on these stories, the author expresses the sentiment that he is passing on tradition, continuing to preserve the ways that he learned from his family. Thus, though Sicilians mixed into mainstream American society, this document expresses the desire to maintain traditional ethnic heritage.

OLD TALES AND NEW TONGUES

by Anthony Navarra

A benevolent fate has made me a teller of tales. After all, it was too much to escape, for I was too deeply involved with a genetic fatality. My grandfather, Padre Gilardi (Grandfather Gerard) was the village story teller in the hill town of Poggio Reale, Sicily.

My grandfather was a splendid human being. Mother never tired of talking about him. Slim, blue-eyed, and fair, he was born in the lovely Greek town of Agrigento, Sicily. His life had a fairytale quality about it. His father, a small merchant and a widower, remarried. The second marriage proved unwise because, like the stepmother in Cinderella, she had two daughters whom she pampered and favored at the expense of Padre Gilardi. When my grandfather (at age 18) could stand her injustices no longer, he gave his stepmother a sound thrashing, packed his clothes, and left Agrigento for Poggio Reale, a village in the north-western part of the golden isle. Family history relates that my great-grandfather rued his marriage and died neglected and impoverished by the exploitation of his second wife.

Padre Gilardi's fortunes, on the other hand, prospered in Poggio Reale. Here he not only met and married Mamma Pippina (my grandmother) but entered into one successful enterprise after another. Here he raised a family of five sons and one daughter. And here he was alive to see all his children, as leaves fall in autumn, depart to seek their fortunes overseas (one as far as Australia where he is today a prosperous merchant in Sydney).

My mother never stopped talking about her father. He was the village story teller. Of a winter's night all the neighbors gathered in his house to hear him, a born raconteur, tell stories. Later my mother narrated all of these tales to me. What a store of tales he knew! "The Barber's Secret," "The Mushroom Man," and "The Trouble Makers"—to name but three. These are folk stories, of course, going back to who knows what European of Asiatic origin.

His favorite adventures, however, centered in the Carolingian cycle. He would pace up and down the room, mother says, puffing gently on his pipe and accompanying his words with appropriate gestures. His voice was pleasing and listeners hung on every magic word. Time and again he told of the treachery of the Duke of Mayence. Rolands last trumpet call sounded through the house on many a winter's eve. In your mind's eye you saw the furious gallop of Bayard, Roland's matchless steed, and the flash of Durindana, the unconquerable sword.

Padre Gilardi's love of stories and his sociability were bequeathed to my mother. She inherited her father's intelligence, curiosity, and spirit of enterprise. She has remained young in heart and in mind to this day. Her strength and integrity moved mountains. Raised in a houseful of boys, she was beloved and cherished by all of them, but because she was a girl, she was given no schooling. At twenty-one she couldn't read or write. Faced with the necessity of writing to my father who had preceded her to America, she taught herself to read and write. Years later she went to school and learned to read and write English.

Her life was filled with work. Boarders, raising her own family, factory work, sewing, never-ending housework—these were her lot. She bore hardships as if she were made of steel. In moments of great stress and tension, it was her equanimity and faith that kept the family together. "We shall not perish," she used to say. And if as a family we did not perish, it was due to her strength and determination.

My brothers, Charles and Joseph, and I passed an enchanted childhood. For mother told us all of her father's stories. How can I recapture the sense of warmth and love as, on a cold December night in Auburn, New York, we huddled around the coal stove, with hot faces and cold backs. Then, impatiently waiting for a few chestnuts or filberts to roast, we would urge her to tell us another story. Ah! The smell of orange peels toasting on a hot lid and the thought of Bayard champing furiously as he waits for Roland to mount him and ride victorious again. Ever victorious Roland, our shining champion!

Seated around my mother we listened and by listening grew wiser. We fashioned, woven from the fabric of many a winter's tale, some permanent values to guide us through this labyrinth we call life.

We learned about the value of friendship (Roland and Oliver), about the ultimate triumph of good over evil ("The Trouble Makers"). We stored up a lesson to be used later when we became fathers and about the importance of loving and accepting children for what they are and as God made them ("The Barber's Secret"). We learned that there may sometimes be wisdom in folly (in the character of that peasant rogue, Berthold). Mother taught us that the greedy are really blind and that this kind of blindness is its own worst punishment ("The Peasant and the Golden Mortar"). Secure at her knees, we could enjoy terror in her stories about "lu lupu manaru" (the werewolf) or that wicked female creature "la mamm'Adraia" (the Hydra).

Years later, as a teacher, I found a wonderful use for these stories. From time to time as I have "covered" a class for a teacher, for any number of reasons, I would ask the class, "Do you want to hear a story?" You can imagine the chorus of yesses. Thus the chain of story-telling remained unbroken. From my grandfather across the seas, to his daughter in a beautiful upstate town, to her son, a teacher in the big city.

I've told my mother's stories to all kinds of boys and girls having all levels of intelligence. The reaction is always the same. "When will you tell us another one?" I found, too, that even the most rebellious and difficult groups would be quiet, cooperative, and would do the lesson willingly if I said to them, "Let us do our lesson well and I'll begin another story at the end of the period."

What these stories may have meant to the listeners I cannot tell. I have, naturally, never allowed them to interfere with the immediate work at hand. Judging by the rapt look on their faces and the ripple of smiles expanding across the whole room as the stories would come to a close, the boys and girls *enjoyed* the stories. One boy did say to me once,

"You know, we don't fight at our supper table any more—I tell your stories!"

But I can say what telling them has meant to *me*. I tell these stories to my classes mainly to give them the kind of pleasure that my mother gave to me. I tell them as a tribute to my mother and my grandfather. I tell them because, as with lovers, all the world loves a story. I dread (don't all teachers?) the moment when some pupil will come to me at the end of a folk tale and say teasingly with a furtive glance at the frost on my temples: "Mr. Navarra, my mother says that you told her that story. Did you?" When that day comes I promise, like Prospero, to put aside this magic (unless some kind publisher invites me to do otherwise) and leave these old tales to newer tongues. Perhaps one of my students (perhaps many) will continue to tell my stories. To be sure, they will not be told as my mother told them to my brothers and me long ago in her sweet and gentle Sicilian cadences. What does it matter?

Let them be told in our glorious English tongue. The tellers pass on and the tongues change, but the tales remain.

Source:
New York Folklore Quarterly, v. XVIII, no. 1 (Spring 1962), pp. 12-15.

Between 1880 and 1930, 4.5 million Italians came to the United States. Nearly one out of four was a Sicilian. Located off the Italian peninsula, the island of Sicily is home to an ethnically diverse people, whose roots are Italian, Arab, Greek, and Spanish. Although Sicilians began coming to the United States in the late nineteenth century, the largest wave of immigration was prompted by agricultural and political crises in the early twentieth century. As these immigrants urgently flocked to America—100,000 came in 1906 alone—they settled chiefly in industrial areas.

From their optimistic expectations to the stark reality of the huge, impersonal city, this essay recounts the attitudes and lifestyles of Sicilian immigrants to New York. Many held overly grand views of what awaited them; upon closer inspection, New York was not paradise. Yet as they settled in the East Side of Manhattan, Brooklyn or the Bronx, the Sicilians swiftly made their boroughs into places resembling—at least culturally—their native Palermo or Naples. The neighborhoods were outposts of the old world, where customs, sayings, and traditions proved to be important links to the life and land which they had left.

As the essay suggests, the ways that Sicilians kept their culture alive were many. They continued the oral tradition of proverbs and riddles, which has links to the old Italian figure of the contastorie or story teller who used to entertain crowds in the town square. The men played the age-old card games scupa and giuoco *avidly into the night. And the women cooked their mothers' and grandmothers' vibrant, sensuous Sicilian recipes, from the gooey cheese-and-sausage of Lasagne Imbotite to the sweet-tasting nougat candy torrone. Long a central part in their village life, churchgoing continued to be devoutly observed in New York, as did the festival atmosphere of carrying statues of the saint through the neighborhoods on holidays. Food became a part of these celebrations, too, and never so dramatically as in preparation for Christmas—when women baked bread at a heroic pace.*

Beneath the outward trappings of the old world, the Sicilians had also brought with them a strong sense of who they were and should be. Family authority rested firmly with the parents. In addition to the family, one had to maintain close social ties with friends, and the essay suggests that Sicilians reserved some of their sharpest scorn for those who failed to participate in the community. Not every aspect of the Old World survived, of course. By the middle of the twentieth century, the superstition which had been a vivid part of Sicilian folklore was less apparent. Only some immigrants still believed in the Evil Eye, a curse by which a hostile person could give someone headaches—or worse. As the belief in such omens faded, fewer New York Sicilians still dressed by putting on their left sock first to ward off bad luck.

SOUTHERN ITALIAN FOLKLORE

Earlier in the present century, during the large flow of immigrants from southern Italy, no Italian ever felt that he should leave behind his precious customs, superstitions, recipes or souvenirs of his complete heritage. With determination, he sought, rather, to manipulate them like dough into his new way of life.

During those thousand of third-class passages, many spoke of New York as the entire America, where the streets were gold-lined and the buildings were taller and whiter than anything they had ever seen in Palermo, Naples or Bagnara. Nevertheless, when they arrived, they were disenchanted upon observing discolored, weathered buildings. Some commented, too, that the closeness of the entrances to city structures would make them lose their way.

Many made a solemn declaration to get rich and return to their homeland; yet they never did, once they became entangled in the tiny condition they called wealth. Envy among their friends back in those southern Italian towns—unfortunates who had not the means to take the voyage to New York—was intense; it was particularly so when children or relatives sent back home small gifts of money.

Today, these same people still reside in New York with very few ideas altered or weakened by the currents of life around them.

Around a table, after a sustaining meal of *Lentichie e Pasta* (lentils and macaroni) *Pesci di Vuova* (a type of omelet with Romano cheese),

black olives and red wine, the light talk is still filled with guessing games such as the entertaining *indovinelli*, or riddles, they brought with them. Some especially favored ones are: "I enter a garden and beautiful women I find with dresses of violet and hats of green. What is it?—Eggplants, of course!" "White mountain, black seeds, the man who sows, always thinks. What is it?—It can be none other but a writer! The white mountain represents paper; the seeds: ebony-inked words; and the sower: a symbol of the author himself." Still another is, "On the mountain of Becafu, there is something that goes voo-oo; it is not a bearded monk, nor is it a goat with horns. What is it?—Naturally, it is a snail!"

Sicilians, who are very easily amused by small things such as these riddles, are also a hard-working people who have been and are generally nicknamed *bruccia la terra*, even in New York. Although literally meaning "burn the earth," it is used figuratively. Its origin began on the old Sicilian farms where the nature of the *contadini* (peasants) was evident. Usually swift and arduous in their labor, they were, in a sense, kindling the soil. Therefore, it is only natural that Sicilians should place the utmost importance on proverbs such as: "The early bird eats the seed."

In Calabrian discourse, there are always sprinkles of proverbs. One can sit with them and be assured of still hearing such statements as: "She who wishes to keep ahead of her neighbor, must go to bed at sundown and get up at dawn," "He who is born round, cannot die square," and "Love who loves you and respond to who calls you."

Calabrians such as those who come from Campo in Calabria are plain, boisterous mountain people whose noticeably brown-stained teeth are attributed to the iron in their drinking water. They fill jobs in the manual trades as do many Sicilian and Neapolitan people in New York. Their superstitions are still apparent, although not so much as they were five decades ago. There are still those who believe in the Evil Eye or *Mal' occhio*. If someone suffers persistently from headaches, the aliment is blamed on contact with this evil. To remove this spell, they would place a small saucer of water upon the victim's head and then proceed to mumble words to drive away the bad spirit. Even though this ritual is no longer practiced in New York, the superstition continues to linger. To this day, some Sicilians who also believe in the Evil Eye try not to forget to put their first stocking on the left leg, in order to ensure a day of good luck. And if, while praying at midnight, they should hear the baying of a dog, they will expect *male notizia* (bad news).

On many a warm summer day or evening on the East Side of Manhattan as well as in Brooklyn and The Bronx, Neapolitan, Sicilian and Calabrian men still play their traditional *Bocci*. They play the game with great interest in empty lots or backyards. Any number can play as long as there is an even number for teams of two men to a team. The score also is indefinite as some prefer to play for a goal of seven while others play for 11 or an even higher number.

One of the diversions that goes on beyond midnight, as in Italy years ago, is the card game called *scupa*. Three cards are dealt to two or four players, and four cards are left on the table. The game consists of adding and matching the right cards; *e.g.* if a man has a king and there is a king on the table, he can pick it up. I he has a queen, which is equivalent to eight, and there is a seven and an ace, these too, can be had, etc. If he can add or match the last cards left on the table, he has *scupa*. He, then, places the adding card, facing upwards, under his winning cards to show he has *scupa*. This is worth a point. However, this does not mean he has claimed complete victory. His goal is to acquire points in the course of the game by picking up either six diamonds, the seven of diamonds, 21 cards or three sevens—all equal to one point each—in addition to *scupa*.

"The Game," any game, has always been a necessity where poverty and lack of progress exist. Therefore, "the game" in those small old towns was an earnest business to be taken seriously. With time and circumstance, that attitude has never altered, even though today no more than a handful play the games. Possibly, the survival of their *giuoco* (game) will be attributed to Italian migrants of coming generations.

Many an old southern Italian still tells his children about the *contastorie* (the story-teller) who, in his day, told actual narratives as well as fairy tales around a wood-burning copper brazier or who sat in the town square in the evening where both old and young men gathered to be entranced by his stories. The *contastorie* was a more familiar figure than the puppeteer because he did not need equipment to convey his art. Amazingly, he was almost always an illiterate who had learned his repertoire, verbally, from another.

In Sicily, it is told, there was once a taboo against the intermingling of the sexes. Hence, only a few of the older women joined the crowds around the story-teller. Only in Neapolitan towns were the younger women permitted to join the audiences listening to the *contastorie*, in his shouting and chanting style, recount adventures of crusaders fighting infidels. There are accounts of how some listeners were so moved that they felt as if they themselves were about to go forth to battle on the side of Christ and would remove their hats or cross themselves.

The religious feasts in their *paesi* (villages) are continued in the Roman Catholic celebration of St. Anthony held in Sullivan Street on the West Side of Manhattan from the first of every June and lasting to the thirteenth. In September, the festival of San Gennaro is held annually on Manhattan's East Side (See illustration on page 222). The commemoration of the twin saints S. S. Cosimo and Damiano is also held in September in Brooklyn; while in the Bronx, a celebration for Our Lady of Mount Carmel in June is another local tradition.

During *la festa* it was a custom to pin on the Saints' vestments valuables such as gold earrings, rings, necklaces or other jewelry as a token of gratitude for a prayer answered by the Saint. Today, only money is pinned to the vestment. Carrying the Saint's statue through streets of the neighborhood on the last day of *la festa* has never varied through the years. Neither has the gaiety, music, spontaneity or the rich smells of *biscotti* (biscuits), *torrone* (nougats) and *caramelli* (candy) disappeared. Nor has there been any change in the *guioco di fuoco* (play of fireworks) which also adds color and zest to the festivities.

But of all the seasonal festivals, Christmas was the one looked forward to with the greatest eagerness and the one which necessitated the greatest preparation. In old southern Italy, it was habitual to retire and rise early during the year. Nevertheless, a few evenings before Christmas meant going to bed late, at least, for the young and older women, who helped one another prepare and bake their traditional *Porcellate* and *Biscotti* which required many hands. There was much rubbing of tired, sleepy eyes, but the pleasure of sharing the festive spirit was immense as goodies were placed one by one on oblong metal trays, then into brick ovens, cleaned of their ashes from burning wood that helped make them white-hot. After inserting the *balata* (a small, iron door) and securing it with wet rags around its edges, to prevent air escaping into those ovens, they chattered about the important day and waited for golden brown delicacies to come from the oven.

Christmas Eve was spent in tranquil dignity and the customary fish supper of *capilone* and *stocco* before everyone attends Midnight Mass.

Then came Christmas morning, in vivid, red-tiled kitchens with burnished copper pots and large wine and water jugs. There they prepared with earnest spirit delightful meals in terra-cotta and clay casseroles. (Christmas was also children squealing happily over their presents of little dolls, toy stallions and Christmas stockings packed with dried figs, chestnuts, confetti candy and cookies by *La Vecchi di Natale*, the old woman of Christmas. The little ones fancied that she had entered under their doors at midnight. With streaming white hair, long nails and bare feet, she tiptoed in to place trinkets beside their beds and fill the stockings.)

The traditions of southern Italian holiday cooking are continued by many in the United States, and the recipes are offerings for rich and delicious holiday eating.

Brodo di Manzo (Beef Broth)

2 lbs. shank beef
1 carrot
1 shank bone with marrow
4 sprigs of parsley
1 ripe tomato
1 potato
1 stalk of celery
6 qts. water
salt and pepper to taste

Place all ingredients in cold water. Bring to boil. Lower flame and cook for 2 hours in covered pot. Remove bone and meat. Then remove marrow from bone. Add marrow to broth. Strain broth and vegetables through colander.

Lasagne Imbotite (Stuffed Noodles)

Meat Sauce:
½ lb. Italian sausage (cooked and chopped)
1 lb. chopped meat (cooked)
2 lb. 3 oz. can of plum tomatoes (strained)
7 oz. can of Italian tomato paste
2 cups of hot water
4 tbs. olive oil
2 cloves garlic salt and pepper to taste

Stuffing:
1½ lbs. ricotta
1 lb. broad noodles (lasagne)
1 lb. cubed mozzarella
1 cup of grated Locatelli cheese
salt and pepper to taste

Brown onion lightly in hot olive oil in casserole. Add hot water with tomato paste. Then add plum tomatoes, garlic, salt and pepper. Boil over high flame for 3 minutes. Lower flame. Partially cover. Stir occasionally. Simmer for 30 minutes. Then add cooked meat. Let simmer for another 30 minutes. When done, remove garlic.

Cook noodles in boiling salted water about 15 minutes or until tender. Drain. Run under cool water for better handling.

Pour ½ cup of sauce into bottom of baking pan. Place layer of noodles, a layer of sauce, a layer of grated cheese, a layer of mozzarella and a tablespoon of ricotta here and there. Repeat this process until all ingredients have been used. Top layer should also consist of all ingredients. Bake in 375° oven for 25 minutes or until crisp and brown. When done, remove from oven and let settle for 10 minutes. Then cut in sections with spatula. Sprinkle with grated cheese. Serves 10 to 12.

Carciofi Imbottiti (Stuffed Artichokes)

4 artichokes
1 cup bread crumbs
4 tbs. grated Locataelli cheese
4 chopped anchovy fillets
2 cloves garlic (chopped)
2 tbs. parsley (chopped)
6 tbs. olive oil
½ tsp. salt
2 cups water
salt and pepper to taste

Cut off stems and about ½ inch tips of artichokes. Remove tough outer leaves. Wash well. Spread leaves open and remove excess water. In a small bowl, mix bread crumbs, cheese, fillets, garlic, parsley, salt and pepper. Stuff between leaves of artichokes. Press them closed. Place in small pan, allowing them to stand upright. Pour oil on tops of artichokes. Add water and 1/2 tsp. Of salt to the bottom of pan. Cover partially. Cook for 30 minutes, on low flame. If water evaporates, add a little extra. When outer leaf comes off easily, artichokes are cooked.

Insalata Di Gigoria (Dandelion Salad)

1 lb. dandelion greens
4 tbs. olive oil
2 tbs. wine vinegar
salt and pepper to taste

Discard undesirable leaves. Cut greens in small, bite size pieces. Wash thoroughly in cool water. Dry leaves. Add oil, vinegar, salt and pepper. Toss lightly. Serves 6.

Biscotti Italiani (Italian Biscuits)

6 eggs
4½ cups flour
1 cup sugar
4 tsp. baking powder
8 oz. jar of maraschino cherries (chopped)
¼ lb. butter (creamed)
½ tsp. salt
3 oz. finely chopped almonds

Beat eggs with salt. Add sugar and beat thoroughly. Sift flour and baking powder. Add to eggs and sugar mixture. Add cherries, cherry liquid, butter and almonds. Mix well until dough is smooth. Cut dough into 4 even sections. On greased cookie sheets, spoon and shape dough into 4 oblong loaves, 5 inches wide and ¾ inch thick. Bake in 375° oven for 25 minutes. Remove from oven and cut into 1 inch slices. Let bake for another 10 minutes.

Porcellate Siciliani (Sicilian Fruit cookies)

¾ cup of shortening
½ cup of sugar
2 eggs
3½ cups flour
3 tsp. baking powder
⅓ tsp. salt
½ cup lukewarm water
2 tsp. vanilla extract confectioner's sugar

Filling:
1 cup chopped, roasted almonds
3 cups ground dry figs
1½ cups ground raisins
4 tsp. grated orange rind
1¼ cups water
½ cup sugar
1 tsp. cinnamon

Place figs and raisins in casserole with water over low heat. Cook for 5 minutes stirring constantly. Remove from heat. Add almonds, orange rind, sugar and cinnamon. Let cool. Makes 3½ dozen.

Combine all dry ingredients. Add eggs. Blend in shortening with hands until fine. Then add water and vanilla. Knead until smooth. Divide dough. Roll ⅛ inch thick into 3½ inch squares. Fill with fruit. Fold and pinch edges. Make horseshoe shapes. Place on cookie sheets. Bake for 25 minutes in 375° oven. Remove from oven. Cool. Sprinkle with confectioner's sugar.

The southern Italian in New York, as in his homeland, is generally entwined in the affairs of the home where he believes in the practice of a firm matriarchy as well as patriarchy and not merely in the phrases. The word *rispetto* (respect) is one of the most utilized words in their language. Without it, for family and friends, there is nothing, so they claim. Those who do not recognize this value merit the comments, "she lives like a hibernated bear" or "He will die alone like a dog."

Aside from this spiritual dictum, the southern Italian in New York is not greatly involved with the world around him. Although passive in some ways, he is, nevertheless, warm, generous and fatalistic. He is content with the brief conversations he has every day, perhaps at a Bleecker Street fruitstand or fish market, or with the parishioners of his church on a Sunday morning. Appreciative of miracles, large and small, he makes the undeniable statement to his friends, with a lively gesture of outspread hands, "I am alive and healthy, *amico*, that is what counts!"

Source:
Pauline N. Barrese, *New York Folklore Quarterly*, vol. XXI, 1965.

Sioux

Dr. Charles A. Eastman, whose first Sioux name, Hakadah, means "Pitiful Last," was one of the Santee Sioux of Minnesota who fled to Canada in 1852, following an uprising against white settlers in the area in which 450 whites were killed. Eastman was only four years old at the time. He fled with his uncle's family, leaving his immediately family behind. His father had been arrested as a member of the uprising, and Eastman did not see him again until he was sixteen. The meeting was a momentous one. As a prisoner, his father had been converted to Christianity, and to a belief in "the white man's way." He had come for his son in order that the teenager might learn "this new way, too."

Eastman became one of the Indian students at Dartmouth College in New Hampshire, and in 1890 he graduated with a medical degree from Boston University. In 1902, he published his recollections of growing up among the Santee Sioux in an autobiography titled Indian Boyhood. Reprinted here is the final chapter, "First Impressions of Civilisation."

Although Eastman did not meet any white people until he was sixteen, as a boy growing up in his uncle's household he had heard many stories of the wakan, or mysterious, white race. Such stories offered a version of early contacts between his people and whites, as well as "tall tales" about new technologies such as the railroad. They also offered critical assessments of many white practices: slaveholding, taxation, and the tendency to put a price on everything.

Eastman's account seems to end on a regretful note: "Here my wild life came to an end." The admiration of Indian ways as "wild" was a common feature of "civilized" life. Many nineteenth century white authors, including Washington Irving (1783-1859) and James Fenimore Cooper (1789-1851), showed in their writings a deep longing for the freedom they imagined that Native Americans enjoyed. In echoing such sentiments, Eastman has indeed adopted the "new way," along with the constraints of modern life. Elsewhere in his memoir, however, he makes clear just how hard life could be for Plains Indians.

INDIAN BOYHOOD
by Charles A. Eastman

First Impressions of Civilization

I was scarcely old enough to know anything definite about the "Big Knives," as we called the white men, when the terrible Minnesota massacre broke up our home and I was carried into exile. I have already told how I was adopted into the family of my father's younger brother, when my father was betrayed and imprisoned. We all supposed that he had shared the fate of those who were executed at Mankato, Minnesota.

Now the savage philosophers looked upon vengeance in the field of battle as a lofty virtue. To avenge the death of a relative or of a dear friend was considered a great deed. My uncle, accordingly, had spared no pains to instill into my young mind the obligation to avenge the death of my father and my older brothers. Already I looked eagerly forward to the day when I should find an opportunity to carry out his teachings. Meanwhile, he himself went upon the war-path and returned with scalps every summer. So it may be imagined how I felt toward the Big Knives!

On the other hand, I had heard marvelous things of this people. In some things we despised them; in others we regarded them as wakan (mysterious), a race whose power bordered upon the supernatural. I learned that they had made a "fire-boat." I could not understand how they could unite two elements which cannot exist together. I thought would put out the fire, and the fire would consume the boat if it had the shadow of a chance. This was to me a preposterous thing! But when I was told that the Big Knives had created a "fire-boat-walks-on-mountains" (a locomotive) it was too much to believe.

"Why," declared my informant, "those who saw this monster move said that it flew from mountain to mountain when it seemed to be excited. They said also that they believed it carried a thunder-bird, for they frequently heard his usual war-whoop as the creature sped along!"

Several warriors had observed from a distance one of the first trains on the Northern Pacific, and had gained an exaggerated impression of the wonders of the pale-face. They had seen it go over a bridge that spanned a deep ravine and it seemed to them that it jumped from one bank to the other. I confess that the story almost quenched my ardor and bravery.

Two or three young men were talking together about this fearful invention. "However," said one, "I understand that this fire-boat-walks-on-mountains cannot move except on the track made for it."

Although a boy is not expected to join in the conversation of his elders, I ventured to ask: "Then it cannot chase us into any rough country?"

"No, it cannot do that," was the reply, which I heard with a great deal of relief.

I had seen guns and various other things brought to us by the French Canadians, so that I had already some notion of the supernatural gifts of the white man; but I had never before heard such tales as I listened to that morning. It was said that they had bridged the Missouri and Mississippi rivers, and that they made immense houses of stone and brick, piled on top of one another until they were as high as high hills. My brain was puzzled with these things for many a day. Finally I asked my uncle why the Great Mystery gave such power to the Washechu (the rich)—sometimes we called them by this name—and not to us Dakotas.

"For the same reason," he answered, "that he gave to Duta the skill to make fine bows and arrows, and to Wachesne no skill to make anything."

"And why do the Big Knives increase so much more in number than the Dakotas?" I continued.

"It has been said, and I think it must be true, that they have larger families than we do. I went into the house of an Eashecha (a German), and I counted no less than nine children. The eldest of them could not have been over fifteen. When my grandfather first visited them, down at the mouth of the Mississippi, they were comparatively few; later my father visited their Great Father at Washington, and they had already spread over the whole country."

"Certainly they are a heartless nation. They have made some of their people servants—yes, slaves! We have never believed in keeping slaves, but it seems that these Washechu do! It is our belief that they painted their servants black a long time ago, to tell them from the rest, and now the slaves have children born to them of the same color!

"The greatest object of their lives seems to be to acquire possessions—to be rich. They desire to possess the whole world. For thirty years they were trying to entice us to sell them our land. Finally the outbreak gave them all, and we have been driven away from our beautiful country.

"They are a wonderful people. They have divided the day into hours, like the moons of the year. In fact, they measure everything. Not one of them would let so much as a turnip go from his field unless he received full value for it. I understand that their great men make a feast and invite many, but when the feast is over the guests are required to pay for what they have eaten before leaving the house. I myself saw at White Cliff (the name given to St. Paul, Minnesota) a man who kept a brass drum and a bell to call people to his table; but when he got them in he would make them pay for the food!

"I am also informed," said my uncle, "but this I hardly believe, that their Great Chief (President) compels every man to pay him for the land he lives upon and all his personal goods—even for his own existence—every year!" (This was his idea of taxation.) "I am sure we could not live under such a law.

"When the outbreak occurred, we thought that our opportunity had come, for we had learned that the Big Knives were fighting among themselves, on account of a dispute over their slaves. It was said that the Great Chief had allowed slaves in one part of the country and not in another, so there was jealousy, and they had to fight it out. We don't know how true this was.

"There were some praying-men who came to us some time before the trouble arose. They observed every seventh day as a holy day. On that day they met in a house that they had built for that purpose, to sing, pray, and speak of their Great Mystery. I was never in one of these meeting. I understand that they had a large book from which they read. By all accounts they were very different from all other white men we have known, for these never observed any such day, and we never knew them to pray, neither did they ever tell us of their Great Mystery.

"In war they have leaders and war-chiefs of different grades. The common warriors are driven forward like a herd of antelopes to face the foe. It is on account of this manner of fighting—from compulsion and not from personal bravery—that we count no coup on them. A lone warrior can do much harm to a large army of them in a bad country."

It was this talk with my uncle that gave me my first clear idea of the white men.

I was almost fifteen years old when my uncle presented me with a flint-lock gun. The possession of the "mysterious iron," and the explosive dirt, or "pulverized coal," as it is called, filled me with new thoughts. All the war-songs that I had ever heard from childhood came back to me with their heroes. It seemed as if I were an entirely new being—the boy had become a man!

"I am now old enough," said I to myself, "and I must beg my uncle to take me with him on his next war-path. I shall soon be able to go among the whites whenever I wish, and to avenge the blood of my father and my brothers."

I had already begun to invoke the blessing of the Great Mystery. Scarcely a day passed that I did not offer up some of my game, so that he might not be displeased with me. My people saw very little of me during the day, for in solitude I found the strength I needed. I groped about in the wilderness, and determined to assume my position as a man. My boyish ways were departing, and a sullen dignity and composure was taking their place.

The thought of love did not hinder my ambitions. I had a vague dream of some day courting a pretty maiden, after I had made my reputation, and won the eagle feathers.

One day, when I was away on the daily hunt, two strangers from the United States visited our camp. They had boldly ventured across the northern border. They were Indians, but clad in the white man's garments. It was as well that I was absent with my gun.

My father, accompanied by an Indian guide, after many days' searching had found us at last. He had been imprisoned at Davenport, Iowa, with those who took part in the massacre or in the battles following, and he was taught in prison and converted by the pioneer missionaries, Drs. Williamson and Riggs. He was under sentence of death, but was among the number against whom no direct evidence was found, and who were finally pardoned by President Lincoln.

When he was released, and returned to the new reservation upon the Missouri river, he soon became convinced that life on a government reservation meant physical and moral degradation. Therefore he determined, with several others, to try the white man's way of gaining a livelihood. They accordingly left the agency against the persuasions of the agent, renounced all government assistance, and took land under the United States Homestead law, on the Big Sioux river. After he had made his home there, he desired to seek his lost child. It was then a dangerous undertaking to cross the line, but his Christian love prompted him to do it. He secured a good guide, and found his way in time through the vast wilderness.

As for me, I little dreamed of anything unusual to happen on my return. As I approached our camp with my game on my shoulder, I had not the slightest premonition that I was suddenly to be hurled from my savage life into a life unknown to me hitherto.

When I appeared in sight my father, who had patiently listened to my uncle's long account of my early life and training, became very much excited. He was eager to embrace the child who, as he had just been informed, made it already the object of his life to avenge his father's blood. The loving father could not remain in the teepee and watch the boy coming, so he started to meet him. My uncle arose to go with his brother to insure his safety.

My face burned with the unusual excitement caused by the sight of a man wearing the Big Knives' clothing and coming toward me with my uncle.

"What does this mean, uncle?"

"My boy, this is your father, my brother, whom we mourned as dead. He has come for you."

My father added: "I am glad that my son is strong and brave. Your brothers have adopted the white man's way; I came for you to learn this new way, too; and I want you to grow up a good man."

He had brought me some civilized clothing. At first, I disliked very much to wear garments made by the people I had hated so bitterly. But the thought that, after all, they had not killed my father and brothers, reconciled me, and I put on the clothes.

In a few days we started for the States. I left as if I were dead and traveling to the Spirit Land; for now all my old ideas were to give place to new ones, and my life was to be entirely different from that of the past.

Still, I was eager to see some of the wonderful inventions of the white people. When we reached Fort Totten, I gazed about me with lively interest and a quick imagination.

My father had forgotten to tell me that the fire-boat-walks-on-mountains had its track at Jamestown, and might appear at any moment. As I was watering the ponies, a peculiar shrilling noise pealed forth from just beyond the hills. The ponies threw back their heads and listened; then they ran snorting over the prairie. Meanwhile, I too had taken alarm. I leaped on the back of one of the ponies, and dashed off at full speed. It was clear day; I could not imagine what had caused such an unearthly noise. It seemed as if the world were about to burst in two!

I got upon a hill as the train appeared. "O!" I said to myself, "that is the fire-boat-walks-on-mountains that I have heard about!" Then I drove back the ponies.

My father was accustomed every morning to read from his Bible, and sing a stanza of a hymn. I was about very early with my gun for several mornings; but at last he stopped me as I was preparing to go out, and bade me wait.

I listened with much astonishment. The hymn contained the word Jesus. I did not comprehend what this meant; and my father then told me that Jesus was the Son of God who came on earth to save sinners, and that is was because of him that he has sought me. This conversation made a deep impression upon my mind.

Late in the fall we reached the citizen settlement at Flandreau, South Dakota, where my father and some others dwelt among the whites. Here my wild life came to an end, and my school days began.

Source:

Ohiyesa (Charles A. Eastman), *Indian Boyhood*. Boston: Little, Brown, & Co, 1922. pp. 267-276, 279-289.

In 1889, starvation was widespread on the Lakota Sioux reservation in South Dakota. Many began to dance the Ghost Dance that had been introduced by the Paiute Indian Wovoka (1858?-1932), who claimed to have spoken with Christ and offered the promise of deliverance within two years to the Indian peoples of the Southwest. Priests of the cult spread the word, which many Indians in the Southwest and the Great Plains, dispossessed, humiliated, and impoverished, eagerly took up. Local whites, fearful of the new "disturbances," demanded that the dance be stopped. The Indian agent at the Sioux reservations prohibited it, but the Indians, stirred by the fresh vision of new hope, kept dancing. In 1890 the agent called for troops. On December 15, as part of the military effort to repress the Ghost

Dance, the great Hunkpapa Lakota chief Sitting Bull, or Tatanka Iyotake (c.1831-1890), was killed, allegedly while resisting arrest.

Hundreds of Sioux broke out of the reservation and headed southwest, many of them joining up with a band led by Big Foot. Upon hearing of Sitting Bull's murder, he led his enlarged band of 350 Indians, including 230 women and children, toward what he hoped was safety at the Pine Ridge Reservation. On the way, they were overtaken by the U.S. 7th Cavalry, formerly commanded by Colonel George Armstrong Custer (1839-1876). The cavalry planned to take Big Foot's band to a military camp on Wounded Knee Creek. On the following morning, December 29, the soldiers tried to disarm the Indians. During a struggle over a rifle, a shot was fired. The soldiers then raked the camp with fire from their weapons, including four Hotchkiss machine guns that had been positioned on surrounding hills. More than 300 Indians died that morning, about 175 on the scene, another 146 who were killed by pursuers some three miles away, and perhaps others whose bodies were removed by survivors. The soldiers lost twenty-five, mostly by their own weapons.

The commissioner of Indian affairs held a hearing in 1891 to investigate how this had happened. Among those who gave testimony were the four Sioux—Turning Hawk, Captain Sword, Spotted Horse, and American Horse—whose words are given here.

INDIAN SURVIVORS' ACCOUNTS OF WOUNDED KNEE

by Turning Hawk, Captain Sword,
Spotted Horse, and American Horse

Turning Hawk, Pine Ridge (Mr Cook, interpreter). Mr Commissioner, my purpose today is to tell on what I know of the condition of affairs at the agency where I live. A certain falsehood came to our agency from the west which had the effect of a fire upon the Indians, and when this certain fire came upon our people those who had farsightedness and could see into the matter made up their minds to stand up against it and fight it. The reason we took this hostile attitude to this fire was because we believed that you yourself would not be in favor of this particular mischief-making thing; but just as we expected, the people in authority did not like this thing and we were quietly told that we must give up or have nothing to do with this certain movement. Though this is the advice from our good friends in the east, there were, of course, many silly young men who were longing to become identified with the movement, although they knew that there was nothing absolutely bad, nor did they know there was anything absolutely good, in connection with the movement.

In the course of time we heard that the soldiers were moving toward the scene of trouble. After awhile some of the soldiers finally reached our place and we heard that a number of them also reached our friends at Rosebud. Of course, when a large body of soldiers is moving toward a certain direction they inspire a more or less amount of awe, and it is natural that the women and children who see this large moving mass are made afraid of it and be put in a condition to make them run away. At first we thought that Pine Ridge and Rosebud were the only two agencies where soldiers were sent, but finally we heard that the other agencies fared likewise. We heard and saw that about half our friends at Rosebud agency, from fear at seeing the soldiers, began the move of running away from their agency toward ours (Pine Ridge), and when they had gotten inside of our reservation they there learned that right ahead of them at our agency was another large crowd of soldiers, and while the soldiers were there, there was constantly a great deal of false rumor flying back and forth. The special rumor I have in mind is the threat that the soldiers had come there to disarm the Indians entirely and to take away all their horses from them. That was the oft-repeated story.

Yellow Bird, medicine man.

So constantly repeated was this story that our friends from Rosebud, instead of going to Pine Ridge, the place of their destination, veered off and went to some other direction toward the "Bad Lands." We did not know definitely how many, but understood there were 300 lodges of them, about 1,700 people. Eagle Pipe, Turning Bear, High Hawk, Short Bull, Lance, No Flesh, Pine Bird, Crow Dog, Two Strike, and White Horse were the leaders.

Well, the people after veering off in this way, many of them who believe in peace and order at our agency, were very anxious that some influence should be brought upon these, people. In addition to our love of peace we remembered that many of these people were related to us by blood. So we sent out peace commissioners to the people who were thus running away from their agency.

I understood at the time that they were simply going away from fear because of so many soldiers. So constant was the word of these good men from Pine Ridge Agency that finally they succeeded in getting away half of the party from Rosebud, from the place where they took refuge, and finally were brought to the agency at Pine Ridge. Young-Man-Afraid-of-His-Horses, Little Wound, Fast Thunder, Louis Shangreau, John Grass, Jack Red Cloud, and myself were some of these peace makers.

The remnant of the party from Rosebud not taken to the agency finally reached the wilds of the Bad Lands. Seeing that we had succeeded so well, once more we sent to the same party in the Bad Lands and succeeded in bringing these very Indians out of the depths of the Bad Lands and were being brought toward the agency. When we were about a day's journey from our agency we heard that a certain party of Indians (Big Foot's band) from the Cheyenne River agency was coming toward Pine Ridge in flight.

Captain Sword. Those who actually went off of the Cheyenne River agency probably number 303, and there were a few from the Standing Rock reserve with them, but as to their number I do not know. There were a number of Ogalallas, old men and several school boys, coming back with that very same party, and one of the very seriously wounded boys was a member of the Ogalalla boarding school at Pine Ridge agency. He was not on the warpath, but was simply returning home to his agency and to his school after a summer visit to relatives on the Cheyenne river.

Turning Hawk. When we heard that these people were coming toward our agency we also heard this. These people were coming toward Pine Ridge agency, and when they were almost on the agency they were met by the soldiers and surrounded and finally taken to the Wounded Knee creek, and there at a given time their guns were demanded. When they had delivered them up, the men were separated from their families, from their tipis, and taken to a certain spot. When the guns were thus taken and the men thus separated, there was a crazy man, a young man of very bad influence and in fact a nobody, among that bunch of Indians fired his gun, and of course the firing of a gun must have been the breaking of a military rule of some sort, because immediately the soldiers returned fire and indiscriminate killing followed.

Spotted Horse. This man shot an officer in the army; the first shot killed this officer. I was a voluntary scout at that encounter and I saw exactly what was done, and that was what I noticed; that the first shot killed an officer. As soon as this shot was fired the Indians immediately began drawing their knives, and they were exhorted from all sides to desist, but this was not obeyed. Consequently the firing began immediately on the part of the soldiers.

Turning Hawk. All the men who were in a bunch were killed right there, and those who escaped that first fire got into the ravine, and as they went along up the ravine for a long distance they were pursued on both sides by the soldiers and shot down, as the dead bodies showed afterwards. The women were standing off at a different place from where the men were stationed, and when the firing began, those of the men who escaped the first onslaught went in one direction up the ravine, and then the women, who were bunched together at another place, went entirely in a different direction through an open field, and the women fared the same fate as the men who went up the deep ravine.

American Horse. The men were separated, as has already been said, from the women, and they were surrounded by the soldiers. Then came next the village of the Indians and that was entirely surrounded by the soldiers also. When the firing began, of course the people who were standing immediately around the young man who fired the first shot were killed right together, and then they turned their guns, Hotchkiss guns, etc., upon the women who were in the lodges standing there under a flag of truce, and of course as soon as they were fired upon they fled, the men fleeing in one direction and the women running in two different directions. So that there were three general directions in which they took flight.

There was a women with an infant in her arms who was killed as she almost touched the flag of truce, and the women and children of course were strewn all along the circular village until they were dispatched. Right near the flag of truce a mother was shot down with her infant; the child not knowing that its mother was dead was still nursing, and that especially was a very sad sight. The women as they were fleeing with their babes were killed together, shot right through, and the women who

were very heavy with child were also killed. All the Indians fled in these three directions, and after most all of them had been killed a cry was made that all those who were not killed or wounded should come forth and they would be safe. Little boys who were not wounded came out of their places of refuge, and as soon as they came in sight a number of soldiers surrounded them and butchered them there.

Of course we all feel very sad about this affair. I stood very loyal to the government all through those troublesome days, and believing so much in the government and being so loyal to it, my disappointment was very strong, and I have come to Washington with a very great blame on my heart. Of course it would have been all right if only the men were killed; we would feel almost grateful for it. But the fact of the killing of the women, and more especially the killing of the young boys and girls who are to go to make up the future strength of the Indian people, is the saddest part of the whole affair and we feel it very sorely.

> *"I stood very loyal to the government all through those troublesome days, and believing so much in the government and being so loyal to it, my disappointment was very strong, and I have come to Washington with a very great blame on my heart." —American Horse*

I was not there at the time before the burial of the bodies, but I did go there with some of the police and the Indian doctor and a great many of the people, men from the agency, and we went through the battlefield and saw where the bodies were from the track of the blood.

Turning Hawk. I had just reached the point where I said that the women were killed. We heard, besides the killing of the men, of the onslaught also made upon the women and children, and they were treated as roughly and indiscriminately as the men and boys were.

Of course this affair brought a great deal of distress upon all the people, but especially upon the minds of those who stood loyal to the government and who did all that they were able to do in the matter of bringing about peace. They especially have suffered much distress and are very much hurt at heart. These peacemakers continued on in their good work, but there were a great many fickle young men who were ready to be moved by the change in the events there, and consequently, in spite of the great fire that was brought upon all, they were ready to assume any hostile attitude. These young men got themselves in readiness and went in the direction of the scene of battle so they might be of service there. They got there and finally exchanged shots with the soldiers. This party of young men was made up from Rosebud, Ogalalla (Pine Ridge), and members of any other agencies that happened to be there at the time. While this was going on in the neighborhood of Wounded Knee-the Indians and soldiers exchanging shots-the agency, our home, was also fired into by the Indians. Matters went on in this strain until the evening came on, and then the Indians went off down by White Clay creek. When the agency was fired upon by the Indians from the hillside, of course the shots were returned by the Indian police who were guarding the agency buildings.

Although fighting seemed to have been in the air, yet those who believed in peace were still constant at their work. Young-Man-Afraid-of-His-Horses, who had been on a visit to some other agency in the north or northwest, returned, and immediately went out to the people living about White Clay creek, on the border of the Bad Lands, and brought his people out. He succeeded in obtaining the consent of the people to come out of their place of refuge and return to the agency. Thus the remaining portion of the Indians who started from Rosebud were brought back into the agency. Mr Commissioner, during the days of the great whirlwind out there, those good men tried to hold up a counteracting power, and that was "Peace." We have now come to realize that peace has prevailed and won the day. While we were engaged in bringing about peace our property was left behind, of course, and most of us have lost everything, even down to the matter of guns with which to kill ducks, rabbits, etc, shotguns, and guns of that order. When Young-Man-Afraid brought the people in and their guns were asked for, both men who were called hostile and men who stood loyal to the government delivered up their guns.

Source:

Documentary Archives: Multicultural America CD-ROM. Woodbridge, CT: Primary Source Media, 1997.

*O*ne of the most vocal and visible Native American activists today is Russell Means, who has worked on behalf of indigenous peoples throughout the world for more than 25 years. He first rose to prominence during the early 1970s as one of the leaders of the American Indian Movement (AIM), a Minneapolis-based civil rights organization founded in 1968. Eloquent and charismatic with a striking physical presence and flair for drama, he quickly became the symbol of what many admired—and some feared—about AIM and its activities. Although he withdrew from the organization during the late 1980s to pursue other personal and professional interests, Means remains devoted to his original cause. "My ultimate aim," he has said, "is the reinstitution of pride and self-dignity of the Indian in America."

An Oglala Sioux, Means was born in Porcupine, South Dakota, on the Pine Ridge Reservation, but grew up in and around Oakland, California. Trained as an accountant, he also worked as a rodeo rider, Indian dancer, and ballroom dance instructor before returning to his midwest roots in the late 1960s. There he found a job in the tribal office on the Rosebud Reservation. He left South Dakota for Cleveland, Ohio, in 1970, where he headed the city's Indian Center. Around this same time, Means was introduced to the American Indian Movement when he attended an Indian conference in Minneapolis. Founded by activist Clyde Bellecourt and others, AIM operated on the belief that the federal government's supervision of Native American affairs would eventually lead to the total destruction of the Indian people unless they themselves took action to ensure their survival. This message appealed to the aggressively outspoken Means, who bitterly resented the fact that white society had forced him and his ancestors to give up their culture and their language. Upon his return to Cleveland, he established a local AIM chapter and immediately became involved in major AIM demonstrations across the country.

Around 1972, Means grew tired of living in the city and moved back to the Pine Ridge Reservation. There he gained personal fame and increased respect for AIM when he led a caravan of supporters across the state line into Nebraska to protest the brutal death of an Indian named Raymond Yellow Thunder. Two young white brothers had beaten up Yellow Thunder "just for fun" and then paraded him around at a dance in the town of Gordon while inviting onlookers to kick him. They then stuffed him in a car trunk, where he later died. When it appeared local authorities had no plans to charge the brothers with any serious crime, AIM became involved at the request of the victim's family. Means successfully reached a settlement that resulted in the resignation of the police chief and a promise to address the rampant racism that had led to Yellow Thunder's death.

Means went on to play key roles in many other AIM protests, among them the Trail of Broken Treaties march to Washington, D.C., in 1972 and the famous Wounded Knee siege in 1973. In the latter incident, which took place on the Pine Ridge Reservation, several hundred AIM members and sympathizers rebelled against the reservation's head administrator, Dick Wilson, whom some of the tribal elders accused of corruption and strong-arm tactics. In a symbolic gesture of defiance, they occupied the hamlet of Wounded Knee, the site of an 1890 massacre of more than 200 Sioux men, women and children by U.S. Army troops who had been ordered to crush the Ghost Dance spiritual movement. Federal marshals and FBI agents immediately stepped in to re-establish government control, provoking an armed standoff between the Indians and the U.S. government. Means served as one of the major spokesmen for the Native Americans during the 71 day occupation and also helped negotiate with authorities. Afterwards, he and other AIM leaders were arrested on various civil disobedience charges. The eight-month trial ended when the presiding judge threw the case out of court for prosecutorial misconduct.

By then, Means had become an international celebrity. With his solemn and somewhat intimidating looks, enhanced by his rough denim clothes, Indian jewelry, and long dark braids. He remained controversial both on and off the reservation, partly because some people felt he enjoyed being in the limelight too much. In 1974, he lost a close and hotly disputed election for tribal chairman to Dick Wilson, which intensified hostilities between pro-AIM and anti-AIM forces. He also became a target; over the next six years or so, Means survived five shootings, was brought up on criminal charges four times, and spent a year in a South Dakota state prison, where he was stabbed by a fellow inmate.

Means nevertheless continued his efforts to keep the concerns of Native American people in the forefront of the overall struggle for human rights. To that end, in September 1977, he was a principal speaker at a special United Nations conference on discrimination against indigenous people of the Americas. Held in Geneva, Switzerland, the conference brought together more than 100 delegates from over 30 countries. More than 50 years had passed since Native Americans had been given the opportunity to air their grievances before a similar world audience.

Means left AIM in early 1988 but has remained much in demand around the world as a lecturer and spokesman for various Indian causes. He has also testified before numerous governmental bodies, including a special U.S. Senate committee investigating the federal government's relationship with Native Americans. Means has more recently branched out into yet another field of endeavor—acting. He launched his new career with a well-received performance as Chingachgook in the 1992 version of The Last of the Mohicans. In 1995, he gave voice to the character of Chief Powhatan in Disney's animated feature Pocahontas and also served as *a consultant on the project. Future goals include producing and directing his own film that would help educate the American people about Indians. "In America," says Means of his new willingness to enter the mainstream, "you achieve visibility through entertainment or the arts." As the following speech makes clear, time has not dimmed his radicalism—or his bluntness. Delivered September 28, 1988 (the place and occasion are unknown), Means began with an Oglala Lakota greeting, which he then proceeded to translate for his audience.*

THE STATE OF NATIVE AMERICA

What I said is, "Hello, my relatives. I am an ally, and I come from Yellow Thunder Camp in our very sacred holy land, the Black Hills."

Back in 1968-70, the state of the American Indian nations in the Americas of the Western Hemisphere was unchanged from 1492. That's in 1968, 1969, and 1970. This is now 1988, and it still remains unchanged from 1492. In 1492 we were considered an "expendable peoples" by Columbus and the governments of Europe, including the Roman Catholic Church. It wasn't until 1897, thirty-two years after the conclusion of the Civil War, that the Catholic Church declared us to be human beings. Until then, the Marine Corps of the Catholic Church, the Jesuits and the Franciscans, considered us to be "beasts of burden." And now they're going to canonize, make into a saint, Father Serra, a slaveowner, a murderer. That is the state of the American Indian nations. The pope is going to canonize an Indian murderer, an Indian slaveowner, Father Serra, who established these missionary outposts for the Marine Corps, I mean the Catholic Church, along the western coast of Mexico and California.

We are an "expendable people." Go down to Brazil and you will see the government forcibly relocating and allowing miners and forestry employees to massively murder Indian people. Go to Paraguay where they still have bounties on the Aiche. Go to Chile, where Pinochet is officially starving the Mapuche to get their remaining lands. Go to Costa Rica, where Weyerhauser is removing Indian people so they can get at their forests. Go to Nicaragua, where the entire government effort has not only relocated but mass murdered, and it continues to this day, the Indian people. Both the left or the right excuse it and would rather deal with dope dealers. Go to Mexico. Go to Alaska. Go to Canada. Come right here to the United States of America, where this government right here today, at this very moment, is relocating and starving to death and completely destroying an Indian nation, the Navajo, in Arizona. Forced relocation, the same thing the Sandinistas are doing.

Welcome to the Americas. Welcome to the Americas, my home, where the dust that you kick up as you walk is made up of the bones of my ancestors. Welcome. For what you have appropriated and for what we have given to you, I will tell you.

Sixty percent of the world's foodstuffs comes from us. Eighty percent of what the average American eats every day comes from us. Non-Indians are continually asking me, "What's some traditional Indian food?" What did you eat today? Did you go to a salad bar? That's all ours."

We domesticated and developed, for instance, over ten thousand species of potatoes. So when the Europeans came over here, what did they take back? One species. So when the blight hit their potato crop, they had nothing to fall back on, and consequently, we got a lot of Kennedys coming over here. When the blight hit one of our potato crops, we had 9,999 to fall back on. And they call me primitive!

Sewage systems we gave to the Europeans. When Cortez and Pizarro and Coronado and all the rest of the conquistadors were over here destroying Indian people and our records, some of the people with them recognized that, hey, these Indians have sewage systems. Let's take it back to Europe and clean up Berlin and Rome and London and Madrid and Brussels, Paris. And voilà! In less than a generation the amount of disease and the plague that was rampant in Europe dramatically was reduced to less than one percent than what it had been before. Because of the introduction of sewage systems that we gave to the world.

I could go on and on and on. The medicines, the advent of pasteurization, named after Louis Pasteur. B.S.! In his own writings he credits the Indians!

Welcome to natural childbirth. The Lamaze method. A Frenchman comes over here, studies the

Indian way of giving birth, goes back to France, writes it up, and you call it the Lamaze method.

Welcome to the Americas. Welcome. The finest medicines in the world developed here. Developed here! Welcome to the Americas. From quinine to penicillin. Welcome. Codeine.

Welcome to the Americas. But instead of the Europeans, the Asians, the Africans, the Middle Easterners, the Far Easterners, instead of saying "thank you," we are still an "expendable people." Does anyone talk about majority rule in Ecuador or Bolivia or Peru or Panama or the Northwest Territories of Canada or Guatemala? No. You don't hear about majority rule. Because those are Indians, campesinos, peasants. Do you see at the family of nations a red person sitting around the table with the family of nations? We are the only color of the human race not allowed to participate in the international community. That's an insult to your own humanity! Think about it! Look around! Your own humanity is being insulted! You live in this modern day and age when an entire people is not even considered to be a part of the international community.

Welcome to the Americas. The states of the American Indian peoples. You blithely continue on in life without an acknowledgement of Colorado or of any of the forty states whose names are derived from the origin of the Indian language. It's amazing how people are not saying "thank you."

[In] 1968 and 1969, 1970, Indians that protested back east were wearing Plains Indians outfits. American Indian people were attending conferences in ties, shined shoes and suits and bouffant hairdos, with pearl earrings on the women. They were afraid to wear beadwork, afraid to wear silver and turquoise. They were embarrassed to announce to the world that they are proud of who they are. I was fortunate to be in the vanguard of a cultural revolution that took place in the late 1960s and 1970s. That cultural revolution enabled our pride and self-dignity to once again become the criteria of what the American Indian nations are all about. It succeeded beyond our wildest plans and expectations, hopes or dreams.

When I sat in Minneapolis with Clyde Bellecourt and Dennis Banks in 1969 and we took the American Indian movement into a national and then international organization, I remember when we attended Indian conferences and they wouldn't allow us to speak because we looked "ridiculous" in headbands and beadwork and moccasins and we had a drum with us. Our own people. When Dr. Alfonso Ortiz, a Pueblo Indian from New Mexico, who is a doctor of anthropology at the University of New Mexico, was up in his three-piece suit at

Russell Means

the National Indian Education Association, of which I was on the board at the time, he was giving the keynote address at a banquet. The American Indian Movement. We came in. I was sitting up there on the dais with him, and the American Indian Movement came in with all their headbands and all their beadwork and their drum, and we stood, Indian people, at each exit, and wouldn't allow these other Indians in their ties and gowns to leave because they tried to leave. We sang Indian at that conference, the National Indian Education Association, NIEA, which now is somehow wallowing in the left-brain, right-brain arguments. That was the state of the American Indian nations in 1970. The Indian people embarrassed about who they are.

"[Native Americans] are the only color of the human race not allowed to participate in the international community."

It's changed that cultural revolution. We had to challenge the United States government militarily, and we won again! Again! Because we were right and we're still right.

But understand the state of the American Indian nations. Because we know. You see, at the advent of the opening up of half the world to the rest of the world, we allowed disease and overpopulation of Europe to dramatically decrease, as I said, in the matter of a generation. There were diseases that were rampant and incurable in Europe: the plague, everything. They instituted sewage systems and the population density went from thirty-five per square mile in 1492 down to seven in less than a century because of the opening of the Western Hemisphere and the cleaning up of the environment.

What happened? The disease was contained. The diseases were contained. But have you all learned? What's the disease today that's incurable? AIDS. The revolution comes around again, but this time there is no more Western Hemisphere, no more Indians. Because we already told those moon Indians, "Watch out, they're coming." There's no other place to go.

The message is the same: clean up. You want to cure AIDS? Clean it up. You want to cure all the other diseases, the cancers, every one that pops up every day? Clean up. As Chief Seattle said, "Continue to contaminate your bed and one night you will suffocate in your own waste."

The state of the American Indian nations, that cultural revolution I was talking about of the 1970s. Here's the beauty of that experience: our traditional people gained respect. Our culture gained respect. And we're still struggling. We're now embarking on an economic revolution. The Red Nations of the Western Hemisphere.

But let me tell you something about the state of the American Indian nations. There is Indian activism in virtually every Indian community. Wherever there's more than one Indian, there's activism. That goes whether it's Seattle University, the Navajo, Nicaragua, Argentina, Chile, Alaska, Canada—everywhere we live. And it's infected the world. Because of our cultural revolution the onslaught and attack on indigenous peoples worldwide is now pervasive.

They're getting our own people to call themselves "Native American." They're getting our own people to teach in universities like this about "we come from China." Understand that we do not come from China. That is a racist, a very racist concept that began with Thomas Jefferson, and he only wrote about it in passing, because of our physical characteristics. In fact, the reverse is true. Geologists know it's impossible for us to have migrated from the Western Hemisphere west. Because during the Ice Ages, the ice corridors that were formed along the northwest coasts of the Western Hemisphere made it impossible to migrate from here to the west, or, as the Europeans call it, the Far East. I could never figure that one out. In fact, those same ice corridors made migration from here going west possible. Geologists know this.

Where are the anthropologists around here? Don't they ever visit with geologists? The archaeologists, the official grave robbers of intellectual institutions such as this? Any high school students that have aspirations towards robbing graves, I would suggest that it is one of the most disrespectful professions and dishonorable professions, if you want to call it that, in the world today. There are federal laws protecting grave robbers. What kind of ghouls are archaeologists?

I live at Canyon de Chelly, on the Navajo for aeons. Canyon de Chelly is part of a whole tourist route to go see where Indians used to live. Cliff-dwellers, they're called. The Anasazi people, they're called by "anthros" and "archies." And these peoples, the Diné, the Hopi, all indigenous peoples of that area, the Zuni, the Pueblos, the Apache, those ruins that are in the sides of the cliffs. We never go there. We have respect for that. We have respect. But day in and day out tourists, non-Indian tourists are trampling all over those cliff dwellings. Every day of the year. They call them cliff-dwellers. They want to know what happened. But you know that archaeologists and anthropologists will not consult with Indian people because that would prejudice their findings. So they have come to the conclusions by robbing some of our graves, and this is the most recent, that we were cannibals because these bones were all broken up and in mass graves in a mass area.

Of course, these graves are about six or seven thousand years old. They didn't take into account any earthquakes or a coyote or two hanging around digging up the earth or moles or worms, etc. They didn't even go over to the Hopi and say, "Hey, guys, how do you bury your people?" They came to the conclusion we're cannibals. I retorted that if I used the same criteria as anthropologists and archaeologists of these learned institutions, I will go to a Christian gravesite, dig up a grave, find a body in a coffin, and say, "Aha! Aha! The white man is saving his dead for future famines! They have found a way to preserve food." That's how ridiculous this grave-robbing has become in the alleged intellectual community. We have our own people believing this. In the same institutions not even protesting it!

I am sick and tired of the state of the American Indian. We had a beautiful cultural revolution, but you know what happens? The government and all institutions are making it even harder for us to know who we are. You see, in this country, the United States of America, the Indian people, we can be anything we want to be. Anything. We can even become archaeologists. But we can't be Indian. It's against the law in this country to be Indian.

We can't pray. The last six decisions of the Supreme Court concerning our freedom of religion all denied it. The last Rehnquist decision totally obliterated our right to freedom of religion. In the name of "progress."

We do not have the right to pray in the Black Hills. I know. We are still in court. I have argued. I'm the only non-lawyer ever to argue before a U.S. Court of Appeals. I argued on behalf of the Yellow Thunder Camp against the Black Hills National Forest for their refusal to allow us to pray in the Black Hills according to our ways. But we as Indian people are not allowed, and I'm going to give you a view of what American Indian people are doing to themselves, because we've become our own worst enemy.

Understand this about the U.S. government: they practice and perfect their colonialism on us, here, in the backyard of America, and then export it to the world. If you don't believe it, look at the West Bank, look at South Africa, look at Borneo, look at the Philippines, etc. Then look at yourselves, look in the mirror. What do we think? We cannot, we do not have self-determination. It's called "self-administration," and that's my term. We get to administer someone else's policies.

Do you think Indian people are standing up? No. Do you know who they consider our leaders? The ones who suck off of Uncle Sam. Those are our alleged leaders, who are leaders by permission from the federal government. They're not my leader. Understand colonialism, where you're not allowed a choice of who your leaders are going to be. In fact, it insults your intelligence so much you refuse to participate in the society. Is that why only forty-five percent of Americans vote? Because they refuse opportunity, they refuse choices?

We still have a lot to give to the world. To be independent. We're not allowed to know who our heroes are. Our Indian children, every day, are bombarded with white and black heroes on TV and in school. And that's good, for the white children and the black children, and that didn't come without struggle. But our children, and you think our fancy, educated Indians are doing anything about making sure that their heroes are known to our own children? No. The only heroes they know, and that's because of us, AIM, are the ones from the last century.

What about our heroes from the first decade of this century? Or the second decades? Or the twenties? We had heroes, local and national heroes. And in the thirties, and the forties, and the fifties and the sixties and the seventies and the eighties. Our children don't know the names. In 1950 all the sports media in this country got together and they voted on who was the finest athlete in the first half

century. You think they voted Jesse Owens? No! Jim Thorpe. They did it again in 1975.

Who was the finest athlete America produced in the first three-quarters of the twentieth century? Jim Thorpe won again, overwhelmingly so, both times. I go around the Indian nation. I ask Indian teenagers and I ask Indian little kids. Just last week, I asked my daughter, who's in the third grade, "Who's Jim Thorpe?" "I don't know." And yet, one of the high schools on my reservation is called the Thorpes. Nobody on my reservation knows who Jim Thorpe is. None of the children.

I said, "Who's Billy Mills?" He won the 10,000 meters at Tokyo. He's from my reservation. None of the kids know who Billy Mills is. That was just in 1964, for crying out loud.

I say, "Who's the first Indian ever to run for president of the United States?" First I ask, "Who was the first Indian to become vice president of the United States of America?" Charles Curtis. [Curtis served with Herbert Hoover from 1929 until 1933.] Everybody knows that, right? My own kids, other Indian kids don't know that.

"In this country, the United States of America, the Indian people, we can be anything we want to be.... But we can't be Indian."

I said, "Who's the first Indian ever to run for president of the United States?" I asked my daughter. She didn't know. I said, "It's your dad." [During the 1980s, Means ran for president on two different occasions, once as the Libertarian candidate.]

But you see? I tell my own people: "Quit your complaining. You want to complain to somebody? Look in the mirror. And be a little bit independent."

But Indians and non-Indians: You're penalized today for being independent. If you're not part of the masses, you're penalized. Think about it. In every aspect of your life. Just look at the tax structure if you don't believe.

The state of the American Indian nations. I'm sick and tired of our own people. There's an entire people now in North Carolina who have Indian blood in their veins and want to be federally recognized. To me that's the abomination of what Indian people are. They actually believe that if you're federally recognized by the United States government, that somehow is a positive development. To me it is the most negative.

The Mikasukis, the Seminoles, the ones who defeated the United States of America not once, but twice, the ones that had every Indian killed by the United States of America in that Seminole war, who have never been defeated by the United States government, cost the United States government then a million dollars. This is back in the early 1800s, when a million dollars was a million dollars. Now a million dollars in those terms is about 120 million, OK?

Imagine, in a war where for every death you cause it cost you 120 million dollars. Those Seminoles, the Mikasukis, who still live in the Everglades, back in the 1960s, when Buffalo Tiger was looking for federal recognition and got it, half of his nation refused to be enrolled in the federal government, refused to go along with him. They said, "No, that would legitimize the United States government. The United States government isn't legal."

These primitives, who refuse to be enrolled with their national ID number, refuse to recognize the United States of America, that is who our Indian leaders are. Not somebody funded by the federal government, funded by you all. You're the taxpayers. Funded by you. That's not my leader.

One thing about Indian people, and I just want to give you a small glimpse of who we are. Indian people are not tourists. We have homes that we never leave, and those that do are no longer Indian because they have no more connection.

"Our way of life is made up of one word: it's called 'respect.'"

Understand what that connection is. It's that dust I talked about earlier, that dust that comes from our Mother Earth. And only out of respect can you regain that. The Indian people are fooling themselves, not only in their culture, they've dropped their culture so they can call it a "powwow circuit," and they can dress any way they want to be, to the point where they fight their own people and are dependent on the federal government.

I come from the poorest county in the United States of America, the Pine Ridge Indian Reservation. The poorest county. I moved away from there last year to the home of my wife, a Navajo, Diné. Because that culturally is the way we do things. The man always moves to where the woman is from.

In fact, because we are a matrilineal society, if we had the disrespect enough to take another's last name, it would be the woman's last name, not the man's. Because the male lives a shorter life than the female. So it's a natural sense that the man would go where the woman is from so that because the man, when we leave this earth, then our wife and children are around their relatives and friends. So they'll always be in friendly society, never be alone.

But we have a home. We don't have to look for zen. We don't have to look for Franciscans, you know. We have a way of life. We do not have a religion, we have a way of life. Our way of life is made up of one word: it's called "respect." But it means a lot more. Respect for our relatives' visions. When you understand that everything lives and that everything is sacred and the further you get away from what is natural the less important life becomes.

When you get yourselves locked into the asphalt jungles and there is no life, then even the human being's life is no longer important. My son, who is three years old, we live out on the Diné land in the desert, and I take him to the anthills and I show him and we sit there and we watch the ant people and I tell him about the ant people: "Have respect. Don't walk on their homes." He says, "Well, Reba does it." Reba's our horse. I say, "Reba's part of the earth. We know better."

If you have respect for the ant people then you'll have respect for people in Hiroshima. If you have respect for the ant people then you will have respect for people in Nicaragua or South Africa or anywhere else in the world.

The state of the Indian nation. Do you know the names of these mountains that are so beautiful right here, that you're so proud of you even put them on your license plates? When I moved down to Navajo, my wife didn't take me around. Just every time we traveled around she'd tell me the name of that mountain and that mountain and its history and whose land this is and what family has lived on that land and why.

This is the state of the Indian nations, but we're losing that because our educated Indians who have bought the white man's way will not allow our children to know our own heroes, our contemporary heroes, and what is beautiful and natural and respectful.

The state of the Indian nations. It's important that you know that you cannot break a branch when you're a child because you're breaking the arm of a living being. It's important to understand and be thankful for rain and not curse it because you have to walk in it. And to love the winter, not because you can ski on it, but because it makes you strong as a person, as an individual.

If you know who you are I know who we are because I know the sacred colors. I know that pink stands for medicine. So I ask why? So my elders tell me. You go into the medicinal plants, all the plants that are good for you, inside the bud, not available to the naked eye. It's pink. Poisonous plants do not have that pink. Remember that when you're out around here at the rivers, because there's some poisonous plants that'll kill you just like that. It's good to know.

Have respect for colors. I know why orange is the color of water. And they say we primitives are not capable of abstract thought? I say, "Now wait a minute. How do you get orange the color of water? Why does that denote water?" Well, according to my nation, we live in the middle of a plains area. Orange is because when the moon comes up it's orange, and the moon controls water. Voilà.

I know what orange means. To me it means the feminine power of birth. I know what it is to respect life because my grandfather told me my role in life, and I didn't know what he was talking about. I finally figured it out. Unfortunately, it took me thirty-seven years to figure it out. Because I had to go through sixteen years of white man education before I went back to school among my own people.

What I found out is that a long time ago, when the Lakota were sitting around the campfire, the men began to see the women grow with child. As they watched, they witnessed the miracle of life: birth. They watched a little longer and they saw that new life, that birth, being taken in the arms of woman and nurtured at her breast. They watched the child grow and become strong. Then they looked at one another. That was the end of my grandfather's story. I add this: The men looked at one another and said, "What are we doing here?"

So we look for the balance in life, the male-female balance of life which is in the universe, which is trapped in these trees, those grasses. All of life has a male-female balance, even you. If you understand the male-female balance then you don't have to worry about your rights, because every individual has a right.

In the 1970s, when I was younger and a militant and I wanted to change the world today, I went around to my people, advocating they pick up the gun. I said, "If we can't win let's get it over with. It's not worth watching the rape of our mother. It's not worth watching the massacre of her children. Let's get it over with."

But the old people would say, "Have patience, young man. Look around you. Understand who you are, where you come from, and why and where you are going. Understand that time is on your side and just because someone has invented a clock does not mean you have to hurry through life. Clocks are for those who are going to be trained to do the bidding of the master. Time is on your side. If you understand that you'll know how to utilize time. Therefore life is no longer a problem. Today is no longer a

problem. Your teenage years is no longer a problem. Nothing is a problem because you understand that there is no time."

The state of the American Indian nation. It's all good, and we don't have to pick up the gun because we understand about life. We understand that we don't need the gun because if that was true then all the grasshoppers in the world would get together and jump on you all. That doesn't happen. We understand immortality. The next world.

And immortality is today. You don't have to worry about tomorrow for peace of mind. That's why we're not tourists.

The old people will not travel for just any reason. I'll give you an example. [In] 1982, the Bertrand Russell Tribunal, a very formidable, very prestigious international forum put together by intellectuals the world over, "anthros," and "archies," and all the alleged social scientists. They did a heck of a thing for the Palestinians in the 1970s. They decided to have a forum on the American Indians of the Western Hemisphere in Rotterdam in 1982. So they invited us. And they came to us, the Indian people.

I was part of that. We wanted to get the issue of the 1868 Fort Laramie treaty with the Lakota Nation before this international tribunal, and we wanted our elders, our most revered elders, the traditional chiefs of our nation, to take our message over there.

So we arranged for our oldest chief, Fool's Crow, and his interpreter and another chief, Matthew King, a noble red man, to go over. We arranged a first class passage on an airplane. We got the St. Mark's Hotel in New York City to give them a three-bedroom suite free.

I was in our international affairs office at the UN arranging last minute details. I got a call from my home in South Dakota. There were Indians coming from all over the Americas; this is just one story, going to Rotterdam. I got a call and they said, "Fool's Crow and Matthew King, they don't want to go."

So I call and I go around and I get the police to go after Matthew King and get him to a telephone and they get him on a telephone, and I said, "Look, your flight leaves early tomorrow morning. You get into New York City. We have first class. We have everybody ready. The airlines, the hostesses, everybody's going to treat you great. I've got you a suite in Rotterdam, and it's going to be first class passage back."

He said, "Nephew, understand this. We're old people. That's a long way away. We might die over there. We don't want to go there. But you tell those Russell people that if they ever come to the United States and have a meeting, maybe we will attend."

Understand the beauty of that. Talk about individual sovereignty, independence. That was the ultimate statement. Here were all these educated Indians in the United States, Canada and the rest of the hemisphere, all the ones with their degrees, all the ones that like this kind of thing, we're hopping, including myself. I wasn't going, but I was all excited about it.

That really sat me down to look at what we are. All of that materialism, all of that ego tripping, didn't mean a thing to these old people. All of these fancy titles after all of these fancy people that were putting on this tribunal. If they ever decide, they'll never have a tribunal over here.

"If those Russell people ever have a meeting over here, then maybe we'll come." I think that is the ultimate statement of sovereignty, individual sovereignty.

The state of the American Indian nations is an exciting state. I see that what goes around comes around. I understand that, because everything that is holy and sacred and good is round. Understand that also. That's part of the male-female balance. The sun is round, the moon is round. Walk up on a hill and you'll see that our sacred grandmother, the Mother Earth, is round. Everything sacred is round. So what goes around comes around.

Our people accomplished a socioeconomic phenomenon in the 1970s, in one decade, in less than fifteen years, not only in the United States of America but in Canada and the rest of the Western Hemisphere.

It's an exciting time to live, and we're fighting, but I'm sick and tired of the educated Indian, because to me they're not educated. They've educated their wisdom out. It's good. I have confidence in people who have education. I have one; my children are getting theirs. I advocate Indians to go on to institutions of higher learning. I hold seminars on it to those that will listen. Drug abuse and alcohol abuse.

But understand that I know what oppression is. I know what sacrifice is. Understand that peoples who come from the barrio, the reservation, the ghetto, we know oppression. So we know how to struggle. We know what sacrifice is. Ask any mother. It's really that simple. Any mother.

So it's an exciting time. And I see it's time now to go to my own people, slap them in the face and hear them say, "Thank you. I needed that."

Because we did it once before, as I told you, at that convention at the NIEA. Understand that we're not through yet.

The sanctity of life is too precious to allow this society to continue to be disrespectful. I have grandchildren, nine grandchildren, and I fought so that my sons and my daughters would have a better way. And I'm not going to allow my sons and daughters to be satisfied so that their sons and daughters get back in the same old rut.

I'm not going to allow these pseudo-Indians who call themselves leaders, who the white man calls leaders. They're an insult to you and to me and to your government to allow these tribal governments to continue.

Understand that you are the next tribal peoples. You're going to be the new Indians of the twenty-first century. You're already feeling the squeeze. Understand. I know the beauty of the male-female balance. I know my creation story, and those that continue to suck off of Uncle Sam are my enemy and the enemy of everyone. It's not just limited to Indians. Maybe to all Native Americans, huh? The state of the Native American.

So I'll leave you with the words of Chief Seattle, and I quote part of his letter and speech to the then-president of the United States of America. He said, "Wave follows wave, and tribe follows tribe. It's the order of nature, and regret is useless. Your time of decay may be distant, but it will surely come. For even the white man's god who walked and talked with him as friend with friend could not escape our common destiny. We may be brothers after all. We shall see."

Thank you.

Source:
Native American Reader: Stories, Speeches and Poems, edited by Jerry D. Blanche. Juneau, Alaska: Denali Press, 1990.

Although his activist roots go back to the late 1960s, Michael Haney has only recently begun to garner widespread attention for his efforts on behalf of Native Americans. His confrontational tactics and often unpopular views on issues ranging from the display of Indian remains in museums to the use of Indian names for sports teams have prompted some to regard him as a troublemaker. But Haney insists that such practices denigrate native peoples and trivialize their history. He shrugs off attempts to intimidate him and makes it clear that he has no intention of withdrawing from the fray. As he once observed in an interview with Chicago Tribune reporter Wes Smith, "All the scared Indians are dead."

Haney grew up on a reservation in Seminole County, Oklahoma, of mixed Seminole and Sioux heritage.He was drafted into the U.S. Army in 1968, and he spent most of the next two years in Germany. Haney emerged from his time in the service far more politically aware that he had been back home in Oklahoma. Before long, he became caught up in the spirit of activism then taking hold among many young Native Americans. He began taking part in various protests, including the famous occupation of Alcatraz Island (the site of a former federal prison) in San Francisco Bay, where a group of Indians took up residence from November, 1969, until June, 1971, to dramatize their opposition to the U.S. government's policies regarding Native Americans. It was there that he rediscovered his own roots and a sense of spirituality that motivated him to dedicate his life to fighting for change.

Soon after, Haney joined the fledgling American Indian Movement (AIM) and was eventually named state coordinator for Oklahoma, which at the time made him one of AIM's youngest leaders. He participated in most of the group's major demonstrations during the 1970s, including the Trail of Broken Treaties march and subsequent takeover of the Bureau of Indian Affairs offices in Washington, D.C. (1972), the siege at Wounded Knee (1973), and the Longest Walk (1978). His reputation was that of a "warrior," a defiant, hot-tempered, and impatient young man who was quick to question and criticize his elders.

Now, a somewhat mellower Haney directs his energies toward activities that he feels will make a difference in the lives of his children and grandchildren. He is convinced that many of the problems Native Americans face—such as high rates of alcoholism, unemployment, and suicide—can be attributed to the fact that white society still looks at Indians as mere "museum pieces" who are not quite human. This in turn leads to low self-esteem among young Indians in particular, he insists, and it is that sense of worthlessness that he has vowed to combat.

To that end, Haney has fought against those seeking to establish landfills or dispose of hazardous materials on tribal property. He has also challenged non-Indian artists who try to sell their works as "authentic" Native American creations. In addition, he has crusaded on behalf of Indian religious freedom, especially regarding the use of peyote in traditional rituals.

But among his most-publicized battles are those that have centered around the treatment of Indian remains and artifacts. To Haney, digging up and displaying the bones and sacred objects of his ancestors is not only a physical violation of their graves but a spiritual one as well. In an effort to educate as many people as possible about the Indian point of view on what is termed "repatriation", or restoring items to their place of origin, he has traveled across the United States lecturing to a wide range of groups. He has also vigorously challenged scientists and museum officials (including ones at the Smithsonian in Washington, D.C.) to take a closer look at their practices and surrender pieces in their collections that are important to Native Americans.

More recently, Haney has spoken out forcefully against the use of Indian names for sports teams. As in the case of the reburial issue, he maintains that it comes down to a matter of respect. No one, he says, would think of naming a team the "New York Negroes" or the "Chicago Caucasians," yet names like the Cleveland Indians, Atlanta Braves, and Washington Redskins are deemed perfectly acceptable. Furthermore, observes Haney, the cartoonish mascot figures (which may be plastered on souvenirs as humble as toilet paper and underwear), along with stadium cheers and dance routines that feature "Indian" war whoops, tomahawk chops, feathered costumes and so on perpetuate old, racist stereotypes "that tend to keep our people locked in the past."

To address these concerns, Haney founded a protest organization, the National Coalition Against Racism in Sports and Media. It has demonstrated at a number of major events and the group has also sued or threatened to sue several teams to force them to drop their names. While he has yet to persuade any professional teams to see things his way, Haney has enjoyed some success at the college and university level. Despite the uphill climb, it is not a fight he has any intention of abandoning. "We [Indians] have a hard enough time without promoting racism with mascots," he told Wes Smith of the Chicago Tribune. "Our effort is part of a spiritual and holistic approach toward alleviating problems that keep our people from reaching their potential."

Haney addressed these and other issues in testimony he delivered on March 30, 1991, before the United Nations Subcommission on the Prevention of Discrimination Against Minorities. His appearance at the special session (held at the American Indian Community House in New York City) was on behalf of the International Indian Treaty Council, which monitors the status of various agreements between Indian nations and government bodies. Haney's remarks were transcribed from an audiotape he himself provided.

MICHAEL HANEY'S SPEECH BEFORE THE UNITED NATIONS SUBCOMMISSION ON THE PREVENTION OF DISCRIMINATION AGAINST MINORITIES

I want to thank the International Indian Treaty Council for all the work that they have done since their founding. I was at part of the founding conference in 1974 in Mobridge, South Dakota, and it has come a long way. It's certainly a credit to the perseverance of the people that have been involved in this organization [that they have gotten] a consultive status to the United Nations.

We've learned throughout the history of our peoples that we *belong* in that international community. That treaties that were entered into with our governments and the United States were ratified by the Senate [and] signed into law by the president of the United States, just as treaties with NATO and treaties with the Soviet Union and treaties with Panama and other countries that are still valid and in full force and effect. It's no secret that the United States, in our opinion, has reneged on many of the provisions that were stipulated in those agreements.

I would like to point out the conspicuous absence of Dr. Miguel Alfonso Martínez and hope that he is able to join [us at] the other hearing sites as soon as possible. I also want to thank Robert Cruz, the director of the International Indian Treaty Council, for being here. He came a long way—from Scottsdale, Arizona—to be here.

As Robert said, I am a Seminole, born in Oklahoma. However, my mother's a Sioux woman, a Santee Sioux from the Niobara area, Nebraska. And I'm an Alligator Clan. We have a clan system there [that] we still recognize and work within. It's a system that our society has been based on for tens of thousands of years. It's in this role as an Alligator Clan member that I'm chairman of the repatriation committee for these twenty-six tribes and nations in Oklahoma.

Today there are approximately thirty-nine federally recognized tribes in Oklahoma. Almost three hundred thousand Indians are in Oklahoma, all the way from the Seneca, Cayuga, Delaware, Wyandotte, Ottawa, Comanche, Kiowa, Apache, [and] Seminole. We even have an Aztec reservation there.

It seems like almost every tribe that warred against the United States ended up in Oklahoma, like one big huge concentration camp. And at one point, it was called Indian Territory, up until 1906.... It was meant and destined to be the Indian state, a part of the union of the United States. But then they discovered salt, something very needed during that period [as a] preservative. Shortly after that, they discovered oil. And as the Kuwaitis have found out, white people are very thirsty for oil. And we suffered.

Our people were removed during the 1830s, in spite of the treaties. [In] 1832, the U.S. Supreme Court, in referring to treaties made with native governments, describes them as "dependent, domestic nations." In a suit that the state of Georgia attempted in order to pass laws over the Cherokee nations, the Supreme Court says they are equal and on par with the state. And these treaties are equal and on par to the Constitution.... That theory has been of help continually in Supreme Court decisions. Most recently, a Potawatomi decision was issued a month ago dealing with sovereign immunity and jurisdiction and [the] ability to levy taxes, collect money to provide services to citizens.

In Oklahoma, when Congress passed an alien act that allowed Oklahoma to become a state in 1906, they created a congress similar to the Continental Congress—the founding papers [of which], along with the Iroquois Confederacy's great law of peace, the U.S. Constitution is loosely based on. Our people were protected by the Supreme Court

under the Supreme Court ruling. Of course, the famous quote by then-President Andrew Jackson was that "Justice Marshall has made his decision—now let him enforce it." [Jackson] promptly ordered the military to remove all Indians east of the Mississippi, which included the tribe I belonged to (Seminole), Creek, Cherokee, Choctaw, Chickasaw. We ended up in Oklahoma. At one time, all of Oklahoma belonged to [these] five tribes. They called us the "Five Civilized Tribes" because we were, I think, easier to steal from than some of our western brothers and cousins.

We walked to Oklahoma. It was called the Trail of Tears. We lost approximately one-third of our people along the way. The old, the very young perished. And when we got to Oklahoma, we settled in new land there. Some of it was very harsh. Remember those Woody Guthrie songs about the dustbowl days there in Oklahoma? That's where we were sent to. Can you imagine being sent from Florida, where there's a tropical setting? We were hunters and gatherers—didn't know how to plant. A lot of our Creek brothers were planters. But we survived. Still surviving today.

"**A**lmost every tribe that warred against the United States ended up in Oklahoma, like one big huge concentration camp."

I'm very proud of that. [It's] very hard to be an Indian. [I'm] very proud of my ancestors for keeping our religion together. We have what we call Stomp Dances. A mother fire was brought, at great hardship, all the way from the southeast. It was really coveted, what we called the Mother Ground. Our medicine people carried that all the way to Oklahoma. And then from this we had what we call a *tookabatchee* ground, a Mother Ground. And then our different tribes—the Cayuga, the Hitchiti, the Miccosukee, the Alabama, the Koasati—those people took from that a coal and took it back to their grounds and made a fire. And then the camps from those grounds made their fire. So we kept that continual touch with that very important fire.

Then it was outlawed—our stick ball games, our fires. They said, "You're heathens 'cause you dance around a fire all night [and] you sing." Well, we reminded them that the message of the Creator came to these white people through a burning bush, to their Moses. You came here seeking religious freedom and tolerance. Then you outlaw *ours!* It wasn't until 1970—*1970*, a brief twenty years ago!—that my people were allowed to fully elect our leaders (they were appointed before) and exercise our religious rights, traditional customs.

This is why we need help from other sovereign governments, from other indigenous peoples across the world because we feel and we know that we're not alone in this political and religious oppression, and that today, our peoples have survived.

Next year the white people are going to celebrate five hundred years of being here since Columbus. [We've been] asked to take part in that. There's a lot of money for Indians to take to do powwow's, do art shows, to participate in this celebration. Well, we really thought about that. How can we do this? We like to have powwows and we're going to have them whether [they're in] conjunction [with Columbus Day ceremonies] or not. We're going to have them. So we finally decided that we would honor our ancestors by celebrating five hundred years of survival [under] colonialism.

Do you remember when those hostages were in Iran under that student group in the American embassy? We have a brother name John Thomas from the International Indian Treaty Council. He was sitting in one of the student's offices waiting to meet with some of them because we had one Indian in there. He was a quarter Kiowa, a man named Richard Kupke. He wanted help! So John Thomas, representing the Treaty Council, went there. (They trusted the Indians, those students.) He was sitting there, so he looked on the wall and there was a picture of Chief Gall. Have you ever seen that picture. . .? It's wild!. . . That was a real odd place to find a poster like that, [under those] circumstances. So he asked them about it. "How come you've got a picture like that?" And they said, "American Indians are the symbol of resistance for us, because you exist in the belly of the beast, so to speak—right in the heart of Western civilization, right in the heart of colonial tyranny. And today, you still exist. You still speak your languages. You still enjoy and practice your customs and traditions. You give us hope [with] what you're doing."

I'm really proud. I'm really proud of our ancestors, and I'm proud of Robert and others that are here today and others that are out standing up for sovereign rights and standing up for their freedoms and standing up for the right to practice those older ways [and] provide alternatives for their children.

We are told by our elders that it is very important for us to pass on these things to our children. Our elders tell us that we are in danger of becoming the link that is broken between tens of thousands of years of instructions. That's how important *our* responsibility is. That's how important *our* role is. I don't want to be that generation, that link, that breaks the continuity between the original instructions that were given to our ancestors and our chil-

dren. [We] have to continue [to] provide a basis for their spiritual foundation, something they can embrace and come home to.

I tell [that to] these Christians that want so much to save our souls, with good intentions. Often they're the largest landowners amongst our reservations and communities. In earlier times, the 1860s, they passed what they called the Comitty Act [under] which every tribe was assigned one religion. "The Jesuits, you can have the Mohawks. The Episcopalians, you can have the Oglalas over there. You Baptists, you can have the Creeks." There were holy wars back then over our souls. Of course, there were other wars over our lands and mineral rights, too, and timber and all that. This is what our ancestors faced and these are the conditions they lived under. What's so surprising [is] that we exist in such strength today. Because it wasn't meant [to be] so.

I tell [the Christians], if you want to look to help us when we're standing up in Oka [a Mohawk reservation in Canada] up there, when we're standing up for Dave Sohappy over here [in the] fishing rights struggle—*there's* where we need your help. We don't really suffer from a lack of religion, because it's been our religion that's kept us intact all these years. So don't look toward our spiritual needs, look toward our physical needs. I want to see you right alongside of me with your Bible—*that's* where we can use help.

It's really hard for me to understand missionary people. We didn't have—Cheyennes didn't go over to the Crows and try to convert them. Just like the beaver didn't go over to the coyote to try to convert him to be the beaver religion, either. This is how outrageous it seemed to us and still does. That's why it's important.

I want to focus in on what my role is with the tribes in Oklahoma [where] religious freedoms [continue to be] under attack.. . . In 1978, they passed the American Indian Religious Freedom Act. [It] sounded really good, but it didn't have much teeth in it. It doesn't protect the ancestral homelands. It doesn't protect the burial sites. I'll give you an idea of how important it is for this to take place.

In Nashville, Tennessee, today—as we speak— there is a landfill that's going to be [established] on top of five thousand Cherokee graves or mounds, right along the Cumberland River.. . . It makes a loop, there's a little peninsula around there, and those are mounds.

Our ancestors used these rivers as interstates. Those were our first highways, these waterways. And we traveled up and down and visited one another, traded. These dentalium shells that you see on these northern [plains] dresses? We found those in the tar pits down in Florida. There's only one way that you could have gotten those, and that's by physically, intentionally trading. All that comes from one spot, and that's the Pacific Northwest. They found gorgets like this and these crescent-shaped ones there, too.

My people traded—the Seminole people—we navigated the Gulf, we went down in the Yucatán Peninsula, we went to Colombia. But you don't hear about that. White people don't tell you about that in your history books. Even some of our Indians don't learn that because they go to a public school, and that's where they get the basics of their education. (There is a gap we need, of course, to address ourselves—to control our schools, our educational systems.) But they were great navigators and travelers.

My people are Seminole. The beautiful vests and the patchwork that you see, only Seminoles have this. Have you ever seen the patchwork done [by] those people from Ecuador or Colombia [with] those birds and so forth? That's where we got this design, from them. We traded with them. You know what we gave them in return? Feathers. We had beautiful feathers down in the Florida Everglades. We traded for metals with the Aztec people, Montezuma's people. We traded for metals because [they're] not indigenous to our area. So we got tin and gold and silver from the Aztec people. We navigated the Gulf to come up around to what's New Orleans, to the Mississippi, and then down to Texas and down that way. We navigated that, but you don't learn about [it].

I went up to the Long House [on the Onondaga Reservation] one time and danced in their social dances—shake the bush, where you kind of dance backwards, and that one bean dance where you kind of dance with the girl. (I kind of like those!) But they did one kind of alligator dance, and that kind of got me. I said, "Alligator dance? Where do you guys get alligators at up here? The only ones I know of around here are in the sewers of New York City, and I know you're not going to be singing about *those!*" They've got a tiger dance, too. That's because we traded, we traveled.

Our ancestor Tecumseh, that Shawnee chief, [whom] I consider one of the very first AIM people, [tried] to unite all the tribes up and down the Ohio River. [He came] down to Creek country. We listened to him, too. We formed what we called the Red Sticks, or the Miccosukees. We warred against the United States.

When someone passed away, or we wanted to winter or summer along some beautiful valley, we dug mounds—burials—one on top of the other. Now those mounds belong to white people. Now the lands that those mounds are on are individual property in most cases. And they sell them—if you saw that film earlier, and I hope we get to see it later again—as grave robbers. "Artifact hunters," they call them. We buried pots with [the dead], drinking vessels, vessels with food in them, for [their] journey. It's our belief and understanding, as it is of Christian people, that the spirit is immortal, never dying. That when they leave this world, they continue on with what they call a spirit journey. [If] you interrupt their final resting places it interrupts them [and] causes a big friction.

I tell this to archaeologists: "You're getting yourself in trouble, you know. Spirits—they'll get you one of these days! Sooner or later, you're gonna join them, too, and you're gonna have a lot to answer for. A lot to answer for. I'm not trying to frighten you, but those are the things that you can consider before you excavate a mound or unearth a remain just to study. If you want to study, you want to learn about us, ask us! We'll be *really* glad to tell you."

I'm really happy to share the teachings of my people with non-Indians, because I think that we have a lot to talk about. I know a lot about white people—speak your language, been to your colleges, schools, churches. I should have a doctorate of Caucasian studies, [I] know so much about them. But you know very little about my people. Very, very little. I've seen people go spend a couple of years hanging around the res, and the next time you see them they've got a PhD after their name and [a] dissertation about two inches thick sitting around. [But] they know very little about us.

And that's a shame. Because the people that you should learn from are our elders, like Fools Crow, like Henry Crow Dog, Mad Bear Anderson. These people are a wealth of knowledge, and they're passing away. *There's* where you "archs" [archaeologists] ought to go. You sociologists and anthropologists and archaeologists and all you "ologists" ought to go talk to these people. Because when they pass away, they take a whole wealth of knowledge with them, never to be brought again on the face of this earth. Lost forever. It's been said that when one of these elders passes away, it's like a whole library burning completely down to the ground. Gone! And they're passing away at a real rapid rate.

It's important to get to them. Not only you lose, but we lose. It's important that we, too, as young men and women—Indian men and women—we have the responsibility to go to them and learn, too.... So if you want to learn about our ancient Cherokees, go talk to Cherokees. They'll be glad to talk with you about it.

From the burials that I have seen, they buried the people very much like we do today. Our people, we build a little house over the graves. And instead of putting it in the earth with them, we put it outside now. I guess it makes it so [that] you won't disturb the body when you come to steal the artifacts. They must have seen it coming. We give them this and maybe their favorite tool to work with, whether it's a scraper or an axe or something. These are what these pot-hunters are looking for.

Last year, at the Opryland Hotel in Nashville, Tennessee, they had an artifacts show. We came and stopped it. We started taking pictures of their license plates and taking pictures of those people.. . . [They were] trying to hide. But one of those pots.. .went for sixty thousand dollars.

That Slack farm site you saw there, it looked like a bombing range where they had in excess of four hundred and sixty holes in the earth. They rented that site from a farmer. Ten of them paid fifteen hundred dollars each—fifteen thousand dollars they gave to him for two months to excavate it. You saw what they did. They rented a backhoe and just started throwing them up when they saw pots. They threw bones everywhere. They got a big three-inch hose, ran it down to the river [with] a pump, and they just started squirting all that. Bones are sticking out, skulls, everything. But they find a pot—one pot—and they've got all their money back plus some. They got literally hundreds of artifacts. So we need protection from [them].

The state feels that it's their property—"finder's keepers," regardless of who they belong to. The individual landowners are saying, "I bought it, it's mine, and no one's going to tell me how to live or what to do with it."

Our arguments to protect our ancestors were really falling on deaf ears. So we went to the U.S. Congress and lobbied a bill through last year. It's called Public Law 101-601, the Native American Grave Protection and Repatriation Act. We were [trying] to provide protection for burial sites and for remains that are in museums and in vaults across the nation, whether [at] the Smithsonian Museum or the Heye Center right here in Manhattan—they have a huge collection of remains and bones and sacred objects. We want those back. We want them back. We want them back out of those plastic bags and out of those paper sacks and out of those wooden boxes and out of those steel boxes. We want them back into the earth.

We feel—and we've been told—that we, as men and women (particularly men) have a responsibility to protect the defenseless, the youth and elders and those that have passed on before us. A lot of things we attempt to do today are unsuccessful because we ignore and we're not addressing our responsibility to our ancestors. [We must] get those ancestors out of the display cases, out of those vaults, and back into the ground so that they can continue that natural process of decomposing, becoming one with the earth, so that their bodies can provide nutrients for new life. Animals come by and eat that grass, and the whole cycle of life continues. That's why you see us wear things in a circle—to recognize the sacred hoop, the cycle of life. And when it's interrupted by these things being coated or being stuffed or formaldehyded in museums and in medical schools, particularly when they butcher them up by cutting them up for what they call scrapings or marrow testing, it's a desecration to us. It's not educational opportunities. It's not medical science. We're not finding a cure for cancer by digging up twelve-hundred-year-old remains of our ancestors.

I challenge those archaeologists to show me one study—one!—where you have benefitted nationally, medically, scientifically, or educationally from excavating the remains or the burials of my ancestors. They never have. They come up with, "Well, we found that you guys ate a lot of corn and you had arthritis." Well, we still eat corn. And we die from arthritis at about the same age these days, with the Indian Health Service and their budget. So very little has changed.

What we need is help from the United Nations to get the remains from other countries, too. It was really fashionable in the 1700s and 1800s to take Indians back to Europe, to have Indian skulls as ash trays, to have Indian artifacts in the castles in Europe and England.. . . It was a fad. Well, we think that's a very morbid fad, and we think that it's important to our spiritual health that these things be returned to us, that they be reburied so that they can continue that spirit journey. One of my jobs is to do whatever is necessary to get those remains back, whether it's speaking at forums, introducing legislation (state or national), or confronting state officials or archaeologists. I've been working with Robert a couple of times, very successfully, doing just that. But it's a long way to go.

Robert was with me in 1988 [when] we addressed the Society for American Archaeology. In [its] fifty-eight-year existence, [that was] the first time they'd ever heard from Indians. Can you imagine that? Here's a whole community of scientists.

Their sole goal in life is to dig up the remains of my people—Indians—here in the United States, and they've never heard from the Indians!

They were really shocked when we appeared. I had on my name tag, "Michael Haney, Living Artifact." They were scared.... They all had beards and [were] dressed in khakis, and they had that Indiana Jones syndrome.. . . When we walked through there, it was like parting the Red Sea, like [in the movie] *The Ten Commandments*. Boy, they got out of our way! They were afraid to touch us. They were afraid of the Indians! You know [the saying] "the only good Indian is a dead Indian"? Well, they've got a saying that "the only good Indian is an unburied one." Tom Emerson [an archaeologist] from the historical society in Illinois said that. And they believe that! They compare repatriating remains and artifacts to book burning. They call us "anti-intellectual." [I told them,] "We'll see who's dumb [and] who's intellectual when you meet the Creator and you have to answer for all these desecrations that you've done. It'll make you sick."

I'm an Alligator Clan, and like I said earlier, we handle the burials for our people. We dig the grave, but when we do so, we protect ourselves. We sing songs. We take sweat. We have a medicine that we wash off us when we get finished because we're told that dealing with that earth, especially this time of year—spring—life comes from the earth, a very powerful thing. When we plant, as when we dig a grave, we open the earth, the fresh earth. We have to wash off because that earth will draw power from you. It'll make you weak. Sometimes it'll give you a leg cramp or something like that, or it'll make you a little restless. Or maybe [you'll] gripe at your wife or something.. . .

I keep telling [the archaeologists] that. Compare it to handling uranium. It wasn't that long ago they had these Pueblo people digging in uranium mines with no clothing on. Then they found out there's radioactivity there. Of course, it was too late for those Laguna people. They've got a high rate of infant mortality and a high rate of birth defects and a high rate of cancer in that area disproportionate to others that didn't come in contact with that mining. We tell [the archaeologists], this is what you should treat remains like—like it's uranium. Because it'll get you. [They] may be unseen, those spiritual forces, but they're there.

And this is what we do. Our people, we wash off and we pray. But you guys don't do that. And at that Slack farm site that you saw earlier, I was there and I saw some archaeologists in those graves, and they were sitting there with their feet dangling off the edge like kids do. They were drinking a can of beer and they had their lunch over here, just some food, and it was sitting on those graves! I saw that and I told this guy, Chico Dulak, to go in there and run them out of there. They ran them out and, of course, *we* got charged with obstructing justice. And I said, "Well, they were drinking beer in there!" And they said, "Well, it was after hours, you know—after five o'clock."

Desecration is desecration. I don't care if you do it in the name of science or education or in the name of curiosity. But for the most part, it's money. Most of these people who are guilty of looting these graves are artifact hunters, are grave robbers and looters. They call themselves "amateur archaeologists" or "para-archaeologists." But that's just a cover-up for grave robbers.

"Desecration is desecration. I don't care if you do it in the name of science or education or in the name of curiosity."

There's so much money that is paid on the black market for those artifacts that they become reckless. They'll go in the middle of the night, and they'll get these miner's hats, and they'll come along in boats to those mounds and dig them up, find something, take off, and sell it the next day. And they're not prosecuted. You never hear of anyone being prosecuted for desecrating a grave.

We're particularly concerned about that one in Lewistown, Illinois, called the Dixon Mounds Museum. It's the only major museum in the United States today that displays human skeletal remains. They display two hundred thirty-seven American Indian remains there.

If you'll look [at] the aerial view of it, you'll see what they did is excavate into a mound, into a burial pit, and then they built a museum on top of it. Well, from an aerial view you'll see that that's the temple around there, and there's a plaza. At one time, that area—along with Cahokia Mounds, south around St. Louis—was the third-largest city in the world. Nine hundred years ago, around a hundred thousand people lived there. We had temples, we had plazas, we had corn fields, we had wheat fields—a very high level of civilization existed there. These were when Europeans were living in caves, hanging around trees and stuff. Our people were going through a copper period. The copper period of the Mayan people lasted longer than the entire Roman Empire.

Our civilization has a *lot* to offer here. Eighty percent of the foods that are used today are indigenous to the western hemisphere. The marketable cotton comes from here. The beans, the squashes, even "Irish" potatoes came from here. Where would the Russians be without their vodka? It came from here.

The United States is now embarking on a restructuring. Did you know that? They're trying to reorganize the BIA. We call it "Boss Indians Around." They call it the Bureau of Indian Affairs. It was first created in the 1700s, and it was in the department of the Army. That was shortly after the surgeon general issued a letter saying that he wanted to find out why Indians blindly followed or were so loyal to their leaders. Archaeology being a new science, they thought it was because they had large brains. So to study that, the Army ordered that all Indian leaders would be decapitated [if it could be learned] where they were buried. (I hope none were killed just for the science, but I suspect this could have happened.) They were decapitated and all their heads sent to Washington. That's true. We found that memo, and we confronted the Smithsonian Institution with this irrefutable, overwhelming evidence. They finally admitted that they did have a collection of heads from that period [of] Native American people. They were studying the cranium, measuring from ear to ear and from here to here, because they thought they had huge brains. What they didn't realize, it was the heart that was important. It was the love for their people that was important. That's immeasurable by their standards. They still get to measure that.

The Bureau underwent two major reformations. One in 1928, called the Meriam Report, and another one in 1975, called the American Indian Policy Review Commission. It was chaired by the senator from South Dakota at that time, James Abourezk. Last year, the BIA snuck in their appropriations a clause that would have [allowed] them to reorganize without consulting the tribes. One of the tribal organizations—the National Congress of American Indians—caught it, called it to the attention of the chairman of the Senate Select Committee on Indian Affairs, Daniel Inouye (the Democrat from Hawaii, a very powerful senator these days), and they got it stopped with the clause that they would consult with the tribes.

I'd like to submit to this body [an outline of] the structure of the BIA. I didn't know that they had a structure! The people are down here. That's the white people up here. Here's us, down here. I'd like to submit that as evidence to Robert. Also, the tribes have come up with what they call a laundry list of issues they would like to see addressed and kept in this BIA relationship. And here is this year's allocation for the Bureau of Indian Affairs.

Of course, they spent in one day the entire BIA budget during this Mideast crisis [the Persian Gulf War]. I thought it was pretty odd that they would send and spend thousands of troops, billions of dollars, all the way to the Mideast to protect the sovereignty of the Kuwaiti government. Sovereignty!— when they trample on the sovereignty every day of the American Indians here in the United States. They don't have to go far to find sovereign abuses.

We only wish that they would spend some of their attention here addressing the needs of the American Indians, the first Americans. Five hundred years is a long time to conduct an undeclared war. And we feel that that's exactly what has happened. We've had an undeclared war for five hundred years against our people. We think that it's time to stop. We think it's time they left us alone. That instead of self-administration, we should [have] self-determination. That the Bureau of Indian Affairs should be streamlined to the point that all they do is just transfer money to us. Today, eighty-five percent of every dollar is eaten up in administration costs. Only fifteen cents gets to the people. That's outrageous! White people wouldn't allow it, but it's okay for us because we employ a lot of white people in the BIA. Most of the people [who] get kicked out of the Defense Department or get washed out of the Department of Education all come to the BIA to retire. That's okay. These Indians—they're used to being trampled on. It's not going to reduce health care, it's not going to reduce educational opportunities for them because they're at a low. [There's] no place up but up for us, anyway. So they're after a major revision. We're concerned about that.

I want to give Robert one example. The University of Tennessee at Knoxville recently sent me a fax from the Department of Conservation. They said that they have 5,043 human skeletal remains. We *did* pass a law last year that caught these people by surprise. They didn't think we could do it, but we lobbied for it. We got a lot of church groups and a lot of people that were helpful, and we passed a law in Tennessee that said that no human skeletal remains will cross the state line unless they're going to be buried.

So we caught them. They were loaning our remains out to Oxford University! "I'll trade you a few Indians for some Africans. I'll trade you a few Indians for some people from Tibet or from Asia." They trade them like you do baseball trading cards! To me, that's very sacrilegious, and it's very disheartening to us. We want that to cease. We also want those five thousand-plus remains from the University of Tennessee. Now we're going to have to sue them to get [them] back.

I have a letter from the Cheyenne Sand Creek descendants [in] Oklahoma. You know, along with Wounded Knee, [there was] another large massacre called Sand Creek. [I think] it was highlighted in that movie called *Little Big Man*. Well, those descendants now live in Oklahoma. The Army went and dug up all those people that they murdered there and put them in a museum. These people want them back. I have a [letter], signed by the chairman, asking your assistance in getting their remains back. They want them back. They want to put them back in the earth.

I would also like to comment on a couple of pieces of legislation now in the draft stages with several organizations. [In] this new legislation we're going to introduce this year, we're trying to address sacred sites. Last year, we had to compromise in the final stages of the 101st session [of Congress] by [keeping] private lands exempt. We had to do this. The farm lobby just said that they were going to kill it, other groups said that they'd kill it. We had to drop private land, so the bill—the Great Protection Act, or Public Law 601—only covers public land and tribal, federal land. This bill that we're introducing April 15 is going to address sacred sites. So when we find burial mounds and village sites on public *or* private property, this is a mechanism that we can [use to] declare them sacred, and we can go in and take care of them. Now we realize there are times when we are going to have to excavate them, because if we leave them there the looters will be there anyway. So we want to set up a national, federal cemetery for Indians that are indigent or Indians that are like this that need a final resting place.

The second part of this [legislation]—there are four parts to it—the second part is dealing with peyote. Last year, they called the Smith decision, *Oregon v. Smith*. Basically, what it said was that the states can regulate the criminal code on the possession of this sacrament by American Indians—that we're not covered under the First Amendment of religious freedom, that states can pass laws to include Indians as criminals.

We feel that what caused this is a couple of groups called the Peyote Way Church. Back in the '60s, some of these—what do you call them? Hippies? We had a little hope for them because they sounded like Hopis a little bit. They called themselves hippies and said, "Oh, we *like* you, Indians," and they had beads all over the place. And then they asked us for peyote. Well, they started their own church and said that Indians have a special privilege because they're Indians. And that's discriminatory, [the hippies said,] because they have a right that's not afforded all Americans. And they

sued. A lot of these suits reached the federal courts, of course, as they were preempted by state decisions. And now the Oregon case came, where the Smith decision is still a precedent. We need that sacrament protected. We're writing legislation now that would exempt American Indians from criminal prosecution for just the mere possession [of certain items,] including the ceremonial fans like eagle feathers and hawk and scissor tail—those are considered migratory birds [and are therefore protected].

They tried this in Oklahoma about ten years ago. They came in and they busted up ceremonies. They came into the tepees and confiscated fans [and] eagle feathers, [and] they arrested ten people. They prosecuted them for violation of the migratory bird act when, actually, these were fans that were used in ceremonies. They went after the very heart of the religion and arrested some medicine people as well.

Thirdly, [our proposed legislation] deals with political prisoners. Almost every Indian family in North America is affected in one way or another, either directly or indirectly, by the policies of state and federal prisons. We have friends or relatives or acquaintances or people we used to go to school with, go to church with, or dance with, or pray with [who at] one time or another are incarcerated. If you're a Methodist or Protestant or Presbyterian or Catholic, you can readily have access to ministers and clergymen, priests. But if you're a traditional American Indian, they say, "We're not gonna let those heathens in here. We're not gonna be building any sweat lodge over here. We're *certainly* not gonna hold a Sun Dance in here."

But our people really *need* the counseling. It's a very tough time for an Indian. It's like caging up a wild animal—this is how our people feel [behind] those bars, in those cages. They need all the strength that they can possibly derive from their own being. They need access to these spiritual people so they can pray with them, ask for help from the Creator during this real hardship time in their life. Federal law needs to provide the national standard for all the states to look at, sort of a backdrop. Because in Oklahoma, there's three hundred thousand of us. We still make up thirty-six percent of the prison population [even though] we make up around five percent of the total population in Oklahoma. And we're *not* all criminals. It's the judicial system—we can't afford it. We can't afford lawyers. Often, we can't afford bail bondsmen. I know of a couple of instances where people were exonerated, but they still spent six months in prison or in county jail waiting for their case to come up, depending on the public [defender who] was like Monty

Hall—"let's make a deal" all the time. So they need help, and this piece of legislation that we're introducing will do that.

The fourth provision [of our legislation] is a legal cause of action, a vehicle for [gaining] access to the federal courts to provide remedies for these issues.

I realize that the United Nations is a very important body and that there are a lot of human rights violations all over the world and that addressing this is certainly a full-time job. But since this is the first time that they've ever come to the United States—and I know this man will come, this Dr. Martínez, because in five hundred years, this is the first time you've addressed *our* human rights. In an era when this country is looking toward economic development, I think they ought to pay some attention to human development as well. I think they ought to pay attention to the rights of minority people. I think they ought to realize that we all pray to the same holy being, whether we call him Jehovah, Hezaketameze, Wakantanka.. . . They're all the same. And that we're going to have a lot—I know *I'm* going to have a lot to talk about when *I* get up there! So I don't want anyone messing with my bones down here while I'm up there talking about my case, pleading my case! So I really want some protection for these final resting places.

"In an era when this country is looking toward economic development, I think they ought to pay some attention to human development as well."

If the United States can be embarrassed into seriously addressing the concerns of the Native American people, I hope that this hearing, and others like it, will be the beginning of that effort. If President Bush is very serious about sovereignty—and he points to human rights violations of the Soviet Union, the sovereignty of the country of Georgia, the sovereignty of the Balkan areas, the sovereignty of the Soviet nations within them, the sovereignty of the Kurdish people that are locked in war as we speak with the Iraqi people—then he, too, should be concerned about the sovereignty of American Indian nations and governments here in the United States. It's very hard to take him seriously, very hard to read his lips, when he's talking out of both sides of his mouth at the same time.

Our people want very much to co-exist with all other peoples. The four colors is not just a color scheme that we enjoy looking at. The four colors signifies all of mankind that we've always known existed. The hoop of life is something that we recog-

nized when we were first put on this earth. Our people never felt that the world was flat. Next year, when they celebrate five hundred years of finding that lost Italian on our shores, they [should] remember this—they pay tribute to this navigator that was half a world off. You know, that's the most you can be, a half a world off. But there are going to be all sorts of celebrations. And I'd like for some of these energies to be focused on the right of self-determination, the right to protect our religious freedoms and to exercise our traditional ways of worshipping and paying tribute to the Creator and to all those living things. This is important for us, as American Indian people, for our future, for the future of our children, and for the future of our nations.

I'd like to close by expressing my gratitude to the American Indian Community House for providing the facilities here for this hearing and to commend the International Indian Treaty Council for the years of perseverance. I know it's really hard to talk about sovereign rights and international agreements when you've got an overwhelming phone bill to pay and you've got to decide, do I go to this conference or do I pay the rent? We shouldn't have to be faced with those kinds of decisions. But they've made them, and they still are existing and continuing to do the work their elders say *has* to be done in order for us to survive. And I want to thank them for that on behalf of all the tribes in Oklahoma.

I go to a lot of ceremonies back home. Often, I'm in those ceremonies and I hear these elders pray. They'll pray, "I've got a niece in Oklahoma City, got a nephew in Los Angeles, Chicago, New York. Be with them, Creator, because it's so very hard, it's hard to be Indian there. Be with them because they're exposed to a lot of detrimental things. Help them to make the right choice."

I want you to know, you that are here, the Treaty Council and those of the officials of this community house, before I left we had a peyote meeting, the Black Legging Society of the Kiowa nation, a warrior society. They prayed for you. They prayed for the success of this hearing. I want you to know that sometimes when you're faced with these hardships—maybe it's [having] to scramble to pay the rent, pay that phone bill, [or someone saying], "I don't want to hear about another Indian program, I don't want to hear about another Indian project"—that these people are praying for you, are grateful. They're grateful for those organizations that are in Tennessee and Georgia and places that we came from, Chicago, Los Angeles, Seattle, Milwaukee, Twin Cities. Wherever they're protecting sovereignty, these people are praying for me. I want you to know that you're not alone in this.

We've always found strength through unity, strength through spirituality. And this spirituality, this camaraderie that we have amongst all of our Indian people is the strength that has kept us going for all these years, and it's the very thing that's going to keep us going for our future. If there's anything that we can do from Oklahoma, we'd be glad to do that. I extend an invitation for you to come. Let me know when you come. We're very proud. Tonight, in Oklahoma, there are at least three or four pow-wows. Every weekend—they've got so many tribes, Indian clubs. I'll be glad to take you there. Or come to our Stomp Dances. I'd like to dance with you and pray. I'm very proud of the ways of our people and how they've existed throughout these times.

And with that, I want to end the testimony.. . .Thank you very much.

Source:

Michael Haney, transcript of speech delivered on March 30, 1991, before the United Nations Subcommission on the Prevention of Discrimination Against Minorities.

SPANISH AMERICANS

The main thrust of Spanish colonization of the New World, as this map shows, had its roots in Mexico and the Carribean. During the Reconquest, the Christian Castilians of northern Spain reclaimed lands from the Moors in southern Spain. Afterwards, the Spanish found a powerful French kingdom to the north and a solid Muslim wall to the south in Northern Africa. As a result, the only direction that the Spanish determined they could expand was to the west. Sovereignty over new lands had been given by the popes to the Portuguese. However, after Columbus's discovery, funded by Spain, the Spanish wanted to end Portuguese favoritism by the Church, and sent envoys demanding that Spain be granted rights to the explorer's finds. The new pope, Alexander VI (pope from 1492 to 1503), was a Spanish Borgia and Spain consequently found themselves favored by the Vatican.

Now that Spain was assured of control of the Carribean and the Gulf of Mexico, Spain began to colonize the islands in the area, including Cuba, Jamaica, Puerto Rico and Hispaniola. The Spanish wanted to gain trading power, mining the vast mineral wealth of the New World, which included deposits of gold and silver, as well as to bring Christianity to the native peoples they encountered. In the process of their colonization, however, they massacred populations of indigenous peoples as well as exposed them to new, and some fatal, diseases.

MAJOR PATHS OF EARLY EUROPEAN PENETRATION OF THE UNITED STATES

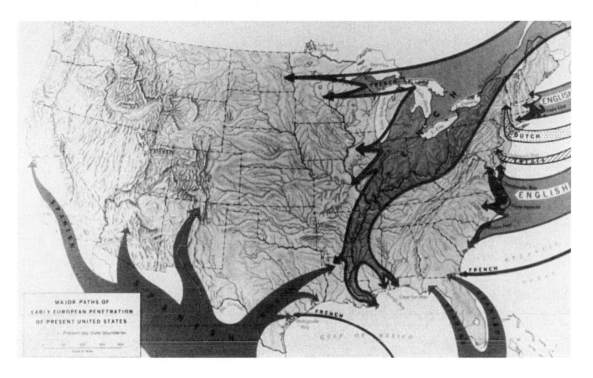

Source:

U.S. Department of the Interior and the National
Park Service.

SWEDISH AMERICANS

In July of 1880, Maine's Swedish colony in Aroostook County, New Sweden, cele-brated its tenth anniversary. This colony was just one of many which formed during the great emigration from Sweden to the United States. Although there was a Swedish and Finnish colony established in the Delaware River area as early as 1638, and though individual Swedes immigrated to America in the eighteenth century, what was seen as the great emigration did not take place until the late-1830s. The cause of this emigration was overpopulation. Sweden's population exploded in the middle of the nineteenth century, more than doubling between 1800 and 1900. Though farming methods had improved and crop yields had increased, the population growth still out-stripped the growth of the farming industry. Because about 75 percent of the population were farmers, the land available for farming became scarce. Sweden faced impoverish-ment; but immigrants were having great success living in America. As a result, many of the new Swedish immigrants to the United States consisted of farmers and their fam-ilies. Between 1867 and 1869, Sweden experienced severe crop failures. Because they already had a history of immigrants to America, and because of the American Home-stead Act of 1862, Swedes began arriving in the United States in great numbers. There were 32,000 immigrants in 1869, and emigration from Sweden continued to increase into the early 1900s. Eventually, some 1.25 million Swedes came to Ameri-can, and approximately four-fifths of them stayed.

In 1870, as Swedish immigration expanded from its original Midwest focus into new locations, the state of Maine encouraged the formation of a Swedish colony in Aroostook County in order to support agricultural development and to increase population. The commissioner of the state of Maine, William W. Thomas, Jr., wrote a New York Times article, "Maine's Swedish Colony," about the travels of the Swedish colonists who came to Aroostook County and of their first ten years of the Swedes in Maine. In it, Thomas described the 51 colonists as farmers and tradesmen who left Gothenburg on June 23 and landed in Halifax, Nova Scotia, on July 13. They arrived in Aroostook County on July 22.

Many Swedish immigrants worked as they had at home, primarily as farmers and as menial labor workers, such as builders. The colonists of Aroostook County were no exception, and worked as the state intended, felling trees, cutting roads, building homes and farming. Often, Swedes would send letters with enthusiastic accounts of their new lives back to Sweden. Some of these were published and aroused interest in the new colonies. In Aroostook County, new members joined the colony soon after its establishment, coming from Bangor and from Sweden. Soon, the United States government recognized New-Sweden, Maine and by 1873, the colony of 50 had grown to over 600. Like many Swedish immigrants, the Swedes in Maine flourished, and on the date of the dedication of the church, they numbered 777 people. They were successful in clearing over 4,000 acres of forest, and they raised many crops and had numerous livestock. Thomas, in his dedica-tion, insisted that "The future of New-Sweden is assured."

Originally published in the New York Times, *on July 27, 1880.*

MAINE'S SWEDISH COLONY

The Hon. William W. Thomas, Jr., who was the agent and Commissioner of the State of Maine in bringing out the colony of Swedish immigrants for settlement in Aroostook County, 10 years ago, gave an interesting account of his labors at the recent decennial celebration of the event, and the dedication of a new Lutheran Church at New-Sweden. In it he said:

"On June 23 the colonists, who came from nearly every province of Sweden, were assembled a Gothenburg, where the Swedish festival of mid-summer eve was observed, and in just 40 days after the first Swedish colonists of our State. The colony was composed of 22 men, 11 women, and 18 children in all, 51 souls. All the men were farmers, but some were also skilled in trades and professions. There was a Pastor, a civil engineer, a blacksmith, two carpenters, a basket-maker, a wheelwright, a baker, a tailor, and a wooden-shoe maker. The women were neat and industrious, tidy housewives, and diligent workers at the spinning-wheel and loom. All were tall and stalwart, with blue eyes, light hair, and cheerful, honest countenances. There was not a physical defect or blemish among them.

"We arrived at Hull Monday evening, June 27, crossed England by rail to Liverpool, and on Saturday, July 2, sailed in the City of Antwerp, of the Inman Line, for America. On Wednesday, July 13, we landed at Halifax, where the agents of the Inman steam-ship lodged the colony in a vacant warehouse. The next day we proceeded to St. John, and on Friday, July 15, ascended the St. John River to Fredericton. Here steam navigation ceased. Two river boats were chartered for the colony, and on Saturday, July 16, we pushed forward. Each boat was towed by two horses. The progress was slow and toilsome, but the weather was fine, and the colonists caught fish from the river, and picked berries along the bank. Six days were spent in towing up from Fredericton to Tobique. The journey is now made by rail in as many hours. Near Florenceville, on Tuesday, July 19, the first misfortune befell the colony. Here died Hilma C. Clase, infant daughter of Capt. Nicholas P. Clase. Her little body was placed in a coffin, quickly constructed, and brought along with the colony. At Tobique Landing we debarked on the afternoon of July 21, and were met by the Hon. Parker P. Burleigh, Land Agent. The next morning, Friday, July 22, teams were provided by Mr. Joseph Fisher, of Fort Fairfield, and the Swedish immigrant train started for Maine and the United States. Mr. Burleigh and your historian drove ahead in a wagon. Then came a covered carriage drawn by four horses, with the women and children. Then two three-horse teams with the men. Followed by two two-horse teams with the baggage.

"So we wound over the hills, and at 10 o'clock reached the iron post that marks the boundary between the dominions of the Queen of Great Britain and the United States. Beneath us lay the broad Valley of the Aroostook. The river glistened in the sun. The white houses of Fort Fairfield shone brightly among the green fields along the bank. As we crossed the line, the American flag was unfurled from the foremost carriage, and we were greeted by a salute of cannon from the village. Mr. Burleigh descended from the wagon and welcomed the colony to the State which was to be their new home. I translated the speech, and the train moved on. The people along the way greeted us with waving handkerchiefs, cheers, and every demonstration of enthusiasm. In ascending a hill the horses attached to one of the baggage wagons became balky, baked into the ditch and upset the wagon. The Swedes sprang lightly from their carriages, unhitched the horses, righted and reloaded the wagon, and ran it by hand to the top of the hill. This was their first act in Maine.

The State extended a helping hand to the infant colony and guarded it with fostering care. But the State only helped those who helped themselves. The passage of the colony of 1870 cost over $4,000, every dollar of which was paid by the immigrants themselves.

"At noon we reached the Town Hall at Fort Fairfield. A gun announced our arrival. Here we dismounted, and a multitude of people surrounded us. The Swedes clustered shyly apart. A public meeting was improvised in the American fashion. The Hon. Issac Hacker was called to the chair, and introduced Judge William Small, who welcomed the strangers in a judicious and eloquent address. He was followed by the Rev. Daniel Stickney, of Presque Isle. The remarks of these gentlemen were repeated to the Swedes in their own tongue by your historian, who then returned thanks at their request. A bountiful collation was served in the Town Hall, and when, at 2 o'clock, the Swedes resumed their journey, it seemed as if half the population accompanied them in carriages and on foot. A Swedish youth of 20 and an American of about the same age ran at the head of the procession, with their arms about each other's waists, laughing and chattering, though neither understood a word of the other's language. Finally they crowned each other with garlands of green leaves.

"As we passed over a hill-top I pointed out the distant ridges of Township 15, rising against the sky, *Det lofvade Landet*, 'the promised land,' shout the Swedes, and a cheer goes along the line. Late in the afternoon we reached the bridge over the Aroostook River. A salute of cannon announced our approach, and a concourse of 500 people turned out with a brass band to escort us to the picturesque village of Caribou. Here the Hon. John S. Arnold delivered an address of welcome, and supper was served in Arnold's Hall, where the settlers passed the night. At this supper one of the ladies of Caribou happened to wait upon our worthy Land Agent, and getting a reply from him in a language which she understood, exclaimed with delight and commendation, 'Why you speak very good English for a Swede!'

"Next morning the train was early in motion. A hundred and fifty Americans accompanied the march. We soon passed beyond the last clearings and entered the deep woods. Slowly the long line of wagons would among the stumps of the newly-cut wood road and penetrated a forest now first opened for the abode of man. At noon, on Saturday, July 23, 1870, just four months after the passage of the act authorizing this undertaking, and four weeks after the departure of the immigrants from Sweden, the first Swedish colony of our State arrived at their new home. We called the spot New-Sweden, a name at once commemorative of the past and auspicious of the future. Here in behalf of the State of Maine I bade a welcome and God speed to these far travellers, our future citizens, and here under a camp of bark the colonists ate their first meal on this township.

"As soon as it appeared from my letters that a Swedish colony would surely come, the Board of Immigration had begun to make preparation for their reception. Under the direction of Mr. Burleigh, the township had been relotted, reducing the size of the lots from 160 to 100 acres. A road was out into the township. Five acres were felled on each of the 25 lots, and 25 log houses would have been built, but the Swedes arrived much earlier than was anticipated, and only six houses were up and only two had glass in the windows. Necessary supplies and tools had also been provided.

"The next day was the Sabbath. The first religious service was the funeral of little Hilma Clase. The services were conducted up the Rev. James Withee, of Caribou.

"On Monday afternoon the farms were distributed. The only fair way of distribution appeared to be by lot; yet this method seemed likely to separate friends from the same province who preferred to be neighbors. This difficulty was finally overcome by dividing the settler into groups of four friends each, and the farm into clusters of four, and letting each group draw a cluster, which was afterward distributed by lot among the members of the group. The division of the farms was thus left entirely to chance, and yet friends and neighbors were kept together. With two exceptions, every one was satisfied and these two were immediately made happy by exchanging with each other. It was determined to set the Swedes at work felling trees, cutting out roads, and building houses, allowing them $1 a day, payable in provisions and tools. Capt. N. P. Clase, a Swede, was placed in charge of the store-house. Every working party was under a foreman, who reported once a week to the storekeeper. The Swedes thus did the work which the State had intended to do for them, and were paid in the provisions which the State would have given them had they arrived later in the season. All through the Summer and Fall there was busy work in this wilderness. In nearly every instance the trees were felled on the contiguous corners of four lots, and a square chopping of 20 acres was thus made, letting the largest possible amount of air and light into each lot, and enabling the settlers to help one another in the clearing. The houses were placed in couples on opposite sides of the roads, so that every household had a near neighbor. It was too late for a crop, but it seemed best to give the Swedes ocular proof that something eatable would grow on this land. So on Tuesday, July 26, the prostrate trees on the public lot were piled; the next day they were burned, and two acres of land were sowed with English turnip-seed. The turnips were soon up, and grow luxuriantly, and in November we secured a large crop of fair size, some of them 15 inches in circumference. This was the first crop raised in New-Sweden. On July 28 we explored an old tote road out off three-quarters of a mile, saved a hard hill and a long pole-bridge, and was at once put in repair and used exclusively. The present turnpike follows this route substantially.

"On July 29 the first letters arrived from old Sweden, and the teamster brought word that a Swede was at Caribou on his way in. The next day Anders Westergren came in and joined the colony. He was a seaman, and had read an account of the colony in Bangor, and immediately decided to join us. On Sunday, July 31, Nils Olsson, the Swedish Pastor, held public religious services in the Swedish language. Tuesday, Aug. 2, the immigrants wrote a joint letter to Sweden declaring that the State of Maine had kept faith with them in every particular, that the land was fertile, the climate pleasant, the people friendly, and advising their countrymen emigrating to America to come to New-Sweden in Maine. The letter was published in all the leading journals in Sweden. On Friday, Aug. 12, the first child was born in New-Sweden to Korno, wife of Nils Perrson. Th youngster is alive today. He rejoices in the name of William Widgery Thomas Perrson, and is happy in the contemplation of the constitutional fact that he is eligible to the office of President of the United States. On Friday, Aug. 19, Andrew Matmqvist arrived from Sweden via Quebec and Portland. He was a farmer and student, 22 years of age, and the first immigrant direct to us from the old country. Saturday afternoon, Aug. 21, Joens Perssons was united in marriage to Hannah Persdotteu by your historian, who luckily happened to be a Justice for the State. All the spoons at the wedding-dinner were of solid silver. Thus, within one month from the arrival of the colony, it experienced the three great events in the life of man—birth, marriage, death. The State extended a helping hand to the infant colony and guarded it with fostering care. But the State only helped those who helped themselves. The passage of the colony of 1870 cost over $4,000, every dollar of which was paid by the immigrants themselves. They also carried into New-Sweden over $3,000 in cash, and six tons of baggage. From 1870 until now, the State has never paid a dollar, directly or indirectly, for the passage of any Swede to Maine.

"In the matter of Government, New-Sweden presented an anomaly. It was an unorganized township, upon which there was not resident a single American citizen through whom the first step toward a legal organization could be taken. For two year the Commissioner found time to settle disputes between the colonists and arrange all matters of general concern. As the colony increased, the work became too great for one man, and a committee of ten was appointed to assist the Commissioner. Nine members of the committee were elected for terms of six months; the Pastor was the tenth ex officio. This decemvirate satisfactorily managed all municipal affairs, until the colonists had completed their term of residence, so as to become citizens and secure a legal organization. The Government of the United States promptly recognized the colony by establishing a Post Office at New-Sweden, and appointing N. P. Clase Postmaster. In the Fall of 1873, the settlement had out grown the township of New-Sweden and spread over adjoining sections of Woodland, Caribou, and Perham. The little colony of 50 increased to 600, and outside of the colony there were at least 600 more Swedes in Maine, drawn to us by our Swedish settlement. The colony was prosperous. The men had

renounced their allegiance to the 'King of Sweden and Norway, the Goths and the Vandals.' Every child that talked at all could speak English. The experiment was an experiment no longer. I was able then to recommend that all special State aid should cease, and that the office which I had held should be discontinued. On the 19th of October, 1873, I laid down the work which for four years had occupied the better portion of my life and endeavor, and took leave of the people of New-Sweden. The colony continued to grow and thrive. Scandinavian immigrants were attracted to other portions of the State. The Swedish example gave a stimulus to the movement of our native population into this fertile region.

"And now, 10 years after the arrival of that little company of 50 in the heart of the forest, we meet in this Christian church. Around us lie pleasant fields, where the tall grain waves in the Summer wind. Sleek cattle and heavy-fleeced sheep graze in the pastures. Great clearings, dotted with cottages, open far into the woods on every hand. The Swedish colony today numbers 777 souls. These Swedes have cleared 4,406 acres of forest. They raised last year 971 tons of hay, 1,304 bushels of wheat, 5,287 bushels of rye, 1,605 bushels of buckwheat, 8,129 bushels of oats, 24,162 bushels of potatoes. They own 166 horses and 661 cattle, besides sheep and swine. In 1879 they made 2,000 pounds of cheese and 13,869 pounds of butter. The value of their farms, live stock, and farming implements and machinery is estimated at $120,000 and the value of their farm products last year at $24,000, where not a dollar was produced 10 years ago. The settlement numbers 163 dwellings and 151 barns. Besides the Capitol, there is a church and five school-houses. Eleven miles of road have been turnpiked, and 31 1/2 miles have been grubbed, an are in a passable condition, with the swamps corduroyed. From the founding of the colony to January 1, 1880, there had been 65 deaths and 216 births in this community. The future of New-Sweden is assured. It will thrive and grow, and push out into the forest. It will continue to attract Scandinavian immigrants to Maine, and will supply a superior and needed class of labor to the older sections of the State. We have no better citizens than those countrymen of John Eriksson, the descendants of the Vikings, and the soldiers of Gustavus Adolphus."

July 27, 1880

Source:
Ethnic Groups in American Life. New York: Arno Press and the *New York Times*, 1978. pp. 65-66.

~

*I*n an effort to counteract the effects of the Great Depression (1929-1941), President Franklin D. Roosevelt (1882-1945; president 1933-1945) instituted a number of programs collectively called the New Deal. Among the many New Deal agencies was the Works Progress Administration (WPA), which gave employment to Americans from a variety of fields and levels of skill.

From 1938 to 1940, the WPA Ethnic Group Survey interviewed a number of subjects in Connecticut as a means of providing documentation regarding immigrant life. Among the people interviewed was a Mrs. S., whose parents had moved to the United States from Sweden. From the interview transcript, it is clear that Mrs. S. had had a difficult life: against her parents' wishes, she married a Norwegian man who turned out to be an abusive alcoholic. By the time of the interview, she had separated from him, and was left to raise three children, one of whom was mentally impaired.

"My father and mother," according to Mrs. S., "were born on the other side"—i.e., of the Atlantic. Though she herself was not raised in Sweden, Mrs. S. seems at times to view herself as a Swede, yet in parts of her interview she refers to "the Swedes" in the third person, as something separate from herself.

Nonetheless, she seems to have retained a prejudice against Norwegians that has its roots in the Old World—though no doubt her ill will was fueled by her experience with her husband. Noting that "Norwegians have a habit of coming to the Swedish affairs" or social functions, she goes on to say of Norwegians that "Most of them seem to remain in the same types of jobs; they don't care about advancing themselves like the Swedes."

From her recollections of her background growing up in Connecticut, it is apparent that Mrs. S. was raised in a traditional manner, and thus is able to contrast herself with the young Swedish American girls she saw around her as a grown woman. She had been brought up to be a homemaker, and her parents had neglected to educate her in other areas simply because they assumed that she would marry a man who would support her.

For Mrs. S., of course, marriage did not bring an end to problems but a beginning, and she speaks wistfully, perhaps a bit enviously, of "The young Swedish girls . . . . who wouldn't take any job, except in business." These girls, she seems to be saying, were more adequately prepared for life than she was. Likewise there is a contrast between the old-style Swedish father and the kind of father Swedes become in the United States. The latter allows his children to "go their own way," mingling with others of their own age group. This of course is the custom in America, but not in Europe, where young and old mix socially on a regular basis.

Concerns about traditional bonds of loyalty—to family, to nation, to religion—permeate Mrs. S.'s discussion of her life. She indicates that for the Protestant Swedes, marrying a Catholic is a serious matter; hence when her brother married one, this upset many in her family. In the old country, this might have caused a great conflict, but the brother and his wife settled their differences like Americans: he went to his church, and she to hers.

Mrs. S. married outside her nationality as well as her religion, though the latter is a curious and unexplained fact, since most Swedish immigrants—and the vast majority of Norwegians—were Lutherans. Perhaps her family embraced one of the denominations that had entered their country in the 1800s as an alternative to the Lutheran Church of Sweden.

Neither religion or nationality were the most serious of Mrs. S.'s problems with her husband. Not only did he beat the children, as she explains early in the interview, but as she notes near the end, he discouraged her attempts to better herself through education. Again and again, she extends her feelings about her Norwegian husband to encompass all Norwegians; hence her final observations about Norwegian men as being weak-willed.

Unconsciously, perhaps, Mrs. S. continually contrasts this alleged lack of resolve on the part of Norwegians with a sort of longsuffering bravery and strength that she attributes to "the Swedes." Thus "if a Swede needs help, he is too proud to say so. They only do it in extreme cases." Though she does not spare the negative details of her own life, perhaps this is a reaction to what she sees as the enforced stoic attitude of the Swedes: "If you're Swedish you get a habit of telling only the good things."

WHAT WOMEN TALK ABOUT

I've had bad breaks ever since I got married. I married a Norwegian and he never treated me right. He was always causing a disturbance in the house, and many times he would scare the life out of my children by beating me or threatening to do something worse. It wasn't that I was so afraid of him, but I didn't want anyone to know about our troubles, least of all my family. They had been opposed to my marrying him because they felt that he had no trade and probably couldn't ever do anything more than work at ordinary labor. I didn't feel this way about it; I thought that someday we would have better times. He had promised to be a good husband and we were expecting to live nicely together. But this didn't happen. When the usual hardships came he took to drink. First he began to feel that he was a failure, then he started to feel sorry for himself, and finally he began to threaten me with injury, saying that I had expected too much from him. I told him many time that this was not so. I told him that he should continue to accept things as they were, and someday we would enjoy better times. This only made him more resentful, and he resorted to many mean tricks. He began imagining things about me and to doubt my fidelity toward him. I was too taken up with the care of the children, and when things got worse I began to feel that life was not worth living. I began to neglect the children, and now they are showing it.

I have three children and they are all underweight. One of the boys is three, and he's very small for his age; the other is five and he's unruly because his health is bad; and the other is . . . eight, but you wouldn't know it—she's mentally defective, and the doctor says that she has a mind of a four-year-old. She never goes out because she is afraid to associate with other children. As far as her mental condition is concerned, she is falling back all the time. She is very small for her age and she looks more like a child of five. She is thin and pale, and the doctor says that we should have her taken away to the institution as soon as we could. All this is the result of my husband's quarrels—they used to be so bad at times that it frightened the children, and now they are suffering for it. If they had the proper nourishment they wouldn't be so bad off.

I have a bad heart condition, and this is the result of my hardships. I started to suffer this way five years after we were married. I don't care so much about myself; it's the children that I'm worried about all the time. If one isn't sick the other one is, and A—is always taking fits and going into convulsions. Lately she's been getting worse and she has me worried so that I don't know what to do with her.

I've been getting city relief now for quite a while. My husband lives somewhere in the city, but he can't help me because he's working with WPA, and he doesn't make enough to support us. We get some aid from a Swedish aid group. It's small help but they do the best they can for us, and they've been very nice right along. I came to live here, in the village [Yellow Mill Village], since about a month ago, and I find it very nice here. It makes the children feel better that they are living in a nice place, and it helps me very much because I don't have to work as hard as I used to before coming here. When I live on M. Street it was very hard because the children were always catching colds and they had no place to play. They were always getting hurt and would have a habit of going out in the street. Here we have none of that danger, and I'm glad I don't have to worry about that anymore.

When my husband first started to give me trouble I never told anyone. Our friends, most of them Swedish people, thought we were getting along very nicely. If you're Swedish you get a habit of telling only the good things. And this is the way I was until I couldn't stand it anymore. Then I told him to leave, and he's been out of the house ever since. If he could have fixed himself I would have taken him back, but he is so far with his drinking that he can't think of anything else. That's the one thing that drove him on the wrong path. He also felt strange because he married me, a Swede, who was used to better treatment.

That's one thing you can give the old people credit for—they are always on their toes about anything and everything. If the young people could convince them about something, they are willing to listen and see if there is some good in it. But regardless of what it is, the parents always have the best answer.

My father and mother were born on the other side. They came here when they were in their thirties, but they didn't come directly to Bridgeport. They had been for some time in New Britain because there were a lot of Swedish friends there. My father was mechanically inclined and on the other side he has been working on machine work. When he came here he did the same thing. Later he heard about Bridgeport—that was about the time of the World War. Then he came here with some of his friends and found work in one of the places here. Since that time he worked in the same shop and never went any place else for work. He was satisfied to stay in the small shop. My father had my brothers take up his trade and they were successful at it. They have been working out of town for quite a few years.

My parents had always advised me to get married to someone who had established himself in some trade. The Swedes are that way, and they feel that their children should marry someone who won't have to worry about supporting the family. I had thought this all along, but then I met my husband and I fell for him. I forgot what I had been told, and the result was that six months later I married him. Norwegians have a habit of coming to the Swedish affairs. They feel that they have something in common with the Swedish people, and the Swedes don't seem to mind their company. But they are a different type of people. Most of them [Norwegians] seem to remain on the same type of jobs; they don't care about advancing themselves like the Swedes. Swedish people have the background and understanding that it takes to make successes of themselves. You very seldom see a Swedish person who doesn't know something about mechanics or some type of skilled work.

When I was a child my mother had all she could do in taking care of the family. We were many and she couldn't attend to us all. She meant well and she helped my brothers in their training. My mother still had the old idea of girls working out as cooks for different families. I worked out for a couple of years, and then I was in charge of the duties in my mother's house. The girls at that time weren't given too much attention. The family felt that the girl could marry some Swedish man who would be able to take care of her. This is the reason why the girl was only taught how to take care of the house. They had the feeling that she would be well taken care of when it came her time to get married. They still do this—the mothers and fathers now feel the same way. The difference is that the girls try to do something for themselves. There are many girls I know who are interested in office work, teaching, and other things. This is something new to the old Swedish parents. Years ago Swedish girls didn't know about these possibilities because she was never told and the family never discussed the possibilities of girls in the professions. The girls now get a lot of that from schools and they see it in movies, and they form their ideas in this way. In my day we either did housework or went to work in the factory. The young Swedish girls don't do that anymore. I know some who wouldn't take any job, except in business. Most of the young girls are now going to high school; I think almost every Swedish girl does the same, but the idea is still the same about Swedish girls marrying for security, and I don't blame them. These days you have to think ahead before you do anything.

The Swedish people are very close together. Everyone in the family tries to understand what the other does. They don't quarrel among each other, and you will never see them shouting or scolding. The parents have everything under control and when there is something that bothers the children, the family decides what to do best. The children usually confide their problems to the mother, and she takes things up with the father. The father has the last word about what is to be done. The father is not stern like some people of other groups, but he is so proud that he wants everybody to know that he is right in whatever he decides.

There is a difference between the old-type father and the parent who is born in this country. The real Swede still holds on to certain Swedish habits, while the American father will do things the American way. In the old days the father would have his children associate with the older people of his organization; you don't find much of this now. The young people go their way, and they very seldom attend the same affairs with the old crowd. In this way they are being separated from the rule of the parents, and they are mixing with people of other nationalities. They are beginning to marry people of all nationalities. You find that most of them strike good marriages, because they expect the husband to be a good provider.

There is another thing that they have to follow, according to the wishes of their family: if possible, they try to marry into the same religion. But there are many who disregard this and they marry Catholics. The older people don't like this, but at least they are open-minded enough to admit that the marriage is a good one if both get along alright, in spite of the differences of nationalities. I know I had the same thing happen in my family—my brother married a Catholic girl. At first my people didn't like the idea because they thought he would become a Catholic, but they realized later that she went to her church an he attended his, and there never was any discussion about this.

My husband was the same—he never let our differences in religion bother us. But that wasn't the trouble that separated us. His was drink, that was his weakness.

Most of the Swedes have the habit of going out to visit one another. Others prefer to associate with their society members. Most Swedish people belong to the lodges and societies and they attend them very often. They like to get together and talk everything there is to talk about. They are no "hotheads" like some people think. They think very hard before they come to any decision, and that's the reason why the Swedes never regret what they do. That's one thing you can give the old people credit for—they are always on their toes about any-

thing and everything. If the young people could convince them about something, they are willing to listen and see if there is some good in it. But regardless of what it is, the parents always have the best answer.

No matter how little money the Swedes have, they are always thinking about providing something for their children's future. They don't actually give them money, but they feel they should provide for furthering their education. This is always the father's responsibility. The Swedish people feel proud when they could say that their child has entered into some kind of training, and some feel that it's a higher honor for them in having their son in a trade than in some profession. They really think it is better for their child to boast a trade. That's one thing I can't understand about them. I always thought that a profession was better than a trade.

When the Swedish men get together at the affairs, they are always talking shop. They talk about what they do and about what they have accomplished. The women talk about the things that all women discuss. When they visit in the house they will get together in card games—this is their favorite pastime. Most of the women either play cards with the men or they spend the time in quilting or crocheting different things. This is the kind of life they spend when they get together. They are always thinking of helping their friends; but even if a Swede needs help, he is too proud to say so. They only do it in extreme cases.

The Swedes like music and athletics. Some of the men join singing groups, others join athletic clubs. They like that very much. In fact, most Swedes feel it is a high honor for them should they join any one of these things. Almost all Swedish children take to studying some kind of musical instrument. Those that do pay a lot of attention to their studies, because they feel proud to demonstrate their abilities. I took up the study of the piano and I always liked it, and music was always appreciated in my people's home. Even now I hear some of the better music over the radio and I never miss the opera on Saturdays.

I like to read very much. My husband hated me for that; he used to think I was crazy—just because I had a love for reading books. I always like reading, and I used to explain to him that I wanted to gain more knowledge for myself, but he used to get mad about it and start to criticize me for it, saying that I was wasting my time. That's because he couldn't understand me, and he was a different type. He was rough, and he used to think that anyone having interests such as mine wasn't in their right mind. He felt that way since the first day we were married, and the only way he could express his resentment was to take it out on me by force and abuse. As I said before, I was never used to this treatment, and I took that sort of punishment for a number of years.

When things became unbearable I decided to put a stop to it. I couldn't tell my friends about my troubles because they wouldn't understand . . . and naturally, he gave them a different impression of what he was really like. Then it was also a question of pride. If nothing else, I always managed to keep my high ideas, and I never wanted to let on how I really felt. Before telling my friends about my intended separation I decided to discuss the matter with my people. They listened to what I had to say, and they were not surprised in the least. They said they had suspected the trouble right along, but they didn't want to say anything because they were afraid of hurting my feelings. They told me that the best thing for me to do would be to get a separa-

tion. I didn't want to air this in any court because I was afraid of such a thing, so the best thing I could do was to tell him to leave the house until such a time as he could see his mistakes. But he never got feeling that way, even after he left.

Almost all Norwegians act that way. They could live and enjoy themselves while there are good times to be had, but when they have to face something they lose their nerve. I have been told that he is just like many other Norwegian men. The women aren't so bad—at least they will admit their faults once in a while. The men are not as strong-willed. I tried to think of asking him back sometime, but I think I have lost all respect for him.

Source:

From the Old Country, edited by Bruce M. Stave and John F. Sutherland, with Aldo Salerno. New York: Twayne Publishers, 1994. pp. 167-171.

SWISS AMERICANS

Between the 1890s and the 1920s, well over 120,000 Swiss immigrants arrived in the United States. Among the immigrants was Mrs. Zimmerman and her family. Based on her experiences, Mrs. Zimmerman drew some strong contrasts between American and Swiss societies in a late 1930s interview.

Born in Switzerland in the 1880s, Zimmerman fondly recalled her earlier days on a small dairy farm in rural Switzerland where her family made cheese and butter. Life seemed happy and complete with gardens, cooking, cheerful cottages, plenty of friends, and economic self-sufficiency. Prior to World War I, she married German Hans Zimmerman and settled in Germany to work on a large farm. But with the outbreak of war, the Zimmermans and their several children returned to politically neutral Switzerland. Upon arriving in Switzerland, the Zimmermans decided to take advantage of a government program designed to relieve overpopulation problems by financially assisting Swiss families permanently immigrating to the United States.

In the early nineteenth century, America's rural Midwest, including Ohio, became a popular area for Swiss settlement. The Swiss Colonization Society was established in the region to provide support to the many newly arriving immigrants. First settling in New England, Zimmerman and her family soon joined the many other Swiss in Ohio. In the interview, Zimmerman briefly described in her broken English their pathway to Ohio,

> Hans had a brother that went to Ohio. . .He said we should come. And the Swiss government was paying fares for people who wanted to go to America. Dey wanted to get rid of us. . .But we had to sign papers that said we would not come back. So we went to Ohio. . .Ach, I love Ohio!

In the interview, Zimmerman pondered the differences between the Americans, whom she perceived as unsociable and reserved, and the more open and welcoming Swiss, strongly lamenting the loss of such warm, friendly human interaction. She also expressed astonishment over the wastefulness of Americans in their daily lives. In middle Europe she described how little was ever discarded:

> In Europe where I lived the farmers tended their land carefully, but here it seems everybody yust tries to see what they can get out of the land. . .Nothing effer wass wasted on our farm in Europe!. . .Lots of women there put food in their soup that Americans—even poor Americans—throw away."

She observed that European farmers were considerably more careful in treating their land and were generally more thrifty and self-sufficient reflecting the conservative, well-regulated manner of Swiss life.

MRS. ZIMMERMAN—AN ALIEN IN YANKEE NEW ENGLAND

Paper One
State: Massachusetts
Name of Worker: Wade Van Dore
Address: New Marlborough
Date of Interview: February 28, 1939
Subject: Living Lore
Name of Informant: Mrs. Zimmerman
Address: New Marlborough

Old Mrs. Zimmerman is Swiss by birth, German by marriage, American by naturalization, and New Englandish by habitation. She is a nice-looking, friendly, motherly woman not much past fifty, but her health is not good and probably she will not live many more years. A result of her ill health is that she is nervous. All the same she has a way of accepting life pleasantly from day to day as people of strong peasant stock often do, taking great pleasure in fancy work, flowers, good cooking, a clean and cheerful home, the kindnesses of friends, and the love and prettiness of her little granddaughter. She is not appreciated by her children, who accept her work for them as a matter-of-fact, and who do not realize the seriousness of her health problems. They are thoughtless rather than deliberately unkind.

Mrs. Zimmerman speaks of Ohio as if it were a village instead of a state. To her Ohio means a small community bounded on all sides by kindliness.

The mother's reaction to this treatment is an intense gratefulness to anyone else who shows the slightest interest in her or sympathy for her. She will talk at great length about her problems, more repetitiously than informatively. She is sincerely bewildered by the tightly closed doors of the neighborhood in which she finds herself in New England. There is no kinship for her with the run-down hill families, and the only others, with one or two exceptions, are summer city people who keep to themselves and do not care for visiting back and forth. This attitude has not been helped by the actions of Mrs. Zimmerman's daughter and son-in-law since buying their country home. They have been rude and unkind to many of the natives, including those whose former home they bought. The few dummer people who know and like the natives resent ill treatment of them and do not care to know such unmannerly folk. They know that Mrs. Zimmerman is not responsible for these actions, but still by force of association she must suffer for them too. Mrs. Zimmerman realizes all this, and her loneliness is doubled. She is so genuine, good-hearted, and wholesome that her daughter seems almost unrelated to her.

The young couple, living in Hartford, bought the old Chase farm for little more than the proverbial song. Besides an old house of great charm, the property included a smaller house where the descendants of the original farm-owners had lived, even after the first sale of the place to a New York doctor. When sold again to the Hartford people, the occupants of the smaller house, were forced out by subterfuge and bullying rather than a straightforward statement that their home was needed for Mrs. Bell's mother. Mrs. Zimmerman had made friends with the former residents of her little house and felt badly to see them treated them so. She remained friendly with them after they moved away, and often visits them.

The Bells, and consequently Mrs. Zimmerman , have not been accepted on social terms by the community partly for these and partly for other reasons. They seem alien to its quiet spirit. They have brought horse-back riding and week-end parties to a neighborhood characterized by flower gardens and book shelves, and feel put out that the flower-lovers and book-lovers have not called on them. They cannot understand an aristocracy of intellect, nor even an aristocracy of kindliness and wholesomeness, from which springs Mrs. Zimmerman . They know only the aristocracy of business and money and property.

In her speech Mrs. Zimmerman has the usual difficulty of the European with the English "th" sounds. Sometimes she remembers to form them and sometimes she says "dat" or "dose." She says "as" instead of the comparative "than." Her "s" sounds are always soft, and "v" is pronounced more like "f," while "j" is said like "y."

Mrs. Zimmerman had brought her blonde, curly-topped little grand-daughter to play with our four-year-old, and while the children were playing together on the floor we offered our guest a cup of tea and a cookie.

"These cookies were made with bacon grease instead of butter for shortening—can you taste it?" I asked her.

"Not so much. I use bacon grease in my cookies too, But we don't have much bacon and I use most of the grease in soap."

"Soap? Do you make your own soap?" I asked, incredulous, in this day of manufactured soaps. "Why, I never knew anyone before who could make soap. How do you make it?"

"Well, first uf all you need a stone crock, and you put a can of lye in that with a quart of cold water. You haf to do that the night before, and let it stand—so. Then you take four pounds of grease—it don't matter what kind, but it should be strained so it is clear, and heat it so it is just melted and lukewarm, not hot. Pour it in the crock with the lye and water, den stir it good for

about five minutes. Den let it get hard, and you can cut it in cakes. I haf enough soap made right now to last a year maybe. Ach? It is easy—you should make it too."

But I always heard that home-made soap was hard on your hands," I said. At this Mrs. Zimmerman spread out hers eloquently.

"Look at mine!" she demanded. It don' hurt mine none. I always used it, since I wass ust a little girl in Switzerland. My mother made all uf her soap that way. Many times haf I been glad to make my own soap, when I hadn't much money. Den I could use what money I had for food. In Germany during the war—"

"Oh—weren't you born in Switzerland?" I interrupted.

"Yes, I wass. On a little farm—oh, a very nice little farm! We had plenty cows, and we made lots of cheeses and butter. Everybody worked,—the children did all the chores. Sometimes we went to school—not very much, dough, but I can read and write. I haf learned many tings since I grew up. On Sundays we did no work at all besides what we had to, and den we wore our best dresses and went happy to church. They were such pretty dresses! I yust wish I had one to save for the baby. An' would you believe it—dey are in style now!—dose striped country skirts and aprons. I wass a pretty girl, people said—like my daughter iss now—and I had a lot of beaux!"

She laughed shyly at her own story, and her fine eyes shone, remembering long-ago sunny Sundays. I could well believe that she had been a very attractive girl—prettier, I felt sure, than her Americanized daughter.

"Den, I met Hans and we right away got married," she went on. "And I had six children. One, the oldest boy, is still in Switzerland, and I haven't

seen him since we left. He hass now a little boy ten years old. My, wouldn't I like to see him, dough! Then I lost two babies. It was a hard thing to have babies den, and lots of times they died, or the women died because dey weren't taken good care of. I never once had a doctor when my babies came— yust midwives, an' sometimes dey were yust dirty an' ignorant women. My babies were all big too—not like dese little seven-pound ones that the girls have now. Eight, nine, ten pounds mine all were! I guess—"she hesitated, then went on bravely—"I guess maybe it wassn't so good for me, dough. I went to the doctor yesterday. He said I haf' some trouble left from one of dose times, an' if I don't haf an operation it will be bad. Well, I've lived long enough anyway. My children don't need me any more."

"But wouldn't you like to see this baby grow up?" I asked, indicating the child on the floor.

I milked eleven cows twice a day, and I worked out in the fields, yust like a man. I used to bring my little girl in a carriage and leave her in it under a tree at the edge of the field while I worked. Den I had to cook and keep house besides. That wassn't eassy either. We had only one room in our cottage. It had a thatched roof and dirt floor and white-washed plaster walls. We all slept and ate and lived in that one room!

"My, yes! but she too can get along without me. Mine got along without their grandmothers. Hans' mother was never friendly with me, and my mother died. We left Switzerland to work a big farm in Germany before the war came. I worked as hard as Hans. Yes, I did. I milked eleven cows twice a day, and I worked out in the fields, yust like a man. I used to bring my little girl in a carriage and leave her in it under a tree at the edge of the field while I worked. Den I had to cook and keep house besides. That wassn't eassy either. We had only one room in our cottage. It had a thatched roof and dirt floor and white-washed plaster walls. We all slept and ate and lived in that one room! I had to carry water to cook with an drink, and do my washing in a river that ran near us. Our house wass much poorer than even the houses that people on relief haf here, but we were always wery, wery clean. And we had money enough too. That was yust the way farmers lived. We got pretty good wages, and saved our money. We had bank accounts and five thousand dollars insurance on every one of the children. But den, the war came, and our money that we worked so hard for, wass soon not worth hardly anyting. So we went back to Switzerland."

"But how did you happen to come here?" I enquired.

"Hans had a brother that went to Ohio' that's why. He said we should come. And the Swiss government was paying fares for people who wanted to go to America. Dey wanted to get rid of us," she laughed. "But we had to sign papers that said we would not come back. So we went to Ohio." Mrs. Zimmerman smiled. Her face shone. I could see that Ohio, not Switzerland, was truly her home-place.

"Ach, I love Ohio! The people, they are so friendly! There wassn't a day I didn't go to Doctor Hoffmeyer's. I would go in, and if dey were haffing supper I would get a plate and sit down right with them. If I didn't go over same days Mrs. Hoffmeyer would send the children to see if I wass sick. And all the neighbors were like that. So good! They had a party for me when I moved away, and all of dem gave me presents. There are no neighbors like dat here. I get so lonesome dat I tink effery day I will go back to Ohio."

Mrs. Zimmerman speaks of Ohio as if it were a village instead of a state. To her Ohio means a small community bounded on all sides by kindliness. She resumed after a short pause.

"Here I don't know hardly anybody but you and Mrs. Cruickshank, and my daughter doesn't want me to go there—or come here, either. She doesn't like it because the people in the big houses haven't come to see her, but I tell her she and James had no right to treat the Cruickshanks like they did, and the people around here don't like it. I yust don't know why they did it. And I don't care if they like it or not—I am going to see Mrs. Cruickshank. She is so nice! I like her. And you too you have been better to me since I have been here as Mary has been herself. She iss so young! Maybe when she iss older she will be better—but den I will be gone! Maybe it iss my own fault, dough—maybe I spoiled her—my only girl, and the baby. But before she got married she was always good to me—cooking and cleaning the house while I worked out."

"What sort of work did you do?" I asked her.

"Well, after we wass in Ohio awhile, Hans he got sick and couldn't work. So I did housework and washing until the children were through school. Then my son got a job in Hartford, and when Mary came to see him she met James, and married him. Then Eric, my son as is still at home, he wanted to come and work in Hartford too. So when Mary and James bought this place up here in the country, they wanted Eric and me to live here. But oh dear, I am so lonesome with no neighbors and no car. I had a car all the time, always, till I came here. Now Eric needs it to go to work. And it iss so far to walk to anywhere. I wish the Cruickshanks could haf stayed in their house! I would haf stayed in Ohio if I knew how lonely it would be! But I am getting too old now to work so hard and make my own living."

Mrs. Zimmerman was on the verge of tears after these assertions, and for some time neither of us said anything. Finally, however, she shrugged her shoulders and smiled.

Look—don't you think this will be pretty?" she said as she spread on her lap the crochet work she was doing. "It is going to be a tablecloth for Mary. She asked me to make it for her. But I can't do it very fast because the thread is so expensive, and I don't have much money to spend. I made Mary some riding breeches last week, and I made a good heavy quilt out of woolen squares—tailor's samples they were, Ach! I keep busy all the time—cooking, cleaning, sewing—and cleaning the big house too. Mary hasn't any help but that nurse-maid, an' she won't even wash the dishes—yust think of that!"

We watched the children building a house of blocks and smiled at their delighted shrieks when it tumbled down.

"Janey luffs to come here and play with Peter. She talks all the time about going to Peter's house. She iss too small to know if people haf a grand big house or not."

There is a growing plant upon the window sill, and our guest notices it.

"You haf a new plant? I haf one like dat too—only mine is much bigger—I've had it so long. It hass grown out of many pots. I brought all my plants with me from Ohio in the car. I couldn't bring many things, but I brought my plants. I luf to haf things growing around me. More than Americans do, I guess. In Europe where I lived the farmers tended their land carefully, but here it seems everybody yust tries to see what they can get out of the land. Almost nothing is put back in, and much is wasted. Nothing effer wass wasted on our farm in Europe! You should see the way people pick up sticks and twigs and dried grass to burn! When I came here I could not understand how the folk could be so extravagant, burning so much wood! It wass the same way in the fields. After the harvest came folk to look for effery small potato or grain of wheat left behind.

"Effery bit of manure wass precious in Germany. We saved it carefully, to spread on the fields. And nobody had garbage to yust throw away. Effery thing wass used for something. Neffer a crust of bread or a cup of sour milk was thrown away. There wass some stuff for the pigs, and what they would not eat was put in a compost heap.

"Lots of women there put food in their soup that Americans—even poor Americans—throw away. Our soup kettle was always on the stove, and we put in it bones, and bits of vegetable or cereal, and boiled it all together and then strained it. Then we put in some rice or barley and cooked that. It makes fine, hearty soup, a whole meal with bread and cheese."

"Aren't you rather shocked, then, by the shiftlessness of same of our neighbors?" I asked.

"Yes, I am! And I think the farmers around here would be better off if dey were more careful of their land and their wood and beasts and all—and if their wives made soap and clothes and rag rugs for their houses, instead of buying so much."

"Some of them are still thrifty, and do these things," I told her.

"But in Europe country people still do the things that their ancestors did, in the same way, for hundreds of years back. And it seems very nice that they do."

"Do you ever wish to be back there again?" Mrs. Zimmerman hunched up her shoulders and slowly smiled in a characteristic way, then answered me.

"Ach, no. I like the comforts we haf here. And they are sure to haf war there soon again. That Hitler hass got the Germans crazy. No, I am lonesome an' sick an' old, but I guess I rather die here in my bed as to be hit by a bomb in Europe."

"And you are alone at night too, aren't you? Are you very afraid to stay alone?"

"No—why should I be afraid? I got a gun under my pillow! Dat fellow Gil Carter came around drunk las' Saturday night about two o'clock in the morning, hollering an' singing an' making a big fuss.

Mary an' James were in the big house, an' James came out with a shotgun an' told Gil to go along home or he would shoot him. Gil was scared, I guess, but he didn't want James to know it. I had opened my window and I heard the drunk one holler, 'You can't shoot me, mister! People around here don't do things like that!' Then he went away. I hope he don't come back again."

Mrs. Zimmerman folded up her crochet and put it into a bag. "Come Janey, it iss time to go home," she said, and started to put on the child's coat and bonnet, encountering considerable resistance as her victim would much rather have continued playing.

"They are going back to Hartford tonight, and I shall be lonely again. Soon you will come up if you can? Please, I would luff to see you. An' I will give you some butterscotch pie an' coffee!"

So the old lady and the little girl started for home, the grandmother with the folkways of middle Europe bred into her bones, and the tiny girl so close to her in blood, but so distant in the way of life she is destined to follow.

Source:

Library of Congress. *American Life Histories: Manuscripts from the Federal Writers' Project, 1936-1940* from the American Memory website (http://memory.loc.gov/ammem/wpaintro/wpa-home.html).

Syrian Americans

Khalil Gibran, the author of this document, was born on January 6, 1883, in Basharri, Lebanon, and was educated in Beirut. Gibran was an American immigrant, arriving in Boston in 1895 with his parents. He continued his schooling in Lebanon in 1898 and returned to Boston in 1903. Gibran settled in New York in 1912 and devoted himself to writing essays, short stories and poetry. A Boston area literary society named al-Rabitah al-Qalamiyah (League of the Pen), which was specifically formed to promote Arabic-language poetry and writing and to preserve Arabic culture, helped further Gibran's career. Gibran is perhaps the best known modern Arabic poet, and his best known work is the widely read The Prophet.

Gibran's text, originally published in The Syrian World in 1926, distinctly spoke to immigrant youths about the opportunities that they have in living in America. He delivered a strong message to Syrian youth:

> It is to be proud of being an American, but it is also to be proud
> that your fathers and mothers came from a land upon which God
> laid his gracious hand and raised His messengers.

Gibran encouraged young immigrants or the children or grandchildren of immigrants to both embrace their adopted country and respect their home land. Syrian heritage is rich and starts in the third millennium B.C. with the Canaanites. Damascus, the oldest living city, was the capital of the Umayyads, who ruled the largest contiguous empire until the Crusades.

It was not until after 1880 that Syrians began to emigrate in large numbers. Immigrants to the United States came primarily for economic reasons, seeking a better life. Gibran was educated when he arrived in America, but most Syrians were not. The majority of immigrants were single men in their late teens and early twenties. When they arrived, they often sought out a relative or acquaintance, settling in industrial cities and working as laborers or becoming itinerant farm workers and merchants. Often, they sent money home and many returned to Syria with their savings. As a group, Syrians moved into the fields of manufacturing and retailing and created several well known manufacturing chains.

Gibran's message to Syrian youth reflects the personal qualities considered important by many first generation Syrian immigrants. The first generation valued hard work and promoted strong moral values of honesty and consideration of others. They held strong family ties and religious faith was of primary importance. While the first generation taught these values to their children born in America, the second generation also assimilated into American culture. A third generation began to re-gain interest in Syrian cultural heritage. It is for this reason that Gibran told young Syrians not to forget their roots. Gibran believed in the possibility of Syrian youths living the lives of good American citizens, while always remembering the Syrian heritage from which they came.

KAHLIL GIBRAN'S MESSAGE TO YOUNG SYRIANS

I believe in you, and I believe in your destiny. I believe that you are contributors to this new civilization.

I believe that you have inherited from your forefathers an ancient dream, a song, a prophecy, which you can proudly lay as a gift of gratitude upon the lap of America.

I believe you can say to the founders of this great nation, "Here I am, a youth, a young tree whose roots were plucked from the hills of Lebanon, yet I am deeply rooted here, and I would be fruitful."

And I believe that you can say to Abraham Lincoln, "The blessed Jesus of Nazareth touched your lips when you spoke, and guided your hand when you wrote; and I shall uphold all that you have said and all that you have written."

I believe that you can say to Emerson and Whitman and James, "In my veins runs the blood of the poets and wise men of old, and it is my desire to come to you and receive, but I shall not come with empty hands."

I believe that even as your fathers came to this land to produce riches, you were born here to produce riches by intelligence, by labor.

And I believe that it is in you to be good citizens.

And what is it to be a good citizen?

It is to acknowledge the other person's rights before asserting your own, but always to be conscious of your own.

It is to be free in thought and deed, but it is also to know that your freedom is subject to the other person's freedom.

It is to create the useful and the beautiful with your own hands, and to admire what others have created in love and with faith.

It is to produce wealth by labor and only by labor, and to spend less than you have produced that your children may not be dependent on the state for support when you are no more.

It is to stand before the towers of New York, Washington, Chicago and San Francisco saying in your heart, "I am the descendant of a people that builded Damascus, and Biblus, and Tyre and Sidon, and Antioch, and now I am here to build with you, and with a will."

It is to be proud of being an American, but it is also to be proud that your fathers and mothers came from a land upon which God laid his gracious hand and raised His messengers.

Young Americans of Syrian origin, I believe in you.

Source:
An Ancient Heritage: The Arab-American Minority by Brent Ashabranner. New York: Harper Collins, 1991. pp. 140-141.

*T*hough he came from Syria, a land faraway and exotic to most people in the United States, the story of Salom Rizk is a thoroughly American one. It calls to mind the many tales penned by Horatio Alger (1832-99), whose novels such as Luck and Pluck (1869) concerned boys who came up the hard way, and through ambition and persistence ultimately realized the American Dream.

Rizk's story, by contrast, is not fiction. Born in 1909, he grew up in a poor village in what was then Syria, though most likely its location was in modern-day Lebanon. Several aspects of his biography suggest this, including the fact that he lived for some time in Beirut, the capital of Lebanon. Also, at the time Rizk arrived in America, during the early 1900s, the majority of Syrian immigrants were

Lebanese Christians. It is clear Rizk was not a Muslim, as most Syrians are, because he herded pigs as a child—something a Muslim would never do, because pigs are unclean according to Islamic law. Furthermore, Rizk dedicated Syrian Yankee to a Christian minister, the Rev. Harold E. Schmidt.

Nonetheless, it is equally clear that he considered himself a Syrian, as his story's title suggests. Lebanon and Syria share much history, dating back to ancient times, when Phoenicia or Lebanon was, along with Syria, one of the dominant civilizations of the Middle East. This relationship continued into modern times, with Beirut and the Syrian capital of Damascus widely recognized as two of the preeminent cultural centers of the Arab world.

At the age of 12, however, Rizk learned that he was not fully Syrian: his mother had been an American citizen, and therefore he could go to America and claim American citizenship as well. With the help of his Syrian schoolmaster, he wrote to his relatives in Iowa, where there was and is a small but significant Syrian community. Eventually they helped him secure passage to the United States, but he had to spend five long years in Beirut waiting for all the paperwork to establish his citizenship.

Not long after Rizk arrived in the United States, the country underwent the Great Depression (1929-1941), in which millions of people lost their jobs and suffered economic hardships. This was also the era of Prohibition (1919-1933), when sale and consumption of alcohol was illegal; hence, as Rizk recalled later, he was wary when some of his friends suggested they buy a pint of "white mule, hooch, moonshine."

The dialogue in Rizk's narrative is full of such expressions typical of the era. His ear for human speech was obviously quite well-tuned, and if his friends sound like characters from an old movie, it is simply because they were a part of the same popular culture that produced those movies.

Rizk himself quickly became disillusioned with that popular culture, as he records in Syrian Yankee. *Like many another immigrant, he responded with shock and some disgust when he discovered the degree to which many Americans took for granted the advantages they enjoyed. Through a series of events that began at a settlement house, a community center for the poor, he discovered his ambition to learn English properly and become a "life servant of the United States."*

Working a variety of odd jobs, he came up with the idea of a free shoe repair service for poor people, and this took hold across the country. Eventually the Rotary Club, a civic organization, invited him to speak before its Ames, Iowa, chapter regarding his experiences as an immigrant. Thus he embarked on a speaking career that brought him to the attention of DeWitt Wallace (1889-1981), founder of Reader's Digest *magazine. As Wallace reported in the foreword to* Syrian Yankee, *after his speech to the Rotary Club, "his audience arose spontaneously and there was prolonged applause, as there has been since in over a thousand auditoriums."*

In April of 1939, Lowell Thomas (1892-1981), a well-known journalist, introduced Rizk to the New York Advertising Club, where members of the Reader's Digest *staff first heard him. Thomas called him the "Syrian Yankee" because his view of the world was so American—more American than that of Americans, in fact, since as Rizk pointed out, his own experience of hardships in Syria helped him to appreciate the freedoms and abundance of American life.*

By the time of his talk before the Advertising Club, Rizk had developed a speech entitled "The Americanization of America." The Reader's Digest *in the*

1930s sponsored him on a speaking tour to 1,495 schools, and at the time Syrian Yankee *was published in 1943, he had addressed more than one million students.*

SYRIAN YANKEE (EXCERPT)

Ambition to Learn English

In my spare time I had been reading a Syrian-language book on American history and how to become a citizen. There were many things not clear to me, and I welcomed every chance to start a discussion on them. One day in a speakeasy booth (to be a good sport I still went out with the gang) I asked this out-of-place question: "What form of government is the American government?"

Said young citizen Number 1, puzzled, as if he knew the answer but couldn't think of it just then: "What form?. . . Form? Form!"—snapping his fingers and repeating, "Form. . .form. . .form," to keep the others from getting their answers in. "Oh yes, we have the best form of government there is."

Said citizen Number 2, "Oh yeah! But he don't mean that, you dope. He means what *kind* of government."

Young citizen Number 3, a girl with artificial cheeks and lips, spoke up: "Well, it ain't no Democratic government, 'cause Coolidge is president and he's Republican."

"Yah, that's it," several shouted. "It's Republican. Yay bo!"

"Well, let's see," one of them said more thoughtfully, hoping to clear things up for me, "sometimes we have a Democratic government, sometimes Republican. All depends on who's president."

A few nights later some of my friends took me to a settlement house; I think they were getting worried about my morals. Anyway, on of the social workers cornered me and with the help of a Syrian-American friend got me to tell my story. She was a very friendly, gracious person. During the whole stumbling recital she kept exclaiming, "How wonderful!" or "How thrilling!" She asked me come back again the next night; said a friend of hers would like to meet me.

The friend was a newspaper reporter. He asked me more questions and made notes on a pad. Next day the picture of a very "immigrantish"-looking fellow appeared in the evening paper with a story that went like this:

Pursuing an ideal set up several years ago when he was a student in the antiquated school systems of Syria, Samuel Rizk now is striving to become an American citizen.

While most American boys may aspire to become a president of his country, a big-league home-run king, or a master of high finance, Samuel will be content to become an educated American, capable of serving his new homeland to the fullest degree.. . . His ambition now, as he declares it, is "to become a life servant of the United States."

When my brother translated that for me, it seemed the most beautiful idea I had ever heard—a life servant of the United States—but I couldn't for the life of me remember having declared it. That newspaperman had a wonderful imagination. And I'm glad he did. His article aroused my spirit from the hapless stupor to which my lack of progress that first year in America had brought me. It inspired me with an overpowering passion to struggle free from the discouraging milieu which made my most urgent ambitions impossible. From now on, if determination counted for anything, I was going to have a more active part in my own destiny.

I began to see my trouble and to search for means to remedy it.

In the first place, I wasn't learning the language. To spare me embarrassment as well as to expedite conversation between us, my Syrian friends were speaking to me in my own tongue. In the packing plant it was no better, for most of the workers around me were foreigners like myself. When they talked to each other they used their own language; when they talked to me they used profanity.

In the second place, I was afraid of Americans. Something in their attitude held me off, made me feel that I was something less than they were. It sometimes made me wonder if I really wanted to meet them or have them as friends. Yet when people like the social worker and the newspaper reporter befriended me, I had a feeling of being on the verge of a great discovery—the discovery of that magic land whose inner spirit my schoolmaster had described so often and so vividly.

But the other though kept coming back over and over again, like steady dripping of rain from the eaves: "You can't be an American without English. You can't be an American without English."

That is really a dreadful feeling. You have America all around you; your feet are on her soil; your ears are filled with the music of her voice; your eyes behold the magnificence and beauty of her material achievements; yet the real America, the America you grasp with the understanding, is always eluding you because you do not have the key.

Desperate and determined, I talked it over with several friends. One of them said, "Sam, why don't you try peddling? Get out of town. Get away from the people you know. Go out to the small towns around here where there aren't any Syrians and sell oriental rugs to the Americans. Then you'll have to learn English."

It sounded like a good idea. Within a few days I had acquired a partner, Joe Solomon by name, who was working his way through school. We arranged for a consignment of rugs and tapestries and bought an old Model-T Ford. It had droopy fenders and doors that refused to stay shut. It was so tentatively hung together that every time something stopped rattling we went back and picked it up. In this seventy-five dollars' worth of mechanical trouble we set out for the hills and prairies of Iowa, Joe to earn next year's college tuition, I to learn English from American housewives in the little country towns.

Source:

Syrian Yankee. Garden City, New York: Doubleday & Company, 1943. pp. 149-153.

TAIWANESE AMERICANS

An interview with Taiwanese American Su-Chu Hadley highlights the dramatic changes in life that immigration to America sometimes poses. Su-Chu was raised in the mid-twentieth century on the densely populated island of Taiwan. Born of poor parents, she was put up for adoption only to join yet another family in poverty. Laboring in agricultural fields as a youngster, she later worked for a Taiwanese family cooking meals, washing clothes and performing other duties. Discovering that similar work for American families could earn a lot more money, Su-Chu learned English and became employed as a housekeeper and cook for an American family.

Despite an ill-fated romance with an American soldier, Su-Chu still hoped to leave Taiwan for the United States, and she took a job as a waitress in an American officers' club. There she met an American civilian whom she eventually married, and they had two children. In 1964, when their children were ready for school, Su-Chu and her family moved to northern California, a common destination for many Taiwanese. Most Taiwanese Americans arrived well educated professionals establishing strong support networks, but Su-Chu, married to an American, was less reliant on such systems. Reflecting the high value of education held by Taiwanese, Su-Chu explained the children would have far better educational and employment opportunities in the United States.

Though not enjoying a good relationship with her Taiwan foster family back home, she continued sending money from the United States, typical of many Taiwanese Americans. Su-Chu often reflected on how vastly improved her life in American compared to her early years in Taiwan. Regarding the happy lives and bright future prospects of her children, Su-Chu commented in seeing her children off to play on the beach,

> You can't know how it makes me feel to see them go off like this. They are ten and twelve, and when I was ten and twelve I was working in the fields all day. . .Sometimes in the evening I cry, thinking of everything that has happened.

Such was the story of Su-Chu, one of many Taiwanese Americans to enter the United States as wives of Americans associated with the U.S. military presence in Taiwan following the Korean War. She was part of the first substantial Taiwanese immigration to the United States spurred by relaxed U.S. immigration controls in the post-World War II era.

SU-CHU HADLEY—FROM TAIWAN, 1964

Where I worked, the man had two wives. The first wife lived on the third floor, and the second wife lived on the second floor. I had to clean, scrub all the bricks of the house, and do the marketing and all the cooking. The first wife was older, and she always wanted me to cook the food longer and softer; and the second wife always wanted me to cook the food quickly and make it crunchy on the outside. I had to please everyone. That's where I learned to cook different styles. And in the nighttime, when I was through cooking, I had to wash all the clothes. I was cooking for thirteen people and washing clothes for thirteen people, and they paid me five dollars a month.

Next door there was an American, and they had two housekeepers and a cook. The cook made thirty dollars a month. I saw that and I started to try to learn English. I wanted to work for an American and make that big money. Every night, when I finished my work—about ten—I would sneak next door and learn English from that cook then come back at eleven-thirty at night. In the morning I would have to get up again at six and start the cooking and the marketing and the cleaning.

After I'd been there for about one year, one day my foster mother saw me in the market and she grabbed me to take me home. I didn't want to go, but she was dragging me. Hundreds of people were standing around and somebody asked, "What's the matter? What's the matter, missus?" My foster mother called out, "This is my daughter and I raised her. I adopted her since she was forty days old, and now look, she doesn't want to go home!" One young guy in the crowd said to my foster mother, "How old is she?" And she says, "Almost twenty-one." And he says, "Too bad! She's twenty-one now, she's free."

When I hear that guy say that, it made me strong. Then I talked to my foster mother and I said, "Okay. Right now I'm making five dollars a month. I will give you four dollars. You will have some money, and I will not go home." She let me go then. So I give them the four dollars a month, and I kept a dollar. Later, I got a raise to six dollars a month, and I got two dollars a month and they got four dollars a month. They were satisfied.

And then one day I became a housekeeper and cook to an American, and I made twenty dollars a month. My first twenty dollars I gave to my foster parents, and then I gave them more money every month. They treated me bad and they beat me, but that was the way things were then. I still think I was lucky that they didn't give me to a teahouse or something like that, because some foster parents, when the girl is old enough, they give her to a teahouse for so much a year. One of my other sisters they gave to a teahouse, and they beat her and beat her there, because she wouldn't do anything. They beat her till she would. Now she has something wrong with her head, because they beat her so much and made her do those things. So I think I was lucky, even though my foster parents punished me so much and beat me. I worked hard and now I'm strong. It was better than the teahouse.

While I was working for this American family as cook, I met my oldest son's father. [*Begins to whisper.*] He was an American and he told me that he wanted me to marry him, but he couldn't while he was in the army. I trusted him. He gave me twenty-five dollars a month to give to my parents, and he asked me if I would stay with him. He said we would get married when he left Taiwan. I lived with him for two years, and then one day I saw him and the next day I didn't. I was looking for him and looking for him. And, finally, I found his army buddy and he told me, "Oh, he went back to the United States. He has a wife and four children back in the States. You want his address?" And I said, "No. I don't want any address from him." At that time I was pregnant, three months pregnant.. . .

Then for a while I was very down—no money, no nothing. I had to go home to the farm with my foster parents until my son was born. That was bad.. . . Afterward, my foster mother took care of him and I went back to Taipei and worked and sent her money. My foster parents were kind of nice to my son, because I sent them money.

I got a job as a waitress in an American officers' club and I stayed there for three years. While I was working at the club I met Tim. He was a civilian, doing some engineering work for the government. He was very, very good to me. We were married there in Taiwan, and he was kind and he wanted me to learn. He taught me a great deal. He sent to the United States for third- and fourth-grade books of mathematics for me to study, and he taught me how to do division, multiplication, how to divide a pie; and he taught me good English—gentle English, because the way I had learned, I learned to talk rough. I didn't learn nice words and I talked very loud. He taught me to speak softly and to use the right words. Every day, when he would go to work, he would say, "Honey, this is your homework today. When I come home, I want to check it." He taught me all these things. He was very good to me.

We took my son to live with us and had two children of our own in Taiwan. Then my husband said, "They should be educated in the United States." So when my oldest was ready for school, we came to the United States. When I came to this country, I heard about all the divorces and I was kind of scared. I wanted to save money in case my husband kicks me out, so I can go somewhere. So I went and scrubbed floors for people, and my husband never knew. He didn't know for four years. I would take my children with me and work for a few days for free to show people what a good worker I was. And then I would work for them from about ten in the morning and come home at three, with the children. And Tim never knew. I saved all that money in case he would kick me out.

Then one day I heard about interest, and so I put my money in a bank. The next month the bank sent me a statement. And that day my husband got the mail. He came in and his face was kind of white. He was so hurt. He said, "Honey, why do you have to do that? Why do you have to sneak money in somewhere? Don't you trust me?" And I say, "I was trying to save money in a corner, in case you kick me out, so I can have a plane ticket to go home." And he said, "You don't have to do that. In the law here, you can take half. If you're mad at me, just take a vacation. Just take the money, take a vacation one week then come home." He said that to me; he didn't say "Go back. Go back to Taiwan." We were both crying. And I thought about it, and then I got the money out of the bank. It was $640 by then, and I let him have it to buy a truck for his work. I didn't sneak around anymore. After that I trusted him, and he trusted me again.. . .

I still send money to my foster parents. Every year I send them money because I understand that they are poor, and I feel, even though they were hard on me, they trained me well. Two years ago I went to visit them, and I felt I have to help them more because their son had drowned and they were alone. And I thought I would take them to the United States and help them. My husband said I can bring them to this country and take care of them if I want to. Then I found that they have kicked me out of their family. They had their little property, their eight acres, and these days property goes up in price. And they thought maybe I would go home to Taiwan and try to divide the property with them, so they went to court and took my name out of their family. When I wanted to bring them over I asked them to send me the household papers, and I find they had canceled my name out. So now I am no longer their child and I cannot bring them over. It's justice. But I still send them money, because I feel they trained me well.

[*At this point in the interview, Su-Chu's two daughters come into the room to say good-bye before gong to the beach. They wear bikinis and carry a picnic basket and a transistor radio. After they leave, Su-Chu looks out the window for a moment. Then she speaks softly*—]

You can't know how it makes me feel to see them go off like this. They are ten and twelve, and when I was ten and twelve I was working in the fields all day. . . . Sometimes in the evening I cry, thinking of everything that has happened, and my children say, "Daddy, how come mommy cry?"

"She's remembering bad things from long ago," he tells them.

And then I look at him and at them and at my house here, and I say, "Well, at least I have a happy ending."

Source:

American Mosaic: The Immigrant Experience in the Words of Those Who Lived It, compiled by Joan Morrison and Charlotte Fox Zabusky. New York: E.P. Dutton, 1980. pp. 331-334.

Like many immigrants, the Lins (the name is a pseudonym) left Taiwan to provide a better life for their children—and to flee political instability at home. But giving their children a better home required great sacrifices. Because he did not know English, Mr. Lin, who was the editor of a newspaper in Taiwan, had to take work as a janitor in America. His wife, a nurse in Taiwan, worked as a waitress in a Chinese restaurant, avoiding at least the garment-industry sweatshops where many Chinese immigrants are forced to work.

In the following interview, Mai Lin (pseudonym), the Lins' daughter, describes her experiences and those of her family as first-generation immigrants to America. The interview was conducted in 1989, twelve years after the Lins immigrated and six years after Mai, her parents, and her older brother became U.S. citizens.

MAI LIN—BEYOND DISNEYLAND

June 1, 1989 Massachusetts Institute of Technology Cambridge, Massachusetts

My parents started off being very poor. They had bought a small house. Apparently they used to eat rice gruel. They saved up money; they tried to save up money and so they scrimped on food.

My father was just getting started in the newspapers, and my mother was starting to be a qualified nurse and getting a job at hospitals. I was sent, because they were both working, back to my grandmother. She raised me, and I saw my parents every two weeks or something like that. They came on weekends. My grandmother lived in the [center] of Taiwan. Taipei is at the very northern tip, and my grandmother lived at least five hours or six hours by train south of that, and so they would come to visit on the weekend. And I have very little memory about my parents in the early stage. One day my grandfather fell pretty badly, either broke his hip or something. At the time I was about two or three, and that was the reason my grandmother had to send me back to my parents. She couldn't take care of me and my grandfather at the same time. I went back to my parents, and I think we had live-in [nannies], both my brother and I. He's four years older than I am. I don't remember what that whole period of time was like, but because of my grandmother and grandfather's influence, I spoke Taiwanese as well as Mandarin, and I was closer to them than I was to my parents while I was small.

I was sent to kindergarten at the age of two and a half because there was nobody at home to take care of me, so I was in kindergarten for three years and I became a bum, kind of. I knew all the ins and outs of the school, knew all the teachers. By the time I left that kindergarten, everybody had seen me for three years. I learned the times table by

the time I entered first grade, and they gave me homework over the summers. You had to write certain characters, certain times with a calligraphy brush. By the time I was in the fourth grade, my parents were well-to-do. My father was the head editor at a big newspaper.

The memories I have about what my parents were doing was when I started going to grade school. I went to the top elementary school in the city of Taipei, and we were driven into the city to go to these schools. My brother was going to middle school that was across a [botanical] garden. Within the garden was a national educational broadcasting system. My father was working in that station every week, putting out his own shows. He would always come and meet us after school.

Two or three times a week he would go on the air and read an article. I used to get out half a day or something when I was in second grade. And then I went there and did my homework. At times I would also go to my mother after school. By the time I was in the fourth grade, she was very well established. She was the head nurse for [one] division of the hospital. She sat in an office and had all these nurses under her. It was quite a luxury in terms of a job for a woman and so it was a really good life.

I have recollections of being able to go to my mom's office and sit in an air-conditioned room, which was a real luxury because most places didn't have air conditioning then, and just do my homework or do whatever hobby things I had. I had a little desk to myself — it was a big office — and we had slippers to put on. I could run around and all the nurses took me everywhere. We'd go and get pastries down the street or something in the middle of the day. It was a carefree life. Or I'd go to my father's broadcast station and he would buy me popsicles, whatever; I'd go out to the garden. Sometimes [my] friends [and I] would go into the ponds and dig for lotus roots to bring home to eat.

It was a pretty happy childhood. I hardly had any worries at all. I was taking piano lessons, I was going to school, and I had different hobby classes that I would attend. I learned how to make Chinese knots, and I was taking calligraphy, brush painting, and things like that.

Both my brother and I, we had a lot of homework. This was in fourth grade. We went to school for five and a half days — half days on Saturdays. My brother was under more pressure because the middle-school kids were ranked, and he was in the top rank. That meant that he was in one classroom with all the top-rank kids. The next thirty were second rank, and they would get a little less better teacher for that classroom, and it goes on down the line. Kids are ranked like this ever since elementary school, middle school, on up to high school and college, so there is a lot of pressure in terms of achieving academic excellence.

My brother was already going to tutoring classes because he was preparing for high-school entrance exams. You have to take a three-day exam, or however many days it is, and it covers all the different subjects and then you get a score. Depending on that score, you file a choice on what high school you want to go to. Depending on those scores, that high school either picks you or else you can't get in if your score is not good enough. Tutoring classes meant that he had to stay in the city until 7 or 8 P.M. School ended at 4 or 5 and then we had to drive him over to the tutoring place. Then we all ate out, usually, 'cause it was too late to go home and cook, and by the time we got home, we were so tired a lot of times we fell asleep doing our homework, but that was the kind of life.

But I didn't feel any kind of pressure at all. I was playing basketball for the school team. I was really short, but I played guard, and we were making our way to the city competition. All of a sudden, my parents decided, "Well, we're going to move to the States." I was nine. By the time we actually left Taiwan, I turned ten, but they were already starting preparations. I was going with them to the immigration officer interviews, and I didn't know what was going on. I was just sitting there and this guy was asking us questions, and I was supposed to answer nicely if he asked me any questions, but other than that I was just supposed to sit there. And we always got dressed up for it, but I didn't know what the heck was going on really.

But my parents one day just decided, "Oh well, would you like to go to America?" I didn't know where it was. I had no concept of what the Western world was like. So I said, "Oh, sure." You know, everybody's heard of Disneyland in Taiwan. My friends were all excited: "Are you going to get to go to Disneyland?" "You're going to have to send us letters and postcards and bring us back souvenirs." I guess we just picked up and went. I remember packing up all my stuff in cartons.

I had my own world. I was concentrating on my basketball. I think we were one competition away from city championships and I left, and that was one of the things that I really regretted. I was so little; I weighed a lot less than all the other kids my age, and I was really short. My mother was actually kind of afraid that, if we came to the United States, health-wise I might not hold up.

I was in this classroom where practically everyone was blond and blue-eyed. There was no other ethnic person in the whole school. Here I was, this oddity. Also, all these kids are curious about me, but then they got rude because I couldn't speak the language. I was wearing weird clothes. I didn't like to eat the food that they had in the cafeteria. I packed weird lunches that smelled weird.

I had an eraser collection. In Taiwan they make a lot of different shapes and different smells and different colors. Every time I'd get an allowance, I wouldn't go and buy candy, I would go buy erasers. I have over 400 of them, but they're pineapples or apples or bananas or little houses and little cars. I just collected them ever since I was five or six. I remember distinctly having to pack away my erasers into these little ice cream holders. My mother was trying to help me pack them as nicely as we could. In Taipei we had originally lived within the city, but then we moved right before we came to the United States to a really nice house on the outskirts of the city and it was a really nice area. It was free from air pollution and woodsy. You walked out of your front door and there was a papaya tree. My father had driven into town to pick us up one day after school, and he had told me and my brother to meet at a particular place, and it was supposed to be a surprise where we were going. He took us up to the new house, and he had these custom-made cabinets for us in our rooms. For me he had made a cabinet with sliding glass doors to display all my erasers. Each one had its own little slot. All of a sudden I had to take them out and put them away. By the time they got shipped over a lot of them had crumbled and got crushed. These are important things to a ten-year-old.

I didn't have any concept that we were really leaving, but when we got to the airport, all the family was there and my grandmother just kept crying. I couldn't figure it out when I was ten years old. I was, "We're going on a plane, we're going to go see Disneyland, we're going to go have a great time, why is she crying?" Maybe cry a little bit because we're not going to see her for a little while, but she kept saying, "I hope I see you soon." And, "Please be good and make sure you write," I started wondering. All of a sudden they called the flight, and they had these glass-enclosed doors to go down into a corridor. For international flights you have to go through these glass-enclosed areas first, and then there was a long corridor down to whatever particular plane you were taking. They called the flight and we started to have to file into the glass-enclosed area. All of a sudden I just didn't want to go! I felt that this was going to be it. I wasn't ever going to see her again, and so I grabbed onto the railing and I refused to let go. They were starting to close the glass doors; they had to file everybody in. I was hanging on and I ran back to my grandmother. My father eventually pried me away. We went on the plane and I still cried for a long time.

We flew from Tokyo to Hawaii. We flew from Hawaii to San Francisco. We were driven [by friends] from San Francisco to Los Angeles, then we went to Disneyland. [Finally] we went from Los Angeles by Greyhound bus up to Spokane, Washington. It was December of '77. My mother's friend was working in this hospital. After a few days there, we went by Greyhound bus up to Vancouver, B.C., and then we stayed with these friends. They said, "Oh, why don't you guys stay around here?

We settled in [a small town in Washington]. [My father became] a janitor. His pride was shot. He had been the head editor of a newspaper. He came and went whenever he wanted to in his jobs, and he had a lot of influence in the community and in Taiwan. All of a sudden he was this janitor, who didn't know the language and a lot of people perceived [of him as] stupid. A lot of people called him names. I remember this man just disappearing. He became very withdrawn and he was depressed. There was no more life in him. He worked the graveyard shift, and so he usually came home when we were already going off to school or else he was sleeping, and so I hardly had any contact with him.

My mother started as a waitress in a Chinese restaurant. It was owned by some of the Chinese people in town, so we got to know some of the Chinese people in the community. My mother was trying to get a job at a hospital. She worked as a nurse's aide then went to be a waitress. They told her, "Your schooling back in Taiwan and your experience there doesn't count as anything because you're a foreigner. You have to be certified in the States." So she had to take L.P.N. exams. There was a Chinese woman who was trying to do the same thing and had books, so my mother was trying to borrow them. She didn't want to lend them to my mother because she didn't want to see us doing better than her own family. There was a lot of competition between Chinese families. My family broke off from all ties with all Chinese. They had no friends except for the people in B.C.

So they settled down in [this town] and you were immediately enrolled in school. What was that like?

Oh, it was terrible. I had a lot of fun traveling around. I hated school. I've always hated school. Ever since I was little. No, it's true! I always hated all the work, but I always did well! I liked learning things, but I didn't always like the work they gave us. All of a sudden I was enrolled in this school. I didn't even know how to say "bathroom" and for two weeks I went around not knowing where the bathroom was, not knowing how to read signs. It was just miserable.

I was in this classroom where practically everyone was blond and blue-eyed. There was no other ethnic person in the whole school. Here I was, this oddity. Also, all these kids are curious about me, but then they got rude because I couldn't speak the language. I was wearing weird clothes. I didn't like to eat the food that they had in the cafeteria. I packed weird lunches that smelled weird. The started calling me names. There were a few kids who were nice that I eventually got to know, but at first everybody said all sorts of weird names. And at first I thought, "Oh, they're funny sounding," and I would just smile. All of a sudden I realized these things are directed toward me. The first words I learned in English were swear words. Everyone else was swearing, and so whenever somebody said something that sounded like something that I didn't like, I would swear back at them, and I didn't know what the heck I was saying. I remember feeling very lonely.

My teacher would be blabbing up there. I didn't know what he was saying. I was just sitting there, bored to death and left there for hours, but eventually the teacher assigned two girls to take me every day to a separate room and show me flash cards and teach me English individually. That was very helpful.

We lived in a motel across the street from the school, and everybody laughed at me because I lived in a motel. Everybody else was going home. Here I was going home to a motel. I didn't have any friends, and in Taiwan I had a lot of friends and I knew where to go. Here I was just going to school and then coming home and that was it, and at school I wasn't even having any fun. So I hated it. I went home crying every single day, and I begged my mother, "Please don't send me back tomorrow! Please, I don't want to go back. All these kids are being horrible to me." But of course she made me go back every single day. Eventually I decided, "All right, I'm going to do something about this. I know I'm not worthless. There must be something that they can like about me."

The starting point was where they were all taking math exams. Numbers were the only things I could read, right? Even though I had gotten perfect scores on these exams, it wasn't until this one day kids were sitting around. There was a free period and the teacher would go around and show people things that they were interested [in]. Some people were playing chess, others were playing checkers, stuff like that. One day he was trying to do this long division problem. He had done it wrong. I kept shaking my head. I kept trying to signal to him, "That's not right." And I guess he figured out what I was trying to say. So he redid it and [said], "Well, yeah, you're right." Because I was trying to do it for him and I had done it in half the time he just did, the kids were like, "Wow!" A couple of kids were like, "Why don't you race her in contest or something?" I guess I got the message somehow. I still didn't know English very well, but there were two old exams from the middle school or high school that he had sitting around. He gave one to me and he was trying to do one himself. We were timed and I beat him easily. The kids were like, "Wow!! This is great!" From then on, "Mai's fine, all right; Mai is this cool person because she beat the teacher!"

After that the kids started showing me how to play checkers. We would have competitions in chess. Then I started playing outside with them in square ball. Eventually I established myself among the kids and things are O.K.

That was middle school. I had this horrible teacher in sixth grade for the first two weeks. Then I got a really excellent teacher when I transferred into this other classroom. She made me do everything that all the other kids had to do. It was because of her that when I entered seventh grade I was getting straight As and I was writing essays just as fluently as everybody else. From then on I was doing well in school; I had a lot of friends, and I was invited to their houses and stuff like that.

Most of the time my parents weren't home and so I would just go over to somebody else's house, but then at home the troubles had started. When school kind of settled down, the home life wasn't so great. Within a year both my parents were very resentful of being in the States and having to work at these lousy jobs; they were obviously overqualified people to be working at menial jobs. Eventually they just started bringing their anger home. I was twelve years old, and they were expecting me to have the dinner cooked, the house cleaned, to take care of myself besides that, and not to have any troubles at all. If I ever brought up any problems, I would always get this lecture how I have to realize that they're very busy, and they're really working very hard, and I have to take care of myself. This is something that a little child gets used to from something that was great and wonderful, a nice family life in Taiwan, and all of a sudden within a year everything has flipped around.

I ended up watching TV a lot of times because there was nobody else home. I was always the first one to get home, so I would just let myself in. We were also being shifted around the first year because we had lived in a motel, then we moved to a rooming house with this other family. By the time I entered sixth grade, we actually purchased a house at the foot of this hill. The hill itself was one of the nice sections of town. For me it's symbolic of the way that our life has changed in the years, because [we moved] form [the] motel to that house and then eventually we bought the house on top of the hill. So financially we were doing a little better, but we always had to scrimp.

I didn't get new clothes. I was always wearing the same things they had brought over from Taiwan. When I went to school, people laughed at my pants. Everybody else was wearing jeans. Here I was wearing these polyester bell-bottom type of things with the elastic. So I was ashamed of where I came from and my parents. In middle school they had Parents Day, where you had a little project to do for the term and everybody exhibited their projects. I didn't want my parents to come. For about two or three years I hated being Chinese, I really did. I wanted to be like everybody else, and I wanted to have a family like everybody else, and I wanted to have a nice home like everybody else, and I wanted to be able to go home and say, "Hello, everybody's going to have dinner tonight at six!" and be able to invite my friends over. I couldn't even do that. I couldn't really invite any friends over because nobody was ever home. Home was really terrible. I didn't want to go home. I always tried to go to a friend's house and stay there as much as I could.

Did you see your grandmother again?

Not until 1981, three or four years later, but I had already known that she was terminally ill. I was becoming Americanized. I didn't have any immediate relatives around except for my own parents and brother, and so the attachment just kind of faded away. She came to visit and she was in a lot of pain. She had cancer. She specifically wanted to come see how we were doing rather than have us go back. At the time we couldn't afford to all go back anyway because my parents still had all their money tied up in the real estate back there. They had paid enough money to get both her and an uncle over so that she would have somebody to accompany her the whole way. This was the second time they bought a house, and it was in the nice section of

town, up a hill, and we had a view. The did that just because they wanted to make sure that she saw we were doing O.K. That was the only time I ever saw her again.

She was only here for two weeks and we had driven her to Yellowstone. She had actually wanted to go down to California to see Disneyland. That's such a symbol of America for some reason for people in Taiwan — kind of an America as a land of fun and of money. Instead we figured that it was better actually to go someplace that was a little more open, so we drove to

Yellowstone. We came back to [Washington]. Then she left and she died.

I just felt very distant. She was stranger to me by the time she came to visit and I remember. . .it was the middle of the night when they called up and told us that she had passed away. I remember my mother crying, and I was just numb. I didn't do anything and she was still the same grandmother. She was still loving and everything, but somehow I had drawn away and put it all away or something. I couldn't figure it out. It wasn't until much later after her death that I went and looked back on things. I had really missed her.

I wrote in a paper recently that if I had known ten years ago what I know now about emigrating to the States I wouldn't have chosen to come. A lot of things have happened to my family that just haven't been worth it, I think. If we had stayed in Taiwan, my parents would have advanced further in their jobs, and they would have been both happier and more relaxed and have a lot of friends. My brother and I would have been under a lot of pressure to get into good schools; it's kind of the same thing here. But it's a different kind of life. In terms of the family, I think it really wasn't worth it. I guess the thing they were really worried about in terms of education was that if we had a bad day at testing and we didn't get into one of the good high schools, then that would practically mean that we were limited to blue-collar life. That's the stratifica-

tion in Taiwan, that people who get into good schools, they're almost assured of a good job and a good life. That was the reason they always gave us as to why we came to the United States.

It wasn't until recently that my mother finally came out and said, "Well, there were also other reasons." All these years they've been making us feel guilty. "It's because of you we're stuck in this rut" and "so you're to blame" kind of thing. During my senior year in high school, I had big fights with my parents. I came out and said, "Look, it's just not fair that you always make us feel guilty for everything that happens and just using the excuse that you came here because of us. It's not like we had a choice." They always came back and said, "That's such a hurtful thing to say to us, after all that we've done for you." It was a no-win situation, but finally she came out and said, "Well, all right, we had our own reasons too."

Eventually [she said] that my father was also very fearful of a Communist takeover in Taiwan at the time, and I remember that as a child. People were angry in Taiwan [when the U.S. pulled troops out of Vietnam]. I remember the discussion about how there was danger of a Communist takeover and also perhaps the United States was just going to abandon us. People were very fearful. And I remember the army and the forts being alerted. More young men were sent to fortify all the coasts. For my father it was like something that he had to live through again and he didn't want to do that. And it was enough, having been separated from his family [once] because of the Communist regime, so that could have been one of the reasons they came over.

So what happened when you were in high school that made you start thinking about something like M.I.T.?

Well, I'd always done well in school, and it just seemed like a natural path. By the time I entered high school, I felt a little bit better in terms of where we were financially. I had started to dress a little more like everybody else; I want to the better high school in town. I mingled with everybody who was really the cream of the crop of the town— everybody who came from doctors' families, lawyers' families. I [was] still kind of ashamed about what my parents were doing. My mother was still waitressing. My father was still being a janitor at the hospital. Whenever people asked me what my parents were doing, because a lot of teachers would ask, I didn't know what to say. I remember I always told them, but I also probably told them with a tone of shame or regret. I remember also by the time I entered high school I had been under about a year's worth of fear that my father was just going to go away one day and not come back because he was under such depression. By this time he'd already felt that in both his workplace and also at home he was losing all authority and all pride. My mother was trying to keep the family together and trying to advance the family within the community, trying to take this test and pass it for her own self-esteem, just to know she could do it. But she had neglected to sense my father's withdrawal. She became very dominant in the family in terms of anything that the kids were involved in. As far as the family as a whole, she was the one who was more outspoken, because she had more contact with the outside world. I just saw my father taking a view that he wasn't important in our lives.

They fought a lot. At one point, by the time I was a freshman in high school, I had really thought that they were going to get divorced. By this time I became accustomed to this idea of divorce. When I first got to the United States, I would ask these kids in the fifth grade, "Oh, so what are your parents doing?" And they would say, "Oh, my stepmother. . ." I didn't know what a stepmother was. That was all very foreign, but by the time I entered high school, I understood and I really saw that if they were really that unhappy together perhaps they would get a divorce. My father all the time said, "We should have never come here." But now they were here, it was too late to go back.

But I went on. I had my own support system, which came mostly from my friends. My parents didn't know half of the time what I was doing except for what I told them about. I got involved in the math club. I was on the math team. I was doing very well. I went to national competitions two times. I was nationally ranked in different areas of mathematics. Also in the sciences I was doing independent study in the high school. I had two years of physics and two years of chemistry. The school itself set the atmosphere for me to excel and a lot of opportunities for me to get into extra things. I took a class in robotics, also a class in optics. Academically and socially I had a lot around me when I went to school, but when I went home it was another story. Nobody was happy, so I stayed away as much as I could. I had good teachers in high school who showed me what was available to me even if we didn't have much money. My math coach was the one who really pushed me to go to a good college and said, "Look, you have all the ability and it's not everybody who has the opportunity to go to a good school." He and my physics teacher both said, "Look, there's M.I.T., and there's Cal Tech, Stanford." They were the ones who really started me looking into different schools.

My parents weren't against me going to a good school. They were very helpful. They were very encouraging in terms of my making something of myself, but at the same time they were also worried about the cost of education. But M.I.T. gave me a good financial deal. My parents said, "Look, if you want to go there, then we'll do everything we can to help you out."

By this time my brother was enrolled in college. He went to the University of Washington. I saw him leave home, but only two hours away. My father wanted him to [major in] electrical engineering, so he took some classes in EE, and he hated it. He didn't want to do that for the rest of his life. He didn't really know what he wanted. He eventually ended up in psychology. My father was going down there every other weekend, telling him what an ungrateful son that he was; they had come over all this way and were trying to give him an education, and here he was going to go into psychology.

It's been difficult. As an adolescent trying to choose what was right from which culture—it wasn't just growing up and trying to choose what's right and wrong. Here you're choosing what's right in which culture and what's wrong in which culture. It was always a struggle.

Here I was in high school. I looked at it and said, "Hey, I'm not going to go through the same thing. I'm going to do whatever I want to do." They have to realize that they brought us over, and they have to accept the responsibility that their kids are not going to be exactly the kind of kids that they had hoped for in Taiwan. It's a different society and different influences, so I decided to come to M.I.T.

By my junior year in high school they had gotten their own business. They went in and they franchised a store in town, and they're doing very well and that's what they're doing now. My father is much happier because he doesn't have to work under somebody else being a janitor, and my mother—well, there's more work for her, at least she sees that my father is getting something out of it, and I think they get along better now, so things have changed a lot. My brother moved back home to help them out with the store.

Tell me about your specialty that you have elected to go into here at M.I.T. Biomedical engineering. When I came here, I wanted to be pre-med because I wanted to go to med school; I wanted to be a doctor—a pediatrician specifically. But then I took some biology courses at M.I.T., and all they have to offer is cellular, molecular kind of biology, which isn't anything I'm interested in. I'm more interested in anatomy and physiology. I started looking into other options. At M.I.T. they have a large biomechanics division within mechanical engineering, where people do rehabilitation engineering [and prostheses design]. I like engineering better than pure sciences. So I decided, "I think I'll switch to being an engineer--be a biomedical engineer and maybe go to grad school.

You're going to be graduating in two days?

On Monday.

So this is an important transition in your life.

Yeah.

You were talking about some of the early times in your life, and it sounded like at certain points you thought you'd better off if you had gone back, but it sounds to me like you have achieved an enormous amount.

Well, I think that at times I have thought it would have been better if I just stayed in Taiwan. I never thought of going back because I knew that my Chinese was deteriorating and I couldn't live within the society as comfortably as I did at one time. I never thought that I would go back except to visit. I didn't go back for ten years. It was just last January that my mother took me back to visit, and it was very strange to see relatives and old houses. Things are so different and I don't know. I don't think that I would go back ever except to visit.

It is a big step, but it's also kind of a difficult time.

You're now a citizen. How do you see yourself, as half of your life was in Taiwan, really, and half of it's been here?

Up until my freshman year in college I had denied the fact that I was Chinese. I just wanted to be American, and it was all I cared about. I didn't care to know about Chinese history. I didn't care [about] my relatives. I didn't really want to know. I didn't even want to know what was happening in my own country. But since I've been at M.I.T., I've been a lot more aware. I have stared to take Chinese history courses and literature. I want to go back and learn Chinese again. So I'm struggling with the fact that I am Chinese and that I am American in my lifestyle and everything else I do, but a lot of internal values I have are still Chinese.

So why is this a struggle?

Anything that is in me that's Chinese is also tied to my parents, and I'm still having a hard time with my parents, even though we get along better now. I still fell very guilty at times for what they've gone through and what they'll still going through.

When I try to define what's Chinese versus what's American and trying to get what's good out of each, it's very difficult. Socially there's different things that are a little difficult. For myself it's certainty a lot more difficult to be an adolescent trying to survive two different cultures. Here the women are just different from Chinese women. Chinese women are supposed to be a lot more quiet and subdued and submissive. Not that you go out of your way to do that, but they just come across that way. In my family it's always been the females who have been the stronger ones. But then just the fact that I also have to take that image and fit myself into this image that Americans have about their women: that they're thin, they're blond—blond is beautiful—blue-eyed, and fair-skinned, although they try to tan themselves. It's been difficult. As an adolescent trying to choose what was right from which culture—it wasn't just growing up and trying to choose what's right and wrong. Here you're choosing what's right in which culture and what's wrong in which culture. It was always a struggle. It was certainly a lot more difficult than if I had either been an American or else just stayed in Taiwan.

If I do have kids here—well, depending on who my spouse is—if I end up marrying someone who is non-Chinese, how do I keep the culture going? Do I want to keep the culture going in the children? I think the one thing that's very important is the language. It's always good to be bilingual or trilingual, whatever you can to learn a different language. And so that if I want to keep the Chinese going, what do you do with your spouse unless they learn the language as well? It's not easy to instill that in your children, who are going to probably speak English most of the time.

And then just different things like the Chinese value of looking after your parents. Usually the son, the oldest son, is supposed to take care of the parents, but, you know, suppose my brother marries somebody who is non-Chinese? My mother isn't going to feel comfortable living with an American daughter-in-law. She's going to think that she's not going to know how to take care of them, and so then it will be up to me to kind of look after them. But suppose I marry someone who's non-Chinese?

I don't know. They're all questions I'm still trying to figure out.

Source:

First Generation: In the Words of Twentieth-Century American Immigrants, compiled by June Namias. Boston: Beacon Press, 1992. pp. 228-244.

TIBETAN AMERICANS

By the late 1950s, monasteries and temples stood in every village and town in Tibet, including over 6,200 monasteries with almost 600,000 monks. Monks were supplied life's necessities by their communities, though they occasionally performed service jobs. Though consideration of a monk's life may bring thoughts of peace and tranquility, an interview with Tibetan monk Labring Sakya provides an exciting tale of harrowing escape from invading Chinese Communist troops and his subsequent fortuitous move to the United States.

Labring was born in the 1920s, just over a decade after Tibet gained independence from Chinese rule. At nine years of age, he entered a monastery in Lhasa where he studied and prayed. Tibet came under People's Republic of China rule in 1949, but the monks, including Labring, who practiced the national Tibetan religion of Lamaism Buddhism were allowed to continue their ancient ways.

Tiring of continued Tibetan rebel resistance, the Chinese Communists in 1960 began to more stringently exert control over the region. With Chinese troops aggressively seeking to capture the spiritual and political leader Dalai Lama, all the monks, including the Dalai Lama, were forced to flee. Some 800 monks were believed killed during the crack down in addition to some 86,000 other Tibetans. Labring survived by crossing rugged mountainous terrain to the Indian border. In total, some 80,000 Tibetans, including Labring, sought political asylum in India and other nearby countries. In a border refugee camp, Labring by chance met a University of Washington professor interested in researching Tibetan grammar and seeking an informant. Labring volunteered and was quickly off to a new home in Seattle, Washington.

Many Tibetans, whose life values are shaped by Buddhist beliefs, find life in America filled with considerable tension, as did Labring. He also found similarities,

> All the time I'm working in the university doing that research on the book, so it's not so very different, except that I go to the little house at night. They brought my niece over here and she stays with me and keeps house for me. I keep up my Tibetan culture and I eat Tibetan style—my niece cooks it. . .Over here there is perhaps more tension, yes, more tension. But on the whole, life is not so different.

Labring continued practicing Tibetan cultural traditions but was unable to visit his homeland since it remained inaccessible to visitors until the early 1980s.

LABRING SAKYA—FROM TIBET, 1960

I was nine years old when I went into the Monastery in Lhasa. I could visit my family and go in and out, but all the boys in the monastery are expected to become monks in the monastery.

In Tibet the monks don't have to do anything, just study and pray. All the food is given by the government, and so much land for the monastery. The land was worked by some laymen, people who lived in the village around. Over here some people say they're like slaves. They weren't like that, actually. We had to pay and we had to give them some land or, if not land, had to give them something. But all we did in the monastery was pray and study.

From the time I was nine, that was the only life I knew, except when I would go sometimes to visit my parents in the town. That was my life.. . .

Then, when I was thirty-four, the Chinese Communists began to take over Tibet. We couldn't stay, you know, couldn't stay there because we were afraid they would kill us. They sent to the monastery and said they wanted our leader, the Dalai Lama, you know. They wanted him to come to their headquarters. They would keep him there, and we didn't want to lose our leader, so we all just came away quickly. We walked from Lhasa to a monastery in the east, about eight days from Lhasa. We got there before the Communists got there It was rough, rough, country and we had to cross a mountain. We had some food, a little food with us, but that was all. We stayed one month in the monastery in the mountains. Then one night the Chinese Communists came there. They were shooting guns, machine guns, you know. So we were all scared. There were eight hundred of us in that monastery—it was a small monastery for Tibet. Only six of us made it away. The others—I don't know if they killed them or captured them. They did capture them at the time, but most are killed now, I'm sure.

The six of us that got away, we had to run right away in the night, fast, you know—fast. [*Snaps fingers.*] There wasn't a road; it was just the jungle, so we came through the jungle. It was very difficult. It took us thirty-six days to come maybe fifty, sixty miles. We had to climb down and up mountains and cross rivers. It took us thirty-six days. Across the rivers there were these bridges; you know, they have those two bamboo lengths going from here to over there. You hold onto one and you walk on the

other, and if the river is long the bamboo bends down. Sometimes you're up to your knees in the water, and it's fast water in those mountain streams and rivers. I was frightened. We had only a little food with us. We passed the local villagers, but they're almost, you know, like animals. They were very primitive. They don't speak Tibetan. They're sort of like half Indian, half Tibetan. They wouldn't look at us. They didn't offer us food. They stayed away from us. I think they were frightened.

When we got near the Indian border, the Indians knew about what had happened. They sent planes, and the planes dropped food to us. Other people were fleeing, too, by then. And when we got to the border, the Indians took us to a refugee camp. I was only in that camp for ten days when a professor came from the University of Washington. He had a grant from the government and from some foundation to work on a Tibetan grammar. He wanted somebody to work on the book with him. And he said to me, "Would you like to come?" And I said, "I'd like to." So I came here. He got the visas very quick—in about fifteen or twenty days. And we flew to Seattle. It was very fast—from the monastery in the mountains to the United States, altogether, in less than three months.

I had a picture in my mind of the United States before I came. I'd heard of such things as washing machines and dishwashers and electric stoves and everything to do the cooking. And I thought to myself when I lived in Tibet, "Well, it must be just like how humans do something." In my mind I thought the machine would come and take your clothes and go somewhere and wash them and dry them for you and fold them and bring them back to you, just like humans doing it. That was my picture in my mind. And I had thought there were lots of houses, very big, very big. And, actually, here the family houses are small! Many of them are smaller than in Tibet. Here I live in a little house on a little street. Of course, the monastery I lived in was very big.

There are monasteries here, too. I went over to a Catholic monastery here—it's almost the same as in Tibet. They're living in the same there. There are the restrictions, the religion, and the study.

All the time I'm working in the university doing that research on the book, so it's not so very different, except that I go to the little house at night. They brought my niece over here and she stays with me and keeps house for me. I keep my Tibetan culture and I eat Tibetan style—my niece cooks it. Things aren't so different here. People have to eat, they sleep, they do some work. Over here there is perhaps more tension, yes, more tension. But on the whole, life is not so different.

Source:

American Mosaic: The Immigrant Experience in the Words of Those Who Lived It, compiled by Joan Morrison and Charlotte Fox Zabusky. New York: E.P. Dutton, 1980. pp. 314-316.

TLINGIT

*T*he Tlingit (pronounced "klingit") are a tribe of Native Alaskans who live in Southeast Alaska. Unrelated to neighboring tribes, they speak their own language and have unique customs and traditions. While they may have occupied the southern end of the Alaskan coastline for as many as 11,000 years, their exact origin is unknown. They are believed to have been the first people to have settled the region.

Notable among Tlingit customs is the way in which they honor their dead. Believing that the dead leave the earth for a new existence in the spirit world, the Tlingit consider it a duty of the tribe to help the deceased make this passage. As such, the death of a Tlingit precipitates a deliberate three-part burial ritual: first, there is a one-to-four day long period of mourning and burial, followed by a party for the deceased's clan, and lastly, the holding of a huge celebratory potlatch which occurs a year or more after the burial.

The final ceremonial potlatch, or koo.éexi, offers the participants a chance to discharge their obligations and even to gain social benefits. At this large feast they pay their respects to the deceased through stories and songs, a process which helps to ease the suffering of loss and let go of the deceased. At the same time, the size of the potlatch is a means for displaying a clan's wealth, by which their social standing can be measured. Both reasons help account for why the potlatch is held many months—and sometimes years—after the funeral: time is required to save for the expense of the celebration.

In the traditional Tlingit folk story, "The Ghost Land," the emotional importance of the potlatch in bringing closure to grief is underscored. It is not a ghost story in the sense of most Western fiction, but rather a symbolic tale about the naturalness of life and death. After the loss of his wife, a grief-stricken young man skips the potlatch in order to wander alone. Wandering along the Death Trail—a path symbolizing his sorrow—leads him to the ghost land, where the dead dwell. There he finds his wife, who tries to instruct him in the separateness of their two worlds by warning him about eating food in the ghost land. Instead of heeding her warnings, he brings her back with him to his village. The results are disastrous. She does not belong among the living, and for his transgressions against the natural order and Tlingit tradition, a terrible price is paid.

THE GHOST LAND

The young wife of a chief's son died and the young man was so sorrowful he could not sleep. Early one morning he put on his fine clothes and started off. He walked all day and all night. He went through the woods a long distance, and then to a valley. The trees were very thick, but he could hear voices far away. At last he saw light through the trees and then came to a wide, flat stone on the edge of a lake.

Now all the time this young man had been walking in the Death Trail. He saw houses and people on the other side of the lake. He could see them moving around. So he shouted, "Come over and get me." But they did not seem to hear him. Upon the lake a little canoe was being paddled about by one man, and all the shore was grassy. The chief's son shouted a long while but no one answered him. At last he whispered to himself, "Why don't they hear me?"

At once a person across the lake said, "Some one is shouting." When he whispered, they heard him.

The voice said also, "Some one has come up from Dreamland. Go and bring him over."

When the chief's son reached the other side of the lake, he saw his wife. He was very happy to see her again. People asked him to sit down. They gave him something to eat, but his wife said, "Don't eat that. If you eat that you will never get back." So he did not eat it.

Then his wife said, "You had better not stay here long. Let us go right away." So they were taken back in the same canoe. It is called Ghost's Canoe and it is the only one on that lake. They landed at the broad, flat rock where the chief's son had stood calling. It is called Ghost's Rock, and is at the very end of the Death Trail. Then they started down the trail, through the valley and through the thick woods. The second night they reached the chief's house.

The chief's son told his wife to stay outside. He went in and said to his father, "I have brought my wife back."

The chief said, "Why don't you bring her in?"

The chief laid down a nice mat with fur robes on it for the young wife. The young man went out to get his wife, but when he came in, with her, they could see only him. When he came very close, they saw a deep shadow following him. When his wife sat down and they put a marten skin robe around her, it hung about the shadow just as if a person were sitting there. When she ate, they saw only the spoon moving up and down, but not the shadow of her hands. It looked very strange to them.

Afterward the chief's son died and the ghosts of both of them went back to Ghost Land.

Source:
Myths and Legends of Alaska, edited by Katharine
    Berry Judson. Chicago: A. C. McClurg, 1911.

In response to the historical exploitation of Native Americans the federal govern-ment has come up with measures designed to protect Indian land rights. The Supreme Court has decided that Native Americans are entitled to "rights of aborigi-nal occupancy," which means that the federal and state governments cannot inter-fere with designated Native American land. The only stipulation regarding the sov-ereignty of Indian land pertains to its impact on economic development. If the occupied territories are impeding the economic progress of a state, the state reserves the right to usurp the land. This loophole was made to account for the discovery of valuable natural resources on Native American territory.

Native Americans own roughly two percent of American land. Land rights is one of the most important issues facing Native Americans today. Native Ameri-cans value their land because of its historical significance as well as what it means to them politically. The historical significance pertains to their repeated mistreatment by the white man. Politically, the issue of self-determination, or having authority over their own affairs without state and federal intervention is extremely important to Native Americans. Self-determination allows Native Americans to develop their communities in accordance with their rich spiritual and cultural heritages. Although having land of their own is important, the real value of the land lies in what it affords them. Land rights enables Native Americans to govern their own affairs as they see fit which means that they can allocate resources that align with their values. Many Native American tribes are hunting, fishing, gathering, or agricultural societies and have stronger ties to nature than white communities.

One of the disputes over land rights in Alaska involves what will be done with valuable natural resources. Native Americans in Alaska feel that just because they prefer not to exploit the land for oil and gas does not mean that they are standing in the way of economic progress—as some state and federal officials contend. Native Americans simply have a different view of the world central to which is great reverence for the land on which we all depend for sustenance. Alaskan tribal leaders are trying to strike some kind of compromise with the white man that will benefit both sides. One of the weapons at their disposal is the use of the U.S. judicial system. Although the American justice system has failed them in the past it does not appear as though political and business leaders who wish to appropriate native land for economic purposes will find much support for their plans in the courts. It would be a tragedy if further harm were done to Native American communities in the interest of economic gain.

NATIVE ALASKANS' LAND RIGHTS

The natives of Alaska (Eskimos, Indians, and Aleuts), who are estimated to number approximately 54,000, today use and occupy extensive areas in Alaska for hunting, trapping, fishing, and other purposes. These are the same lands which they used and occupied for many centuries prior to the coming of the first Europeans.

Today, the descendants of these native groups still continue to hold, by "rights of aboriginal occupancy," the great bulk of the same territory.

Today, Alaska, the last great frontier and wilderness region of our nation, is the sole remaining part of the United States which includes extensive areas still used and claimed by the indigenous inhabitants, based on *rights of aboriginal occupancy.* Except for these large areas in Alaska, the Indian or native title to lands of our nation has, over the years, been acquired by the federal government.

As repeatedly held by the Supreme Court of the United States, aboriginal Indian title to lands embraces the *complete beneficial ownership based on the right of perpetual and exclusive use and occupancy.* Such title also carries with it the *right* of the tribe or native group to be *protected fully by the United States in such exclusive occupancy against any interference or*

conflicting use or taking by all others, including protection against the state governments. In short, as declared by the Supreme Court, aboriginal Indian ownership is as sacred as the white man's ownership.

From some lips fall the familiar complaints that the native occupancy of lands is impeding the economic development and progress of the state of Alaska.

Our answer is that though we have the right of complete beneficial use of our aboriginally occupied lands and all the resources of such lands, we have been prevented and restrained from exercising our rights to deal with and develop such lands and resources. We say that only after we have been permitted the reasonable opportunity to exercise such rights a judgment may fairly be made as to whether our occupancy is hampering the economic development and progress of Alaska.

We believe that we have sufficient leadership ability to direct the development of our lands and resources.

We believe that we have the capacity—at least equal to the federal and state bureaucracies—to make wise selection of experts and technicians to assist us, including engineers, geologists, foresters, managers, investment advisors, accountants, economists, and lawyers.

Some argue that since the discoveries of valuable oil and gas resources on the native lands have been recent and since the natives in their aboriginal way of life did not exploit their lands for oil and gas, the natives have no basis for complaint if the federal government permits the natives to continue to use the land solely for hunting, trapping, and fishing purposes, or if the federal government appropriates the lands for such aboriginal uses without regard to the oil and gas values.

This is an argument which has been repeatedly rejected by the Supreme Court and the court of claims in cases involving Indian tribal lands.

By a parity of poor reasoning, it may be suggested that if Senator Jackson or Congressman Aspinall owned a 5,000 acre tract of mountain lands in his home state, which he used exclusively for hunting and for enjoying its beauty, and then valuable mineral deposits were discovered on the land, the federal government could, lawfully and in good conscience, appropriate the tract and pay Congressman Aspinall only for its value for hunting purposes and for its beauty.

Many have suggested that since the Alaska Statehood Act gave to the state of Alaska the right of selection of some 103,000,000 acres of land, a serious dilemma has been created in that the exercise of such right by the state would necessarily require the selection of much land presently held by the Alaska natives.

Our answer is that Congress was fully aware of this problem when the statehood act was passed. In accordance with the uniform federal policy to honor and protect lands held by aboriginal occupancy rights, Congress explicitly required the state of Alaska in the statehood act to "forever disclaim" all right or title to any lands held by Indian, Eskimo, and Aleut groups.

We say that any state selection of lands which are held by native aboriginal title is violative of the terms, intent, and spirit of the statehood act and contrary to other acts of Congress as well as federal policy.

Alaska natives have assumed a statesmanlike posture, reflective of a conscientious awareness of the welfare of all citizens by their expressed willingness to negotiate on a political or legislative solution through the United States Congress. We, who are the first Alaskans, desire the development of our home state. We only ask that justice and equity be done and that, in the future, Alaska's native people may become active participants in Alaska's development.

Although Alaska natives have agreed to negotiate politically and are, therefore, not making recourse to the courts, we must emphasize that we are negotiating from a position of right and strength. We stress the fact that while we eschew the litigatory route, we still choose to retain the right to define our substantive legal rights, for therein lies the strength of our bargaining position and the basis of our negotiating effectiveness. Nevertheless, *litigation is a viable alternative, which we have, thus far, chosen to avoid.*

We Alaska natives envision that provisions of an equitable settlement of the land claims will enable us to uplift the qualities of life for our people. Recognizing that frustrations may be derived from a minority status due to ethnic origin and economic powerlessness, we anticipate our ability to exercise the *prerogative of choice* within the context of our needs, our goals, and our desires. We will recognize that many of our people will choose life in the villages, because it is, for them, a fulfillment and a satisfaction, while others, desirous of projecting themselves into a competitive society, will have the means to do so.

Source:
Congressional Record, 91st Congress, 1st Session.

TRINIDADIAN AMERICANS

*T*rinidad's history and racial and ethnic make up is diverse. The Spanish first settled Trinidad, followed by the British, who brought blacks from Africa to work on sugar plantations. Slavery was abolished in 1838 and blacks went to urban centers, refusing to work on the plantations. Many left for the United States at this time and immigration continued into the 1920s. The emigration wave of the 1960s was brought on by social problems of many kinds, and the U.S. Immigration and Nationality Act of 1965 eased the restrictions previously imposed on immigration, facilitating Trinidadians' entry into the United States. Most blacks, along with East Indians and other racial and ethnic groups, immigrated after 1965. Immigrants settled primarily in the northeast, in the black neighborhoods of New York, as well as Connecticut, Pennsylvania, and Massachusetts.

In the oral history interview "Trinidad Farewell," Deborah Padmore recounts her impressions as Trinidadian immigrant in the United States. She came to America in the early 1960s with her husband so that he could attend school. They lived in Washington, D.C., and then in New York. Padmore found the American experience to be more racially divided than Trinidad. The racial atmosphere of Washington and Boston in the late 1960s was one of prejudice and separation, and Padmore expresses some disappointment in the racism that she encountered. She concludes that she does not want citizenship, but wants to remember her roots, and wants her daughter, who lives in Trinidad, to stay there, away from the racism of the United States.

DEBORAH PADMORE—TRINIDAD FAREWELL

You Always Have This Black Thing Hangin' Over Your Head"

Trinidad is a small, independent island country off the coast of Venezuela. Like most of the islands in the Caribbean, it has had a history of both colonialism and slavery. Between 1498 and 1797 the Spanish controlled Trinidad and its smaller sister island, Tobago. During the late 1770s the French had economic but not political control, and in 1797 the British took over. The native population was decimated in the first years of foreign occupation, and Africans were forcibly captured and brought to the island to operate a growing sugar-plantation economy. When the British gained control of Trinidad, abolitionism was a growing force, and in 1832 slavery was abolished, although an interisland slave trade continued.

In order to assure a stable and docile labor force, the British in Trinidad imported large numbers of indentured workers from India in the late nineteenth century. One hundred and forty-three thousand Asians entered Trinidad between 1845 and 1917.1 By the end of World War I, the growing Indian nationalist movement began to protest Britain's treatment of Indian immigrants on the island. At the same time, a growing black nationalist movement in Trinidad indicated that independence and better economic conditions were on the minds of its people. In August 1962 Trinidad became independent.

British colonies in the Caribbean, like Jamaica, Barbados, and Trinidad-Tobago, have contributed to the United States immigrant population since the beginning of the Republic. Prince Hall, an ex-slave from Barbados, fought at Bunker Hill; Denmark Vesey, from the Virgin Islands, tried to start a slave rebellion in the Carolinas during the early 1820s; Marcus Garvey, a Jamaican, formed the black-nationalist Universal Negro Improvement Association in the 1920s; Stokely Carmichael, a Trinidadian, was a major force behind the Student Nonviolent Coordinating Committee in the 1960s; and Shirley Chisholm is of West Indian origin.[2]

Black immigrants from the English, Spanish, and French Caribbean were living in New York and other major American cities in the early part of this century. Those from the British West Indies brought to the United States a combination of British and African traditions. In fact, it was their British citizenship that allowed them to continue to enter the United States after the passage of the quota laws in the 1920s; they entered on never-filled British quotas.

Though entrance was easy, adapting to American society was not. As one early student of black immigration noted in the late 1930s, "The Negro enters in the dual role of Negro and immigrant."[3] Black immigrants carry the dual burden of being foreign and being black in a society where whiteness is prized. There is a new country, in some cases a new language, and there is also a different and discriminatory pattern of social relations. As Ms. Padmore said, "You always have this black thing hangin' over your head."

The rise in West Indian immigration to the United States since 1960 has been attributed to rising populations and economic problems, as well as changes in British immigration policy. After World War II, a growing number of British Commonwealth citizens from the Caribbean immigrated to the United Kingdom. By 1961 close to forty thousand West Indians were requesting permanent residency there. According to one study of Jamaican immigrants, those entering Britain were young, often skilled, and better educated than those back home. Almost half of them were women, seventy-five percent of whom left children on the islands.[4] During this same period a growing number of Indians and Pakistanis were also entering Britain. A slackening British economy could not absorb this new population growth. As more blacks and Asians entered England, a racial reaction set in and in 1962 the Commonwealth Immigrants Act was passed, placing strict limits on further immigration to Britain.

It is ironic that as various pressures led West Indians to seek their fortunes abroad, Britain began closing her doors and the Untied States and Canada began liberalizing their earlier racially oriented laws. Between 1966 and 1975 close to two hundred thousand people from Jamaica. Trinidad-Tobago, and Barbados entered the United States legally, with Jamaica accounting for about three-fourths of that figure.[5] At this time figures for all three countries are sharply rising.[6]

Deborah Padmore came to the United States from Trinidad in the early 1960s. She works as a secretary at an economic-opportunity agency in Cambridge, Massachusetts. Although her real ambition is to become a marine biologist, she is attending nursing school. She has one daughter, who lives in Trinidad.

When asked if she visited Trinidad frequently she replied that the $450 fare made it difficult to do so. "And you would be amazed at this anxiety that you have when you get on the plane to go back to Trinidad, hopin' that your friends would be there, and the place would be the same as you left it, and when you go back, it's not there. People have grown up; everything is changed."

July 26, 1976
Cambridge, Massachusetts

Who would want to write a book about immigrants? Everybody got the same thing to say—they want to go back home but—there's always this *but*. "Why don't you want to go back home if you're not satisfied with the United States?" And I think this is the struggle that you go through every day, havin' this yearnin' to go back since you came because, although you have lived here and you have accepted a lot of American customs, you still have ties with your *roots*. Take, for instance, me. I have been away since 1960; and I always think of Trinidad as when I left it. But then you go home periodically and you see that things have changed! It's not like what you left it as, but you still have that *yearnin'* to go back home and try to fit in, although I know I can't fit in. When I go back home, I'm too accustomed to this life here in America: getting up in the morning, goin' to work, hustlin', hustlin', hustlin'. I think it's something that I trained myself into, and I wouldn't be able to go back home and be relaxed as I was when I was there a kid.

How did you happen to first get here?

I was married at this time. I got married at eighteen. My husband came to go to Howard University, and I followed after him. *An old story.* [Laughs.] It was a big world, I wanted to see what it had in store for me. I think he felt the same way. He never got around to tellin' me. I ventured out, to learn as much as I could. It was rough.

It was about '61. Really at the height of everything, with Stokely Carmichael and the whole thing. I was not part of it. I was still learning. I was still in the grass roots, coming from Trinidad, not knowing *anything*.

You know, you have this *vivid* imagination of America being the most beautiful land in the world. You respected Americans, for some reason. They came down as tourists, and they portrayed America as a fantastic place to live in, where you always had money, and everything was beautiful. They tell you these stories, and it's like you *should* come here. Most of the time they came from places like Harlem, where you really had to save for five years to get a vacation around the '50's, '60's, and you're *not conscious* of this. You never hear them thinking of going to Paris or going to the Riviera, where *rich* people go. But they come down to the West Indies. They build you up. They give you this big impression that America is *it*. You never think about the racial tension and the intensity that you have to live with. They never talk about it. So I wanted to see for myself, and I saw a lot. It was a great deal.

Being by myself, I had more time to meditate or concentrate, and I was able to see different people, and I learned a lot. It started fascinating me, how *could* one place be so different from another, and when it's not too far away, just four hours' ride? The workin' pressure in New York is not half as bad as here in Massachusetts.

I went to Washington, D.C. My husband, he went to Howard. We got an apartment, and we lived there. [Later we moved to New York.] I worked and he worked. We went through our changes—a whole lot of them—and we just finally split up. I didn't stay with him that long, about five years, off and on, off and on.

I had just migrated from Trinidad; the atmosphere I was living in was *not* an American life-style. I'm not sure whether you are hip to Trinidad, but they do have a cosmopolitan culture. And you sit there with Indians, and you sit with Chinese children, and you sit there with so-called "Trinidad white people," and you never have a problem! You never *think* about it bein' a problem, because you are in this little country. When you come abroad, it takes you a while for you to see certain things.

At that time I didn't know what the hell was happenin'. I was hearin' so many things, and I couldn't *see* exactly where Stokely Carmichael was comin' from, where Rap Brown was comin' from. And even though you pick up a book and you read, you read, you read, things ever did fall into place until after you started growin' and seein' things.

I'm not a racist. I cannot say that I'm a racist, that I hate people, white people, and that I *hate* the government, because the American government had done a lot for *me*—much more I think, than any other, or even my little country, will do for the people. I was able to go to school and get an education, which I know damn well my country would not be able to give. But there is good and bad in everything, and I don't think it's the government, really, I think it's the people.

Did breaking up with your husband have to do with you're being thrown into a whole new culture?

Well, it did and it didn't. Maybe if I was in Trinidad, I would have had to depend on him, he being the sole breadwinner of the family, because I know jobs are hard to get in Trinidad. And coming here and earning my own money made me more independent than I was born, and I was a very independent person. But that had a *lot* to do with it, coming here. I started working for my own money, and I started making a lot of friends and seeing and observing, reading a lot of magazines. Those things like *Redbook, Woman's Day,* they have a lot to contribute to divorces, too, you know. [Laughs.] You read them and you say, "Wow! What the hell's wrong with me! Why am I puttin' up with this shit? This man was goin' to school. I'm bustin' my ass to send him to school. He's screwin' all over me." Sometimes he slept home, sometimes he didn't. It got to a point where he gambled a lot, too, and well, of course, he was in America. I don't know where the man's head was at, to tell you the truth.

I think it was my husband who really eased me out of New York. He kept tormentin' me, tormentin' me, all the time, that I should come back to him.

I wasted too much time. If I had the man behind me, you know what would have happened? It would be cool sailin' for me, but then life is a different thing. You have to live it in stages. You can't push nothing, and things come along, just as you hoped they would. Now, looking back at it, I don't think I went through a lot. I think I made a good move coming to Boston. Seventeen years, you think you're in love, in love with what? I believe it was my mother and father both died. I thought I was very independent, and my sister got married, and I was sort of left alone. And I could remember me sayin', "What's the best thing for you to do? Get married." The first man came along I got married. I didn't stop and think who he was, where he came from, what's his background, anything. I don't think they make seventeen- and eighteen-year-olds like that anymore. I think I was the last batch of the stupid ones.

I think Boston, Cambridge did a lot for me. More enlightenment, because I was away from my people in New York, and I was able to see the world. Being by myself, I had more time to meditate or concentrate, and I was able to see different people, and I learned a lot. It started fascinating me, how *could* one place be so different from another, and when it's not too far away, just four hours' ride? The workin' pressure in New York is not half as bad as here in Massachusetts.

What kind of pressure?

I'm talkin' about racial pressure. In New York, as a black person, you could work freely. But here, apart from you not being able to work as you want to, you always have this black thing hangin' over your head. You know, that you are *black*. I think if there is one place that reminds you of *who* you are is working in Boston. And this hostility that people have to acquire to *survive* in a small place like Boston. The ignorance that you hear, for a place with leadin' colleges, M.I.T. and Harvard.

I had a lot of experience here—especially as a worker. When I started working, I worked at the hospital. I was a technical assistant—*supposedly*. Ended up to be a charwoman. They would like to impress you that you are one notch on top of a nurse's aide, but break it down. They have you so uniformed. You have to have this pinstriped blue uniform. They keep you in your place. Apparently when the authorities come, they say, "Well, we have a couple of hundred black people. Look at *them*." Shit work! And the racist nurses. I don't know whether it's racism, stupidity, or just plain ignorance. Well, racism is ignorance, so I have to call it ignorance.

It was nasty—the way they treat the patients comin' in there, as though they were not supposed to come into a hospital. And if you are on welfare, they have to look down at you because you don't have money to come into [that hospital] so you will get the worse care possible. Very few doctors and very few nurses that I was with were sympathetic. They *push* for this power and recognition.

And the black people that come in there are supposed to go start in the kitchen. And if they had any potential at all to be anything else, they would have to go through this world rigamarole even to get a transfer.

The minute you walk in there you think that these people goin' to help you. The only time they would get anxious or interested in you—if you had some rare disease or if you're the son of somebody that they want recognition from. It's just sickening.

But there are some nice people. They're hard to find, but somebody's out there. They have to lead this intense, nontrustin' life. This is something that the people in Trinidad do not live.

They never listen to anybody, Americans, never, to hear what people have to say—even around here. They call you a Turk. I don't know where the name derived from, but as long as you're a West Indian, you're a Turk. I do not know if it's jealousy, but West Indians have no place in America. They're not white, so they can't fit in with white people. And they're stupid, according to the black American. If I was takin' a poll, maybe I'll go around interviewin' people, but my *observations*—I do not know if it's because West Indians came here as skilled laborers. Most of them are. And the jobs that they can get, most Americans are not skilled. Only now, they are able to train black people, but before, you'll find a West Indian coming here as a carpenter, a painter, which he had to do.

I found so much ignorance when I came here. It was amazing. I was very much surprised that the standard of education was so low among black people, because in Trinidad, they tend to give you a British education, which covers everything, from A to Z. And I was surprised to see big people, grown people, not even knowing where Trinidad was. Since 1965 most black people are more aware.

Do you think you'll get citizenship some time?

I don't want citizenship. You still want to know where your roots are. I could tell you who my great-great-grandfather is. Although everybody came from Africa, those who landed in the West Indies were the much more fortunate ones. They came there first. The first stop was in Barbados, and Trinidad, and they probably kept their families together much more than when they were scattered throughout the South, although they had a lot of bartering slavery in Boston from Barbados here. I could still remember my great-grandfather, not really remember, but hear my mother talk about my grandfather and her father, and he talking about *his* father. And you know they had some sort of definite *link*. But when you hear people from America talk, they could only go back to one generation, or two generations, maybe. You don't see them gettin' that real link-up, "My father's father," unless they do some heavy research.

Do you think you'll bring your daughter here?

Tracy? She would come here on vacation, but I don't think America's a nice place to bring up a kid. She'd have no freedom. Maybe if I lived in the country where she is able to walk outside. And the crime rate is so high here. I don't think I would like her to go through the same shit that I went through. She has a big house in Trinidad, she has the nieces and nephews. And the freedom that she has. It isn't worth it. Especially in Boston, for her to go through that busin' business, it would just freak me out. I don't think that children should have to go through this bullshit in the first place. I think if they get some good teachers and put them in the school, the kids won't have to be used, especially in places where people don't want you.

Look at the dangers these kids have to go through to go to different parts of the country. The stoning of buses. It's ignorance, plain ignorance. I can't see the head nor tail of it, up to now. And it's a big, wide world, and all of sudden, everybody's gainin' territory. You can't go down to South Boston, because South Boston is predominantly white; you can't go down to Roxbury, because Roxbury is predominantly black. So nonsensical.

I think that part of me still remains with me from Trinidad. That's still what remains with me. People not bein' able to integrate and talk to one another, because it's the life that you live, and everybody has their ups and downs. And poverty is something that everybody goes through, unless you are super rich. Poor black and poor white. Everybody's poor. I don't know what the fight is all about. Somebody of a different nationality than me, unless he's coming in to rob *me*, then I might be defensive! Other than that, could I say that I hate this person because he's black, or I hate this person because he's white? It's very illiterate.

Source:

First Generation: In the Words of Twentieth Century American Immigrants, compiled by June Namias. Revised edition. Urbana: University of Illinois Press, 1992. pp. 187-195.

TURKISH AMERICANS

*F*olktales play a larger role in Turkish culture than they do in American culture. Folktales are a timeless, universal, yet distilled collective experience of an ethnic group. Stories become a form of communication as they provide a backdrop for characters and personality types often encountered in daily life. Turkish folktales are similar to anecdotes and some jokes in American culture. Turkish folktales convey anecdotal and stereotypical characterization. Styles and topics fall into several categories, but the most widely known are Nasreddin Hodja tales and Bektashi stories.

Nasreddin Hodja is almost 700 years old as a literary character, and he has been riding his old donkey since the thirteenth century. The character is based on an actual person. Nasreddin Hodja lived in Aksehir between 1208 and 1285. He was educated in the Muslim theological school but was partially self-trained. There is not much historical information on his life but evidently he was a folk philosopher and a humorist. His personality became the center of Turkish folk humor, with new stories based on his personality originating century after century.

Nasreddin Hodja (sometimes called Hoça) is a beloved character of ancient folktales, a modest hero who is the wise fool, a master of humorists. Usually, the word Hodja means a stranger out of his little village. But Nasreddin Hodja is a household name in caravans, urban centers and palaces. Sometimes he is a simple old man facing the ordinary irritations of life, like dealing with an obstinate donkey, a babbling wife or stingy neighbors. In other stories he is an almost shady trickster who comes awfully close to being a scoundrel. Sometimes he is a teacher, preacher, or wit and wise man with the pure logic of a genius. Or he is a raconteur and good company or a fair judge with common sense and the best part of human nature.

In all incarnations, Nasreddin Hodja possesses a delicate, merciful and optimistic personality but he does not guard his tongue against the great sultans or cruel kings. He can be courageous or simple but he speaks his mind in both circumstances. He loves life, talks with children, nature and animals. He is the champion of the truth, justice, peace, and jokes. He enjoys music, traveling and being with people. He does not enjoy meanness, bigotry, corrupt judges, or insolence.

This much beloved Turk has no enemy and many friends in a vast geographic area extending from the West China and East Turkmenistan to Balkan, Eastern Europe and up to Hungary, from Southern Siberia and Caucasus to North Africa and Arabia. Hodja stories travel throughout the Arab speaking cultures, enjoyed by folk groups of these regions though they may differ in religion, language, or ethnic background. Nasreddin Hodja is everyman; he is the folk himself. Turks will say that right now Hodja is causing laughter somewhere on this planet.

Bektashi stories are based on the wandering holy man, Haji Bektash Veli, who was born in 1248 A.D. and who founded the Bektashi Order of Dervishes. A Dervish is a member of a Moslem religious order that engages in whirling dances. Haji Bektashi Veli was said to ride lions, talk with birds and deer, walk on the sea, raise the dead, cure the sick and give sight to the blind. Tradition says he flew to *heaven on a lion skin. Bektashi stories have spiritual truths that are illustrated in daily life.*

The Arab culture values literary cleverness and poetic expression. Most Turks know many tales and stories. The stories told may be centered on a neighbor or a nationally known figure. Within Turkish publication, folktales are collected and used as part of calendar information as well as magazine and newspaper fillers. But the great majority of Turkish folktales are simply part of the oral tradition that continues to adapt to modern life. Nasreddin Hodja tales are told by second-generation Turkish Americans who bring the beloved old character into American trappings where he displays the irresistible wit and wise personality that keeps him alive in folk culture.

Additional resources for Turkish folklore can be found in Tales Alive in Turkey by Dr. Warren S. Walker and Dr. Ahmet E. Uysal (Lubbock, Texas, 1990, More Tales Alive in Turkey by the same authors, published in 1992, and Tales of the Hodja by Charles Downing (New York, 1965).

NASREDDIN HOCA TALES

1. "Borrowing a Pot"

Informant: Ozdemir Korurek.

One day Nasreddin Hoca wanted his neighbor's big saucepan and after one week he sent it back to his neighbor. But he had put a small saucepan in the big saucepan.

After several days his neighbor asked him.

"There was another little saucepan in mine—why?"

Nasreddin Hoca answered him.

"Because your saucepan bred in my home."

"O. K., this is very good," said the neighbor.

After several weeks Nasreddin Hoca wanted it again from his neighbor. But this time he didn't want to give it back. After several days his neighbor wanted his own saucepan fro Nasreddin Hoca.

"Nasreddin Hoca, our saucepan is necessary today to us."

Nasreddin Hoca answered him.

"But your saucepan died."

"Oh Nasreddin Hoca, do saucepans die at any time?"

Nasreddin Hoca answered him.

"Sure, if it breeds, why doesn't it die?" Accordingly, he had a big saucepan with a little one.

2. "Mourning Mother's Death"

Informant: Sinasi Aykin.

One day Nasreddin Hoca and his wife were at the table for lunch. That day they had a soup that looked very good.

At first time, Hoca's wife took a spoon of soup but she began to cry because the soup was very warm. When Hoca saw (this), he asked his wife:

"Why are you crying?" Then Hoca's wife answered:

"I remember my mother, because she liked this soup. But now she is dead."

Hoca can't understand and he took a spoon of soup but he began too to cry. Then his wife asked Hoca, because of his tears,

"Why are you crying?"

Hoca answered:

"I am crying for your mother's death who gave you to me before (her) death."

3. "Hoca and Timor"

Informant: Bedi Dincel—oral transmission.

Hoca was living in Anatolia at the time of Timor (Tamberlaine). Timor heard of how clever Hoca was and sent for him. He invited Hoca to dinner. When Hoca came to eat, Timor showed him out the window the hens in the garden. They were standing on one foot.

Timor said, "Why do hens have only one foot in your country?"

Hoca said, "All people in my town have only one foot."

Timor said, "That is impossible. We, all men, have two legs." Timor realized Hoca was lying. So he called to his gardener to chase the hens out of the garden. He did, and the hens ran away using two legs.

Timor said, "You see you were lying. If you lie to Timor, you will have to run away fro her not on one or two feet but on all four feet."

4. "Noah's Dove a Male"

Informant: Kilic Solu.

One afternoon, when the sun was going down, Nasreddin Hoca met his friend and they talked everything over; then his friend said to Nasreddin Hoca.

"Do you know what kind of bird took the branch of olive to (the) ship of Noah? I mean, was the bird feminine (woman) or masculine (man)?"

"I suppose he was (the latter)!"

"How (do) you know?"

"If the bird should be (a) woman, then she would want to say everything—I mean, women can not be quiet (for a) long time—and so maybe the branch of olive should go down (would have been dropped)."

5. Forty Years' Vinegar

(i.e., vinegar that is forty years old.)

Informant: Dogan Kabalak.

One day a man asked Hoca, "Mr. Hoca, do you have forty years' vinegar?" Hoca said, "Yes, I have."

"May you give me a small piece?"

"No, I may not."

"Why?" asked the man and he took this answer.

"If I gave it to everybody, I would not be able to have forty years' vinegar now."

6. A Bag of Gold

Informant: Dogan Kabalak.

Everyday Hoca prays (to) God and he wants so much money. One of Hoca's neighbors sees that and he wishes to jest with Hoca. One day Hoca was praying again. He heard a noise in the fireplace. This noise was the noise of a bag of gold which the neighbor threw down the chimney. Hoca took it with pleasure and delight.

Next morning the neighbor came to control (to check upon) Hoca's position. Hoca could not stay in his place. The neighbor saw Hoca's seriousness and he began to explain this incident. Hoca did not

believe him. They could not understand each other and the neighbor proposed to go to a judge to solve this problem. Hoca told him that they could not go like that. If the neighbor would buy a horse and a fur coat (for him), then he would go. Then man bought them. Then they went to the judge.

The poor man told the judge with a great sorrow all (the) events. At this time Hoca interrupted his neighbor. "This is a foolish man; don't believe his talking. If you will ask him about my coat and my horse, I fear he will say that they belong to him."

The man who became bewildered said: "Sure, those are mine."

The judge who heard this sentence said to him, "You are talking through his hat, get out!"

7. "The Lost Mind"

Informant: Ozdemir Korurek.

One day people say, "Your wife lost her mind," to Nasreddin Hoca.

Nasreddin Hoca begins to think.

The people ask him, "Why do you think?"

Nasreddin Hoca answered: "That is because my wife had no mind. I wonder what she did lose."

8. Nasreddin Hoca and Beggar

Informant: Ozdemir Korurek.

One day, while Nasreddin Hoca is sitting in his home, some beggar knocks on his home's door. Nasreddin Hoca is on the second floor. When the door is knocked, he looks out of the window. And he asks him: "What do you want?"

The beggar answered: "Please, come here, just one minute."

When Nasreddin Hoca gets to the door, the beggar wants alms from him. Nasreddin Hoca becomes angry, but he doesn't show his own anger. And Nasreddin Hoca said to him, "Come upstairs." When the beggar came upstairs Nasreddin Hoca said to him, "Let God give."

9. Medicine for the Eyes

Informant: Ozdemir Korurek.

Someone asked a medicine for his eyes from Nasreddin Hoca. And Nasreddin Hoca said, "Several days ago, my tooth pained. The best medicine was to pull it out. And I pulled it out."

10. Nasreddin and the Robber

Informant: Ozdemir Korurek.

One day, a robber entered Nasreddin Hoca's home. The robber had taken all Nasreddin Hoca's luggage. But the robber in going awakened Nasreddin Hoca and Nasreddin Hoca saw him. As the robber left, Nasreddin Hoca got up and took up his bed and he put it on his own back. And he went after the robber. Accordingly, they went a long time. But the robber felt that someone was following him. When the robber looked backwards, he was Nasreddin Hoca; and he was confused. But the robber worked to make it appear that he was not confused.

The robber asked Nasreddin Hoca:

"Where are you going, Nasreddin Hoca, at midnight?"

Nasreddin Hoca answered him.

"I don't know, but I think, we are moving my home."

Source:
William Hugh Jansen, *Hoosier Folklore*, vol. V, Dec. 1946, No. 4. pp. 138-141.

UKRAINIAN AMERICANS

*U*kraine at the end of the nineteenth century was strife-ridden. The revolution of
1848 had sought to unite the Ruthenians with the Ukrainians under Russian rule
and divide Galicia into separate Polish and Ukrainian provinces. The revolution
was suppressed and the imperial regime made an agreement with Polish nobility that
ceded political control of Galicia to the Poles. The government reforms that were
put in place neglected to pay attention to land reform, rural overpopulation and
lack of industry. As a result, Ukrainian peasants became progressively more
impoverished. This began the large scale emigration of Ukrainians to the Americas,
which lasted from the 1880s until World War I.

At the beginning of the twentieth century, ethnic conflict became more pronounced. Peasants held strikes against Polish landlords, university students demonstrated, and in 1908, a student assassinated the Galician governor. In 1914,
World War I pitted Russia against Austria-Hungary, and Ukrainians on both sides
were adversely affected. In Russia, Ukrainians were suppressed, arrested or exiled.
When Russian troops advanced on Galicia, retreating Austrians executed thousands of Ukrainians, who they suspected were Russian sympathizers. Although the
Austrians re-conquered the area in 1915, there were still military operations taking
place in western Ukraine. It was not until the Russian Revolution in February of
1917 that restrictions on the Ukrainian press and freedom of speech were lifted.
The eased restrictions allowed for a Ukrainian representative body to be formed in
Kiev, but this body refused to accept the Bolshevik's authority over Ukraine after
the November coup. On November 20, 1917, Ukraine proclaimed the creation of
the Ukrainian National Republic. The Western Ukrainian National republic was
formed in October, 1918.

People fled Ukraine to escape the continuing war. Many of them had come to
America from a life of poverty as peasants. Those in New Jersey and Pennsylvania
often were employed in mines and factories. In 1917, the Reverend P. Poniatishin
made a plea to Congressman James A. Hamill for aid for Ruthenians and Ukrainians suffering from the consequences of the war. The measure, which sought to designate a day for the collection of funds for Ukrainians throughout Ruthene and
other parts of the Austrian Empire, was taken by Hamill and Senator Hughes from
New Jersey. In this document, Hamill makes an impassioned plea for its passage in
the House as a great act of charity; the measure was unanimously passed by the
Senate of Foreign Relations.

CONGRESSMAN HAMILL'S REMARKS ON RESOLUTION TO PROCLAIM UKRAINIAN DAY

Extension of Remarks of HON. JAMES A. HAMILL, Of New Jersey, In The House of Representatives,

Wednesday, February 21, 1917.

On Senate joint resolution (S. J. Res. 201) requesting the President to appoint a day for the relief of the Ruthenians (Ukrainians).

Mr. HAMILL. Mr. Speaker, this resolution was conceived in a spirit of humanity. It explains its own purpose. Millions of Ruthenians have been sorely oppressed and scourged by the ravages of war in eastern Europe, and no helping hand had thus far been extended to them, save the feeble assistance which a few of their own people from the Ukrain now residing in America have been able to render.

The matter was first brought to my attention by the very reverend administrator of the Ruthenian Catholic Diocese in the United States, the Rev. Father P. Poniatishin, through his counsel, Mr. William J. Kearns, of the New Jersey bar. Before the Christmas holidays Mr. Kearns consulted me with reference to the adoption of some measure of relief for the Ukrainians, especially for those in war-stricken Galicia, Bukowina, and other Provinces of Austria. Then I received a letter from the very reverend administrator, which I beg to insert, as follows:

NEWARK, N. J., *December 27, 1916.*
Hon. James A. Hamill, M. C.
Jersey City, N.J.

MY DEAR CONGRESSMAN: I have to thank you most cordially for the deep interest you are taking in the cause of our Ruthenian war sufferers, and to say that the Ruthenians who have made their homes in this country will always feel that they owe you a sincere debt of gratitude. In our diocese in the United States there are at least 600,000 souls from Galicia, besides some 500,000 more Ruthenians, who are also of Ukrainian origin, from Hungary, Bukowina, and other parts of Austria. I know I speak the true sentiment of my people in expressing our warmest appreciation of your efforts in their behalf. These people deeply sympathize with their afflicted brothers, but have been unable to render them much practical assistance in their great misfortunes and terrible sufferings. Millions of our people in Galicia have been deprived of all their property and belongings and are in actual need of the necessaries of life. In Galicia alone, prior to the war, there was a Ruthenian population of some 4,000,000. At least 1,000,000 of these former inhabitants have been driven out of their country through the scourge of war, and are wandering without home or friends through other parts of the Austrian Empire. These Ukrainians seem to have been forgotten, or overlooked, for notwithstanding that measures of relief have been undertaken for other nationalities, nothing whatever of a systematic, regular character has yet been done for them. If the President of the United States would designate a day for the collection of funds to relieve their destitution I feel that America out of its great, generous heart would respond nobly. May I, therefore, supplement the request of my counsel, Mr. Kearns, that you stand sponsor for a resolution requesting the President so to act?

With sentiments of deep respect, I am,

Very sincerely, yours,

P. PONIATISHIN, *Administrator.*

On January 3, 1917, Very Rev. P. Poniatishin, with his counsel, came to Washington with reference to this measure and enlisted my interest more thoroughly. On January 23, 1917, they visited the Capitol again, and on January 24, 1917, the resolution was introduced in this House and simultaneously in the Senate. Senator HUGHES of New Jersey stood sponsor for it in the other House, and the Senate Committee on Foreign Relations reported it with unanimous approval. It passed the Senate and has now been substituted on the House calendar for my measure. It appeals to the humanitarian instinct of every Member of this House. It breathes the spirit of a broad charity. The great American heart will unquestionably respond with a warm and generous sympathy, and prompt the citizens of our country, irrespective of racial origin, to aid materially millions of their fellow human beings whose sufferings are simply incredible and who are unable to help themselves.

Probably no section in all war-stricken Europe has undergone so terrible an affliction as has the country inhabited by the Ruthenians in eastern Galicia and the northwestern part of Bukowina. Before the war, in Galicia alone there dwelt 4,000,000 of these people. Their country has been so terribly ravaged by war that it may be regarded as almost irretrievably ruined, for its people are scattered and hundreds of thousands of them are today homeless and lack the very necessaries of life. College professors, clergymen, lawyers, doctors, and merchants have been deprived of their all and their families reduced to destitution, and compelled actually to beg for bread. They lack necessary clothing to protect them against the cold of an Austrian winter, and many of them, according to reliable reports, are absolutely without shoes and stockings. Their country has been overrun and raked fore and aft by the most terrible war ever known, not only three or four times in general military movements, but by innumerable deadly and devastating minor skirmishes, entailing vast suffering and destitution. Since the taking of Lemberg and its recapture, and both prior to and since the siege and fall of Przemysl, there has been an uninterrupted, desolating warfare raging throughout this region, which has told most terribly upon the Ruthenian population.

No contributions or measures of relief collected or intended for the other war sufferers ever reach these Ruthenians. Theirs is a typical instance of a people who have been actually submerged; they are, in fact, a forgotten race, and yet these Ukrainians constitute a nation just as clearly and sharply defined as do the Poles, the Russians, or the Bulgarians. There are few people who understand that the Russian tongue is a language as foreign to a Ruthenian as French is to an Italian. Unfortunately these people and their country are little known either in Europe or America, although they have existed for centuries as a distinct race and nation, while their ancient capital of Kiev, on the river Dneiper, rivaled at one time in wealth and magnificence the capital of the Eastern Roman Empire, but that was before it was pillaged and destroyed by the Muscovites.

The Ukraine covers about 828,185 square miles, and its territory is therefore one and one-half times as large as the present-day Germany. In eastern Galicia, the northwest of Bukowina, and the northeast of Hungary there is a Ruthenian population of 4,200,000 souls, or rather there was such a population there before the war began, while the Ruthenian race, populating the Ukraine, numbers, or rather did number prior to the war, nearly 40,000,000 souls. Millions of them have been slain, maimed, crippled, and irreparably ruined by the belligerents on both sides, and no hand has been raised as yet in any regular or systematic way to relieve the distress of this particular people.

The first Ukrainian immigrants came to America about 40 years ago. Many of them came here to better their economic conditions; some of them fled before the political and religious persecution. This tide of immigration has immensely increased in late years, and continued until the war began. At present there are a million Ukrainians in the United States, and 200,000 in Canada. In Canada they are mostly farmers, having settled in the great wheat-producing Provinces of Manitoba, Saskatchewan, and Alberta. In the United States they are laborers, miners, farmers, skilled workmen, and business men. The conditions in America from the very beginning favored the development of the Ukrainian immigrant. The man that under the oppressive circumstances in the old country seemed doomed to eternal dependence had here in America a chance. As it is usually the case with all the Slavonic immigrants, the Ukrainians settled in large colonies in different industrial centers. Having provided homes for their families, their next endeavor was to provide for their own spiritual needs, and on this they never spare money and sacrifice. So the churches were built, beneficial and educational organizations were founded, economical, cooperative institutions were started, and many Ukrainian papers founded. The Ukrainians are very much interested in all these institutions, and it is considered as a national duty to be the member of at least one of them. Usually at the churches parochial schools are organized, for the purpose of teaching the children the Ukrainian language as well as the principles upon which the American civilization is built. The Ukrainians have a full confidence in the American schools, and are eager to send their children there.

Conclusion

Now, however, that the terrible plight of these people, who were almost a forgotten race, has been brought to the attention of the American Congress, and that the American President has raised his voice in behalf of the submerged peoples of the world, a glimmer of hope has even come to the Ruthenians, who were well-nigh on the brink of despair—in fact, who were actually in despair—of their receiving some temporary provisional relief. Therefore, may they hopefully look forward to some amelioration of their present condition of misery and wretchedness. Hence, Mr. Speaker, I bespeak for this resolution the unanimous vote of the House. In this appeal I am joined by my colleague Mr. FARR, of Pennsylvania, who has enthusiastically supported and aided me in all my endeavors to have this resolution enacted.

Source:

The Ukrainians in America, 1608-1975: A Chronology & Fact Book, compiled and edited by Vladimir Wertsman. Dobbs Ferry, NY: Occana Publications, 1976. pp. 33-35.

*E*aster is perhaps the most revered holiday among practicing Christians. The event celebrates the crucifixion, death, and resurrection of Jesus Christ. Easter was formally recognized as a day of observance by the Council of Nicea which is one of the earliest forms of organized Western Christianity. The Council of Nicea was formed by Emperor Constantine in 325 A.D. The day of celebration was designated at the first Sunday after the first full moon after the vernal equinox. Eastern churches subsequently included Easter as a festival in the Church year. According to an English historian called "the Venerable Bede" (672-735) the term "Easter" derives from "Eostre," who was the Anglo-Saxon goddess of Spring (Easter is celebrated in the Spring.

One of the forms of expression practiced by Christians in honor of the holiday is the decoration of Easter eggs. The egg signifies fertility among many cultures and has come to symbolize the resurrection of Christ. Ukrainians, who have elevated decorating Easter eggs to an art form began the practice in roughly 988 A.D. The decorated eggs are called pysanky among Ukrainians. The term pysarka in Ukrainian originally referred to women who were expert Easter egg decorators. Some of the more common images painted on the eggs are ribbons which are connected to symbolize the ring of eternity; plants such as periwinkles, pine trees, and roses; and animals such as chickens, birds, sheep, and reindeer are also commonly represented.

Another common decoration seen on Ukrainian Easter eggs is geometric shapes. Often triangular baskets are represented which signify the Holy Trinity and fire, water, and air. Today one of the most common images found on Easter eggs in the United States is that of a bunny. Prior to the advent of Christianity the rabbit symbolized the beginning of life and was subsequently incorporated into the Easter tradition for this reason. In modern day America the Easter Bunny has grown inseparable from the holiday. The art of decorating Easter eggs in the United States has been adapted into a family event similar to carving a pumpkin or decorating a Christmas tree. Many Christian families in the United States purchase food coloring kits for children who soak the eggs in a vinegar based solution to form pastel colors such as yellow, blue, and pink and place the eggs in Easter baskets.

Although there are many methods used to paint Easter eggs, the most common is called the "wax resist method." This method involves using bees wax to prevent the different dyes from bleeding into one another. Among Ukrainians it is more common to use raw eggs (rather than hard-boiled eggs) because the texture of the raw egg more thoroughly absorbs the dyes. One of the most prominent Easter egg painting artists was Nicholas Mulicky, who was a Ukrainian immigrant who resided in Hartford, Connecticut.

DECORATING EASTER EGGS

Generations of Ukrainians have decorated Easter eggs. Indeed, the decoration became such an art that in the Ukraine a woman who was particularly skillful was called a *pysarka* and was asked by people in neighboring villages to decorate special eggs for them. After the colored eggs had been blessed, they were often presented as gifts. One of the hard-boiled eggs was cut into pieces at the beginning of the Easter dinner, and each member of the family ate a portion in token of the end of Lenten fasting. The gaily decorated eggs might also be used in a game as part of the Easter festivities. Young people would try to strike each other's eggs with their own. The owner of the unbroken egg would win the cracked one, thus eliminating from the game those who lost their Easter eggs. Because of the religious significance of the eggs, however, the shells of even the cracked ones were never just dropped on the ground; they were thrown into fire or water.

These Easter eggs are so rare in America that they are not ordinarily either eaten or used in games. Among the Ukrainians in the Triple Cities, though, many people decorate Easter eggs with the traditional designs, for Mrs. Frank Lawryk, wife of St. John's Ukrainian Church, has taught the young people the art of Easter egg decoration. Almost any design may be used: for instance, I have seen a large egg with the picture of the Last Supper done in reverent detail. Most of the designs, however, are geometric, often giving a kaleidoscopic impression because of their brilliant colors and tiny shapes.

These eggs are not cooked because the raw egg shell absorbs the color better than a cooked one. In fact, while a person works on the egg, he holds it with a cloth or tissue so that the oil from his hand will not keep the dye from being absorbed. The egg is not blown out of the shell, either, for a blown egg shell is fragile. In the whole raw egg the albumen eventually dries to the shell, making it stronger.

A batik process is used by the Ukrainians in decorating their Easter eggs. To do this, one holds the egg gently and sketches lightly the main lines of his design. Then he draws on the shell the first lines of the design with a *pysar*, or small, metal-tipped writing tool, dipped in melted beeswax. These lines will be white, the original shell color, when the design is completed, because they are protected by the wax from any dye. When these lines have been completed, the egg is dipped into the lightest vegetable dye, probably yellow. As soon as the egg is dry, the designer covers with wax the parts he wants to stay yellow, and dips the egg into the next darker dye, usually orange or red. This process is continued with each color desired except for a few, like blue or green, which cannot be covered completely with other colors. These, if used, are laid on with a toothpick.

After the design is completed, the egg is held over a candle flame to melt off the wax. Then the egg is shellacked or varnished, and this miniature work of art is complete, ready if carefully handled to brighten Easter for ten or twenty years. Such eggs, or *pysanky*, are presented to friends and relatives on Easter morning with the greeting, "*Krystos voskres* [Christ is risen]" and are received with the reply, "*Voistynu voskres* [He is risen, indeed!]"

Source:

"Easter Eggs in the Triple Cities," by Edith E. Cutting. In *New York Folklore Quarterly*, vol. XII, 1956. pp. 23-24.

Oksana Roshetsky displaying decorated Easter eggs. The custom of decorating Easter eggs is a popular tradition among children during the holiday.

VIETNAMESE AMERICANS

Prior to 1975 there were very few Vietnamese Americans. On April 18, 1975, less than two weeks before Saigon fell to the North Vietnamese following the American withdrawal, President Ford authorized the entry of 130,000 refugees from the three countries of Indochina, 125,000 of whom were Vietnamese. This marked the beginning of a massive immigration movement. While only 3,200 Vietnamese arrived the next year, and only 1,000 came in 1977, the number dramatically increased in 1978 as American citizens and organizations pushed the government to allow resettlement of a people some felt the U.S. government had failed. That year, 11,100 Vietnamese entered the United States.

When war broke out in 1979 between Vietnam and Cambodia, then between Vietnam and China, conditions became desperate for Vietnamese trying to flee. As a humane gesture, the United States accepted 44,500 more immigrants that year. The United Nations assisted the U.S. government and the Vietnamese government in setting up the Orderly Departure Program to help 1,000 Vietnamese leave their country each month. During this time the United States and Vietnam had no formal diplomatic relations, yet the program functioned from 1979 through 1987 to allow 50,000 Vietnamese, especially children of American soldiers and former South Vietnamese soldiers, to escape Vietnam.

But refugees pouring in from camps in other countries did not have ties with the United States. Many of these immigrants were actually Chinese citizens of Vietnam. Public opinion began to shift, calling for a change of policy to slow the flow while admitting those who were truly in danger in Vietnam. Congress passed the Refugee Act of 1980 to systematize the admission of refugees to the United States. The Act spells out the intention of the United States to accept any person who is outside her or his country and unable to return on fear of persecution; in other words a political refugee. This policy was accepted by the American public because it offered help to people with whom the United States had been involved in the Vietnam War, while not opening the doors to everyone.

By 1980, the immigration wave became a flood of Laotians, Cambodians, and Vietnamese, some 167,000 desperate people, many of whom pushed away from Vietnamese shores in unseaworthy boats. The U.S. media named them the "boat people" and in 1981, more than 132,000 immigrated to the United States. In 1981, Californian officials estimated that 5,000 to 6,000 Southeast Asia refugees moved to that state each month. More than half sought public financial assistance. Of the 7,500 refugees in Sacramento County, 5,500 were on welfare, and in Orange County, more than 20,000 of the 50,000 Southeast Asia refugees received welfare payments, according to the New York Times. California was thought to have more than 60 percent of the 450,000 refugees who had come to the United States since the end of the Vietnam War in 1975. This was not intentional. Six camps in the United States received refugees and prepared them for resettlement. After a medical examination, each refugee was assigned to living quarters and sent to one of nine voluntary agencies, the largest of which was the United States

Catholic Conference. The agencies found sponsors who would assume financial responsibility for refugee families. A secondary migration that began in the early 1980s concentrated the Vietnamese in California, a state that always had a high Asian population. The immigrants selected California because of the moderate climate, and in many case, the presence of relatives.

During the spring of 1981, American immigration officials began to apply more strictly the distinctions made in the 1980 Refugee Act between political and economic immigrants. Vietnamese people simply seeking a better life were discouraged from applying for admission to the United States. Those who sought to immigrate were required to have family in the United States or be able to show that to remain in Vietnam could result in prison or death. In addition, the United States no longer accepted Vietnamese who were refugees in other countries.

By December of 1982 the flow of immigrants had dropped 20 percent. The number of Vietnamese and other Indochinese coming to the United States never again reached the high points of the immigration waves of 1980 and 1981. Around 24,000 Vietnamese immigrants came to the United States each year up until 1986. The Refugee Act of 1980 helped provide a policy with which the United States could regulate its immigration obligations.

REFUGEE ACT, 1980

Title I—Purpose

Section 101. (a) The Congress declares that it is the historic policy of the United States to respond to the urgent needs of persons subject to persecution in their homelands, including, where appropriate, humanitarian assistance for their care and maintenance in asylum areas, efforts to promote opportunities for resettlement or voluntary repatriation, aid for necessary transportation and processing, admission to this country of refugees of special humanitarian concern to the United States. The Congress further declares that it is the policy of the United States to encourage all nations to provide assistance and resettlement opportunities to refugees to the fullest extent possible.

(b) The objectives of the Act are to provide a permanent and systematic procedure for the admission to this country of refugees of special humanitarian concern to the United States, and to provide comprehensive and uniform provisions for the effective resettlement and absorption of those refugees who are admitted.

Title II—Admission of Refugees

Section 201. (a) Section 101 (a) of the Immigration and Nationality Act (8 U.S.C. 1101 (a)) is amended by adding after paragraph (41) the following new paragraph:

"(42) The term 'refugee' means (A) any person who is outside any country of such person's nationality or, in the case of a person having no nationality, is outside any country in which such person last habitually resided, and who is unable or unwilling to return to, and is unable or unwilling to avail himself or herself of the protection of, that country because of persecution or a well-founded fear of persecution on account of race, religion, nationality, membership in a particular social group, or political opinion, or (B) in such special circumstances as the President after appropriate consultation (as defined in section 207(e) of this Act) may specify, any person who is within the country of such person's nationality, within the country in which such person is habitually residing, and who is persecuted or who has a well-founded fear of persecution on account of race, religion, nationality, membership in a particular social group, or political opinion. The tern 'refugee' does not include any person who ordered, incited, assisted, or otherwise participated in the persecution of any person on account of race, religion, nationality, membership in a particular social group, or political opinion."

(b) Chapter 1 of the title II of such Act is amended by adding after section 206(8 U.S.C. 1156) the following new sections.

Annual Admission of Refugees and Admission of Emergency Situation Refugees

Section 207. (a)(1) Except as provided in subsection (b), the number of refugees who may be admitted under this section in fiscal year 1980, 1981, or 1982, may not exceed fifty thousand unless the President determines, before the beginning of the fiscal year and after appropriate consultation (as defined in subsection (e)), that admission of a specific number of refugees in excess of such number is justified by humanitarian concerns or is otherwise in the national interest.

"(2) Except as provided in subsection (b), the number of refugees who may be admitted under this section in any fiscal year 1982 shall be such number as the President determines, before the beginning of the fiscal year and after appropriate consultation, is justified by humanitarian concerns or is otherwise in the national interest.

"(3) Admissions under this subsection shall be allocated among refugees of special humanitarian concern to the United States in accordance with a determination made by the President after appropriate consultation.

"(b) If the President determines, after appropriate consultation, that (1) an unforeseen emergency refugee situation exists, (2) the admission of certain refugees in response to the emergency refugee situation is justified by grave humanitarian concerns or is otherwise in the national interest, and (3) the admission to the United States of these refugees cannot be accomplished under subsection (a), the President may fix a number of refugees to be admitted to the United States during the succeeding period (not to exceed twelve months) in response to the emergency refugee situation and such admissions shall be allocated among refugees of special humanitarian concern to the United States in accordance with a determination made by the President after the appropriate consultation provided under this subsection.

"(c)(1) Subject to the numerical limitations established pursuant to subsections (a) and (b), the Attorney General may, in the Attorney General's discretion and pursuant to such regulations as the Attorney General may prescribe, admit any refugee who is not firmly resettled in any foreign country, is determined to be of special humanitarian concern to the United States, and is admissible (except as otherwise provided under paragraph (3)) as an immigrant under this Act.

"(2) A spouse or child (as defined in section 101(b) (1)(A), (B), (C), (D), or (E)) of any refugee who qualifies for admission under paragraph (1) shall, if not otherwise entitled to admission under paragraph (1) and if not a person described in the second sentence of section 101(a)(42), be entitled to the same admission status as such refugee if accompanying, or following to join, such refugee and if the spouse or child is admissible (except as otherwise provided under paragraph (3)) as an immigrant under this Act. Upon the spouse's or child's admission to the United States, such admission shall be charged against the numerical limitation established in accordance with the appropriate subsection under which the refugee's admission in charged.

"(3) The provisions of paragraphs (14), (15), (20), (21), (25), and (32) of section 212(a) shall not be applicable to any alien seeking admission to the United States under this subsection, and the Attorney General may waive any other provision of such section (other than paragraph (27), (29), or (33) and other than so much of paragraph (23) as relates to trafficking in narcotics) with respect to such an alien for humanitarian purposes, to assure family unity, or when it is otherwise in the public interest. Any such waiver by the Attorney General shall be in writing and shall be granted only on an individual basis following an investigation. The Attorney General shall provide for the annual reporting to Congress of the number of waivers granted under this paragraph in the previous fiscal year and a summary of the reasons for granting such waivers.

"(4) The refugee status of any alien (and of the spouse or child of the alien) may be terminated by the Attorney General pursuant to such regulations as the Attorney General may prescribe if the Attorney General determines that the alien was not in fact a refugee within the meaning of section 1019(a)(42) at the time of the alien's admission.

"(d)(1) Before the start of each fiscal year the President shall report to the Committees on the Judiciary of the House of Representatives and of the Senate regarding the foreseeable number of refugees who will be in need of resettlement during the fiscal year and the anticipated allocation of refugee admissions during the fiscal year. The President shall provide for periodic discussions between designated representatives of the President and members of such committees regarding changes in the worldwide refugee situation, the progress of refugee admissions among refugees.

"(2) As soon as possible after representatives of the President initiate appropriate consultation with respect to the number of refugee admissions under subsection (a) or with respect to the admission of refugees in response to an emergency refugee situation under subsection (b), the Committees on the Judiciary of the House of Representatives and of the Senate shall cause to have printed in the Congressional Record the substance of such consultation.

"(3) (A) After the President initiates appropriate consultation prior to making a determination under subsection (a), a hearing to review the proposed determination shall be held unless public disclosure of the details of the proposal would jeopardize the lives or safety of individuals.

"(B) After the President initiates appropriate consultation prior to making a determination, under subsection (b), that the number of refugee admissions should be increased because of an unforeseen emergency refugee situation, to the extent that time and the nature of the emergency refugee situation permit, a hearing to review the proposal to increase refugee admissions shall be held unless public disclosure of the details of the proposal would jeopardize the lives or safety of individuals.

"(e) For purposes of this section, the term 'appropriate consultation' means, with respect to the admission of refugees and allocation of refugee admissions, discussions in person by designated Cabinet-level representatives of the President with members of the Committees on the judiciary of the Senate and of the House of Representatives to review the refugee situation, to project the extent of possible participation of the United States therein, to discuss the reasons for believing that the proposed admission of refugees is justified by humanitarian concerns or grave humanitarian concerns or is otherwise in the national interest, and to provide such members with the following information:

"(1) A description of the nature of the refugee situation.

"(2) A description of the number and allocation for the refugees to be admitted and an analysis of conditions within the countries from which they came.

"(3) A description of the proposed plans for their movement and resettlement and the estimated cost of their movement and resettlement.

"(4) An analysis of the anticipated social, economic, and demographic impact of their admission to the United States.

"(5) A description of the extent to which other countries will admit and assist in the resettlement of such refugees.

"(6) An analysis of the impact of the participation of the United States in the resettlement of such refugees on the foreign policy interests of the United States.

"(7) Such additional information as may be appropriate or requested by such members.

To the extent possible, information described in this subsection shall be provided at least two weeks in advance of discussions in person by designated representatives of the President with such members.

Asylum Procedure

Section 208. (a) The Attorney General shall establish a procedure for an alien physically present in the United States or at a land border or port of entry, irrespective of such alien's status, to apply for asylum, and the alien may be granted asylum in the discretion of the Attorney General.. . .

Adjustment of Status of Refugees

Section 209. (a)(1) Any alien who has been admitted to the United States under section 207—

"(A) whose admission has not been terminated by the Attorney General pursuant to such regulations as the Attorney General may prescribe,

"(B) who has been physically present in the United States for at least one year, and

"(C) who has not acquired permanent resident status, shall, at the end of such year period, return or be returned to the custody of the Service for inspection and examination for admission to the United States as an immigrant in accordance with the provisions of sections 235, 236, and 237.

"(2) Any alien who is found upon inspection and examination by an immigration officer pursuant to paragraph (1) or after a hearing before a special inquiry officer to be admissible (except as otherwise provided under subsection (c)) as an immigrant under this Act at the time of the alien's inspection and examination shall, notwithstanding any numerical limitation specified in this Act, be regarded as lawfully admitted to the United States for permanent residence as of the date of such alien's arrival into the United States.

"(b) Not more than five thousand of the refugee admissions authorized under section 207(a) in any fiscal year may be made available by the Attorney General, in the Attorney General's discretion and under such regulations as the Attorney General may prescribe, to adjust to the status of an alien lawfully admitted for permanent residence the status of any alien granted asylum who—

"(1) applies for such adjustment,

"(2) has been physically present in the United States for at least one year after being granted asylum,

"(3) continues to be a refugee within the meaning of section 101(a)(42)(A) or a spouse or child of such a refugee,

"(4) is not firmly resettled in any foreign country, and

"(5) is admissible (except as otherwise provided under subsection (c)) as an immigrant under this Act at the time of examination for adjustment of such alien.. . .

Section 202. Section 211 of the Immigration and Nationality Act (8 U.S.C. 1181) is amended—.. . .

Section 203. (a) Subsection (a) of section 201 of the Immigration and Nationality Act (8 U.S.C. 1151) is amended to read as follows:

"(a) Exclusive of special immigrants defined is section 101(a)(27), immediate relatives specified in subsection (b) of this section, and aliens who are admitted or granted asylum under section 207 or 208, the number of aliens born in any foreign state of dependent area who may be issued immigrant visas or who may otherwise acquire the status of an alien lawfully admitted to the United States for permanent residence, shall not in any of the first three quarters of any fiscal year exceed a total of seventy-two thousand and shall not in any fiscal year exceed two hundred and seventy thousand."

"(b) Section 202 of such Act (8 U.S.C. 1152) is amended—.. . .

"(e) Subsection (h) of section 243 of such Act (8 U.S.C. 1253) is amended to read as follows:

"(h)(1) The Attorney General shall not deport or return any alien (other than an alien described in section 241(a)(19)) to a country if the Attorney General determines that such alien's life or freedom would be threatened in such country on account of race, religion, nationality, membership in a particular social group, or political opinion.

"(2) Paragraph (1) shall not apply to any alien if the Attorney General determines that—

"(A) the alien ordered, incited, assisted, or otherwise participated in the persecution of any person on account of race, religion, nationality, membership in a particular social group, or political opinion;

"(B) the alien, having been convicted by a final judgment of a particularly serious crime, constitutes a danger to the community of the United States;

"(C) there are serious reasons for considering that the alien has committed a serious nonpolitical crime outside the United States prior to the arrival of the alien to the United States; or

"(D) there are reasonable grounds for regarding the alien as a danger to the security of the United States.

Title III—United States Coordinator for Refugee Affairs and Assistance for Effective Resettlement of Refugees in the United States

Part A—United States Coordinator for Refugee Affairs

Section 301. (a) The president shall appoint, by and with the advice and consent of the Senate, a United States Coordinator for Refugee Affairs (hereinafter in this part referred to as the "Coordinator"). The Coordinator shall have the rank of Ambassador-at-Large.

(b) The Coordinator shall be responsible to the President for—

(1) the development of overall United States refugee admission and resettlement policy;

(2) the coordination of all United States domestic and international refugee admission and resettlement programs in a manner that assures that policy objectives are met in a timely fashion;

(3) the design of an overall budget strategy to provide individual agencies with policy guidance on refugee matters in the preparation of their budget requests, and to provide the Office of Management and Budget with an overview of all refugee-related budget requests;

(4) the presentation to the Congress of the Administration's overall refugee policy and the relationship of individual agency refugee budgets to that overall policy;

(5) advising the President, Secretary of State, Attorney General, and the Secretary of Health and Human Services on the relationship of overall United States refugee policy to the admission of refugees to, and the resettlement of refugees in, the United States;

(6) under the direction of the Secretary of State, representation and negotiation on behalf of the United States with foreign governments and international organizations in discussion on refugee matters and, when appropriate, submitting refugee issues for inclusion in other international negotiations;

(7) development of an effective and responsive liaison between the Federal Government and voluntary organizations, Governors and mayors, and others involved in refugee relief and resettlement work to reflect overall United States Government policy;

(8) making recommendations to the President and to the Congress with respect to policies for, objectives of, and establishment of priorities for,

Federal functions relating to refugee admission and resettlement in the United States; and

(9) reviewing the regulations, guidelines, requirements, criteria, and procedures of Federal departments and agencies applicable to the performance of functions relating to refugee admission and resettlement in the United States.

(c)(1) In the conduct of the Coordinator's duties, the Coordinator shall consult regularly with States, localities, and private nonprofit voluntary agencies concerning the sponsorship process and the intended distribution of refugees.

(2) The Secretary of Labor and the Secretary of Education shall provide the Coordinator with regular reports describing the efforts of their respective departments to increase refugee access to programs within their jurisdiction, and the Coordinator shall include information on such programs in reports submitted under section 413(a)(1) of the Immigration and Nationality Act.

Part B—Assistance for Effective Resettlement of Refugees in the United States

Section 311. (a) Title IV of the Immigration and Nationality Act is amended—

(1) by striking out the title heading and inserting in lieu thereof the following:

Title IV—Miscellaneous and Refugee Assistance

Chapter 1—Miscellaneous; and (2) by adding at the end thereof the following new chapter:

Chapter 2—Refugee Assistance Office of Refugee Resettlement

Section 411. (a) There is established, within the Department of Health and Human Services, an office to be known as the Office of Refugee Resettlement (hereinafter in this chapter referred to as the 'Office'). The head of the Office shall be a Director (hereinafter in this chapter referred to as the 'director'), to be appointed by the Secretary of Health and Human Services (hereinafter in this chapter referred to as the 'secretary').

"(b) The function of the Office and its Director is to fund and administer (directly or through arrangements with other Federal agencies), in consultation with and under the general policy guidance of the United States Coordinator for Refugee Affairs (hereinafter in this chapter referred to as the 'Coordinator'), programs of the Federal Government under this chapter.

Authorization for Programs for Domestic Resettlement of and Assistance to Refugees

Section 412. (a) Conditions and Considerations.—(1) In providing assistance under this section, the Director shall, to the extent of available appropriations, (A) make available sufficient resources for employment training and placement in order to achieve economic self-sufficiency among refugees as quickly as possible, (B) provide refugees with the opportunity to acquire sufficient English language training to enable them to become effectively resettled as quickly as possible, (C) insure that cash assistance is made available to refugees in such a manner as not to discourage their economic self-sufficiency, in accordance with subsection (e)(2), and (D) insure that women have the same opportunities as men to participate in training and instruction.

"(2) The Director, together with the Coordinator, shall consult regularly with State and local governments and private nonprofit voluntary agencies concerning the sponsorship process and the intended distribution of refugees among the States and localities.

"(3) In the provisions of domestic assistance under this section, the Director shall make a periodic assessment, based on refugee population and other relevant factors, of the relative needs of refugees for assistance and services under this chapter and the resources available to meet such needs. In allocating resources, the Director shall avoid duplication of services and provide maximum coordination between agencies providing related services.

"(4) No grant or contract may be awarded under this section unless an appropriate proposal and application (including a description of the agency's ability to perform the services specified in the proposal) are submitted to, and approved by, the appropriate administering official. Grants and contracts under this section shall be made to those agencies which the appropriate administering official determines can best perform the services. Payments may be made for activities authorized under this chapter in advance or by way of reimbursement. In carrying out this section, the Director, the Secretary of State, and any such other appropriate administering official are authorized—

"(A) to make loans, and

"(B) to accept and use money, funds, property, and services of any kind made available by gift, devise, bequest, grant, or otherwise for the purpose of carrying out this section.

"(5) Assistance and services funded under this section shall be provided to refugees without regard to race, religion, nationality, sex, or political opinion.

"(6) As a condition for receiving assistance under this section, a State must—

"(A) submit to the Director a plan which provides—

"(i) a description of how the State intends to encourage refugee resettlement and to promote economic self-sufficiency as quickly as possible,

"(ii) a description of how the State will insure that language training and employment services are made available to refugees receiving cash assistance,

"(iii) for the designation of an individual, employed by the State, who will be responsible for insuring coordination of public and private resources in refugee resettlement,

"(iv) for the care and supervision of and legal responsibility for unaccompanied refugee children in the State, and

"(v) for the identification of refugees who at the time of resettlement in the State are determined to have medical conditions requiring, or medical histories indicating a need for, treatment or observation and such monitoring of such treatment or observation as may be necessary;

"(B) meet standards, goals, and priorities, developed by the Director, which assure the effective resettlement of refugees and which promote their economic self-sufficiency as quickly as possible and the efficient provision of services; and

"(C) submit to the Director, within a reasonable period of time after the end of each fiscal year, a report on the uses of funds provided under this chapter which the State is responsible for administering.

"(7) The Secretary, together with the Secretary of State with respect to assistance provided by the Secretary of State under subsection (b), shall develop a system of monitoring the assistance provided under this section. . .

"(b) Program of Initial Resettlement.—(1)(A) For—

"(i) fiscal year 1980 and 1981, the Secretary of State is authorized, and

"(ii) fiscal year 1982 and succeeding fiscal years, the Director (except as provided in subparagraph (B)) is authorized, to make grants to, and contracts with, public or private nonprofit agencies for initial resettlement (including initial reception and placement with sponsors) of refugees in the Unites States. Grants to, or contracts with, private nonprofit voluntary agencies under this paragraph shall be made consistent with the objectives of this chapter, taking into account the different resettlement approaches and practices of such agencies. Resettlement assistance under this paragraph shall be provided in coordination with the Director shall jointly monitor the assistance provided during fiscal years 1980 and 1981 under this paragraph.

"(B) The President shall provide for a study of which agency is best able to administer the program under this paragraph and shall report, not later than March 1, 1981, to the Congress on such study. . .

"(2) The Director is authorized to develop programs for such orientation, instruction in English, and job training of refugees, and such other education and training of refugees, and such other education and training of refugees, as facilitates their resettlement in the United States. The Director is authorized to implement such programs, in accordance with the provisions of this section, with respect to refugees in the United States. The Secretary of State is authorized to implement such programs with respect to refugees awaiting entry into the United States.

"(3) The Secretary is authorized, in consultation with the Coordinator, to make arrangements (including cooperative arrangements with other Federal agencies) for the temporary care of refugees in the United States in emergency circumstances. . .

"(c) Project Grants and Contracts for Services for Refugees.—The Director is authorized to make grants to, and enter into contracts with, public or private nonprofit agencies for projects specifically designed—

"(1) to assist refugees in obtaining the skills which are necessary for economic self-sufficiency, including projects for job training, employment services, day care, professional refresher training, and other recertification services;

"(2) to provide training in English where necessary (regardless of whether the refugees are employed or receiving cash or other assistance); and

"(3) to provide where specific needs have been shown and recognized by the Director, health (including mental health) services, social services, educational and other services.

"(d) Assistance for Refugee Children.—(1) The Director is authorized to make grants, and enter into contracts, for payments for projects to provide special educational services (including English language training) to refugee children in elementary and secondary schools where a demonstrated need has been shown.

"(2)(A) The Director is authorized to provide assistance, reimbursement to states, and grants to and contracts with public and private nonprofit agencies, for the provision of child welfare services, including foster care maintenance payments and services and health care, furnished to any refugee child (except as provided in subparagraph (B)) during the thirty-six month-period beginning with the first month in which such refugee child is in the United States.

"(B)(i) In the case of a refugee child who is unaccompanied by a parent or other

close adult relative (as defined by the Director) the services described in subparagraph (A) may be until the month after the child attains eighteen years of age (or such higher age as the State's child welfare services plan under part B of title IV of the Social Security Act prescribes for the availability of such services to any other child in that State).

"(ii) The Director shall attempt to arrange for the placement under the laws of the States of such unaccompanied refugee children, who have been accepted for admission to the United States, before (or as soon as possible after) their arrival in the United States. During any interim period while such a child is in the United States or in transit to the United States but before the child is so placed, the Director shall assume legal responsibility (including financial responsibility) for the child, if necessary, and is authorized to make necessary decisions to provide for the child's immediate care.

"(iii) In carrying out the Director's responsibilities under clause (ii), the Director is authorized to enter into contracts with appropriate public or private nonprofit agencies under such conditions as the Director determines to be appropriate.

"(iv) The Director shall prepare and maintain a list of (I) all such unaccompanied children who have entered the United States after April 1, 1975, (II) the names and last known residences of their parents (if living) at the time of arrival, and (III) the children's location, status, and progress.

"(e) Cash Assistance and Medial Assistance to Refugees.—(1) The Director is authorized to provide assistance, reimbursement to States, and grants to, and contracts with, public or private nonprofit agencies for to 100 per centum of the cash assistance and medical assistance provided to any refugee during the thirty-six month period beginning with the first month in which such refugee has entered the United States and for the identifiable and reasonable administrative costs of providing this assistance.

"(2) Cash assistance provided under this subsection to an employable refugee is conditioned, except for good cause shown—

"(A) on the refugee's registration with an appropriate agency providing employment services described in subsection (C) (1), or, if there is no such agency available, with an appropriate State or local employment service; and

"(B) on the refugee's acceptance of appropriate offers of employment; except that subparagraph (A) does not apply during the first sixty days after the date of the refugee's entry.

"(3) The director shall develop plans to provide English training and other appropriate services and training to refugees receiving cash assistance.

"(4) If a refugee is eligible for aid or assistance under a State plan approved under part A of title IV or under title XIX of the Social Security Act, or for supplemental security income benefits (including State supplementary payments) under the program established under title XIX of that Act, funds authorized under this subsection shall only be used for the non-Federal share of such aid or assistance, or for such supplementary payments, with respect to cash and medical assistance provided with respect to such refugee under this paragraph.

"(5) The Director is authorized to allow for the provision of medical assistance under paragraph (1) to any refugee, during the one-year period after entry, who does not qualify for assistance under a State plan approved under title XIX of the Social Security Act on account of any resources or income requirements of such plan, but only if the Director determines that—

"(A) this will (I) encourage economic self-sufficiency, or (ii) avoid a significant burden on State and local governments; and

"(B) the refugee meets such alternative financial resources and income requirements as the Director shall establish.

Congressional Reports

Section 413. (a)(1) The Secretary, in consultation with the Coordinator, shall submit a report on activities under this chapter to the Committees on the judiciary of the House of Representatives and of the Senate not later than the January 31 following the end of each fiscal year, beginning with fiscal year 1980.

"(2) Each such report shall contain—

"(A) an updated profile of the employment and labor force statistics for refugees who have entered under this act since May 1975, as well as a description of the extent to which refugees received the forms of assistance or services under this chapter during that period;

"(B) a description of the geographic location of refugees;

"(C) a summary of the results of the monitoring and evaluation conducted under section 412(a)(7) during the period for which the report is submitted;

"(D) a description of (I) the activities, expenditures, and policies of the Office under this chapter and of the activities of States, voluntary agencies, and sponsors, and (ii) the Director's plans for improvement of refugee resettlement;

"(E) evaluations of the extent to which (i) the services provided under this chapter are assisting refugees in achieving economic self-sufficiency, achieving ability in English, and achieving employment commensurate with their skills and abilities, and (ii) any fraud, abuse, or mismanagement has been reported in the provisions of services or assistance;

"(F) a description of any assistance provided by the Director pursuant to section 412(e)(5);

"(G) a summary of the location and status of unaccompanied refugee children admitted to the United States; and

"(H) a summary of the information compiled and evaluation made under section 412(a)(8).

"(b) The Secretary, in consultation with the Coordinator, shall conduct and report to Congress, not later than one year after date of the enactment of this chapter, an analysis of—

"(1) resettlement systems used by other countries and the applicability of such systems to the United States;

"(2) the desirability of using a system other than the current welfare system for the provision of cash assistance, medical assistance, or both, to refugees; and

"(3) alternative resettlement strategies.

Authorization of Appropriations

Section 414. (a)(1) There are hereby authorized to be appropriated for fiscal year 1980 and for each of the two succeeding fiscal years, such sums as may be necessary for the purpose of providing initial resettlement assistance, cash and medical assistance, and child welfare services under subsections (b)(1), (b)(3), (b)(4), (d)(2), and (e) of section 412.

"(2) There are hereby authorized to be appropriated for fiscal year 1980 and for each of the two succeeding fiscal years $200,000,000, for the purpose of carrying out the provisions (other than those described in paragraph (1)) of this chapter.

"(b) The authority to enter into contracts under this chapter shall be effective for any fiscal year only to such extent or in such amounts as are provided in advance in appropriation Acts.". . .

Title IV—Social Services for Certain Applicants for Asylum

Section 401. (a) The Director of the Office of Refugee Resettlement is authorized to use funds appropriated under paragraphs (1) and (2) of section 414(a) of the Immigration and Nationality Act to reimburse State and local public agencies for expenses which those agencies incurred, at any time, in providing aliens described is subsection (c) of this section with social services of the types for which reimbursements were made with respect to refugees under paragraphs (3) through (6) of section 2(b) of the Migration and Refugee Assistance Act of 1962 (as in effect prior to the enactment of this Act) or under any other Federal law.

(b) The Attorney General is authorized to grant an alien described in subsection (c) of this section permission to engage in employment in the United States and to provide to that alien an "employment authorized" endorsement or other appropriate work permit.

(c) This section applies with respect to any alien in the United States (1) who has applied before November 1, 1979, for asylum in the United States, (2) who has not been granted asylum, and (3) with respect to whom a final, nonappealable, and legally enforceable order of deportation or exclusion has not been entered.

Approved March 17, 1980.

Source:
Asian American Almanac, edited by Susan Gall.
Detroit: Gale Research, 1995. pp. 250-257.

*L*ang Ngan, a long time employee of the United States embassy in Saigon, left Vietnam on April 25, 1975 in a military airlift during the first wave of evacuees from Vietnam. Ngan and her family left her homeland to escape the persecution of a military government that was established after the South Vietnam government surrendered unconditionally to the North Vietnamese on April 30, 1975. North Vietnamese tanks moved into Saigon, the major city of South Vietnam. The Vietnam War, which began in 1955 and ended only with the surrender of South Vietnam to North Vietnam, was a tremendously destructive war for Americans and Vietnamese alike. There were more than 58,000 American casualties and more than 303,000 were wounded. While casualty figures are less certain for the Vietnamese, estimates range from 185,000 to 225,000 killed and 500,000 to 570,000 wounded. About 900,000 North Vietnamese and Viet Cong troops were killed and more than 1,000,000 North and South Vietnamese civilians were killed. Bombing and defoliation heavily damaged the land and its cities, towns and villages. Agriculture, industry and business were disrupted. Refugees fled Vietnam, seeking an escape from the devastation and the new government.

The evacuations in April of 1975 were the first major wave of emigration from Vietnam. This group, primarily consisting of those who worked for the United States government and high-ranking members of the military, numbered about fifteen thousand people. During the last part of April, another 80,000 Vietnamese were evacuated. In total, approximately 125,000 Vietnamese arrived in the United States in 1975. A second wave of immigrants followed this first wave. This group primarily escaped in boats, earning the refugees the nickname "boat people." These people included farmers, merchants, and fishermen as well as military and government officials. Foreign or naval ships picked up some of these people, but other ships sank, were overrun by pirates or were refused landfall in ports such as Malaya or Indonesia. The emigration of the "boat people" from Vietnam began in 1975 and lasted into the 1980s. A more organized effort in 1979 called the Orderly Departure Program (ODP) provided clearances from the Vietnamese government and U.S. Immigration. A primary effort of this program was to reunite families.

The circumstances under which many Vietnamese left Vietnam were traumatic and dangerous, and for most of them, immigration was not planned or voluntary. Orientation to and settlement in the United States was difficult. In The Success Story Ngan describes the experience of the April, 1975 evacuation as she and her family left Vietnam with only the clothes that they wore, in secret, without saying good-bye to friends or relatives. She also recounts the hardships that she and her family endured and the sacrifices they made in the United States. It took over two years, but Ngan and her family became successful members of the community, with several of her siblings earning scholarships and the family purchasing a two family home. Ngan credited their success to tenacity and persistence, saying "We went through all those difficulties, so when we have a chance, we grab it."

THE SUCCESS STORY

by Lang Ngan

Lang Ngan came to the United States in July 1975 by military airlift during the first wave of evacuees from Vietnam.

"On April 25th, near the end of the war, my supervisor called me in, and told me that by six o'clock that evening, we had to meet, to get to the airport by nine the next morning. I had worked for the U.S. embassy in Saigon for seven years. If we had stayed, we would have been persecuted by the new government.

"There was no time to talk to friends or relatives because the evacuation was supposed to be secret, and we were not allowed to tell our relatives. We couldn't even take our money out of the bank. We weren't prepared to come to this country. It was a last minute thing. We had to make our decision overnight. We didn't have any time to think about it.

"I was allowed to take my family, because I was single. My father, my mother, myself and six brothers and sisters—the nine of us. We were so frightened because we didn't have any friends or relatives in this country to help us. We couldn't sell our property. We literally left with the clothes on our backs. I was twenty-nine when I came to the U.S., one brother was twenty-three, and one was nineteen. The youngest was only eight. The rest were in their teens.

"I didn't have the Golden Mountain dream (a Chinese term for America, where making lots of money fast is believed possible). I knew life wouldn't be easy, especially since we didn't receive a high education in Vietnam. I told my brothers and sisters on the plane coming here that I didn't know whether I could support all of them. If not, then I would have to give them up for adoption. They said they understood but asked that before I left, I give them my address so that when they grew up, they could look for me.

"We were transported by military cargo plane. At the time, the evacuation was so sudden the U.S. government didn't have a chance to prepare for our arrival. So we were taken to a military camp in the Philippines for a few days. From there, some of the refugees were sent to Guam. We were sent to Wake Island, and screened for admittance. We left Vietnam April twenty-fifth. We arrived at the camp in Arkansas on May fourth.

"At the beginning, there wasn't enough food. There was a shortage because the U.S. government wasn't prepared for us. But really it wasn't bad. It was actually much better than the first asylum camps in Malaysia and Thailand. We felt we were the luckiest. A month later, the government contracted a company to provide food for us, so after that, there was plenty of food. The living situation wasn't bad. The housing was used by soldiers in training, and the facilities were good like staying in dorms. There were bunk beds. The volunteer agencies—refugee resettlement agencies—started sending people to process us. Some of the agencies, such as the one I work for now, are partially funded by the State Department. Currently, they provide five hundred twenty-five dollars for the initial resettlement cost. Part of the funding is also provided by public donations, or foundations. These resettlement agencies and the immigration office sent people in to screen us, to see if the refugees have relatives or friends in this country they could go to, and to process them. Because I could speak English, I started helping many of those who couldn't, translating for them. I met the representative from the International Rescue Committee, and started to work as a volunteer for IRC. I ended up in New York because the IRC offered me a job. Southeast Asian refugees were calling the office, and no one could understand what they were saying. I was so happy that I could get a job right away. I asked my boss if he thought that I alone could support a whole family of nine. And he said, 'Probably not. Why don't I hire your sister, too?' She was only nineteen at the time, and we've worked for the IRC ever since.

"My sister and I left the camp first, and we started work as soon as we got to New York. We started looking for apartments, but at the time, my salary was only one hundred fifty dollars a week, and my sister made one hundred twenty-five dollars. Someone took us to look for an apartment in Flushing, Queens. A two bedroom was two hundred fifty dollars, and a one bedroom was one hundred ninety dollars, and even with a family of nine, we took the one bedroom, because we tried to save as much as possible. Fortunately, the building superintendent was a refugee—from Cuba—and he helped us. He said he wouldn't tell the landlord that there were nine people living there as long as we didn't make any noise, and kept the children quiet. So he helped us get the apartment. He lied to the landlord for us by saying there were only two girls in the apartment—my sister and myself. The superintendent was very helpful. He tried to get some used furniture for us, and used clothes and dishes. He collected them from other tenants and his friends. That is how we started.

"Half a month later, we had the rest of our family join us. Even though there was only my sister and I working to support nine, life wasn't bad. We were quite happy. But the only frustration was our parents. They had a lot of difficulty adjusting. They felt isolated, because there were no Cantonese-speaking people in the building, and in the daytime, when all the children were in school, there was nothing for them to do but sit. In the beginning, I wanted to go back to Vietnam, because life was easier there. Here, we had no friends or relatives, and the lifestyle was so different. Even the mailbox was different. Every evening, we opened it and it was full of papers and envelopes. I was afraid to throw away anything in case it was important, so I would read every word—thinking they were letters—not realizing that this was advertising, junk.

"As for my siblings, they knew that if I couldn't support them I would give them away. So they were happy when I didn't have to do that. They felt lucky. So they worked hard. They didn't think about many of the things children think about today—expensive toys, expensive clothes, fixing their hair. We wore whatever people gave us. Today I tell my refugee clients, I wore the same used clothes people gave me until two years ago. I finally threw them out because they were so worn.

"The first books we bought were dictionaries. We got three or four of them. We used them a lot. We didn't have any friends or relatives here, but at least we were together as a family. The children studied very hard to catch up in school. We had only one table, and they all had to study together around the same place, and all of them still feel this closeness to this day. We helped each other. I helped the children at that time, but not now. Now they correct my accent.

"We had no furniture—just a few chairs and a used sofa that the supervisor gave us, and broken TV. And the rest were mattresses. We had no beds, only mattresses. In the evening, we had to carry all the mattresses to the living room for the males to sleep. All the females slept in the bedroom. And we lived in this condition for two and a half years, until we were able to get a two-bedroom apartment. We waited till we felt financially secure to do this. We had saved money over the two and a half years, and because I was getting married, I felt that with my husband's income, we could afford to move. My husband and I got a one bedroom apartment and my family moved to a two bedroom place in the same building. We were very happy. We felt that we were one family unit. We were really together, and sharing. There was no privacy, but we all remembered the times we had gone through together, and we were able to work things out with each other without problems.

"All my younger sisters and brothers have done very well in school. And the teachers and school counselors have shown them what is the best way for them to go. Actually, we didn't give them that much counseling. They got it all from school. Even though they don't act the same way I did when I was going to school in Vietnam, they still have certain values—such as respect, and obeying teachers, and therefore the teachers liked them, and tried to help them. My sister got a full scholarship to MIT from Bell Labs. I have one brother who got an electrical engineering degree from Columbia, and the other finished at City College. One other brother is going to medical school at New York Med.

"I think the problems we had when we first came to this country helped our success. We're not like other people who were born here, and had everything. We went through all those difficulties, so when we have a chance, we grab it. We now own a two family house. My husband and I live in one side, my parents in the other."

Source:

Asian American Experiences in the United States: Oral Histories of First to Fourth Generation Americans from China, the Philippines, Japan, India, the Pacific Islands, Vietnam and Cambodia, edited by Joann Faung Jean Lee. Jefferson, NC: McFarland & Co., 1991. pp. 62-65.

Hoang Khoi Phong was born in Hai Duong, Vietnam, in 1943. He served in the Army of the Republic of Vietnam. His first major work, The Rising Sun, *was published in 1967 in Vietnam. He left Vietnam in 1975 and currently lives in southern California, where he cofounded the Bo Cai publishing company in 1977. Since his arrival in the United States, his published work includes* Days N+, *a war memoir, the short story collection* Letters Without Destination, *and* Men of a Hundred Years Ago, *a novel.*

"Twilight" surveys the landscape of a mobile-home park populated by refugees, veterans, and indirect participants in the Vietnam War (1964-1975), all of whom were emotionally or physically handicapped by the experience. The narrator is a veteran of the Army of the Republic of Vietnam who interacts with an African American veteran unable to resist the seduction of drink, a refugee couple from Armenia who lost a son to the war, and a nosy but well-meaning neighbor who served in Vietnam. All of them are connected in this mobile-home park, a strange kind of American Main Street. But as the name suggests, mobile-home parks are just transitory places, somewhere to stop before heading elsewhere, for better or worse.

TWILIGHT

by Hoang Khoi Phong

Finally, after three days, my bewilderment faded and I found myself growing accustomed to my new neighborhood. Such a strange concept: a "mobile home" park. This particular one had been designated for people over fifty-five. But the natural instincts of owners to make the best use of an empty property conspired to make me a resident in an area from which—since I didn't meet the simple criteria of age—I should have been excluded.

About a hundred trailers were parked in the complex. As a newcomer I thought I should take some time to introduce myself to my neighbors or at the very least get to know the faces and names of those living on both sides of my fence and in the trailer facing mine.

And that was where I stopped, right in front of a "single-wide" mobile home supported about a yard and a half off the ground by six stone blocks. The house had an air of genteel shabbiness about it, from the exposed wheels that the owner hadn't thought to conceal, to the empty aluminum cans scattered in the shadowed spaces near the base of the trailer. In the garden next to the house, I saw the owner sleeping soundly in a wheelchair, under the shade of several peach trees laden with fruit. A thin blanket covered his legs and lying on his lap was a bag of seeds brought to feed city birds too lazy to forage on their own. As I watched a bold squirrel snuck up and surreptitiously gathered the corn kernels strewn across the lawn, now and again cautiously standing up on its hind legs and listening for a sound, watching for a movement. I turned back and sat on the rattan chair on my porch, looking at my sleeping neighbor and wondering how much longer it would take before I could go over and perform the small yet obligatory act of greeting that seemed required in my adopted land.

I wondered how old the man was. It seemed as if the color and weight had been leached out of him, leaving him wrinkled and spent. The lines on his face and neck were as pronounced as the carvings on an old sculpture. Yet even though time had atrophied his body, leaving only a layer of skin over a framework of brittle bones, he still managed to fill the entire chair. He must have been a strong and forceful man when he was young.

The old man suddenly stirred and opened his eyes. He seemed dazed. I should give him a couple of minutes to regain his bearings, I thought. But even as I watched, he shifted and went back to sleep. Fifteen minutes later, I saw him wake and grope for the whistle he had around his neck. As soon as he'd found it, he blew long and hard. The sudden noise startled me. The door behind him opened and out came an old woman who quickly asked: "Honey, are you OK?" She bent down to whisper in his ear, then turned and kissed him lightly on the forehead.

Gathering my confidence, I went over and introduced myself, explaining that I was a new arrival to the neighborhood. The old man, incapable of speech, bade me welcome with his eyes. But not his wife. The eyes that a moment before had gazed upon the old man with warmth and pity clouded over into two pools of indescribable darkness when they looked at me. I wondered if it would be wise to greet any of my other neighbors.

The next day was a Saturday, and I decided to do some laundry. I had just put two large bags of dirty clothes into my car when I saw another old man approach, his walk energetic, his eyes mischievous, his voice booming. "Good morning, son!" he called. "You Vietnamese?"

I felt annoyed. If he knew I was Vietnamese, then he should have understood that the diminutive "son" didn't appeal to us, particularly when coming from a foreigner, I was still debating how to reply when the man, nonplussed, continued:

"My name's Bill—I'm your next door neighbor. I was in your country for three years, '69 to '72."

"My name is Nguyen."

"You a vet too? ARVN?"

"I served in the army."

In the morning, I went to the convenience store to pick up a few things and saw Mr. White, paying for a gallon bottle of whiskey. When he saw I'd noticed him, his eyes clouded with uneasiness. I drove back home, haunted by his look.

I resigned myself to making the best of his visit—at least it meant one less person to whom I'd have to introduce myself. We exchanged some pleasantries about the weather and then our biographies. Bill had retired from the Air Force; he'd been stationed in many places. He actually knew quite a bit about Vietnam and had a good grasp of the kind of Vietnamese vocabulary not used in polite society. While he'd been in Vietnam, he'd supported a "little wife," he told me. Although he was sixty-five, he seemed to me to have the vigor of a man in his fifties.

After that first meeting Bill would often come by to chat with me through the fence, and even, occasionally, visit my house. He'd appointed himself as the bearer of news about what was happening in the neighborhood for me. For the most part, our conversations were one-sided—I let him do most of the speaking, since I was insecure about my English. Through him I learned about everything that was happening in this little world of ours.

"Hey, Nguyen, you coming to the party at the clubhouse this weekend?"

"What party?"

"Steve and Laura's two year anniversary."

"I don't know them—I wasn't invited."

"Hey, don't sweat it—parties around here are open to everyone. Come on; there'll be free food, music; it'll be fun. Steve and Laura got married right here. They're both in their late eighties. Hell, they both got great-grandchildren."

Changing the subject abruptly, he said: "Listen, do you know that guy White in F8."

"I haven't met anybody except the couple next door and you."

"He's a black guy; a vet—he was in Vietnam too. You know, the first five years he's here, I never even knew he had a son. Then the kid starts coming over, spending his nights here. One night, two AM, he breaks into Mrs. Barbara's trailer, M4, steals about two hundred dollars. Then he rapes the old woman and stabs her to death. Then the nervy little bastard comes back the next week, probably to do in someone else. That's when they got him. Since then White hasn't dared to show his face, case someone thinks he's an accessory."

"Nine out of ten his son just took advantage of him to scope out the area," I said. I felt a twinge of sympathy for White.

"Well, I guess the police thought the same thing—they asked him a few questions, then let him go. But I'll tell you, Nguyen, no matter what, I just don't trust any of those people."

That night, when I arrived with my bouquet of flowers and a greeting card, the clubhouse was filled to capacity with fifty or sixty elderly couples. Some of them were in wheelchairs, though I saw no sign of the couple next door to me. As soon as he saw me, Bill rushed over and introduced me to everyone. I felt awkward and out of place among this gathering of elders. Steve and Laura, the anniversary couple, denied the passage of time with brightly colored clothing that was too young for them. His hand trembling, Steve took the bouquet I brought and muttered an almost unintelligible thank you. I mumbled my best wishes back, but the atmosphere depressed me. As soon as Bill brought me a paper plate, I took a sandwich and retired to a chair in the corner. Soon after I sat down, a black man entered, carrying a beautifully wrapped gift. His entrance reduced the commotion in the room to soft murmurs of surprise. The man's face was marked with loss and suffering. He brought the gift to the wedding table, put it down and gave his best wishes to the couple. Ignoring the stares of the other people, he settled into the empty chair next to mine and introduced himself.

"Hi, My name's White."

"Nguyen."

I gave him a firm handshake, and I was abruptly conscious of the few furtive glances thrown in our direction. Then someone must have given a sign, for suddenly an old lady sat down at the piano and began to caress the keyboard. Songs about youth and love tumbled from her lips. Bill, full of energy, seemed to grow younger; he was at his most entertaining. He hugged one person, swung another one out on the floor to dance. Some of the dancers were to heavy to even walk; others were fragile and thin as toothpicks. Many of them left the dance floor wheezing or consumed by fits of coughing. As the noise abated, Mr. White got up and went to the piano. He bent and whispered to the pianist, who flipped through her songbook and tested a couple of chords before she started to play. Her music blended with White's voice and an indescribably sad song filled the air. All of the people seemed visibly moved. As the song went on, I got up and snuck out, uncomfortable with all of the signs of mortality around me. My mind was haunted with images of withered bodies, of snowy white hair, of the elegance of the lady pianist. I felt mesmerized by the way clouded eyes were able to shine for a brief moment of happiness before returning to their distant dullness.

For several days soon after, the guest parking lot outside the complex filled up with cars bearing out of state license plates. Young couples and sometimes even small families complete with chubby, rosy-cheeked babies, roamed the compound. In the morning, I went to the convenience store to pick up a few things and saw Mr. White, paying for a gallon bottle of whiskey. When he saw I'd noticed him, his eyes clouded with uneasiness. I drove back home, haunted by his look. As I stepped out of the car, Bill came over to me.

"Hey, Nguyen, any visitors today?"

"I have many friends, but they were afraid they wouldn't be able to find parking here. Anyway, usually we just meet at Vietnamese restaurants."

"Well, I didn't mean your friends. It's almost Father's Day—everyone's expecting their kids. Except me. I got a card from my son yesterday, says he can't make it this year."

"Where is he?"

"San Francisco. After he finished up at U.C.-Davis he decided to stay up there, on account of his job. Been there about ten years now; he's thirty-two. By the way, that couple next door to you? They haven't had a visitor in the last five years."

"I tried to visit them when I first moved here. But up to now I haven't even been able to find out their name."

"Sarkissian, that's his name. Armenian. He's a doctor, or was a doctor—he came to the states in 1945, when he was thirty-five. So he's what now, close to eighty? I heard he left a wife and son behind back in Armenia; his wife now's a nurse who worked with him in a hospital. They had a son too. But he was killed in your country, in the war."

It was as if he had cleared up a nagging mystery and opened up a whole new line of thought for me. I remembered the dark glance the old woman had given me that first day when I went over to make their acquaintance. In my mind, I heard again that whistle, saw clearly the lazy city birds and squirrels that fed on the old man's sorrows. Even those seeds made perfect sense now. And yet I remembered also, very clearly, how the old man's eyes, when they fell on me, had been much gentler than his wife's.

"Hey, you know why my kid isn't coming up this year?" Bill interrupted my thoughts.

"I imagine he's probably just busy. The holidays are perfect for making money."

"Nothing that exciting," Bill said. "It's because of his worthless new wife. The fat b——. You know, his first wife wasn't only very pretty—she was real nice. Brought me tons of gifts every time they came up. But the one he has now is not only fat and ugly—she's lazy as hell. She makes me feel like hating my son."

"Well, look, at least we're both luckier than White. I saw him buying a whole gallon of whiskey this morning."

"His son just got sentenced—life in prison. About half this trailer park went to the courtroom the day they announced the verdict."

Soon the excitement of Father's Day passed and the parking lot returned to its usual emptiness. The sight of relatives wheeling their loved ones in the dying light of the sunset became less frequent. Now in the evenings, as the sun moved level with the windows, the old folks searched for companionship at the public beaches near the complex. In t his way their lives passed by, a calm seclusion interrupted only by the periodic need to say farewell to a departing neighbor. There were only two reasons for leaving the trailer park: death or nursing homes for those unfortunate ones who could no longer prepare their own meals or care for their own most basic needs.

So the days passed until one evening I came home to a great commotion. Police cars, ambulances and fire trucks had filled up the parking lot and my neighbors were clustered around F8, Mr. White's trailer. From the look of them, I know that something serious had occurred. The lady pianist, her face stained with tears, was being comforted by Bill, who'd put his arm around her and was leading her over into the shade of the peach trees. The police had cordoned off F8 with a yellow tape. Emergency medics entered and exited while the firemen, deprived of an opportunity to ply their trade, squatted down and leisurely puffed at their cigarettes.

It was Veteran's Day, and I knew that Bill and the other veterans had planned to throw a party. Those who had managed to preserve their old uniforms and ribbons had taken them out of their closets to display to one another. As I found out later, the old timers had visited each other all morning, telling their war stories. Bill had been everywhere and had gone to see everyone—except White. Perhaps it had slipped his mind. Finally, just before five in the afternoon, when the party was to have started, he remembered White and decided to go to this trailer and drag him along. He knocked, but there was no answer, so he'd gone to check the car shed. Sure enough, White's Buick was there. Bill went back and knocked again. Still no answer. He circled around to the back door. Noticing a little space where the blind didn't quite meet the bottom of the window, Bill peeked inside. White was hanging in a corner of the bedroom, his face bloated and pale, his tongue sticking out at least an inch. Bill felt faint and had to sit down for a while to regain his composure. After several minutes, he got up and went to the home next door and called the police.

A half an hour later, the party began as scheduled. Bill stood next to the piano, but the pianist sat motionless. No one played, no one sang. All that could be heard was Bill's agonized voice recounting over and over the day's events, reproaching himself. He should have dropped in on White sooner. If he had, if he'd said hi to White, had a drink with the black veteran, he knew he could have stopped him and White would have been here, at the party, singing God Bless America with everyone else.

Time slipped by and before I knew it I had been at the trailer park for more than a year. White left behind nothing more than a few belongings and his trailer was sold quickly and cheaply in order to pay off his debts. The new owner was Korean. He was about my age and very well-mannered.

Soon he made the acquaintance of all the families in the park. He seemed better than me in all ways. He drove a shiny new Hyundai, repainted his house in a bright color and hung a poster of the 1988 Olympics on the wall. Backing him was a country embarked on a successful road to development. Once in a while, I saw Bill stop by the Korean's for a drink.

At that time I was working the second shift. After getting home from a full day of work, I'd clean up, read the newspaper and watch a program or two on TV; by then it would be three in the morning and time to sleep. But whenever I woke up, still cocooned in the comfort of my bed, the first image of the day I'd see through my window would be the old man next door, motionless on his wheelchair, his back supported by an air pillow, his body curved against the chair, his eyes looking up at the sky. Once in a while, one hand would grope for the feeding can fastened on the armrest. With a flicking motion, his hands would direct the birds first to one side, then to the other to snatch their much awaited seeds. I became thoroughly familiar with his system of whistles. A long steady sound signalled his need for water, two shorter ones a wish to be moved into the shade, three and he needed to go inside the house; I imagine to take care of bodily needs. Each time he gave the three whistle sequence, his wife would appear immediately and wheel him inside. At noon he left the peach trees and went inside for his nap, then appeared again after four o'clock in the winter and after five-thirty in summer. That old couple cared for each other with a tender love that was greater than any other love on earth. Often she would sit beside him and whisper into his ear. If she was inside, his whistle invariably brought her smiling face back outside. And when she came, she never failed to kiss his forehead or his cheek.

Since I'd learned he was a refugee from Armenia, I'd felt close to the old man. He had left his country against his will, and then his son had died on the soil of my land. I felt I understood him and I longed to speak to him, but his circumstances prevented me. Even with his wife, he could only whisper, and more often than not he just had to signal his needs. Besides, the woman's coldness towards me hadn't dissipated. Perhaps I was a reminder to her of her present childlessness, her future loneliness. Many times I helped her carry her laundry bags from the car to their trailer, or lifted some heavy articles for her, only to receive a curt and cold thank you. She gave no sign of thawing, of forgiving. But I became used to it and continued to help her without hope of receiving any acknowledgment.

At Christmas I took a ten day vacation. Feeling that I'd been isolated for too long, I decided to visit old friends, many of whom lived around the Washington D.C. area. By coincidence, Gorbachev was visiting the United States and the media was filled with stories about glasnost and the two superpowers bringing peace to the world. But suddenly Heaven was angered and disaster struck Armenia. The same land ravaged by the hands of man, the land oppressed by the Russians for close to half a century, now became the victim of violent earthquakes which claimed hundreds of thousands of lives. Gorbachev cut short his visit and hurried home. But Heaven must have no eyes and the old Earth gods must have no ears, for why did they wait until the exact moment when the Armenians were about to demand their independence to rain such calamities on them? The images I saw on my television and in the newspapers reminded me of my neighbor. Having himself survived intact, was he now thinking about his homeland? My meetings with my friends were bittersweet, as we told each other the old stories and talked about Vietnam. For a while I pushed the images of a distant city covered with debris and rubble out of my mind.

But the minute I returned, even as I turning my car into the complex, an uneasiness came over me. It was ten o'clock already, yet the old man wasn't in his wheelchair under the peach trees. The door to his trailer was closed tightly. As soon as he spotted me, Bill ran out of his house like a whirlwind.

"Did you hear? Sarkissian dropped dead."

I was stunned to the point of speechlessness. The only person here with whom I'd felt a sense of connection had vanished to the Ninth Cloud. After a long while, I was able to ask Bill when it had happened.

"Three days after Christmas."

"Was it an accident, or did he fall ill?"

"Hell, Nguyen—he was just old."

"Where's his wife?"

"Right after the funeral, she moved to Fresno to live with her sister."

"Has someone else bought the place yet?"

"No, not yet. You know, Nguyen, I helped her pack. She had all of these stacks of books and magazines and photo albums, and a box of old letters she'd hung onto. All this stuff. She told me that towards the end, the old man wanted to hear her read all those old letters from forty or fifty years ago from relatives and friends. He couldn't see a thing, so he'd ask her to flip through the pages in the photo albums one by one, then read him aloud the name in each caption under every picture. I got a look at the album. He was a great-looking guy when he was young, handsome, full of muscles. A veteran, like you and me, only he was a doctor. All those old books and magazines had stuff about his country in them."

"Did you go to his funeral?"

"Sure. Everybody here went, except the people in wheelchairs."

"Where's the cemetery?"

"Down at the corner of Bolsa and Beach."

"Do you know where his grave is located?"

"Naw, I never remember stuff like that. Check in at the cemetery office—they should be able to give you the fine details."

I visited the cemetery that evening and found his resting place. And there I lit some incense, to commemorate a compatriot.

Finally, I moved out of the "mobile home" park. A friend had bought a small house near the place I worked and asked if I would move in with him, to share expenses and keep him company. The rent was cheaper, so I left. But I miss that place, miss the old couple, the nosy insensitive neighbor with his secret good heart, the elegant pianist, the tragic black man. The man who took over my 1969 model mobile home was yet another Korean, even younger than I, and fresh off the boat. I moved out in the morning and he moved in that afternoon. He too drove a Hyundai and had in his possession a large poster of the 1988 Seoul Olympics. The difference between us was that he always with his head high, while for the last ten years it seemed that I had always looked down.

Source:

The Other Side of Heaven: Postwar Fiction by Vietnamese and American Writers, edited by Wayne Karlin, et al. Willimantic, CT: Curbstone Press, 1995. pp. 266-273.

INDEX

*P*ersonal names, place names, events, organizations, and various subject areas or key words are listed in this index with corresponding page numbers indicating text references. Page numbers appearing in boldface indicate the page range of a specific document.

Immigrants, professionals 191
Islam 194
Marriage 192
Memoirs 196-199
Servants 192
Traditional clothing 194
Treatment of the elderly 193
Eighth Moon: The True Story of a Young Girl's Life in Communist China 103
El Saadawi, Nawal 195-196
Elderly, treatment of
Egyptian Americans 193
Elementary and Secondary Education Act 419
Employment
Afghan Americans 2
Chinese Americans 91
Colombian Americans 119, 125
Palestinian Americans 603
Peruvian Americans 609
Polish Americans 617
Salvadoran Americans 675
Taiwanese Americans 758
Engagements
Macedonian Americans 486
English Americans 200-214
Colonization 201, 770
Chicago, Illinois 211
Immigration quotas 204
Indentured servants 202
Laborers 202
Pauperism 205
English as a Second Language (ESL)
Japanese Americans 418
Englishwoman in America (autobiography) **207-214**
Equal Rights Amendment 232
Erik Christian Jensen—Danish Steel Worker (oral history) **177-180**
Eritrean Americans 215-218
Assimilation 215, 217
Child care 217
Cuisine 217
Immigration quotas 215
Traditional roles 217
Espada, Martín 636
Estonian Americans 219-221
Asylum, political 220
World War II 219
Ethnic "cleansing." *See* Genocide.
Ethnic identification
Chinese Americans 102
Ethnic intimidation 10
Executive Order 589. *See* "Gentlemen's Agreement."
Executive Order 9066 **409-412**, 430
Exiles
Cuban Americans 161-163

F

Factory workers
Sicilian Americans 693
Faleomavaega, Eni F. H. 682-688
Family relationships
Afghan Americans 1
Egyptian American 192
Greek Americans 280
Hungarian Americans 345
Polish Americans 621, 623-629
Samoan Americans 680
Swiss Americans 744
Taiwanese Americans 754, 759
Family structure
Creeks 127
Family traditions
Asian Indian Americans 57
Farewell Letter to the American People **113-114**
Farm workers
Filipino Americans 224
Farmers
Austrian Americans 60
Blackfoot 67
Cypriot Americans 166-167
Czech Americans 171
Icelandic Americans 351
Laotian Americans 463
Navajos 537
Samoan Americans 680-682
Swedish Americans 734
Farrakhan, Louis 19
Feast of San Gennaro in Little Italy (periodical article) **399-400**
Feast of the Epiphany 45
Federal training programs
Laotian Americans 464
Federation for American Immigration Reform (FAIR) 521
Female firsts 231
Feminism
Jewish Americans 446
Festival of Flowers 594
Fiction
Vietnamese Americans 797-801
Filipino Americans 222-234
Discrimination 228
Grape pickers 224
Hawaii 225
Immigration quotas 222
Five Civilized Tribes
Chickasaws 118
Choctaws 112, 114-116
Creeks 128
Flemish Folklore in Kansas (journal article) **63-65**
Folk arts
Belgian Americans 64

R

Rabbi Isaac Mayer Wise and Order No. 11
(newspaper editorial) **439-440**

Race relations
African Americans 20
Asian Indian Americans 58
Cuban Americans 154

Racial discrimination. *See* Discrimination.

Racial identity
Chinese Americans 99

Racism
African Americans 20
Apaches 35
Asian Americans 687
Japanese Americans 422
Mexican Americans 499
Native Americans 713

Ranching
Samoan Americans 681

Ravage, M(arcus) E(li) 658-659

Recipes. *See* Cuisine.

Refugee Act of 1980 **786-793**

Refuse to Kneel (oral history) **128-138**

Reina, Ernesto 139

Religion
Albanian Americans 28
Jewish Americans 434
Korean Americans 456
Macedonian Americans 484
Swedish Americans 741

Remembering Hungary (oral history) **345-348**

Rennie Stennett, from Panama, 1969 (oral history)
605-607

Repatriation
Native American property 721

Reservation communities/lifestyles
Navajos 537
Oneidas 589, 590

The Reservation School (oral history) **329-332**

Restaurants
Korean Americans 460

Revolutions
Hungary 345

Rita Flores, from Colombia, 1965 (oral history)
125-126

Rituals
Iroquois Confederacy 384
Mexican Americans 514

Rizal, José 222

Rizk, Salom 749-750

Rodolfo de León—Leaving Cuba (autobiography)
144-149

Roles of women
Navajos 549

Roma Americans. *See* Gypsy Americans.

Roman Catholicism
Argentinean Americans 44
Creeks 131

Romanian Americans 658-666
Christmas 659
Cultural differences 663

Roosevelt, Theodore 453

Russian Americans 667-672

Russian Old Believers in Pittsburgh (periodical
article) **667-672**

Ruthenians. *See* Carpatho-Rusyns.

Ryu, Charles 457

S

Sackett, S. J. 63

St. Joseph's Day (journal article) **694-698**

St. Patrick's Day Parades (periodical article) **374-
377**

St. Paulinus Festival
Italian Americans 401

Salvadoran Americans 673-679
Cultural differences 676
Employment 675
Undocumented immigrants 677-679

Samoan Americans 680-688
Athletes 683-685
Atisanoe, Salevaa 683, 685

Santa Claus
Belgian Americans 64

Schmidt, Fritz and Frieda 273 276

The Schmidts (oral history) **274-276**

Scottish and Scotch-Irish Americans 689-691
Buildings 689-691
Marriage 690-691
Traditional clothing 689-691

Seder 443

Segregation
Chinese Americans 99

Seguín, Juan N. 499

Self-employment
Italian Americans 394

Senator Lehman's Speech Against Deportation of
Estonians **220-221**

Sequoyah 76

Serbia
Albanian Americans 25

Servants
Egyptian American 192

Settlement patterns
Czech Americans 172
Icelandic Americans 349
Laotian Americans 464
Nepalese Americans 554

Seven Days: Diary of a "Rafter" **140-143**

Sheep herders
Navajos 537, 548, 550

Violence
    against Chinese Americans 107
Vlach, V. V. 172
Vocational Education Act 420

W
Wagner, Robert 270
Wagner/Nourse Rogers Bill **271-273**
Wars
    Albanian Americans 26
    in Afghanistan 1, 4
    in Armenia 49
    in Cambodia 73, 74, 785
    in China 785
    in El Salvador 673, 677
    in Eritrea 215
    in Ethiopia 215
    in Vietnam 785
War Relocation Authority (WRA) 409
Weddings
    Lithuanian Americans 479
    Macedonian Americans 484-495
Welfare and immigration reforms 467
Welfare. *See* Government assistance.
West Side Story (oral history) **95-98**
What Women Talk About (oral history) **739-742**
Where Korean Food is Just Waiting to Be
    Discovered (periodical article) **460-462**
Where the Twain Shall Meet—Lebanese in
    Cortland County (journal article) **473-478**
White Dog Feast
    Iroquois Confederacy 383-388
White Dog Feast at the Onondaga Reservation
    (journal article) **385**
White Dog Feast, Games At (journal article)
    387-388
White slavery
    Jewish Americans 442
White supremacy 20, 521
White, Elizabeth Q. *See* Qoyawayma, Polingaysi.
Whitehorse, Emmi 548
Whiteman, Roberta Hill 589

Why Farmers Have to Work So Hard (story) **323-325**
Wilma Mankiller's Inaugural Address **82-84**
Winnemucca Hopkins, Sarah (Thocmetony) 593
Women in politics 231
Women travelers
    English Americans 208
Women's movement 232
Women, contributions of 548
Work ethic
    Dutch Americans 186
Worker's compensation 469
Works Progress Administration (WPA) 738
World War I
    German Americans 264, 266
    Greek Americans 282
    Palestinian Americans 602
World War II
    Estonian Americans 219
    German Americans 266, 270
    Japanese Americans 409, 427, 686
    Jewish Americans 270
Wounded Knee Massacre (1890) 597, 708-712.
    See also Indian Survivors' Accounts of Wounded
    Knee.
Wovoka 593, 597, 708
Writing systems
    Cherokee 76

Y
"Yellow Peril" 85
Yiddish 343
Young, Brigham 523, 528
Yup'ik 135

Z
Zeytoun (village), Turkey 47
Zia, Helen 106-108
Zoot Suit Riots 496
Zoot Suit, Prologue (stage play) **497-498**